San Diego Christian College
2100 Greenfield Drive
El Cajon, CA 92019

The Megamusical

Profiles in Popular Music

Glenn Gass and Jeffrey Magee, editors

Unlocking the Groove: Rhythm, Meter, and Musical Design in Electronic Dance Music
Mark J. Butler

Neil Young and the Poetics of Energy
William Echard

Jazzwomen: Conversations with Twenty-one Musicians
Wayne Enstice and Janis Stockhouse

Choro: A Social History of a Brazilian Popular Music
Tamara Elena Livingston-Isenhour and Thomas George Caracas Garcia

Five Percenter Rap: God Hop's Music, Message, and Black Muslim Mission
Felicia M. Miyakawa

The Megamusical
Jessica Sternfeld

792.6
SB39m

26.96
EP

The Megamusical

Jessica Sternfeld

Indiana University Press | Bloomington and Indianapolis

Publication of this book is made possible in part with the assistance of a
Challenge Grant from the National Endowment for the Humanities, a federal
agency that supports research, education, and public programming in the
humanities. Any views, findings, conclusions, or recommendations expressed in
this publication do not necessarily reflect those of the National Endowment for
the Humanities.

This book is a publication of

Indiana University Press
601 North Morton Street
Bloomington, IN 47404-3797 USA

http://iupress.indiana.edu

Telephone orders   800-842-6796
Fax orders   812-855-7931
Orders by e-mail   iuporder@indiana.edu

© 2006 by Jessica Sternfeld

All rights reserved

No part of this book may be reproduced or utilized in any form or by any
means, electronic or mechanical, including photocopying and recording, or by
any information storage and retrieval system, without permission in writing
from the publisher. The Association of American University Presses' Resolution
on Permissions constitutes the only exception to this prohibition.

The paper used in this publication meets the minimum requirements of
American National Standard for Information Sciences—Permanence of Paper
for Printed Library Materialshalf*, ANSI Z39.48-1984.

Manufactured in the United States of America

Library of Congress Cataloging-in-Publication Data

Sternfeld, Jessica, date
  The megamusical / Jessica Sternfeld.
       p. cm.—(Profiles in popular music)
  Includes bibliographical references and index.
  ISBN-13: 978-0-253-34793-0 (cloth)
  ISBN-10: 0-253-34793-9 (cloth)
  1. Musicals*—History and criticism. I. Title. II. Series.
  ML2054 .S74
  792.6—dc22
                                2006013537
1 2 3 4 5 11 10 09 08 07 06

for alan

CONTENTS

APPENDICES

Acknowledgments

Musical examples in this work are based on scores which have kindly been made available to me by those who hold the rights to the materials. I created my examples using Finale 2000 software, based closely on the scores to which I had access. I made occasional reductions or editorial changes for ease of reading, but otherwise the musical material is unaltered. Any inaccuracies in the music or lyrics are my own. Any quotations of lyrics from musicals not listed below came from published libretti (usually contained in CD booklets) and are cited within the text.

I cannot express strongly enough my gratitude to The Really Useful Group (especially Head of Publishing David Robinson) and Music Theatre International. They gave me access to extremely closely guarded unpublished material, and enthusiastically supported my request to make excerpts available here.

"Heaven on Their Minds," "Blood Money," "Superstar," "The Temple," "Everything's Alright," "The Last Supper," "Damned for All Time," "Trial Before Pilate," "Gethsemane" from JESUS CHRIST SUPERSTAR
Words by Tim Rice
Music by Andrew Lloyd Webber
© 1969, 1970, 1971 LEEDS MUSIC LTD.
Copyrights renewed
All Rights for the U.S. and Canada Controlled and Administered by UNIVERSAL MUSIC CORP.
All Rights Reserved. Used by Permission.

"King Herod's Song"
from JESUS CHRIST SUPERSTAR
Words by Tim Rice
Music by Andrew Lloyd Webber
© 1971 Norrie Paramor Ltd.
Copyright Renewed
This arrangement Copyright © 2005 by Norrie Paramor Music Ltd.
All Rights Administered by Chappell & Co.
International Copyright Secured. All Rights Reserved.

EVITA
Words by Tim Rice
Music by Andrew Lloyd Webber
© 1976, 1977 Universal / Evita Music Ltd.
All Rights Reserved. International Copyright Secured.

JOSEPH AND THE AMAZING TECHNICOLOR DREAMCOAT
Words by Tim Rice
Music by Andrew Lloyd Webber
© 1969, 1973 The Really Useful Group Ltd., London.
All Rights Reserved. International Copyright Secured.

"Jellicle Theme," "Overture," "Invitation to the Jellicle Ball," "The Naming of Cats," "Jellicle Songs for Jellicle Cats," "Old Deuteronomy," "Macavity: The Mystery Cat," "Mr. Mistoffelees," "Gus: The Theatre Cat," "Growltiger's Last Stand," "Grizabella: The Glamour Cat," "Memory" from CATS
Music by Andrew Lloyd Webber
© 1980, 1981 Andrew Lloyd Webber assigned to The Really Useful Group Ltd. and Faber Music Ltd.
All Rights for Faber and Faber Ltd. Administered for the United States and Canada by R&H Music Co.
Text by Trevor Nunn and Richard Stilgoe after T. S. Eliot ("Jellicle Songs for Jellicle Cats")
© 1981 Trevor Nunn, Richard Stilgoe, and Set Copyrights Ltd.
Text by Trevor Nunn after T. S. Eliot ("Memory")
© 1981 Trevor Nunn and Set Copyrights Ltd.
All Other Texts by T. S. Eliot
© 1939 T. S. Eliot; this edition of the text © 1980, 1981 Set Copyrights Ltd.
All Rights in the text Controlled by Faber and Faber Ltd. Administered for the United States and Canada by R&H Music Co.
International Copyright Secured. All Rights Reserved.

"Prologue," "Look Down," "Lovely Ladies," "Do You Hear the People Sing?" "Bring Him Home," "Master of the House," "One Day More" from LES MISÉRABLES
Music by Claude-Michel Schönberg
Lyrics by Alain Boublil, Herbert Kretzmer, and Jean Marc Natel
Music and Lyrics © 1986 by Editions Musicales Alain Boublil
English Lyrics © 1986 Alain Boublil Music Ltd. (ASCAP)
Mechanical and Publications Rights for the U.S.A. Administered by Alain Boublil

Music Ltd. (ASCAP) c/o Stephen Tenenbaum & Co., Inc., 1775 Broadway, Suite 708, New York, NY 10019, Tel. (212) 246-7204, Fax (212) 246-7217
International Copyright Secured. All Rights Reserved. This music is copyright. Photocopying is illegal.
All Performance Rights Restricted.

"Poor Fool, He Makes Me Laugh," "The Phantom of the Opera," "Notes," "All I Ask of You," "Little Lotte," "Don Juan Triumphant," "The Music of the Night," "Masquerade" from THE PHANTOM OF THE OPERA
Music by Andrew Lloyd Webber
Lyrics by Charles Hart
Additional Lyrics by Richard Stilgoe
© 1986 Andrew Lloyd Webber assigned to The Really Useful Group Ltd.
International Copyright Secured. All Rights Reserved.

The Megamusical

Introduction

What is a megamusical? Like many neologisms, the word may sound funny, but it is probably the most accurate term for the repertoire discussed in this book. "Megamusical" describes a kind of musical theater that rose to prominence in the 1970s and 1980s and that remains a dominant force on Broadway today. I am not the first to use the term; it began to appear in the *New York Times* during the 1980s. The label was picked up, sometimes derisively, by various critics and reporters and has found its way into theater histories and surveys. It has synonyms—"spectacle show," "blockbuster musical," even "extravaganza"— but "megamusical" is the most pervasive and describes the repertoire effectively.

The features that make a musical a megamusical come both from within the show itself and from its surrounding context. The most influential megamusicals date from the 1980s and sport the style of that decade, but the genre has evolved into newer, thriving forms. No megamusical exhibits all the features of megamusicals generally, but as a group, a strong consistency emerges, especially in the 1980s: *Cats, Les Misérables, Starlight Express, The Phantom of the Opera, Miss Saigon, Chess.* Perhaps the most obvious feature is that all these shows were imported from England. Indeed, the megamusical "invasion" of Broadway began with British composer Andrew Lloyd Webber, followed by the French team of Claude-Michel Schönberg and Alain Boublil, who arrived on Broadway from Paris by way of London. For the first time in modern American musical theater, a dominant style emerged that was not American. London had sent New York some delightful shows over the years, and indeed European influence on the New York theater scene was strong in the nineteenth and early twentieth centuries (especially in realms like operetta), but Broadway in the last eighty years had always been perceived as an American institution, born in New York and almost exclusively made up of American composers, lyricists, producers, directors, and performers. Then, with *Cats* in 1982, British composer Andrew Lloyd Webber

1

started to become the most successful writer of musicals in America. And he wasn't American.

While foreign roots are an obvious feature, they do not make the megamusicals "mega." Clearly something very large must be present, and in fact megamusicals are large in several respects. First, the plots of megamusicals are big in scope: they are epic, sweeping tales of romance, war, religion, redemption, life and death, or some combination of these and other lofty sentiments. They do not tell contemporary stories of, say, New Yorkers with relationship issues. Rather, a megamusical tends to be set in the past, often the distant past, yet it grapples with such broad, universal issues that audiences tend to relate more to the concepts than the specific location. *The Phantom of the Opera* concerns obsessive love far more than the details of Paris in 1861. And *Les Misérables*, while containing a fair amount of French revolutionary history, focuses rather on basic human desires for freedom and forgiveness. These are big plots that sweep across years, even decades, and feature broadly drawn characters in dramatic, sometimes melodramatic, situations. Emotions run high; the tears tend to flow both onstage and in the audience, and comedy takes up relatively little time, though it does provide some much-needed relief from the drama.

Just as the plot of a megamusical is big, so too the music: a megamusical has little or no spoken dialogue, but is typically sung throughout, in a combination of set songs, linking and transitional material, and recitative-like material. Characters do stop and sing numbers as in the musical comedy tradition, but they also sing virtually everything else, including their dialogue with each other, and the orchestra plays constantly. Everything is fluid, underscored, tied together by the music. This musical style makes the megamusical seem much more like opera than other forms of Broadway musicals; in fact, some consider megamusicals to be operas.

If the plot is big and the music is big, it follows that the sets and staging are big as well. Impressive, complicated, expensive sets became one of the defining characteristics of the megamusical. In the glitzy 1980s, in fact, some megamusicals focused more on the twinkling, moving, distracting sets than the story or the music. Spectacle became crucial to the making of a megamusical, although the best remain grounded in the elements of plot and music as well; shows that primarily concern sets that move and sparkle tend to be unsuccessful both as drama and as business ventures. Still, the style seems to demand some sort of physical hugeness, to accompany the hugeness in the plot, the emotions, and the music. Again, a comparison to opera arises: a similar emphasis on spectacle defined Italian opera of the seventeenth century, as well as French *grand opéra* of the mid-nineteenth century.

A megamusical, then, is usually sung-through and features an epic, historically situated, but timeless plot staged on a fancy set. Of course, the composers of megamusicals did not invent these features; plenty of earlier musicals used grand epic plots and broad emotion, and musicals have often been staged on a large scale. But the megamusical is the first twentieth-century musical theater genre to combine these factors with such consistency, and to add some equally important extramusical features.

A megamusical is not just big inside the theater; it is big outside it as well. New megamusicals, especially in the 1980s, were cultural events marketed with unprecedented force. British producer Cameron Mackintosh led the way; a front-line British "invader" as important as Andrew Lloyd Webber, he sold megamusicals like any other product, complete with logos, theme songs, and advertisements saturating newspapers, radio, and television. By the time a new megamusical opened, massive advance ticket sales testified to the effectiveness of these intense marketing campaigns. It was also often the case that music from the show, a single song or sometimes the entire score, was already well known to the audience because the creators and producers had released a recording before the show opened. Both the pre-opening publicity and the pre-opening release of the music grew out of trends set by *Jesus Christ Superstar* in the early 1970s, though neither maneuver was entirely intentional. But by the 1980s, the formula had been proven, and strong marketing became a staple of the megamusical.

Responding to the publicity wave, the press followed the process of mounting the show; issues of casting, staging, and backstage gossip became regular topics in the newspapers, and the hype, whether positive or negative, was good for business. This leads us to another major element of the megamusical: it is financially successful. It is, in fact, a money-making machine of unprecedented proportions in the history of the theater. There have of course been megamusical-style shows that have flopped, but the most "mega" of megamusicals are those that run for years, even decades, and continue to draw audiences until they become veritable institutions on Broadway. Three of the main focuses of this book (*Cats, The Phantom of the Opera, Les Misérables*) are the strongest examples of this longevity and financial success, while others, especially some that have followed the megamusical model in the 1990s, are bound for equal or perhaps greater financial success, with *The Lion King* leading the way.

The large qualities of the megamusical make it a phenomenon not just in New York and London, but around the world. In the 1980s a pattern developed in which a megamusical opened successfully in London, then New York, then around the United States, and finally all over the world. Now, London often follows New York, megamusicals being more often created in America than in Britain, but the eventual goal of opening in cultural capitals like Vienna, Sydney, Toronto, and Tokyo still holds. Like the most successful Italian romantic operas, megamusicals are extremely exportable. Their epic plots allow people of various cultures to relate to the stories. Unlike older musicals in which spoken dialogue helps to move the plot forward, in the megamusical it is the music that carries the story, thus easing potential language barriers for international audiences, even when the lyrics are translated into the local language. And, perhaps most significantly, the marketing that accompanies a megamusical around the world makes it an easy commodity to sell; the logo, theme song, and slogan seek to assure a foreign audience that it gets exactly what was produced on Broadway. This is indeed the case; unlike musicals of earlier decades, which could be staged in any way a local director chose, the megamusical has been reproduced in foreign cities with meticulous care to ensure that it resembles its Broadway incarnation as closely as possible.

One final feature helps to define the megamusical: it is generally not loved by critics. Audiences may flock to see the latest spectacular show, lured by the hype and then returning year after year, even across decades, because they love the music, the story, and the atmosphere of these powerful, escapist pieces of theater. But critics generally tend to give megamusicals mixed, lukewarm reviews. A few American critics, especially in the 1980s, hated them on principle: created by foreign invaders, these shows had no substance, just pretty tunes and shiny sets. But most critics found megamusicals disappointing rather than insidious; here were crowd-pleasing, enjoyable shows that did little to educate or challenge, though they were admittedly effective theater.

In the era of the megamusical, the role of the theater critic has changed significantly. Before the 1980s, theater critics wielded a great deal of influence over the success of musicals, and more often than not a mixed review or a pan could close a production. *Cats* proved that a show could receive rather poor reviews and become the longest-running musical of all time; a number of me-gamusicals since have experienced similar success in the face of negative reviews. Critics, in the case of the megamusical, largely ceased to matter. The new ad-vertising style generated so much interest in a show that poor reviews, and a lack of pithy positive quotes attached to a show's ad campaign, went unnoticed. And audiences kept coming, long after the initial hype had subsided. Were the critics missing something? How could they dislike a show that audiences so wholeheartedly embraced? Were they out of touch, no longer able to relate to the taste of the average theatergoer? The dichotomy between audience and critics forms a fundamental element of the megamusical, and an ongoing theme in this book.

As with any genre of music, defining the megamusical remains an inexact science, and exceptions to any definition abound. Nevertheless, the features mentioned above should begin to form a picture of the megamusical: in short, it features a grand plot from a historical era, high emotions, singing and music throughout, and impressive sets. It opens with massive publicity, which usually leads to millions of dollars in advance sales. Marketing strategies provide a recognizable logo or image, theme song, and catch phrase. Successful (re-)productions spring up all over the world. Audiences rave; critics are less thrilled. It runs for years, perhaps decades, becoming a fixture of our cultural landscape.

Next to no musicological scholarship exists on the megamusical. This is not simply because the genre arose only recently, but because many scholars dismiss, disdain, and purposely ignore the genre. Like the critics who dislike megamusicals by virtue of their popularity, most musicologists and theater scholars develop an arrogant, even disgusted tone when mentioning the megamusical, if they mention it at all. In contrast, some wonderful scholarship has been written on the work of Stephen Sondheim, clearly an acceptable—often revered—figure. Andrew Lloyd Webber, whose works are contemporary with Sondheim's, exists in a research vacuum. Yet *The Phantom of the Opera* is the longest-running Broadway musical of all time, breaking the record of *Cats* in 2006. That fact alone makes it worthy of study.

A great deal of the scholarship on musical theater (much of which concerns Golden Era musicals of the 1940s and 1950s) discusses issues of form. Scholars debate things like the integration of songs into a show's plot development, the response of the musical styles to the story or the setting, and the amount of disruption various numbers cause in a show's theatrical arc. There are integrated musicals, stop-and-sing musicals, concept musicals, and musical comedies, to name a few genre labels, all defined slightly differently by various historians.[1] Each retelling of the history of musical theater champions certain composers and shows, with varying degrees of consensus; everyone feels that *Oklahoma!*, for example, was pivotal, but some scholars cast Sondheim in the role of Broadway's savior while others declare Broadway to have been dead by 1970. Arguments over the canon then arise: how much attention do Rodgers and Hammerstein, or Cole Porter, warrant? Does *Porgy and Bess* count as a musical? Is financial success a factor, or critical reception, or long-term reputation?

Two points, then, emerge from current musical theater scholarship: one, the sung-through megamusical represents a new form that has gone largely undiscussed; and two, the megamusical is virtually never mentioned in debates over canonization.[2] This seems to be the result of a combination of factors: loyalty to the Golden Era or to Sondheim or to America, resentment of foreign invaders, resentment of Lloyd Webber's success, and resistance to anything so popular that it feels unscholarly to discuss it. Scholars seem to understand that the material demands investigation, thanks to its success and impact; they simply do not want to do the investigating themselves. Michael Walsh, author of the only solid critical biography of Andrew Lloyd Webber's life and music, found himself in a similar position: "When the first edition of this book appeared in Britain in 1989, the author was widely taken to task by critics for the effrontery of treating Lloyd Webber and his work seriously."[3]

The most valuable sources for the study of megamusicals, one might then imagine, come from outside musicology. The main secondary materials are reviews and articles in the media and coffee table books. Critics' reviews of a new megamusical are of course fundamental, but the continuing coverage in the *New York Times* and other periodicals of each show's creation and run allows me to recount a production's history. Also, big books full of glossy photos, intended for fans, occasionally offer more insight than one might imagine.

In this work I examine the phenomenon of the Broadway megamusical. I investigate two main aspects of this genre: its theatrical style and techniques, and its function as a socioeconomic force. The two threads—the shows themselves and the larger social context of the shows—run parallel to one another, and indeed cannot be separated. Since the qualities that make a musical a megamusical include both internal features (a sung-through score, an epic plot, large sets) and external ones (aggressive marketing, economic success, unenthusiastic critical reception, cultural currency), this study addresses both categories and how they interact.

In chapter 1, I examine *Jesus Christ Superstar,* the first megamusical, which (in some ways accidentally) gathered the elements of the genre together. It seemed at the time that what *Superstar* brought to Broadway was rock music, but as the 1980s arrived, it became clear that what it really brought was the megamusical. Chapter 2 addresses all the musical and cultural qualities of the megamusical with a focus on its chief creators: composer Andrew Lloyd Webber, lyricist Tim Rice, and producer Cameron Mackintosh. In chapter 3, we look at *Cats,* the second-longest-running Broadway musical of all time. In chapter 4, I turn to a new team of megamusical creators, composer Claude-Michel Schönberg and lyricist Alain Boublil; influenced by Lloyd Webber, they created the most successful musical in history, *Les Misérables. The Phantom of the Opera,* the subject of chapter 5, marks for many critics and historians Lloyd Webber's maturity as a composer. Chapter 6 moves to a more far-reaching, less exhaustive survey of other megamusicals in the 1980s, focusing on Tim Rice's *Blondel* and *Chess* and Andrew Lloyd Webber's *Starlight Express,* and also briefly on the context in which all the 1980s megamusicals existed. Chapter 7 moves on to the 1990s, recounting what became of the megamusical as time marched on. An unavoidable force after its success in the 1980s, the megamusical in the 1990s (with shows such as *Aspects of Love, Sunset Boulevard, Miss Saigon, Jekyll and Hyde, Titanic, Beauty and the Beast, The Lion King, Rent,* and *Ragtime*) morphed into new styles in a number of ways. In chapter 8, I recount the history of the megamusical, and of Broadway generally, since the turn of the twenty-first century (with brief looks at shows such as *Aida* and *The Producers*). I also discuss here the history of Broadway since September 11, 2001. Few industries were more directly affected by the attacks than Broadway, and Broadway—as both a business and a cultural institution—continues to recover.

My primary goals in this study are history and analysis—to gather in one place information about an unexamined genre, to shape that information into a narrative history of sorts, and to examine (in varying amounts of detail) the repertoire along the way. I am not particularly interested in arguing that the megamusical is the greatest genre ever created, although I am a fan of many of these shows. I do argue that the genre is undervalued both as worthy of critical discussion and as an undeniable influence on all musicals that have been written since its advent in the 1970s. When you hear "Memory" in *Cats,* you might cry, or you might roll your eyes. Millions cried during the show's record-breaking eighteen-year run, so something powerful must be at work. This book tells the history of the megamusical, and makes an effort to explain all the factors that make people cry during "Memory."

"Why'd You Choose Such a Backward Time and Such a Strange Land?"

Jesus Christ Superstar

When you're just sitting around and nobody knows
who you are, you look for something that will
bring you attention.
Andrew Lloyd Webber

The new era announces itself in the opening notes of *Jesus Christ Superstar:* over a low tritone pedal point, an electric guitar begins to wail. It is a dissonant, serious line, free in tempo, and immediately unsettling. It rises, pulling the pedal point with it. The electric guitar then grows insistent, launching into a driving tempo. A full orchestra and a full rock band join. The overture proper has begun, progressing through a series of melodies that will reappear over the course of the musical. This foreshadowing is normal procedure for an overture, of course, but here the melodies are hardly the typical love songs and dance numbers. The meter keeps shifting, the mood is consistently tense, and nothing feels settled until the electric guitar begins to play an ostinato, a riff, which it goes on to play twenty-seven times in succession. Eventually the full orchestra settles into a majestic D major, to which will be sung the words "JE-sus Christ . . . SU-per-star." But in mid-phrase, this line is dropped, the off-stage chorus sings an unstable phrase that suggests D but also G, and the strings softly intone a set of chords in D-flat major.

This music prepares us for what is to come, and this radically unusual overture opens a show that was, in 1971, beyond unusual; it was revolutionary. It marked at once the end of what many felt was a rather weak and old-fashioned decade of musicals (despite a few notable exceptions such as *Cabaret*) following the "Golden Age" of Broadway (ca. 1943–1964), and the beginning of a new era, one which remains as yet unnamed and which we are still experiencing. Many critics refer to those shows of the 1970s and 1980s which descended from *Jesus Christ Superstar* as "megamusicals." *Jesus Christ Superstar* demonstrated many of the elements that would define megamusicals and make them so successful: a sung-through score with no spoken dialogue, lavish and complicated sets, and an extremely emotional, larger-than-life plot. The composer was Andrew Lloyd Webber, whose influence on the musical in the last three decades cannot be overstated. That wailing electric guitar signaled his arrival on Broadway, and Broadway would never be the same.

Jesus Christ Superstar was not without precedent. Several musicals had already featured some of the elements that made it unusual. *Hair,* a recent Broadway hit, featured a rock band complete with electric guitars. *Godspell* even featured Jesus Christ. But *Hair* had no real plot and no orchestra, just an onstage rock band accompanying a series of songs about modern hippie life. And *Godspell* was running off-Broadway and also had little plot, just a series of songs, many of them comic, loosely related to biblical teachings and events. These somewhat remote influences were far less effective in paving *Jesus Christ Superstar*'s path to Broadway than the music and text of the show itself. Before coming to Broadway, a double album of the entire score of the "rock opera" had sold with huge success. Millions of people already knew the words and music. There were even several touring companies traveling the country. Nevertheless, this was Broadway, that great American institution, home to Rodgers and Hammerstein, Lerner and Loewe, Gershwin, Porter, Loesser, Styne, and the heir apparent to their throne, Stephen Sondheim. And in swept a very young Englishman and his young lyricist, Tim Rice, to upset the line dramatically, with a rock opera driven by plot and character, with astounding sets and a rock band sharing the pit with a full orchestra. One critic, writing before "megamusical" was a word, called *Superstar* "the first of the prepackaged blockbusters," the first "all-new transatlantic long-playing mega-hit" that offered traditional American Broadway its first real challenge.[1] From this point, the line of Broadway history would split into two branches: the American musical, usually about American people in a dialogue-with-songs format, and the imported megamusical. The two paths, distinct for years afterward, have become increasingly blurred in recent seasons: megamusical and other musical theater styles have influenced one another, creating new blended styles, and the creative team of a new show can include both Americans and non-Americans. Perhaps we are heading toward another revolutionary moment now, more than thirty years after the one begun by *Superstar.*

Broadway BC

Richard Rodgers and Oscar Hammerstein composed their most lauded and enduring hit musicals in the 1940s, and so great was their influence that Broadway rode their wave for two decades. *Oklahoma!* (1943), the musical most scholars cite as the start of the Golden Era, was not the first show that successfully integrated songs into a solid, sometimes serious plot, but it was considered the landmark musical that made this style the norm. Earlier examples of this so-called "integrated musical," such as Jerome Kern and Oscar Hammerstein's *Show Boat* (1927), were exceptions in a genre otherwise populated by revue-oriented song-and-dance shows in which fancy but unmotivated production numbers stopped the action with little advancement in plot or character development. With the coming of Rodgers and Hammerstein's successful formula, musicals were strongly based on plots (known as "books"), and the musical numbers, both songs and dances alike, had to fit into the overall trajectory of the drama. *Carousel* (1945) and *South Pacific* (1949) confirmed Rodgers and Hammerstein's position as kings of the Golden Era, and their influence is clearly seen in the work of other creative teams, who continued the development of the integrated book musical through the 1940s and 1950s in their own ways: Lerner and Loewe (*Brigadoon, My Fair Lady*), Loesser (*Guys and Dolls, The Most Happy Fella*), Porter (*Kiss Me, Kate*), Styne (*Gypsy*), and Bernstein and Sondheim (*West Side Story*), to name a few.[2]

The 1960s began with more of the same, although the number of hit shows turned out by the leading creators declined sharply. The first half of the decade saw several encouraging new teams and a respectable handful of hit shows, although most worked within the now old-fashioned stop-and-sing musical comedy formula. Among these shows were *Bye Bye Birdie* (1960) by Charles Strouse and Lee Adams, Jerry Herman's *Hello, Dolly!* (1964), and Mitch Leigh and Joe Darion's *Man of La Mancha* (1965). The most successful show of the decade, *Fiddler on the Roof* (1964), by Jerry Bock and Sheldon Harnick, marks, for many scholars, the end of the Golden Era and the last of the classic book musicals in the Rodgers and Hammerstein style.[3] John Kander and Fred Ebb presented the eerie *Cabaret* in 1966, but they would not have another hit until 1975 with *Chicago*. Similarly, Stephen Sondheim, student of Hammerstein and successor to his (and Rodgers') throne as the next great Broadway writer, produced only one hit in the 1960s, *A Funny Thing Happened on the Way to the Forum* (1962); he would not have another until the 1970s, and his career would be plagued by the occasional flop and uneven reception.

In short, by the late 1960s Broadway musicals were in a serious slump.

Critics declared Broadway dead or dying, a cry which, although voiced throughout the history of the institution, seemed quite justified at the time. Musical Broadway had fallen behind the times; its music, stories, and style were out of fashion. In the 1940s and 1950s, Broadway music and popular music had been the same thing; cast albums were regular chart-toppers, as were singles from musicals. Now, show music was relegated to the older generation—the youth of America had moved on to rock 'n' roll. On Broadway, and also in out-of-town tryouts, failures abounded. Costs to mount a show rose, and audiences dwindled.[4]

But one area in which musicals continued to do well, and even improve their situation, was in export abroad. England had a long history of welcoming Broadway shows, and with *Fiddler on the Roof* and *Man of La Mancha,* some continental European cities opened their theaters to American musicals as well.[5] England, unlike the United States, had a patchy, largely unsuccessful history with its home-grown musical theater, partly the result of a different mindset toward the genre. Sheridan Morley, a historian of the British musical, explains:

> Hit musicals in London were still regarded as lucky accidents that came out of nowhere and went nowhere; the idea of having a support system of the kind that Broadway has always given its musicals and that in the British theatre has only ever been given to Shakespeare at Stratford, the idea of a continuous policy of training and reviving and rehearsing, is still oddly alien to the world of musicals and it was not until twenty years after *Oliver!* that [Lionel] Bart's one true successor as a sole creator of hit musicals which could also make an impact on Broadway, Andrew Lloyd Webber, would begin even to think about the possibility of a permanent London musical theatre company.[6]

Lionel Bart's *Oliver!* (1960) was indeed a full-fledged British hit, both in London and New York, but like many other composers around this time, Bart had no follow-up. His next show, *Blitz!,* was the most expensive British musical to date, and in an odd foreshadowing of the reception of many Lloyd Webber shows, the spectacular sets were the only thing critics or audiences remembered. Other British composers were inspired by the success of *Oliver!* to write tame, pleasant scores based on old-fashioned books; still others wrote interesting, effective shows that failed to find a place in the Broadway repertoire. Unlike their American counterparts, however, the British had not fallen from a great height, a Golden Era; instead, their situation was—as Morley dramatically asserts—"yet another reminder that at that point there was really no such thing as a reputable British stage musical."[7] There would not be one for several more years, and that show would have to come to London by way of Broadway, despite being created by a British team.

In 1968, the first step toward updating Broadway was taken: *Hair* featured rock music, bridging the gap between popular music and show music. Although the show was a success—it ran for five years and, like many successful musicals, lives on in regional productions—it was not an integrated musical. Gerome Ragni and James Rado based the show on their research among the hippies living in Greenwich Village; as a result the slight plot is more like a series of unconnected elements that make up the hippie lifestyle, such as drugs, free love, rebellion against their elders as manifested by long hair and baldly sexual language, and, perhaps most important, resistance to the war in Vietnam. Ragni and Rado wrote the lyrics, and Galt MacDermot added music in various popular styles, mostly with a basis in rock, to suit each topic.

When *Hair* transferred from off-Broadway to Broadway, it gained director Tom O'Horgan, who had already made his mark with other innovative, experimental off-Broadway productions. O'Horgan's directorial style was well suited to the show: he worked a great deal from improvisation, he spent much rehearsal time having the cast bond together, and he was a hippie himself, with strong political ideas and unusual ways to stage them. The show's group atmosphere was clear in *Hair*'s subtitle: it was billed as "an American tribal love-rock musical," and although a few of the characters interacted in plot points, the show was more hippie experience than story.[8]

The lack of plot is not necessarily a negative feature, and plenty of successful examples of musical theater work this way. However, at the time *Hair* was something of a novelty in the way it pulled out all the stops, including explicit language, drug use onstage, and a group nude scene. Many critics and historians saw the show as insincere and motivated by the urge to shock, rather than a genuine celebration of counter-culture (although the desire to shock was itself often a motivation for some hippie activities). As one historian describes it, this was a "low-energy, hedonistic group, with not much on its communal mind except free love (i.e., sex), free drugs, and free anything else."[9] In a foreshadowing of critical reactions to come, the *New York Times*'s Walter Kerr found O'Horgan's direction too heavy-handed, trampling on the mood of innocence and the air of subtle humor with strange and irrelevant trickery.[10] Not everyone was so hostile toward *Hair;* overall it received mixed reviews. The review that mattered the most, that of Clive Barnes of the *New York Times,* was quite positive. He called it "the first Broadway musical in some time to have the authentic voice of today rather than the day before yesterday."[11] Audiences at *Hair* were much younger than at most other Broadway shows, so it did succeed in bringing new people into the theater. No one had yet discovered how to merge recent popular music with effective drama, rock with plot. Theater historian Mark Steyn calls *Hair* "muddled and undisciplined," and summarizes, "It was left to the British to develop a more efficient fusion of musical theatre and the Top Forty: *Hair* proved to be the dawning of the Age of Lloyd Webber."[12]

Two other endeavors attempted to fuse pop music and theatricality. In 1969, the rock band The Who released *Tommy,* a "concept album" in which all the songs were linked by a theme, like a song cycle, about a blind deaf-mute boy. Events of plot were sometimes manifested in individual songs, but there was no overall dramatic arc, just a thematic thread. The Who called their album a "rock opera," which implied a staged production, but they did not pursue a staging for many years, intending the music to stand as a concept album. A drama would not be supplied until twenty-four years later, when *Tommy* opened on Broadway in 1993.

Structurally similar to *Hair* was *Godspell.* The show, directed by book writer John-Michael Tebelak with music and lyrics by Stephen Schwartz, opened off-Broadway in May 1971 and moved to Broadway after a successful five-year run. Based on the idea of conversion, *Godspell* was a series of songs that included psalms and hymns performed by a group of young, trendy people about events in the life of Jesus as told in the Book of Matthew. Everyone wore casual modern clothes and clown make-up. Even more than in *Hair,* there were no real characters (sometimes cast members represented biblical figures, but most went by their own first names) and few plot points. The sweet songs were in a mixture of popular styles, the language cleverly slang yet biblical. *Godspell* received positive reviews but little general attention, due to its small scale, off-Broadway home, and modest ambitions.[13] No one had yet changed the face of the Broadway musical, integrating new musical styles, inventing a new form, and making Broadway relevant and appealing to a wide audience once again.

The Single and the Album

> There are some people who may be shocked by this record. I ask them to listen to it and think again. It is a desperate cry. Who are you Jesus Christ? is the urgent enquiry, and a very proper one at that. The record probes some answers and makes some comparisons. The onus is on the listener to come up with his replies. If he is a Christian, let him answer for Christ. The singer says he only wants to know. He is entitled to some response.[14]
>
> Dean Martin Sullivan, St. Paul's Cathedral, London

This disclaimer-disguised-as-challenge, appearing on the record which first introduced *Jesus Christ Superstar* to the public, was one of many careful gestures meant to dispel potential controversy over the subject matter. The topic of the last seven days of the life of Jesus, no matter how it was handled, was bound to upset some people, and the creators and recording executives spent much time and energy explaining themselves. In fact, this fear of potential resistance to the show prevented Lloyd Webber and Rice from finding producers for a staging, so they recorded the album first, with the qualified support of the record company. In the long run this process probably only increased the attention the show received once it had made its way from successful single to extremely successful album to live production. And the executives were more inclined to back a stage production knowing that a market for it existed.

The cultural climate in America was such that they need not have worried so much. Jesus, it seemed, was in fashion. In popular music of the late 1960s and early 1970s, references to Jesus and to religion in general were becoming increasingly frequent. Oft-cited examples of this spiritual "Jesus Rock" movement include the Beatles' "Let It Be," Simon and Garfunkel's "Bridge Over Troubled Water," and Neil Diamond's version of "He Ain't Heavy, He's My Brother."[15] These singles dealt with the idea of brotherhood and a general spirituality. More specific examples of "Jesus Rock" abounded in songs like "Remember Bethlehem," "Will the Real Jesus Please Stand Up," and "Jesus Is Just Alright."[16] *Time* magazine pointed out that Jesus could be found not only in pop music but on all sorts of merchandise like bathing suits and wristwatches; he was a fad among America's youth.[17] For some more liberal-minded churches, this was a boon, as they drew new worshippers by incorporating popular music into their services and classes.

This was the market into which Andrew Lloyd Webber and Tim Rice thrust their new rock opera. The two young Englishmen had had some minor success at home with their first musical, but they knew that to achieve a breakthrough, they had to conquer the United States.

Lloyd Webber came from several generations of musicians on both sides of his family. His father, William Lloyd Webber, was an accomplished organist and had longed to be a successful composer himself, but for practical reasons had turned to teaching and administration instead.[18] By the time his son was grown, William was the director of the London College of Music.[19] He and his wife, Jean, a piano teacher, singer, and violinist, led a somewhat bohemian household, filled with guests, cats, and music of all kinds. Born in 1948, Andrew studied violin, piano, and French horn, but did not play any particularly well; his younger brother Julian would take to the cello and become a well-known virtuoso. Andrew's passion lay instead in composing, which he began to do at age six, and in staging musicals in his toy theater which, because of his other love, architecture, was an impressive structure in itself. Musical theater was his genre from the beginning; as a child, he saw *South Pacific* a dozen times at the movie theater.

In his teens he wrote the scores for three musicals at school, and sold a song to Decca record producer Desmond Elliott. Elliott had in his employ a young gofer, Tim Rice, and encouraged the two to meet. Rice wrote to Lloyd Webber in April 1965, in a now legendary letter:

> Dear Andrew,
>   I have been given your address by Desmond Elliott of Arlington Books, who I believe has also told you of my existence. Mr Elliott told me that you were looking for a "with-it" writer of lyrics for your songs, and as I have been writing pop songs for a short while now and particularly enjoy writing the lyrics I wondered if you consider it worth your while meeting me. I may fall far short of your requirements, but anyway it would be interesting to meet up—I hope![20]

Rice, at twenty-one about four years older than Lloyd Webber, had studied at the Sorbonne, pumped gas, and begun to study law, but finally had given in to his true dream, to become a pop star or at least have a hand in pop music. They met and liked each other enormously, despite the contrast of their personalities: Lloyd Webber leaned toward theater and had a restless drive to compose, while Rice's interests lay in popular music and in gaining wealth and fame.[21] Lloyd Webber began his studies at Oxford but lasted only a semester before the pull of composing became too great; he finished his schooling with a token year at the Royal College of Music but had already begun working with Rice. From 1966 to 1968, the duo wrote four singles that were recorded and released but gained little notice, and a mediocre musical in the English tradition of *Oliver!* that was never staged.

Their work together had nevertheless prepared them for their first commission. A family friend of Lloyd Webber's, Alan Doggett, music master at Colet Court prep school for boys, asked the pair to write a short work on a religious story for the boys to perform for their parents at the end of the term. The result, which parents enjoyed on 1 March 1968, was the first version of *Joseph and the Amazing Technicolor Dreamcoat,* at this time a fifteen-minute cantata which tripped breezily through the story of Joseph and his brothers with pop music. William Lloyd Webber liked it so well that he helped restage it in May at Central Hall, Westminster.

It just so happened that the pop and jazz critic from the *Times* of London, Derek Jewell, had a son in the chorus. This little school show so impressed him that he wrote an article on it, and thereby Lloyd Webber and Rice won some attention. The show was expanded gradually as more school and community theater groups performed it. Novello and Company published the songs and Rice's boss at Decca recorded it. They also got an agent, David Land. A third, well-publicized performance took place at St. Paul's Cathedral in November 1968. Fourteen years later, having become a fully staged two-act musical with an adult cast, *Joseph* made it to Broadway.

But for the young pair of creators in 1968, getting *Joseph* seen by several thousand people, as well as recorded, was quite a victory. It was also enough to inspire David Land to go ahead, tentatively, with their new idea, also based on a biblical theme.

In 1969, it seemed to Tim Rice that many people, especially rock stars and celebrities, were being referred to as "superstars." The term implied not only fame, but a certain over-hyped, over-marketed quality that suited Rice's evolving philosophy about the story of Jesus. When their record company, Decca (part of MCA-UK at the time), asked for a single to test the market before agreeing to bankroll a whole opera, Rice chose "Superstar" for the song's title. It was an impressive effort for a single. Lloyd Webber composed and arranged it for fifty-six-piece orchestra, rock band, solo singer, three backup singers, and chorus. Both men were meticulous about the recording quality, and produced the song themselves. Although the song would, in the context of the show, be sung by Judas from beyond the grave, at this stage it was marketed as if sung by an Everyman, a questioning persona who was meant to stand in for anyone. The soloist was Murray Head, a British pop singer with a powerful rock-style wail who was appearing in London's production of *Hair* at the time. At twenty-three, his was an appropriately young, handsome image for the single's cover.[22]

To write some sort of rock opera seemed an obvious step, Rice explained. "We naturally considered rock with my background and opera with Andrew's knowledge of the classics. Then we had this idea. 'Why not combine the two?' The Who had caused quite a stir by calling their *Tommy* a rock opera. That's how it all came about."[23] The term "rock opera" is perhaps no worse than most for the show, but much of the music is not strictly rock music, and identifications of operatic elements are subjective and debatable, as we will see. But before they could complete their rock opera, MCA tested the waters with the single.

On 21 November 1969, the single "Superstar" was released in England, complete with the endorsement of Dean Sullivan of St. Paul's Cathedral and a promise of a forthcoming opera, *Jesus Christ.* Not much happened. But when it was released in the United States on the first of December, it generated contro-versy everywhere, with voices both for and against it. Some radio stations read Dean Sullivan's statement before playing it; others refused to play it at all. Dis-cussion groups sprang up almost instantly, on radio panels consisting of clergy members and teenagers, and in church groups and classes all over the country. Protests rolled in to the record company's American distributor. Lloyd Webber, in a rather telling choice of words that revealed his creative and economic sides at once, hoped that the controversy would not overshadow his "very serious attempt to stimulate discussion about Jesus Christ among record buyers."[24] There were indeed record buyers, raising the single into the top eighty hit singles on the *Billboard* chart by February 1970. It was not the all-out victory the executives had hoped for, but was solid enough for them to send Lloyd Webber and Rice off with a contract to write the whole opera in preparation for a full-length recording.

What was it, besides the simple mentioning of Jesus in a rock song, that made the single "Superstar" instantly controversial? The focus of discussion was almost entirely on the lyrics. A man leads a chorus, and both he and the group question Jesus. The speaker wonders:

> Every time I look at you I don't understand
> Why you let the things you did get so out of hand.
> You'd have managed better if you'd had it planned,
> Why'd you choose such a backward time and such a strange land?
> If you'd come today, you would have reached a whole nation.
> Israel in 4 B.C. had no mass communication.
>
> *With backup singers, repeated:* Don't you get me wrong, I only want to
>   know.
> *Backup singers alone:* Jesus Christ, Jesus Christ, who are you, what have you
>   sacrificed?
> Jesus Christ Superstar, do you think you're what they say you are?
>
> *Solo speaker:* Tell me what you think about your friends at the top
> Who do you think besides yourself's the pick of the crop?
> Buddha, was he where it's at, is he where you are?
> Could Mohammed move a mountain or was that just P.R.?
> Did you mean to die like that, was that a mistake, or
> Did you know your messy death would be a record breaker?

According to this text, then, Jesus seems to have led a mismanaged movement that succeeded despite some of his actions. From his vantage point in the present, the singer feels that Jesus' movement was haphazard, and would have been more convincing with the benefits of modern life. As it is, the singer cannot tell if Jesus really was a god, or if he had any reasons for leading his movement the way he did, or even if he died on purpose as some sort of publicity stunt. Evident in this first single is Rice's flair with slang; although his tone is generally modern, he often reserves the truly trendy for moments of irony or sarcasm. The speaker's thoughts on whether the Buddha was "where it's at" or whether Mohammed's mountain-moving was "just P.R." are particularly biting examples of Rice's efficient, pointed slang. The chorus, sounding jubilant, is nevertheless as unresolved as the speaker, helping him ask the questions over and over. There is no final word; although everyone seems content to enjoy the moment by song's end, no answers have appeared. These demanding, audacious questions were bold and interesting to some, scandalous and horrifying to others. Rice claims in his autobiography to have been wary about the controversy that they knew would arise, but he also wanted the song to have an attention-grabbing edge of uncertainty and modernism: "I knew exactly the sort of questions I wanted Judas to ask, and by setting it in the twentieth century rather than in the first, the questions struck a strong contemporary chord."[25]

Lloyd Webber's music for the single is one of the most rock-like rock songs he has ever written, with a healthy dose of funk and an emphasis on text and beat rather than melody. Walsh declared it his best song to that point in his career, "a three-chord rocker" (though it has many more than three) that sounds uncomplicated but nicely contrasts the soloist with the simple and somewhat simple-minded chorus sentiments.[26] The presence of rock music, no matter its quality, pleased supporters and upset detractors; nevertheless, the text and the philosophical position it espoused were the elements that mattered at this point.

Through a combination of their own genuine interest in the story and exquisite timing, the duo had hit upon the best possible topic with which to launch their careers. America, with its Jesus fad in full swing, was primed for this modern, rock-oriented, youthfully worded examination of Jesus. Inspired by the success of the single, the MCA executives gave Lloyd Webber and Rice a contract for a recording of the full opera, *Jesus Christ Superstar*. The resulting double album did relatively poorly back home in England, which Rice (often the spokesman for the two) explained away as a demonstration of the difference between being a young adult in America and in England. Americans are activists, he explained, discussing religion, going to war, protesting the war, or fighting for their rights; English youth are much more easygoing and uninterested in engaging in politics and social issues, or in the nature of religion.[27]

Jesus Christ Superstar delves headfirst into the nature of religion by its very subject matter, but, as Lloyd Webber and Rice were quick to point out, the rock opera was not really about religion. Their Jesus is a flawed man, struggling with the conflicts and pressures of his life. This does not mean they were unaware of the instant controversy the show would cause; as Lloyd Webber said, in one of his rare candid moments, they were "looking for something that will bring you attention."[28] Neither man was particularly religious, having been raised in the

Anglican church but having become, like some of the youth of America, more interested in the idea of Jesus as man than as God or son of God. This did not mean, as Rice said repeatedly, that they were making any sort of definitive statement about what they believed or what others should believe. The story was just more interesting their way. A man with a mission to spread peace, healing, and understanding finds himself with far more power than he imagined, and another man, Judas, is conflicted about how to help. Rice points to lyrics in the song "Superstar" as being the essence of the story's theme. "We were simply trying to express our feelings about Christ at the time," Rice told a reporter, "trying to tell His story and make suggestions for the gaps. We weren't trying to make a comment. Who are *we* to make a comment? The whole thing is summed up in Judas's lyrics . . . 'Don't you get me wrong—I only want to know.' "[29]

The story is told largely from Judas's perspective; it is he who wants the answers, who wants to know. As the show begins, he has already become separated from the other apostles; while they continue to follow Jesus with un-wavering glee, he sees the larger picture. Their movement has grown far larger than they expected, and they are attracting the distrustful attention of Caiaphas and the other Jewish priests, who represent local authority. Jesus, who needs his apostles, knows they hold overly simplistic views about their present and future situations. For what little comfort his tense life has, he looks to Mary Magdalene, who is often referred to in the musical simply as Mary; his mother, Mary, is not present in the story at all. Jesus' movement grows, from a core group to tens of thousands of followers. Caiaphas threatens his life; the needy demand his healing touch. Jesus becomes somewhat disillusioned and tired. Judas does the only thing he feels will save both Jesus' life and any hope of the message's continuation: he tips off the priests. At the last supper, a tired and angry Jesus questions his own role in the story, his worth whether dead or alive, his God. Judas hangs himself in an angry, grief-stricken haze; he loves Jesus, and he is tormented by the knowledge that Jesus seems not to understand his actions. Later he returns from the dead, or from the future, to question Jesus about his actions—and here he sings "Superstar." The story ends with the crucifixion; there is no resurrection in the score, although it can be implied to various degrees through staging.

This was the humanizing story that Lloyd Webber and Rice set out to dramatize. The result is a largely character-driven show, one which spends its time examining the thoughts and actions of its players and sketches events only in a general way. As Joseph Swain points out, because the story is familiar, there is plenty of time for such close character development.[30] As Lloyd Webber put it,

What we are trying to do is bring Christ home to people; to make Him more real, and bring Him down from the stained glass windows. . . . In the opera He's fallible, human, never sure of himself, whether or not He is God. He decides that He must die to attract more attention to His movement, which has gone as far as it can.[31]

This is actually only part of what happens in the show; in fact, there is plenty of evidence to suggest that the decision to die is at least partly out of Jesus' hands, left to fate, to Judas, to God. At times Jesus does appear to be more than a regular man—he sees the future, he heals the sick—but he is always self-doubting, confused, and struggling, just as Judas is. Rice explains that Jesus' human suffering is the heart of the show, that "it is Jesus as a man facing death who is the protagonist in *Superstar*. He is greater because, whether God or not, he had human failings and fears, and these must have dominated his final days on earth."[32]

These questions, these human experiences, were what fascinated Rice (the primary book writer and the source of the ideas for all three Lloyd Webber/Rice musicals) and Lloyd Webber. Jesus, Judas, Mary Magdalene, and Pilate were all multi-dimensional, fallible, interesting characters to them. Some of the relationships in the show remain ambiguous, unless they are staged in a particularly clear way. One especially tricky topic is Jesus and Mary. They are clearly close, but it is uncertain whether they have a sexual relationship. Almost every audience member and critic assumes so because they are affectionate with one another, they touch each other, and she declares—to us, not to him—that she loves him, though she does not know *how* to love him. Her profession as a prostitute, as Judas snidely points out, inclines everyone to assume the obvious. Rice, in an odd display of conservatism and somewhat in conflict with his own lyrics, maintained throughout that "only a moron or a gorilla could say that Christ and Mary had an affair."[33] Her love is mental, not physical, he insisted; she is amazed and confused by him. She can of course feel this and still be engaging in a physical relationship, as implied by various productions and the movie. It would in fact be rather difficult to imply the opposite, given the personal moments between them that are built into the work.

All these elements of the story were falling into place as Lloyd Webber and Rice wrote the opera from late 1969 to March 1970. Rice used the Bible as his source for organizing the events, but he relied more on the book *The Life of Christ* by Bishop Fulton J. Sheen for the details of the Gospels.[34] He then proceeded to dismiss or alter many of those details, creating characters and events of his own.

The story in place, the team wrote the rock opera with relative ease. Rice's modern, occasionally casual lyrics suited Lloyd Webber's music, mostly rock and pop, occasionally humorous in style. When they emerged from seclusion they had a major work for eighty-five-piece orchestra, seven rock musicians including one playing Moog synthesizer, a church organ, eleven principal singers, sixteen chorus singers, and three backup choirs.[35] Murray Head was retained to sing Judas, and Ian Gillan of the British rock group Deep Purple was cast as Jesus. There were also two members of the cast who would stay with the show through every 1970s incarnation: Yvonne Elliman, a seventeen-year-old club singer discovered by Lloyd Webber, became Mary Magdalene; and Barry Dennen, an experienced American musical theater actor working at the time in London, portrayed Pilate.[36]

The album was slowly, meticulously recorded at great expense from March to July of 1970; its excellent quality stands up today. Decca boldly staged the U.S. premiere in a church, inviting the press to hear it on 27 October 1970. Now officially called *Jesus Christ Superstar,* the London release had caused little stir, but that was hardly the case in the United States: the album was a smash hit. After the successful launching and a great deal of early buzz, Decca went on to promote the album with gusto. A two-page advertisement in *Record World* emphasized the youthful, modernized version of the story: "Andrew Lloyd Webber and Tim Rice have made the most awesome seven days in the history of man meaningful to our time." And, just to make sure to avoid controversy once again, they added that the creators "have received the endorsement of England's and America's leading clergymen." This show, Decca proclaimed, would do no less than bridge "the musical—and scriptural—generation gap."[37] The reviews came in, and they were almost all positive. By February 1971, the hype and the raves made the album number one on the *Billboard* chart. It hovered in the *Billboard* top five for months, reached the top spot again in May, lingered in the top ten until September, and only in May 1972 slipped from the top one hundred albums.

William Bender of *Time* magazine gave the album a rave, considering it in a league with Bach's passions "in ambition and scope if not in piety or musical exaltation."[38] This passion play was full of youth and would surely intrigue "the agnostic young" with its bold take on the story. Bender found Lloyd Webber's music clever and varied, and also mentioned a quality which would appear in much of Lloyd Webber's music henceforth: pastiche. Eventually, Lloyd Webber's use of recognizable musical styles, set up against one another over the course of a show—a technique as old as music theater, but one to which Lloyd Webber is particularly partial—would become an object of criticism. But here, in what Bender felt could have been a rather monotonous, repetitive rock score, Lloyd Webber's mixing in of other elements made for a refreshing and even daring technique. Bender mentioned Prokofiev, Latin music, ragtime, Puccini, gospel, the

Beatles, Orff, and Stravinsky, among others, and asserted that all these influences combine with great effectiveness. "*Tommy*," Bender wrote, "was the first, flawed suggestion that rock could deal with a major subject on a broad symphonic or operatic scale. *Superstar* offers the first real proof."[39] Hubert Saal of *Newsweek* agreed that the album was spiritual in a human, fresh way, and praised Rice and Lloyd Webber lavishly. Again the musical stylistic borrowing came in for high praise, as did another Lloyd Webber trait, melodic beauty: "Though rock is the opera's dominant beat, it is still fairer to call the work a pop opera. Webber is quick to use all kinds of musical forms including rhythm-and-blues, old-fashioned torch songs, simple ballads, as well as anthems and hymns, often changing speed and course in mid-song in response to the dramatic demands of the libretto. His boundless store of melody is spread around impartially."[40]

Alan Rich, lively arts critic from *New York* magazine, was unimpressed. The rock music was not real rock, but pop, which would be fine if it were not filled with the "trickery" of mixed styles and unusual meters, tied to overly slangy lyrics.[41] This review was one of the very few to pan the album completely, and several more moderate voices emerged. Carl LaFong of *Record World* knew a landmark had been created; *Superstar* "could conceivably even be the greatest-selling album of all time. It will eventually be promoted from many pulpits; it is bound to provoke concern and controversy; and it will probably be staged hundreds of times." Despite this largely accurate prediction, though, LaFong found Jesus' emotions a bit high for a man of peace, and thought the work more a novelty than a true trend.[42] He would only be partly right: while rock operas in the strictest sense were few, the changes that the show would lead to as a staged musical would be far-reaching and irrevocable.

Many of the album reviews saw parallels with contemporary politics, social issues, and modern superstardom. Rice made contradictory comments about whether he intended such parallels, but it certainly was not his primary goal.[43] Nevertheless, the protagonist struck many as a social crusader unable to survive the passage from local leader to overly famous hero, a figure exemplified in contemporary times by Martin Luther King. "The character called Jesus," wrote one commentator, "is, to those of us who were involved in the civil rights and antiwar struggles, every sacrificing man of God we ever followed, from Martin Luther King to Dan and Phil Berrigan. Each started out teaching truths, basic and important truths. Each spoke of peace and equality for all men, of feeding the poor, housing the homeless, curing the sick. Each became the center of a cult. Centers of cults tend to fail, for no one man can bear the responsibility for all mankind."[44] Others saw parallels with temperamental rock singers whining about being too famous, too loved. With this kind of superstar at the center, another writer demonstrates, the other characters fall into place: "Mary Magdalene as his chief groupie, Judas as conniving manager, the Apostles his turned-on band, the priests the blind guardians of rigid law and order, Pilate a kind of smooth university president, Herod, governor of the state."[45]

Both the music and lyrics fit this interpretation. Rock music had always been the music of rebellion, the way to fight the establishment, to shock and change and stimulate. And the show's lyrics, while generally conversational and natural-sounding in tone, are at times quite riddled with slang that screams "1970s." It was only natural to see the parallels.

En route to Broadway

If you knew the path we're riding, you'd understand it less than I.

Jesus in *Jesus Christ Superstar*

The massive success of the album made *Superstar*'s trip to Broadway a sure thing; it also made it very big business. Into the picture came Robert Stigwood, whose name would become linked to large Broadway ventures, and who at this point was already a reasonably successful producer. Lloyd Webber and Rice, having no idea how to take a show to Broadway, needed someone bold and experienced. To make matters more complicated, unauthorized productions of the work as a staged show abounded. Stigwood was more than prepared to take on the large tasks. He became their producer and agent, not by unseating the one they already had in England, but by buying that company outright and incorporating it into his own. After this purchase his moves continued to be bold, generating great profits for everyone as well as a few artistic disasters.

Stigwood's first job was to put a stop to the unauthorized performances being mounted by groups all over the country. There was much confusion about rights: first, it was unclear whether the album represented a full organic musical or was simply a collection of songs, and different laws applied to each; and second, Lloyd Webber and Rice had, generously but naïvely, allowed churches to perform the songs if no fee was charged. Groups took advantage of these gray areas, cutting one song to avoid claims that they were doing the whole work and asking only for donations and raking in a fortune. Eventually almost all these productions were shut down through Stigwood's battles in the courts, and he quickly made it clear that there was only one official production so far: the tour he launched in July 1971.

Both the tour and the eventual Broadway show were cast more or less simultaneously, resulting in a tour that was treated like out-of-town tryouts, with the same cast as that which would appear on Broadway, though with a different director. Rice and Lloyd Webber wanted to keep Elliman as Mary and Dennen as Pilate, which was not a problem because, as Americans, they gave Actors' Equity no reason to bar them.[46] Stigwood, in his first unsuccessful foray into the artistic side of the enterprise, cast Jeff Fenholt as Jesus; as it turned out, Fenholt was not well received.[47] Eric Mercury played Judas on tour, but Ben Vereen, only twenty-three but already seasoned, was to take over on Broadway. After the tour was launched, the team had two months to get it to Broadway. Meanwhile, several other tours were launched, in the United States and abroad, all with great success (about $3.5 million worth before New York's opening night), and the Broadway opening had the largest advance sale to date, over one million dollars. The album continued to sell well, reaching about 2.5 million sold by the time the show hit Broadway.

Tom O'Horgan: "I like to fill the stage with lots of things to look at"

Stigwood's second disastrous foray into the artistic side of things, after the unfortunate casting of Fenholt as Jesus, was his choosing Tom O'Horgan to direct the Broadway production. A performer and director for several decades, O'Horgan had made a name for himself with avant-garde off-Broadway productions. His shows often featured sets which changed shape and purpose, large onstage metamorphoses of scenery and lighting. His direction of actors was considered just as bold, but lacking subtlety or depth. "O'Horgan is the great exteriorizer," one critic proclaimed.[48] His work had recently gained great attention and success, and when *Superstar* opened, he had two shows already running on Broadway, *Lenny* (about Lenny Bruce) and *Hair.*

O'Horgan was comfortable among the hippies of *Hair,* as he led something of the bohemian lifestyle himself, and the sensibilities of it fit nicely with his directorial technique. Rehearsals were called "group encounters"[49] and featured as much discussing, touching, improvising, and sharing as they did blocking and practicing. He brought these avant-garde ideas to Broadway, which in effect ended the avant-garde movement by making it mainstream. "There just isn't any point going into some loft now," he said upon arriving on Broadway, "and putting on some crazy play. We did all that when you couldn't do crazy things anywhere else. I'm probably more outrageous on Broadway than I ever was downtown."[50]

Crazy and outrageous were indeed the words for his production of *Superstar,* but while his style worked in his other productions, problems of blending his vision with the score of *Superstar* arose immediately. It would be O'Horgan's contribution to the show above anyone else's, including Lloyd Webber and Rice's, that the critics would discuss and deride.[51]

O'Horgan made his mark from the beginning by demanding that he have "total creative control over all aspects of the production, including casting, sets, lighting, and costumes." Also, the production would carry the credit "conceived for the stage and directed by Tom O'Horgan" in letters at least as big as the names of Lloyd Webber and Rice.[52] His vision involved huge moving sets, transforming costumes, and large symbolic props. He employed these elements to serve the "totally spiritual experience" he hoped the show would be.[53] His group encounters, in an effort to get the cast in touch with this spirituality, involved activities such as blindfolding Fenholt and having the cast lick honey off his body.[54]

Eventually the massive moving sets were built, and before opening day most of them worked. The sound system was the final problem: microphones were required since no singer could compete with the electric guitars and other rock instruments in the pit, instruments which were by definition amplified. Most Broadway shows had just a few mikes or none at all, so while this was by no means the first show to boost sound, it was among the first to boost it to rock concert levels. This was also the first show that was under some obligation to re-create the experience of a well-produced and popular album. This exigency led to the use of a term that was prominent in pop music but new to theater— "concept album"—and also to some very high expectations. The sound not only had to be clear and balanced, but actually sound like a record. Body mikes kept picking up the noise of police and taxi radios, forcing a last-minute switch to hand mikes that led O'Horgan to cancel the first two previews on 27 and 28 September 1971.[55]

Protests: "Jesus Christ ~~Superstar~~ Lamb of God"

On the day the show opened, protest began. Outside the theater a group of rather disorganized picketers held signs that crossed out the "Superstar" of the show's title and replaced it with phrases affirming Jesus' divinity, such as "Lamb of God." Only one group mounted a calculated, organized protest. The American Jewish Committee, with backing from the Anti-Defamation League of B'nai B'rith, released a statement which spelled out their concerns: the show "unambiguously lays the primary responsibility for Jesus' suffering and crucifixion to the Jewish priesthood. The priests are portrayed as hideously inhuman and satanically evil: contemptuous, callous and bloodthirsty."[56] The AJC made it clear that censorship was not their goal, nor was any implication of antisemitism, but they felt obligated to speak out against a show that could have damaging effects on America's freethinking and impressionable youth. The musical "is at the center of the creation of a set of cultural images in the counterculture of America. It is the creation of a religious counterculture."[57] With Caiaphas and Annas as unmistakable villains, the AJC felt that both the New Testament and more modern interpretations of Jews' role in the event had been dismissed in favor of a view similar to centuries-old passion plays.

The protest garnered much attention in the press but did not rally any other Jewish groups, nor did it result in any changes to the show. The album, while generating protests by various individuals from the time of its release, had garnered no negative reaction from anyone in the Jewish community, and Israel was currently hosting a very successful touring company.[58] Stigwood, for his part, never met with the protest leaders and released a statement saying that the show was "an affirmation of humanity. It is not a literal representation of the passion of Christ as revealed by the New Testament. It views, in contemporary style, the timelessness of a legend, a myth, and the confrontations of a reformer and the Establishment which continually recur in the history of man. No man is guilty—not even Judas—no man is innocent."[59] While conveniently steering the issue away from the entirely guilty Caiaphas and Annas to the more complex Judas, the statement also encouraged the increasingly popular interpretation that the show was about any charismatic social leader, including those of modern times.

Lloyd Webber concurred: "The priests represent the establishment. They're establishment people, not Jewish people." Rice pointed out that every character in the show except Pilate is Jewish, including Jesus: "There are some good Jews and some bad Jews."[60] Almost all critics and commentators saw this point, and did not quibble with the content from a sectarian point of view. "The high priests," *Time* magazine argued, disagreeing with protestors, "are not so much Jews as caricatures of all officials whose job and ambition is to suppress disorder."[61]

Jews were by no means the only group with a complaint; during the opening night protest, most major American religions were represented. The Catholic protesters were offended by the show's implication that Jesus was not godly. Some Protestants disapproved of Jesus' more than platonic relationship with Mary Magdalene. Baptists and Mormons listed various other problems. And a group of African Americans was offended that Judas, the bad guy (or one of the bad guys, at least), was portrayed by a black man.[62] But each group of protesters represented only a small minority of its larger social group, most members of which throughout the country were grateful to *Superstar* for opening up new discussions, bringing any sort of attention to religion at all, helping to kindle an interest in such issues among young people. The smallish group of picketers outside the theater on opening night was more an amusement to theatergoers than anything else.[63]

The Score's Techniques and Styles

Though from early in Lloyd Webber's career, the score of *Jesus Christ Superstar* employs techniques and styles that have remained in the composer's works ever since. On the surface, with its hard rock edge, wailing electric guitars, and shrieking tenors, *Superstar* sounds quite different from his other shows. His next production, *Evita,* would include more pop-oriented and Broadway-derived orchestrations, voices, and styles, although a rock element remained. But beneath the seemingly unique sound world of *Superstar* lay a number of structural and stylistic devices that both dramatized and unified the songs, devices that would become hallmarks of Lloyd Webber's style and of the megamusical in general.

Three main musical characteristics of *Superstar* would become defining traits of the megamusical. First, the recurrence of musical material in different guises over the course of the show, though not new to music theater or even to Broadway musicals, is manifested in three somewhat idiosyncratic ways. First, short motifs or themes used as symbols, which carry emotional or character-related meaning, appear at key moments; second, sung melodies return in new contexts with new lyrics, sometimes related to the original lyrics and sometimes completely different; and third—and most unexpectedly—songs receive brief previews before being sung in their full forms. Each of these techniques brings added emotion and layers of meaning to the story and characters.

For example, a short motif that symbolizes an emotion or represents a character's struggle adds depth to the moment in which it appears, especially if the association between the motif and the dramatic moment is not obvious. Also, the recurrence of melodies serves to draw large connections across the story. Why might two characters share the same melody, for example, especially if their situations seem unrelated? Or why might a character offer a short excerpt from a song he will not sing for some time? These techniques set up expectations and associations among situations and characters that help to tie the entire show together as a dramatic whole.

The second musical technique that pervades *Superstar* involves long scenes made up of smaller sections of musical material; lengthy scenes such as "Judas's Death" and "The Last Supper" feel like one section of music and one dramatic event, but they are built from a series of linked set numbers, recitative-like passages, orchestral transitions, and other short items. Often, this technique and the first technique go hand in hand: some of the smaller sections of a larger scene are occurrences of musical material pulled from elsewhere in the show. Indeed, it is often impossible to separate the two techniques—recurring musical material and scenes made up of short sections—because they so smoothly coexist. The second technique creates powerfully dramatic passages that can dwell on one scene or set of characters without becoming musically dull. Such long, uninterrupted sections of dramatic material—a staple in certain operatic traditions like the Italian Romantic operas of Verdi—would become a defining characteristic of the megamusical in the 1980s, especially in Lloyd Webber's *The Phantom of the Opera* and Schönberg and Boublil's *Les Misérables.*

Third, Lloyd Webber employed a technique perhaps more common to musical theater than the first two, but in a way that would help define the megamusical nonetheless. Each major character is defined by his or her own musical style or genre, which helps to give that character a memorable personality with his or her own personal musical signature. King Herod is perhaps the most obvious example, but Mary and Jesus each have a personal sound, as do the priests. This technique allows Lloyd Webber not only to make each character distinctive, with a personal vocal style and musical genre, but also to use a variety of musical genres other than rock. In the case of the priests, this third musical technique combines with the first, because the priests usually reuse not only their distinctive sound but their melodies as well. A few examples of each of these three musical features, with adequate concessions made for the frequent overlap of categories, demonstrate how each feature works.

RECURRING MUSICAL MATERIAL

Perhaps the most obvious of these structural devices involves recurring music. The first form this takes is moveable motifs or short themes which arise in different, usually dramatically linked, contexts. The most prominent recurring motif by far is the guitar riff that underpins the overture, Judas's "Heaven on Their Minds," and important parts of "Trial Before Pilate" and "Judas's Death." It makes its first appearance partway through the overture. The overture, as mentioned, consists of music that is sung later. In fact, almost all the musical events in the overture occur in "Trial Before Pilate," just as presented here. The guitar ostinato that accompanies the thirty-nine lashes Jesus receives is played in the overture twenty-seven times (for no obvious reason) under an increasingly wild guitar solo and, eventually, a counterpoint line in the strings. The riff lowers the second degree of its minor key, a device, along with a flattened seventh in major keys, that Lloyd Webber uses regularly.

The guitar riff, abandoned toward the end of the overture, returns almost immediately to become the basis for the first song, "Heaven on Their Minds." This links the riff not only with Jesus and Pilate, as will be seen in the second act, but with Judas; this is almost too many associations to serve any sort of leitmotif function other than representing a general feeling of anguish, pain, and torment both physical and psychological. Also, its driving beat lends it an air of aggression and strength, a certain forward-rushing, out-of-control feel. This seems fitting for Judas's sense of unrest and pained stress, already evident in the opening number, "Heaven on Their Minds" (see ex. 1.1).

The guitar riff, with its tension and drive, becomes particularly appropriate when it arises in two highly charged moments of drama. First, the riff pursues Judas to his suicide, as part of the climax of "Judas's Death." The riff also accompanies the thirty-nine lashes Pilate inflicts on Jesus during "Trial Before Pilate"; in that instance, the riff is played exactly thirty-nine times, a fact made painfully clear as Pilate counts the lashes Jesus receives, one for each repetition of the ostinato.

Example 1.1. "Heaven on Their Minds"

In its final moments, the overture presents another recurring theme. This theme strays from the path it eventually takes in "Trial Before Pilate" only at the end, where it features the bitonal juxtaposition of two elements. Off-stage chorus voices—an unusual feature for an overture—clash with the ironic major chords that taunt Judas at several key moments. These major chords make up another motif. At the end of the overture the chords appear in the orchestra, but later the chorus intones them, in the final moment of act 1 after Judas has betrayed Jesus to the priests (see ex. 1.2). Similarly, they chant "Poor old Judas, so long Judas" just after Judas hangs himself. The purity and simplicity of the major chords, especially when surrounded by the context of anguished minor keys that dominate the score, give this recurring phrase an eerie, disturbing feel. Rice's somewhat flippant, dismissive lyrics add to the uncomfortable effect. The chords reappear once more, at the end of the show, played by the orchestra alone; as they did at the end of the overture, the chords bring a closure, albeit a bitonal, unsettled one, to the moment (and, in this case, to the entire show). The chords, then, are indelibly linked to Judas, but also to moments that generally feel conflicted and unresolved.

A third recurring short musical motif is also, like the first two, presented in the overture, although in an incomplete form. It is presented complete in its original home, the song "Superstar," in which the chorus and the "soul" girls ask the key questions of the show (see ex. 1.3). Having already had a successful life as a single, "Superstar" was well known to the audience. Its catchy refrain becomes a particularly recognizable motif in other contexts, even when presented quite differently. In fact, the melody of this refrain appears in two locations, played majestically by the full orchestra. Its appearance toward the end of the overture, after the guitar riff section but before the final major chords, cuts off in mid-phrase (as if singing, "Jesus Christ, Jesus Christ, who are you, what—"). The second time the orchestra states the line, it plays through the phrase twice in full, then immediately launches into the funky rhythm of "Superstar" itself. It

Example 1.2. "Well done Judas" chords

Example 1.3. "Superstar" chorus

provides a segue, then, from the final fate-sealing moments of "Trial Before Pilate" to Judas's reappearance from the beyond.

The second subcategory of recurring music involves songs that reappear with different lyrics. Sometimes the return happens quite soon after the original song, and the effect is obvious, but at other times the association of the two statements are less clearly linked. One particular reuse of a melody with new words carries quite a clear meaning. The scene "The Temple" opens with the orchestra, then the chorus, on a two-phrase melody that accompanies the buying and selling of secular, even sinful goods and services (see ex. 1.4). This melody is set to a rollicking 7/4 rhythm built on two chords, and it repeats many times as the selling and calling and general noise gradually increase.

Jesus interrupts them. "My temple should be a house of prayer," he shrieks, touching on the uppermost reaches of the rock tenor range. "But you have made it a den of thieves. Get out!" He then sings a few short, soft phrases that later become part of his solo "Gethsemane." The 7/4 chorus then rejoins him in a new guise. Vendors and traders have become lepers and beggars. Singing the

Example 1.4. Vocal parts from the beginning and end of "The Temple"

same two phrases from the beginning of the temple scene, but slower and to little accompaniment, they gradually surround Jesus and list their woes. (Both the vendors' lyrics and the beggars' lyrics can be found in ex. 1.4.) The tempo gradually pushes faster, to a near frantic pace, and the volume increases, as the chorus begins to list their ailments as a group while strange voices slide and wail in the background. The 7/4 now seems frantic, aggressive, allowing no room to breathe on the "missing" eighth beat of an expected common (or 8/4) time. Phrases cascade one after another. Jesus, surrounded, smothered, angry, and afraid, cannot reach them all. "There's too many of you," he cries. "Don't push me! . . . There's too little of me. . . . Heal yourselves!" This last is screamed, suddenly silencing the mass of noise.

These two occurrences of the same music with different lyrics form bookends to the scene contained under the umbrella title "The Temple." The effect is bold—the aggressive, sinful vendors and consumers are linked to the aggressive, needy lepers in a way that makes both groups, drawn from the same population of those he attempts to help, seem greedy and unthinking. Both groups anger and disappoint Jesus, pushing him further toward disillusionment.

A second example of a number returning with different words first appears in "Everything's Alright," the tense trio for Judas, Jesus, and Mary that later returns as a section of "The Last Supper." A characteristically catchy Lloyd Webber melody is arranged into clear but varied verses in a loose AB'A'B"A" form, and the conflicts among Mary, Jesus, and Judas are spelled out. The 5/4 meter feels smooth and inevitable. Joseph Swain, partial to this number, says the meter erases "the strong sense of regular strong beats and divisible rhythmic groupings [and] gives the melody an almost chant-like flow."[64] Mary sings a lilting E major melody with bluesy touches, backed softly by the women in the area. Judas quickly invades the relaxed mood, forcefully singing his complaints. His is a minor and upward-driven variation of her melody, with faster harmonic motion and more push than lilt to it. His text, in a subtle but telling move, shifts almost imperceptibly from the ostensible object of his anger (Mary) to the real one (Jesus) (exs. 1.5a, 1.5b). Swain writes that the increased harmonic activity in the accompaniment and stronger rhythmic accents help characterize the difference between Judas's approach and Mary's to similar melodies.[65] A huge orchestral climax meets Judas at the end of his tirade. Mary tries to restore calm by repeating her verse, but Jesus cannot resist the urge to respond to Judas's accusations. Like Judas's verse, Jesus' turns from the ostensible topic of conversation, the plight of the poor, to the underlying problems which, from Jesus' point of view, are Judas's current state of bitter inertia and his own limited time on earth.

Example 1.5a. Mary's verse in "Everything's Alright"

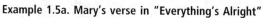

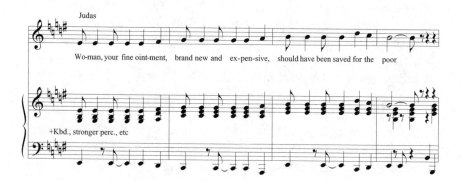

Example 1.5b. Judas's verse in "Everything's Alright"

He seems already to know, and here mentions almost in passing, that he will be gone soon. Jesus' verse matches up to Judas's exactly, until he reaches the final line and begins to wail freely over the accompaniment.

> *Jesus:* Surely you're not saying we have the resources
> To save the poor from their lot.
> There will be poor always, pathetically struggling,
> Look at the good things you've got.
> Think while you still have me, move while you still see me,
> You'll be lost, and you'll be so sorry when I'm gone!

Both men's verses grow in intensity and rise in pitch, and both end with hard-rock wails of emotion, demonstrating the frustration they feel with one another. Rational thought once again degenerates into crying and yelling by the end of Jesus' verse. The orchestra once again builds to a climax, and Mary, for the third time, asserts her presence and sings her version of the melody. This time she succeeds in controlling the conversation somewhat; Judas drifts away, and Jesus remains with Mary.

An extremely long fadeout follows; Mary repeats, many times, her minor-tinged line "close your eyes, close your eyes and relax," and the chorus women do similarly. The men of the crowd, as is their wont, become swept up in the fun of singing and lose the message; they repeat "everything's alright, yes" with increasing volume and joy, and the mood, while happy on the surface, is energized also with unsettled tension lingering in Judas's wake.[66]

This dialogue between Jesus and Judas is the most overt confrontation of the entire first act, and its driving, rising line displays their anguish with great effectiveness. Lloyd Webber capitalizes on the association of this music with confrontation during "The Last Supper," at the beginning of act 2. As we shall see, "The Last Supper" is formed out of sections of musical material; one of these sections is a recurrence of Jesus and Judas's verses of "Everything's Alright." In their second heated confrontation, it seems quite fitting that they revisit the music through which they argued earlier. The verse is less tightly structured here than before; it gets interrupted and extended, as it follows the somewhat erratic flow of Jesus' thoughts and actions. First, he launches into the melody when he turns on his apostles, singing the first five of six lines before the apostles interrupt him.

> I must be mad thinking I'll be remembered,
> Yes, I must be out of my head.
> Look at your blank faces, my name will mean nothing
> Ten minutes after I'm dead.
> One of you denies me, one of you betrays me

Ignoring the apostles' protests, Jesus picks up his vocal line in the middle of the verse, rounding first on Peter (who will deny him), then Judas (who will betray him). At this point, the music of "Everything's Alright" becomes stuck in a loop, a circular confrontation that becomes suspended, unable to be resolved. The structure of the original verse is lost, and the orchestra cycles through the three chords of the verse many times, reflecting the men's inability to reach an agreement. With no Mary to intercede, Jesus goads Judas into committing the betrayal they both know is coming, and Judas spits hostile words back (ex. 1.6).

Finally reaching the orchestral climax which arrived at the end of the men's verses in "Everything's Alright," this "Last Supper" version moves on to a new musical idea rather than back to Mary's relaxing major-key version of the verse. The conflict in "The Last Supper" is longer, less tidy, and far angrier than the conflict in "Everything's Alright." The balance, the intermediary forces, and the fairly rational tone of discussion are lost now, and these two men have nothing else to say to each other for the rest of Judas's natural life. Clearly Jesus knows, even understands, Judas's actions, but he resents them nonetheless, and Judas cannot seem to explain to Jesus why he feels he must betray him. In "Heaven on Their Minds," Judas sang, "My admiration for you hasn't died." Now, he spits at Jesus, "To think I admired you, for now I despise you!" The use of their earlier music of confrontation, which now explodes thanks to the out-of-control nature of their argument, makes this a particularly powerful recurrence of the same music. One can also read the reuse of "Everything's Alright" ironically: the

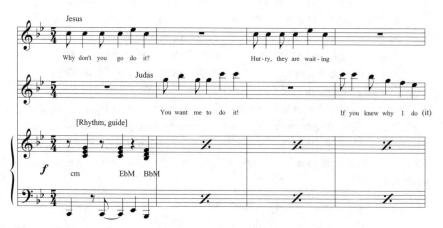

The score notes that in this section, "the interpretation must be very free" in the voices and the orchestra

Example 1.6. Jesus and Judas in "The Last Supper"

music that was once associated with at least a semblance of peace and civility now represents its complete loss.

A third example of a melody returning in a context which relates to its original dramatic use actually alters the lyrics only slightly. Instead of having characters revisit their earlier melody with new words, this example reassigns the melody to a new character, with subtle changes in the lyrics. The original is Mary's gentle solo, "I Don't Know How to Love Him." She sings her big number after rescuing Jesus from the demanding hands of the beggars and lepers and putting him to bed.[67] Set in a simple country-inflected ballad style, the song begins with folk-like guitar accompaniment and builds gradually. Like Judas, Mary best expresses her feelings for Jesus when he is not there; like Pilate, Mary is given this one moment of reflection alone. Her second verse:

I don't know how to take this
I don't see why he moves me
He's a man, he's just a man
And I've had so many men before
In very many ways
He's just one more.

As Rice adamantly asserted, Mary makes it clear that Jesus has not said he loves her, but it is also clear that the two have a relationship already. The risk, for her, is not in sleeping with him, but in telling him how she feels about him. She wonders how this strange, powerful man would react, and whether it would do her any good to tell him. Her song clearly stands apart from the material before and after it as a set piece, and it has enjoyed a successful career as a pop single. The lyrics are quite specific to Mary's dilemma, and the music suits her gentle nature (as already heard in "Everything's Alright").

Her struggle to love Jesus nevertheless finds a parallel with Judas's struggle much later. In one section of "Judas's Death," the anguished man shifts from an angry tirade into a quieter mood and reprises Mary's "I Don't Know How to Love Him," which with slightly altered words and melody fits Judas's situation perfectly. Swain calls this "the most important reprise of the opera,"[68] by which we can assume he also includes all the revisited melodies with new words. All along, Judas has not understood the powerful hold that this more-than-a-man has had on him. He chokes out a verse and the bridge before a sob overcomes him and the tune is lost. His verse fits Mary's melody, and the lyrics make strong reference to hers: "He's a man, he's just a man / He is not a king, he is just the same / As anyone I know / He scares me so." Like Mary, Judas loves Jesus but has never understood how to be close to him, or why he feels so strongly about him.

Interestingly, *Superstar* contains one example of a recurring melody that carries with it no apparent dramatic motivation at all. Early in the first act, Judas comes on the scene of Jesus and his followers and directs his hostility, already voiced to the audience in "Heaven on Their Minds," directly at its target, Jesus. But instead of criticizing the movement, he focuses on Mary, surely the least of the problems at hand. This is "Strange Thing Mystifying." (Note that the second part of his brief song, beginning with "It's not that I object to her profession," makes use of Lloyd Webber's fondness for a flat seventh degree.) This music returns in the seemingly unrelated context of "Peter's Denial." Confronted by several people about the recently arrested Jesus, Peter (just as Jesus predicted) claims he never met the man, as Mary looks on. He uses the same melody, accompaniment, tempo, and even mood. There is no clear reason for the reuse of this melody, no obvious dramatic link. It actually functions better in the second context, where its rather cheerful 1950s stroll-feeling seems appropriate for Peter's meeting with three curious strangers. One can nevertheless speculate about some dramatic justifications. It is plausible that the fairly light, pleasant feel of the song is an attempt on the part of its singers to cover up teeming emotions beneath the surface. In Judas's case, his anger and frustration toward Jesus have just begun to find a voice, but so far he remains fairly civil; in Peter's case, he makes a noble effort to appear casual and ignorant in the face of what could be life-threatening accusations. Perhaps both men employ a smooth, upbeat song to hide their inner turmoil.

The third and final subcategory of recurring music that Lloyd Webber employs would become one of the most notable elements of his most famous megamusical, *Cats.* This technique involves presenting a short portion of a song before the song is sung in full, acting like a preview of a big number yet to come. The well-known and much-maligned "Memory" from *Cats* receives several such previews that act like teasers to build anticipation for the show-stopping song. In *Superstar,* two songs receive previews; neither is quite so bold or obvious as for "Memory," but both help to foreshadow songs and dramatic situations that lie ahead.

The first instance of a previewed song appears in the middle of the scene "The Temple." In between Jesus' confrontation of the merchants and his struggle with the lepers discussed above, he has that quiet moment to voice his disenchantment with his calling as the leader of these unrepentant people; it is the opening of his later solo, "Gethsemane." It will also be the music for the instrumental closing of the whole show, in "John Nineteen Forty-One." In "The Temple," he sings:

My time is almost through,
Little left to do
After all I've tried for three years,
Seems like thirty, seems like thirty.

By the time Jesus reflects on his time on earth again, in "Gethsemane," the three years will seem like ninety rather than thirty. Other than this subtle but very telling change of lyric, the passage is unchanged in its second occurrence. Here at its first occurrence, it hints at Jesus' growing disillusionment so that when the moment of pause is interrupted by the greedy lepers, we get the sense that Jesus will return to these musings.

The second preview of a later song occurs in "The Last Supper," when Judas presents the beginning of "Superstar." This moment arises toward the end of the long confrontation between Judas and Jesus, just before a resigned Judas leaves the garden of Gethsemane and the apostles begin to drift off to sleep. In a slow and anguished manner, Judas cries out the first three lines of a six-line verse, before breaking off into a wail of anguish: "Every time I look at you I don't understand / Why you let the things you did get so out of hand. / You'd have managed better if you'd had it planned—." Later, in its complete form, the verse is funky and fast-paced. Judas, no longer tortured by his earthly concerns, now sings the lines in a raucous, almost flippant manner, and has no trouble rattling off the wordy lyrics about choosing "such a backward time and such a strange land."

The preview of "Superstar" thus demonstrates that Judas's most pressing questions, about why Jesus did what he did, remain with him both before and after his death. The difference is one of attitude: when Judas is still on earth, tortured by the choices he has to make and unable to understand his friend's actions, he can only choke out the first few lines of his thought process. Later, freed by death from his emotions, he returns and asks his questions in a bold, almost condescending way, with support from a chorus of funky angels. (See appendix A for a listing of recurring musical material.)

LONG SCENES MADE FROM SMALLER SECTIONS OF MUSICAL MATERIAL
We have already seen indications of the technique of building scenes from smaller units of material in the examples above, since the smaller sections that become part of a long scene sometimes come from elsewhere in the score. Breakdowns of four of these long scenes will help demonstrate what other sorts of smaller items make up their structures, and how the items are held together.

In "The Last Supper," one of the most complex and lengthy collections of ideas, new material is mixed with old melodies (but with new words), and the sections range in length from brief transitional material to quasi-set pieces. The sequence of events runs as follows:

1. Apostles' refrain
2. Jesus' slow solo referring to communion; uses new musical material
3. Jesus' accusations and confrontation with Judas; borrows the music of Jesus and Judas's verses of "Everything's Alright"
4. Apostles' refrain
5. Jesus and Judas continue their argument using new musical material
6. Judas previews "Superstar"
7. Apostles' refrain
8. Jesus' short coda

As the scene opens, the apostles lounge about, musing happily on their coveted roles in a drama they do not understand.

> Always hoped that I'd be an apostle
> Knew that I would make it if I tried
> Then when we retire, we can write the gospels
> So they'll still talk about us when we've died.

This is sung gently, to a folk-like accompaniment, in a blissfully ignorant mood. As usual, Rice has reserved the comic lyrics for appropriately light characters; this is also the only moment in which the Bible is mentioned.

After two verses their idle thoughts fizzle out, and Jesus turns sadly, then angrily, on his dim-witted friends. Included in his thoughts is a cleverly bitter twist on the origin of the wine and bread of communion.

> The end is just a little harder when
> Brought about by friends.
> For all you care, this wine could be my blood
> For all you care, this bread could be my body

After Jesus' death, Rice imagined "the Disciples half-remembering these words and interpreting them, through guilt and confusion, as an instruction to commemorate Jesus through bread and wine."[69] Jesus next launches into the "Everything's Alright" section of the scene, confronting Judas. The argument eventually reaches a climax, but it cannot return to Mary's music as it did in "Everything's Alright"; instead, it returns to the apostles' song. This material therefore takes on the function of a ritornello;[70] another confrontation will follow, then a third statement of the apostles' song.

In this second version of their verse, the apostles sing full-voiced, with the entire orchestra in support. They burst into harmony. It is grandiose and funny, but also somewhat desperate, as if they hope to drown out the sound of the fighting around them with sheer volume. After their requisite two verses and a new section for Judas and Jesus, Judas launches into his preview of "Superstar." The electric guitar finishes the melody for him as he runs off. The apostles drift in for a final, sleepy, drunken statement of their song. The whole sequence has a coda tacked on at the end, as Jesus gazes at his sleeping men and asks, futilely, if none of them will stay awake to wait with him for the next event. "The Last Supper" is a powerful series of musical moments that moves, sometimes smoothly, sometimes in lurching jerks, through the action. Most interesting, it includes sections that both refer back to earlier material ("Everything's Alright") and preview things to come ("Superstar").

"Judas's Death" is structured in a similar manner. Judas has not been seen since Jesus' arrest five numbers previously, and it is clear that in the interim he has panicked about his actions and their consequences. Frantic, Judas begins the number by running to Caiaphas and the priests, just as he did at the beginning of "Damned for All Time," and indeed the same music accompanies him here (in yet another example of a melody revisited). First, a brief look at "Damned for All Time": in three frenetic verses, with one verse inserted for solo saxophone, he spells out the scope of his dilemma (see ex. 1.7 for the end of the first verse, repeated at the end of the other two as well). "Jesus wouldn't mind that I was here with you," Judas asserts desperately—a complete fabrication on his part, a manifestation of his desperate need to convince himself that he is doing the right thing. Interestingly, it is he who first broaches the subject of payment for his information, in the same breath that he asserts he had no choice. Attached to these somewhat contradictory sentiments is a third, the fear that he will be punished. Predictably, but effectively, Judas's vocal line grows increasingly unrestrained, until his final "damned for all time" is stretched, cried. Walsh writes that "philosophically, it is the opera's central number, expressing Judas's terrible existential dilemma."[71]

The music of "Damned for All Time" opens the complex number "Judas's Death," the sections of which can be labeled as follows:

1. Judas confronts priests; music from "Damned for All Time" (as in ex. 1.7)
2. Priests respond with their melody from "This Jesus Must Die"
3. Judas sings verse and bridge of "I Don't Know How to Love Him," with lyrics related to Mary's earlier version
4. Brief ominous orchestral transition

Example 1.7. "Damned for All Time"

5. Guitar riff; Judas refers briefly to "Heaven on Their Minds" (as in ex. 1.1)
6. Chorus sings "So long, Judas" chords (as in ex. 1.2)

When Judas reuses the music of "Damned for All Time" at the beginning of "Judas's Death," he rails at the priests for their treatment of Jesus, which proves to be a defense against his own guilt for turning him in:

> My God! I saw him! He looked three-quarters dead!
> And he was so bad, I had to turn my head.

You beat him so hard that he was bent and lame
And I know who everybody's going to blame.
I don't believe he knows I acted for our good
I'd save him all this suffering if I could.

The priests respond to Judas's outburst with insincere words of comfort set to their trademark music from "This Jesus Must Die." Caiaphas tries to convince Judas that he has in fact saved Israel; he says, with mock jocularity, "You'll be remembered forever for this." The next section is Judas's version of "I Don't Know How To Love Him." A segue is provided by an electric organ playing sustained chords as a soft percussive tap sets the new tempo and a guitar slides ominously around its notes. Soon, the familiar guitar riff begins circling endlessly. Judas, weeping, chokes out a few lines related to "Heaven on Their Minds" with altered lyrics that now address God, or Jesus, or both:

"Judas's Death":	original, in "Heaven on Their Minds":
My mind is in darkness now	My mind is clearer now
God, I am sick, I've been used	At last, all too well, I can see
And you knew all the time	Where we all soon will be

His thoughts are scattered, he is no longer capable of singing much by way of tune; the score suggests rhythms for only some of his phrases, and there are almost no pitches indicated. The form of the vocal line is lost. His phrases float unsteadily over the grinding stability of the ostinato, which grows in volume and force beneath his words. As it continues, Judas begins to sing, over and over, referring to Jesus, "You have murdered me, murdered me, murdered me." Another element is added: the crowd, elsewhere, intones, "So long, Judas. Poor old Judas," in the major chords they used after Judas informed the priests of Jesus' location at the very end of the first act (see ex. 1.2). Here, in their third incarnation, the chords offer a nauseating clash with the persistent ostinato not only because of their entirely independent rhythm, but because of their key, G-flat major, against the orchestra's G minor. By the time the chorus has intoned their slow "So long, Judas. Poor old Judas," five times, the guitar riff has faded out, and Judas has hanged himself. Silence is all there is now between the chorus's last few repetitions of the phrase. It is a frightening, effective moment. "Judas's Death" contains, therefore, a number of the techniques with which Lloyd Webber has become associated: several symbolic motifs representing emotions and character (the guitar riff that stands for tension and pain, and the major chords intoned by the chorus which are tied to Judas), melodies reused with new words (the material from "Damned for All Time" and "This Jesus Must Die"), and both melody and lyrics borrowed from earlier ("I Don't Know How to Love Him").

Each of these sections, along with the new material, is linked together in a chain of events that combine to create the whole number.

A third example of a scene made up of smaller items works in a somewhat different manner. Rather than using a series of unrelated ideas, this scene ties together some very closely related ideas in an interlocking web. It begins with "Simon Zealotes" and includes the two numbers that follow, "Poor Jerusalem" and "Pilate's Dream." The links can be demonstrated as follows:

1. Simon and crowd sing "Simon Zealotes"
2. "Poor Jerusalem" part one: Jesus borrows Simon's melody from "Simon Zealotes"
3. "Poor Jerusalem" part two: Jesus previews the melody of "Pilate's Dream"
4. Pilate sings "Pilate's Dream"

Before they transform themselves into greedy tradespeople and lepers, the crowd, led by the apostle Simon, gleefully sings its love for Jesus. At the top of "Simon Zealotes" the chorus bursts into a funky dance number (marked "quasi 'soul' " in the piano score). Another side of the crowd's personality emerges here: not only do they follow blindly and have fun doing it; they seem to be more interested in proving how hip they are than in learning anything. Simon emerges from the crowd and points out to Jesus the benefits of Jesus' current position. Over fifty thousand people would follow your lead, he says, so why not turn them against Rome? Jesus would gain power and glory; the people would gain a home. As in "Heaven on Their Minds" and "Everything's Alright," this number has a long repeated section at the end in which the basic chord progressions and choral parts are repeated and the solo singer, Simon in this case, freely improvises on his main idea, working himself up into high emotion.

Sadly, softly, Jesus tells Simon and the crowd that none of them knows anything about the power and glory they wish for him; this is "Poor Jerusalem." Jesus turns Simon's music into his own, in an effort to explain his peaceful message, in contrast to Simon's. This new, poignant version of Simon's music about power and glory demonstrates that Simon's raucous, dangerous ideas do not fit Jesus' philosophy at all. "Neither you, Simon, nor the fifty thousand," Jesus sings, "understand what power is, understand what glory is." The music sounds quite different in Jesus' voice. He then sings two verses of melody from a larger number that belongs to Pilate. "Poor Jerusalem," Jesus sings, has no idea what awaits it.

A scene change takes us immediately to Pilate who, singing the same tune Jesus has just previewed, tells us his perspective in "Pilate's Dream." Thus ends a series of thematic threads pulling one number into the next: Simon's verse in the larger choral number becomes the first part of Jesus' solo, and the second part of that solo becomes the main theme of Pilate's, yet all three numbers feel like set pieces. The thematic thread makes especially meaningful sense in the case of Jesus and Pilate, who are linked at this moment by a sense of impending doom, or perhaps by what Walsh calls a "fateful, psychic connection between the two powerful men."[72] Pilate, in a simple song with an acoustic guitar/folk music feel, has dreamed he met a silent, haunted man from Galilee, whose death will be blamed on Pilate. This is our only view of Pilate until the second act, and our only view in the entire show of him alone with his thoughts. Later he will be loud, frustrated, and hostile toward Jesus. But he seems already to know that Jesus will die partly because of him, and he already regrets it. The calm and simplicity of "Pilate's Dream" show Pilate to be a sympathetic figure, knowledge that will help the audience understand his torment in the second act.

Fourth, and finally, "Trial Before Pilate" is the umbrella title for perhaps the most complicated, dissonant collection of musical elements in the show. Although this scene lends itself less to sectional labels than the previous three, the scene can be divided as follows:

1. Tritone drone and Pilate's dissonant melody, borrowed from the opening of the overture (which there featured electric guitar on melody)
2. Pilate confronts Jesus in a rhythmically unpredictable section (as in ex. 1.8)
3. Orchestral ostinato underpins confrontation among Pilate, Jesus, and the crowd (as in ex. 1.9)
4. The thirty-nine lashes, each lash set to one repetition of the guitar riff (as in ex. 1.1)
5. Pilate questions Jesus using music heard at the top of "Pilate and Christ"
6. Orchestral ostinato returns as the crowd goads Pilate (as in ex. 1.9)
7. Pilate disavows responsibility for Jesus, using music that the orchestra presented at the end of the overture
8. Grand version of "Superstar" chorus (the funky version of which is ex. 1.3)

The scene opens with the tritone drone in the bass and the winding dissonant line heard at the top of the overture and at the top of "This Jesus Must Die," here sung by Pilate. (The overture has already laid out most of the music in this scene.) Next, in an unstable 5/8 marked by unexpected percussive orchestral comments, Pilate turns to Jesus, dropping his sarcastic, showy public persona in favor of a more genuine approach that reflects the sympathetic Pilate we met in the first act (see ex. 1.8). A wordy exchange between Pilate and Jesus, then Pilate and the crowd, follows, all held together by an ostinato in the orchestra (see ex. 1.9). The scene loses all sense of tonal center; instead, we get this frantic

Example 1.8. Pilate in "Trial Before Pilate"

Example 1.9. Crowd in "Trial Before Pilate"

undulating figure. Eventually this figure will step up higher several times, changing from single notes to note clusters. The tension mounts each time as the figure is hoisted up another notch. Pilate and Jesus discuss the nature of truth, but are interrupted by the crowd calling for crucifixion. "You'd crucify your king?" Pilate asks them incredulously. "We have no king but Caesar!" they respond. Eventually, he bends partly under pressure from the mob. "To keep you vultures happy," Pilate says, "I shall flog him."

What follows is one of the most terrifying moments in the show, largely because of the music to which it is set. Each of the thirty-nine lashes receives one repetition of the guitar riff, heard also in the overture, then in "Heaven on Their Minds," and also in "Judas's Death." Pilate counts in time with the riff. Gradually the brass section enters, adding harmony to the riff, and the electric guitar and electric bass dance wildly around the figure.

A sudden halt after the thirty-ninth repetition (and a two-measure tag) finds Pilate once again appealing to Jesus for information and guidance. He sings now the melody that was the slow orchestral introduction to the song "Pilate and Christ."

> Where are you from, Jesus?
> What do you want, Jesus? Tell me.
> You've got to be careful
> You could be dead soon, could well be.
> Why do you not speak when I have your life in my hands?

Softly, but with more of the forceful and unpredictable comments from the orchestra, Jesus informs Pilate that he does not hold any power at all: "Everything is fixed, and you can't change it." The crowd, whose comments have continually interrupted Pilate and Jesus, grows persistent once again and the undulating eighth-note figure returns, higher now. Over and over, higher and higher, they goad Pilate (see ex. 1.9).

Pilate snaps. He sings, screaming, his final words on the situation, washing his hands of this "misguided martyr." This is the music which comes toward the end of the overture, but instead of leading into the eerie major chords associated with Judas as it does there, here it segues into the grand opening of "Superstar." Walsh calls this moment "the score's most chilling and dramatically apposite."[73] It puts a bold, and disturbingly definitive, ending on "Trial Before Pilate," perhaps indicating that Jesus' fate is now sealed, thanks to Pilate's decision to distance himself from the situation. With hardly any sections that feel like set numbers, "Trial Before Pilate" is the most complex but also the smoothest of the large scenes built out of smaller sections.

MUSICAL STYLES THAT DEFINE CHARACTER

Despite the numerous instances of large scenes made from small sections of musical ideas, *Superstar* also contains a number of fairly traditional set pieces. Often, such a song serves to define a character's personality and emotional state, and therefore the sound of that song becomes associated with that character. *Superstar* employs a number of pop music styles and theatrical styles, despite its label as a "rock opera"; Lloyd Webber uses this variety of musical styles and vocal types to help draw sharper images of each character. We have already seen this in the case of Mary; her gentle music, colored with both a folk and a blues feel, pervade both her sections of "Everything's Alright" and her solo, "I Don't Know How to Love Him."

Similarly, the high priests have a distinctive sound all their own; in fact, not only does this sound follow them through their numbers, but the melody of their first number, "This Jesus Must Die," often follows as well. The first major change of setting in the show takes us to the lair of growling bass-voiced Caiaphas and his screechy tenor minions for "This Jesus Must Die."[74] The priests complain about Jesus and his crowds in recitative-like passages, interrupted by the mob outside, until the song proper kicks in. As is always the case, Rice reserves his casual lyrics for the less important and less sympathetic characters, lending a moment of humor to his otherwise bleak text:

> *Priests (variously):* What then to do about this Jesus mania?
> How do we deal with the carpenter king?
> Where do we start with a man who was bigger
> Than John was when John did his baptism thing?

This tactic actually helps fit his lyrics more appropriately to the rather bouncy pair of tunes Lloyd Webber spins. It also helps characterize these priests as the lesser threat, for despite Caiaphas's deep voice and his bold threats ("Like John before him, this Jesus must die"), it will be Pilate who has the actual power to decide Jesus' fate.

The priests (in an example of the first musical technique, melodies reused with new lyrics) reprise the music of "This Jesus Must Die" twice, in "Blood Money" and "Judas's Death." Both times, the return is paired with music that belongs to Judas. The first time the priests revisit the music of "This Jesus Must Die," in "Blood Money," they use it to convince Judas to do their bidding. Annas's lines in "Blood Money" borrow the melody of the beginning of "This Jesus Must Die."

> Cut the protesting, forget the excuses
> We want information, get up off the floor

We have the papers we need to arrest him
You know his movements, we know the law.

The "protesting" and "excuses" to which Annas refers have just been presented
by Judas in "Damned for All Time." This links the two songs, "Damned for All
Time" and "Blood Money," together as a pair, even though the music of "Blood
Money" has a previous home in "This Jesus Must Die." The pair occurs again,
as the first two sections of the lengthy "Judas's Death." Judas first uses his
"Damned for All Time" melody to express his new grievances, after which the
priests respond with their now-signature melody (with lyrics that match up with
both of the instances above):

Cut the confessions, forget the excuses
I don't understand why you're filled with remorse
All that you've said has come true with a vengeance
The mob turned against him, you backed the right horse.

Not only do the priests have their own sound, therefore, they also have their
own oft-repeated music, with its sarcastic, bouncy tempo and flippant lyrics.

One other number helps to define character, but this one occurs only once.
King Herod, a more obvious villain than the priests, has an even more distinctive
sound. "King Herod's Song" is a stylistic exception to everything that has come
before or is yet to come, and a shocking, bizarre exception it is. Although Herod
sings to Jesus, Jesus does nothing in the scene but watch passively. Herod's song
boldly invokes an out-of-place musical style: it is a bouncy ragtime number full
of honky-tonk piano, vaudeville sensibility, and a campy Herod. (In various productions Herod has been played as a full-out drag queen, a Vegas crooner, a
smarmy sort of used car salesman, and everything in between, but in no way
can he be played straight; this Herod must, by dictate of the music, be showy.
Even the tamest interpretations set Herod out from his context; the song does it
for him.)[75] He begins calmly enough, but then the oom-pah tuba and the rag
piano kick in, and Herod gleefully dances about (see ex. 1.10). "Change my water
into wine," "feed my household with this bread," Herod demands. Getting no
reaction, Herod opts for the big finish. The tempo slows, a kick-line rhythm grinds
into gear, and the orchestra modulates dramatically, a step higher.

Hey . . . aren't . . . you . . . scared of me Christ?
Mr. Wonderful Christ?
You're a joke, you're not the Lord!
You're nothing but a fraud!

People often do not know quite what to make of this anomaly, and indeed
it is shockingly different from the rest of the show. Critics made much of the

Moderato, Ragtime style

Example 1.10. "King Herod's Song"

extreme change of pace: "As unexpected as it is, introducing this kind of musical anomaly so far into the evening leaves the audience feeling disoriented and sometimes more hostile toward Rice and Webber than toward Herod."[76] Lloyd Webber and Rice clearly felt that some sort of comic relief from the drama was needed, and their view is certainly sound, though this particular respite can feel quite dated. However, allowing the show to date itself is not necessarily a bad quality, and many other musical and textual moments do so anyway. Nor does

Herod need to be played in a campy way; his over-the-top personality can take any number of forms. Also—and this is overlooked by critics and scholars when discussing the anomaly of Herod—the complete change of mood to one of gleeful silliness is, in its context, quite disturbing. How can this man be so oblivious to the seriousness of the matter placed before him? Does he treat all serious matters of government this way? If one keeps an eye on Jesus during the song, the radical juxtaposition of the two men becomes representative of Herod's general inability or refusal to understand the issue, the man before him, the decision he might make. Instead he tosses Jesus out, back to Pilate, and the whole scene feels rather like a dream, or a bad nightmare.

As a final example of a number that helps to define not only the personality but the sound of a character, we turn to Jesus' solo, "Gethsemane." It is a long, difficult number with several subsections and a large overall arc of emotion, from doubt to anger to resignation. As Swain points out, this is the first time that Jesus' usual "indignant tone of righteousness" is replaced in more than a passing way with "indecision, near failure of nerve, and [an] almost childish pout."[77] To the soft tune previewed in his section of "The Temple," Jesus begins to talk directly to God. Finally, he gives full voice to his doubts, his resistance to his death, and his anger, which all become apparent as the orchestra gradually swells beneath him.

The second section begins. Over a slow, bold repeated pattern of descending tetrachords—a standard musical topos representing sorrow—then over a rhythmically jarring, lurching pattern, Jesus starts making demands. If Jesus lets them "hate me, hit me, hurt me, nail me to their tree," then God must show Himself. Will it make a difference if he dies? "I'd wanna know my God," he says. In perhaps Rice's only misguided moment, Jesus becomes sarcastic, obnoxious, and in the process, dated (see ex. 1.11). Jesus, over a restatement of the descending tetrachords, gives in: "Alright, I'll die!" he wails, in long, high, hysterical notes. "Just watch me die!" First there is an orchestral climax, then a softer section, then the orchestra swells again, supporting Jesus' newfound determination in a coda-like section:

> I will drink your cup of poison,
> Nail me to your cross and break me,
> Bleed me, beat me,
> Kill me, take me now
> Before I change my mind.

The orchestra closes with an eerie phrase first heard at the end of the overture, sung then by off-stage voices, here played by high shimmering strings. No real

Example 1.11. Late in Jesus' solo "Gethsemane"

closure exists, although a silence, after the strings finish their phrase, vaguely marks the end of the number. "Gethsemane" contains all the aspects of Jesus' personality, from gentle to doubtful to angry, and all of his sounds, from sweet to crying to hollering. This and its pivotal position in the drama make the number Jesus' strongest defining moment.

One number embodies not a character, but an event. "Crucifixion" is not a set number, or a series of sections, or like anything heard to this point. It is more a series of frightening, surreal noises, only some of them musical. The score offers a rather loose guideline, inspired in part by the recording rather than by any fixed rhythms or melodies. Strings and woodwinds sustain a bizarre dissonant chord that contains half-steps and tritones. Soldiers hammer Jesus to the cross. Strange percussive noises emanate from the orchestra at seemingly random times. Girls laugh maniacally. "God forgive them," murmurs Jesus. "They don't know what they're doing." Gradually, chorus voices enter, singing "ah" on a dissonant chord that changes, one pitch at a time, slowly. Cymbals play a lewd strip-tease beat. The piano quickly plays arpeggios in no particular key. Jesus continues to murmur to himself sporadically, speaking rather than singing his words, a practice which up to this point has happened only for a shouted word here and there. Animal noises, strange cries and laughs, and random percussive claps join the dissonant voices. The orchestra abandons its sustained dissonant chord and begins a long, slow rise, a cluster of sound sliding up and getting louder. As it reaches its peak, Jesus whispers, "It is finished." The thick texture of sound hovers, suspended, waiting. Jesus says, "Father, into your hands I commend my spirit," and the orchestra falls suddenly silent. It is a terrifying scene; nevertheless, there is also something obvious about it. One can imagine Lloyd Webber and Rice thinking, "It's supposed to be horrifying and eerie, so let's just make scary noises." But perhaps this was unavoidable. Faced with the almost impossible task of representing the crucifixion of Jesus onstage, in music, Lloyd Webber and Rice had few options. Surely Jesus could not hang on the cross and sing a proper song. The chorus could have sung something, but this would be a step back for them; they have already deteriorated into an angry, thoughtless mob, capable of singing little but "Crucify him!" over and over again. Judas has said his piece, and Mary is not central enough to carry the moment. Perhaps terrifying noises and music intentionally designed not to sound musical are the best ways to represent the basically unrepresentable.

Also, and perhaps this is the root of the terror in this scene, the noises are best interpreted as coming through Jesus' own ears—we hear what his own death sounds like to him. Unrealistic, bizarre sounds are mixed with inappropriate music and warped everyday noises. The concept album certainly suggests this interpretation, since it puts Jesus' soft voice very near to us, with the strange noises washing in and out of the foreground. Lloyd Webber, the melody man, and Rice, provider of the perpetually clever lyric, have both stepped back and allowed for a different sound space entirely. It is possible, in fact, to argue that everything from "Superstar" onward takes place in Jesus' mind. Perhaps Judas does not actually return from the future to confront Jesus, but rather Jesus, in his final moments, embodies his own doubts and fears in the form of Judas, with whom he had such a tortured relationship. Jesus' doubts in "Gethsemane" bear a striking resemblance to Judas's oft-repeated worries, and since "Superstar" has an out-of-body air to it already, the song may be Jesus' supernatural experience, not Judas's. By the time we reach the "Crucifixion," certainly, we hear at least partly through Jesus' ears.

"John 19:41" follows "Crucifixion"; it is an orchestral postlude, played while the audience gazes at the final visual image onstage, whatever that might be. The rock band is largely silent; the strings, warm and rich, take over. They play the opening melody of "Gethsemane." The melody soars, but at its final moment, a deceptive cadence takes us to the dissonant tune sung by off-stage voices at the end of the overture, played here by a solo flute, with chromatic wanderings in other winds accompanying it. As the melody settles to a halt, part of the orchestra joins it in B-flat major, but the others settle softly in G major, in a tiny reminder of the "Good old Judas" chords. B-flat major does have the last chord, but the G major chords still ring, and the show ends on this bitonality, as if reminding us that we are to make up our own minds about what we have just seen. For Walsh, the bitonality represents the questions, "Was Christ God? Or did he just think he was?"[78] But other ambiguities resonate in this final sonority, including Jesus' reluctant decision to die, Judas's actions, and Pilate's responsibility for the crucifixion.

Jesus Christ Superstar is among Andrew Lloyd Webber's tightest, most consistent scores, and of the many elements of the megamusical it put into place, the most important contributions are its completely sung story, its use of the rock idiom alongside pop and theatrical styles, and all its techniques of musical return. Each of these elements would influence later megamusicals. Most remember Superstar as rock-oriented, but as we have seen, few of the numbers truly fall into the rock category; various lighter pop music styles abound, as do more dramatically structured scenes in a mixture of styles (such as "Trial Before Pilate"). Significantly, the rock sound falls completely away by the end of the show. "Crucifixion" sounds, at times, like the choral works of Gyorgy Ligeti or Luciano Berio, invoking recent post-tonal musical ideas. "John 19:41" uses the orchestral instruments, but not the rock ones, creating a rich symphonic sound. This rock opera, therefore, is better understood as an opera that uses rock styles, as well as pop, modern, and classical/romantic sounds. Such a mixture of musical styles would become a defining trait of Lloyd Webber's music, one that critics discussed at length. But perhaps what Superstar does best is to tell a dramatic story effectively, as musical theater should. Lloyd Webber admires its straightforwardness and drive: "The important thing about it for us was that we attempted a lot of things which we'd never attempted before, and the greatest quality it has for me is that it knows exactly what it is going to do and does it. I still feel that, in an extremely dramatic way, it runs in a straight line from A to B. And that makes it work in some kind of operatic terms, however naively."[79]

Reviews: A Large Slice of Eggplant and an Auto-Erotic Silver Artichoke; or, "What the Hell Is He *Doing*?"

The fate of Jesus Christ Superstar, like most shows on Broadway and certainly like all shows by newcomers, rested largely in the hands of critics. The myth that the New York Times can make or break a show is based on a long list of cases in point; there were few exceptions in the early 1970s, and it would take Lloyd Webber several more shows to become one of those exceptions himself. For the very young, completely unknown Lloyd Webber and Rice, reviews were crucial. Happily for them, the show mostly received reviews which were mixed or even positive, and critics usually had kind things to say about Lloyd Webber's and Rice's contributions as compared with their reactions to the rest of the creative team. Unfortunately, critics unleashed some of their most scathing prose on this show, and, even if it was aimed at director Tom O'Horgan rather than Lloyd Webber and Rice, the show suffered greatly for it.

The *New York Times,* in 1971, meant Clive Barnes. He found the show intriguing in its novelty, but he had to "confess to experiencing some disappointment." He knew the album had been selling well, and while the show was "less than super," he was sure that the "novelty of its aspirations should win it many adherents." It was like, he summarized, seeing the Empire State Building for the first time: "Not at all uninteresting, but somewhat uninspiring and of minimal artistic value."[80]

Alan Rich, lively arts critic for *New York* magazine, had disliked the album intensely and was not at all inclined to change his mind now. O'Horgan's staging just made it worse.[81] John Simon, theater critic for *New York,* had also not liked the album, and had the same reaction as Rich: staging did it no good.[82] Richard Watts of the *New York Post* agreed: he found the score fine, if dull, but found the live version "flat, pallid, and actually pointless."[83] Most critics, however, had liked the album and enjoyed the music in the show, but were distracted by the staging, which led to mixed reviews; the *Village Voice,* among others, falls into this category.[84]

Because of the controversial staging, few critics turned in unqualified rave reviews. Douglas Watt of the *Daily News* was beside himself: the show "is so stunningly effective a theatrical experience that I am still finding it difficult to compose my thoughts about it. It is, in short, a triumph." The story, "almost unbearably moving" to begin with, became "strikingly immediate" in the hands of Lloyd Webber and Rice. Watt even praised O'Horgan and the generally hated sound system.[85] Another unqualified rave—sincere but reading rather like a book report—came from George Melloan of the *Wall Street Journal,* who felt that it was a perfect combination of rock and the Jesus fad: the creators had "adapted the powerful religious and cultural emotions of the Christ story to a vigorous musical idiom, rock, which is new in the historical sense. The Broadway production adds the further dimension of advanced theater arts and dance."[86] The overall assessments, then, added up to a mixed package. But they do not, by any means, represent the most memorable ink spilled on this show.

A reporter for the *New York Times,* John Gruen, looked back at the reviews of the Broadway opening of *Jesus Christ Superstar* several months after the fact: the "high and mighty of New York theater criticism," he summarized, "suffered what might be described as a collective fit." While critics disagreed about many elements in the show, they were almost entirely of one mind about the role of director Tom O'Horgan. "Their high-voltage invectives, hurled primarily at

O'Horgan's direction and concept, all but charred the pages they were printed on."[87] Although Gruen seemed to think much of the problem stemmed from O'Horgan's treatment of a sacred subject, this was not at all the case. Almost every critic understood that this was a humanized, youthful telling of a historical story with religious overtones, and many enjoyed this perspective on the events. Their invectives, hurled with great force, were entirely for O'Horgan's choices: he had thoroughly and boldly wounded, many said even killed, the material. No matter how good the score was, and many thought it quite good, this misguided, pointless, bizarre, overly large staging buried, confused, and ruined the material it was meant to showcase. Gruen pointed out that no one should have been surprised by O'Horgan's work, given his previous history, but that did not make the show any better. The mistake was not in misunderstanding O'Horgan, or disliking him, but in hiring him in the first place. The mistake was Stigwood's. As Scott Miller points out, there was no saving the show once O'Horgan got his hands on it and molded it to his own strange taste for things large, symbolic, and odd. "The audience should not be *impressed* by the crucifixion of Christ," he says, summarizing the basic conflict between O'Horgan and his material, "they should be *upset* by it, *disturbed* by it."[88]

Critics were more than disturbed by what they were seeing, because it was nonsensical and weird and because it obliterated the score. The stage, for example, instead of a curtain, sported a wall with wavy lines that were meant to look like muscle tissue.[89] As the show began, the wall tilted backward and became the floor. Throughout the story, Judas had four tormentors, meant to be his conscience, men in puffy suits that danced about him silently. As Judas's opening number ended, Jesus rose up through a hole in the floor in a huge silver goblet, wearing a beaded cape.

Caiaphas and the other priests entered from above, riding on a flying bridge made out of large white animal bones. This was meant to represent their "feeding off the carcass of mankind."[90] In "Hosanna," instead of carrying palm fronds, the crowd carried cymbals, plastic tambourines, fish, enormous protozoa-like creatures, representations of the man in the moon, strings of beads hanging from poles, boulders, and a gigantic set of false teeth.

Pilate, in a distinctly non-O'Horgan-like moment, sang his dream on a bare stage in one spotlight. But by the second act, things were back to "normal": banners hung in front of the stage in place of a curtain (or wall), which depicted a see-through Jesus, muscles and organs visible, doing a headstand. These banners became the canopy over the last supper scene. During "Gethsemane," Jesus stood in front of a large box which contained twinkling lights meant to represent stars, referred to by O'Horgan as the "universe box."[91]

Pilate's residence featured a huge sculpture of the head of Caesar, the forehead of which rose to reveal two extra sets of eyes. Herod, not to be outdone, entered while lounging inside a giant hollowed-out dragon's head. And he was, infamously, in full transvestite gear: "ornamental tiara, six-inch platform shoes, long dangling pearls for earrings, necklace, and a heavily painted face with elongated, polished fingernails."[92]

Judas, preparing to die, surrounded by his now-frantic puffy tormentors, had a whole host of ropes from which to choose his noose. He chose one, it pulled him up to the flyspace, and from there the audience lost sight of him but heard his neck snap. During the thirty-nine lashes, soldiers carried Pilate around the stage, as he counted into a large horn or perhaps an elephant's trunk, with a red tongue lolling out its wrong end. Judas later returned from the dead in a silver lamé bikini, descending from above on a huge stained glass butterfly. His backup singers wore gold sequined gowns and frosted afro wigs.

Crowning the spectacle was a moment rife with O'Horgan's favorite scenic device: things that completely transformed before the audience's eyes. For the crucifixion, Jesus rose up through the floor hidden inside a cocoon-like pod, which the chorus pulled apart in layers. Judas lowered a crown of thorns onto Jesus' head. The cast pulled ropes that caused the pod to be replaced with layers upon layers of robes, until eventually Jesus was wearing a hundred yards of gold lamé which tumbled from his perch fifteen feet in the air to cover the stage floor. The chorus covered this stage picture with another large banner, through which Jesus, now wearing only a loincloth, flew forward. He hung, crucified, not on a cross but on a golden inverted triangle, which eventually fell away, leaving him suspended in flames. The critics had a great deal with which to work, to say the least.[93]

Clive Barnes led the way in denouncing O'Horgan's efforts. "There were too many purely decorative effects, artistic excrescences dreamed up by the director and his designers," Barnes said. He mentioned the moving platforms, flying bridges, the stars of Gethsemane in a blue plastic box. "The total effect is brilliant but cheap—like the Christmas decorations of a chic Fifth Avenue store."[94] Walter Kerr, second theater critic for the *Times*, was significantly less calm in his assessment (and Barnes had been only semi-calm). He paved the way for the collective fit that most critics joined. A fan of the album, he was disappointed to glimpse only a bit of it "through the hallucinatory gyrations onstage."[95] Instead of keeping it simple and allowing the text to be clear and the message clean, as he should have done, O'Horgan adorned it: "Oh, my God, how he has adorned it." Jesus, rising in his chalice at the beginning, reminded Kerr of "Dolores in the Ziegfeld Follies of 1924." Later Jesus was dragged offstage "on what seems a large slice of eggplant." Judas's tormentors, "loin-clothed creepy-crawlers," served only to announce O'Horgan's presence in the theater. Kerr was puzzled by the false teeth, the cornucopia with a lizard's tongue hanging out of it, a set of giant caterpillars which are covered by fog "before they have acquired any conceivable significance," and, worst of all, the crucifixion, which "is Death in 3-D."

Regarding Herod, Kerr raised a slightly deeper, less openly hostile point: an over-the-top Herod like O'Horgan's loses all subtlety. Had Herod eased into the number, gradually breaking out into a full dance-hall moment, the humor would remain intact. "A more or less traditional Herod doing a kick-step would be amusing and suggestive," Kerr pointed out. "This one looks as though he had never done anything else." Kerr took issue with some other directorial decisions made for actors, especially Jesus, whom O'Horgan had directed "to be simultaneously fidgety and limp." Driving his point home, Kerr lamented the disservice O'Horgan did to the material: "It is not simply that Mr. O'Horgan's impositions are irrelevant, though they are that; it is a deep mystery to me how this man has been able to identify himself with a counter-culture that prides itself on 'relevance.' The worst—or next to worst—of it is that they deliberately interfere. In both the most obvious and the subtlest ways Mr. O'Horgan is eternally bent on cutting across what is good, or might be good, severing head from body."

Time magazine devoted a cover story to the show, full of background on the creators and glossy photos, but its main point was to deride O'Horgan. The article opened with four quotes that gave away the game:

> *Shaw:* "Must then a Christ perish in torment in every age to save those that have no imagination?"
> *Jesus:* "You cannot serve God and mammon."
> *Webster:* "Vulgarity: something vulgar—for instance, seating a chimpanzee at a formal dinner."
> *O'Horgan:* "I just like to stir people up."[96]

The oddities were listed: the layered robe that cost $20,000, the bone bridge, the six-eyed Caesar head through which Pilate enters, the box of lights which might be God, or a computer, or "the ark of the covenant as crafted by Magnavox."

John Simon of *New York* magazine, known for being harsh, did not disappoint. O'Horgan, "patently the Busby Berkeley of the anti-establishment," here having embraced the establishment with his move to Broadway, was the focus of this show. Again, he listed the strange images, the "giant gimmickry signifying nothing" such as "merchants selling what appear to be mummified babies and soldiers in armor cunningly designed to facilitate instant sodomy." Jesus' big number inspired Simon's most creative interpretations: "Twice during the Gethsemane song, there is lowered over Christ's head what looks like a huge box of candy in translucent wrapping, which, according to Clive Barnes, represents the stars over Gethsemane, though I would have sworn it was the bonbons over Gethsemane. (My date claimed it symbolized the squareness of God.)" In an unusual break from most critics, Simon's favorite moment in O'Horgan's staging was King Herod's song, but mostly because it had awareness of its own strangeness: "Here at least the show espouses its freakish sensibilities with brazen forthrightness and earns a rowdy, raucous laugh or two."[97]

The *Village Voice* went beyond blaming O'Horgan to blaming producer Robert Stigwood for turning this oratorio-like album into pointless "ocular dazzle." Stigwood was deemed responsible for hiring O'Horgan and letting him take over "because that's the kind of conventionally stupid decision commercial producers make." The *Voice* suggested crucifixion of them both.[98] Jack Kroll of *Newsweek*, like most, took delight in listing O'Horgan's odd symbols, such as Jesus appearing like a "deus ex Dixie Cup" in his chalice, and his layers of robes that peeled off like an "auto-erotic silver artichoke."[99]

How had such a previously successful director, praised from many sides for his work on *Hair*, gone so clearly wrong? First, the main difference between *Hair* and *Superstar* was that the former had virtually no plot, leaving plenty of room for fun, inventive staging without fear that the audience would miss the story or lyrics. *Superstar*, on the other hand, featured a serious and character-driven story which needed clarification onstage, not decoration, especially since the audience already had an emotional investment in the story. Also, O'Horgan's work on *Hair* and other shows had not been nearly so large in scale or invasive to the eye; for this show, he had clearly gone too far. There may also have been some bias against unusual stagings in a traditional Broadway theater, as opposed to O'Horgan's usual off-Broadway home, where audiences and critics expected experimental theater. Still, even the most open-minded critics, who would have happily embraced innovation on Broadway, balked at this production. Historian Denny Martin Flinn summarized the problem succinctly: "O'Horgan failed to realize that his directorial approach was really a style, and he did not express the content of other musicals [as opposed to *Hair*] well at all."[100]

A small minority of critics had praise for O'Horgan, usually contained within a general rave review (such as those by Douglas Watt of the *Daily News* and George Melloan of the *Wall Street Journal*). Martin Gottfried of *Women's Wear*

Daily was fascinated by O'Horgan's "trying to alter the SCALE of theatre."[101] Coming from relatively unimportant sources, these raves did little to restore O'Horgan's shattered reputation.

Lloyd Webber and Rice, for their part, had quite different reactions to the director's interpretation of their work. Having relinquished all control to O'Horgan, who had "conceived and directed" the show without their input, both were surprised by the staging. Only Lloyd Webber, however, disagreed with the results. In an interview with the *New York Times* several days after opening night, they revealed their opinions with relative openness. Lloyd Webber tried to remain tactful: "Let's just say that we don't think this production is the definitive one." Rice, immediately contradicting the "we" of Lloyd Webber's statement, cheerfully put in, "I enjoyed the show very much." Their exchange continued:

> *Lloyd Webber:* Well, it's not the way I envisioned it. I saw it more as an intimate drama of three or four people.
> *Rice:* We're just a couple of English lads and we don't know Broadway. But it does seem to us to be good Broadway entertainment.
> *Lloyd Webber:* I do think the music has suffered a little.
> *Rice:* O'Horgan did a *great* job.

Though Rice may have been motivated in part by the suspicion that a negative review of a production from one of its own authors would not be good for business, he seems also to have taken the production in stride. Lloyd Webber, protective of his work and less tactful in the area of public relations, could not fully endorse it. While he pointed out moments he enjoyed, and credited O'Horgan with having an admirably deep feeling for the material, he also admitted, "O'Horgan's production has posed problems for me. I won't tell you what some people have told me they think of it, because it would only cause trouble. When I saw Judas coming down in that *butterfly,* I thought, 'What the hell is he *doing*?' " Lloyd Webber expressed confusion and dismay regarding Herod the drag queen, which Rice explained away as dramatic license and an effort to create an air of general debauchery.[102]

Michael Walsh claims that Rice and Lloyd Webber's disagreement about O'Horgan's work created the first wedge between them. Lloyd Webber had wanted something simple that would work with the score, not against it (although his claim of hoping for an intimate three- or four-person show is surely hyperbole). The critics' reactions realized his fears, and he "began to project how this catastrophe (for so it was already in his mind) would adversely affect his and Tim's chances for success with their next show. It would, he decided, take them years to live this down."[103] In fact it was O'Horgan's career that never recovered. The generally positive reaction to Lloyd Webber and Rice's score and lyrics meant that they would indeed have the opportunity to prove themselves again.

Clive Barnes had mixed but milder things to say about Lloyd Webber's music than about the staging. Using a theme that critics would talk about in association with every subsequent Lloyd Webber show, he noted—and did not seem to mind—the extraordinarily wide range of musical styles contained within this "rock" opera. "John 19:41" reminded him of Vaughan Williams and Massenet, and (unnamed) numbers of the Beatles. He enjoyed "Superstar" with its energy and "almost revivalist fervor," and found "I Don't Know How to Love Him" a sweet ballad. In general, though, Barnes was underwhelmed: "Most of the music is pleasant, although unmemorable."[104]

Walter Kerr liked the music more than Barnes did, saying that the "score functions well . . . using rock as a frame rather than an obsession." The borrowings of a wide range of mostly popular musical styles seemed well suited, Kerr argued, to the show's atmosphere of extraordinary events taking place in an ordinary world full of regular people. He found it "a pop opera about pop attitudes, and I think it works."[105] Bill Bender and Timothy Foote of *Time* magazine called the stylistic borrowings "pastiche," a term that many critics would later use in a derogatory manner in criticisms of Lloyd Webber, but here Bender and Foote felt it succeeded. It was not quite rock, and certainly not show music, but offered something for everybody: blues, torch songs, camp, references to the Rolling Stones, the Beatles, Ray Charles, Prokofiev, Orff, Richard Strauss, all fused "into a new kind of thespic amalgam that has high dramatic point[s], melodic joy, and rarity of rarities, wit."[106]

A similar range of comments, from mixed to positive with a few dissenters, surfaced for Tim Rice's lyrics. Barnes felt that while record sales proved that Rice's goal of reaching the youth of America had clearly succeeded, his lyrics strayed too often into the unforgivably pedestrian and slangy. He also felt Rice was trying too hard to be clever.[107] Kerr disagreed: "The tone of voice is not merely mod or pop or jauntily idiomatic in an opportunistic way. It sheathes an attitude. It speaks, over and over again, of the inadequate, though forgivable, responses ordinary men always do make when confronted by mystery." For Kerr, Rice's lyrics demonstrated the effectiveness of the show's characterizations of the shallow, selfish reactions many of the characters exhibit. The chorus, after offering Jesus their love, turn to each other and ask, "Did you see I waved?" Rice conveys all of this with "blunt, rude, pointedly unlyrical lyrics, not meant to coat any period with a little literary flavoring but to catch hold of thought processes—venal, obtuse, human. Delivered in the jargon we more or less live by, they become woefully and ironically recognizable."[108]

For many critics, the most interesting aspect of the pair's project, for better or worse, was their perspective on the story. "They are young Englishmen of obvious talent," summarized Barnes, "and it is apparent that this midcult version of the Passion story is seriously and sincerely intended."[109] Yet Barnes did not care much for the approach; he called the work "the best score for an English musical in years," but felt that its attitude contained "coyness in its contemporaneity, a sneaky pleasure in the boldness of its anachronisms, a special undefined air of smugness in its daring." He was probably right to say that Lloyd Webber and Rice were sincere, but he was also right to believe the creators were rather cheerfully being bold for its own sake, hoping to make their mark with this great-man-as-average-guy approach. Alan Rich agreed, but he laid the blame at the feet of a wider group of culprits, pop culture in general. Marketing Jesus like a fad, which indeed happened in so many arenas, represented a profit-seeking, corrupt cultural attitude. Manifested in musical form, the work came off, to Rich, as "cheap, shoddy, vulgar and, worst of all, cynical."[110]

Critics achieved a clear consensus regarding the performances in *Superstar*. There were raves all around for Ben Vereen as Judas (despite the melodramatic contortions O'Horgan put him through) and Barry Dennen as Pilate, and Yvonne Elliman's voice made Mary Magdalene likable. Jeff Fenholt as Jesus fared less well; his voice was strong but his acting was considered rather weak, a situation made worse by O'Horgan's having him play the role limp and whiny.[111] The chorus of young, strong singers received admiration from all critics ("All the lepers are first-rate," said the *New Yorker*).[112]

Most reviews demonstrated a massive but probably unavoidable imbalance: a great deal of space was devoted toward O'Horgan's monstrosities, leaving less for Lloyd Webber and Rice. The existence of the album, the controversy over the material, and the publicity caused by the protests meant that in the end, far less than usual was said about the music. But thanks to revivals and continued familiarity, *Jesus Christ Superstar* took its place as the first influential proto-megamusical. Indeed, the show's reputation has risen in the light of megamusicals that followed. This first true example of the megamusical stood up well in comparison with those of the 1980s and 1990s, since it could boast a stronger score and a more powerful plot than many of them.

"Who Says the British Cannot Write Musicals?"

The critics had a strong effect on ticket sales. About eight months' worth of tickets had been sold in advance; after that sales dropped sharply, and by eleven months into the run discounts were offered. The show ran a rather disappointing twenty months. The Tony Awards also brought disappointment. The show was nominated in five categories (three heavily influenced by O'Horgan—lighting, costumes, and scenic design—one for best score, and one for Ben Vereen for best supporting actor), but won none, which was not a surprise. In fact, it lost all five to shows by Stephen Sondheim, four of them to his latest, *Follies,* directed by Hal Prince, the fifth to a revival of *A Funny Thing Happened on the Way to the Forum.* No one knew it yet, but this competition laid the ground for what would be, at least to critics and the press if not to the composers themselves, a long-standing rivalry between the Lloyd Webber and Sondheim camps.

A cast album of *Jesus Christ Superstar* was recorded in the traditional way, with the Broadway cast and orchestra in one day. However, sales of the concept album had been so strong that it was deemed foolish to market a similar but less well-engineered recording, and so a one-disc abridged version was released with no fanfare.[113]

Despite *Superstar*'s rather limited run on Broadway, it has continued to enjoy a successful life on tour in the United States and abroad. The first stop after Broadway was Los Angeles, where O'Horgan, despite Lloyd Webber's protests, directed a new version for an open-air arena that seated nearly four thousand people. The L.A. staging was much different from that of the Broadway production, though by most assessments equally strange, and critics responded more positively; perhaps O'Horgan's large gestures were better suited to a venue this size. The production opened on 28 June 1972, and featured two understudies from the Broadway cast: Carl Anderson as Judas and Ted Neeley as Jesus. Both were well received and would go on to do the film version.[114]

The year 1972 brought many other versions of *Superstar* to the world, in addition to international tours that had already been launched. Dozens of countries would eventually host productions, and successful runs in Australia, France, and Scandinavia were already under way when the show made it to London in August 1972. Stigwood, despite having brought O'Horgan on board and endorsing him in New York, knew that it would be box office suicide to allow him to direct the show in relatively staid England. A contractual loophole allowed him to use someone else, and he chose Jim Sharman, who had directed the Australian version. Sticking closer to Lloyd Webber's vision of the show than to O'Horgan's, Sharman staged a somewhat less glitzy, more accessible version which opened at the Palace Theatre on 9 August 1972. Critics generally liked it, some adored it, and the public embraced it wholeheartedly. It ran a then-unprecedented eight years.[115]

Many British critics hailed the show's arrival as the first great British contribution to the genre; we can "stop apologizing for the British musical," said Irving Wardle, chief drama critic for the London *Times.* He did not love the show by any means; he found the story rather shallow and not particularly touching, but his reaction to the score was positive and he enjoyed most of the performances. Wardle and others did not find favor with Paul Nicholas as Jesus, leading to speculation that hardly anyone could garner great reviews in such a demanding role.[116] (Ted Neeley, however, would do so in the film and onstage for years to come.)

Harold Hobson for the Sunday *Times* had nothing but glowing things to say; for him, it changed the musical and England's place in it forever. "Who says the British cannot write musicals?" he demanded, and described the coming of this show as being "like a great river in flood, like an army with banners. If the kingdom of God could be taken by storm, this would take it."[117] A second Sunday *Times* critic, Derek Jewell, who had discovered Lloyd Webber and Rice with *Joseph,* had liked the New York production so well that this one paled in comparison. The deliberate toning-down of the sets and wild emotions struck him as something of an acquiescence to British sensibility: "The singing and the playing generally need more spunk and there's no reason why more work and less uptightness shouldn't generate it."[118]

A film version of *Superstar* had been planned almost from the beginning, well before the show had begun rehearsals on Broadway.[119] Having learned their lesson, Rice and Lloyd Webber became very involved in the movie, working closely with director Norman Jewison, whose previous foray into the movie musical was the successful *Fiddler on the Roof.* Jewison promised and delivered a much more naturalistic look, and began by getting permission to film on location in Israel. This was encouraged both by the Israeli Film Centre, which knew that such arrangements were good for the local economy, and by the mayor of Jerusalem, the city in which some scenes would be filmed. The Israeli Parliament was troubled by the content, however, and eventually the Israeli government politely dissociated itself from the film entirely.[120]

Meanwhile, filming continued, from August to December of 1972. The cast pre-recorded the soundtrack, and Andre Previn did the orchestrations. Rounding out the cast, along with Los Angeles stars Ted Neeley and Carl Anderson, were Yvonne Elliman and Barry Dennen, back once again, and a new Herod, Joshua

Mostel (son of Zero). Jewison used a mostly natural look for the movie, with earth-toned (if bell-bottomed) costumes and stark desert and cave settings. A few moments made clear a theme that the score and other productions had only suggested: what happened then could happen now. To remind viewers of this, Jewison had the Roman soldiers carry modern machine guns, and sent a line of tanks to help push Judas to the priests' temple, where he reveals Jesus' location. The truly flashy, over-the-top moments arose for appropriate numbers: Judas, speaking from modern times in "Superstar," entered on a helicopter and wore a sparkly funky jumpsuit; and Herod, decadent as always, wore medallions, showed too much skin, and had the company of a colorful harem. Most significantly, the entire movie was framed by the arrival and departure of the cast on a bus. During the overture they rolled into the desert and disembarked in modern dress, laughing and dancing, to set up the sets and don their costumes. At the end, sober, tired, and silent, they reboarded the bus, Anderson and Elliman looking back wistfully over the land. Neeley, not seen since the crucifixion, did not board the bus. One particularly insightful editorial about the film championed the idea that *Superstar* was about modern social leaders, the immense pressure they felt to live up to expectations, and peoples' need to believe in such charismatic figures. The movie's frame story made this explicit: the bus brings the young people to "re-enact the story of the greatest cult leader of them all, to see it for themselves and learn from it." When they leave, disappointed, they have realized that "in the matter of improving the human condition there can be no miracles, no leaders who can rise up after dying, no man who cannot die, and, above all, no man who can carry the whole load unaided by the people."[121]

Opening on 8 August 1973, the film inspired a fresh wave of protest. There had already been resistance in Israel during the filming, although it was more scattered and unorganized. "We already had one Jesus here," a policeman was quoted as saying, "and he gave us more than enough trouble."[122] The National Jewish Community Relations Advisory, a group which represented a number of smaller Jewish groups, including the American Jewish Committee, released a statement similar to the one which had appeared on Broadway's opening night. Again, they disliked the evil portrayal of the Jewish priests, which could be bad for Jewish/Christian relations, and they objected to an African American Judas portrayed as a "dupe of the Jewish priesthood," fearing it could be bad for Jewish/black relations.[123] Universal Pictures released a statement politely denying the validity of any protests.[124]

The film fared rather poorly. Perhaps the controversy it had inspired in each new incarnation had finally run its course. The *New York Times* was unimpressed, finding the score too loud, frenzied, and gaudy when set against the bare landscape of the vast desert. The show may simply have played more effectively as an album or a stage vehicle (when staged well) rather than as a film. Still, the cast and several moments in Jewison's version came in for high praise,[125] and it is fair to say that the film deserves far more attention than it has received, especially because the Broadway production was so unrelated to the original intentions of the score's creators. *Superstar* was realized in so many forms, including concept album, tour, and Broadway production, that it is difficult to call one incarnation the original, best, or most authentic. Certainly the concept album had great impact on the show's popularity, but the film provides viewers an excellent production, embodied and complete. It may have fared poorly in 1973, but thanks to continuous airings on television and the availability of video and DVD, it is in this form that most people (and certainly most young people) know the show at all. The film boasts superb performances, a soundtrack (also available as a recording) which rivals the concept album in quality, and powerful visual images. Lloyd Webber biographer Michael Coveney argues that the film "stands up today as both theatrically intelligent and cinematically interesting."[126]

Thanks to *Superstar,* in its embodiments as concept album, Broadway musical, and film, there would be no forgetting Lloyd Webber and Rice now. The young team had arrived, and would now be faced with the daunting task of proving themselves and their staying power. No flash in the pan, they would impress again with their next work, and the one after that. With the experience of *Superstar* behind them, they knew how to mount a show, and they had learned about directors, staging, money, albums, ticket sales, critics, and public relations.

More important, the megamusical had arrived. Its first outing as embodied by *Jesus Christ Superstar* had been full of hits and misses, and the "mega" quality provided by O'Horgan had been a disastrous miss, but the concept was now in place. Over the course of the 1970s, audiences and critics would grow accustomed to the idea that Broadway musicals were sometimes big, expensive, emotional spectacles full of fancy sets, amplified sound, and melodramatic stories. Most audience members would be pleased by this development; most critics would not. Within two weeks of the release of the album in the United States, Rice realized he and Lloyd Webber had created "a work of massive cultural impact. I am of course not claiming that *Jesus Christ Superstar* is a sophisticated composition of genius but, stone me, it was popular."[127] The split between critical reception and popular appeal had begun to settle into place. So too had the idea of exporting, as *Superstar* so quickly reached many cities in Europe and Australia. It would take a decade for the megamusical to become firmly established as a full-fledged genre, but the trend that began with *Superstar* already pointed toward the 1980s.

"Humming the Scenery"

The Megamusical Ascending

To a lot of Americans, he is an alien odd-ball at best, a
raving English eccentric at worst.
Gerald McKnight in his biography, Andrew Lloyd Webber

He may be beloved as a composer, but Americans' views of Andrew Lloyd Webber the man are a different matter. The same is true in his home country, where the media have given his personal life massive, mostly negative, attention. He has never dealt particularly well with the press or the public, especially in the early phases of his career, nor is he known for being easy-going and charming, like Tim Rice. In his autobiography, Rice recalls meeting Lloyd Webber for the first time: "He oozed contradiction. Aspects of this were instantly apparent; he seemed at once awkward and confident; sophisticated and naïve; mature and childlike. Later I discovered he was also humorous and portentous; innovative and derivative; loyal and cavalier; generous and self-centered; all these characteristics to the extreme."[1] Even early in his career, Lloyd Webber was determined to become a wildly successful theater composer. His brother, Julian Lloyd Webber, recounted to biographer Michael Coveney how an aunt had said, after *Jesus Christ Superstar* opened successfully in London, "You must feel you've really done it now, Andrew."

> Andrew replied, in total seriousness, "I shall never think that I've done it unless I can go into the record stores and see the shelves packed with the Greatest Hits of Andrew Lloyd Webber. Like Richard Rodgers." Julian knew his brother well, but even then he was struck with the way he said this without a trace of emotion: "Writing one hit show for him, if that's what it was going to be, wasn't going to mean very much. He wanted, even then, to be the best there had ever been."[2]

By all accounts, Lloyd Webber still seeks this goal and does not feel he has achieved it yet, although his frenzied race to get there seems to have slowed since the 1980s. In the meantime he has become more accustomed to the high-profile aspects of a public career, and has learned how to live within the system rather than stumble awkwardly along its boundaries. As Coveney notes, "Tim Rice had been the relaxed, easily approachable one for a couple of years with Andrew looking surly and unsure of himself with his floral shirts and curly long hair. But increasingly Andrew revealed a flair for public utterance and over the years would slowly become an adept manipulator of the media and eventually, like Rice, a polished exponent of the opportunities that opened up the print and other media."[3] By the time Lloyd Webber learned these skills, he was wealthy beyond imagination, a former hippie turned conservative, the owner of many houses and, eventually, many theaters. He learned a great deal about how to present himself to the public from producer Cameron Mackintosh, who opened his eyes to the world of marketing. In order to understand the media's fascination with Lloyd Weber, we take a brief look at his private-as-public life to date, and then discuss the major areas of contention regarding his music and the mega-musical generally.

After the initial success of *Jesus Christ Superstar,* Lloyd Webber and Rice spent a great deal of time working with productions all over the world, learning how to solve problems of translation, casting, and staging in any given city. Meanwhile, Rice dabbled in all sorts of nontheater activities in his spare time, and Lloyd Webber wrote scores for two films, *Gumshoe* (1971) and *The Odessa File* (1975). Most of the music he wrote for these films was cut, but Lloyd Webber enjoyed the experience of working in a new medium. The latter film featured a piece for cello and rock band, a sound to which Lloyd Webber would return in *Variations.*

Lloyd Webber also spent the mid-1970s dealing with his newfound wealth. He founded the Really Useful Company, a production company that would manage all his interests not already controlled by Robert Stigwood, with whom he was under contract until 1979. Although Stigwood had been invaluable to Lloyd Webber in the beginning of his career, the two had been drifting apart, and Lloyd Webber now understood the value of controlling his own money and producing projects for himself. In May 1979, Lloyd Webber and Rice let their contract with Stigwood expire; Lloyd Webber then hired former MCA associate and *Superstar* supporter Brian Brolly to run the Really Useful Company. He also bought Sydmonton Court, a country estate which featured a chapel-turned-theater. This building would become the home of Lloyd Webber's annual Sydmonton Festival, a testing ground for new material (his and others') for an audience of friends and theater associates.[4]

Lloyd Webber spent profusely in the 1970s, beginning what would become an impressive collection of property and art. Over the decades he acquired, besides Sydmonton Court, a house in London, an apartment in Trump Tower in New York, a villa in Europe, and a string of thoroughbred horses. His shows, of course, have produced record-breaking income over the years, and he manages his fortune closely and expertly. And yet, he continues to maintain, "Money is not of great importance to me." Indeed, for many years he would downplay and even deny his wealth, but by now this is no longer possible.[5]

In the 1970s he was able to maintain a relatively low profile, for despite the success of *Jesus Christ Superstar,* he and Rice had not become household names overnight. The show was famous, but for the pair of young, hip rockers to become equally well known they would have to prove their staying power. At first, this looked unlikely; Lloyd Webber's first show after *Superstar, Jeeves* (with a book and lyrics by Alan Ayckbourn), was a disaster. He returned to Rice for *Evita,* which, while controversial and not without its detractors, was well received and certainly assured the world that the pair were no flash in the pan. But *Evita* also marked the third and final show the two would create together. Their first, *Joseph and the Amazing Technicolor Dreamcoat,* would eventually reach Broadway in 1982, but this was a matter of expanding on a score that Lloyd Webber and Rice had written in the late 1960s. After *Evita,* the men parted on mostly amicable terms and Lloyd Webber began a new phase of his career. It was this phase that would make him a household name and make his personal life fodder for tabloid headlines. Two items initiated this frenzy: *Cats,* which opened in London in 1981 and in New York in 1982, and Sarah Brightman.

Andrew Lloyd Webber married Sarah Hugill in 1972, and they had two children. Sarah Brightman, meanwhile, spent her youth as a dancer and had success with the pop music and dance group Hot Gossip. She sported blue hair and a racy punk style, and had a hit with "I Lost My Heart to a Starship Trooper." By her early twenties, she decided to try her luck as a singer and dancer in the theater, and answered a cattle-call audition for *Cats* in London. Lloyd Webber liked her and cast her in a relatively minor role, as a sweet-voiced young kitten with several featured moments of wide-eyed innocence. She later moved on to another show, which Lloyd Webber saw; he was apparently enthralled by her— her voice, her personality, her evident talent. Within months, he began dating her and soon announced he was leaving his wife for her.

The press, needless to say, had a field day. They immediately dubbed the newcomer Sarah II, and branded her a young, home-wrecking theater gypsy, while they championed the steadfast Sarah I, homemaker and mother. The press followed the new couple everywhere, reveled in Brightman's saucy past, and speculated about the couple's future. "In Britain," writes Michael Walsh, speculating as to the cause of the media frenzy, "successful men simply didn't ditch their long-suffering wives—they had met when she was *sixteen,* for God's sake."[6] On 22 March 1984, two days after his divorce was final, Lloyd Webber married Sarah Brightman. That night, he presented the new Mrs. Lloyd Webber to the Queen of England at the royal opening of *Starlight Express.* Lloyd Webber and Brightman began to get accustomed to unrelenting media attention, but also took to suing the tabloids for their wilder acts of creative journalism. The couple won their cases, but the papers cheerfully paid the settlements and then continued fanning the often false gossip flames. Brightman would stay at the forefront of the news throughout the next few years, mainly because of the starring role her husband wrote for her in *The Phantom of the Opera.* After six years, Lloyd Webber announced that he and Brightman would divorce.

Business continued to boom for Lloyd Webber in the 1980s. The Really Useful Company branched out, producing some of Lloyd Webber's own work but also getting involved in recording, publishing, film, and television, as well as the productions of plays and musicals by other people, such as the well-received musical *The Hired Man* by Howard Goodall and Melvyn Bragg. Cameron Mackintosh co-produced several of Lloyd Webber's first efforts without Rice (*Cats, Song and Dance, The Phantom of the Opera*) and helped Lloyd Webber learn the business to the point that he no longer needed a production partner. In December 1985, the Really Useful Company went public, becoming the Really Useful Group. Lloyd Webber continues to run his business expertly, claiming all the while that if he had a choice, he would stay out of it and get back to his music.[7] All the same, his keen business sense has enabled him to buy a string of London theaters, starting with the Palace Theatre in 1983, where *Les Misérables* opened two years later, and also the Adelphi and the New London Theatres, both of which he restored. In 1987, the Really Useful Group won the Queen's Award for achievement in export. "Musicals were the new diplomacy," remarks Coveney.[8] In January 2000, Lloyd Webber bought ten West End theaters at once, for a total of about $145 million. In partnership with an outside corporation, Nat West Equity Partners, and under the heading Really Useful Theaters, Lloyd Webber now owned—in addition to the Palace, the Adelphi, and the New London—the London Palladium, the Garrick, Her Majesty's, the Lyric, the Apollo, the Gielgud, the Queen's, the Cambridge, the Duchess, and Theater Royal Drury Lane. He explained his purchases as resulting from a desire to put theaters in the hands of those who know theater, not in the hands of giant business ventures interested only in earning money. He spoke of filling those houses with some less obvious, more experimental shows, and was quick to point out that *Evita* and *Cats* had been huge risks and looked like extremely unlikely hits on paper, succeeding only because people took a chance on them.[9]

In 1992, Lloyd Webber was knighted for his service to the arts. In 1993, his name was inscribed on a star on the Hollywood Walk of Fame. In 1997, the royal family promoted him again, making him the Baron of Sydmonton Court and Lord Andrew Lloyd-Webber.[10]

Having triumphed so thoroughly in the 1980s with *The Phantom of the Opera,* Lloyd Webber spent the early 1990s on the poorly received *Aspects of Love* and the triumphant *Sunset Boulevard.* Two of his recent London shows, *Whistle Down the Wind* and *The Beautiful Game,* have not been seen on Broadway. His newest, *The Woman in White,* ran for only three months on Broadway starting in November 2005, causing very little stir and closing partly because of an ailing leading lady. In addition to his real estate ventures and stretching the Really Useful Group into pursuing home video versions of *Cats, Joseph,* and *Superstar* and a film version of *The Phantom of the Opera,* Lloyd Webber has written a "restaurant and free-wheeling opinion column" weekly in the London *Telegraph.*[11] Despite a comfortable lifestyle and his other interests, he remains a ruthlessly ambitious composer, striving for both a hit and critical esteem by turns. And despite the fact that his personality and private life often get the media's attention, he would receive no attention at all but for his controversial, popular music.

Critics and Audiences

> *Andrew Lloyd Webber:* Why do people take an instant dislike to me?
> *Alan Jay Lerner:* It saves time.

This apocryphal exchange[12] would perhaps be more apropos if "critics" were substituted for "people." While theatergoers like Lloyd Webber, critics as a group seem annoyed by him, bitter about his success, and sarcastic about his alleged talent and penchant for creating spectacle-driven shows. Walsh, the most thorough of the few writers who deal with Lloyd Webber, points out this disparity, and Coveney follows suit, but neither entirely explains it. There may be no single reason why a composer is popular yet disliked by critics, other than the fact that critics often dislike (even consciously choose to dislike) composers who gain popularity. As Walsh explains:

> Rarely does musical history offer such a disparity between a composer's popular reputation and his critical estimation. Despite his indisputable box-office prestige

... Lloyd Webber repeatedly has seen his works critically disdained (indeed, savaged), especially in the United States. Their plots are scorned, their musical content derided as the meretricious parroting of Lloyd Webber's Broadway betters and higher-toned operatic antecedents. There is even one school of thought that considers Lloyd Webber fundamentally derivative—nearly a plagiarist—who preys on his audience's ignorance and childish love of spectacle.[13]

It is rare for critics and audiences to disagree so strongly about a composer; interestingly, another of these rare instances concerns reactions to the operas of Giacomo Puccini, whose style Lloyd Webber has admired and occasionally emulated. In fact, critics often complain that Lloyd Webber sounds too much like Puccini, even when the music does not support this, as if they are considering instead reputation and their own role as critics deriding a popular composer. Fausto Torrefranca, Puccini's most passionate critic, cited among Puccini's flaws a number of qualities also associated with Lloyd Webber: "Puccini . . . embodies, with the utmost completeness, all the decadence of current Italian music, and represents all its cynical commerciality, all its pitiful impotence and the whole triumphant vogue for internationalism."[14] Torrefranca, like Lloyd Webber's harshest critics, could abide neither works which achieve great popularity (surely a result of "cynical commerciality") nor works with international qualities and appeal. Arthur Groos and Roger Parker note that this bias against Puccini's style and its success, coupled with Torrefranca's "anti-feminism," actually undermines some valid criticisms of Puccini's music.[15] As is the case with Lloyd Webber's strongest detractors, Torrefranca loses credibility thanks to his overly harsh language and obvious hostility for his subject. As with Lloyd Webber, Puccini's fame brought him massive media attention; Alexandra Wilson notes that Puccini's "personality and physique were subject to as much scrutiny as his music."[16]

Walsh refers to critics who consider audiences ignorant and childish; he himself gives credit to Lloyd Webber, and indeed to the average audience member, for more than a mere love of spectacle and mindless simplicity of plot and music. His explanation, however, seems to presume that critics do not understand Lloyd Webber. What is it, then, that critics seem to miss? Why do Lloyd Webber's musicals speak to the same audiences sitting all around the critics, while the critics themselves remain grumpily unmoved?

One reason is obvious. Lloyd Webber became a natural target of critical volleys by virtue of his very success. Any artist, upon achieving domination in his field and popularity of such consistency, will automatically find himself the rebels' favorite artist to hate. If regular folks like him, surely he cannot be smart enough for the educated, or hip enough for the "in" crowd. In addition to simple popularity, Lloyd Webber's work has been highly influential; Broadway would not have taken the path it has taken had he not launched the sung-through epic musical. Broadway has already welcomed successors in the megamusical genre, reinforcing the resentment of those who were happy with the state of Broadway before Lloyd Webber, or those who had envisioned it taking a different path. "Hero, villain, savior, or scoundrel," summarizes one historian, "Andrew Lloyd Webber has been responsible for a collection of musicals that have changed the face of Broadway."[17] The very conspicuousness of his shows has made them an easy target for sneers: they were the most "successful export of the Thatcher years, gargantuan, hollow, triumphalist, a soundtrack for our times and easily despised."[18] This implies the unspoken idea that Lloyd Webber encounters resentment not only for being successful, but for being wealthy as a result. He was clearly much easier to champion when he was a young, unknown hippie, but there is little reward for a critic who endorses an artist long ago embraced by everyone else.[19]

A more subtle explanation for the distance between critics and audience attacks not Lloyd Webber, but his admirers. A number of critics and historians praise Lloyd Webber for his achievement while simultaneously insulting the audiences of the last several decades. They admire his ability to please audiences so consistently, but they disparage those audiences' tastes. His music speaks simply and directly to the masses, these writers believe, and he fills their minds with pretty tunes and lovely high-tech imagery. It's all pop music, film-like effects, loudspeakers. These critics imply that Lloyd Webber dumbs down his work for television-minded dolts who want to be amused by shiny things. The problem with this charge is simply that audiences are not that inept. All musicals take work to watch. It is entirely possible to turn one's brain off at a musical, but then one will get nothing in return. A musical, at least a good one, involves some combination of an interesting story, new music, intriguing things to look at, many words to hear. Indeed, it takes concentration to follow a musical, to take in the dancing, the music, the story, the words, the scenery, and still be so involved in the show that tears flow and standing ovations erupt. Audiences will not give a sincere, spontaneous standing ovation to a mildly diverting, simple-minded night at the theater. They will not cry over the scenery—although admittedly they do occasionally applaud it. They come prepared to focus and to receive all that the creative team is about to throw at them.

My defense of the intelligence of the audience is corroborated (with slightly less fervor) by Michael Coveney, who points out that the fact that Japanese tourists flock to see *Cats* does not "in itself contaminate the original undertaking," although high-minded cultural critics believe it does. Coveney argues, "Innocent audiences might first be seduced by the publicity and the hype. But that doesn't form their responses once they are inside a theatre."[20]

Legend has it that a critic can make or break a show, that a production with an uncertain future can be saved or closed by one review. There are also examples to prove the opposite. A panned show can run for years; a critical favorite can close quickly. There are too many other factors involved: word of mouth, or reviews that contradict one another, or aggressive advertising campaigns. Nevertheless, the press and potential audiences still consider critics one of the most powerful factors in the future of a new show, and the most powerful of these in the United States is the critic at the *New York Times.* Frank Rich, the *Times*'s theater critic through much of Lloyd Webber's career to date, has had mixed feelings about his supposed power as a critic, denying it, resisting it, yet knowing it was real, at least in many cases.[21] Rich rarely wrote anything better than a mixed review for Lloyd Webber's shows, and by the time *Aspects of Love* reached New York, a feud of a rather personal nature had arisen between the two men.[22] Director Trevor Nunn, in part responsible for the successes of *Cats* and *Les Misérables,* finds the *Times*'s power "destructive and undignified" even when it works in his favor. He resents the fact that one paper seems to have an overwhelming, emperor-like thumbs-up-or-down power over a show, revealed to the world on the morning after opening night.[23] In London, no single paper reigns supreme, nor are opening nights considered quite the life-or-death moment they are in New York. On the other hand, critics in both cities do have some powers in common: if a paper likes a show, it will run follow-up pieces, interviews, background stories, features on the creative team and the performers; this is wonderful free publicity. Any good review, moreover, is fodder for quotation: a nice phrase about a show often finds its way onto posters and newspaper and television ads for a show.

There has always been debate over the qualifications of critics, the chief charge being that, in the case of reviewing musicals, they know theater but not music. There is something to this complaint: it is rare indeed to find a morning-after review that discusses the music of a show in any depth. On the other hand, the critic is expected to discuss performances, staging, story, all the elements which might interest readers, who are usually not trained musicians. Nevertheless, ideally theater critics should have some musical training to review musicals at all, and if possible extensive training. This will allow critics to discuss, even briefly, all sorts of things about music and lyrics that might go unnoticed by less qualified observers.[24]

Many critics, whether they know music or not, have adopted an anti-Lloyd

Webber stance and stuck with it for years. In the 1980s it became extremely hip to hate Andrew Lloyd Webber. It was "fashionable to dismiss" his work as pandering to the lowest common denominator, implying somehow that critics, apparently smarter than audiences, were above his works.[25] Michael Coveney speculates, quite reasonably, that backlash against the too-popular Lloyd Webber probably set in during the peak of fame he experienced in the 1980s. The "tone of envious jeering and childish rudeness that characterizes quite a lot of press comment" from around this time is difficult to take seriously.[26] Critics may have had valid points to make, but the tone certainly made them less effective. "It's just jealousy, and isn't that too damn bad," opines director Hal Prince dismissively.[27] It wasn't long before rude remarks about Lloyd Webber extended beyond theater reviews into popular culture in general. Nasty comments about Lloyd Webber popped up in the 1980s in movie reviews, worst-dressed lists, and stand-up comedy routines.

Despite the critical trend against Lloyd Webber, the idea that all critics dismiss or detest his work is more cultural stereotype than truth. As other chapters of this book discuss, almost every Lloyd Webber show receives at least a few raves, and most garner mixed reviews rather than outright pans. Nevertheless, since the 1980s it has been the norm to dislike Lloyd Webber's contribution to a show more than to praise it. But by the time of *The Phantom of the Opera,* his shows required no reviews at all to be financial successes, and bad reviews rarely hurt them. Walsh calls him "perhaps the only critic-proof composer in the world," which was certainly true for about twenty-five years, and he points out that his shows rarely run critics' raves in his advertising; there is little need to do so.[28] Cameron Mackintosh helped Lloyd Webber reach this critic-proof status with *Cats;* catchy quotes in advertisements could be disregarded in favor of a simple pair of yellow cats' eyes. Indeed, *Cats* received mixed reviews, including Frank Rich's distinctly less-than-thrilled observations in the *New York Times,* and yet it remains the second-longest-running show in Broadway history.[29]

Our culture tends to separate forms of musical theater into two categories: high art intended to be intellectually and creatively fulfilling, and popular shows intended to entertain. I have already argued that this construct is largely a result of critical rhetoric, and that shows can be both smart and entertaining, and that audiences can be both smart and entertained. Nevertheless, the idea of high versus popular persists, to the point that Lloyd Webber himself has occasionally spoken in these terms, and on both sides. He is sometimes proud to be an entertainer, and casts some of his shows in this light, but at other times he complains of being misunderstood, that he is a serious composer with some respectable works to his credit that somehow fly under the critics' radar.

As we see later in this chapter with the discussion of the emphasis on spectacle and marketing in the musicals of the 1980s, for some historians Lloyd Webber has come to represent the commercializing and simplifying of a formerly noble and meaningful genre.[30] Lloyd Webber knows and loves popular music— he grew up on rock 'n' roll—just as he knows and loves classical music. He is aware that most of today's audiences know pop music too, and they know movies, and they expect spectacular modern trappings, and he happily gives them what they want. But to Lloyd Webber, those things are also the stuff of art, and his works help to prove that an invented line between art and entertainment can and should fade away.[31] Lloyd Webber can be "the Ziegfeld of his day" as he "gives people what they want," and yet he can still be artistically fulfilled, and fulfilling.[32]

The Tony Awards demonstrate the unstable standing Lloyd Webber has between art and popularity. The awards are voted on by about 700 theater insiders, including the board of the American Theatre Wing, the board of Actors' Equity, members of societies for performers, directors, choreographers, and producers, and all the important critics. A Tony, then, is a powerful mark of respect from knowledgeable voters, plus it often generates excellent publicity for a show, especially a struggling one; a nomination, and especially an award, can provoke a vast increase in ticket sales and keep a closing at bay. Lloyd Webber, not surprisingly, has an uneven Tony history, one that generally follows the critical receptions of his shows. *Superstar,* nominated for a few important awards, won none. *Evita* did extremely well, winning the crucial awards: best musical, book, score, director, and lead actress. *Cats* also won for best musical, book, score, director, and lead actress, and for costumes and lighting as well; the Tonys were far kinder to *Cats* than the somewhat hostile press had been. *Starlight Express* received nominations in all the major categories but won only for costumes, a fate quite in keeping with its critical reception, and even less surprising considering that its chief competition was the most successful megamusical of all time, *Les Misérables. The Phantom of the Opera* won best musical, director, lead actor, and many technical awards, but lost the crucial book and score awards to Sondheim's *Into the Woods. Sunset Boulevard* won virtually all the awards, but it was an embarrassingly weak year for musicals, so the victories in best musical, book, and score felt rather less weighty. *Aspects of Love,* on the other hand, was virtually ignored.[33]

There is no easy way to separate high and popular art in the case of recent musical theater, nor any reason to attempt to do so. Musical theater has always mixed the idea of hope for artistic fulfillment with hope for commercial success. The balance has shifted in emphasis over the centuries; some composers, in some eras in some countries, seem more concerned with one than the other. But every form of music theater requires an audience, and all creators hope viewers will enjoy their work, their art. So too Lloyd Webber.

The Marketing of International Successes

It's vital you sell me, so Machiavell-me

Eva Peron in *Evita*

Megamusicals travel well. They translate well; they can be marketed effectively in many countries; they speak to people in a clear way without too many culturally specific references. Some historians believe megamusicals are successful because they have no plots, and focus instead on spectacle, to suit dimwitted audiences. *Cats* and *Starlight Express,* one writer believes, do not have plots "which would occupy more than the back of a matchbook."[34]

A more accurate evaluation would be that megamusicals feature plots which are intended to be universal in nature. While it is true that *Cats* and *Starlight Express* are short on story, *The Phantom of the Opera* is quite full of plot, but despite its Parisian venue, it tells the familiar cross-cultural tale of beauty and beast. *Evita* and *Jesus Christ Superstar* both recount the rise and fall of a leader who came to power without complete preparedness, a story with parallels in many cultures. And *Les Misérables* has about as much plot as a musical can have, yet its themes of rebellion, revolution, loyalty, and true love are certainly ones to which almost any culture can relate. The choice of these plots over others which may have been more typical in the past has been noted by critics and historians, sometimes with dismay. What indeed seems to have been lost, both in England and in America, is the sense of local and contemporary flavor; instead, the shows depict ages past, lands far away. Before Lloyd Webber and Mackintosh, musicals did not regularly travel in either direction across the Atlantic. Some American musicals were too full of local humor and characters, local problems and (especially with recent composers such as Sondheim) New York angst. "The problem with the classic American musicals," Walsh explains, "was that they were too, well, *American.*"[35] Specifically American and also specifically English musicals were still being produced, but they simply were not being aggressively marketed to foreign countries. For the most part the two styles managed to coexist; English theater historian Sheridan Morley points out that the theater community should happily embrace an international hit like *Starlight Express* (a shallow but popular and enjoyable megamusical) if it means that Lloyd Webber can then finance a "specifically British musical" like *The Hired Man* (a small-scale musical about a British family, by Howard Goodall and Melvyn Bragg, from 1984).[36]

Historian Mark Steyn laments the loss of humor with the coming of the megamusical; he argues that humor is local and wit is embedded in tight little song forms. Megamusicals instead give us broad emotions and generic lyrics, and a paucity of jokes.[37] This is true to a certain degree; megamusicals by definition are usually serious, in keeping with their epic plots. But they contain without fail moments of comic relief, ones which play just fine all around the world. *Superstar* introduced this precedent with a mixture of lighthearted moments and heavy drama, and, of course, the over-the-top "King Herod's Song." A more traditional use of comic or light numbers exists in *The Phantom of the Opera* ("Notes," and the scene from *Il muto*) and *Les Misérables* ("Master of the House"). Some of the second-generation megamusicals, such as *The Scarlet Pimpernel* and *Beauty and the Beast,* are generally more comic than serious.

The new megamusical, with universal plot and concomitant potential for international appeal, was marketed using the methods of Lloyd Webber and Mackintosh. With *Cats,* Mackintosh introduced a marketing strategy which would prove successful to an unprecedented degree, not only for that show but for his future megamusicals. First, a very simple, memorable image represented a show: for *Cats,* two yellow cats' eyes on a black background, their pupils formed by shadowy dancers; for *Phantom,* a plain white mask and a red rose on a black background; for *Les Misérables,* a simple lithograph of a sad-faced waif in a beret. These recognizable images became fodder for vast amounts of merchandising: coffee mugs, T-shirts, books, refrigerator magnets, perfume, jewelry, key chains, posters, music boxes, snow globes. Items were available not only in the theater lobby but in souvenir shops and department stores. Mackintosh was not, of course, the first producer to sell show-related merchandise; Steyn traces his model to Lehár's *The Merry Widow* in 1905, which offered *Merry Widow* "gowns and gloves and broad-brimmed hats and corsets and trains and cocktails and cigarettes."[38] Mackintosh simply marketed more aggressively than anyone ever had before. He advertised to the point of saturation, on television, on radio, and in print ads. Commercials began to run long before opening day, so that by the time the show arrived, anticipation had built up (as had advance ticket sales).[39] Also, Mackintosh encouraged Lloyd Webber's strategy of releasing a single as a pop song long before the show opened; Lloyd Webber had tried it with *Superstar,* and Mackintosh would boldly capitalize on the idea for *Cats.* A hit song from a musical before it even premiered created an aura of "hit" around the show in general.

By the time *Cats* came along, Mackintosh's methods of promotion had joined with Lloyd Webber's own ideas about marketing, and the two formed the most powerful advertising team in Broadway history. In typical fashion, Lloyd Webber often downplays his interest in, and talent at, marketing and promotion. He often claims to be uninterested in such commercial activities and acts surprised when his songs become successes as singles. Yet his marketing skills are on a par with his talent at running a business.

Mackintosh cheerfully agrees. "Andrew is a brilliant natural exploiter of his own shows," he says, by way of compliment. "It runs parallel with his creative talent. He understands showmanship: knowing how to launch a song, finding the right artist to promote it, doing the right [television] programs and interviews. All of these things he does with consummate skill."[40] One statistic has Lloyd Webber doing over a hundred interviews on BBC television and radio alone, all before 1984.[41] And it is surely true that in the pop-oriented 1980s, only Lloyd Webber could have had a hit single from a Requiem mass. His "Pie Jesu" topped the *Billboard* charts in 1985, a feat which some saw as an example of great marketing skills, others as crass exploitation and calculation. Lloyd Webber, typically, expressed surprise: "It was not in one's head that one could have a Top Ten hit from a piece in Latin," he said, and his surprise may be genuine in this case. He added, "But that doesn't mean I'm not delighted that it happened."[42]

Soon after MCA released *Jesus Christ Superstar* as a concept album, an executive there lamented, "It's not a record, it's an industry."[43] This can be said of any megamusical; while the experience of seeing the show should be, and usually is, an emotional and fulfilling one for most audience members, the whole endeavor also demonstrates a calculated business side. Mackintosh's marketing skills are eerily powerful tools that create seemingly unavoidable urges to go see these shows; like the latest movie everyone must see, megamusicals are the shows that can't be missed. Also, his reach stretches beyond the London and New York openings. In the 1980s, after Mackintosh's most successful megamusicals opened, he sent the shows abroad. Unusual for traveling productions, these stagings were virtually identical to the original mountings in London and New York. The *Phantom of the Opera* you saw in New York was the same as that in Australia or Germany, and if you did not see it in New York, you could be assured that what you saw on your home turf was the genuine article. This created an "aura of celebration" when the "cloned" productions arrived in a foreign city.[44] Meanwhile, the powerful advertising of megamusicals meant that in "the tri-state area [New York, New Jersey, and Connecticut] of approximately 15 million people," *Cats, Les Misérables,* and *The Phantom of the Opera* became "the one event they had to experience on their birthday, anniversary, honeymoon, prom night, etc. It became a new lifestyle rite of passage."[45] The same has become true in cities all over the world.

On Sets, Hostility, and Money

> The so-called British musicals are not musicals. They have music that people have heard before, though they may not realize it. They have a story taken from a pop movie or *Madame Butterfly*. They have chandeliers, helicopters landing. As I said, and I was the first person to write it, you come out humming the scenery.
>
> Clive Barnes, quoted in Frommer and Frommer, *It Happened on Broadway*

Barnes's regard for the megamusical is shared by many critics who believe that a show with an emphasis on fancy scenery and visual trickery must be seeking to compensate for deficiencies of plot and music. As we have seen, such critics wrongly assume that stage spectacle alone is sufficient to dazzle audiences in what is otherwise an unsatisfactory evening of musical theater. While it is true that megamusicals lavish much attention on their visual components, the spectacle usually serves the story. The over-the-top effect of a helicopter landing onstage is undeniable, but that stunt's role in the overall success of *Miss Saigon* was much less than the publicity surrounding it might have suggested. Only a few shows could be called fundamentally visual. From the outset, Lloyd Webber and his team intended *Starlight Express* to be a show which allowed the audience to watch moving trains onstage. The way to execute this goal developed along with the creation of the score and the other elements of the show. In the case of *The Phantom of the Opera, Les Misérables,* and most other megamusicals, there is no reason to believe that source material was chosen based on its visual possibilities. Lloyd Webber chose *The Phantom of the Opera* for its romantic story, not its falling chandelier (like *Miss Saigon*'s helicopter, an overhyped but entirely integrated moment of visual spectacle). However, Barnes and his peers have a point: the megamusical is regularly executed with huge stagings that are not entirely necessary, even if they serve their plots well. Certainly small-scale stagings could dramatize the same stories. Nonetheless, since the stories themselves are of epic proportions, it is only logical that megamusicals match them in scale.

As noted, critics are often reduced to explaining the new theatrical style by insulting the audience, and they often use spectacle as the means to do it. Howard Kissel of the *New York Daily News* is typical in his comments: "The Andrew Lloyd Webber shows and the like fulfill many people's idea of what an evening in the theater is supposed to be: spectacle, constantly changing panoramas, theater as a movie. The average person doesn't know that something should happen to him while he's watching a play."[46] But Kissel seems unaware of the weeping in the audience that inevitably accompanies the end of *Les Misérables*—during which nothing in particular happens visually—or the cheering that erupts after the Phantom sings "The Music of the Night" standing still on a mostly unmoving set. Something does happen to many people while watching these plays, belying his characterization about what "many people's idea" of theater is, and their emotional reactions can hardly be credited to the sets alone. Instead of examining the audience's motivations for their positive reactions, he remains steadfast in his commitment to his own negative one. Presenting his reaction is certainly his job, and he is welcome to ignore the reactions of those around him, but his views demonstrate the expanding gulf between critic and audience—or between the editors who employ the critics and the theatergoers they putatively serve. Kissel laments the loss of the Golden Era of the 1940s, he resents the influence of television and (for no apparent reason) Bob Dylan, and he projects onto the audience the exhaustion that he describes himself feeling after seeing a megamusical. Mimi Kramer, writing in the *New Yorker,* feels that megamusicals are driven by the urge to try to pull off something difficult technically, without bothering to worry about the quality of the score or talent on the stage: "Achievement here lies not in ingenuity or skill, or even in the gimmick concept, but in the idea of extravagance itself."[47]

Some of this hostility toward the new large plots and sets comes from a resentment of any change in the style of musical theater. Some critics seem unwilling or unable to adjust to new styles, even when well executed, and their reviews make them sound old, tired, rigid, out of touch. Others have happily (or even unhappily) kept in touch with the changes, and therefore can evaluate with more discrimination each megamusical on its own terms rather than dismissing megamusicals as a group. More objective critics point out that visual effects have always been part of musical theater, the history of which includes eras in which plot or words or music or spectacle is emphasized over other elements. Steyn offers as evidence an extensive list of musical theater that used water and boats in various ways, from the interesting to the all-out distracting.[48] He argues that musical theater, including opera, has always been visual first and foremost; this is why we prefer to see the show live, rather than listening to a recording or studying the score. We expect dancing, singing, and interesting things to look at that support the story being unfolded. "By definition," Steyn summarizes, "all musicals have to be large," at least in spirit. Musicals, unlike plays, require a large heart, a grandness of gesture, something other than a flat presentation of story.[49] Like nineteenth-century French grand opera, the megamusical represents a particularly large phase in the history of an always large genre.

In the last several decades of the twentieth century, grandness of spirit required money, as it had in the second half of the nineteenth century. In the 1980s, with Broadway enjoying one of the peaks of spectacle in musical theater that Steyn mentions, the cost of mounting such elaborate shows skyrocketed— not only because it took far more money to mount and run the technology, but because of a whole series of other factors: massive advertising; demands from unionized actors, instrumentalists, and stagehands; the inevitable hike in ticket prices; and a sudden rise in theater rental prices.[50] Rosenberg and Harburg argue that the cost of mounting a show also rose partly as a result of having multiple producers on a show. For the most part, shows since the 1980s no longer have one producer at the helm, Cameron Mackintosh excepted. In the old days, a producer would gather small amounts of money from multiple investors, traditionally called angels, but would do the actual producing himself. Now he or she is more likely to accept huge donations from a few corporations which, because of their steep investment, wish to be involved directly as producers themselves. When a show is produced by this unqualified, cumbersome committee, Rosenberg and Harburg point out, the result is loss of control over the budget, as well as poor artistic choices and lack of clear leadership. A strong director can often correct this, as can a producer such as Mackintosh, who retains his leadership despite the presence of demanding investors.[51]

With the rise of the megamusical as a durable genre, producers and directors had to look for ways to guarantee a return on investments despite the enormous initial costs. Advertising, chief among these, led to many an expensive musical becoming a hit. But the most reliable way to make a profit on the megamusical was to export it. When producers understood that the megamusical traveled well, they saw that even a show which was risky on Broadway could pay off in national and international tours.

Cameron Mackintosh and the "British Invasion"

> Other than Cameron Mackintosh's and Andrew Lloyd Webber's, all British musicals are weird.
>
> Mark Steyn, *Broadway Babies Say Goodnight*

Theater historians agree that until the megamusical, British musical theater failed to impress. While of course the British created a few wonderful gems and occasionally exported these to the United States, England did not nurture a community of musical theater creators churning out show after show. Instead, British musicals tended to be created by ever-changing teams of unlikely artists, and critics almost always saw these as lagging behind Broadway: "British musicals, when they were considered at all, conjured up images of aging vaudevillians with straw boaters and canes barking strophic ballads at nodding pensioners."[52] It was simply not an artistic field at which the British seemed interested in excelling; the musical was an American genre. Steyn points out that despite the copious talents of a few artists (Noel Coward, Lionel Bart, Anthony Newley), until the 1970s British musicals still tended to have clunky lyrics by playwrights, not lyricists, and old-fashioned scores moving awkwardly through weak plots.[53] Lloyd Webber and Rice, then, sprang from almost no tradition in their home country. They knew some American musicals and loved a few, but were far more interested in pop music and opera than in the stop-and-sing style of earlier musicals. They invented the megamusical, or at least what would become the megamusical, by mixing the elements from all their musical influences and making the rest up, and thus began the British Invasion.

Sheridan Morley declares that the changes in British theater in the 1970s, thanks to *Superstar* and *Evita,* were equivalent to "getting from the Stone Age to the Restoration in a single weekend." While *Superstar* was exciting, it had its start in America; historians considered the new British trend real only after *Evita* was successfully mounted in London and exported to New York. Morley notes, "For the first time in the eighteen years since *Oliver!* London could actually boast a musical which could be exported across the Atlantic with a feeling of pride instead of the usual deep embarrassment." By the time Lloyd Webber sent *Cats* and *Phantom* across the ocean, the British leadership of the world of musical theater was obvious to all. Not only were British shows being staged beautifully in London and shipped overseas to great acclaim, but back in London, British teams restaged American musicals in interesting, successful new ways. "As a result," notes Morley, "London almost overnight became the capital city of musicals, both old and new, minuscule and massive, native and foreign."[54] Lloyd Webber was rewarded for making his mark by watching his original London *Superstar* run for ten years, and *Evita* for eight; *Cats* (the record-holder at twenty-one years) closed finally in May 2002, and *Phantom* continues to run strong.

It did not take long for it to become clear that what seemed like a British invasion was really just the invasion of three men: Andrew Lloyd Webber, Cameron Mackintosh, and Trevor Nunn. Director Nunn worked with Lloyd Webber and Mackintosh on *Cats,* with Mackintosh on *Les Misérables,* and with Lloyd Webber on *Sunset Boulevard.* (Also, Tim Rice, though largely absent from the megamusical in its 1980s heyday, was crucial to its creation in the 1970s and returned to it, with new partners, full-force in the 1990s.)

Cameron Mackintosh was apparently a born producer. By the time he was eight, he had already developed a knack for persuading people to give him money so he could put on shows. As a young man he learned as much as he could about stage managing, bookings, publicity, tours, program notes, advertising, and performing. Success came in 1976 with *Side by Side by Sondheim,* followed by several hit revivals. Lloyd Webber, knowing what a tough sell *Cats* would be, asked Mackintosh to produce it, and Mackintosh rose to the challenge.[55] Mackintosh would follow *Cats* with the biggest international hit of all time, *Les Misérables,* among other successes.

Resentment toward the invasion of these men can be strong indeed. As people flocked to see *The Phantom of the Opera* and *Les Misérables,* one historian opines, the megamusical trend "almost choked the theatre to death."[56] Less expensive, less spectacular shows could not compete, while megamusicals set up shop in a theater and stayed for years. Historian Richard Kislan concedes that the British imports did wonders for a struggling Broadway economy, but he portrays the British as interested only in money, not theater.[57] Jack Kroll, theater critic for *Newsweek,* took a particularly bold stance against the British invasion by writing a feature article about the "debacle" of these "foreign devils." Writing in 1987, after *Cats* had "secured the beachhead" and *Starlight Express* and *Les Misérables* followed, Kroll's tone was sarcastic but heartfelt. Kroll's military invasion metaphor continued: filling in the bomb craters left by flops from Hal Prince, Charles Strouse, Bob Fosse, and Marvin Hamlisch are the hits by Lloyd Webber, Mackintosh, and Nunn. At this rate, Kroll predicted, Lloyd Webber would be the most successful stage composer of all time and Mackintosh would be "just about the most powerful, enterprising and sought-after producer in Western civilization." Kroll explained with more reasonable objectivity the reason why the British were succeeding where natives could not: first, the new composers gave audiences an emotional, direct musical style that they seem to want; and second, the stagings were incredibly innovative. Speaking for many critics, Kroll both praised some of the British shows and lamented their existence on formerly American-dominated Broadway.[58]

The rise to prominence of Lloyd Webber, Mackintosh, Nunn, and the British musical theater in general had some happy results in England. As Sheridan Morley argues, now that the British theater had joined modern times, producers and creators developed an interest in reviving and cultivating home-grown musicals of the non-mega sort. In true testament to his reach, even the credit for this goes partly to Lloyd Webber. In the 1970s and 1980s, Lloyd Webber and Rice stirred up an interest in British musical theater and tried to create a few local-flavored shows of their own; unfortunately, both Lloyd Webber's *Jeeves* and Rice's *Blondel* flopped. Lloyd Webber's Really Useful Group also backed a number of plays and musicals in which he was involved only as a hands-off producer (as he still does with, for example, *Bombay Dreams,* which reached Broadway in 2004; Lloyd Webber is given co-credit only for producing and for the "idea"). The British musical theater also received a strong boost from traditional theatrical organizations becoming involved in musicals: Trevor Nunn brought his Royal Shakespeare Company team with him when he directed *Cats* and *Les Misérables,* for example.

Still, the British musical theater beyond Lloyd Webber, Nunn, and Mackintosh has continued to struggle. While some new composers have achieved success in the West End, none have made a lasting impact in New York since Lloyd Webber and the *Les Misérables* creators Schönberg and Boublil (from France by way of London). British creators are still making their mark, to be sure, like Elton John with his contributions to *The Lion King* and *Aida*—both with Tim Rice's lyrics—but there remains little musical theater on Broadway that originated in England. Even in the 1980s, when Broadway seemed filled with imported shows, London was filled with Broadway shows. In 1982, with the industry beginning to feel the impact of *Cats,* there were more Broadway shows running in the West End than vice versa. By 1985, American musicals constituted the major force other than Lloyd Webber: London had ten American musicals running (such as *West Side Story, Barnum,* and *Guys and Dolls*), plus three Lloyd Webber shows (*Cats, Evita,* and *Starlight Express*), and one other original British musical plus two revivals.[59] The British Invasion, then, boiled down to Lloyd Webber and his team, and London was overrun in return by American offerings. Soon, the lines between the two countries would blur almost out of existence; teams of creators were made up of people from both countries, and musicals would not be so easily labeled "British" or "American."

"Want to Hear Some Tunes?"

Andrew Lloyd Webber studied music from early on, classical music formally and popular music rigorously on his own. Biographer Michael Coveney notes that Lloyd Webber cites his two favorite pieces as being Prokofiev's *Love for Three Oranges* and Bill Haley's "Rock Around the Clock." As Coveney suggests, this nicely encapsulates Lloyd Webber's musical influences and his resulting style, which mixes classical and pop traditions.[60] Lloyd Webber always knew he would be a composer and was writing music by age six. His *Toy Theatre Suite* was published in a magazine in 1959 when he was eleven, and, in an interesting example of his tendency to reuse his own tunes, one of the songs from the suite made its way into *Joseph.* By his teens, Lloyd Webber was composing musicals for his classmates, beginning with *Cinderella Up the Beanstalk and Most Everywhere Else!* in 1961. He saw some West End shows with his Aunt Vi, but none made a particularly strong impression on him; more important was what he learned from her about fine wine and food. He did adore the movie version of *South Pacific,* and he was highly influenced by seeing Maria Callas in *Tosca.*[61]

At first, the Broadway world seemed to ignore his classical training, as they often saddled him with an orchestrator, despite the fact that he does all his own orchestration expertly, only occasionally with the input of a co-orchestrator. Most of the work that outside orchestrators have done on his scores has amounted to little more than arrangements, adapting the score to fit the live orchestra rather than the orchestra Lloyd Webber used on the concept album, for example. Lloyd Webber is an avid student of musical structure, and often studies scores of other composers to analyze their forms, shape, and technique.

"Pastiche" has become a word used so often in association with Lloyd Webber's music that it almost ceases to have meaning. There are some blatant, usually humorous, pastiches of musical styles in Lloyd Webber's work, and he fully intends audiences to notice and enjoy them. These pastiche numbers stand out from the rest of the score, and yet critics often simply dismiss Lloyd Webber as a pastiche artist, somehow misunderstanding the deliberately derivative music while ignoring the rest of the score. The pastiche numbers are intentionally clear. In *Joseph and the Amazing Technicolor Dreamcoat,* there is a country song, an Elvis rock song, a calypso number, and a French chanson. In *The Phantom of the Opera,* Lloyd Webber parodies Meyerbeer in the *Hannibal* scene and Mozart in *Il muto.* And in *Cats,* he presents an even more extensive opera parody, this time of Puccini, the composer most often cited as Lloyd Webber's strongest influence. He became so tired of being accused of writing Puccini-like music, in fact, that he added to *Cats* the Puccini scene, "Growltiger's Last Stand," on purpose. "Everyone says it's Puccini-esque because it *is,*" said an annoyed Lloyd Webber of "Memory," which he had set up as a Puccini-like moment of heightened drama.[62] *Cats* also features a dance-hall tap number, a rock song, and a few other purposely identifiable styles. In other works, such as *Evita* and *Sunset Boulevard,* references to musical styles are more fluid; *Evita* features some Latin rhythms and flavors in various songs, and *Sunset Boulevard* evokes the sounds of late 1940s Hollywood.

All this tends to annoy Lloyd Webber's stronger critics, who feel that his music sounds no more than cobbled together from other sources, rather than reflective of a personal style of his own. "If imitation is the sincerest form of flattery," wrote one critic on *Phantom,* "Puccini must be in hog heaven."[63] Another opined that Lloyd Webber can "assume but not assimilate imitations of all sorts of other music with disastrous ease."[64] Other oft-cited influences besides Puccini include Prokofiev, Stravinsky, Ravel, and Richard Rodgers. As Walsh astutely points out, what this means is that people say "(a) his music all sounds the same, and (b) it all derives from elsewhere—even though that elsewhere is only rarely specified, and when it is, it is usually wrong."[65] Critics often simply complain that Lloyd Webber's music sounds vaguely familiar. When critics or historians do go hunting for actual stolen tunes, they rarely find any, and when they do, the results do not amount to much. He borrows from himself all the time, usually using tunes he has written for unfinished projects or for no particular project at all; occasionally, one of these tunes will actually show up in two successful works. But despite the critics' cries of "I hear Puccini!" Lloyd Webber does have a style that is fundamentally, recognizably his, one which incorporates all his classical, popular, and theatrical influences. He is exceedingly well trained and constantly aware of what he writes. "Whatever else one might accuse him of," summarizes Walsh, "to accuse him of being a mere pastiche artist or plagiarist is purely an expression of historical ignorance."[66]

Other than the occasional hostile critic, few people have openly accused Lloyd Webber of outright plagiarism, and their efforts to prove it have come to naught. In 1990, a man named Ray Repp, who composed religious folk music, sued Lloyd Webber, claiming that the song "The Phantom of the Opera" had been taken from his 1978 song "Till You." The suit was quickly thrown out; there was no evidence that Lloyd Webber could have known the obscure song, which had earned a total of $78.09 for Repp over the years, nor was there much to support Repp's claim that the songs sounded similar. In court, Lloyd Webber cheerfully admitted to the influences of a Bach Preludium, Grieg's "Melodie," and Holst's "Glittering Sunbeams," but he had never heard of Repp or his music. When Repp threatened to appeal the ruling, Lloyd Webber countersued, claiming that "Till You" in fact stole from his own earlier song "Close Every Door." To Repp's chagrin, the case went to trial, because there were actually vague similarities between these two songs. Eventually the court ruled in Repp's favor, a result that Lloyd Webber had fully intended, with the hope that it would inspire Repp to drop his appeal; Lloyd Webber was far more capable of keeping this up for years than Repp was. But Repp pushed onward, and everyone from Sarah Brightman (for the defense) to musicologist H. Wiley Hitchcock (for the prosecution) testified. The jury came back with a "not guilty" ruling in just over an hour. "I have been totally vindicated," said Lloyd Webber. "Perhaps we will now see the end of these money-grabbing spurious cases."[67] Despite the fact that the case was, indeed, spurious and highly frivolous, the media had a field day, reveling in the accusation that Lloyd Webber might indeed be stealing rather than inventing his catchy tunes.

When critics review a new Lloyd Webber show, and when historians write about one in retrospect, they focus their attention on those moments in the score that are readily recognizable as purposeful pastiches. This is understandably true of morning-after reviews. The critic's ear, especially if untrained in music, latches onto what it knows, and the result is often a lopsided review, focusing on a few numbers to the detriment of the work as a whole. The majority of the music in a Lloyd Webber show, even a pastiche-filled show such as *Cats*, still bears the stamp of Lloyd Webber's style. Lloyd Webber himself offers an explanation for this critical fixation on the catchy and dismissal of everything else: "The trouble is that the moment you give people a lot of melody in one evening it's awfully difficult for them to take in. Their normal view would be that it's either 'unmelodic' or 'derivative' or whatever. They will *not* take a vast amount of melodic invention in an evening."[68] There is too much going on, he implies: if you throw too many melodies out there, critics will write some of them off as too hard to process. More important, when a melody returns in a new context, and usually with new words, it will have a different, deeper meaning. This is a favorite technique of Lloyd Webber's; all his shows feature a number of melodies which return in different contexts. Tim Rice admires this aspect of Lloyd Webber's approach to a show's overall structure: "In all his work reprises of principal tunes have been his trademark, and frequently the cause of unintelligent criticism. This practice makes the whole much more than a string of tunes and can often make points that mere words cannot, such as the physical decline of a star [as with the return of 'Don't Cry for Me, Argentina' in *Evita*]."[69] Mackintosh supports Rice in his assessment of the value of Lloyd Webber's reprise technique as part of his large-scale thinking about structure: "He's a great respecter of craft. It's just nonsense when people say his shows have only one tune. Andrew will plot every single note from the outset to the play-out in a theatrical arc. He likes to build what he calls an unsinkable boat, constructing and butting everything together."[70] Lloyd Webber is a master of the "melodic invention" he mentioned above, and he masterfully regulates its flow.

Melodic invention in fact is where it all begins for Lloyd Webber; he writes tunes first. His harmonies, orchestration, changeable rhythms, all can be surprising, inventive, beautiful, but the tunes come first. To interviewers and guests, he asks, "Want to hear some tunes?" and then plays them on the piano and sings along (badly).[71] As Walsh points out, he can "whip up a song, or dive into his drawer to retrieve one, in practically no time."[72]

As with the pastiche issue, the melody issue has become oversimplified in writings about Lloyd Webber. More than that, scholars admire his simple tunes, when in fact many of his melodies do not fit this description. Musical supervisor David Caddick speaks highly of Lloyd Webber's simplicity: "Andrew writes very simple, beautiful melodies. They're not complex, they're very forward and direct. That is a style that is very appealing to the public because it's conveyed in a very simple and direct message. What confounds the critics is the simplicity. It doesn't have pretensions of being other than it is."[73] It is true that the music does not sound pretentious, and it is indeed sometimes true that Lloyd Webber writes simple and clean melodies. "Memory" could be described as straightforward in its prettiness. So too "I Don't Know How to Love Him" from *Superstar,* "The Music of the Night" from *Phantom,* and any number of pleasant examples. But Lloyd Webber's melodies are also often intricate, free-formed, and complex. The chorus of "Hosanna" from *Superstar* features many unpredictable turns. The refrain of "Goodnight and Thank You" from *Evita* rests on strange leaps and dissonances as well as uneven phrase lengths. The title song from *Sunset Boulevard* lurches into unexpected rhythmic and melodic territory throughout. Lloyd Webber can be even bolder when he writes for more than one voice; the quartet "Falling" from *Aspects of Love* is as dissonant a piece as Broadway has ever heard. And all these, too, are typical Lloyd Webber melodies. He knows how to use dissonance and atonality, and, as he puts it, he has "no fear about where I will make harmony go, so long as I can make melody take it there naturally."[74] Unfortunately, Lloyd Webber has said very little about the complexities of his music, as few have bothered to question him about it. When given the chance, Lloyd Webber speaks eloquently about the intricacies in his scores (in this case, *Evita*):

> I don't expect people to recognize what's going on in the score at first hearing—how the motifs are planted, how they lie in the orchestration. If that is what you *had* to understand to appreciate *Evita,* it would fail for you. But without those interwoven musical elements, the work would be much less effective and interesting. They are catalysts for what is happening on the stage.
>
> If there's no musical subtext, a work will be shallow. In *Evita* there are moments when the various themes of the piece begin to combine. In the end, they combine to kill her. The first time we hear the death motif is when she meets Perón. There's a harp interlude when she turns the girl out of Perón's apartment. It's implied Evita and Perón have made love, or are about to. It's

the first time for the death theme, so I've musically doomed her at this point. And that death theme starts to take over the others. It becomes more and more twisted. In the end it becomes quite obvious, so that death seems inevitable.[75]

In another interview, Lloyd Webber does a tidy job of defending both the complexity of his work and the intelligence of his audences: "I put an awful lot into these scores. It is not a matter of two or three songs repeated and repeated. If people think it is, they are crazy. The reason why the public responds is that the pieces are very rich."[76]

While Lloyd Webber may be known for his lovely melodies, Broadway has never been lacking in these. More important has been his enormous influence on the structure of the Broadway show: because of his work with Tim Rice, many new Broadway musicals were largely sung-through. There is little dialogue in most of Lloyd Webber's shows—the only exceptions being *Sunset Boulevard* and *Whistle Down the Wind,* though these too are still largely sung—nor in those of his primary megamusical followers Schönberg and Boublil.[77] But the influence of the sung-through style reached beyond this first generation of composers, into the 1990s, with shows entirely or almost entirely sung: *The Secret Garden* by Lucy Simon and Marsha Norman, *Ragtime* by Stephen Flaherty and Lynn Ahrens, *Rent* by Jonathan Larson, *Marie Christine* by Michael John La Chiusa, *Parade* by Jason Robert Brown, *Titanic* by Maury Yeston, *Jekyll and Hyde* by Frank Wildhorn and Leslie Bricusse, and *The Scarlet Pimpernel* by Wildhorn and Nan Knighton, to name a few. These musicals, moreover, feature a number of other megamusical elements in various combinations, such as epic plots, historical settings, and large stagings.

While there were occasional sung-through shows in the past (Loesser's quite operatic *The Most Happy Fella,* for example), *Jesus Christ Superstar* made the absence of spoken dialogue intrinsic to the megamusical style. Lloyd Webber decided that with his vast knowledge of opera, especially when weighed against his relative lack of experience in book-based musical theater, an opera-like sung-through form made sense. Also, he reveals himself to be something of a control freak, and the sung-through style suits him: "The most important thing for the composer is to be able to control the piece from A to B. If you have any dialogue, no matter how brilliant, that interrupts the flow, it means the composer is not in the driver's seat."[78] Opera taught him this. He and Rice agreed from the start that this was a more effective structure, and if one wanted to call *Superstar* and *Evita* operas, that was fine with them. Rice was a lyricist, not a playwright, and felt he was most effective writing lyrics, not dialogue. He and those who followed found endless ways to give a sung-through show just as much structure and variety as a stop-and-sing show. Don Black, a lyricist who worked with Lloyd Webber on *Aspects of Love* and *Sunset Boulevard*, feels that although a show may be sung throughout, there are still countless ways to set up a separate number, a dramatic moment, a change of mood.[79] In partnership with Lloyd Webber, the lyricists have found interesting ways to make sections that clearly function as set pieces, and recitative-like sections, and all manner of transitional, amorphous, loosely structured material in between.

In his *Musical! A Grand Tour*, historian Denny Martin Flinn, no fan of the megamusical, finds the sung-through style unimpressive and detests the "poperetta" of Lloyd Webber and the like.[80] The biggest problem, he claims, is that it forces the characters to sing even the most trite ideas. Steyn argues a longer version of the same view, but with more sympathy.[81] The sung-through form works quite well for Lloyd Webber's shows, he points out, because the big emotions and grand stories leave little to chat about in dialogue. Steyn argues that the hardest thing to write in a musical is the book, not the music or the lyrics, and that sung-through musicals (and opera) avoid this challenge by ignoring the book. (By book, typically, Steyn means spoken dialogue, although book credit in the case of sung-through musicals goes to whoever crafted the plot.) He believes the rise in tension from dialogue to underscoring to song is gone. But surely the rise from recitative to scena to solo or duet or ensemble is just as effective. Still, Steyn concludes, "Whether you think Jule Styne is a better composer than Verdi is up to you; but it's not difficult to argue that, in the relationship between the elements and in the fusion of music and lyrics, the American musical is formally more sophisticated, more discriminating, than opera." It surely goes without saying that these anti-opera views reflect an enormous bias toward early musical theater and a distinct misunderstanding of opera. A show without dialogue has different challenges, but not fewer challenges; there is nothing inherently more or less sophisticated about one or the other genre.

Many operas feature dialogue, and a lack of dialogue does not automatically make a piece of musical theater an opera. *The Phantom of the Opera*, for example, is a musical that has much in common with certain types of opera, with its Mozartean ensembles and its *verismo* spirit. Lloyd Webber has clearly learned much from opera, reflected in the way he strings together solo numbers, ensembles, and transitional material. The most useful course of action would be to stop distinguishing between opera and musical theater altogether; in this era, Broadway musicals are the popular musical theater form, as opera of previous centuries had been. Critics use the term opera in association with Lloyd Webber in order to link his works with a lineage inherited from Meyerbeer, Verdi, and Puccini. Calling Lloyd Webber's works operas does not relate them to, say, Philip Glass or John Adams; it merely evokes a superficial air of classiness and artistic merit. As Walsh argues, regarding the actual difference between opera and musicals, "There isn't any."[82] However, there are a few features of Lloyd Webber's style other than the mere lack of dialogue that provide more legitimate reasons to ponder opera's influence.

One obvious link to opera is the use of operatic voices in the megamusical, a convention that Lloyd Webber himself did not come to until *The Phantom of the Opera. Jesus Christ Superstar* is comprised entirely of pop voices, from sweet ballad singers to hard rock tenors, and *Evita* and *Joseph* feature Broadway belters. With *The Phantom of the Opera,* and with the arrival of Sarah Brightman in his life, Lloyd Webber developed an interest in the classical soprano voice, and created a show with a mixture of operatic and Broadway voices. *The Phantom of the Opera* therefore features a lyric soprano and two Broadway-style tenors, backed by a caricatured dramatic soprano and various other standard Broadway voices in all ranges. Schönberg and Boublil went one step further a year sooner, giving each character an even more distinct vocal style, one in keeping with his or her character, until they had populated the cast of *Les Misérables* with one of every possible vocal type: a pair of young lovers, lyric soprano and lyric tenor; a jaded, smoky alto; a spunky girl belter; a dramatic baritone villain; a dramatic tenor hero. Broadway had featured, of course, lyric soprano voices of the Julie Andrews sort in the 1940s and 1950s, not to mention operetta voices since the early twentieth century, but it also gave a home to the belters (Ethel Merman, Mary Martin, Gwen Verdon) and the actor-singers (Rex Harrison, Robert Preston, Richard Burton, William Daniels). By the 1970s, Broadway and pop voices had pushed operatic and lyric voices firmly out of the way; it was Christine in *The Phantom of the Opera* and Cosette in *Les Misérables* that integrated the operatic voice into the megamusical.[83]

Historians of the musical mention other operatic features which make their presence felt in the megamusical. Stephen Citron argues that the love song— the straight-ahead, sincere, guileless love song—returned in the megamusical after an absence since the days of operetta. Songs like "A Heart Full of Love" from *Les Misérables* and "All I Ask of You" from *The Phantom of the Opera* are entirely without the doubt or reflection one finds in earlier musicals or in musicals of the non-megamusical sort, like Stephen Sondheim's.[84] Steyn argues that megamusicals feature bland, interchangeable lyrics that sound more like opera than like the lyrics of the witty wordsmiths of the Golden Era. While examples of generic love song lyrics can certainly be found in the megamusical (Steyn's example: "Say you'll share with me one love, one lifetime / Say the word and I will follow you" from "All I Ask of You" in *Phantom*), it is easy to counter with examples of the character-specific lyric in the megamusical: "A Heart Full of Love" from *Les Misérables* is an equally corny love song, yet it is appropriate only to the characters involved. By the same token, examples of the generic and interchangeable love lyric abound in the older musical; "Some Enchanted Evening" from *South Pacific* and "Till There Was You" from *The Music Man* come to mind. Still, Steyn's analogy of Lloyd Webber to some operatic composers is well taken; musicals to this point had always been a collaborative effort, and few composers, even those who wrote their own lyrics, seemed as interested as Lloyd Webber in maintaining artistic control of a project. Not unlike Verdi or Wagner, Lloyd Webber the composer sees himself as the leader of the creative team and often chief dramatist as well.[85]

For Lloyd Webber, the distinction between opera and musicals is no more than a matter of where they are performed. He is usually content to have his works called operas, and in fact he encouraged the term with *Evita* and *The Phantom of the Opera,* in an effort to get his works taken more seriously. But people consider them musicals, he argues correctly, because they run eight times a week in Broadway theaters rather than eight times a season in an opera house. The label "musical" annoys him at times, despite the fact that it has always been his life's work, for he feels that it has limited his ability to become known as a "serious composer."[86] He said back in 1981 that he was annoyed by *Jesus Christ Superstar*'s massive popularity and strong pro and con reactions because it pigeonholed him as a writer of musicals; his instrumental work *Variations* went unnoticed, for example. This is another of Lloyd Webber's self-contradictory moments; in other discussions he embraces musical theater wholeheartedly and expresses delighted surprise over his popularity. All the same, his desire for legitimacy, respectability, a more classical and sophisticated reputation, is undeniable.[87] Verdi, Puccini, and Mozart may have been show business composers of musical theater in their time, but their enduring historical importance under the "opera" heading means that any new works listed under the same heading automatically gain a certain weight.

Just as the word "opera" hovers about Lloyd Webber's work, so too does the word "rock." *Jesus Christ Superstar* managed to combine the terms, and its label of "rock opera" was as good as any for the unusual style. Certainly the score, while not consistently rock-like in the strictest sense, drew more on popular musical styles than on theatrical ones. But Lloyd Webber would never be so rock-oriented again; while his music always draws on popular musical styles, it rarely delves into hard rock. A number of scholars find this inevitable, given the nature of rock music; by strict definition, rock is repetitive, and rather stagnant in terms of chords, beat, and form. It does not make particularly interesting theater music. But the massive impact that rock had on popular culture could not go ignored by Broadway, and eventually the megamusical absorbed its influence and altered it to make a modified Broadway-rock-pop style. As Steyn summarizes, "only on Broadway could Andrew Lloyd Webber be considered a rocker."[88] But Lloyd Webber's attention to current trends was one of the crucial factors to his success with *Jesus Christ Superstar,* and his continuing commitment to the use of popular music styles is fundamental to his own popularity. His overall musical style, and that of his immediate followers like Schönberg, mixes pop music of a broader-based sort with theatrical music. Megamusicals feature ballads, tinged with pop, country, blues, or cabaret influences; they also offer hard-driving up-tempo numbers, songs in an early rock 'n' roll style, and love duets that could work just as well in the movies or on television as they do onstage. All these appear alongside quasi-operatic ensembles and purely theatrical styles.[89]

Tim Rice

This mix of Broadway and opera, of rock and classical music, massively staged, make the megamusical for which Lloyd Webber has become so famous. But Lloyd Webber did not invent the musical style of the megamusical alone; in fact, he was not even the primary instigator of the form. Tim Rice's role to this point in the history of the megamusical has been understated; it was largely his idea, for example, to through-sing *Jesus Christ Superstar, Joseph and the Amazing Technicolor Dreamcoat,* and *Evita.* He could not have predicted the megamusical in its later embodiment as the epic, spectacle-driven, melodramatic style it became. In retrospect he can take some credit for its invention:

> Whether we knew what we were doing or not, Andrew and I effected an important and lasting change in British musical history, and even in world musical history, as writers. After *Evita,* the producer has been king [referring to matters of marketing, money, and leadership] and the only major change has been in the audiences. These have been vastly increased, in the traditional musical centers such as London and Broadway, and in new ones such as almost every civilised capital city in the world.

He goes on to note an unexpected side effect of his preference for shows without dialogue: they play well to audiences who might not speak the language of the show. The "sheer spectacle compensates and the basic storyline is pretty obvious," even if the lyrics are witty or complex in themselves. "So, by introducing a new era of popular musicals without books, I have contributed to the down-grading of the importance of lyrics in the contemporary musical—as Homer Simpson would say: 'Doh!' "[90]

By all accounts, including his own, Tim Rice is a relatively easy-going person. Sometimes he seems to lack the drive of his former partner Andrew Lloyd Webber; while he is a gifted lyricist, there seem to be plenty of other things he happily does with his time. Some of this attitude is for show; he feels passionately invested in each of his projects, and he leaves if he does not. Still, he is more at ease in the world, more charming than Lloyd Webber has ever been. Michael Coveney calls Rice "tall, blond, confident, easygoing and blazingly genial. He loved cricket, pop music, pretty girls and gave a good impression of taking nothing at all very seriously. He was the absolute antithesis of everything in Andrew's rather more tortured temperament and conditioning."[91] Upon meeting Lloyd Webber, Rice was impressed and also confused by Lloyd Webber's intense drive to become a successful composer of musicals. As a young man, his own dream was to be a pop star, but this was "never life or death to me," nor was his new dream, to write musicals with Lloyd Webber.[92]

Born in 1944, Tim Rice was a bright and easily bored child who worked far ahead of his age in math and astronomy. He loved manipulating numbers and had a passion for statistics and lists such as cricket scores or the tracking of songs on the pop charts. He also enjoyed word manipulation and crossword puzzles. In his autobiography, he points out that it is unlikely to encounter a lyricist as a child prodigy; while Lloyd Webber was capable of composing moving music as a schoolboy, Rice had not had any life experience yet and therefore had nothing to write. "Words are too specific, too clear, to give the receiver any significant variation of interpretation, so they must be well-crafted, knowing, mature."[93] His school music lessons gave him an admiration for Gilbert and Sullivan, especially for Gilbert's lyrics, and he enjoyed a trip to see Julian Slade and Dorothy Reynolds's *Salad Days* in the West End in 1954, but he had no real interest in musical theater until Lloyd Webber brought it out.[94] Rice makes an exception for *My Fair Lady,* the original cast album of which he wore out as a pre-teen. He speaks glowingly of Lerner's lyrics for the show, ones whose meanings continue to evolve in Rice's mind today. Lerner's wit and complexity inspired him, he reports, to toss words like "fratricide" (in *Joseph and the Amazing Technicolor Dreamcoat*) and "quid pro quo" (in *The Lion King*) into even his child-oriented musicals.

A six-month stay in Japan with his family gave Rice his first intense lesson in American pop culture, as he was enrolled in a largely American school. He was also intrigued by his biblical studies there, and already at age ten began pondering the more shadowy figures in the stories. By his teens, Rice had joined the first of what would be many pop/rock bands, and in a foreshadowing of his impact on Broadway, his first group developed a following because they were the first school band to use electric instruments. It having not occurred to him that there might be a career in pop music, Rice drifted into law school and was thoroughly uninspired. Without his realizing it, his gift for lyrics, storytelling, and word manipulation began to develop.

> I was polite; I was very good at adapting my attitude, manners and even accent to suit the occasion (a creep anxious to be liked?); I was witty (if sometimes childishly so) and had a great love of word-play. I so often found myself listening to conversations in two ways; interpreting them the way the speaker intends and at the same time in a literal way, analysing and playing with the speakers' words to set them spinning off into unintended meaning and complication.

Eventually he realized that the law was not for him, and he had more or less failed out of law school in any case. He began to pursue a career in pop music, a process which, he admits, sometimes involved "going to a pub and/or movie every night," but by age twenty-two he had sold the rights to three original pop songs.[95] These all went nowhere, a fate that would befall a long string of singles Rice would pen (with or without a composing partner) over many years. Rice later saw that his singles tended to fail because they lacked the emotional power that a song can have within the context of a larger show; all his hit singles would come from musicals.[96]

Inspired by his love of the pop charts, Rice approached a friend of the family who had publishing connections, Desmond Elliott, proposing a book of pop charts from years past. Elliott, thoroughly unimpressed by the idea, suggested instead that the young songwriter contact a young composer he had met, Andrew Lloyd Webber. Within days, they were at work on their first musical, *The Likes of Us.* It was never performed; having visions of the West End, they refused to accept more humble staging venues. But the experience demonstrated that the duo had excellent chemistry and compatible talents. Rice, meanwhile, had taken a job at a law firm but grew increasingly careless about the work, until finally he was motivated to pursue a job he liked and joined the staff at EMI Records.[97] He and Lloyd Webber wrote a handful of unsuccessful singles for EMI, and Rice used his job as talent scout there to make a number of connections which would be helpful later. Then his boss at EMI resigned and took Rice on as an employee of his new company, the Norrie Paramor Organization.

The duo's second endeavor, *Joseph and the Amazing Technicolor Dreamcoat,* would prove a very slow-building success. Rice and Lloyd Webber did gain some local attention after a few successful performances in 1969, though, and this won them an agent and a steady income. For three years, they would be paid to write, and for the first time since he had met Lloyd Webber four years previously, Rice embraced the creation of musicals as his full-time job. Their first attempt at a follow-up to *Joseph* failed to get off the ground, but the idea would stick with Rice until it was fulfilled many years later. The show, *Come Back Richard, Your Country Needs You,* was a delightful romp through the crusades of King Richard; it would eventually become Rice's musical with composer Stephen Oliver, entirely reworked and called *Blondel.* After tossing around a few other ideas, most of them biblical (it had worked with *Joseph*) and most of them Rice's, he and Lloyd Webber settled on the story of Jesus. Rice's interest in the mysterious figures of Judas and Pilate inspired him to create the imaginative, potentially scandalous retelling of the end of Jesus' life that became *Jesus Christ Superstar.*

The success of *Jesus Christ Superstar* made Tim Rice suddenly wealthier than he had ever imagined being, and it made him somewhat uncomfortable at first. He claims never to have been a great money manager, and would surely have made more from his wealth had he taken a page from Lloyd Webber's book and become an astute businessman and investor. But it did not interest him, and he enjoyed the early days of celebrity unabashedly, becoming a regular on television and radio, tolerating the occasional need to attend to the business end of things. While Lloyd Webber formed the Really Useful Company, Rice became Heartaches Ltd.

The pair were not quick to move on to their next project, still reeling from the international success of *Jesus Christ Superstar.* They began work on *Jeeves,* but Rice soon dropped out of the project and left Lloyd Webber to work on the endeavor alone, which failed in due course. Rice pursued his pop interests by producing some work for other artists and his love of cricket by forming his own team. In 1977, Rice fulfilled his ambition to publish a book of pop charts, *The Guinness Book of British Hit Singles,* which became the first of over thirty best-selling versions. Rice married Jane McIntosh in 1974 and they had a daughter, Eva Jane, a name which Rice says was chosen "sort of after Eva Peron."[98] His autobiography ends on 21 June 1978, the night *Evita* opened in London. It was a logical stopping point, since *Evita* does mark the point at which his work with Lloyd Webber ends, and the first phase of his career along with it, but there is much more to tell. The opening of *Evita* also marks the point at which Rice's relationship with *Evita*'s star, Elaine Paige, became romantic, a scandal which would go on so long that it would in fact cease to be scandalous.

Rice has gone on to achieve great success in the musical theater, although it was much slower in coming than for his former partner. His first two major theatrical endeavors after *Evita, Blondel* with Stephen Oliver and *Chess* with Benny Andersson and Björn Ulvaeus, were not considered successes, although both have excellent scores. Rice continued to pursue his interest in pop music; he wrote the lyrics for Elton John's song "The Legal Boys" on his 1982 album *Jump Up,* and he followed that by working with everyone from Freddie Mercury to Celine Dion. He found a home once again in musicals, although they were movie musicals at first, when Disney composer Alan Menken lost his lyricist partner Howard Ashman. Menken and Rice won an Oscar for the theme from *Aladdin* (1992), "A Whole New World," and they went on to work on the staged version of *Beauty and the Beast,* for which they added new songs not found in the movie; the show opened in 1994 and continues to thrive on Broadway. Another Disney movie, *The Lion King,* won Rice and new partner Elton John another Oscar, and *The Lion King* also made a wildly successful transition to Broadway in 1997. In 2000, Rice and Elton John wrote the successful rock-style retelling of an operatic story, *Aida.* Just two years behind mega-star Lloyd Webber, Rice was knighted and became Sir Tim Rice in 1994.

After some rocky years, then, Tim Rice is enjoying an extremely successful career in musical theater, with plenty of rock music in the mix. The men did not realize it at the time, but *Evita* would be the final show Rice and Lloyd Webber created together. Lloyd Webber would next choose to set a book of poetry—no lyricist needed, at least at first—and he had already branched out into instrumental music with *Variations.*[99] Rice, looking back, remembers that he and Lloyd Webber fought while working on *Evita,* something they had never done before: "I became less tolerant of his exaggerations and tantrums, he less so of my apparently casual approach to our partnership." It was not that Rice's approach to his work really was casual, just that "Andrew's passion encouraged my show of indifference."[100] They reunited for a short piece commissioned by the British royal family in celebration of Queen Elizabeth's sixtieth birthday in 1986. Directed by Trevor Nunn, the show, *Cricket,* with eleven songs, was performed at Windsor Castle on 18 June 1986 but, other than a staging at a Sydmonton Festival, it was never performed again. They also worked together on a new single for Madonna, for the film version of *Evita.*

Rice, while grateful for the opportunities to work with wonderful composers over the years, expresses some regret that he and Lloyd Webber did not stay together longer and speaks of his former partner's talent with respect. Lloyd Webber may have been a difficult person to work with at times, Rice tells us, but he was gifted and destined for greatness, through a combination of drive, talent, and luck.

Obviously Andrew had a great gift for melody and I had a feel for a turn of phrase that occasionally amused or intrigued, but so did many others. Our good fortune was that we chose an unusual way of displaying our wares, at least for songwriters starting out in the mid-Sixties when everyone else wanted to be the Beatles. I did too, actually, but Andrew's ambition to write musicals, already long-established when I met him shortly after his seventeenth birthday, distracted me from my futile (and admittedly half-hearted) quest to be a teenage idol, and had us operating in an arena where there was less competition. This was a fantastic stroke of luck for me, but on the other hand my unconventional and thus original approach to the theatre, founded on pure ignorance, was the one missing element in his precocious armoury of musical talents.[101]

Lloyd Webber achieved his massive fame in the 1980s without Rice, but Rice was the driving force behind Lloyd Webber's first three musicals. Rice continues as a successful, truly gifted lyricist, and his influence on the styles of musical theater in the last thirty years should be treated with far more attention than it has received.

Evita

> Instead of government we had a stage,
> Instead of ideas a prima donna's rage.
> Instead of help we were given a crowd.
> She didn't say much but she said it loud.

Cats, the most popular of Lloyd Webber's megamusicals, opened ten years after *Jesus Christ Superstar.* In between the two shows, Lloyd Webber opened three other musicals: *Jeeves,* a small-scale show that became a large-scale flop; *Evita,* Lloyd Webber's third and final project with Tim Rice; and *Joseph and the Amazing Technicolor Dreamcoat,* his first staged project with Rice that was written for children but eventually found its way to Broadway.

Jeeves, like *Superstar* and *Joseph* before it, and like the upcoming *Evita,* was Tim Rice's idea, but he left the project when he saw that its overall story and shape would never work. Based on the novels of P. G. Wodehouse, *Jeeves* acquired a new lyricist and bookwriter, comic playwright Alan Ayckbourn. The match seemed ideal in theory, but the unhappy results were some vaguely 1930s-sounding but rather dull songs with lyrics that did not nearly match up to Wodehouse's original wit, all laid rather uncomfortably over Ayckbourn's mock-Wodehouse play. *Jeeves* opened in April 1975 to unanimous pans, and limped along for less than five weeks.[102]

Lloyd Webber learned quickly from this experience; *Jeeves* had been staged and opened to the public without any testing at all, there was no concept album, no out-of-town tryouts, not even a private preview for friends. Lloyd Webber was inspired to invent such an arena as soon as *Jeeves* closed: he created the Sydmonton Festival, a venue for testing new material for friends and business associates in the comfort and privacy of his own country estate. He also returned to *Jeeves* many years later, when he and Ayckbourn released a drastically downscaled version, *By Jeeves,* to a friendly reception in 1996 in England. It enjoyed a number of regional U.S. productions before its limited run on Broadway in late 2001.

After *Jeeves,* Lloyd Webber returned to Tim Rice for his next project, which Rice had already begun. Back in 1973, Rice had been struck by the story of Eva Peron, the beautiful, conniving woman who had fought her way to the top and become the first lady of Argentina. He plunged into research, traveling to Argentina and reading what little he could find in English about her. As *Superstar* had been a huge scandal in Argentina (the theater had been burned, the movie house bombed), and as he was "never quite sure whose side my musical [*Evita*] was on," he conducted his research there quietly so as to avoid attention.[103] He surmised that Argentines would not take kindly to a musical about their former first lady, no matter whether the musical was sympathetic or damning. When he took the idea to Lloyd Webber, the composer was somewhat enthusiastic, especially because the story would require some experiments in Latin music, but he was wary about writing another show about a leader who had come to power too quickly and had died at thirty-three. But Rice, on some level, was in love with the glamorous Eva Peron and knew Lloyd Webber would come around. It proved quite complicated to write a musical about a dictator and his equally immoral wife, and Rice understood perfectly well that Eva Peron was no saint, but he was fascinated by her charm, her charisma, her ability to snow an entire country into loving her while she went about her nefarious ways. "I think I was as captivated as the descamisados [the lower-class 'shirtless ones' that Eva Peron claimed as her followers]. All that style hoodwinked me as much as it did them. It was an act of seduction, which she was very good at and which we decided should always be in the show, until you came to the point where you actually saw what else she was doing."[104] For many critics, the "what else" would not be revealed with nearly enough force, and controversy swirled around this musical for seeming to glamorize a tyrant.

Rice had already written a plot and some lyrics when Lloyd Webber joined him. *Evita* is the story of Eva Duarte, poor country girl, whose ambition took her to Buenos Aires, then to a career in radio and film, and eventually to a position as wife of dictatorial president Juan Peron. She became beloved by her people for (what appeared to be) acts of generosity toward them; she was called Evita, even Santa Evita, with affection. Rice added a strong figure to counterbalance Eva's seeming seduction of her people in the character of Che, who points out, in scathing asides to the audience and in occasional confrontations with Eva herself, that she is a corrupt, lying cynic. He is not the historical Che Guevara, but Rice took advantage of the fact that Guevara was Argentine and lived in his homeland during Eva's reign. In actuality there is no evidence that he had any opinion about her whatsoever. Rice simply speculated that he would have seen through her and so set him up as a symbolic counterpart. Otherwise, Rice stands completely behind his historical research and even takes credit for the enormous revival of interest in the history of Argentina during the Peron years.[105] (Appendix B contains *Evita*'s full plot and song list.)

Lloyd Webber contributed what would eventually become the emotional center of the work. Feeling that Eva needed both a crowning moment of achievement and, when she is dying and frail, a pathetic attempt to re-create that moment, Lloyd Webber wrote a song that would be called "Don't Cry for Me, Argentina."[106] At first Rice considered the song a potential hit single, but as the number began to take shape he decided it was far too specific to stand alone. He also thought it was problematic that Eva's lyrics are deliberately insincere: she woos the crowd, seducing them with a mock love song. But Lloyd Webber's melody was stunning, and "Don't Cry For Me, Argentina" became the duo's biggest hit single ever.

Lloyd Webber wrote an extremely strenuous part for Eva. She is a belting alto, required to shriek shockingly high chest notes before turning around and seducing sweetly with her voice.[107] Che is written for a rock-based tenor, Peron for a more traditional acting-oriented baritone. Almost the entire score is sung by these three characters and a prominent chorus.

Having seen it work so well for them in the past, the duo agreed to make *Evita* an album before taking it to the stage. By early 1976, the score was complete and the recording process began. They hired singer Julie Covington to portray Eva, and a demo tape containing a few songs landed them a recording contract with their old colleagues at MCA-UK, who had supported the *Superstar* album. Singer Paul Jones was cast as Peron, and the largely unknown C. T. Wilkinson as Che. (Wilkinson had played Judas for a time in the London production of *Superstar*, but would not find true fame until, as Colm Wilkinson, he created the role of Jean Valjean in *Les Misérables*.) Recording took place through the summer of 1976, and sections of the score were played to an appreciative audience at the second official Sydmonton Festival. The album was released in England in November 1976 to very positive reviews (including a glowing one from long-time supporter Derek Jewell in the *Sunday Times*), and it enjoyed a respectable run up the charts to number twenty-four. "Don't Cry for Me, Argentina" was released as a single and clawed its way slowly to the number one spot, where it remained for a week. In the United States, the album fared much less well, thanks in part to new leaders at MCA who did little promotion. Nevertheless, the album made the charts, and singles of "Another Suitcase in Another Hall" and "Oh What a Circus" won some air time.

Lloyd Webber had sent a copy of the concept album to director Hal Prince, who had recently expressed interest in working with him. After listening to the album, Prince sent Lloyd Webber and Rice a lengthy letter full of suggestions for changes which, while setting the duo back a bit, seemed logical. Eventually, schedules were coordinated, Prince was hired, and the London opening was set for the summer of 1978.[108] Lloyd Webber was particularly pleased to have such a well-respected and trustworthy director on board, never having lost his wariness after the Tom O'Horgan disaster. With such important shows as *Cabaret, Company,* and *A Little Night Music* behind him, his presence vastly reassured Lloyd Webber. (Prince would go on to direct Sondheim's *Sweeney Todd* and Lloyd Webber's *The Phantom of the Opera,* as well as several important shows of the 1990s, among them *Kiss of the Spider Woman, Parade,* and a successful revival of *Show Boat.*) Prince's particular skills have always lain in the areas of structure and stage image; he makes interesting, effective stage pictures, and these carry a story along smoothly and creatively without getting in the way of the material. He envisioned a biting, raw mood, embodied in Che especially, so that Eva's seductive charms would have a stronger counterpart than on the album. Critics, generally positive about Prince's contribution to the show, mentioned almost without fail two of his more clever moments of staging: the revolving door through which Eva's lovers cycle during "Goodnight and Thank You," and the symbolic game of musical chairs which results in the elimination of Peron's rivals in "The Art of the Possible." The staging in general was stark, full of black, white, and red; Prince filled the stage with placard-wielding protestors so aggressive that they occasionally wound up in Eva's bedroom.

When casting began, the press latched onto the great search for Eva with gusto, to the point where the creative team feared an overdose of publicity would cause any woman to fail to measure up to the pressure; the relative unknown Elaine Paige would succeed. She became a star in the media even before the show opened. Rice's autobiography does not discuss his relationship with Paige that developed at that time, but he freely admits his admiration for her talents: "I found her too good to watch sometimes, spine-tinglingly irresistible."[109] Prince felt neither Wilkinson nor Jones looked right for their roles from the album, and hired instead David Essex, a pop star and actor, as Che, and Joss Ackland, a respected actor, as Peron.

Evita opened at the Prince Edward Theatre in London on 21 June 1978, to fairly positive reviews and great public acclaim. The show ran a very healthy eight years in London. But the move to New York was more of a risk; the singles and album had never quite taken hold there, and Elaine Paige, as a foreigner, was barred by Actors' Equity from reprising her role in New York. Eventually, a more than suitable Eva was found: Broadway belter Patti LuPone. Like Paige, she was relatively unknown but had been paying her dues for some years. Prince made a few changes for the New York version, having more time to rehearse and some ideas about how to strengthen the story as well as offset critics' accusations of glamorizing a fascist. The role of Che was strengthened, made even more cynical and aggressive, and put in the hands of the frenetic Mandy Patinkin, then an unknown, but destined for Broadway stardom in shows including Sondheim's *Sunday in the Park with George.* Broadway actor Bob Gunton was cast as Peron. Producer Robert Stigwood, who had shied away from backing the London production, cheerfully backed it in New York by himself, knowing it was a sure thing. The show toured Los Angeles and San Francisco, where it was a smash hit, before opening to a massive amount of buzz on Broadway at the Broadway Theatre on 25 September 1979.[110]

Despite a few rather bad reviews and mixed notices overall, the public embraced *Evita.* It ran for four years in New York, and Lloyd Webber's critic-proof status began to cement itself. In a strange turnabout, the same collection of critics gave *Evita* the New York Drama Critics' Circle Award, and the show also won seven Tony Awards, including all the crucial ones: best musical, best director, best book, best score, and best leading female. In 1981, the Broadway cast album won a Grammy, and the film rights were bought by Paramount. It would take them seventeen years to make the movie. Rice recalls that, despite some pans, he and Lloyd Webber knew they had written something great. "We both genuinely felt it to be our most mature and polished work, the most original in style and content."[111]

Evita is indeed mature, polished, and original, although the adjective that springs most strongly to mind is "disturbing." *Evita* is often upsetting, harsh, and unpleasant, populated as it is by bitter characters often singing in dissonant, angry ways. It is just as powerful in its way as *Superstar,* but not nearly as much fun; there remains a distance between the audience and the characters, an overall sense of distaste. We feel for Eva to a degree, but we are also shown all too clearly that she is an evil person. And we feel for Che, who is routinely silenced and beaten throughout the show, but since his job is to detach himself from the action and report the news to us, he is never given the chance to become a real person. Drawing the story from real life robbed it of a certain amount of drama; Eva has no catharsis, no change of character. She simply pushes on with her ambitions until she dies. There is no one to turn on her as in *Superstar,* no Judas or crowd to feel conflicted about her power, only the fundamentally uninvolved Che. This starkness was exactly what Rice and Lloyd Webber had in mind, and they accomplished it so thoroughly that *Evita* is fascinating to watch, but not necessarily moving.

The score is their most complex work as a pair. Less sectionalized than *Superstar* and *Joseph,* it moves from number to number smoothly, with all sorts of recurring melodies, transitional material, and amorphous moments, as well as a few symbolic motifs. Most importantly, it is Lloyd Webber's most dissonant score, with Rice's most cynical and bitter lyrics. Joseph Swain, one of the very few writers to examine the score in any detail, notes that the moments of honesty in the story, those moments when Eva, Che, and Peron are speaking the truth to each other rather than snowing their people, are rendered in a consistently harsh, dissonant musical language. "Goodnight and Thank You" is the prime example, and Eva's theoretical confrontation with Che, "Waltz for Eva and Che," is equally complicated and jarring. Things become much more melodic when deceit is involved, as in "Don't Cry for Me, Argentina," or when Eva is out to be the center of attention, as in "Buenos Aires."[112] Biographer Michael Coveney, in a brief discussion of *Evita,* notes that what makes the score so effective is that it is genuine theater music, that each song suits its character and moves the duo's style from oratorio to opera. The team was doing its best work yet, somehow blending "the latin mass and the Latin dance."[113]

But most critics reserved little time for a discussion of the score, having been almost entirely preoccupied by the treatment of the subject. John Simon of *New York* magazine was particularly offended: "It is hard to say from their trashy work whether they actually admire her, which would be reprehensible, or are merely exploiting, without any moral point of view, her sensational story, which is, if anything, more loathsome."[114] A number of other critics, especially in New York, were also offended by what seemed to them to be a glamorizing of the story of Eva, an implicit admiration for her style, her spunk, her clever mind. At the very least, critics felt, the authors did not take a strong enough stand against her. By showing off her powers, the authors were implicitly praising them. Lloyd Webber and Rice consistently denied this, especially Rice, who was held more responsible: "If your subject happens to be one of the most glamorous women who ever lived, you will inevitably be accused of glamorizing her. The only political messages we hope will emerge are that extremists are dangerous and attractive ones even more so."[115] Nonetheless, Rice harbored a rather obvious admiration for Eva's style. Still, he asserted repeatedly, it was not him who made Eva look glamorous; she *was* glamorous, and that was the whole crux of her power. Lloyd Webber had no such attraction. "The basic point of *Evita*," he told the press, "is that it's very anti-Eva."[116] And, "I cannot imagine any intelligent person going to *Evita* and coming away with anything but the idea that she was a fairly grisly piece of work."[117]

The press chose to ignore these explanations, and dwelled instead on the idea that what they saw was a show examining the workings of a beautiful fascist. What was one supposed to feel, for example, when Eva rallied her people so effectively at the end of the first act, solidifying her power? Is one meant to applaud the song, the character? One *New York Times* article pointed out that London audiences had handled the issue much more calmly: "Personality and performance can be separated from morality."[118] But Americans, especially New Yorkers, apparently could not divorce show tunes from politics. The *Times* actually fed the fire by writing about Eva's fascist and dictatorial activities in their usual pre-opening feature story.[119]

Walter Kerr, the *Times* theater critic, wrote a mixed review, arguing that the main problem with the show was not that it glamorized Eva, but that the creators, in an effort to preempt claims that it had, had removed all her appeal. Somewhere between the concept album and the New York staging, the show had taken on such a brittle, removed quality that Kerr found it hard to feel involved.[120] Julius Novick of the *Village Voice,* on the other hand, read the creators' intentions just as they were meant, and enjoyed how the show revealed fascism as a kind of show business.[121]

Almost every critic agreed that Prince's staging was brilliant. His stage images encapsulated each moment, and his ideas were clever without being distracting or overly large. The score was granted mixed reviews, and of course charges of derivativeness and pastiche arose. Kissel managed to find the music borrowed, pre-familiar, and characterless all at the same time. But Kerr and several others, even while expressing their distance from the show in general, found Lloyd Webber and Rice's work quite admirable, full of innovation, mood, and subtlety.

After mixed reviews, a great deal of free publicity, and successful runs in both London and New York, *Evita* might have inspired Lloyd Webber and Rice to move on to another project together. However, tensions had arisen between them during the later stages of the creative process, and both were looking toward other creative outlets. Soon, Lloyd Webber would be immersed in *Cats* and Rice in *Blondel*. It would come as something of a surprise to both of them, then, when a third show of theirs made it to Broadway several years after *Evita,* seemingly all on its own. It was the culmination of a long, meandering trip taken by their first staged show together.

Joseph and the Amazing Technicolor Dreamcoat

> Don't give up Joseph, fight 'til you drop.
> We read the book, and you come out on top!

Joseph and the Amazing Technicolor Dreamcoat had been Rice and Lloyd Webber's second show together, after their failure to stage *The Likes of Us.* At the time they considered it simply a job, a way of practicing their skills and getting something mounted, no matter how humble the arena. The arena was quite humble indeed: Alan Doggett, a friend of the Lloyd Webber family, had asked the pair to write a little piece for the boys in his music program to sing at an assembly. Doggett was the head of music at Colet Court, a prep school for boys, so Lloyd Webber and Rice found themselves composing for a few dozen eight- to thirteen-year-olds. Perhaps a Bible story would be appropriate. The year was 1967.

With no major emotional investment in the work and nothing to lose, the young pair wrote *Joseph* quickly and easily. Lloyd Webber invented a host of bouncy tunes, and Rice unleashed some of his wittiest lyrics. Rice realizes now that without intending to, they had followed a few critical rules for the making of a good musical: they picked a good story, complete with flawed hero, re-deemed villains, some great plot twists, and plenty of humor; they created a unique style full of lighthearted irreverence; and they got the show performed, which is crucial to assessing its viability.[122] Also, and entirely by accident, they established the sung-through style that would become their trademark and the basis of the megamusical. The boys were young and had been singing as a chorus, not as theater performers, so Rice suggested that they often sing together and sing throughout. Rice's rather lowly connections from EMI Records allowed him to round out the performers' ranks with a few adults, mostly out-of-work EMI talent: David Daltrey sang Joseph's solo lines, and a band called the Mixed Bag joined Lloyd Webber (on piano) in the pit. Rice himself played the rock 'n' roll Pharaoh.

Joseph tells the story of Jacob's favorite son, the one on whom he bestows a fancy multicolored coat. (See appendix C for a plot summary.) The boys served as a group narrator, which worked very well for this cantata-like piece. The show, running about fifteen minutes, premiered on 1 March 1968 at Colet Court School, in front of a group of enthusiastic parents. It was so well received, in fact, that the group decided to perform it again in a larger venue, a Methodist church. They added the Colet Court orchestra to the pit, plus Lloyd Webber's father on organ, brother on cello, and family friend John Lill on piano. This performance, in May 1968, was also greeted with raves from parents and friends, but it appeared that none of the invited critics or music industry leaders had come.

It turned out that one had. Derek Jewell, the music critic for the *Sunday Times,* happened to have a son in the chorus, and he subsequently wrote a glowing review, becoming the first to bring the duo to wide public attention. The article brought interest from a record company and a publisher, and suddenly their agent, Desmond Elliott, was fielding his first legitimate offers for the young writers. The record company at which Rice worked, the Norrie Paramor Organization, recorded a version of *Joseph* which featured a new song, "Potiphar," and a few other extensions. The album was released in early 1969. In November 1968, *Joseph* enjoyed its third live performance at the invitation of the Dean of St. Paul's, the Very Reverend Martin Sullivan. He would soon become a key player in support of *Superstar.* This third performance went quite well, but a fourth was uninspired, and the duo began to suspect *Joseph* had run its course.

The reins were then taken up by an outside party, director Frank Dunlop, who staged a theatrical version in September 1972 at the Edinburgh Festival. Rice notes that Dunlop's production was creative and delightful, and showed that the material could easily be made into an effective theater piece rather than an oratorio. This production, sporting a few more additions, traveled to several other venues before making its way to the West End in 1973. It was a campy staging, full of scantily clad actors and a Pharaoh in a full Elvis costume. Because the show was still so short, Dunlop had added another piece (unrelated to *Joseph*) to make it a full evening of theater. By the time this production was headed for the West End, Lloyd Webber and Rice felt compelled to provide a first half of their own, and they wrote *Jacob's Journey,* an unsatisfactory play with a few unsatisfactory songs that never met anyone's expectations (including the critics'); eventually, to their surprise, they realized the solution to creating a full-length evening lay in stretching *Joseph* yet again. The brothers gained their three pastiche numbers, among other additions. The show had already closed in the West End after seven months, but now, with *Jacob's Journey* out and a full *Joseph* in place, things began to get moving once again.

The first American version was staged in December 1976, at the Brooklyn Academy of Music; it featured a strong Narrator (one soloist long since having taken over for a chorus of boys) in the form of Cleavon Little, and future Broadway star David Carroll (Tim Rice's *Chess*) as Joseph. In 1980, the *New York Times* announced that the rights to *Joseph* had been rented from Robert Stigwood by a new young team of producers, and they hoped to bring their version to Broadway eventually.[123] Tony Tanner, director of this version, had what would prove to be an inspired idea: he made the Narrator a woman, and he cast Laurie Beechman. Suddenly *Joseph* featured a virtuoso part for a woman, otherwise sorely lacking in the show, and Beechman was stunning in the role. A belter of the best sort, she became a Broadway star; Rice opines that the Narrator can make or break a production of *Joseph,* even more so than the talents of Joseph himself.[124] This version opened first in Washington, D.C., then at the Entermedia Theater in the East Village, before transferring to Broadway on 27 January 1982.[125]

The *Joseph* that arrived on Broadway featured a number of megamusical elements, but also contained elements not usually found in other megamusicals by Lloyd Webber or anyone else. It was sung from beginning to end, made use of pop music styles, and featured a fairly flashy staging. But, unlike other megamusicals, *Joseph* was mostly a comedy, telling a potentially grand, epic story in a decidedly down-to-earth, light way. It simply does not have the scope or weight of a megamusical like *The Phantom of the Opera* or *Les Misérables.* Like Lloyd Webber's other smaller works (*Song and Dance,* for example), it bursts with the wit and charm that his bigger shows can lack. *Joseph* also arrived on Broadway in a non-megamusical way, which is to say fairly quietly.

New York, critics and audiences alike, embraced *Joseph.* Laurie Beechman was fast on her way to stardom, and Bill Hutton as Joseph, while receiving some less than glowing notices, would soon become a teen idol.[126] Eventually, in 1991, *Joseph* returned to the West End, in a huge, flashy staging at the Palladium, where it ran for a strong three years; the closing song "Any Dream Will Do" rose up the pop charts. By now, the score of *Joseph* had been more or less settled once and for all; the version sung on Broadway in 1982 is the one that stuck, and the one that continues to be performed today in theaters large and small.

The Broadway version even won over John Simon, who a few years before had complained so bitterly about *Evita.* He was thoroughly charmed, proclaiming it the duo's best work, and reveled in the funny anachronisms and the purposely unpretentious air. He admired how the music and lyrics managed to be "simple, but . . . not simpleminded" and how the story contained just enough irony to avoid sappiness.[127] In short, he liked most of the elements that made the show *not* a megamusical. Mel Gussow of the *New York Times* was also charmed, stating that the "young, classically trained, popular composer is one of the most inventive artists in contemporary musical theater."[128] The only important voice of doom was Clive Barnes, newly appointed to the *New York Post* from the *Times*, who found the show better off left unstaged and preferred the duo's other works.[129]

 Joseph sparkles from beginning to end, even when it grows still and hushed. The music is simple in its clean melodies and great stretches of tunefulness, but its energy and bounce are not at all easy to explain. Rice's lyrics are hilarious, complicated, and touching. Many of the best numbers in *Joseph* are action songs, ones in which the Narrator tells us stories while Joseph, the brothers, and other characters act them out and chime in. The mood is firmly set in "Jacob and Sons," which introduces us to the family ("Depended on the farming to earn their keep. . . . / Spent all of their days in the fields with sheep"). Similarly, "Potiphar" manages to compress an enormous amount of information into a fast, funny number ("Potiphar was cool and so fine, / But his wife would never toe the line. / It's all there in chapter thirty-nine / of Genesis"). The rousing "Go Go Go Joseph" manages to combine Joseph's interpretations of the baker's and butler's dreams with the Narrator's cheerleading on Joseph's behalf, and has to rank among the most energetic, applause-inspiring act-one finales.

 The spark that lights up these energetic numbers is still present in the calmer moments, which are all the more striking for their contrast. "Close Every Door" is one of Lloyd Webber's most effective tunes from any show: it is haunting and sad, with a turn toward hopefulness at the end, all within the simple shapes that pervade *Joseph*. Rice paired it with a beautiful lyric about an otherwise-unmentioned issue in the show, Joseph's role as a Jew without a homeland: "Close every door to me / Keep those I love from me. / Children of Israel are never alone. / For I know I shall find / My own peace of mind, / For I have been promised / a land of my own."[130] Joseph leads the cast in the show's closing number, "Any Dream Will Do," which is also a rather slow ballad, making for an unexpected twist. One might expect another peppy show-stopper, but instead we get this poignant reflection on the necessity of dreams, even unfulfilled ones: "The world and I / We are still waiting / Still hesitating / Any dream will do." Rice ranks this number the best "by far" in the show and among the best four or five he and Lloyd Webber ever wrote. He speculates in his autobiography that he must have been thinking of Paul Simon when he came up with such a sad, obscure lyric for Lloyd Webber's sweet tune.[131]

 The four pastiche numbers are, of course, the ones that everyone remembers. "One More Angel in Heaven" is a full-on cowboy number, which allows the brothers to do some nifty heel-clicking dance moves. "Those Canaan Days" is a silly French chanson, complete with accordion and goofy French accents. They lament, "No one comes to dinner now / We'd only eat them anyhow." Their third pastiche, "Benjamin Calypso," is adorable in its flavor but less effective in portraying its message, namely that Benjamin must be innocent of the crime of which Joseph has accused him. Most obvious of the pastiches, "Song of the King" is an Elvis song; it cannot be performed without doing an Elvis impersonation, but a bad impersonation is perfectly fine.

As is often the case with Lloyd Webber's music, some of the most interesting passages are embedded within more complicated numbers, as opposed to the obvious stand-out songs or the pastiches. "Grovel, Grovel" is one such passage in *Joseph;* as the brothers beg for food from their long-lost sibling, Joseph gloats about his power over his former tormentors. The whole sequence has a delightful swing to it, and the lyrics that fly by are concise and effective. They beg: "Grovel, grovel, cringe, bow, stoop, fall. / Worship, worship, beg, kneel, sponge crawl. . . . Life is slowly ebbing from us, / Hope's almost gone. / It's getting very hard to see us / from sideways on."

Despite the rampant silliness of some of these passages, *Joseph* never becomes campy (although it can certainly be staged that way). It remains, more than anything, charming. It has achieved far more than its humble beginnings would have suggested, and it works wonderfully as a megamusical, but it need not be big. In fact, it is extremely popular now among school groups, in keeping with the show's humble roots.

On to the 1980s: "Isn't the Curiosity Killing You?"

Joseph and the Amazing Technicolor Dreamcoat opened on Broadway, largely without any direct involvement of Lloyd Webber or Rice, in January 1982. *Cats* would open that October. Lloyd Webber had moved on since *Evita,* away from Rice, and taken up a project entirely of his own devising. After three relatively successful Broadway shows, Lloyd Webber was ready to go it alone, and to bring to Broadway a show born of his own unique vision. He was about to change Broadway forever; after *Cats,* the megamusical would be here to stay, and Andrew Lloyd Webber would be the most famous Broadway composer of the 1980s—the peak decade, so far, of his career. In the 1970s, the megamusical began to make its mark; in the 1980s, it would take over. In the 1970s, critics noticed the first infiltration of the British into Broadway; in the 1980s, the invasion would be undeniable. And it would be *Cats* that marked—as one reporter described it—the "era of the megaspectacle, the heavily merchandised and immensely profitable model for a succession of lavish British musicals that in the

1980s and early 1990s not only came to dominate Broadway, but also shifted the balance of creative power in the musical theater from Times Square to Leicester Square."[132]

Andrew Lloyd Webber was about to make a bizarre idea for a musical into the second-longest-running Broadway show of all time. As a result, he would be, as Walsh puts it, "the most popular and the most reviled man in the musical theater. Nobody, it seemed, was neutral about him."[133] Critics would label his works "Mediocrity Incarnate but terribly commercial."[134] Audiences would come by the millions.

"Well, the Theatre Is Certainly Not What It Was"

Cats

It's a terrifying thought, but could they have really meant
"now and forever" *literally?*

This is a favorite joke about *Cats.* When the show broke the record for the longest-running musical in Broadway history, advertisements gained a new tag line: "now and forever." Until just a few months before it finally closed in September 2000, television commercials continued to advertise *"Cats.* Now and forever at the Winter Garden Theater." When comedians interpreted the slogan as a threat, it always got a laugh.[1]

What makes *Cats* the show that critics and comedians, and anyone trying to be hip, love to hate? And how is it that everyone in the know understands that anti-*Cats* jokes are funny, yet the show continued to sell out for nearly eighteen years? Clearly there is a dichotomy of reactions to this show: amid continued mockery, *Cats* has become a culturally shared joke, but more important, due to its wild success, it has also become a cultural icon.

A number of factors have contributed to the creation of this culturally understood entity. In many cases, the elements that went into the making of the *Cats* phenomenon had never been seen before. It was the first all-dancing show from England, a country hardly known for its hoofers. It garnered great success in London before arriving in New York, more so than Lloyd Webber's previous imports. It was Lloyd Webber's first musical without Tim Rice. It took over a radically redesigned Winter Garden Theater with impressive sets that moved and twinkled and oozed smoke. It featured grown women and men in tight stretchy

112

outfits and full cat make-up. It was marketed more heavily and more adroitly than any show before it, with a simple poster sporting only two yellow cats' eyes. It featured a hit song of massive proportions, by some estimations the most successful song ever from a musical. In short, *Cats* was the first true mega-musical.

It is no wonder, then, that the show has become a favorite target.

> Recently, *Cats* celebrated 5,000 performances at the Winter Garden. This also marked the 5,000th occasion that a guy had turned to his wife and said: "What the hell is this?"[2]

As Bruce Handy wrote in 1994, "[*Cats*] has transcended Broadway spectacle, taking on the added social burden of being an easy punch line. It is the reference of choice for conjuring up an especially redolent-of-the-80's (*furry leg warmers!*), beloved-by-Hoosiers (*hydraulics!*) brand of theatrical experience."[3] The reference to Hoosiers implies that only simple-minded farm folk of Indiana (and other out-of-town visitors) are impressed by the staging in *Cats*, especially the levitating tire featured at the end. Indeed, by the end of its run, *Cats* had come to seem almost quaint in its 1980s-style "mega" qualities. The arrival of newer and in many cases even more spectacular shows, plus the sheer staying power of *Cats*, contributed to this change in perception. And yet it is hard to remember now just how innovative, how adult, how influential *Cats* seemed when it arrived—and how the concept, the marketing, and the music all shared in making *Cats* the cultural icon it has become.

"That Moment of Mystery, When I Made History . . ."

Cats, like any musical, was the work of many hands. Critics and audiences alike were well aware of the formidable contributions of the director, choreographer, and set designer, as well as the role played by T. S. Eliot's verses, which became the show's lyrics. But it was only Lloyd Webber who became a household name afterward. The show was his brainchild from the start and bore his mark through-out, not only in the nonstop music but in the concept itself. It was he who pushed to get the show mounted, and he who won the support of a valuable ally—Valerie Eliot, T. S. Eliot's widow—that made it happen. In addition, without a partner in the traditional sense—meaning a lyricist with whom to collaborate and compromise—Lloyd Webber's name stood alone. Of course there was as much input from the rest of the creative team as with any show; director Trevor Nunn, in fact, stepped beyond the traditional bounds of director into the realms of book writing and lyric writing. Nevertheless, it was Lloyd Webber who received almost all the publicity.

The attention reflected a recognition that Lloyd Webber stood at a critical juncture in his career. Before *Cats,* he and Tim Rice were a very successful writing team, but still somewhat unknown by name or reputation, especially in the United States. "I feel like an outsider," he said, referring to being in New York. "In London, I'm the only fish in a very small pond."[4] After *Cats,* as biographer Michael Walsh puts it, "he was wealthy beyond the dreams of avarice and the centerpiece and chief tangible asset of an entertainment empire that stretched around the world." When *Cats* opened on Broadway, neither side of the Atlantic could deny his impact, since he then had three musicals running in each of the two centers: *Cats, Evita,* and *Song and Dance* in London, and *Cats, Evita,* and *Joseph* in New York. This was a first in the history of musical theater. He had conquered both Broadway and the West End, and in doing so went from being a successful composer to a famous personality in his own right, proclaimed as "Andrew Lloyd Webber, Superstar."[5] *Cats* and its success became irrevocably tied to Lloyd Webber's public persona. As John Rockwell of the *New York Times* wrote, "It is the key musical in his career, the show that defined him on his own, established the very idea of a new English musical . . . and crystallized the controversy that has swirled around him ever since."[6]

The coming of *Cats,* then, meant not only the establishment of Lloyd Webber as a dominant composer in the world of musical theater, but also the establishment of the megamusical as a dominant style. *Jesus Christ Superstar* and *Evita* had been flawed but interesting, unique experiments. *Cats* was a force to be reckoned with and was here to stay, forcing those that followed to deal with its impact. Musical theater historian Mark Steyn, with some bitterness but complete sincerity, divides the history of musicals into eras BC and AD—Before *Cats* and Andrew Dominant.[7]

The Making of *Cats:* Subtext by Trevor Nunn

Andrew Lloyd Webber had grown up hearing his mother read T. S. Eliot's light book of children's verse about cats to him; he had also grown up with actual cats, and adored them. When he found a copy of Eliot's collection *Old Possum's Book of Practical Cats* in an airport in 1972, he bought it. Around 1977 he began sketching a few settings of the poems, imagining them to be a suitable text for something like a song cycle, similar to his show *Tell Me On A Sunday.* He was also eager to tackle the challenge of setting finished poetry, rather than working with a lyricist (which, in Lloyd Webber's case, almost always meant writing a melody, and having Rice fit lyrics to his music).[8] The poems were also natural choices for musical settings, since, as director Trevor Nunn would later note, they contained musical structures already: "Not only were the metres inventive, the rhyme schemes full of wit and the beat unfailingly maintained, but also the poems abounded in colloquialisms, catch phrases and choruses."[9]

The "Old Possum" of the title was Eliot himself; friend and fellow poet Ezra Pound had given him the nickname. The "practical cats" in the poems come from all walks of British life, and only British life; despite Eliot's St. Louis birth, he had "transformed himself into a pillar of the English establishment"[10] through his poetry and residence in England. The poems are light and often quirky; some critics embrace them as representative of Eliot's fun side, while others dismiss them as a lesser effort. They certainly evolved from a lighthearted source: about eight years before the collection was published, Eliot wrote to his godson (a relation of his publishing team, Faber and Faber) about his remarkable cat Jellylorum. Over the years, letters to the boy featured various Jellicle Cats and Pollicle Dogs, and Eliot began naming other people's cats for fun: Carbuckety, Tantomile, Sillabub, Pouncival (a cat with ties to King Arthur).[11] A volume about cats and dogs had been planned, but eventually Eliot decided to focus on the cats, and Faber and Faber published the slim volume, with Eliot's own cat cartoons on the cover, in 1939. The idea of setting Eliot's poetry to music, be it the light or the challenging, had been bandied about in Eliot's own day, partly a result of the strong rhythms inherent in much of his work. He apparently preferred the notion of having his poems read against background music, rather than having them sung, and before *Cats* no attempt to set them had met with any particular commercial or critical success.

Lloyd Webber, nevertheless, began setting the texts, inspired by love for the words. By the time he held the Sydmonton Festival at his home in the summer of 1980, he had enough settings of the poems to present a song cycle. He knew he needed several things before the project could go any further, not the least of which was a plot and a main character or two, to hold the cycle together. But more important, he needed the endorsement of Eliot's estate, which would come from Eliot's widow, Valerie. To his joy, Mrs. Eliot adored the settings and gave the project her full support; she also assured Lloyd Webber that despite Eliot's stated resistance to musical settings of his poems, she was sure he would have loved these. She volunteered an eight-line poem fragment that Eliot had not published, deeming it too sad for children; this was "Grizabella the Glamour Cat." This and other fragments, correspondences, and insights from Mrs. Eliot would transform *Cats* from song cycle into staged musical.[12]

Valerie Eliot's endorsement of Lloyd Webber's work inspired him and Cameron Mackintosh to believe that a real musical could emerge from the poem settings. A director could make this leap, and Mackintosh suggested Trevor Nunn, director with the Royal Shakespeare Company. This seemed an odd choice, as Nunn had basically no experience with musical theater, but Mackintosh reasoned that his experience with poetic British language and his flair for staging would make him suitable. Nunn's first vision upon hearing the music would have suited a song cycle: "Something in a very intimate hall. Five actors, two pianos—a chamber piece that could mirror Eliot's charming, slightly offbeat, mildly satiric view of late-1930's London."[13] But Lloyd Webber had something bigger in mind, and Nunn happily went along with it, never imagining the show would not only become huge in production, but huge in influence: "Certainly I found it hard to reconcile this material with dreams of creating a popular show which could dismantle class and ethnic barriers, and which would be celebratory and uplifting, the familiar fantasies of all who set out to conquer the British Musical."[14] Nunn, nevertheless, demonstrated as much ambition and vision as Lloyd Webber, and dove into the project. He added the other two key players to the creative team, choreographer Gillian Lynne and designer John Napier, both of whom he had worked with previously.

Nunn already knew from working with Lloyd Webber on the material so far that they needed a theatrical space in which all the various cat characters could meet. The eclectic mix of personalities in Eliot's poems was unified by their cat focus, and the show needed a set that could not only reflect but help create a cat world for all of them. Napier had the vision that would accomplish this unity: a garbage dump, some sort of urban alley in which piles of trash created shapes, shadows, spaces in which cats could cavort. It would all be rendered in cat perspective, huge, so that the performers would look cat-size in comparison.[15] Napier, then, did more than just meet the demands of the show, he actually helped create its center. The look of the show, the mostly unchanging and very imposing set, is fundamental to the experience of *Cats*. His vision of a cat-perspective world filled with trash would affect the show's story, direction, and choreography. In London, the set also featured a three-quarters in the round staging, which helped greatly in making the audience feel involved. During the overture, the first few rows of the audience actually moved; the floor swung them from the back of the room to the front, so that they were in place by the time the opening number begins. In New York, other methods of involving the audience would be devised.

With much of the music written and a general idea of how the show would look, it was time to seek investors. Mackintosh faced an uphill battle, to say the least; he found it nearly impossible to sell a show that featured a dead poet as lyricist, Lloyd Webber without Rice, a director who had never done a musical, songs about cats sung by people in cat suits, a massive amount of dancing in a country distinctly known for its inability to do dance musicals, and—to top it off—a cursed theater. The New London was notorious for flops, to the point that it often housed ventures other than live theater (many of which were equally unlucky). In addition, the presence of Mackintosh himself did not inspire total confidence; he had had his share of flops, and had done only a handful of musicals, whereas Lloyd Webber's previous producer, Robert Stigwood, had been consistently successful. Stigwood's ten-year contract had run out, however, and he was permanently out of the picture. Eventually Mackintosh, getting desperate for backers, took out advertisements in financial newspapers, asking for only £750 per person; in the end it took two hundred and twenty investors, plus Lloyd Webber's personal funds, to finance the show.[16]

Soon, the new team of Lloyd Webber, Nunn, and Mackintosh would prove to be a winning one. *Cats* would make stars out of both Mackintosh and Nunn, who would go on to great success in musical theater afterward. Mackintosh would produce Lloyd Webber's *The Phantom of the Opera* and *Song and Dance*, as well as the smash hits by Schönberg and Boublil, *Les Misérables* and *Miss Saigon*. Mackintosh would work with Trevor Nunn on *Les Misérables*, and Nunn would go on to direct Lloyd Webber's *Starlight Express, Aspects of Love*, and *Sunset Boulevard*.

With the team in place, what *Cats* needed now was a plot of some sort, an arc, a thread to hold the disparate songs together. Most of the poems in Eliot's book are accounts of individual cats: Growltiger, the intimidating pirate cat; Skimbleshanks, who helps out on trains; Mungojerrie and Rumpelteazer, who torment their family of owners with petty theft and vandalism. Each character exists in different times and places, and they do not interact. Nunn began to see several ways to unite these tales into something of a community of cats. One way was obvious: besides individual tales, Eliot's volume also contained several poems about cat nature as Eliot fancied it. In "The Song of the Jellicles," Eliot describes Jellicle cats (his name for this group) gathering under the Jellicle Moon to celebrate the Jellicle Ball. This, then, would be the reason all the different cats were in one place, Nunn reasoned: it was the night of the Jellicle Ball. The poems also provided a character whom Nunn cast as a village elder, the leader of the group. Old Deuteronomy is described in a poem as being worthy of the respect of even the oldest locals, so he was a natural father figure. Valerie Eliot provided the groundwork for another plot factor when she supplied "Grizabella the Glamour Cat": the story of a down-on-her-luck, tattered cat with something of a scandalous past became the central plot point. Nunn added the final, and most crucial, element to the plot when he gave the Jellicle Ball a purpose besides sheer revelry: at the Ball, Old Deuteronomy chooses one cat to be reborn, to start anew. Eliot had provided, in a letter, a couplet of poetry mentioning the Heaviside Layer, something like a cat heaven or paradise. Nunn decided that this would be the place to which the chosen cat would go, in order to be reborn. Playing on the notion that cats have nine lives, the device justifies the introduction of each cat in turn, so that the most worthy may be chosen. It is not unlike the plot device in *A Chorus Line;* in both shows, each character introduces himself or herself through song, and at the end, the man in charge chooses who is in and who is out.[17] In the case of *Cats,* though, there is little suspense: the only cat with real problems is Grizabella, and it is she whom Old Deuteronomy selects to be reborn.

All of this required some additional text, which Nunn provided, with a small amount of help from lyricist Richard Stilgoe. An opening number, "Jellicle Songs for Jellicle Cats," was modeled loosely after the style of Eliot's "The Song of the Jellicles" and also incorporated some of the unpublished poem "Pollicle Dogs and Jellicle Cats." The "Grizabella" fragment, combined with some loosely interpreted excerpts from an outside Eliot poem, "Rhapsody on a Windy Night," became the song that introduces Grizabella. "Rhapsody on a Windy Night" features a reference to a worn out, broken woman and, later, a vicious cat. From this Nunn created a worn out, broken cat: Grizabella. The sad cat herself sings "Memory," which features lyrics by Nunn that are also loosely based on sections of "Rhapsody on a Windy Night." Nunn and Lloyd Webber then constructed an entire song around Eliot's one couplet concerning the Heaviside Layer, which is Grizabella's destination for her rebirth. Finally, Old Deuteronomy was given a song, "The Moments of Happiness," which featured text excerpted from Eliot's poem "The Dry Salvages" from his collection *Four Quartets.*[18] Other than these sizable additions, almost all of the text in the show is Eliot's, with only occasional minor changes in pronouns to accommodate various speakers. *Cats* resulted, incidentally, in a huge increase in sales of *Old Possum's Book* and a boon to Eliot's estate.[19]

While the creative team worked out the details of plot, text, and structure, choreographer Gillian Lynne began giving the show movement. Because the music never stops and much of the cast is onstage almost continuously, Lynne's job was a massive one. By British standards, she met with great critical success; she would fare much less well with critics in America. Whatever the opinions about her choreography, nevertheless, it was clear that she had done what had never been done before: she had pulled together a full company of British dancers, all of whom were excellent, to pull off a dance musical unprecedented in its vigor. One British historian called it "a vivid and marvellous gesture of transatlantic defiance," which proved, for the first time, that England could rival Broadway in dance.[20] Before *Cats,* as Walsh notes, it was almost unheard of for a British company and a British choreographer to attempt a dance musical: "The decision to hire a British choreographer was a calculated dare: everyone knew that the English couldn't write musicals, and they were positively certain that the Brits couldn't do dance musicals."[21] Still, Lynne found about thirty dancers who could also sing and act, and almost every British critic embraced this talented group as champions of the newfound British dance musical. Among the young hopefuls who came to the open call for dancers was Sarah Brightman, later the second Mrs. Lloyd Webber and star of *The Phantom of the Opera.* Her pure, youthful voice and sexy dancing won her the role of Jemima, a young kitten with several featured moments in the show. (The part would be renamed Sillabub in New York but was largely the same.) The only cast member trained as an actor rather than as a dancer was Judi Dench, who was cast as Grizabella, a role that requires little dancing. By February 1981, with three months until opening, the show was cast.

Nunn, having already crafted lyrics for an opening number and several other additional songs, decided that the Eliot text was still missing one more thing: a poem that could become a hit song. Unlike *Superstar* and *Evita,* which had partly grown from the idea of a hit central song outward, *Cats* as yet had no obvious stand-out pop song begging for radio airplay. Lloyd Webber was actually taking a much more conventional approach to the preparation of this show; it had no concept album, and no single reached the charts in London. He released a single, "Magical Mr. Mistoffelees" sung by Paul Nicholas (the first Jesus in London's *Superstar*), and it received some airplay and probably helped ticket sales in London. Still, a real hit song would not emerge until after the London opening.

Neither Lloyd Webber nor Nunn saw the potential for a hit song in Eliot's book. Lloyd Webber reverted to his pre-*Cats* style of working: he wrote a melody (or, in this case, borrowed a melody he had already written but had never used), and hoped to have a lyricist write something to fit it. On and off, he had pondered a musical about the rivalry between Puccini and Leoncavallo, when both opera composers had been working on versions of *La Bohème.* From his drafts Lloyd Webber pulled out a Puccini-like melody, which provides a very simple explanation for why so many critics would feel "Memory" sounded like Puccini: it was originally meant to. However, one anecdote suggests that Lloyd Webber feared he had outsmarted himself: "Indeed, the melody was so Pucciniesque that Andrew worried it might be a real Puccini tune. He asked his father, 'Did I steal it?' Bill assured him that he had not, and added: 'It's going to be worth two million dollars to you, you fool.' "[22]

When Lloyd Webber played the new song for the assembled cast, Nunn is reported to have said, "What is the date? The hour? Remember, because you have just heard a smash hit by Andrew Lloyd Webber."[23] Nunn set about penning lyrics for the song, using bits from "Rhapsody on a Windy Night," but when he began changing them repeatedly, even in previews, it became clear that a professional needed to be summoned, and Lloyd Webber turned to his most reliable of lyric writers, Tim Rice.

Rice wrote a complete set of lyrics in thirty-six hours, and everyone but Nunn was greatly relieved. Nunn, for his part, was in the strange position of being a competitor in this lyrics contest as well as one of the judges. But he, Mackintosh, and Lloyd Webber agreed in the end that Rice's lyrics were not cat-oriented enough, as well as being somewhat depressing and confusing, and they agreed to use Nunn's mostly complete lyrics. It was rumored in a gossip-mad press that Rice was furious about the seeming snub, that he had refused to make changes and had therefore been dismissed, that he and Lloyd Webber were no longer speaking. In reality it is unlikely that any of this was true; it must have been somewhat annoying to Rice to have been called upon in a crisis and then have his product remain unused, but he had never minded making revisions, and he and Lloyd Webber were still on good, if somewhat distant, terms.[24]

By the time the song was placed in the show, with its lyrics still in debate, it was clear that Judi Dench was a fine actress but only a passable singer. Still, Nunn was pleased with her, when fate intervened to remove her. She injured a tendon quite suddenly and, after three weeks of convalescing, returned to rehearsals only to injure it again. It was clear she could not perform. Previews were a few days away. Meanwhile, Elaine Paige, London's Eva Peron, happened to hear the "Memory" theme, played without lyrics, on the radio, and thought it lovely. Paige told herself she would call her old friend Lloyd Webber in the morning and ask to record the song as a single. Instead, she was awakened by a phone call from a frantic Cameron Mackintosh, begging her to take over the role of Grizabella. That day, she was in rehearsals, in, as Nunn described it, "littered rooms with rickety furniture and naked light bulbs. Grizabella rooms. Ah, the glamour of the theatre. Crisis is a great leveller."[25] At this same moment, Rice, Paige's lover, was invited to write a lyric for "Memory." In a matter of days his work was out, but Paige stayed. The song suited her perfectly and became forever associated with her.

London Opening: "Don't Miss It"

Cats opened at the New London Theatre on 11 May 1981. Already a high-profile event, the opening won extra publicity thanks to a bomb threat phoned in by a man with an Irish accent. The performance had just ended, and the audience was in the middle of its standing ovation, when Brian Blessed, playing Old Deuteronomy, interrupted and asked the cast and crowd to file out onto the street. No bomb was found.[26]

Almost every critic, even those who did not care for the show, championed it as a great event in British musical theater. The mere fact that the cast pulled off the dancing was a victory in itself. Critics universally praised the whole cast for being energetic, convincing, and talented, as singers and actors as well as dancers. Also—and this would not be the case in New York—the choreography by Lynne was hailed as unique and exciting with almost total consistency. The "Jellicle Ball," one critic wrote, was "a driving ecstatic ballet that must be the most exciting number ever seen in a British musical."[27] Sheridan Morley, in *Punch* magazine, went so far as to claim that the whole night really belonged to Lynne, who turned in the most impressive work of the entire creative team and who proved that the English could dance like Broadway while still remaining faithful to the piece.[28]

While Morley found the plot thin and unconvincing, he did not seem bothered by it. He accepted the show as a celebration, with some dramatic flavor, of Eliot's poems, which were showcased beautifully. The atmosphere the show created matched Eliot's "weird mix of menace, melancholy and mayhem" and it drew in the audience. Morley predicted a smash hit that would run at least four years (a bold estimate before the era of the megamusical truly took hold).

Like Morley, Robert Cushman of the London *Observer* found the plot little more than "a series of charming vignettes" that went nowhere; unlike Morley, he seemed to want it to go somewhere. There was no suspense surrounding who would be chosen to ascend, nor subplots involving the criminal kidnapping cat Macavity and the disappearance of Old Deuteronomy. But this was his only real reservation; otherwise, he found the Jellicle Ball and the special effects alone worth the price of admission. He had nothing but praise for Lloyd Webber's mix of musical styles, a compositional technique which gave each cat a distinct sound. " 'Cats' isn't perfect," he declared. "Don't miss it."[29]

The *Guardian*'s Michael Billington wrote a pure rave. The dancing, the treatment of the Eliot texts, the mix of musical styles that define each cat, the newly added plot: all were successful.[30] Derek Jewell of the *Sunday Times* was similarly dazzled, not surprising considering Jewell had "discovered" Lloyd Webber and had been the first to write about him. His praise was rendered so gushingly that it ceased to have much meaning as criticism, but its intent was clear: this "triumphant piece of musical theatre fashioned against the odds" was successful thanks to the "sheer volume of impeccable high talent which has been so generously poured into the show."[31] By this point in Lloyd Webber's career, American critics commonly argued that his music was too full of other people's styles, all cobbled together in a row, rather than integrated into one personal style. Jewell led the British critics—almost all of whom agreed with him, but were less forceful about it—in interpreting Lloyd Webber's style in a more positive light: "He has drunk in the popular sounds and styles of this and other centuries to produce evocative melodies and fine orchestrations which bear his highly individual stamp. You recongise [sic] his touch at once, and as he waves his wand the various ingredients, no matter how disparate, surprisingly coalesce." Jewell concluded by placing *Cats* "among the most exhilarating and innovative musicals ever staged."

The two major voices of dissent both came, rather unfortunately for the show's reputation, from one of England's more respected newspapers on theater, the London *Times*. Irving Wardle, in a foreshadowing of the New York reviews, predicted that it would be the sets that audiences would remember. The oversized junkyard, the spaceship-like tire which delivered Grizabella to the Heaviside Layer, and the fancy lighting overwhelmed most everything else. He agreed with others that the plot seemed too forced and contrived, and he found that more bothersome than most; there seemed to be "an attempt to press the poems into the service of Mr. Nunn's warm-hearted style of community theatre" and an effort to propel them toward an unnaturally happy ending. Not only was he unimpressed by Nunn's new lyrics, he felt that having the cats recite Eliot's poems put them in the awkward position of having to talk about themselves, "a self-cancelling task." Wardle enjoyed much of Lloyd Webber's music, particularly some of the different popular styles used to represent various cats, as well as two motives (he does not define these; there are many phrases to which he might be referring) used as "dramatic binding agents." Despite a lack of detail, Wardle's criticism was one of the more specific in terms of music; he was the only major British critic to address the idea of themes and the importance of the orchestration. "What remains," he summarized in regard to the whole show, "is a vast input of talent, which never succeeds in taking fire into an organic work."[32] James Fenton of the *Sunday Times* submitted a similarly mixed review, reserving his most negative comments for the poetry itself, which he had always disliked. He agreed that the plot's climax felt forced, and was motivated by an air of "spiritual pretentiousness" through all the talk of rebirth and redemption.[33]

It soon became clear that the rave reviews far outweighed the negative ones, and it became even more obvious that reviews probably did not matter at all. The show was sold out for many months in advance, audiences embraced it wholeheartedly, and it ran in London for twenty-one years. "Memory" became a hit song in England the month after the show opened, and two months after that, the cast album reached the charts as well. The following year, some of the music for the Jellicle Ball reached a huge audience when it became the theme music for the BBC's broadcast of the 1982 World Cup.[34]

En Route to Broadway

It took over a year for *Cats* to find a home on Broadway, but by August 1982, the production had taken up residence at the Winter Garden and casting was complete. Some of the featured cast members were Broadway regulars, but none were major stars. Grizabella proved by far the most challenging role to cast; the creative team had spent the first half of 1982 searching for the right woman without success. Betty Buckley had sung exceptionally well at her audition but had been deemed too strong for the role, which called for someone less healthy, more waif-like. Buckley had had great luck in her early career—she had, in fact, landed her first Broadway role on her first day in New York, originating the part of young Mrs. Jefferson in *1776*—but since then her work onstage had been intermittent. Legend has it that at her callback for *Cats,* she declared boldly but with trepidation to Trevor Nunn that it was her time to shine. Now thirty-five, she was due, she insisted, for this high-profile role. She got the job.[35]

Lloyd Webber, Nunn, and Lynne enthusiastically praised the talent pool in New York. "I hate to knock my own country," Lloyd Webber told the *New York Times,* "but we don't really have the dance training in depth that you do here. The sheer depth of talent at the auditions has been humbling; I never saw anything like it."[36] Between 1,400 and 1,500 performers showed up for the auditions, not a surprisingly high number considering that a job in a Lloyd Webber show probably meant steady employment for at least a few years to come. Hopefuls were somewhat surprised by the demands of the show, since not only did this British musical make them dance in a very strenuous, nonstop way, it also asked them to sing high Ds while doing it. Still, Lynne, Nunn, and Lloyd Webber were thrilled to find at least eighty singer/dancer/actors who were entirely castable, and were free to choose about thirty.[37]

Another step which proved much easier in New York than in London was finding financial backing for the production. The fact that *Cats* was already a huge hit in England meant that Mackintosh financed the show with only four backers: the Shubert Organization, ABC Entertainment, the Metromedia Corporation, and Geffen Records. Two of these, the Shuberts and David Geffen, were listed as actual producers on the show, in conjunction with Mackintosh and with Lloyd Webber's Really Useful Company (a company which, despite its rapid growth, was not yet big enough to handle a project of this magnitude).[38]

With money pouring into their theater and a sure hit on their hands, Lloyd Webber, Mackintosh, Nunn, and the rest of the team felt able to make some significant changes in the new version. They spent four times as much money as in London, in part simply to accommodate the Winter Garden's shape but also to make the set, effects, and technology more impressive. A hole was cut into the roof of the theater and a dome was added, to allow for Grizabella's ascension. Junk covered the theater from front to back, top to bottom. The first seven rows of seats were removed and the stage extended, so that the audience wrapped around more than three quarters of the stage, and a back section of the set opened out and became a pirate boat, the setting for a completely reworked "Growltiger's Last Stand."

Lloyd Webber significantly reworked two numbers, and performed the usual cutting, stretching, and tinkering that comes with any new production. Growltiger's big number now featured a humorous parody of a Puccini love duet, and Lloyd Webber rewrote "Mungojerrie and Rumpelteazer" with a completely new tune. Two acrobats became eight, and a few parts were combined and underwent name changes (although the audience is unaware of the names of most players in any case). The orchestra, now hidden offstage behind the junk and behind a clump of audience members who sit more or less upstage right, was increased from sixteen to twenty-five members.[39]

When *Cats* opened in New York on 7 October 1982, it boasted the highest ticket advance in history, $6.2 million. The audience, a jubilant Valerie Eliot among them, felt the show fully lived up to its hype.

And the hype was indeed massive. Neither Mackintosh, nor any producer before him, had ever advertised a show so heavily or so consistently. Wherever the ads went, all over the country and eventually around the world, that yellow pair of cats' eyes with vague images of dancers silhouetted within were instantly recognizable. *Cats* was "a product, a trademark," claims Michael Walsh, and Mackintosh plastered it on anything he could find, from billboards to T-shirts.[40] He put a huge display on the theater itself, in June 1982, a full four months before opening. Print ads began running in newspapers as early as April, and in August, when the box office opened, Mackintosh added radio ads. The print ads featured the eyes, the radio ads had "Memory" playing in the background; both featured only one line of text: "Isn't the curiosity killing you?" By this time,

"Memory" was already very familiar to American listeners, as Barbra Streisand had had a hit with it and Barry Manilow, Judy Collins, and Johnny Mathis led the pack of hundreds of other artists who would record it as well.[41] All through the summer of 1982, planes trailing banners flew over the beaches of the New York area announcing the arrival of *Cats* in the fall. Mackintosh arranged for magazines from *Smithsonian* to *Penthouse* to run feature stories on the show.

The show itself was a star even before it opened. The curiosity was indeed getting to thousands of people, who cheerfully paid a whopping $45, then a record high, to witness this new phenomenon. Advertisements never carried photos or film footage of the performers. They also never carried quotes from critics, something every other show did and which this one easily could have done. Before the New York opening, there were plenty of London accolades from which to choose, and American critics supplied dozens more. Mackintosh deemed this unnecessary; he pushed, with record force, only the idea of the show itself, and Lloyd Webber's name.

Mackintosh was not only being business-savvy; his strategy of marketing the whole show as a concept ideally suited this particular show. There was no one star, not even a clear group of featured players. Betty Buckley was relatively unknown as a theater actress. The only truly bankable name in the bunch was Lloyd Webber, and even that was a bit of a leap unless he was identified with his previous works, though in many ads that was the case.[42] *Cats* was an ensemble show which created a mysterious, shadowy world, and the cats' eyes, the teasing slogans, and the spare advertisements prepared audiences perfectly for what to expect. Mackintosh would find that variations on this marketing technique would prove ideal for all his future megamusicals.

While Mackintosh controlled many of these factors, a few lucky twists of fate also helped make the show such a hit. He had encouraged Streisand to record "Memory," but he could not have guaranteed it would chart. Also, and this was not at all Mackintosh's doing, cats were "in." Cats were all the rage in the early 1980s, just as the figure of Jesus had been experiencing an upswing in popularity during the coming of *Superstar*. At the time of *Cats'* opening, there were no fewer than five books of cartoons about the cartoon cat Garfield on the bestseller list.[43] Everyone from children to their grandparents loved cats and owned cat merchandise. In another example of uncannily good timing, Lloyd Webber had chosen a topic with which Americans were fascinated.[44]

If all these marketing strategies and twists of fate helped make *Cats* a hit upon opening, what allowed it to endure for eighteen years? In fact, some of the reasons that made it a hit in 1982 are the same ones that kept it a hit through 2000. There was always an audience that was drawn to those cats' eyes, so recognizable, so promising about what was in store. A large percentage of that audience in recent years, however, consisted of foreign tourists. The phenomenon that Americans were so eager to witness became one that visitors to New York had to experience. One reporter estimated that in 1997, about 80 percent of the audience was from out of town, and 40 percent from foreign countries.[45] Several critics have argued that *Cats* particularly appeals to non-English-speaking tourists, since the dancing, set, and action account for a great deal of the show's effect. This may seem a rather tough argument to support considering how complex Eliot's poetry is, but in fact a large number of English-speaking audience members also seem to miss a great deal of the text. Anecdotal evidence suggests that most people get the essence of each cat's personality and the point of each number without effort, but are hard pressed to explain or recall the text in any detail. Also, it is a decidedly child-friendly show, although only in recent years has it been marketed as such. Children abound in the audience; there are *Cats* dolls and toys now, and kids (or adults) are welcomed up onstage during intermission to meet Old Deuteronomy. All these new methods of marketing, both at opening and over the long haul, add up to what became the longest-running musical in history. "The show itself is the star," the *New York Times* summarized several years ago, "and like a certain kind of celebrity, it managed to become not only famous but also famous for being famous."[46]

The Experience of *Cats:* "What's a Jellicle Cat?"

Seeing *Cats* at the Winter Garden was an intimate experience. The theater is relatively small and quite shallow, so that even the back row feels close to the stage. As modified for *Cats* it seated 1,482 on the orchestra and mezzanine levels, which is about average for a Broadway house. But because the stage jutted out into the audience, the seats bent in rainbow formation around the stage in long curves, resulting in an average depth of only twenty-two rows. Also, running behind approximately the fifth row of the orchestra level, an aisle cut a wide path through the seats, taking up the space of several rows. Numerous wide aisles ran from front to back as well. The result was an audience divided by many crossing aisles into small clumps, somewhat unevenly spaced, so that no audience member was very far from an open space. There was no orchestra pit; the musicians were hidden off stage right, and the performers watched the conductor on closed-circuit television monitors mounted on the balcony. Front-row ticket holders sat directly in front of the stage. The knees of the taller audience members actually touched the oversized fish bones, cereal boxes, dead batteries, and other set decorations which adorned the low wall in front of them. The stage was raked sharply and ended quite low, so that when performers sat at its downstage edge, they were nose to nose with the audience. It was as if the plane of the stage continued directly into the laps of the front row spectators. There was no "fourth wall"; performers spent a great deal of time singing directly to the audience, their eyes boldly focusing on one face after another. They used the many aisles almost as often as the stage itself. They entered and exited through the house, they sang certain sections in the aisles, and if they had nothing featured to do at a given moment, they slipped out into the audience for a cuddle. In fact, even spectators not in an aisle seat might have been sniffed at, rubbed against, smiled at, flirted with, or sat on by at least one cat: frisky performers crawled over audience members from time to time.

And if perchance no cat came near, spectators still could not help but feel drawn in. The small theater's shape was crucial to the sense of intimacy, and the entire place was part of the set. The oversized junk (empty cans of beans and cat food, crumpled newspapers, broken luggage, bent gasoline cans, dirty rags, wooden beams and scrap metal lying askew, hatboxes and bottles) was everywhere, from the back wall of the house to the balcony railing to the stage. Huge torn scraps of formerly colorful paper covered the stage floor. It felt as if a junkyard had been half-heartedly cleared out, so that some seats could be put in. Visible in the background was the night sky, with the Jellicle moon glowing full, and many twinkling stars. Also, during the overture and at several other times, the lighting design included the audience. Strings of tiny Christmas-like lights crossed overhead in a messy web; lights glowed and pulsed from all sides. During the overture, while the audience was still gazing upward at sparkling overhead lights, the performers slipped into the aisles from the back and sides of the house, often surprising many audience members. The cats slunk about, eventually winding their way onto the stage and finding hiding places in huge pipes, an abandoned car, and hidden crevices around the stage. Then hundreds of pairs of cats' eyes lit up, glowing greenish-yellow in the almost total darkness, peering out from every possible nook and shadow. The audience was now initiated into the universe of the Jellicle cats.

The opening number, "Jellicle Songs for Jellicle Cats," welcomes us into this world and explains what sort of creatures inhabit it. This is the first of several crucial numbers in which the cats engage in detailed group self-definition. Here, they explain in countless ways what Jellicle cats are, boisterously listing numerous cat accomplishments and qualities and celebrating their cat-ness. The next number, "The Naming of Cats," serves as the consequent to the first. The mood turns hushed and serious, and the cats chant in unison the reasons why a cat must have three names. Seven numbers later, "The Jellicle Ball" appears, and in its first section the cast describes Jellicle cat qualities and habits much as they did in "Jellicle Songs for Jellicle Cats." The second act has only one of these group-description numbers, the final number "The Ad-dressing of Cats," performed mostly by the Jellicle leader, Old Deuteronomy, rather than the entire company. In it he reminds the audience how best to relate to our cat friends.

These sorts of numbers, at least in quantity, are unusual for a musical. If a musical contains a self-descriptive number, it is usually dispensed with right away, so that a background can be prepared against which individual characters will interact. "Another Op'nin', Another Show" from *Kiss Me, Kate* lets us know that this is a backstage musical. "Tradition" from *Fiddler on the Roof* could not set up the value system of Anatevka and Tevye more clearly. "Iowa Stubborn" from *The Music Man*, "Age of Aquarius" from *Hair*, "At the End of the Day" from *Les Misérables*, "Prologue: Ragtime" from *Ragtime*, and "Before the Morning" from *Marie Christine* all set the stage. Full-company numbers that come later in most musicals, rather than returning to this kind of self-identification, will instead reflect plot developments, changes the characters have undergone, or evidence of the passing of time.

This is not the case in *Cats*. While all the self-defining numbers are quite different from one another, they still all serve the same purpose: examining Jellicle cat-ness. They build and ebb in terms of intensity, in keeping with the dramatic arc of the show, but this group of creatures still spends an exceptional amount of time talking about itself. In fact, the celebration of Jellicle cats is the chief reason they (and we) are there. They celebrate themselves as a group in each of the numbers already mentioned, and they celebrate some individual members of their group in all the other numbers in between.

After "Jellicle Songs for Jellicle Cats" and "The Naming of Cats" have allowed the audience some time to get used to this cat culture, the score moves on to a few individual personalities. Each featured cat gets his or her own song, corresponding to one of Eliot's poems. The cats themselves often sing the numbers in the first person, but sometimes other cats describe the personality in question, and in many cases a song features both first-person and third-person delivery of the lyrics. Between the opening set of group numbers and the "Jellicle Ball," we meet Jennyanydots the Old Gumbie Cat, the Rum Tum Tugger, Bustopher Jones, Mungojerrie and Rumpelteazer, and Old Deuteronomy. In the second act, numbers introduce Gus the Theatre Cat, Skimbleshanks the Railway Cat, Macavity, and Mr. Mistoffelees. When characters are not featured in their own numbers, the actors usually take their place in the chorus, either retaining their featured character or taking on the guise of a different cat. (Menacing Macavity or fat Bustopher Jones, for example, do not join the chorus.)

These individual numbers make up a large portion of the show, just as their corresponding poems make up much of Eliot's book. They are held together by the general Jellicle songs at beginning, middle, and end. One more element adds development and drama throughout the whole show. In the middle of the first act, while various cat personalities cheerfully emerge, Grizabella the Glamour Cat staggers onto the scene. Unlike all the others, she is depressed, tattered, weak, and unhealthy. The cats avoid her, taunt her, coldly shun her. Two step forward to sing about her, and she has a few lines herself; this is the song "Grizabella the Glamour Cat." Later, at the Jellicle Ball, Grizabella can be seen in the background, watching while all the others dance and revel with abandon. In the final scene in act one, she takes the stage alone, trying to no avail to imitate what she saw, imagining she might join them. Toward the end of the second act, she drags herself in once again, and sings her own song of introduction, much as the others have done, although hers is more a poetic musing on her sad life than a literal description of her cat activities or personality. This is "Memory." The others, having seen her several times now and having been moved by her tragic song, follow Old Deuteronomy's lead and support his decision to allow her to be reborn into a better life. They welcome her and encourage her to move on; tentatively, but eventually joyfully, she does so.

This, then, is the extent of the plot, and one can see how critics, with great consistency, found it too thin. There is hardly anything to it. (Appendix D offers a more complete description.) We meet a bunch of cats, and the saddest one gets to be happy. But the plot, in a strict sense, is by no means the point of the show; its continuous thread, its dramatic arc, relies far more on themes, ideas, and moods. These themes include many reflections on memory, on the past; there are old and young characters, happy and sad ones. They express resistance to the unknown, then acceptance; they experience hopelessness, faith, and redemption. Nunn knew from the beginning that the "plot" he created was a simple one, but hoped that the philosophical ideas which sustained it would become the focus. He hoped he "would achieve the sense of progression through themes more than incidents."[47] These themes are unmistakable, and do indeed create a dramatic thread. Despite the thinness of the traditional plot, the show conveys a wealth of actions, characters, and relationships.

The nature of the plot points to one of the most important elements of *Cats:* almost none of this plot is expressed in words. A vast amount of information is imparted through action, mood, and music only. Every cat has a personality, but only a handful is given songs in which to express it. The rest of the personalities and relationships are made clear through continuous acting and interacting among the cast. The acting which conveys this information was both created by and directed by Nunn, with input from Lloyd Webber and Lynne. Nunn's job as director, then, was a rather unusual one. *Cats* is danced throughout; there is virtually no dialogue; almost all information about how the cats feel about each other, treat each other, react to things, and behave is conveyed without words. Nunn described his job as one which involved "writing and structuring material, conducting improvisations, delineating character, finding and communicating textual meaning and marrying the text with physical expression, pacing and phrasing the various sections of the show, arbitrating and adjudicating, connecting the many collaborators together by attempting to describe the intention of the whole, and carrying the can."[48] Nunn's hand in creating characters and making them work within the text was strong and effective. He had the cast improvise for weeks, so that they could bring some of their own personality traits to their portrayals of cats, and so that those traits would shine through the makeup, wigs, and dance steps. And he was not the least bit shy about taking credit for his powerful influence over the show: "[Lynne] has a teeming and inventive mind, but what you must focus on is this: on day one of rehearsals what we had was 15 poems set to music and five weeks later we had a show with characters, relationships and stories running from beginning to end. Those things don't get there by osmosis. They get there because a director is working them out and making them happen. Perhaps one day there will be credit for all musicals that says 'subtext by so-and-so.' "[49] An interesting proposition, to be sure, but one that would make less sense for a conventional show that does not sport the complexities of subtext of *Cats*.

What do we learn about the individual cats merely from subtext? Munkustrap is the active leader and guardian of the group. Although Old Deuteronomy is the spiritual leader and honored father figure, Munkustrap is in charge of the day-to-day protection of the Jellicles; he also narrates a number of songs and delivers the exposition of several key plot points. In the opening number, during which virtually every cat has a solo line to sing, he sings the first line. In the final section of "The Naming of Cats," after the poem proper has been recited, he steps forward and prepares us for the story to come:

> Jellicle cats meet once a year
> At the Jellicle ball, where we all rejoice
> And the Jellicle leader will soon appear
> And make what is known as the Jellicle choice

When Old Deuteronomy, just before dawn,
Through a silence you feel you could cut with a knife,
Announces the cat who can now be reborn
And come back to a different Jellicle life.

Munkustrap is extremely protective of Old Deuteronomy, for whom he has great respect. He also watches out for the younger kittens, who tend to leap without looking. He has many friends among the other male cats, although he is often annoyed by the Rum Tum Tugger, who enjoys calling attention to his sexy self and therefore gets in Munkustrap's way. And all this is made clear through action alone; not only are these relationships left unexpressed in words, Munkustrap's name is in fact never spoken in association with him. Only the cats with individual songs have names attached to them; the rest can only be found in the audience's programs. Many of those names are derived from Eliot's "The Naming of Cats," which lists a number of possible cat names ranging from the common to the exotic. Nunn and the rest of the creative team used mostly the unusual ones to name some of the cast: Munkustrap, Demeter, Alonzo, Coricopat, Jellylorum, Plato, Bombalurina. They invented names for the remaining cast members: Victoria, Tumblebrutus, Cassandra, and others.

Every one of these has a personality, even if the audience would have to engage in some detective work with their programs to link that personality with a name. They exhibit their individual styles through actions, as Munkustrap does, and also through their costumes and makeup, dance styles, singing styles, and mannerisms. Every performer wears a body stocking made of shiny spandex and each is colored differently. Each cat has a wig which suggests ears and a fur-covered head, and many have tufts of fur in clumps on various body parts. Many also wear leg warmers on their legs and arms, the fuzzy thickness and tube-like quality of which suggest paws rather than hands and fingers and feet. Every cat has a personality, a voice, and a style of movement to match his or her costume and makeup design.

For example, Munkustrap, in addition to his role as guardian and leader, dances powerfully, fights, and has a warm baritone voice and a sense of humor. He is costumed in bold splashes of black and white. Bombalurina is one of the sexier cats in the group: she sings, with Demeter, the slinky song "Macavity"; she flirts with the Rum Tum Tugger; she wears a spiked collar around her neck and fingerless gloves; her multicolored costume has subtle swirls around her breasts. The all-out sexy cat, however, is Cassandra, rarely featured but unmistakable thanks to her sleek, furless maroon body suit and slinky, cool movements. Victoria is the only cat in an all-white costume; she is a featured dancer with a slow, impressive solo, but she is also still young and frightens easily. The youngest of the group is Sillabub (called Jemima in London); she is tiny, has a shorter wig, wears a collar with short spikes, sports lines on her costume that look like random crayon scribbles, and sings in a high, youthful voice.

Those cats who have featured songs offer much more concrete glimpses into their personalities, but even then, their costumes, voices, and mannerisms throughout the show are highly informative. The Rum Tum Tugger stands out: he wears an all-black suit with a wide, flashy fur collar and a silver rhinestone belt. His suit is unbuttoned, so to speak, suggesting a visible furry chest beneath. He swaggers, he seduces, he shows off. He was taken by many to be a cat version of Mick Jagger, a logical conclusion given his flashy performance style and his signature rock song.[50] During his own song, young girl cats swoon over him and men disdain him. But as the show progresses, he becomes a valued member of the community. Mr. Mistoffelees, too, has a featured song but joins with the company the rest of the time. His costume suggests a tuxedo, with its black suit and white bib, which matches his role as a cat capable of great feats of magic, including at one point the retrieval of the temporarily missing Old Deuteronomy. He is fun-loving and energetic, and is the most featured male dancer, often a counterpart to Victoria. Skimbleshanks works on the railroad and wears a stiff collar, fancy brown vest, and pocket watch. Mungojerrie and Rumpelteazer, mischievous thieves, wear matching costumes and stolen jewels. Old Deuteronomy wears not a bodysuit but a full loose coat of stringy fur and a beard.

It takes multiple viewings to sort out each of these personalities; only a few capture the audience's attention at first. For the most part the audience experiences a journey into the world of Jellicle cats, and the structure of the show's score helps them understand what this means.

The Score: "Jellicle Cats Come Out Tonight"

In *Jesus Christ Superstar*, Lloyd Webber used recurring musical ideas, sometimes moving a short motif into new locations, other times revisiting a melody with either related or new lyrics. In *Cats*, Lloyd Webber created a great many more musical motifs than in *Superstar*, using them as fodder for development and manipulation. When he revisits entire melodies, he uses both a reprise technique unique to *Cats*, as well as a previewing technique employed in *Superstar* but exploited to its maximum impact here. Another musical choice that comes to the forefront with *Cats* involves pastiche.[51]

JELLICLE-DEFINING SONGS AND MOTIFS, AND THEIR RECURRENCES

As mentioned, *Cats* features an unusually large number of songs which define the group. This consistent revisiting of self-defining songs helps unite the numbers of the score into a whole, so that the songs for individual cats feel like temporary pauses in the evening's main activity: understanding Jellicle cats. Most of the numbers that unite the separate cats into a Jellicle whole share a recurring musical theme, which comes in several major forms and countless variations, diminutions, and fragmentations. When Lloyd Webber presents this Jellicle theme in full, it comes in three basic versions. The simplest is a two-phrase version which moves from tonic to dominant and back again; the two melodic phrases are almost identical. The second version is four phrases long and visits the supertonic before moving to the dominant and back to the tonic. The second phrase has more upward motion than downward, whereas the other three phrases move down. The third version is eight phrases long, visits some new key areas, and features a melody which moves up, down, and back on itself again. Example 3.1 shows the simple two-phrase form. All the takes on the Jellicle theme appear in various orchestrations, and the two-phrase version is not always used strictly, but the theme is always clearly recognizable (and almost always has B-flat major as its tonic). The theme also serves as inspiration for entire numbers full of fragmentations and development.

In the overture, Lloyd Webber opens with an agitated, chromatic fragment of the theme over an ostinato figure. It is not clear at first that the line derives from the Jellicle theme, but over the course of the overture, Lloyd Webber builds it and manipulates it into its complete form. The short chunk from the opening measures eventually gains extensions, and is later treated fugally in a dense, dissonant passage. This drives toward the first full statement of the theme, in four-phrase form, which in turn leads to a grand, slow statement of the theme in eight-phrase form with accompanying fanfares and majestic percussive emphasis. The eighth phrase turns back on itself a number of times, gaining momentum and driving to the sudden ending of the overture (see ex. 3.2).

Like all overtures, this piece prepares us for what is to come. But while traditional overtures visit the songs that will be heard later, this one visits none

Example 3.1. Jellicle theme in two-phrase form

Example 3.2. End of overture (Jellicle theme in eight-phrase form)

Example 3.2. (*continued*)

Example 3.2. (*continued*)

of them; instead it is built entirely on the Jellicle theme. In this case, that is perfectly appropriate, since the exploration of Jellicle cats is the show's main purpose. The overture prepares the audience for music both dissonant and grandly melodic, and this theme will recur in these and many other forms. The theme's connection with the essence of Jellicle cats becomes clear later when Munkustrap sings it while describing the Jellicle Ball (to the text quoted in part, above, from "Invitation to the Jellicle Ball"). The theme is in eight-phrase form there, although it fizzles out in the sixth.

But even though "Invitation to the Jellicle Ball" is only the fourth number, the Jellicle theme has already been heard in association with several important self-describing moments. Just before Munkustrap's stanza, the orchestra intones the theme slowly and softly while Victoria, glowing white in the spotlight, dances an almost impossibly difficult solo. It is the two-phrase version of the theme, played through twice and gaining a sultry rising clarinet line the second time. Next, a perky Mr. Mistoffelees shatters the hushed mood, bounding forward and singing the most basic of Jellicle texts set to the four-phrase version of the theme (see ex. 3.3).

Even before this sequence of events, however, the Jellicle theme has already undergone manipulations since the overture. "The Naming of Cats" is based entirely on bits of the theme, fragmented and dissonant, much as in the beginning of the overture. This is an unusual number for several reasons. Although the music has roots in the Jellicle theme, it has no solid key signature or harmonic stability. It begins with Jellicle theme fragments, wanders into some new variations and smaller, disjointed fragments, and eventually dwindles away to nothing. Meanwhile, the cast does not sing at all, but rather speaks the entire poem in unison, with a soft chant-like quality (see ex. 3.4). The entire number answers a crucial question, introduced by Munkustrap, who gazes out at the audience and asks, "Do I actually see, with my own very eyes, a man who's not heard of a Jellicle cat? What's a Jellicle cat?"

One of the most engaging things about the text of "The Naming of Cats" is that it is delivered in perfect unison, but in natural speech rhythms. The score renders much of the vocal line in even eighth notes, but in reality the cast almost never holds to this. Also, the performers never speak on the same pitches as one another; their voices visit different vocal ranges, peak and recede at different times, and never fall into any matching sing-song shapes. As they speak, they drift out into the audience, so that audience members can hear the individual voices nearest to them. By the end, the cats have slipped back onto the stage and into the shadows to make way for Victoria's solo dance.

The Jellicle theme having largely saturated the three early numbers (the

Example 3.3. "Invitation to the Jellicle Ball" (Jellicle theme in four-phrase form)

Example 3.4. "The Naming of Cats"

overture, "The Naming of Cats," and "Invitation to the Jellicle Ball"), it recedes into the background. After Old Deuteronomy's arrival (which takes place during the song "Old Deuteronomy"), Munkustrap makes the transition to the next number, "The Pekes and the Pollicles," by intoning one quatrain derived from his earlier exposition during "Invitation to the Jellicle Ball." With the two-phrase version of the theme slowly descending behind him, he says, "Jellicle cats meet once a year / On the night we make the Jellicle choice / And now that the Jellicle leader is here / The Jellicle cats can all rejoice." The Jellicle theme recedes once more.

It emerges again in "The Jellicle Ball," a number which is perhaps best understood as the theme's true home, for here it undergoes almost every manifestation touched on throughout the score. This is the longest, most complex production number in the show, lasting approximately fourteen minutes. For the first few minutes, there is text, Eliot's poem "The Song of the Jellicles." The cats speak each line in ever-changing groups of one, two, or three, while the entire company moves and dances in complicated patterns.

> *Cats, variously:* Jellicle cats are black and white
> Jellicle cats are rather small
> Jellicle cats are merry and bright
> And pleasant to hear when we cat-erwaul

The music here replicates that found at the top of the overture, the same music that has already been revisited at the beginning of "The Naming of Cats." Lloyd Webber then begins to reuse certain sections of music, usually in multiples of eight bars. For example, an eight-bar phrase of music as found in "The Naming of Cats" is repeated immediately after it appears, but with added instruments, new passing tones, and other small changes. As the speaking voices become more intense, the music continues to borrow and develop sections of music both from the overture and from "The Naming of Cats." Occasionally, Lloyd Webber puts a new twist on a borrowed element; for example, he reuses the ostinato figure which opens the overture and "The Naming of Cats," but here it accompanies a new set of melodic gestures. In another case, only the bass line from the fugal section of the overture plays, while the other orchestral voices move on to new ideas. The cats, meanwhile, work themselves up into something of a frenzy, eventually erupting into singing. They intone, not surprisingly, the Jellicle theme in two-phrase form, to the most typical of couplets: "Jellicle cats come out tonight / Jellicle cats come one, come all / The Jellicle moon is shining bright / Jellicles come to the Jellicle Ball."

The final invitation having been issued and the Jellicles having finished describing their breed, it is time for the ball to begin. The orchestra returns to the beginning of the piece, and plays, almost exactly, the same music, but without the speaking or singing. Each of the small borrowed sections, then, has now combined into one large unit, revisited, slightly reorchestrated, and newly choreographed. Without the voices, and with so much choreography to look at, it is not particularly noticeable that these particular arrangements and fragments of the Jellicle theme have just been heard. Most of this section features the entire cast dancing in unison, with Victoria often downstage center. When this large section of music finishes, the ball continues on smoothly to new fragmentations of the materials. We hear, for example, a new arrangement of the Jellicle theme; it is in standard four-voice form, but is played in a perky swing and radically shifts the mood of the piece from eerie and dark to bright and energetic, almost saucy. As befits this mood, this version features Bombalurina and Cassandra, along with some of the other sexy female cats, and eventually the Rum Tum Tugger and other manly cats join them. The lighting shifts from the almost always-present blue glow to a raunchy red one.

Next, the refrain of "Old Deuteronomy" (which was heard in its original form several songs earlier; see ex. 3.6) emerges from the orchestra, punctuated by snippets of the Jellicle theme in its more dissonant, agitated forms. The blue nighttime lighting returns. The "Old Deuteronomy" refrain plays through three times, with increasing insistence on the Jellicle theme. Old Deuteronomy enters, is greeted gleefully by a spinning, twirling group, and takes his usual seat upstage center. The "Old Deuteronomy" music reaches a climax, signaling the mid-point of the number. A few very soft, dissonant chords step slowly down and up, and then the Jellicle theme, loosely presented in two-phrase form, enters in cascades of synthesized bell sounds. This soft, slow section features Victoria lifted, turned, and touched by several dancers in one of the most sensual moments in the show. As the cascades of the Jellicle theme end, the entire company has piled together on the floor.

Having reached the gentlest point of the number, the energy now builds to the end of the ball. First, the orchestra revisits material from "Jellicle Songs for Jellicle Cats," in a loose series of variations. This builds in enthusiasm until the final section: the Jellicle theme, in full eight-phrase form, played almost exactly as it appeared at the end of the overture (as in ex. 3.2), drives with gusto to a sudden finish. This long, challenging dance, impressive and exhausting to watch, is the ultimate celebration of and by Jellicle cats. Lynne hoped to make it "exciting theatre whilst showing the cats at the height of their passion, dancing their most private, energetic and anarchic rituals."[52] The Jellicle theme, which ran throughout almost the entire number, will not reappear in full again until the climax of the show.

The Jellicle theme serves, in the meantime, only as transitional material and orchestral fodder for dance music. The slowest, quietest moment of the ball appears briefly at the top of the second act, helping introduce "The Moments of Happiness." After "Macavity," when that evil cat emerges at last and fights Munkustrap and others, the orchestra plays the fugal version of the Jellicle theme, as heard in the overture and the ball. In its two-phrase form, the Jellicle theme also acts as bookends to "Memory." It is intoned sweetly and reverently on bells, actually played by a synthesizer on a setting that the score labels "Jellicle Bells."

The Jellicle theme in grand eight-phrase form arises only once more in the show, as Old Deuteronomy and the others escort Grizabella to the Heaviside Layer. She joins Old Deuteronomy on the giant rubber tire toward the back of the stage. As the orchestra swells and crashes, the stage fills with smoke and the tire rises straight up. Lights from beneath it create patterns in the smoke. By the fifth phrase of the Jellicle theme, a glistening golden staircase has descended from the ceiling, coming to rest with its first step on the raised tire. Old Deuteronomy encourages a wary but willing Grizabella onto the staircase. She steps on and climbs; the staircase folds back up into the heavens, taking Grizabella with it. The orchestra, having now reached its sixth phrase, pivots into a quote from "Jellicle Songs for Jellicle Cats" and the voices join in to celebrate the moment.

Other self-defining moments in the show do not employ the Jellicle theme, but discuss Jellicle traits nonetheless. The long opening number, "Jellicle Songs for Jellicle Cats," has a complex structure and many subsections. The song opens with vague, loose phrases in the orchestra, spread out among long silences. A clarinet offers up four notes; after a pause, a flute offers four more. A trumpet and xylophone play an odd phrase which quickly fades away. This continues until eight phrases have been offered and the cats have begun to emerge from the hiding places which they found at the end of the overture. Munkustrap is spotlighted, and after him there are spotlights on other cats alone, in pairs, or in threes. The eight lines of the verse loosely follow the shape of the eight orchestral phrases that opened the piece. Then the entire company sings the chorus, which has somewhat different lyrics each time it occurs but always features an engaging rhythmic syncopation (see ex. 3.5 for a verse and chorus).

As the piece continues, the verses gain momentum, the choruses gain harmony, and the entire piece gains volume with the gradual addition of voices and instruments. Neither the verses nor the choruses repeat exactly; each has variations in melody, rhythm, voicing, instrumentation, and lyrics, submerging the underlying structure beneath this variegated surface. Also, inserted into the piece is a completely new section. The cast stops dancing momentarily and gathers in a tiered clump like a choir, folding their paws before them. An organ introduces their hymn in four-part harmony:[53]

> The mystical divinity of unashamed felinity
> Round the cathedral rang "Vivat"
> Life to the everlasting cat!

A transition leads the choir back to the refrain, and after several more verses and choruses, the number suddenly stops and makes the transition to "The Naming of Cats." The opening number is abandoned, with no closure.

Lloyd Webber does not use material from "Jellicle Songs for Jellicle Cats" nearly so often as the Jellicle theme, but it does emerge in several places. He

When you fall on your head do you land on your feet? Are you tense when you sense there's a
B   Em   F   F   D7

Accompanied by piano and elec. bass, using guide chords: Very sparingly, funky

storm in the air? Can you find your way blind when you're lost in the street? Do you know how to go to the -
Em7   Em   C7   F7   Bb7   B

Heav-i-side Layer?   Be-cause   Jel-li-cles can   and Jel - li-cles do   Jel-li-cles do and Jel-li-cles can
E   p

Drum pick-up
Piano, Elec. piano, Gtr., high hat
Bass
p

Jel-li-cles can and Jel - li-cles do   Jel-li-cles do and Jel-li-cles can   Jel-li-cles can and   Jel-li-cles do.

Example 3.5. "Jellicle Songs for Jellicle Cats"

reworks at length the opening eight phrases, the verse material, and the chorus material in the "Jellicle Ball," often to points of unrecognizability. He revisits the first eight phrases soon thereafter, accompanying Grizabella's weak attempt at dancing. The verse material appears in the music that accompanies "Macavity's Fight." Finally, and most effectively of all, the grand hymn section returns to mark the moment of Grizabella's apotheosis. She rises to the sounds of the eight-phrase Jellicle theme, but at the moment she disappears from view, the full company turns from watching her departure to face the audience. Boldly, in full voice, they celebrate with the hymn to "the mystical divinity of unashamed felinity" for the last time.

This leads directly into the final number of the show, "The Ad-dressing of Cats," the last of the Jellicle-defining numbers. In it, Old Deuteronomy, still perched above the others on his tire, sings directly to the audience about what they have learned and how they might apply it to future encounters with cats. "Cats are very much like you," he points out, saying that if one treats them with respect and feeds them what they like, eventually one will be honored to call them by their names. The chorus echoes, in a hymn-like moment similar in spirit to the one from "Jellicle Songs for Jellicle Cats," the final lesson: "A cat's entitled to expect these evidences of respect, / So this is this and that is that, and there's how you address a cat." The stacks of harmony and the full-throated singing make this an effective closing moment. The chorus is somewhat more still than usual; they simply watch Old Deuteronomy during the first verse, and during the second they face stage front, posing and stretching as fog billows out over the audience. This final Jellicle-defining moment does not appear before its position at the end of the show; instead, Lloyd Webber gives us this new material for the last Jellicle moment.

OTHER RECURRING MUSICAL IDEAS

Other themes, fragments, and motifs recur throughout the show, but none with anything like the variation or frequency of the Jellicle theme or the music of "Jellicle Songs for Jellicle Cats." They usually have significance related to plot or character, rather than a generally Jellicle meaning.

The song "Old Deuteronomy" is simple and beautiful; it features two verses, a bridge, and a refrain, and the refrain finds its way into later moments in the show.[54] The song proper opens with the refrain, after one of the cats announces that Old Deuteronomy approaches. Munkustrap sings the first verse, and the Rum Tum Tugger the second. It makes for a touching moment; Munkustrap is surprised when the Rum Tum Tugger steps forward to help recount the story of Old Deuteronomy, and the two find a shared value in their respect for their leader. The chorus repeats the refrain four times; it modulates after the second, and builds in emotion and volume each time. During the verses and the first two repeats of the refrain, the cats lounge about sensually on the floor, stretching and rolling. By the third refrain, Old Deuteronomy has made his way through the audience to the stage, and the cats rush to greet him. The young cats jump all over him, Munkustrap clears a path through the bodies for him, and he exchanges warm nods with the Rum Tum Tugger. The orchestra supplies a swelling, moving climax under the fourth repetition, which it suggests earlier with a counter-melody during the second repetition (see ex. 3.6).

Example 3.6. Refrain, "Old Deuteronomy"

This refrain melody becomes Old Deuteronomy's motif, used in conjunction with appearances by him or thoughts of him. It is played through three times during the Jellicle Ball, in a section during which Old Deuteronomy stands proudly among the reveling dancers. It is clearly audible there, while the Jellicle theme fills the spaces left by the sustained chords with agitated fragments. The refrain melody returns again at the beginning of the second act, before Old Deuteronomy's solo song "The Moments of Happiness."[55] After several measures of introduction, the orchestra revisits a few chords borrowed from the slow middle moment of the ball, then moves into (instead of away from, as in the ball) Old Deuteronomy's melody.

His theme returns once more during the cats' fight with Macavity, who has kidnapped Old Deuteronomy. Just before the song "Macavity," the mysterious, evil cat creates havoc and drags Old Deuteronomy away. Demeter and Bombalurina then sing about Macavity's acts of crime in the past. Once the number ends, Macavity returns, disguised as Old Deuteronomy. The Old Deuteronomy theme occurs here, but is interrupted first by the eight orchestral phrases which open "Jellicle Songs for Jellicle Cats," and then, when Macavity is revealed, by a pounding rendition of the verse material of "Jellicle Songs." The fight music uses the Jellicle theme in various forms, but it ends with a return to Old Deuteronomy's refrain played on a solo flute, and then the company sings the last line on the text, "We have to find Old Deuteronomy."

Like Old Deuteronomy, Macavity also has his own music, representing his sneaky, mysterious abilities and his habit of never being where he is thought to be (see ex. 3.7).[56] This motif has roots in the song "Macavity," where it serves as the music of the fifth verse, the only verse to have a significant change in melody: "He's outwardly respectable. / I know he cheats at cards. / And his footprints are not found in any files of Scotland Yard's." The motif is played in its instrumental form whenever Macavity is suspected to be about and causing trouble, appearing twice in the first act, introduced by a sudden loud crash and sounds of breaking glass. In both cases the crash interrupts the action and the cats rush about in fear, searching for Macavity, for the site of the crash, for shelter, while Munkustrap stands at the ready, prepared to protect his charges.

Example 3.7. Macavity's motif

But no one can be found and the moment passes. In the second act the crash and Macavity's music interrupt yet again, and this time the music leads directly into the song "Macavity" itself.

One final recurring theme seems to have no particular association with a character or event, but serves as a simple mood-breaker. It is a cheerful fanfare, played through several times whenever it occurs, and it usually acts as a transition from a darker, hushed moment to a sunny one. After the rather eerie "The Naming of Cats" and Munkustrap's expository verses, the fanfare bounds in for the first time. This prepares us for the perky cat Jennyanydots, in "The Old Gumbie Cat." The fanfare serves a similar function after "Old Deuteronomy." It again shatters the mood, which at that moment is somewhat reverent and subdued, and makes the transition to "The Pekes and the Pollicles," which is a light-hearted legend recounted by Munkustrap and acted out by the others. The fanfare makes a final appearance in its role as transition tool in the second act, where it serves as a direct introduction to "The Journey to the Heaviside Layer." It moves the music away from the emotional "Memory" with its Jellicle theme ending, and into the bright world of Grizabella's ascent. Interestingly, the fanfare appears in one other place, where it serves not as transitional material, but rather becomes a somewhat buried layer within the refrain of a song; in "Mr. Mistofelees," the fanfare sounds beneath the much-repeated celebratory chorus (see ex. 3.8).

PASTICHE AND SONGS FOR INDIVIDUAL CATS

More than half the numbers in the show are devoted to an individual cat (or, occasionally, a pair of cats or the tale of a cat of ages past) rather than to the Jellicle cats as a group. It was the preponderance of this kind of number that led many critics to complain that *Cats* was nothing more than a revue, a series of songs strung together with a bare thread of a plot. Though it is true that more than half the set pieces concern one cat or another, these songs add up to less than half the running time of the show. The numbers about Jellicles in general are much more involved and much longer than the individual numbers, and when Grizabella's series of numbers is added in, the songs about the other individual cats look more like welcome diversions from the general evening of Jellicle celebrations rather than the focus of the show.

Most of the songs devoted to singular cat personalities feature the cat in question, showing us his or her talent as described in the poem while singing and dancing about it in an appropriate style. It was in discussing these numbers that critics came to use the word "pastiche" frequently, and usually as an insult. Michael Feingold of the *Village Voice* would contend in his review that Lloyd

Webber's music wandered in its "usual fashion through scraps of old show tunes, old pop tunes, and old light classics" and sounded as if Lloyd Webber had cobbled together the sounds emanating from a hallway full of practice rooms.[57] He offered no specific examples. John Simon of *New York* magazine likewise thought the music full of various pastiches, and though he was less bothered by it than Feingold and thought the score worked as a whole, he too exudes a somewhat hostile air:

> And what of the tunes? In his usual fashion, Lloyd Webber has contrived melodies that vary from the catchy to the merely serviceable, from the vaguely Puccinian to the less categorizably derivative, but very much—including even the mercilessly miked hit, "Memory"—purrloined. Never have I had such a yen to hire a private tune detective to track down the provenance of these songs, but mongrels though they be, they manage to work as a score.[58]

What, then, is the problem? If none of the tunes are borrowed from any obvious source, if they form a genuine pastiche collection of a variety of genres as opposed to being thefts of specific songs, and if they work as a score, why is pastiche a negative quality? Critics have a resistance to recognizable things, outside things. They seem to prefer that a composer have a sound exclusively his or her own, one that can be identified as belonging to that composer and no one else, no matter the circumstances. In the case of the individual cat songs, Lloyd Webber strove to do the opposite, to cater his musical style to the dramatic or characteristic moment at hand. This does not mean that his music has no signature sound; he, like most composers, displays consistent traits. One of them, in fact, is that very mix of styles. But this compositional device continued to bother critics who would have preferred his songs to sound more like each other, and his scores to sound more like each other.[59] Their distaste for this practice speaks to their distaste for Lloyd Webber in general, as the practice of invoking a variety of musical styles over the course of a show has been standard musical theater practice for virtually all theater composers since the vaudeville days—and indeed happens often in some operatic traditions as well.

Michael Walsh, while unimpressed by *Cats*, offers a more thoughtful explanation for Lloyd Webber's use of a variety of musical styles in the score. "The fact was," he wrote, "that Lloyd Webber was an agglutinative composer, not a thief." Lloyd Webber purposely composed pastiches of various genres and styles. The problem with this technique, Walsh stresses, is that Lloyd Webber did not then synthesize these songs into something "new and vital" but rather simply assembled them into something "popular."[60]

In the cases of the songs written for the individual cats, this may be a valid point. These songs do feel like separate units, each with a separate style, matching the cat in question. The posing Rum Tum Tugger gets flashy rock music, the mysterious Macavity a slinky blues song. The separateness of each number is reinforced by Lynne's choreography, which is quite literal. Where Lloyd Webber wrote old tap-style vaudeville music, Lynne designed a traditional tap number. The bluesy "Macavity" involves a great deal of arching, stretching, and sexy gesturing. Lynne's translations of texts into movement was intentionally obvious, since she was responsible for conveying a large part of the text and book.[61] Her approach led to reviews which called her choreography unoriginal, traditional, repetitive. This resulted from her creations not only being literal, but also not always being well suited to the material. There are traditional tap numbers and there are boring tap numbers; Lynne's example tips toward the latter category, relying on fairly simple tap steps and slow-moving stage pictures. However, these individual numbers that drew the critics' attention still add up to less than half the score, and Lynne's work in the larger half—the Jellicle numbers—was much more engaging. Indeed, although most of the musical pastiche numbers work well, Lloyd Webber's work, too, is consistently better in the Jellicle numbers. And in any event, most of the critics (Feingold and Simon aside) found the pastiche numbers delightful. As one historian aptly puts it, "Lloyd Webber happily indulged his propensity for amiably gentle musical parody as each cat was given a tune and a style with just enough familiarity about it to help point up his parallel with a certain kind of human being."[62]

"The Rum Tum Tugger" is among the best of these songs. The music, a rock tune set to a delightfully funky beat, can make audiences groove in their seats. One lucky ticket-holder, in fact, gets to groove out of her seat: during the dance break toward the end of the song, the Rum Tum Tugger bounds into the aisles and selects a woman to dance with him. His charisma spills beyond the stage and into the house. He is a rock star, flashy and arrogant, and milks his sex symbol status so skillfully that by the end of the number, the young girl cats sigh and mew in rapture. Eliot's text fits the mood nicely: this cat is impossible to please, disagreeable at every turn, and quite aware that, as he says, "There's no doing anything about it." Strong rhythmic gestures and the engaging pop beat accompany his declarations, which he accents with many pelvic thrusts, hip shakes, and proud struts.

Other numbers for single cats are slightly less over the top, and although excess might not be required to make the other numbers equally engaging, few of them are. "The Old Gumbie Cat," while not transporting, is pleasant; Eliot tells us that this cat, whose given name is Jennyanydots, lazes about during the day but at night spends her time training the house's mice and cockroaches to be productive and kind. Munkustrap is aided in his recounting of her story by a trio of women in tight three-part harmony, Jellylorum, Bombalurina, and Demeter,[63] as well as by Jennyanydots herself. Meanwhile the rest of the cast dons makeshift costumes representing mice and roaches, and taps with her. The music is in a traditional dance-hall style, reminiscent of vaudeville, and comes complete with a tap breakdown.

"Skimbleshanks: The Railway Cat," known as Skimble, is described by Eliot as being essential—from the cat's point of view, at least—to the workings of the railroad. He sees to the comforts of the passengers, helps with the work, keeps an eye out for trouble. Skimble himself describes much of his doings, acting them out as he goes, with support from a group of women. At one point the entire cast builds a train, complete with moving parts, out of the junk at hand, which soon collapses on top of the delighted cats. The music is stridently high and repetitive, featuring many verses with few brief refrains. Also, and perhaps inevitably, it is set in a chugging 4/4 meter. The poetry practically insists on this; it would be difficult indeed to maintain the structure of the poem without using the rhythm and meter inherent to the text itself.[64] Lloyd Webber was likely thinking of "Skimbleshanks" when he wrote that the poems were already inherently rhythmic and "dictate to some degree the music that will accompany them," although happily most of the other poems fell into his second category, those "frequently of irregular and exciting metre" which makes them "very challenging for a composer."[65]

"Bustopher Jones" is among the more forgettable of the individual songs. Jennyanydots, Bombalurina, and Jellylorum introduce him as the cat about town, a fat, pampered fellow who spends much of his time at his clubs, dining extravagantly. He is costumed in a huge black suit, with white spats, huge silver spoon as a cane, silly moustache, and monocle. The music that accompanies the women's verse about him is light-hearted but repetitive and a bit plodding, and his own verse is a slower, wordier version of it. The text, especially in his verse, surely escapes much of the American audience, or indeed any non-British audience: "My visits are occasional to the Senior Educational / And it is against the rules / For any one cat to belong both to that / And the Joint Superior Schools."

"Mungojerrie and Rumpelteazer," though almost as full of wordy British references, does a much better job of conveying its point and entertaining the audience than "Bustopher Jones." This pair of exceptionally perky cats enters on an empty stage, carrying a bag full of loot. For this number Mungojerrie wears a t-shirt that matches his costume's patterns, and Rumpelteazer wears thigh-high stockings and garters over her cat suit as well as a fat strand of stolen pearls. They dance constantly, eventually achieving applause-worthy feats of acrobatics, while relating their exploits. Mungojerrie, the male cat, and Rumpelteazer, the female, look remarkably alike to their human family, such that when things go missing and turn up broken, no one can be sure which cat to blame. The duo giddily reveals their secret: they're in it together. The music adds variety to the wordy verses by dividing the text into several musical sections. Each verse begins with a somewhat controlled melody set to common time, but with the second half set in a frantic 7/8 over which the voices bounce and roll. A half-step rise in tonality and a big finish bring the song home, which, when coupled with the astounding dancing, makes for a sure hit. (Lloyd Webber completely rewrote this number for New York; in London the tune was rather monotone and unvaried. The London cast soon incorporated the New York version.)

Even more impressive dancing sells "Mr. Mistoffelees," which features the principal male dancer. Narrated largely by the Rum Tum Tugger, the song features an oft-repeated catchy refrain (see ex. 3.8). Note that the recurring fanfare representing good cheer, used elsewhere for transitions, appears here in the trumpet part as part of the song's accompaniment. The music for the verses moves away from this straightforward perkiness and instead touches on funky pop. Mr. Mistoffelees, the Rum Tum Tugger tells us, is a magician, conjurer, and inventor of great skill. While dancing and sporting a special tuxedo-like jacket with twinkling lights on it, Mr. Mistoffelees performs some magical feats: he causes small explosions of smoke and fire, he trails a seemingly endless ribbon around the stage, and, best of all, he finds Old Deuteronomy by revealing him hidden in a huge pipe. Thrilled to see his leader again, Mr. Mistoffelees actually manages to leap

Example 3.8. Refrain, "Mr. Mistoffelees"

on him and land such that his entire body is curled up in Old Deuteronomy's arms, while he licks his leader's face with glee. The moment is an audience favorite.

"Macavity" is among the best and most unusual of the numbers about individual cats. The cat in question is not onstage at all, having already kidnapped Old Deuteronomy and fled the area, during the third instance of his theme music. Instead, a knowing Demeter and Bombalurina recount his story to us, which makes for a nice change of pace, even if it shatters the scary mood by being far too much fun. This bluesy, sexy number has a striptease beat under a slippery minor melody punctuated by brass comments. Demeter and then Bombalurina, and eventually both plus some of the other women, slink about throughout the song. Strangely, the two women seem terribly knowing about this evil cat, and their sexy demeanors make them come across as admirers, like gangsters' molls. Normally, they are terrified of him. Yet the music is so seductive that audiences are not bothered by the girl cats' temporary change in attitude.

Two rather extensive songs recount tales of past glories. The simpler and far less engaging of these is "The Pekes and the Pollicles," narrated by Munkustrap and pantomimed by the cast. It tells of a confrontation between two groups of dogs, the Pekes and the Pollicles, and the interference of two other groups, the Pugs and the Poms. Like "Skimbleshanks," Eliot's poetry for this number has a strong rhythmic element, such that its translation into a rolling 6/8 meter is almost inevitable. This makes for such an onslaught of words that the audience invariably loses the plot. The cast dresses up in makeshift dog costumes assembled from scraps of fabric and old boxes, and their confrontation is clear, though not its details. Only Munkustrap's narration and a few interruptions by the Rum Tum Tugger save it from being a nonsensical number, at least up until the entrance of the Great Rumpuscat, who saves the day merely by arriving. While the Rumpuscat's appearance entertains, and he enters impressively by flying up from a hole in the stage, the fight's resolution feels anticlimactic and the whole number falls flat.

The other cat legend is far more engaging, partly because it is framed by one of the songs about individual cats, "Gus the Theatre Cat." Gus, Jellylorum tells us, is an old cat actor, now weak and a bit feeble, but in his day the star of the stage. Taking over the singing, Gus tells us that he played many roles, knew how to act with his tail and his voice, needed little rehearsal, and was quite famous. He laments the downfall of theater in these modern times, making for a delightfully ironic moment that seems to speak perfectly for those critics who resisted *Cats* itself. Indeed, it is easy to imagine the critics mentioned in this study agreeing with Gus: "Well, the theatre is certainly not what it was."

The melody is one of Lloyd Webber's gentlest, a simple lilting line featuring an unexpected major triad built on the subtonic in the accompaniment as the antepenultimate chord (on the word "Fiend"), one of the few times *Cats* sounds at all like *Jesus Christ Superstar* (see ex. 3.9).

Refreshingly, there is no choreography at all for this number. Jellylorum simply stands beside Gus, patting his hands occasionally, as the others sit around on various levels of the set to watch. As Gus continues to reminisce, he recalls playing the role of Growltiger the pirate cat, and as he imagines that he could do it again, the scene fades and "Growltiger's Last Stand" begins without pause. In Eliot's book, these two poems are unrelated, but Nunn and the rest of the creative team decided to make Growltiger into Gus's favorite role. The few lines in which Gus mentions Growltiger are Nunn's invention. As the lights come up on a pirate ship, which has folded out from the back of the set, a youthful and strong Gus emerges in his Growltiger costume, complete with eye patch. Jellylorum will be his true love, Griddlebone, in the enacted scene.

As this ballad-like poem tells us in its thirteen short verses, Growltiger was a mean-spirited cat with a torn coat, a missing ear, and a vengeful attitude toward the Siamese cats who had once attacked him. His crew, made up of cast members including Munkustrap, the Rum Tum Tugger, Mr. Mistoffelees, Skimbleshanks, and other men, narrates this for us while they stalk about their ship. It seems that this gruff pirate has a sentimental side when it comes to his true love, who emerges in sparkling white fur. Meanwhile a band of Siamese prepare to board the ship, but their invasion gets postponed until after the love duet.

Here we have Lloyd Webber at his most blatantly Pucciniesque. After countless critics had accused him of borrowing Puccini's music specifically or his style generally, Lloyd Webber decided to treat them to an all-out parody. This number had not been in the London version, but for the New York opening, he replaced the song sung by Growltiger and Griddlebone in the London show (Eliot's rather unromantic "Ballad of Billy McCaw") with a completely new text set to new music. He set Italian verses based on a translation of the Growltiger poem to a tune dripping with sentiment and featuring a vaguely Orientalist pentatonic melody (see ex. 3.10). After this Puccini-like respite, the Siamese cats invade, Griddlebone is lost at sea, the Siamese force Growltiger to walk the plank, and citizens from England to Bangkok rejoice to hear that the evil pirate will menace them no more.

As the music of jubilation fades, Gus the old theater cat reemerges, a kindly Jellylorum again at his side. He reprises a bit of his gentle song, lamenting the state of theater today and letting his voice fade to nothing as he recalls past glories. The whole sequence works well emotionally, all the more in that the

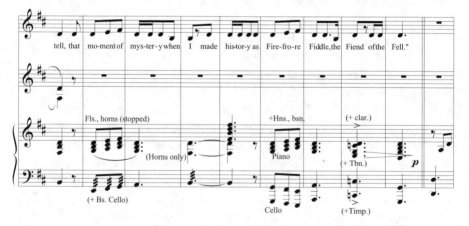

Example 3.9. "Gus the Theatre Cat"

Example 3.10. "In una tepida notte" from "Growltiger's Last Stand"

slow, sweet song for Gus makes the audience feel more invested in the tale of Growltiger, and the parody of opera is delightfully broad. However, anecdotal evidence suggests that the onslaught of action and text conveyed through most of "Growltiger" sometimes overwhelms those not paying attention, and few in the audience understand why there are sections in Italian, much less that Lloyd Webber intends to parody Puccini.

REPRISES AND PREVIEWS

Gus's reprise after "Growltiger's Last Stand" is by no means the first reprise of the show; in fact, many songs feature reprises immediately after they finish, one of the more common and more awkward techniques Lloyd Webber uses to link one song to the next in *Cats.* These immediate reprises exist solely to provide a time during which the audience may applaud before the score moves on to the next cat. Lloyd Webber therefore breaks one of his own rules: usually, he does not create closure at the end of numbers for applause; in the few places in which he does, he never launches into an immediate reprise. In *Cats,* this strange reprise technique feels disruptive to the flow and manipulative of the audience. At the end of the first song about an individual cat, "The Old Gumbie Cat," for example, there is a clear big finish and full stop. The audience claps. Then the orchestra strikes up the opening verse again, intoning the first few lines, only to be interrupted suddenly by the first notes of the next song, "The Rum Tum Tugger." Nothing in particular justifies the reprise of the Gumbie Cat's music other than it gives her time to be escorted out of the way so that the Rum Tum Tugger can make his flashy entrance. The interruption seems appropriate enough, though, for such is his way. He will do it again. At the end of his own song, he too achieves full closure, drinks in his applause, and then fires up the orchestra for a reprise, which in turn is interrupted by the sudden entrance of Grizabella. The same reprise-as-segue technique returns after "Mungojerrie and Rumpelteazer"— a shattering crash and Macavity's sneaky motif interrupt their reprise—and "Skimbleshanks," whose lengthy reprise of most of a verse is also interrupted by Macavity's crash and motif. Mr. Mistoffelees receives a full reprise without an interruption. By the time his song proper has ended and he has received his applause, he has already rescued Old Deuteronomy and shown us his prowess as a dancer, but more lies in store. During the ensuing reprise, which repeats the refrain of his song seven times, Mr. Mistoffelees demonstrates some of the most impressive dancing in the show, finishing with a bang and a puff of magical smoke, into which he disappears. The reprise is fun, but like the others, there is little dramatic justification for it.

The reason that many people know *Cats,* and one of the major reasons that audiences filled the theater for eighteen years, is "Memory." In its context, this is one among many songs about individual cats. Granted, it stands out in that it is delivered with more drama than the others, is unaccompanied by dancing, and leads directly to Grizabella's being chosen for rebirth. Still, the main reason the song is so familiar to spectators is that it achieved unprecedented success as a pop song, independent of the show. This is exactly what Nunn intended when he and Lloyd Webber were in the midst of putting the show together. There was no hit song, no great showstopper, no (as they called it in the old days) eleven o'clock number. "Memory," once Lloyd Webber added it, became not only the second-act powerhouse that it is, but a thread that runs throughout the show. As he had done with "Gethsemane" and "Superstar" in *Jesus Christ Superstar* and "Don't Cry for Me, Argentina" in *Evita,* Lloyd Webber previews "Memory" several times before it is sung in full, priming us for a big moment to come.

The first time Grizabella enters, a ground bass figure in the cellos accompanies her; it represents, powerfully, the dark mood which surrounds her.[66] She is a fallen woman. Her costume resembles a tattered mink coat, and reveals a once-elegant but rather too short black sequined dress beneath. She has long curly hair, now mussed into an untidy frazzle, that hints at cat ears. She wears gray sparkling gloves, long fingernails, and uncomfortably high heels that cause her to wobble shakily. As she moves across the stage, the other cats flit about in fear and agitation, unsure whether to flee or attack. Munkustrap stands tall, clearing her a path, keeping both the curious and the hostile at bay. The young cat Sillabub approaches Grizabella, but is pulled away. Alonzo scratches Grizabella's arm. Bombalurina and Cassandra are aloof and condescending. An English horn plays a forlorn tune (based loosely on the shape of the melody of "Memory," but barely recognizable here), and then Grizabella sings this tune to them all, bitterly, about herself in the third person as the ground bass continues (see ex. 3.11).

The ground bass dissolves when Grizabella's anger overcomes her. The music becomes grating and harsh. All this is actually the introduction to the body of the song about her, "Grizabella the Glamour Cat." A more steady tempo asserts itself as Demeter steps forward to relate Grizabella's story. The song is among the best of the show. It is sultry, minor, tinged with a sexy blues feel, but remains poignant and sorrowful as well (see ex. 3.12). It conveys perfectly this once-glamorous cat, fallen since her glory days into a pathetic life that suggests prostitution. Demeter is later joined by Bombalurina, her partner in "Macavity." The

Example 3.11. Opening of "Grizabella the Glamour Cat"

group, staring after Grizabella as she makes her way off the stage, echoes the final lines of the verse. There is a small silence, and then the mood is shattered, somewhat jarringly, by the opening notes of "Bustopher Jones."

Grizabella can be seen hiding in the high shadows during the "Jellicle Ball," watching the others celebrate. When the dance is complete, she enters, accompanied again by her dirge-like cello ground bass and a brief reprise of the introductory lines concerning her torn coat and her twisted eye, sung this time by a somewhat sympathetic Jellylorum and a youthful, almost friendly Sillabub. Grizabella's presence (and Munkustrap's wariness of her and protectiveness of the others) clears the stage and she comes to stand alone except for Old Deuter-

Example 3.12. "Grizabella the Glamour Cat"

onomy who, unbeknownst to her, watches from upstage. As Grizabella attempts to imitate some of the dance moves she saw, the orchestra loosely revisits the opening eight phrases of "Jellicle Songs for Jellicle Cats," here played poignantly mostly by clarinet. Grizabella is too weak, stiff, and ashamed to dance any more; she stands still.

Next the orchestra introduces the first preview of "Memory." She sings a verse, a bridge section, and another verse, dwelling on the silence, the moonlight. "I remember the time I knew what happiness was," she sings. "Let the memory live again." She comes to a calm finish as the orchestra slides into a full statement of the Jellicle theme in two-phrase form, hushed. She moves slowly off the stage, and this ends the first act.

Grizabella is not seen again until the end of the second act, but "Memory" is previewed toward its beginning. Directly after Old Deuteronomy's introductory song, "The Moments of Happiness," the young Sillabub stands and sings one simple verse in a high, sweet D major (as opposed to the song's usual home in B-flat major). The others, mostly sitting or lying about on the floor around her, repeat it softly. They sing of the new life that can begin. The orchestra then takes over, playing the bridge section and another verse, the final downbeat of which becomes the first note of the next song, "Gus the Theatre Cat." There are several reasons why "Memory" is revisited in this way. Sillabub, fresh-faced and innocent, free of prejudices, seemed to like Grizabella when they met in the first act, and here seems to be demonstrating an understanding for the unhappy woman and her needs. She may also represent Grizabella's lost youth, her innocence and joy demonstrating to the audience how broken Grizabella is now. This contrast of age will become clearer during the full statement of the song; here, it seems to serve as a suggestion of what is to come, lest we forget about Grizabella over the course of the second act.

In preparing the full statement of "Memory," Lloyd Webber brings together a number of elements at once. After the jubilant "Mr. Mistoffelees," the orchestra plays the Jellicle theme on the Jellicle bells, in soft cascades of two-phrase form. This moves directly into a verse of "Memory," sung again by Sillabub in D major.[67] "I am waiting for the day," she sings, her face uplifted joyously to the sky. This moves into more cascades of the Jellicle theme, as Munkustrap reminds us one final time why we are here. Speaking in a hush, he intones, "Now Old Deuteronomy, just before dawn / Through a silence you feel you could cut with a knife / Announces the cat that can now be reborn / And come back to a different Jellicle life." The moment is interrupted by Grizabella's ground bass line in the cellos, up a half-step to B-flat minor rather than the original A minor, to accommodate the coming song. Grizabella enters for the final time and comes to stand downstage center. The others simply watch, waiting to see what will happen, not bothering to welcome or snub her. The ground bass line is played twice, then pivots to B-flat major and begins the arpeggios that open "Memory." It is not hard to see why Lloyd Webber thought this a particularly Puccini-like melody; like Puccini, and indeed like his own parody of Puccini, it tends to avoid the seventh degree, it features a somewhat circular, floating melody, and it ebbs and flows in romantic swells (see ex. 3.13).

Grizabella sings two verses, the bridge section, and another verse, then collapses, seemingly drained, onto the floor. The orchestra takes over, playing half a verse in G-flat major, then moving to the bridge. Here, Grizabella begins to sing again, but is soon joined an octave above by Sillabub, perched high on the junkyard piles. Like the crowd's assistance during Evita's "Don't Cry for Me, Argentina," this support seems to give Grizabella strength; as the bridge comes to an end and the orchestra grinds into a powerful key change, she stands. Now in D-flat major, she belts out the last verse.

> Touch me, it's so easy to leave me
> All alone with the memory
> Of my days in the sun.
> If you touch me you'll understand what happiness is.
> Look, a new day has begun.

No matter how many times one may have heard the song, this is an irresistible moment in the show. This sad, pathetic woman fills the house with high D-flats and E-flats, begging for happiness, longing for understanding. For the final line of text, she drops down to a softer tone, seeing with wonder that a new day is coming. Thunderous applause, guaranteed. The orchestra slips back in, and adds its final tag: the Jellicle theme, in soft two-phrase form, on the sweet Jellicle bells, as Victoria slips forward and places her hand, curled like a paw, into Grizabella's. As the cheerful fanfare motif eases the mood from darkness to sunlight, the entire cast surrounds Grizabella, welcoming her, touching her, embracing her. They lead her to Munkustrap, who bows respectfully, then gently turns her over to Old Deuteronomy. She is dazed and shocked throughout, but happiness begins to blossom as well. Old Deuteronomy leads her around the stage and up to the tire, and "The Journey to the Heaviside Layer" begins.

Walsh contends that what sells "Memory" is its chord structure, which he labels a "standard romantic-era harmonic progression" with an English feel. Moving every bar, the chords are I-vi-IV-iii-ii-vi7-V7-I.[68] While it may be common in romantic music, the progression is also not at all far from the standards of rock and pop music. It flows down and up again, predictable but sustained long

Example 3.13. "Memory"

enough to remain interesting. Coupled with a melody that floats rather circularly over it and including some unexpected rhythmic and metrical variations (note, for example, the 10/8 bar in the middle of the verse), it makes for an effective song in and out of context. Theater producer and historian Stuart Ostrow labeled "Memory" Lloyd Webber at his best, with its "soaring melody, complicated rhythmic cadences . . . and a modulation to lift the last chorus to the heavens."[69]

While some critics were aware that the tune had its origins in Lloyd Webber's abandoned Puccini musical, others did not. And most of them charged Lloyd Webber with pastiche or stealing, even if they liked the song. John Simon wrote, "Betty Buckley, as the aging beauty Grizabella, keeps the pathos within bounds and sings 'Memory' (damn it, where was that tune lifted from, anyway?) with commendably understated wistfulness."[70] It was called "soupily derivative" (of nothing specific) by another critic,[71] and reminiscent of Ravel's *Bolero* by a third.[72] All the same, most critics thought it a lovely song, moving in its context, and of course millions of audience members around the world embraced it wholeheartedly.

It has been recorded an estimated six hundred times, in versions ranging from easy listening to techno.[73] It also became the most requested song of the 1980s at piano bars, lounges, and (it has been estimated) weddings, concerts, and gatherings of countless sorts. Setting aside the usual critical disdain for things so wildly popular as "Memory," it is clear that the song works beautifully in its context. It is, in fact, a rather traditional "eleven o'clock number," placed at the show's emotional peak, with its great belted high notes and interesting but memorable melody. Lloyd Webber's previews of the song, moreover, have primed the audience's ears for the full number, and expectations are at last fulfilled. It is Lloyd Webber at his best, delivering melody and well-crafted drama together. But if that is his blatant best, there is even more to be said for his subtle best. The Jellicle themes, the mobile sections of music, the less show-stopping but complex Jellicle-defining numbers are often the more interesting elements, more rewarding upon investigation and multiple viewings.

Reviews in New York

The *New York Times* had a new chief drama critic in 1982, Frank Rich. He brought no particular admiration for Lloyd Webber to his new job, and eventually he would be openly hostile toward the man and his music. Rich had some aesthetic criteria for disliking Lloyd Webber, but it was not just that he did not care for his style; it was also that he liked Stephen Sondheim's far more. In fact, Sondheim became Rich's main cause in the 1980s, and in turn Rich, backed by the *Times,* became Sondheim's most ardent supporter in the media. The praise and attention he lavished on Sondheim's *Sunday in the Park with George* became a major factor in the show's success. It is partly because of Rich's love for Sondheim and distaste for Lloyd Webber that the two composers came to be seen as opposites and competitors. But at the time of *Cats,* Rich was still something of an unknown factor and Lloyd Webber was not yet a target.

Rich's review of *Cats* was mixed, though generally more positive than negative. Still, had Lloyd Webber not been at the point in his career at which critics ceased to matter much, Rich's review could have hurt the show. Rich had already seen the show in London and formed opinions about it that changed little in New York. His main issue matched that of some London critics: it was a show that had "nothing, but nothing on its mind except cats."[74] This stemmed from a perceived near absence of plot, a void filled with poetry and continuous dancing. Rich confuses the situation by misusing the word "bookless," by which he means continuously sung, in the same breath as the idea of plotlessness, by which he means lacking in dramatic action. He defines *Jesus Christ Superstar* and *Evita* as bookless, but then compares them to *Cats* in terms of plotlessness, which makes for messy reading. This running together of a number of ideas (lack of dialogue, the function of a plot structure, the degree of plot complexity) is a common symptom of analysis of megamusicals by critics, although Rich would rarely make such mistakes again.

Rich's review of the New York opening predicted a long run for *Cats,* not so much because it was great theater, but because it was so appealing as escapism.

> It's not that this collection of anthropomorphic variety turns is a brilliant musical or that it powerfully stirs the emotions or that it has an idea in its head. Nor is the probable appeal of "Cats" a function of the publicity that has accompanied the show's every purr since it first stalked London 17 months ago. No, the reason why people will hunger to see "Cats" is far more simple and primal than that: it's a musical that transports the audience into a complete fantasy world that could only exist in the theater and yet, these days, only rarely does. Whatever the other failings and excesses, even banalities, of "Cats," it believes in purely theatrical magic, and on that faith it unquestionably delivers.[75]

The transporting, the theatrical magic, were aided greatly by Napier's set, Rich wrote, along with his costumes and makeup. This was a complete cat world that never stopped engulfing the audience. Nunn and Lynne successfully gave each cat a personality while also uniting them into a "cohesive animal kingdom" of superb singers and dancers. Lloyd Webber's score also came in for high praise, for in this case, unlike in his reviews to come, Rich enjoyed the composer's mix of styles. "The songs are often pastiche," he wrote, "but cleverly and appropriately so, and, as always with this composer, they have been orchestrated to maximum effect." Rich singled out "Gus the Theatre Cat" as an effective melody, and Stephen Hanan's portrayal of Gus as touching. He also praised Betty Buckley as Grizabella, who could "rattle the rafters" with her singing while also being a "poignant figure of down-and-out catwomanhood." Generously taking his time, he singled out a number of less featured players.

Having warned us about failings, banalities, and excesses, Rich went on to list them. As he had reported from London, he found the plot basically absent, and the dancing aspired to fill the void, but failed. He was certain that when the audience cheered Grizabella's ascent, it was not because of the choice of the fallen character, which was obvious, but because of the fancy spaceship. Rich voiced an opinion about Lynne's choreography that almost every other New York critic would share, seeing it as basically dull and conventional. Although the cast slithered delightfully, "such gestures sit on top of a repetitive array of jazz and ballet clichés, rhythmically punctuated by somersaults and leaps." The result was a number of dragging moments which more varied and creative choreography could have saved; among these were sections of the very long "Jellicle Ball" and the number for the Pekes and Pollicles, which "could be an Ice Capades reject." Rich singled out only Terrence V. Mann's Rum Tum Tugger as a less than successful performance, arguing that his Mick Jagger impersonation did not work, yet Mann received high praise from virtually every other critic and would go on to a successful Broadway career. Rich's "excesses" included lighting that often flashed and twinkled, which sometimes broke the spell of the magical cat world.

Rich closed his review of *Cats* as he opened it, with high praise for its theatrical magic. Later, he and other critics would regularly lament the emphasis that megamusicals placed on spectacle, but here, in the megamusical's early days, the spectacle was "wondrous" and made the theater "an enchanting place to be."[76]

Walter Kerr, Rich's *Times* colleague, came close to panning the show in the Sunday edition of the paper. His main problem lay in what he saw as a massive miscalculation of proportions. The lights, the spectacle, the sets were all perfectly enjoyable, until they became too much to take, becoming "so much bigness, so much busyness, such a massive sweeping of sounds and bodies from the back stage wall to the lobby doors" that he was exhausted.[77] His fatigue resulted not only from the saturation of the senses, but from the mental struggle to link the spectacle to the texts. "The connection is just not there," he wrote. "[T]here is a staggering disproportion here—between the ballooning-out of the effects onstage and the simple lines that have supposedly begat them." Kerr probably would have been much more enthusiastic about Nunn's original vision as a chamber piece with two pianos. No great fan of the Eliot poems to begin with, Kerr argued that the show chose to "inflate them beyond all reason" until any meaning was lost.

He found a few moments quite enjoyable, especially the parody of nineteenth-century Orientalist opera which is at the center of "Growltiger's Last Stand." He also enjoyed Lloyd Webber's score, delighted when he heard it "cheerfully helping itself" to styles including Puccini, burlesque, marches, light rock, and hymns. He lamented that the show was not content to stay lighthearted, but rather its creators felt the need to add depth. Old Deuteronomy's role as holy beloved leader, for example, is demonstrated almost entirely by the music, Kerr pointed out; Lloyd Webber and Nunn worked too hard to add meaning that should not have been added. Lynne, for her part, did not work hard enough, and the choreography was ultimately just repetitive: "The first cat to arch its back or stretch its belly along the floor is charming; the 65th needs a brand new repertoire."[78]

Returning again to the notion that this was too much spectacle covering up too little substance, Kerr saw *Cats* as a sign of a recent trend: "[M]ore and more, and perhaps most obviously in 'Cats,' we are making our theatrical mountains out of less and less solid rock." Kerr, it should be remembered, had been chief theater critic for the *Times* and was now representative of an older school of criticism which resisted the megamusical. This does not necessarily make his argument less valid, at least in this case, for *Cats* is indeed more concerned with spectacle than with plot. Kerr's argument against spectacle in general, however, and his resistance to extravagant visual stimuli would come to bear on his reviews of all megamusicals and was an opinion shared by a number of more conservative critics.

Interestingly, the voice at the opposite end of the theatrical-political spectrum also panned *Cats;* Michael Feingold, for the *Village Voice,* unleashed some of his nastiest language on the show. "*Cats* is a dog," the headline summarized, and it got worse: "To sit through it is to realize that something has just peed on your pants leg. For two hours."[79] Feingold tidily listed each disastrous element and how it contributed to a show clearly doomed to failure, and yet, for some reason he could not fathom, others declared a success. The poetry itself, Feingold began, struggled painfully and unsuccessfully to be innocent and nonsensical. The calculated cuteness, like naming two cats Mungojerrie and Rumpelteazer, made Eliot "guilty as hell."

Lloyd Webber's score constituted Feingold's "disaster element number two." He argued that Lloyd Webber suited the 1980s, apparently a decade with no redeeming features: "His music is such inane, characterless drivel that only a generation of stoned clones and TV drones could have summoned it up. I use the word 'composer' only as a courtesy; in fact, the one thing Webber's music doesn't sound is composed. It doodles randomly from chord to chord, never developing a theme or shaping a structure." This is a remarkably odd criticism: Lloyd Webber's music is filled with catchy, obvious melodies and themes, and critics almost always point out that his music is anything but random. Structure, chord progressions, and themes are more than evident. Feingold did not further explain his problems with the music, but moved on to his third horror, Lynne's choreography, which looked borrowed and represented all too well her "utterly undistinguished career." Nunn, next on Feingold's list of the damned, was accused of substituting cute gestures and special effects for real characterization. Unlike other critics, but in keeping with Feingold's ever-present resistance to the megamusical, he was unimpressed by the set, and found the atmosphere lacking in style or character. He suggested, "It ought to be retitled *101 Uses for a Dead Musical*," a reference to the popular book *101 Uses for a Dead Cat*.[80]

The bulk of the opening night reviews fell into the mixed category. A mixed review can result from a critic's lukewarm attitude toward a show overall, or it can result from a critic's particular enjoyment of certain elements of a show and strong distaste for other elements. In the case of *Cats*, the latter sort of mixed review was the norm. Clive Barnes, late of the *Times* but now at the *New York Post*, advised his readers to see the show, which automatically colored his review in a positive light overall. He found the added plot "portentously philosophical" but thought it did a fine job of binding the show together. Lloyd Webber's score was "breathtakingly unoriginal yet superbly professional." He admired the singable tunes, the lovely orchestration, and the "ghosts" of other composers who influenced Lloyd Webber (although he thought the Puccini parody a mistaken addition).

What made the show a must-see, for Barnes, was the "mad authority of its staging." It was a slick, unbroken blend of movement and atmosphere and image, creating one thorough mood: "These are cat people in a cat world, and despite all the tumultuous theatrical shocks and show-offs, most of them are piercingly enjoyable. It is the simplicity that gives Nunn's work its ultimate gleam." "Simplicity" was hardly a word others used to describe flashing lights and a rising spaceship tire, but Barnes was correct in that *Cats* created an all-encompassing, inescapable world that surrounded the audience from start to finish. His point is similar to Rich's notion of theatrical magic and transportation. *Cats,* argued Barnes, was greater than the sum of its parts. It was not quite genius, it was not a great show in itself, but it contained miracles.[81]

John Simon of *New York* magazine agreed that the powerful atmosphere was the center of *Cats,* although he focused more on the special effects than the overall mood. This was "kitty-litterature at its grandest," and it reminded him of Disneyland. He tried hard to resent the "overblown" spectacle based on a thin plot, but in the end he succumbed: "You cannot help experiencing surges of childish jubilance, as cleverness after sleek cleverness rubs against your shins." He praised many cast members, the song "Old Deuteronomy," the lighting, the sets, the direction, yet refused to admit that the whole amounted to anything important. It all merged "into a delightful albeit trivial *Gesamt*almost-*kunstwerk.*"[82]

For a few enthusiastic critics, the spectacle and everything else *Cats* had to offer was entirely satisfying. Brendan Gill, writing for the usually less effusive *New Yorker,* penned an all-out rave. The "triumph" of the spectacle was supported by a strong cast and "brilliant" contributions by Nunn, Lynne, and Napier. He was convinced by the "pathos" of the show, as embodied by Grizabella and Gus the Theatre Cat, and felt certain Eliot "would have rejoiced to see his cats in glory on Broadway."[83]

Jack Kroll (with Constance Guthrie) wrote a feature for *Newsweek* which contained a somewhat calmer but almost equally committed rave review. In a savvy prediction into the future of its marketing, Kroll labeled *Cats* a show suitable for the whole family. Adults could see the subtexts not made explicit in the words, but which were present onstage, like Old Deuteronomy's role as a deity-like figure. These elements gave the show "guts as well as flair" and helped to reveal the darker meanings within Eliot's seemingly light poems. Credit for this bold addition of a "thirst for transcendence" went to Nunn, who understood, according to Kroll, that "it's in everything that Eliot wrote." Kroll admired "Memory" as a wonderful theater song.[84]

Later History: Eighteen Years of "Forever"

The opening night audience, by all accounts, loved the show. Tickets continued to sell well in advance, and began to flag significantly only after seventeen years. For the 1982 season, *Cats* won the Tony Awards for best musical, book (the award went to T. S. Eliot, in spirit, though it was Nunn's creation with Lloyd Webber), score (Lloyd Webber and Eliot), direction (Nunn), costumes (Napier, who was also nominated in the scenic design category), lighting (David Hersey), and featured actress (Betty Buckley).[85] Despite an enormous initial production cost of over four million dollars, the show easily recouped this investment in only forty-one weeks. Within the decade, the show would return about six times the amount each backer had invested.[86] Producer David Geffen, encouraged by sales of the imported London cast album in the United States, produced the American version of the cast album and was rewarded with excellent returns.[87] Lloyd Webber had clearly triumphed beyond all expectations in the United States despite mixed reviews. "Nothing, and no one, could stop him now," Walsh summarizes dramatically. "Maybe he *was* critic-proof."[88] Clearly Lloyd Webber did not need Tim Rice, or Robert Stigwood, or rave reviews.

Over the years, the *New York Times* ran articles about long-running shows and the issues which arose regarding them, especially *Cats*. The show became an institution, and reporters developed a cottage industry of *Cats*-related journalism, checking in on the show and finding new angles to investigate. In 1983, injuries to dancers were the focus; in 1985, the subject was various ways that the show was kept fresh. For example, *Cats* had two production supervisors (most shows had one, if any) continually monitoring the quality of the shows both on Broadway and on tour, which so far had meant Los Angeles, Chicago, and Toronto.[89] The *Times* interviewed Terrence Mann, still playing the Rum Tum Tugger after three years, and Laurie Beechman, formerly the Narrator in *Joseph* on Broadway, now in the role of Grizabella. A later article spotlighted Liz Callaway, a Grizabella of the mid-1990s.[90]

Other follow-up articles often disclosed that the same issues which swirled around *Cats* upon opening remained with it. "It's accepted as spectacle," wrote one reporter, marveling at what he saw as the audience's passive joy.[91] A 1997 article that revisited long-running shows to see how they held up reported that although it was in good shape after fifteen years, " '*Cats*' is still stuck being '*Cats*.' "[92] It suffered from a bit of fatigue ("You're paying $70, you want your cats perky") but featured some superb performances.

In 1984, a music video of "The Rum Tum Tugger" was released; it was the first rock video from a musical. The rock element was hardened by a five-piece band rather than the usual orchestra.[93] The *Times* enjoyed reporting *Cats*-related trivia and statistics from time to time, including the amount of yak hair in performers' wigs, the pounds of dry ice used, the number of condoms needed in the show (they protect body mikes), and the amount earned by Eliot's estate. An avid fan ran *The Cats Meow*, a *Cats* newsletter.[94]

Cats broke a whole series of records. In 1989, it became the longest-running musical in British history, breaking the record held by *Jesus Christ Superstar.* A celebration was thrown in 1991 in honor of the ninth anniversary of the opening of *Cats* on Broadway, to mark its "nine lives." In those nine years, a host of new musicals had opened, many of them modeled in at least some ways on the *Cats* formula. Its influence was clear. Lloyd Webber had gone on to several new shows, and other composers had entered the megamusical arena. With this perspective, the *Times* looked back and called *Cats* "the first of the British megamusicals." By this time, *Cats* was the third-longest running show on Broadway, but would soon pass *Oh! Calcutta!* and looked primed to pass *A Chorus Line* as well. There had been, over the years, twenty-one productions around the world, many of which continued to run. Thirty-nine million people had seen it, and the show had grossed a billion dollars.[95]

On 7 October 1992, the tenth anniversary, the *Times* again called *Cats* "the first of the British megamusicals." Almost six million people had seen it in New York alone.[96] In October 1996, the *Times* traced the history of the entire original company as pictured on a poster that had become, over the years, ubiquitous on trains and in theater district windows.[97]

The press had an opportunity to report one of the more bizarre stories associated with a musical in February 1997, when a woman sued the Rum Tum Tugger. One Evelyn Amato, who had been in the audience the previous year, had been targeted by the Rum Tum Tugger for his mid-song dance with an audience member. As was the Rum Tum Tugger's custom, actor David Hibbard had bounded into the audience during the orchestral interlude in his number and cajoled Ms. Amato to dance with him. She claimed that when she would not, he did some bumping and grinding in close proximity to her face and pulled her hair. She filed a lawsuit claiming assault, battery, invasion of privacy, violation of civil rights, negligence, and intentional infliction of emotional distress. She sued Hibbard, the Shubert Organization, Trevor Nunn, Cameron Mackintosh, and Andrew Lloyd Webber. The *New York Times,* not bothering to hide its amusement, added that the suit "does not name T. S. Eliot, whose poems supplied the show with its lyrics." She asked for six million dollars. She lost.[98]

On 19 June 1997, *Cats* broke the record as the longest-running musical in Broadway history, with 6,138 performances. Peter Marks, a theater writer for the *Times,* noted that seeing the show now was like going back in time to 1982, like seeing an artifact. No staging, he believed, could look fresh after more than about five years, not only because of the look of a show, but as a result of cultural changes.[99] Nevertheless, the occasion called for a celebration by all concerned. On its front page, the *Times* declared that *Cats* had now been seen by over eight million people in New York, and fifty million around the world. It had grossed $2.2 billion, and "almost single-handedly revived the sagging road business" with its touring companies and regional productions. *Cats* had channeled over three billion dollars into New York City's economy, thanks to tourism.[100] Mayor Rudolph Giuliani proclaimed 19 June *Cats* Day. In attendance at performance number 6,138 were Lloyd Webber, Mackintosh, Nunn, Lynne, and former cast members. Amazingly, one cast member, Marlene Daniele, was still in her role as Bombalurina, a role she had taken on mere months after the show opened, having been bumped up from an understudy position; she would remain in the role for the rest of the show's run. Laurie Beechman, who had played Grizabella for a record of almost five years, returned for several months and sang the role at the special performance.[101]

On 2 November 1998, PBS televised a new staging of *Cats* and subsequently released it on home video. Lloyd Webber weighed in on all aspects of the production, including some new orchestrations. The show was newly directed (by David Mallet) for television, with many close-ups and fast camera cuts and few long shots. As a result, it has a different feel than a filmed live performance. This has advantages and disadvantages; the close shots of the performers' faces make it easier to tell them apart, see their personalities through the make-up, and keep up with their interactions. The pre-recorded and nicely mixed soundtrack also makes the words and stories perfectly clear, something that audiences sometimes find difficult to achieve at a live performance. However, the camera work is rather frantic, and rarely do we get a sense of the choreography, since the editing makes us feel as if we are running around onstage with the cast rather than watching them. This is in keeping with the interactive spirit of the live staging, but it makes for some confusing moments. The cast, assembled from various recent companies and new additions, is excellent. Featured were the original London Grizabella, Elaine Paige, the popular Old Deuteronomy of Ken Page, and British actor John Mills as Gus the Theatre Cat. Regrettably, there are some significant cuts, especially the complete excising of "Growltiger's Last Stand"; Gus no longer relives his youth in flashback.[102]

On 20 February 2000, the *New York Times* announced on its front page that *Cats* would be closing in June. Rumors to that effect had been circulating for months; ticket sales were finally beginning to fall off significantly, and the road production had just closed. Apparently its time had finally come, after $380 million in ticket sales and ten million Broadway viewers. But thousands more suddenly clamored to see it. Just after the announcement, ticket sales surged; lines at the box office—which meant tickets were being bought by locals, not tourists—ran down the block. A million dollars in tickets were sold in just five days. The closing date was pushed back to 10 September, and this date would stick.[103] That day marked performance number 7,485 and passed with relatively little fanfare.

The Impact of *Cats*: "These Modern Productions Are All Very Well . . ."

While most critics gave *Cats* a mixed review, almost all of them credited the show with being innovative and unusual at least in some aspects. There had never been a musical on quite so grand a scale in terms of the visual, and when this atmosphere was then filled with an engaging, nonstop score performed by an excellent cast, factors upon which most critics agreed, it became obvious to even the grumpiest of critics that *Cats* would be influential. The question became whether that influence was a positive one. Members of an older school of thought, perhaps best represented by Walter Kerr, resisted the newness of fancy spectacle on principle and longed for the less flashy musicals of ages past. Another school, including Michael Feingold of the *Village Voice*, speciously argued that spectacle automatically meant lack of emotional or intellectual depth. Most critics contended that although *Cats* indeed focused on exciting spectacle instead of complex character development or personal drama, that did not necessarily make it a bad show. Indeed, *Cats* entertained, most agreed, and there was nothing necessarily wrong with that. Trevor Nunn argued that this magical air, not plot or drama or character, was in fact the goal of *Cats,* and that the spectacle was an integral part of pulling it off: "*Cats* sets out to transport its audience to a world in which plot and conventional character development are rendered unnecessary by the experience of a fantasy without human circumscriptions. All fine and dandy until the hydraulic ramp gets stuck or a colour changer develops a death rattle, or the speakers go into feedback or a million and one other devices don't deliver."[104]

Not surprisingly, *Cats* was a show whose formula could not be imitated with ease, and only some of its elements went on to become staples of the megamusical. The later shows satisfied critics even more than *Cats* had, for they would find ways to combine stunning spectacle with real people. Megamusicals would remain sung-through and would feature impressive sets and effects, but the plots would become more engaging, and the characters real humans.

Nonetheless, many critics were unable or unwilling to ride with this transition and were stopped in their tracks by *Cats,* refusing to see how its influence would flow into the next generation of musicals. Denny Martin Flinn, an opinionated theater historian with a particular hostility toward megamusicals, noted that "*Cats* marked the beginning of the megamusical, wherein spectacle not only superseded but *replaced* drama."[105] It is almost impossible to argue with this fairly common view; Flinn did not see drama in *Cats,* even though other critics and millions of audience members did. Flinn claimed that many older audience members disliked *Cats,* implying that it was due to the show's low quality. There is no evidence that older theatergoers resisted *Cats;* in fact, anecdotal evidence suggests strongly that it was quite popular with people of all ages. Flinn, then, comes to represent the sort of critic and historian who resists *Cats* and other megamusicals largely because they differ from what preceded them. When *Cats* became the longest-running Broadway musical, William Grimes of the *New York Times* summarized the view of the resisters: "There are more than a few who see the 'Cats' phenomenon as the theatrical equivalent of the rise of the megabudget Hollywood action film. For them, 'Cats' is a soulless money machine." He argued, rightly, that *Cats* would never have been successful had it not been innovative in its time.[106] "I can find no rational explanation for *Cats,*" historian Mark Steyn writes in the flippant tone of many critics, but then goes on to put forth a perfectly reasonable explanation, with which many critics agreed: *Cats* is not a normal show. It is an experience, difficult to define and thoroughly entertaining.[107]

Michael Walsh argues that this resistance was due to a Broadway that was conservative, nostalgic, and rigid:

> Although it was nice to revel in glorious reminiscence of the great days of Rodgers and Hammerstein, those days were gone for good, and there was no use trying to recapture them. For some reason, composers and critics in America could not get this simple principle into their heads, as the annual yammering about the Decline of Broadway proved. America was supposed to be a young country, brimming with fresh ideas, but on Broadway everybody was either old (the ninety-two-year-old George Abbot, for example, was still active) or acted old. Here it was, 1980, and no other Broadway composer [besides Lloyd Webber] had yet admitted that Elvis or the Beatles existed.[108]

For Cameron Mackintosh, this void clearly needed filling. This backward, stodgy Broadway scene could be revolutionized by the influx of some fresh voices with some modern ideas. Lloyd Webber had begun the process already with his first three musicals, but it was clear that *Cats* was the one that would force Broadway to admit there would be no going back. Lloyd Webber and eventually others like him would write innovative musicals that featured new structures, modern popular sounds, and creative visual elements. Mackintosh would then market these musicals as never before, packaging them like any other product and exporting them around the world. This meant that not only were the older styles of musicals left behind, but so too were the older ways of doing business.

> Just as Andrew and Tim [Rice] had put the ghosts of Rodgers and Hammerstein behind them by forgetting all about the Broadway model and forging ahead with *Superstar* and *Evita* on their own terms, so Lloyd Webber and Mackintosh had stumbled onto a new formula for musical theater success. The trouble with Broadway—the trouble with the Shuberts and the Nederlanders and the others—was that they were too shortsighted. Their world was delimited by New Haven, Philadelphia, Washington, and "the Coast." London was a transatlantic rival, France was a place you went on vacation, and as for Germany, forget about it. Mackintosh, however, saw all those places as potential markets, and Japan, too.[109]

Mackintosh felt that to make musicals fresh, and to keep them in business, the whole world had to become their audience. For better or worse, in the 1980s, people expected big entertainment—big sets, big songs, big stories. This meant spending big money, which in turn meant having to earn big money back. Megamusicals could do that. Not only were they clearly successful with New York audiences, they were also hits in London and all around the world. This is largely due to the fact that with constant music, and in the case of *Cats* a simple plot, audiences could understand enough to enjoy the show thoroughly.[110] In this sense the megamusical is like opera, which for hundreds of years did excellent business all over Europe and America, sometimes translated into the local language, sometimes not. As Walsh points out, opera, "the original bookless [he means dialogue-less] musical," does fine in Japan. What Lloyd Webber and Mackintosh had created, then, was an "all-purpose, exportable, international entertainment marked by brilliant scenic design and told entirely through music."[111] The megamusical had arrived and it was here to stay. As Clive Barnes wrote of *Cats,* "Its importance lies in its wholeheartedness. It is a statement of musical theater that cannot be ignored, should prove controversial and will never be forgotten."[112]

Lloyd Webber, treading as he rarely has into the fray of the debate over the "mega" aspect of musicals, argued in support of *Cats* as a unique experience: "If you look at it as an *experience* (which incidentally is how theatre is going to be increasingly looked at in my opinion, because seats are so expensive) then surely it is *hugely* for the medium? It's no good putting on something nowadays which people can see just as well on their video. That's why *Cats* is so popular. They can't get to see anything like it, not at all. It doesn't exist."[113]

4

"To Love Another Person Is to See the Face of God"

Les Misérables

> Once in every five years or so, given average theatergoing luck, a musical soars out, providing a feast for the eyes as well as the ears, and this show is one such: a great blazing pageant of life and death at the barricade of political and social revolution in Victor Hugo's nineteenth-century France.
>
> *Sheridan Morley,* Spread a Little Happiness: The First Hundred Years of the British Musical

Les Misérables was one of the first megamusicals created by a team that did not include Andrew Lloyd Webber. In fact, *Les Mis*,[1] as it came to be known, would go on to become not only the most successful megamusical of the decade, but the most successful musical of all time. Although the team behind *Les Mis* included Cameron Mackintosh, it is nevertheless remarkable that a relatively unknown composer and lyricist, aspiring to Lloyd Webber's model of the megamusical, surpassed him in international success with this "great blazing pageant of life and death."

Les Mis sprang from a virtually musical-free zone. The lyricist and composer were distant from the Broadway scene of the 1980s, and from British and American musical theater in general. In France, the home-grown musical had never really taken root; no French creators had mounted a successful Broadway-style musical either within France or as an exported show. Musicals simply did not register on the French cultural radar, although American and British musicals did occasionally visit.

Like the proto-megamusical, *Jesus Christ Superstar, Les Mis* was the brain-

175

child of its lyricist and bookwriter, in this case Alain Boublil. A fan of American musicals, Boublil had seen *West Side Story* in Paris in 1959 and had thought theater music might be in his future. In a life decision similar to Tim Rice's, Boublil studied more practical fields (business and banking) but began writing lyrics on the side. He got a job at a radio station and soon became a record producer. Boublil would alter his career path when he saw the original Broadway production of *Jesus Christ Superstar* in New York. That night, the megamusical gained an important adherent:

> The Lloyd Webber-Rice musical represented an art form Boublil had instinctively been drawn to, without ever believing it could be realised in a world increasingly dominated by pop and disco music: an all-sung musical with an historical theme, mixing the tradition of Italian opera with contemporary musical and literary styles. After the performance, he walked the Manhattan streets in a daze, unable to sleep. As Boublil recalls, he felt an overwhelming compulsion to keep walking until he'd thought of a suitable theme for a rock opera that might compare in scope and emotional intensity with the subject matter of *Jesus Christ Superstar*. Inspiration came at dawn: why not deal with the single most important event in French history—the French Revolution?[2]

The result was *La Revolution Française,* the first megamusical by Boublil and composer Claude-Michel Schönberg. They had met years earlier through Boublil's wife when Schönberg was also working as a record producer; subsequently Boublil started a publishing company and wrote songs.[3] Schönberg, like Lloyd Webber, had been something of a prodigy and studied music throughout his childhood. He composed works by age six and had extensive knowledge of the classical and operatic repertoire, but he did not focus on a career as a composer for a number of years.[4] It was Boublil, inspired by *Superstar,* who took his idea to Schönberg and another composer, Raymond Jeannot, and also a co-writer, Jean-Max Rivière. They followed the megamusical model closely, creating a sung-through score dealing with, as one might imagine, an epic plot strong on drama and emotion. In another *Superstar* move, they released an album before the show opened, and it was a hit. The show ran for a successful season in 1973 at the Palais des Sports, which by Broadway standards was not nearly long enough to count *La Revolution Française* as a megamusical hit, but for France it was quite respectable. Schönberg himself made an entertaining Louis XVI.

Encouraged by this first attempt and clearly thinking in the megamusical vein now, Boublil had another revelation while seeing a revival of *Oliver!,* which happened to be produced by the young Cameron Mackintosh. Boublil's focus rested not on the production in general but on the character of the Artful Dodger, who reminded him of Gavroche from Hugo's novel *Les Misérables.* An entire musical based on Hugo's epic quickly took shape in his mind, and his enthusiasm and ideas persuaded Schönberg to retire from producing records and join Boublil full-time.[5]

As with Boublil's first topic, using *Les Misérables* as the basis for a musical was a specifically French choice. As he later told the *New York Times* when the show headed for Broadway, he never imagined that it would achieve international success. Although its universal themes eventually became clear, he chose it for its specifically French nature: "In order to be able to have musical theater performed in France, a country where the genre does not exist, you have to touch something that is deep in the heart of the people."[6]

From Hugo to *Les Mis*

Victor Hugo's *Les Misérables* tells many stories, but centers on the tale of good-hearted parole jumper Jean Valjean and his tireless, honor-bound policeman pursuer, Javert. The climactic action of the novel takes place in 1832, during the uprising of students and workers which resulted in students building barricades— and getting slaughtered—in the streets of Paris. All the characters converge here, and a historical context frames the fictional story. Bits of the characters' lives also stemmed from events Hugo witnessed: he saw a man arrested for stealing bread, which is Valjean's original crime, and he drew on information gathered from many prison visits and walking journeys through Paris's poor streets. Hugo himself once defended a prostitute who fought against the attacks of a wealthy and abusive would-be customer, as does Valjean in defense of the fallen Fantine. Young student Marius, who is among those who take to the barricades in a bid for social freedom, is thought by many critics to represent a young Hugo.

In 1832, Hugo was a young playwright who followed the uprisings with interest. He began his epic novel in 1845, but dropped it for many years and did not finish until 1861, thanks in part to distractions from an ever-changing French government. Hugo alternately served those in charge and fled the country, depending on the circumstances. During these years he became a liberal reformer, and by the time he resumed his work on *Les Misérables,* his work clearly embodied his leftist politics.

Interestingly, the publication of the novel demonstrated a distinctly "mega" spirit. As Edward Behr describes it, Hugo launched the book with Mackintosh-like production values, and it received a distinctly Lloyd Webber-like critical and popular reception. "Victor Hugo launched *Les Misérables* in Brussels in 1862 with the practiced skill of the born media star. It became an instant literary phenomenon, making Hugo enormously rich once more. It was, however, a popular rather than critical success: most French literary critics attacked it for its excessive sentimentality."[7] Indeed, the popular impact of the novel was so great that the riots of 1832, considered minor events until then, became part of the national psyche, and people's knowledge of that time in history merged with their affinity for the characters in the novel. The first edition of 7,000 copies sold out the day it went on sale, and the novel has remained successful ever since.[8]

The story's themes—freedom and justice for the poor, crimes committed by good people for good causes, young love, relentless pursuit in the name of heavenly justice—made the novel an obvious choice for dramatic adaptation. The first staged version was mounted in 1863 by Hugo's son, and the first of many dozens of films was a silent, in 1906. The first version with sound, in French, was released in 1933, and others in America, Russia, Mexico, Italy, Japan, and India followed. *Les Misérables* clearly told a story with global resonances. Perhaps the most famous film version came in 1958, from France, and there have been many since, as well as television versions (even the long-running series *The Fugitive* was loosely based on the Valjean/Javert chase).[9]

Like all these adaptations, the musical crafted by Boublil and company focuses more on the events of the novel than the lengthy philosophical and historical musings Hugo provides. Boublil and his team excised Hugo's essays on religion, Napoleon and Waterloo, politics, and slang language, as these do not concern the characters at all, although the philosophies behind them find their way into the action at times. Also missing are the extensive family histories of the characters which Hugo often traces back many generations. The musical's creators also chose to leave out some of the less credible coincidental character interactions; players in the novel meet numerous times without ever being aware of it, which all agreed would have been far too confusing for audiences to follow onstage. They knew it was risky to alter such a well-known classic, but eventually they shaped a retelling of the story that looked plausible for musicalization; their book of the original novel seemed to work.

Like Lloyd Webber and Rice, Schönberg and Boublil (now working as a duo, without their initial collaborators) worked in a music-first manner, though less strictly and with more back-and-forth interaction between them. Schönberg worked long hours tirelessly and recorded anything he thought might be decent for Boublil to fit with lyrics. They critiqued each other's work throughout, making multiple drafts, cuts, and revisions. After two years, the duo emerged with a two-hour demo tape, featuring Schönberg at the piano and singing every role.[10]

The demo impressed record executives enough to record a full version, orchestrated by John Cameron and released in 1980. In a savvy Mackintosh-like move, the team made a crucial marketing decision. The record jacket featured the image that would come to represent *Les Mis* around the world—a lithograph done by the nineteenth-century illustrator Emile Bayard of the child Cosette, pouty and waif-like; Bayard had been a favorite of Hugo's who created representations of all the main characters. The album sold an impressive 260,000 copies, which helped in finding support for a full staging. *Les Misérables* opened at the Palais des Sports in September 1980, under the direction of Robert Hossein, and was seen by a respectable 500,000 people. A few producers from outside France made hesitant queries about producing the show elsewhere, but nothing came of these.[11]

It was when Mackintosh heard the French concept album in November 1982 that things began to move quickly. He was not the first important producer to admire the work; James Nederlander had already paid Schönberg and Boublil a small deposit toward an investment in a possible American version. The Nederlander family, along with their rivals the Shubert Organization, controlled virtually all of Broadway producing and theater ownership between them. But the Nederlanders' initial investment, intended to retain Schönberg and Boublil for a year, came to nothing. Mackintosh, however, having already led the creative team of *Cats* to remarkable megamusical success, arrived with both momentum and a proven formula. Knowing that the Nederlander family had formerly shown interest in the project, Mackintosh agreed to produce a staging in London himself, then share production credit and duties in New York.[12] Eventually Mackintosh secured financial backing for the London staging from the Royal Shakespeare Company, though he retained sole credit as producer.[13]

The RSC would become greatly involved in *Les Mis* in another capacity. In early 1983 Mackintosh chose for director his fellow megamusical veteran Trevor Nunn, a director for the RSC who had been borrowed for *Cats;* the same arrangement applied here, except that Nunn retained his affiliation with the RSC while working on *Les Mis* and brought with him a number of team members from that organization. *Les Mis* in London became, therefore, a production of the Royal Shakespeare Company, staged at their London theater, the Barbican. If things went well, the production could be moved to a West End theater. Nunn brought on board his usual RSC co-director, John Caird, for *Les Mis;* Nunn and Caird had developed a successful system of team-directing, and Nunn felt it both more beneficial and fair to continue the partnership despite the unusual task of directing a musical for the RSC. John Caird actually had musical experience; he had directed Lloyd Webber's *Song and Dance* in 1982, which Mackintosh had produced.

As *Les Mis* grew successful in London, a good deal of commentary swirled around Nunn's dual affiliation with commercial theatrical undertakings and the "legitimate" government-subsidized world of the RSC. The idea of legitimate theater implied not only governmental endorsement, but a certain weightiness not associated with popular new musicals. Nunn himself always made it clear that he saw no real division between commercial theater and whatever was meant by the term legitimate theater, and he found it perpetually annoying that there remained a "prejudice that says that if a show makes money it can't be any good."[14] This largely media-generated distinction is a limitation that virtually all the creative players behind megamusicals have experienced, but Nunn, unlike many others, has participated equally in both types of theater. Nunn and Caird had already crossed over, if accidentally, with their production of *Nicholas Nickelby* for the RSC in 1980, which was "legitimate" subsidized theater that had become an unexpected commercial success. Nunn moved from this to *Cats* and other diverse projects while still directing for the RSC and also for opera companies, Broadway, and film.

Mackintosh and the RSC team of Nunn and Caird amicably divided the directing and producing duties. Mackintosh retained final word on the hiring of RSC musicians, and both Mackintosh and Nunn had veto power over casting decisions. Mackintosh made it clear that the RSC should dispense with its general attitude toward musicals, which was to treat them in a lighthearted and unprofessional manner, inappropriate for *Les Mis:* "We didn't want the traditional, slightly amateurish British aspect of musical theatre where brilliant classical actors let their hair down."[15] This was no end-of-season revue for fun, but a serious play that happened to be sung.

Mackintosh brought in Schönberg and Boublil, impressing and pleasing them by asking them to be involved deeply in the process of expanding, translating, and staging *Les Mis;* they had expected him simply to buy the rights from them. They also marveled at the facilities the Barbican had to offer, compared to the plain staging arena they had used in Paris; they began envisioning scenes that took place in the sewers, for starters. It became clear that both the story currently told by the musical and its lyrics would require major reworking. The French version assumed the audience knew the story, and a great deal of action happened offstage; Nunn described it as scenes or impressions from the novel, rather than a full telling of it. The team returned to the novel, pulling from it all the pertinent action, emotions, and plot points, and removing the specifically French colloquialisms and references that did not translate well.

Mackintosh hired James Fenton, a poet, drama critic, and opera translator, to write English lyrics that would both reflect Hugo's literary style and convey an enormous amount of information and emotion. Things seemed promising at first; Fenton added a prologue to the musical which featured Jean Valjean being freed from prison and encountering the bishop who altered the course of his life, and he added the scene that would become Marius's song "Empty Chairs at Empty Tables." (For a full plot summary of Les Mis, see appendix F.) Meanwhile, Nunn and Caird worked on making fuller characters out of what felt like flat melodrama types, and they cut some of Schönberg's long symphonic interludes in the interest of drama and clarity. They also added a theme that they felt needed strengthening from the French version: the role of religion in the main characters' lives. Jean Valjean believes in a redeeming God, Javert believes in a vengeful one, and Thénardier declares that God is dead, a trio of ideals that drives each of them. Eventually, the creative team added three songs, "Bring Him Home," "Stars," and "Dog Eat Dog," each a religious statement by one of the three.[16]

Around this time, the contributions of Fenton, promising at first, began to frustrate and disappoint the rest of the creative team. He wrote with unbearable slowness, and his results thus far were far more intellectual, poetic, and unsingable than Mackintosh and Nunn had envisioned. The original opening date of October 1984 had to be postponed for a year due to the unsatisfactory lyrics. All agreed it was time to replace Fenton, who stepped down with civility but with a demand for a small cut of all future grosses of the show, as payment for his dedicated, if unsuccessful, efforts. Theater historian Michael Coveney calls Fenton the "richest unsung lyricist" of all time as a result of this deal.[17] The team replaced Fenton with veteran Herbert Kretzmer, who boasted strong credentials for the job: besides being a songwriter and lyricist, as well as a former drama critic for the Daily Express, Kretzmer had successfully adapted into English a number of songs for French singer Charles Aznavour. By early 1985, Kretzmer began working madly on what he described as three separate tasks: loose translating of Boublil's lyrics, free adaptation of ideas and events in the novel, and new lyrics for recently composed or relocated music. He also struggled to match English words to what he called Schönberg's "decidedly Gallic" score, which seemed more suited to French.[18] But by July 1985, when casting began, Les Mis had a detailed book and most of a score with completed music and lyrics. As had been the case with Cats, Nunn became involved in the book, again overstepping the traditional boundaries of a director in order to shape the story.

Besides the three solo songs added for Valjean, Javert, and Thénardier, the score eventually gained a song for the chorus women in the second act, "Turning." This gave the women, featured in "Lovely Ladies" and other first-act numbers, more of a presence late in the show. Also, Eponine's strongest manifestation of her personality and beliefs, "On My Own," grew out of several other places.

Schönberg had used the melody in a song for Fantine in the French version, called "La misère," but he replaced that song with a new anthem for Fantine, "I Dreamed a Dream." The creators relocated the melody to Fantine's death scene with Valjean, and also rooted Eponine's "On My Own" in this melody. Kretzmer points out that the "melody is one of the seminal pieces of music in the entire show," which is to say it generates other material and carries importance when it appears.[19] Other material also began to take on symbolic or philosophical weight. Now that Javert's "Stars" was in place, Nunn came to see its importance: " 'Stars' for me was a fundamental element of the whole show: without it Javert is a cipher, a shadowy figure, and without it there is no tragic dimension to his suicide. The song makes the audience aware of a man broken on the wheel of the intractability of his beliefs."[20] Without "Stars," Javert is simply a villain, and the audience would not sympathize with his motivation to hunt Valjean or his suicide.

Now that the score boasted full characterizations and all the songs necessary to the drama and the emotional arc of the book, a practical problem arose: the show ran too long. Three and a half hours was not only rather unusual for a musical, but Mackintosh, for once acting more like a bottom-line producer than a member of the creative team, argued that they would never be able to afford to pay the musicians the necessary overtime if the show did not do well. Nunn, out of loyalty to his work, refused to make any cuts while the show still resided at the Barbican, but told Mackintosh that if they did well enough to move to the West End, they could consider cuts. When the production was indeed moved to the Palace Theatre, a few sections of scenes and songs were excised, a process which continued through the out-of-town tryouts in Washington, D.C., up to the Broadway opening. Technical tightening also helped, and the current *Les Mis* runs three hours—long for a musical, but not exceptionally so.[21]

Casting began. Hopefuls performed for the weighty lineup of Schönberg, Boublil, Mackintosh, Nunn, Caird, musical director Martin Koch, and musical supervisor and orchestrator John Cameron. Nunn invited any actors from his players at the Royal Shakespeare Company to audition if they wished, and three landed sizable roles: Roger Allam as Javert, Alun Armstrong as Thénardier, and Sue Jane Tanner as Madame Thénardier. The other RSC players who might have been interested did not sing well enough for featured roles, and none were willing to join the chorus. The search for other performers widened. Nunn sought Tim Rice's advice about finding a Valjean: did Rice know an actor who could look like a convict, carry a man around on his back, and sing beautifully? Rice sent them Colm Wilkinson, a move that both boosted the show's success and made Wilkinson a star. He had sung Che on the concept album of *Evita* and had taken a turn in the long-running London production of *Superstar,* but he was not at all well known. Nevertheless, he won the role instantly upon singing for the team, and Schönberg, Koch, and Cameron cheerfully rewrote the role for tenor rather than baritone to suit Wilkinson's strong but sweet voice.

One of the show's most moving and popular songs, Valjean's statement of faith and prayer for Marius, "Bring Him Home," came to the score quite late. The idea for a dramatic solo for Valjean at this point in the story dated back to Fenton's time as lyricist, but the melody did not gain words until late in Kretzmer's working schedule. After Kretzmer heard the music, he altered his original plan to write a song for a lonely Valjean who feared losing Cosette to another man, and instead wrote Valjean's selfless prayer for Marius's safety. Like "Memory" from *Cats,* "Bring Him Home" had a huge impact on the cast when they first heard it in rehearsal. With "Memory," Nunn had told those present to note the date and the time, for they had "just heard a smash hit by Andrew Lloyd Webber." Now, with Wilkinson singing "Bring Him Home," "There was a hush throughout the theatre," writes Edward Behr, "eventually broken by Trevor Nunn. 'I told you the play was all about God, that it was a deeply religious experience,' he told the assembled cast. 'Yes,' said one of the actors, 'but you didn't tell us you'd engaged Him to sing it.' "[22]

Rounding out the twenty-seven member cast were Frances Ruffelle, who would come with the production to New York, as Eponine, and romantic, strong-voiced Michael Ball, later of Lloyd Webber's *Aspects of Love,* as Marius. The final addition was the only cast member who brought a major theatrical "name" to the show: Patti LuPone, Broadway's Evita, as Fantine. She happened to be in London performing in Blitzstein's *The Cradle Will Rock,* and she signed on as Fantine after hearing the French recording.

Details of blocking and costume changes were greatly complicated by the fact that almost all the actors played multiple roles, and although the cast would grow with future relocations, multiple roles remain in current productions. The cast began with several weeks of improvisation, French history lessons, and an introduction to Hugo. Critic Jack Kroll notes that in London, each member of the cast researched an area of nineteenth-century French life, such as the church, the police, education, or medicine. When the show moved to New York, Nunn and Caird would ask each cast member to explain from where his or her family had come. Everyone told similar stories of injustice and poverty, and could relate strongly to the material; according to Kroll, this research and discussion lent the cast "fierce gusto" in their powerful performances.[23] The London cast, after sharing their research, began rehearsals in a space that included a revolving stage floor, which would accustom them to the set design.

Designer John Napier had entered the picture. Having staged the massive *Nicholas Nickelby* for Nunn and Caird at the RSC, as well as having designed the colossal junk heap that is the set of *Cats,* Napier was a natural choice for this sweeping and complicated story. Nunn and Napier decided that a revolving floor would help a show requiring so much sense of motion, including chase scenes, passages of time, and cinematic changes of locale. Strolling around Paris, Napier had a revelation about what to put on top of the revolving floor, at least some of the time: two large pieces of clearly manmade structure that would merge and separate. This would be the barricade, made from a puzzle-like pile of furniture, wood, stairways, and crates built by the revolutionary students, but it would also represent the poor side of town where Eponine and Gavroche live.

Napier colored the barricade and his other set pieces gray and brown, and costumer Andreane Neofitou followed his lead, putting the factory workers, convicts, and poor people in dusty gray tones. The whores added a rare spot of color, in raunchy costumes that reminded Nunn of saloon girls in a Western, but Neofitou argued that the costumes made the character types easily recognizable. Lighting designer David Hersey, like Napier a veteran of *Cats* and *Nicholas Nickelby* as well as *Evita,* invented several pivotal visual images. His lighting, plus the revolving stage, gives Valjean's trudge through the sewers a realistic look, for example. The revolving floor also allows the audience to see both sides of the barricade. Usually viewers see the students' side, as they shoot at upstage enemies, but after the massacre, the entire barricade swings slowly around, revealing those victims caught on the enemy's side, now draped over the jagged set. Hersey provides a bright white light at moments of death throughout the show, an obvious but effective gesture that reminds the audience of the underlying goal of heavenly redemption for which many of the characters wish.

Javert's suicide proved one of the cleverest solutions to a staging problem. Napier and Hersey had to make Javert's leap off a bridge look realistic, and Napier realized the solution lay not in having the actor really leap down, but in having the bridge fly up just after he steps off it, and Hersey clarified the image by turning the stage floor into a rushing river.[24] But often, the simplest staging ideas prove the most memorable and effective: "One Day More" ends the first act with all the characters at their most uncertain, yet hopeful. The students, led by Enjorlas, rally the people behind them and march in time to the music. Since the stage revolves as they march, and the chorus remains on it, their marching pattern involves a step forward, then a step back—symbolic, in a subtle way, of the uphill struggle they face and their constant setbacks after every step ahead. These motions also convey a sense that the world is moving in one direction, the students and the crowd in another, and that only bald, ill-fated enthusiasm keeps them facing toward their path; though they make little progress, at least they continue to march.

In London and En Route to Broadway: Songs of Love and War and Death and Desperation; or, a Spreading Quicksand of Romance

Les Misérables opened at the Barbican on 8 October 1985. Scheduled to run ten weeks there before moving to a West End theater, it was not clear after opening night if the show would run even another few days, much less survive until the move. The opening night audience cheered with uniform enthusiasm, but the morning-after reviews tipped toward the unimpressed, with a few painful pans. That day, Mackintosh had apparently pondered allowing the show to fizzle out after its Barbican run, when he heard the startling news: ticket sales had just achieved a record-breaking level. The box office sold five thousand tickets on 9 October, selling out the Barbican run; word of mouth and a few glowing reviews had clearly overcome the pans and mixed reviews.

Despite encouraging sales, and some much more positive reviews that came in over the next few days and weeks, a move to the West End still had its risks. Their target theater was the Palace, which, by coincidence, Andrew Lloyd Webber's company, the Really Useful Group, had just bought. Mackintosh had made a sizeable deposit toward reservation of the theater, which meant that Lloyd Webber, theater owner, had to like the show fairly well if things were going to continue smoothly. It marks a strange and extremely rare moment in the history of the megamusical, when the fate of Lloyd Webber's chief followers—or competitors—in the megamusical style actually rested partly in his hands. In the end, however, Lloyd Webber's personal opinion of *Les Mis* mattered little to its economic standing; he did not particularly care for the show, and told Mackintosh it was a huge risk to pursue it. He apparently even offered to give Mackintosh his deposit back. But the financial backers and the rest of the creative team encouraged Mackintosh to take the plunge, and Lloyd Webber, without hesitation, welcomed *Les Mis* to the Palace, where it remained for eighteen years.[25] In April 2004, Mackintosh revamped and refreshed the show by moving it to the nearby Queen's Theatre; Nunn and Caird were on hand to restage some of the blocking, the score was reorchestrated for fewer players (but alas, more electronics), and the set underwent some alterations to fit it into a larger, more modern theater. The move generated increased ticket sales and, as of this writing, the show's run remains open-ended.

What caused the initial disappointment of a handful of negative critics? In his review for the London *Times,* a newspaper that usually carried a fair amount of weight, Irving Wardle moved beyond disliking *Les Mis* to complaining about musicals in general. He found the storytelling shallow and overblown, despite his claim that the score was rather good; he grumpily asserted that the problem lay in the "general rule that musicals trivialize everything they touch." Action, he felt, was continually interrupted by a "spreading quicksand of romance" that slow things down, resulting in a combination of "spectacle and push-button emotionalism at the expense of character and content." The spectacle, he admitted rather grudgingly, was quite well done, as was the adaptation of the novel, but he remained unmoved by what he saw as the overly sentimental tone of the show.[26]

Michael Billington of the *Guardian* wrote a review colored entirely by his reverence for Hugo's "towering masterpiece," and therefore he found that the musicalization failed to live up to the novel. He invoked the societal classification of theater in declaring the show "fine middlebrow entertainment rather than great art." The plot remained, but Billington felt the spiritual conflict was "barely existent"—as if he resented that Hugo's fourteen pages of musing on class structure could be boiled down to a rhyming couplet. Billington then went on to praise a number of elements, including the ambitious if imperfect music, the "highly proficient" lyrics, the excellent cast, and the staging which ranged from dramatic and large to subtle and clever, but in general he seemed incapable of enjoying any musical adaptation of his revered text.[27]

Like Billington, Michael Ratcliffe of the *Observer* used his *Les Mis* review as a pretext for entering the high art/low entertainment debate, with plenty of space devoted to deriding the RSC for taking on *Les Mis* at all. If the RSC wants to do musicals, he argued, which would be an admirable goal, they should do serious musicals by people like Offenbach, Weill, Bernstein, or Sondheim. Instead, they were seduced by spectacle. Oddly, having just argued in favor the separation of high and low forms of musical theater, Ratcliffe then attempted to recombine them and review *Les Mis* as both a high-art adaptation of a classic novel and as a catchy piece of musical theater. *Les Mis* failed on both accounts: the creators "emasculated Hugo's Olympian perspective and reduced it to the trivialising and tearful aesthetic of rock opera and the French hit parade of ten (15?) years ago," using melodies too synthesized, driving, and ineffective. A great cast and the impressive barricade could not save the show, which for Ratcliffe remained rooted in the RSC's strange choice to do *Les Mis* in the first place: "It is less depressing that the RSC is presenting this witless and synthetic entertainment in the hope of making money (why not?) than that they appear to believe it is a piece of quality and an exciting development of their best work. It is a parody of it."[28]

Balancing these negative reviews were several raves that often argued the exact opposite points. John Peter, following Wardle's review in the Sunday *Times*, felt that *Les Mis* managed to turn "one of the great pseudo-classics of literature" into a "gripping, brilliantly paced and thrillingly organised" musical. It certainly helped that Peter had no allegiance to the novel, but he also argued that the score boasted effective music and lyrics, and that every number "makes robust contributions to character and drama."[29] Michael Coveney waxed even more enthusiastic in his *Financial Times* review, declaring that this example of a new genre of musical/opera/rock opera broke "brand new ground somewhere between Verdi and Andrew Lloyd Webber." He found the story and the emotional situations powerfully conveyed, and was particularly impressed with ensemble numbers, including trios, quartets, and "One Day More," which he labeled "one of the best" first act finales of all time. Like almost all critics, Coveney praised the directing and staging, and also devoted a good deal of space to praising all the leading players individually. In a foreshadowing of Broadway reviews, he devoted particular attention to Colm Wilkinson as Valjean.[30]

Sheridan Morley in the *International Herald Tribune* declared *Les Mis* the "musical of the year, if not the half-decade," and if the reader failed to agree, Morley suggested he or she be "locked in a cupboard" with the soundtrack from *Starlight Express* (evidently Morley's least favorite megamusical). Morley admired the show's organic nature, which, rather than being structured in a way that set up and delivered hit songs, worked more like pieces of a puzzle. "There are songs of love and war and death and restoration: there are patter songs, arias, duets and chorus numbers of dazzling inventiveness and variety. For this is not the French 'Oliver' or even the musical 'Nicholas Nickelby,' though it owes a certain debt to both. Rather it is a brilliantly guided tour of the 1,200-page eternity that is Hugo's text, and indeed there is no way that in three orchestral hours we can ask for more than that." Morley felt that the sung-through nature of the score allowed little time for deep characterization, but the emotions and the story came through, and the cast shone.[31]

Several years later, Morley would continue to praise *Les Mis* in his book *Spread a Little Happiness*. By then, he found *Les Mis* not only thrilling, but innovative in its use of megamusical elements. It "sets out to redefine the limits of music theatre" with its quasi-operatic through-sung score and its "universal themes of social and domestic happiness" and "individual despair." With its lavish yet appropriate staging, score, and plot, *Les Mis* used the best of the megamusical qualities: "It relies on no scenic or choreographic gimmicks, no repetitive phrasing, no simplistic homilies." Morley declared it a great achievement for musical theater, attainable only outside his native England, despite his fondness for Lloyd Webber: "There is an energy and an operatic intensity here which exists in the work of no British composer, past or present: the sense of a nation's history being channeled through trumpets and drums and violins and guitars and 'cellos."[32] That it would take someone other than Lloyd Webber to create the most successful megamusical yet may be correct, though not, as Morley implies, because the British lack the passion or nationalistic fervor that suits the megamusical's epic nature. Rather, critics and a few cynical theatergoers were more willing to embrace a megamusical that did not have Lloyd Webber's name on it, since after *Cats* the resentment toward his success had firmly cemented itself in the media.

Offers to mount *Les Mis* in other countries arose immediately, but Mackintosh, true to the megamusical formula, headed to Broadway next. When he had originally expressed interest in *Les Mis,* he discovered that the Nederlanders had done the same, and so agreed to produce the Broadway staging together. Now, Mackintosh expressed doubt about the usefulness of the Nederlander team; he had been disappointed by their handling of his revival of *Oliver!,* which had experienced a lackluster run in one of their theaters. The Nederlanders agreed to pull out, and Mackintosh became the first solo producer to mount a show in decades. Indeed, shows with a single producer remain extremely rare; much more commonly, a show lists several corporations and production teams as producer, including the formidable Walt Disney Company.

What Mackintosh needed, rather than co-producers, were investors. This model had been the norm in Broadway's "Golden Era" of the 1940s and 1950s, but over the years, theater owners had become increasingly involved in production. Rather than simply renting their theater to a producer and his show, they became producers themselves, putting money into the production and, in an effort to see their money well spent, becoming involved with artistic decisions. This led to strong complaints that unqualified businessmen had snuck their way into areas like casting and directing, which was indeed sometimes the case. Mackintosh returned to the earlier model, which meant that a single producer raised money from investors, or "angels," while maintaining complete control over how to spend that money. "Single-handedly," the *New York Times* reported, "he has restored the balance of power between producers and theater owners at a time when the independent production of Broadway musicals has gone virtually the way of new musicals themselves. Because Mr. Mackintosh doesn't need their investment money, he is free to pick and choose the right theater at the right terms for his shows."[33] *Les Mis* was Mackintosh's first solo-produced show; *Cats,* for example, had been produced by Mackintosh, Lloyd Webber's Really Useful Group, and the Shubert Organization, who owned the Winter Garden Theatre.

Now, with *Les Mis* predicted to be a sure hit in New York, Mackintosh easily persuaded investors simply to back the show silently.

A striking difference between the old angel investment system and Mackintosh's modern version involved the nature of the angels. In the earlier era, money came from many people offering small investments; as little as a few thousand dollars could help a production and might, with luck, pay off. Now, with expenses soaring but with huge potential rewards, Mackintosh turned to large corporations, a practice that has become common in the megamusical. The biggest angel behind *Les Mis* was Mutual Benefit Life Insurance, which enjoyed good publicity and little risk.[34]

Mackintosh's ingenious marketing strategy was now unleashed with greater force than ever before. The main task involved saturating the market with publicity well in advance of opening night. He put tickets on sale ten months in advance (rather than the usual two or three, or five in the case of *Cats*), targeting the mail order market, especially those buying in large groups. Individual customers could buy tickets by phone with Telecharge five months in advance. Also, as had come to be expected with Mackintosh, the advertising blitz began early and hit the newspapers, radio, and television intensely. The radio voiceover promised an epic in true megamusical style: "From despair comes hope. From adversity comes triumph. From struggle comes glory. From across the ocean comes the theatrical event of a lifetime."[35]

Meanwhile, the creative team took over the Broadway Theater, owned not by the Nederlanders but by the other dominant theater-owning group, the Shuberts. The theater suited the show's needs better than either the Barbican or the Palace had, since it featured computerized motion of the revolving floor and the sets and a much better lighting system.[36] From London, the team brought Colm Wilkinson as Valjean and Frances Ruffelle as Eponine, both having won high praise in their roles. New additions included *Cats* veteran Terrence Mann as Javert and Judy Kuhn (who would play the lead in the Tim Rice/Benny Andersson/Björn Ulvaeus show *Chess* the following year) as Cosette. The creative team made only one significant change to the score between New York and London: Valjean gained a deathbed confession scene, to explain his actions to Cosette and to reassure the audience that he felt at peace with all he had done.[37]

Five weeks before *Les Mis* opened in New York, it had already broken the record for advance ticket sales formerly held by *Cats*. *Les Mis* also broke *Cats*'s record for first-day sales.[38] The buzz on the show was perhaps the strongest that Broadway had ever seen, for several reasons: word of mouth from both London and D.C., where *Les Mis* had enjoyed a wildly successful tryout, was extremely positive; the London cast album was released in the United States, so familiarity with the score began to grow; and the Broadway season offered little else of note. The *New York Times* also speculated that the story of *Les Mis* appealed to audiences, filled as it was with humans in dramatic situations, rather than non-humans (cats or trains, for example) in less moving situations.[39]

Les Misérables opened at the Broadway Theater on 12 March 1987.

The Score and the Show's Structure: "Do You Hear the People Sing?"

More than *Cats, Jesus Christ Superstar,* or other sung-through megamusicals before it, *Les Misérables* embodies the word "sweeping." Even *The Phantom of the Opera*, which Lloyd Webber would take to Broadway a year after *Les Mis* arrived, featured a less epic plot and sensibility. The plot is certainly the most obviously grand, sweeping feature of *Les Mis*—it covers about twenty years of the characters' lives, smoothly played out in an almost seamless series of scenes. This seamlessness adds to the sweeping sensation: with almost no pauses for applause, and constant underscoring during set changes, passages of time, and other transitions, the story moves perpetually. The revolving stage rolls new sets on and off and carries people with it. Things swing in and out of view; days and years fly by. The momentum pauses for important events and reflections, but then continues to carry us forward before we have a chance to wonder what might come next.

Demonstrating his knowledge of Lloyd Webber, Schönberg borrows some of his structural techniques, incorporating them into a distinct musical language. The score of *Les Mis* features a great deal of recurring music, a device that helps to unify the show and give it a consistent (though satisfyingly varied) musical signature. In *Superstar* and *Cats,* we saw that Lloyd Webber used several kinds of recurring material, two of which are prominent in *Les Mis:* first, motifs or recitative-like melodic shapes which pop up in different forms, lengths, and guises; and second, complete vocal melodies reused with new lyrics. These two types of recurring music are examined below, along with two other prominent musical features that make *Les Mis* distinctive. First, we look briefly at the seamless, continuous structure of large sections of the show, in terms of their dramatic flow. Then, after an examination of how the recurring music works, we look at the dramatic center of the entire score, the ensemble/choral number "One Day More." This number, perhaps more than any other, invokes the idea of an oratorio, a sensibility which runs strongly throughout *Les Misérables.* Unique to this megamusical, the influence of oratorio can be felt not only in the structure and staging of "One Day More," but also in the distinctly hymn-like quality of "I Dreamed a Dream" and the battle cry of "Do You Hear the People Sing?" Most significantly, the idea of an oratorio—a work for soloists and chorus on a religious theme—is carried throughout *Les Mis,* since the show features its spiritual threads so prominently. This makes *Les Mis* unique; *Cats* offered a vague theme of rebirth, but *Les Mis* rests its plot—and, to some extent, its musical sensibility—on religious ideas of justice, forgiveness, and heaven.

THE "SWEEPING" EFFECT: LARGE SEAMLESS SECTIONS OF DRAMA

The seamless transitions between scenes weave together everything in the show, including songs that can be considered set pieces with somewhat closed forms, as well as the less tidy, more recitative-like or action-packed material that comes between set pieces. The same would be true of *The Phantom of the Opera,* with its mixture of clear songs and more amorphous transitional material, but it has more static sets and a less sweeping plot. If one considers the nonstop sung-through element of the megamusical to be its most defining characteristic, *Les Mis* is the genre's best example.

Both of the long acts have four or five sections each, marked by significant set changes or large leaps ahead in time. But no pause in the music marks these sections; stops come only for the occasional applause break and never accompany a set change. The comic relief of "Master of the House" garners applause, for example, but the actors simply hold their positions during it, and the scene continues. Similar pauses for applause occur after Fantine's "I Dreamed a Dream," Javert's "Stars," Eponine's "On My Own," Valjean's "Bring Him Home," and Marius's "Empty Chairs at Empty Tables," but virtually nowhere else (although enthusiastic audiences occasionally try to applaud over the orchestra's continuing underscoring). Often, even significant solo numbers do not warrant an applause break from the orchestra, even if otherwise the number feels like a set piece. Valjean's dramatic "Who Am I?" and the rousing "Do You Hear the People Sing?" offer no rest before running onward, and the same is true for the duet "A Little Fall of Rain" and the number "Javert's Suicide." Instead, these and all the other numbers, along with all the musical material generally, are held together by orchestral underscoring, sets that roll in, out, and around, and other "sweeping" gestures.

One large section joined by such techniques occurs early in the first act, under the umbrella title "Lovely Ladies." Here we meet the whores of Montreuil-sur-Mer, and we watch Fantine become desperate enough to join them, so that she may support her daughter Cosette. "Lovely Ladies" consists of a number of catchy refrains, but also contains recitative sections as Fantine sells her necklace, then her hair, and eventually her body. She then encounters an abusive aristocratic customer, whom she resists. Javert wants to arrest her, but Valjean, now the mayor, intervenes on Fantine's behalf and has her sent to the hospital. All this is accomplished with a combination of recitative and sections of set numbers, some of which have been heard in full form already, others of which are yet to come. On the final note of Valjean's solemn vow to help Fantine, the orchestra launches into frantic music for the runaway cart, which leads in turn to a discussion between Valjean and Javert about the supposed recapturing of prisoner 24601—Valjean, of course. Their discussion uses several recurring recitative patterns as well as more metrically regular recurring materials. The stage clears behind Valjean as he ponders in "Who Am I?" whether to come forward. When he decides he must tell the truth, a courtroom, complete with judge, bench, jury, prisoner, and spectators, rushes downstage to meet him. Suddenly Valjean confronts Javert in the courtroom that had not been there when he began the number. As he rushes out, the orchestra plays a ten-measure transition to the hospital, and the stage rotates Fantine into view. "Fantine's Death," for Fantine and Valjean, becomes "Confrontation" between Valjean and Javert. Finally, the orchestra has a brief but full stop as the set rotates to reveal the Thénardiers' inn. Thus, continuous, smooth action has presented and linked several major plot points and dramatic peaks. The effect carries the audience members along, pulling them effortlessly through the drama with little time to reflect.

The other large sections of *Les Mis* work much the same way. For example, after the plot leaps forward ten years toward the end of the first act, we meet the rebellious students. Their scene at the ABC Café becomes "Red and Black," which becomes "Do You Hear the People Sing?" Then the attention shifts without an orchestral pause to Cosette's front yard; she is now grown and in love with Marius, who appears and begins to woo her. Their love scene includes "In My Life" and "A Heart Full of Love." After the briefest of pauses, which sometimes draws applause, an eavesdropping Eponine spots her father, Thénardier, and his cronies; this is "The Attack on Rue Plumet," an action-filled passage which lands breathlessly on the first note of the act 1 finale, "One Day More." Thus, the entire section from the introduction of the students to the end of the act feels like one dramatic gesture.

Perhaps the most extensive section of seamless action begins at the top of the second act, and might be thought of as ending when we move from above ground into the sewers, although the music carries even this transition without pause. Until the sewer scene, the entire act features the barricade on which a whole series of events and numbers occur. When the act begins, the students are building the barricade; the action cuts away briefly to follow Eponine but soon returns. The events on the barricade include Javert's arrival as a spy, Eponine's arrival and her death, Valjean's arrival and his freeing of the captured Javert, several quiet moments of pre-battle reflection, and three complete battle scenes in which the authorities kill almost everyone present, including the helpful street urchin Gavroche, the student leader Enjorlas, and all his men except Marius. The whole section, with its broad drama and its tragic conclusion, feels emotionally draining and relentless in its focus on the events at the barricade.

These large sections feel complete only when time takes a leap forward, or when a significant set change occurs—from Fantine's scenes to the inn, for example, or from the barricade to the sewers. How do Boublil, Schönberg, Nunn, and Caird make the transitions of scene and time? As mentioned, the seams are often covered by Schönberg's virtually continuous orchestra that picks up a tune or motif and develops it, preparing the mood of the next scene. For example, after Valjean has successfully bargained for Cosette in "Waltz of Treachery," he carries her off to a better life, and ten years pass. As Valjean and Cosette rotate toward the dark back of the stage, a projection tells us that Paris in 1832 is now the setting, while the orchestra plays an expansive, unsettling line from "Waltz of Treachery" that will blend into the top of "Look Down." In seven measures of music, ten years pass. Now we see a filthy street filled with beggars.

The prologue offers less dramatic but almost constant examples of the musical's scene change methods. Valjean, freed from prison, walks for what feels like miles, both with and against the flow of the revolving floor, as he encounters various groups. A farmer denies him his full wages for work because he is a parolee, and an innkeeper turns him out. These characters, and various bystanders, rotate on with a few pieces of furniture, creating simple settings that last only a few lines each. After more walking, Valjean encounters the bishop, who swings on with his nicely set table and silver candlesticks. As the bishop rotates out again, Valjean reflects on his new life on a bare stage. The motions and props are simple, but the fluidity of the staging manages both to hold the whole prologue together and to convey the passage of time as Valjean grows increasingly frustrated. Until the barricade takes over the revolving floor in the second act, such simple sets and smooth revolving transitions carry much of the action. Later, the barricade transports people and action just as the floor did.

RECURRING MOTIFS, FRAGMENTS, AND RECITATIVES

Besides this fluidity of time, space, and constant music, the main technique that binds the musical together is recurring musical ideas. With *The Phantom of the Opera* yet to come, though, *Les Mis* was the first megamusical score to use such an extensive and complex set of motifs, themes, melodic contours, bits of songs, and full reprises. A melody that makes up the heart of a set piece also becomes fodder for motivic manipulation and fragmentation; other musical shapes never find a settled home in a set number but rather float among sections of recitative and transition.[40] First, we look at six examples of material that is fragmented and motif-like (as opposed to the more complete, melodic material discussed below).

Perhaps the show's most recognizable piece of musical material comes from the very beginning. The opening set of descending dotted-rhythm chords moves into a song for the prisoners, underpinned by a distinctive steady beat and minor-mode melody; this moves in turn to Valjean and Javert's first conversation. While the prison scene is contained in the prologue and has no title of its own, it shares much of its music with "Look Down," a number late in the first act. Indeed, even the prisoners' lyrics are similar:

Look down, look down, don't look 'em in the eye
Look down, look down, you're here until you die.

The transition from the opening chords into either the "Look Down" music or another musical idea happens several times, and each time the bold rhythmic chords mark moments of importance. These moments include the building of the barricade and the beginning of the final battle, as well as the top of the show (as in ex. 4.1).

By the time we reach the number "Look Down" itself, its music has already been heard in the opening of the show, "Confrontation," and several segues elsewhere. The melody plays softly, for example, in the flutes and reeds as Valjean walks during the prologue, and it clashes with the vamp of "Master of the House" as Valjean arrives at the Thénardiers' inn. Nevertheless, when the melody and its distinctive vamp accompaniment receive full choral treatment in "Look Down," the song feels like this material's true home (see ex. 4.2).

The number "Look Down" introduces us to Gavroche, who sings his own melody over the vamp, a melody which as the scene progresses gets taken up by Enjorlas and his followers, then by Marius and Eponine. The chorus also has a second melody, a more active line used for the confrontation of several whores, plus the crowd's frustrated longing for something better ("it'll come, it'll come, it'll come"). All these sections of "Look Down" are interspersed with others, including a section in which Thénardier and his group attempt to wheedle money out of Valjean and Cosette, to the tune of their "Waltz of Treachery."

All parts of this "Look Down" music find their way into later scenes. The tune Gavroche introduced accompanies Eponine's arrival at the barricade, for example, and the dotted-rhythm orchestral chords intone softly as the students honor Eponine's death. With nearly twenty references to some element of the

Example 4.1. Top of "Prologue"

"Look Down" music, some subtle, others obvious, the score uses this material for serious, weighty moments of all sorts.

A second melodic line with a distinct driving accompaniment recurs frequently, but never finds a home in a set number. It first appears in the prologue, when the police catch Valjean with the bishop's silver and accuse him of lying about how he came to have it. Their forceful, hostile melody is answered by a consequent line, a more gentle and far-reaching tune that the bishop presents (see ex. 4.3). Because this musical idea first appears when the police accuse Valjean of theft, and because in fact it accompanies a number of similar situations, I have dubbed this material "accusation music." It will next appear when Javert demands an explanation for the scuffle between Fantine and her violent customer; the customer sings the consequent phrase in an obsequious tone. Javert responds with the first melody, then Fantine (in an effort to stay out of

Example 4.2. "Look Down"

jail so she may continue to pay for Cosette) answers with the second. Javert rounds out the section with the first melody plus a short tag phrase ("Honest work, just reward / That's the way to please the Lord").

The accusation music also accompanies Javert's description of the prisoner accused of being number 24601, as well as Javert's intervention in the Valjean/Thénardier scuffle during "Look Down." Gavroche sings the first part of the accusation music as a coda to Javert's "Stars," mocking the inspector and claiming to know far more about local events. Finally, the accusation music pops up when the students have Javert in their custody at the barricade, and accuse him of being a spy. Javert uses the consequent tune to counter with an accusation of treason.

In a third example, a piece of musical material with a defined function, but one less structured in style than the accusation music, occurs more often. It accompanies encounters, usually hostile ones, between characters, and it is usually in a free, recitative-like unmetered tempo; it might therefore be called "recitative encounter music." The vocal line is jagged, marked by dissonant leaps (including an opening tritone leap, often revisited), and ending with a tight re-

Example 4.3. Accusation music in "Prologue"

peating figure that tensely steps down inside a diminished fourth (as in the Old Woman's "No more than five. / My dear, we all must stay alive"; see ex. 4.4). This encounter music first appears in the prologue, when the farmer dismisses Valjean: "You'll have to go / I'll pay you off for the day." Valjean exchanges similar recitative with the prologue's innkeeper and his wife. Next, Fantine has a series of three encounters during "Lovely Ladies," as she grows step by step more desperate for money. She uses the recitative encounter music to sell her necklace (as in ex. 4.4), hair, and virtue. The encounter music also appears in an in-tempo form (for the first and last time) in "Lovely Ladies," as the local pimp spies Fantine and invites her to join him and his whores.

Other encounters that are achieved with this music include Fantine's meeting with her violent customer, and the meeting between Valjean and the man he has just saved from the runaway cart ("You come from God, / You are a saint," the man tells Valjean, using the encounter music's final falling line). Javert appears just after this moment, and uses the same music to approach Valjean, now the mayor, with his memory of the strength of prisoner 24601. After several other appearances, the encounter music disappears for most of the second act, although it is put to effective dramatic use during one of the most significant encounters late in the show, when Valjean meets Javert, in the students' custody, at the barricade. It develops a prominent rhyme scheme this time, especially noticeable with the rhyme of "life" and "knife."

> *Valjean:* We meet again.
> *Javert:* You've hungered for this all your life.
>   Take your revenge.
>   How right you should kill with a knife.
> *Valjean:* You talk too much.
>   Your life is safe in my hands.
> *Javert:* Don't understand.
> *Valjean:* Get out of here.
> *Javert:* Valjean, take care, I'm warning you.
> *Valjean:* Clear out of here.

The score uses a number of other musical ideas, some of them more recitative-like than others, to convey exchanges, information, and plot. For example, Valjean uses a melodic shape that steps up in fast waves, then moves back down more calmly, to convey his feelings or circumstances. During the prologue, for example, he expresses his frustration about life as an ex-con: "And now I know how freedom feels, / The jailer always at your heels, / it is the law." He uses the shape again to inform the Thénardiers of his intentions regarding Cosette:

Example 4.4. Encounter music in "Lovely Ladies"

"And I am here to help Cosette / and I will settle any debt / you may think proper." While the vocal line is sung in a strict tempo, it has a conversational, recitative-like feel to it, and only Valjean sings it.

Similarly, Eponine is assigned two melodic shapes which she uses to express her feelings and desires in fairly conversational tones; these two shapes always come together. She shares the material with others, usually Marius or Thénardier and his men, but the music is always hers. It makes one of its most complete appearances just after Eponine has realized who Cosette must be:

> *Eponine (singing the first melodic shape):* Cosette, now I remember.
>   Cosette, how can it be?
>   We were children together,
>   Look what's become of me.
> *(To Marius):* Good God, ooh, what a rumpus!
> *Marius:* That girl, who can she be?
> *Eponine:* That cop, he'd like to jump us
>   But he ain't smart, not he.
> *Marius (moving on to the second melodic shape):* Eponine, who was that girl?
> *Eponine:* Some bourgeois two-a-penny thing.
> *Marius:* Eponine, find her for me!
> *Eponine:* What will you give me?
> *Marius:*   Anything!

One final musical idea that recurs belongs entirely to the orchestra; it is a falling arpeggiated figure that links several significant moments. It marks the top of the first act proper, after the prologue, introducing "At the End of the Day." But usually it accompanies key moments in Valjean's life; it runs throughout "Who Am I?" for example, and since the music of "Who Am I?" becomes Valjean's opening of "One Day More," the figure runs throughout much of that number as well. It also signals the magical moment in which Marius and Cosette first spot each other; Marius sings a single line of melody from "I Dreamed a Dream" over the figure. Finally, it runs throughout Valjean's deathbed confession to Marius (see ex. 4.7 for this figure in "One Day More"). These cascading four-note arpeggios lend an air of freshness and excitement to the scenes in which they appear, marking, for example, Valjean's new start as mayor, the discovery of true love, and the immediacy and tension which carries "One Day More."

RECURRING MELODIES THAT MAKE DRAMATIC AND EMOTIONAL LINKS
Schönberg and Boublil use a number of songs in the same way they use the material of "Look Down"; set pieces get reprised, reworked, and fragmented, with varying degrees of recognizability. As we have seen, Lloyd Webber had

already become well-known for this technique of revisiting melodies with completely new lyrics, in new (but usually related) dramatic circumstances. Most obviously in *Les Mis,* the music of "Fantine's Death" is the same as that of Eponine's showstopper, "On My Own." Slight reorchestration and a very different mood help Fantine's gentle lullaby become Eponine's poignant profession of unrequited love. This is the most complete reuse of a song; its emergence as Eponine's lonely love song helps to link her tragic situation to Fantine's. Fantine used the melody to profess her love for her daughter Cosette, whom she will never see again. Eponine, who never knew Fantine, uses her music to declare her devotion to the unattainable Marius.

More commonly, set numbers are revisited with new words in brief restatements. "At the End of the Day," "Who Am I?" "A Heart Full of Love," "Drink with Me," "Castle on a Cloud," "A Little Fall of Rain," and "I Dreamed a Dream" experience such revisitations in either semi-complete or quite fragmented forms. Sometimes the songs follow characters quite logically; "Castle on a Cloud," for example, is almost always associated with (and sung by) Cosette. Similarly, Marius and Eponine preview their upcoming duet "A Little Fall of Rain" before they sing it, in the only example of Schönberg's use of the preview technique that Lloyd Webber made so prominent with "Memory" in *Cats.* The melody of "A Little Fall of Rain" also accompanies the students' reverent removal of Eponine's body from the barricade after she dies. "Drink with Me" and "A Heart Full of Love" receive brief yet easily recognized reprises, with virtually the same lyrics.

The rousing anthem of the students' rebellion, "Do You Hear the People Sing?" recurs a number of times. Schönberg puts it to effective use particularly during the battle scenes, in which he fragments and upsets its tidy structure, turning it into fodder for orchestral development. Enjorlas presents it the first time it appears, and rouses the rabble to join; they burst into glorious, enthusiastic harmony (as in ex. 4.5), but this momentary happy stability does not last. Just at the chorus's final chord, the orchestra pivots away, stepping off the stability of C major immediately. Interestingly, the dotted-rhythm chords that opened the show (see ex. 4.1) here close "Do You Hear the People Sing?" and serve as the transition into the next number, Cosette's "In My Life." The chords' appearance therefore facilitates a sizeable scene change, from the crowds marching in the streets to Valjean's quiet front garden (see ex. 4.5 for the last few bars of the students in harmonious optimism, plus the beginning of the transition).

Another dramatic high point, Valjean's prayer "Bring Him Home," also serves the drama well in a later context. This song has had perhaps the most successful life outside the show, similar to Lloyd Webber's hit singles, if slightly less widely

Example 4.5. "Do You Hear the People Sing?"

known. When Valjean first presents the song, he asks God to deliver Marius safely from the violence at the barricade. The number makes effective use of Valjean's upper register; though it is a tenor role, Valjean has aged, and his often-gruff voice reaches heavenward—especially at this song's end—in a gesture sure to evoke an audience's tears.[41] Ironically, while critics love to search for famous borrowed melodies in Lloyd Webber's music, almost all failed to note the similarity between "Bring Him Home" and the music to which Cio-Cio-San waits for Pinkerton's return (the famous "Humming Chorus") in Puccini's *Madama Butterfly*. The similarity, if intentional at all, can be seen as quite appropriate, as both characters are keeping an overnight vigil on behalf of those they love, and an air of tense hushed expectation dominates the scenes. The orchestra revisits "Bring Him Home" during the most boldly tragic moment in the show; after the students have all died in the final battle, the barricade slowly rotates and shows the audience each man that has fallen. The orchestra accompanies this with a reprise of "Bring Him Home," the vocal line played by a mournful oboe.

Thanks to Valjean's prayers and, on a more practical level, his long trip through the sewers with Marius in tow, Marius survives his wounding at the barricade. But he suffers from a severe case of survivor's guilt, and he expresses it in his own featured solo number, "Empty Chairs at Empty Tables." When Schönberg, Boublil, Nunn, and Mackintosh added a prologue to *Les Mis* during rehearsals for the London opening, "Empty Chairs at Empty Tables" gained a second airing, placed well before its original location. In a reprise of a tune that does not seem particularly motivated by drama or character, the bishop uses Marius's tune to "buy" Valjean's soul for God. This odd dual use of a melody is reminiscent of the "Strange Thing Mystifying"/"Peter's Denial" melody in *Jesus Christ Superstar,* as there seems little dramatic motivation for making the bishop's kindness sound like Marius's grief. Despite the dramatic distance between the scenes, however, both moments feel quiet and personal, making them similar in mood. The melody suits the bishop's scene perfectly well, but it makes its true home—thanks to its bold presentation—in expressing Marius's grief over the loss of all his friends.

Perhaps one of the most memorable set numbers introduces the evil yet entertaining Thénardier. "Master of the House" is the only fully comic number in the entire first act, and indeed Thénardier and his wife carry the only one in the second act, "Beggars at the Feast," which reprises the music of "Master of the House." With "Master of the House" marking the Thénardiers' first appearance and "Beggars at the Feast" marking their last, the melody helps characterize the nefarious duo—the tune becomes their catchy theme song. In between this first and last appearance, Thénardier reveals his hateful side, as he begs for money under false pretenses, then attempts to rob Valjean, and finally pilfers jewels off the dead while expressing his atheism in "Dog Eats Dog." But "Master of the House" and "Beggars at the Feast" act as comic bookends to Thénardier's evil ways, so that in the end audiences shake their heads ruefully, amazed and not entirely sorry that this villain has triumphed. Child abuse and other felonious crimes forgotten, Thénardier ends as he began, skimming money from the rich. His characteristic music, presented in "Master of the House," invokes a bouncy vamp and a rousing chorus of grudging support (see ex. 4.6 for the top of the refrain).

The music of "Master of the House" is one of the few examples of a melody always associated with one set of characters; "Castle on a Cloud" is another. But more commonly, melodies change hands in accordance with dramatic or emotional situations; for example, it becomes appropriate for Fantine and Eponine to share a melody (in "Fantine's Death" and "On My Own"). Unlike Lloyd Webber's *Cats,* in which each character has a distinct musical style or genre, the players in *Les Mis* mostly share musical material and styles; the accusation music,

Example 4.6. "Master of the House"

encounter music, and melodies of songs such as "Empty Chairs at Empty Tables" change hands fairly freely.

Instead of assigning each character a musical genre, therefore, Schönberg focuses more on shared moods and moveable musical material. This does not mean that the characters do not sound distinctive; in fact, each has a vocal quality and range which helps define him or her. Valjean, as we have seen, is a tenor who strays both into gruff baritone areas and an ethereal, light falsetto register when the drama calls for it. By far the most demanding part vocally in the show, the role of Valjean also involves a great deal of onstage time and formidable physical strength. Marius is a typical Broadway-style tenor, who can move between belting and lighter love songs. Schönberg and Boublil pair him with Cosette, a light operatic soprano who harkens back to similar voices of the Golden Era and also foreshadows other operatic soprano roles in mega-musicals such as Christine in *The Phantom of the Opera*. Eponine and Fantine, Broadway belters, balance her. But adding weight to the operatic side of the spectrum, Javert is a baritone whose role, especially in dramatic peaks such as "Stars," calls for a more classical and less brassy sound than is typical on Broadway.[42]

One feature of Broadway musicals that *Les Mis* takes to the extreme is its use of the chorus. As a group and in ever-changing subgroups, these several dozen players become one of the most important unifying features or "characters" of the show. Their most important function is to become the miserable people of the title, first in "At the End of the Day" and then, years later, in "Look Down." It is they who voice the problems which the students rally to fight—poverty, starvation, poor treatment of workers, prostitution, injustice. The men also voice the grievances of the prisoners in the prologue, and the women become factory employees and whores in the first act and grieving widows in the second. When the chorus emerges as a clean, well-dressed bunch at Marius and Cosette's wedding feast, it is a bit startling, for we have no previous evidence of any well-heeled friends. Most importantly, the students rally the poor men and women to their cause in "Do You Hear the People Sing?" and it is these formerly miserable, now hopeful people who step forward in the final moments of the show, ending on a stirring reprise of their anthem.

THE UNIQUE STRUCTURE AND DRAMATIC HIGH POINT OF "ONE DAY MORE"

The most complex and effective number in the score combines all the main and secondary characters with the chorus. "One Day More" combines reprises, reworked references to earlier numbers, new material, and several motifs en route to its rousing climax. It takes place in something of a frozen moment, when all the plot lines have reached maximum tension, and gives each character the opportunity to reflect on choices to be made. At the start of the number, Jean Valjean thinks (wrongly) that Javert has hunted him down at last, and that he and Cosette must leave the next day. The distinctive four-note arpeggios open the number just as they opened "Who Am I?" and Valjean's music begins much the same as that earlier song. Next, Marius, having just helped to disperse Thénardier and his men as they attempted to rob Valjean of his wealth and his daughter, reflects on his new-found love. "I did not live until today. / How can I live when we are parted?" he sings, using the melody of "I Dreamed a Dream" that Fantine sang earlier. Cosette joins him, in harmony, and they come to stand together in this moment of suspended time despite the actual physical distance now between them. Next, Eponine picks up the melody of "I Dreamed a Dream" with the bridge, as Marius and Cosette insert comments between her lines. Eponine expresses her lovelorn predicament: "One more day all on my own. / One more day with him not car-ing." She reaches a high point in the melodic line, which inspires a key change and the entrance of a new character, Enjorlas. He restates the bridge of "I Dreamed a Dream" with some alteration, urging Marius to leave Cosette and join the fight; Marius inserts comments between Enjorlas's lines, uncertain about which path to take.

As he has done several times already, Valjean bridges the seam from this last section to the next with his cry of "one day more." Javert enters, on a new melody but still over the arpeggiated figure in the orchestra, expressing his dedication to undermining the student revolution the next day. Next up are the Thénardiers, popping their heads up through a hole in the stage floor, to put in their two cents—they are eager to reap whatever financial benefits will result from what will surely be a massacre of the young students. "Most of them are goners so they won't miss much," they cackle. They reprise, in somewhat altered form, the melody of the refrain of "Master of the House," their theme song.

Finally, the chorus emerges as a group, revisiting the bridge of "I Dreamed a Dream" now in its alternating-line form that has already appeared twice in "One Day More." "One day to a new beginning," they cheer, "raise the flag of freedom high." At the last moment, Marius joins in their march, vowing, "My place is here, I fight with you!" It is perhaps at this point, as the chorus joins the soloists, that "One Day More" most strongly demonstrates an interesting parallel: Arthur Honegger's oratorio, *Le Roi David* (1921), features in its final number "La mort de David" a soloist, a four-part mixed chorus, and a remarkably similar orchestral figure to that which underpins "One Day More" with its four-note descending shape. The largely static staging of "One Day More" also invokes the idea of an oratorio, as does the spiritual theme of the entire show.

The final sections of "One Day More" weave together all the vocal lines sung by the lead characters up to this point. Schönberg alters some of the lines slightly to make them fit, and to allow each to be heard from time to time, but the melodies of Valjean, Marius and Cosette, Javert, and the Thénardiers remain recognizable. Eponine fits in her comments where she can, which suits her anguished state appropriately. As the climax of the number nears, the music that began the song, borrowed from "Who Am I?" reasserts itself, and the entire ensemble (including the chorus) joins in on an ending related to that of "Who Am I?" The orchestra, with a brief reference from the brass to Marius's first line in the song, drives its arpeggios to the end. Example 4.7 shows the juxtaposition, then the unification of all the melodies and the momentum that closes the number.

Example 4.7. "One Day More"

New York Reviews: "Too Inspirational"

Frank Rich of the *New York Times* praised *Les Mis* so enthusiastically that his review stands as an almost unqualified rave. His mixed and negative reviews of previous megamusicals gained a context: it was not that he disliked megamusicals, only Lloyd Webber's megamusicals. This show, including its megamusical-style sets, plot, score, and emotions, was in his view quite moving. He particularly appreciated the inventiveness and original elements that *Les Mis* brought to Broadway, and how the creators fused these with more traditional techniques. This "gripping pop opera" managed a "fusion of drama, music, character, design

Example 4.7. (*continued*)

Example 4.7. (*continued*)

rall. molto – – – –

known.   To -

and yet   with you   my world   has   start - ed.   To -

and yet   with you   my world   has   start - ed.   To -

To - mor - row we'll be far a - way, to - mor - row is the judge - ment day, to -

bud,   we'll   be   read - y   for these   school   boys.   To - mor - row is the judge - ment day, to -

all.   To -

To -

To -

rall. molto – – – – – – –

Example 4.7. (*continued*)

210   "TO LOVE ANOTHER PERSON IS TO SEE THE FACE OF GOD"

Example 4.7. (*continued*)

Example 4.7. (*continued*)

Example 4.7. (*continued*)

and movement" that "links this English adaptation of a French show to the highest tradition of modern Broadway musical production." The show successfully combined a sociology/history lesson, "unashamed schmaltz," and creative staging to tell its story. For Rich, the act 1 finale "One Day More" summarized the show's accomplishments, proving that "the contemporary musical theater can flex its atrophied muscles and yank an audience right out of its seats." The number managed to convey the states of mind of all the main characters clearly and simultaneously, and then Schönberg, having given each of these characters a musical theme, "now brings them all into an accelerating burst of counterpoint." Aided by Napier's design for a Paris about to revolt and by Nunn and Caird's clear, fluid staging, the moment worked for Rich.

Rich praised the creators' adaptation of the novel, which managed to keep Hugo's "thematic spirit" intact, even if it often glossed over plot points. The staging helped convey this spirit: the piles of junk that became the barricade represented how the city treats its poor; the sets were almost devoid of color and very realistic, the only burst of color coming from the students' red flag of revolution; Valjean's dilemma in "Who Am I?" was resolved when he sprang into action and the courtroom suddenly zoomed into focus behind him; and the audience traveled from the stars to the sewers along with Javert when he jumped off the bridge.

Schönberg's score also came in for high praise. Rich admired numerous melodies as well as the successful mix of madrigals, rock, Bizet, Weill, and the worlds of "harpsichord and synthesizer." These features (notable melodies, a mix of musical styles) were often mentioned by Rich and other critics when reviewing Lloyd Webber, but here Rich felt they worked to great effectiveness. Similarly, the notion of recurring musical motives, which Rich usually found troublesome and pointless in Lloyd Webber's work, impressed him in *Les Mis:* "Motifs are recycled with ironic effect throughout, allowing the story's casualties to haunt the grief-stricken survivor long after their deaths." Rich found the lyrics clever and never too sentimental, always carrying a harsh edge.

Rich led the way in praising Colm Wilkinson's performance, describing him as "convincingly brawny, Christlike without being cloying, enraged by injustice, paternal with children." He also admired Terrence Mann as Javert and Frances Ruffelle as Eponine, as well as Judy Kuhn as Cosette and Leo Burmester as Thénardier. He voiced complaints about Randy Graff's Fantine, David Bryant's Marius, and Jennifer Butt's Madame Thénardier, but these were Rich's only slight disappointments beyond a brief reference to undisclosed slow spots early in act 2. The power of the show in general was so strong, Rich argued, that the cast needed only to walk forward toward the dawn at the end of the show to convey perfectly a sense of hope for the future.[43]

Other important critics turned in rave or near-rave reviews, although, as several of them pointed out, it would probably make little difference what they said. As Jack Kroll described it in *Newsweek*, *Les Mis* would become a success based only on word of mouth. Even after the mixed reviews in London, it would still, he rightly predicted, become "the biggest hit in theater history" around the world. Kroll also correctly predicted that the show, which might seem a delightfully sentimental adaptation of an old-fashioned classic to us, would genuinely stir people to political action and social change in other countries.[44]

William A. Henry III of *Time*, who had admired *Les Mis* in London, now offered a slightly less glowing rave than Rich or Kroll, finding a few of the performances disappointing, although he admired Wilkinson's impressive ability to come across as both saintly and enraged. He argued that it mattered little if we never quite know what the students are fighting for; some sort of "generalized populist sentiment" is moving enough. The show's most impressive accomplishment, he felt, was its ability to convey a depressing story in which politics interrupts romances, the good die, and the bad thrive, and yet audiences leave feeling "exalted." The whole thing added up to a "thrilling emotional experience."[45]

Clive Barnes situated his positive review for the *New York Post* in an odd context. He argued, without quite stating it openly, that theater had been on a downward slide toward unimaginative lowbrow art for hundreds of years: "Go with the proper expectations, and you will have a lovely evening. And before we get stuffy about it, remember in the good old days you never went to Richard Rodgers expecting to hear Mozart"—meaning that Mozart is better than Rodgers, who in turn is better than Claude-Michel Schönberg? It was an odd argument from a theater critic who often embraced big, emotional musicals, and not just for their crowd-pleasing qualities, but as innovative, respectable art. Despite this curious stab at musical theater in general, Barnes called *Les Mis* "simply smashing" and "magnificent, red-blooded, two-fisted theater" that "lives up to its hype." He admired the staging and all the leading players, as well as the lyrics. He found the score rather monotonous, though, too full of a few "decent tunes" repeated far too often; he suggested, in a nasty backhanded compliment, that Schönberg could "even learn from Andrew Lloyd Webber."[46]

John Simon of *New York* gave *Les Misérables* the ultimate mixed review, declaring it half good. He found the plot too lurching, a quick trip through Hugo's highlights, and the score disappointed him. The second act entertained him far more than the first, and he found some cast members lacking. Some of the stage effects worked, others did not. The ending, he felt, was "too inspirational," by which one must assume he was left uninspired, rather than overly inspired.[47]

Considering Simon's pointed distaste for Lloyd Webber's megamusicals, this review could have been much worse.

Not surprisingly, Michael Feingold of the *Village Voice* led the negative reviews. Inclined to detest both Lloyd Webber and popular megamusicals in general, Feingold, unlike Rich, panned *Les Mis* as vehemently as he had its predecessors. In fact, Feingold scolded Rich in his review for enjoying "One Day More," and for daring to compare its technique to that used in the ensemble version of "Tonight" from *West Side Story*. Feingold opined that Hugo, a good author whose dramas could look great in the hands of talented adapters such as Verdi, fares poorly here. In a particularly mean-spirited mood, even for Feingold, he complimented yet insulted Schönberg condescendingly while sneaking in a tasteless jab at Lloyd Webber: "Though Claude-Michel Schönberg's music is to Verdi's as an ant is to the World Trade Center, he writes nicely shaped little tunes, much more listenable than Andrew Lloyd Webber's streams of musicalized pee. If they're mostly second-hand or unmemorable, their plainness suits Hugo's mawkish little-people attitude, and they keep the enormous, busy story rolling along." Unlike virtually all other critics, even those who disliked the show, Feingold found the staging an annoying series of tableaux, the sets the "most grandly wrongheaded of the production's hollow grandiosities." This led Feingold to his final point, that going to see *Les Mis* was, he felt, an action laden with social meaning for all who attended; in essence, only rich people go to see the show, and they do it to look good and feel good about themselves. The fact that most Broadway audiences are solidly middle-class or that his take on attending the show is as insulting and stereotyping to the poor as to the rich seems not to occur to him. "That throngs of affluent theatergoers will pay fifty dollars a pop to squint at a black hole full of poor people crawling over a huge junk sculpture seems to me the most hilarious specimen of radical chic in years," he explains. The show's "posture of proud poverty gladdens the heart of the wealthy, and makes the liberal mistake it for serious art. The poor, who like their theater full of color and liveliness, would know better."[48] Feingold was wrong, at least in several cases. When the Washington, D.C., company invited one hundred and fifty homeless people to a performance, the show's "toughest audience" gave quite positive reviews. One man noted, "It reminded me of a lot of things that I was going through: coming out of prison not having a job or a home . . . then having someone help me like that priest."[49] The social relevance to people around the world engaged in various economic, social, and political struggles would eventually become clear.

The few negative reviews had no effect on the success of the show. *Les Mis* was, briefly, the second-longest-running show to have played on Broadway (after

Cats, a record recently passed by *The Phantom of the Opera*), and it remains the most successful international musical of all time.

"Eternal Truths about Human Nature"

In a preview of the Tony Awards, *Les Misérables* won five Outer Critics' Circle Awards (which are voted on by journalists) in May 1987. Nominated for twelve Tonys, the show won eight: best musical, director (for which Nunn was also nominated that year for *Starlight Express*), book, score, scenic design, lighting design, best actress Ruffelle, and best supporting actor Michael Maguire as Enjorlas. Surprisingly, Colm Wilkinson lost best actor to Robert Lindsay of *Me and My Girl,* as did fellow nominee Terrence Mann. Judy Kuhn as Cosette lost best actress to fellow castmate Ruffelle; costume designer Adreane Neofitou also earned a nomination but no award.

Thanks to a perpetually sold out theater, *Les Mis* recouped its investment in an impressive twenty-three weeks, earning Mackintosh and his angels their $4.5 million back; everything earned since then has been profit. The *New York Times* attributed the financial success of the show to excellent word of mouth, the successful Washington, D.C., tryout, good reviews, and, as always with Mackintosh, publicity that began early and seemed relentless. The show's success led to strong sales of the American cast album, released in May 1987.[50]

The creative team behind the writing, staging, and producing of *Les Mis,* now veterans of the megamusical, always planned on sending the show around the world. Perhaps more than any other recent musical, they hoped, this one would translate well. Its themes of religion, forgiveness, and revolution for the sake of freedom seemed universal, despite their specifically French context. Certainly the actual translation of the lyrics would be tricky, but Mackintosh and company were committed to sending full productions to each foreign city, complete with moving barricade, carefully translated score, and full production staff. *Les Mis* in Japan, and in Japanese, seemed odd at first, but soon Mackintosh and the others developed smooth working methods for bringing the show into other cultures.

Les Mis has opened in more cities in less time than virtually any musical, and it has generated more income than any show of its time. Only a few musicals by Rodgers and Hammerstein, with a forty-year head start—but usually much less expensive tickets, even adjusting for inflation—have earned more money overall. The international success of *Les Mis* can be attributed to several factors already in place for megamusicals, but handled particularly well in this case. First, the plot and emotions translate into other cultures with remarkable effectiveness, so much so that the show has occasionally instigated political and social change. Mackintosh's marketing strategies also come into play in each new location as well; as it did in New York, Les Mis tends to become an event in any city that the locals feel they must experience. The lithograph of little Cosette's pitiful face is everywhere.

In its first ten years, Les Mis arrived in Tokyo, Tel Aviv, Budapest and Szeged in Hungary, Sydney, Reykjavik, Oslo, Osaka, Vienna, Toronto, Gdynia, Stockholm, Amsterdam, Brisbane, Auckland, Prague, Madrid, Copenhagen, Dublin, Edinburgh, the Philippines, Singapore, and Helsinki, among other locations. In some cities, especially those without experience in the Western musical theater tradition, the appointed directing and producing team did far more than mount the show in a local theater. They drastically altered and occasionally built theaters from scratch, and they trained local performers in the Broadway style of the show. The text, translated for each new language, had to remain true to the story and emotions of the original while making sense grammatically and culturally in its new locale. Tokyo, an extreme case in point, became host to a Les Mis "school," which trained performers in everything from singing, movement, and acting to French history, the notion of revolution, and the basics of Christianity in Europe. John Caird directed the production through a translator. It turned out to be an unprecedented hit.[51]

Occasionally, Les Mis has received a one-time staging for a special event; Mackintosh, for example, mounted an outdoor version in Australia in January 1989 to celebrate the country's independence on Australia Day. French and Australian patriotism blurred, in a telling example of the universal appeal of the themes in Les Mis. Cameras projecting images onto huge screens helped involve an audience of 125,000.[52]

In October 1991, Les Mis returned home, opening in Paris to uncharacteristically enthusiastic crowds and strong positive reviews in influential papers like Le Monde and Figaro. The expanded English version, retranslated into French, looked like it might finally win the French over to musicals of the English/American sort. Mackintosh and his team knew the step was a risk, but sixty other cities worldwide had already embraced the show thus far. Unfortunately, French audiences remained true to their tastes; after a strong first month, sales dropped off, and the show closed after seven months, suffering a loss of $3.7 million— the first time the show lost money. The New York Times speculated that despite consistently enthusiastic (if ever shrinking) audiences, word of mouth never gained enough momentum to overcome Parisians' general lack of enthusiasm for imported musical theater. Also, research suggested that the French resisted Les

Mis because it told a depressing and familiar story foisted on them as students, and seeing it in musicalized form did not appeal.[53]

Historian Mark Steyn points out that musicals with political themes (and political results) have arisen at various points in the past, but *Les Misérables* is a particularly strong example. While we might be cynical about seeing people wear the image of poor little Cosette on their overpriced T-shirts (a view certainly taken by Michael Feingold in his review in the *Village Voice,* for example), the show and its recognizable symbol served as a real call to arms in some Iron Curtain countries. In Poland, for example, the story struck independence-minded audiences as so relevant to their changing political situation that they used the image of Cosette superimposed not over a shredded French flag, but rather over the Solidarity flag.[54] When the events in China's Tiananmen Square became international news in June 1989, audiences and cast members felt a strong similarity between real life and the recreated historical events in the show. The company in Vienna, for example, dedicated a performance "to the memory of the Chinese people fighting for democracy."[55]

As *Les Mis* expanded around the world, it also traveled across the United States. Productions quickly opened in Boston, Los Angeles, Philadelphia, Chicago, Detroit, and Baltimore, among other urban centers, but Mackintosh also sent out an elaborate bus and truck tour. This road company was old-fashioned in that it traveled to smaller cities, lugging cast, crew, and set to areas that otherwise would not likely have had the exposure. But, remarkably, this included every element of the production, complete with full cast, orchestra, and revolving-barricade set. Audiences understood that they were getting the Broadway treatment, not a scaled-down version.[56] This stemmed not only from the commitment of Mackintosh, Nunn, and Caird to deliver a Broadway experience to every audience, but also from the team's desire for creative control. In order to keep the quality high, they reasoned, they would not simply license the rights to any interested group, but rather would authorize and monitor each new production themselves, supplying each with a now-standardized and easy-to-assemble set and a team of trained leaders. Caird defended the practice against charges that they stamped out productions like cars on an assembly line. Certainly this sort of quality control is better than allowing shoddy tours to go out, he argued; in addition, while the sets, makeup, and other technical elements remained the same, every cast is different. Each new company had the chance to improvise and become familiar with the story, just as Nunn and Caird did with the original RSC cast. Individual personalities were clear, Caird argued; he and the other consulting team members were there simply to make sure the turntable worked.[57]

Meanwhile, the Broadway production continued to roll on. Frank Rich visited the show after it had been running for a year, and enjoyed it just as much the second time.[58] After two years, the occasional ticket became available, but scalpers ran rampant. Mackintosh ran notices featuring the Cosette waif sporting a Mohawk haircut, urging patrons not to get scalped.[59] But in 1997, Mackintosh, Nunn, and Caird felt that in order to keep those seats filled, they needed to take a drastic step. In an unprecedented and highly controversial move, they fired much of the New York cast and replaced them with fresh faces, to revitalize the show on the occasion of its tenth anniversary on Broadway. Mackintosh and Caird had seen a disappointing performance in September 1996, and spent several weeks studying each cast member and working with the other producing and directing team members to evaluate what to do. Eventually, they fired twelve cast members, asked nine to reaudition for the same or other roles, and allowed nine to remain in their roles. The story broke in October 1996, and the current cast would stop performing the following January; the touring company would take over until March, when the new cast would "reopen" the show.

Some musicals have cast turnovers built into their performers' contracts, for the express purpose of keeping the production fresh, but this was not the case with *Les Mis.* Actors' Equity immediately raised protests and began investigating the legality of the move. But the inquiry revealed that Equity's executive secretary, Alan Eisenberg, actually knew of the impending firings for some weeks, and did not warn the cast, who now had an additional target for their anger. Legally, only those playing Valjean, Javert, and Fantine were considered "principal" roles, because all the other actors played multiple parts. Even those playing Cosette, Marius, and Eponine, who only appear late in the first act, pop up earlier in the show in the chorus. All three actors in principal roles had been about to renew their contracts, but Mackintosh, Nunn, and Caird invited only Christopher Innvar as Javert to do so. They demoted the current Valjean to his earlier set of roles in the chorus. In a lateral move, the woman playing Eponine took on Cosette; almost all the other featured roles were recast. Chorus members could not be fired without just cause, and this need for refreshment, Mackintosh admitted, did not qualify. As compensation, Mackintosh offered those who were let go the maximum severance pay plus $25,000. *New York Times* reporter Mel Gussow pointed out the impact this maneuver would have on these actors, many of whom had been in the company for nine years. Here were Broadway's hardest workers, playing multiple roles, largely uncredited, and paying their mortgages with their salaries.[60] But despite these sad tales of performers, the move appeared to have worked for the show.

Les Misérables reopened on its tenth anniversary, 12 March 1997. Peter Marks, now the chief drama critic for the *Times,* declared the recasting entirely necessary and quite successful. Just before the opening, he feared the changes would not help a show that looked boring, labored, and lacking in passion; he thought that no show, no matter how good the cast, could feel energetic after ten years. He lamented, "Old mega-musicals, it seems, never die. They just fade away."[61] But he cheerfully declared himself mistaken in his review, and found the show's original emotional impact entirely intact.[62] Perhaps most important, recasting and reopening served to remind potential new audience members of Les Mis's existence, generating a fresh wave of publicity and interest long after the show had settled into a quiet life as a seemingly permanent tourist attraction. Sixteen years is certainly almost permanent, in Broadway terms; Les Mis closed in May 2003, after 6,680 performances; it currently ranks as the third-longest-running show on Broadway, behind Phantom of the Opera and Cats. And if that were not enough, Cameron Mackintosh announced in early 2006 that the show would return to Broadway at the end of the year for a six-month run with the national touring company. The production re-creates the original Broadway version, but any show absent from New York for more than three years is eligible for the Tony Awards as a revival.

Productions continued to open abroad. Mackintosh generated excitement at home about foreign openings of Les Mis, which helped to support the notion that Les Mis was the event to see, no matter the location; by going, one participated in a worldwide cultural experience. When the show opened in Oslo, for example, the New York Times ran an ad that featured the waifish Cosette sporting a horned metal helmet over the headline, "invading Oslo tonight." The Tel Aviv opening inspired an image of Cosette in front of the Israeli flag, rather than the usual tattered French one. She gained earmuffs and a scarf for Reykjavik, a mountie uniform in Toronto, and a Sound of Music–like hill on which she cavorted for Vienna. For Australia, she was printed upside down.

Several other factors helped to make Les Mis an international cultural phenomenon. In 1988, David Caddick produced a recording of the complete score of Les Mis, performed by an international cast, marking the first time a mega-musical had been recorded in this way. Previous cast albums had included most of the music, but Les Misérables: The Complete Symphonic Recording, filling three compact discs, included every moment of the show. The London Philharmonic Orchestra backed up a cast assembled from productions in London, New York, Sydney, Los Angeles, and Tokyo; Caddick recorded the various performers separately and later put it all together. Gary Morris, a successful New York Valjean, sang the role in the recording, and Philip Quast of Australia sang Javert. Kaho Shimada, Eponine in Japan, learned her role in (slightly accented) English for the recording. Michael Ball, an original London cast member, returned as Marius.

Chorus members and bit players came from London and Los Angeles, making a total of seventy-five singers. While the availability of the complete work is a plus, the quality of the recording and the performances are uneven. Occasionally, the spliced-together nature becomes evident through changes in sound quality, and some of the performances are stiff and less impressive than those captured on recordings of performing casts.

Fast becoming an institution, *Les Mis* was celebrated with unprecedented pomp and circumstance upon the occasion of its tenth anniversary. Ten years to the day from its London opening at the Barbican, a group rightly billed as the "dream cast" gathered at Royal Albert Hall on 8 October 1995 for an elaborate concert performance. Colm Wilkinson, generally agreed to be the definitive Jean Valjean, reprised his role, as did favorite Marius Michael Ball. Eponine was played by a newer star, Lea Salonga, who had found fame in the second musical by Schönberg and Boublil to be given the British/American megamusical treatment, *Miss Saigon.* The cast, in full costume, sang oratorio-style, without staging. Images were projected behind them, and footage of staged versions was cut into the video version of the concert. The Royal Philharmonic Orchestra and a chorus of about two hundred and sixty, almost all of those who had ever been in the London production, completed the group. The evening closed with what proved to be a moving idea that inspired a half-hour standing ovation: seventeen Jean Valjeans, gathered from productions around the world, entered one at a time, each singing one line of "Do You Hear the People Sing?" in his native language. Despite some frustrating cuts in the score, the quality of this recording in audio or video format proves more satisfying (and more helpful for teaching purposes) than the complete symphonic version.

One final element that added to *Les Mis* becoming such a lasting cultural phenomenon is usually discussed with a rather cynical tone. From the beginning, and in each new city, Mackintosh's advertising and marketing machine proved remarkably effective. "More than any other musical," Joe Brown wrote in the *Washington Post,* " 'Les Miz' is marketed as an Event."[63] This self-proclaimed "musical sensation" has a certain "McMiz" feel to it, he argued, served up to seventy million audience members. The merchandise bearing Cosette's pouty face included all the usual suspects (sweatshirts, beach towels, a re-release of the novel in English), and was actually quite tastefully done, Brown felt. The difference between *Les Mis* and other megamusicals was not the merchandise or the pre-opening blitz of advertising, but the tone of the advertising that convinced millions that *Les Mis* was not just a musical, but a moving, powerful, life-changing journey. Promising this sort of atmosphere proved extremely effective in selling tickets, but had the show not delivered on its promise, the long runs in almost all cities around the world would not have happened. Again, the idea of spiritually themed oratorios and choral works comes to mind; like audiences attending performances of Handel's *Messiah* or Beethoven's Ninth Symphony, audiences at *Les Mis* speak of a spiritual uplifting and an emotional journey. The show proved as powerful as it claimed, judging from the unflagging attendance of audiences, and the idea of *Les Mis* as an event became self-perpetuating.

Les Mis, then, is a cultural institution thanks to a combination of international success, a plot that resonates with cultures worldwide, accessible and memorable music, the ability of productions to reach not only most countries but most little American towns, and the idea of *Les Mis* as an event (including occasions celebrating its milestones in grand fashion and the ever-vigilant marketing campaigns). Perhaps the most interesting and important aspect of the cultural life of this musical concerns its effects on world events and social issues. As already noted, *Les Mis* resonated with events in China and Poland, but more than just reflecting events, the show seems to do cultural work. Author Edward Behr notes that *Les Mis* has raised more money for charitable organizations than any other show. Various companies have contributed profits to the homeless, to victims of accidents and terrorism, to rain forest preservation, and to AIDS treatment. The themes of *Les Mis*—the call for social justice, the need for aid to the poor—often seem to speak directly to local or current situations. The AIDS crisis affected the Broadway community strongly, especially in the 1980s, and organizations trying to raise awareness and funding for AIDS embraced "Empty Chairs at Empty Tables" as one of their theme songs. It works remarkably well in that context.

Les Mis has found its way into American politics on several other occasions, its music used for rallies and gatherings. Most notably, *Les Mis* can claim credit for helping elect Bill Clinton president in 1992: campaigning in New Jersey, and knowing he needed that state's support to win, Clinton asked Mackintosh to lend him the Broadway cast. They sang "One day more! Clinton, Gore!" and helped lead Clinton to a victory in that state.[64]

Behr's book on *Les Mis* is meant for fans, and he gushes about the musical's wonderful attributes accordingly. But despite the sentimental language, his take on why *Les Mis* works as drama, why its impact has been the strongest of any musical internationally, has truth in it. First, he cites the show's themes of injustice and senseless death: "Though not all countries have directly experienced revolution, barricades or insurgencies, we can all identify with the social injustice *Les Misérables* condemns and we all aspire to the perfect world Victor Hugo hoped time would usher in. The memories of the dead linger in any society, in any family: we all feel guilt at one time or another for surviving adversity, disease or war, while others less lucky have perished." Behr goes on to describe that we all share in this "family of humankind," and that the show speaks to things beyond politics or even death: "The universal aspect of *Les Misérables,* though, has less to do with political upheavals and revolution than with the eternal truths about human nature—and belief in God. In essence, the story of Jean Valjean is that of a sudden, Pauline conversion, and a determination to retain the almost impossible ethical standards he has set himself. The quest for saintliness is the one thing all religions have in common."[65] It is likely, then, that any audience member with spiritual leanings can relate to Valjean's hope of redemption and his quest to do good for others. This combination of themes—overcoming social injustice, the call for freedom, the hope of a spiritual reward—is probably the most important factor in the success of *Les Mis.* Mackintosh, describing the appeal of *Les Mis,* similarly links it to the broad megamusical quality of its plot and themes: "Whatever their age, audiences all seem to appreciate *Les Misérables'* sweeping emotions, its powerful depiction of the human character and, above all, its uplifting example of man's ability to triumph over adversity."[66] Hugo himself had explained the nature of his story, in language more flowery than Behr's or Mackintosh's or that of any impressed critic, but that still manages to touch on these shared ideals. He wrote to a publisher:

> You are right, Sir, when you say "Les Misérables" is written for a universal audience. I do not know whether it will be read by everyone but it is meant for everyone. . . . Social problems go beyond frontiers. Humankind's wounds, those huge sores that litter the world, do not stop at the blue and red lines drawn on maps. Wherever men go in ignorance or despair, wherever women sell themselves for bread, wherever children lack a book to learn from or a warm hearth, "Les Misérables" knocks at the door and says: "open up, I am here for you."[67]

When the first national tour of *Les Mis* opened in Washington, D.C., *Washington Post* theater critic Joe Brown gave it a rave, because it told a great story in a great way. He recognized its megamusical elements, including an abundance of sentimental plot points with a story based on grand and simple ideas such as good, evil, and true love. He had even written his rather cynical article just the week before about the "McMiz"-like nature of the marketing machine behind this event. It won him over nonetheless. "Sure you're being manipulated," he noted. "But when has it been done this well?" With such effective staging and powerful performances, Brown could easily forgive the elements of the megamusical about which others chose to be cynical: "So let the nay-sayers call 'Les Miserables' a monolithic money-making machine. It is. But it deserves every centime it earns."[68]

5 "The Angel of Music Sings Songs in My Head"

The Phantom of the Opera

His face . . . looks like a mild case of albinism, with a few
blotches any dermatologist could cure.
Michael Feingold, "The Ghosts of Music Past," Village Voice

When [the Phantom's mask is] at long last removed, it
reveals something that looks like an unfinished face-lift, not
so much repulsive as improbable.
John Peter, "There Is a World Elsewhere," Sunday Times
(London)

What is it about this musical with a hero who has a face
like melted cheese, and a 1,000-pound chandelier for second
lead, that lures audiences in droves, including people who
rarely go to the theater?
Dinitia Smith, "The Chandelier That Earned $1.5 Billion,"
New York Times

As much as critics enjoy describing the Phantom's deformed face in colorful terms, people do not flock to see Andrew Lloyd Webber's megamusical *The Phantom of the Opera* for this sight. It could be argued that they go to see the chandelier, falling as it does almost on top of the front rows before veering toward the stage to land, but even this is a passing and entirely predictable thrill. They go, critics agree, to experience more pervasive qualities of the show: romance and lovely melodies. The latter quality had been in Lloyd Webber's work from the first, but the romantic, human, sometimes erotic story was a new feature. He wanted to write a romance, a story of grand emotions and intriguing characters. This work is a significant turning point in Lloyd Webber's career, marked both by a mature compositional style and a story with adult themes.

For their part, critics generally treated this show more kindly than the two preceding Lloyd Webber shows, *Cats* (the lack of plot in which seemed to disturb many) and *Starlight Express* (about which the critics were more justifiably hostile; unlike *Cats*, it has few redeeming qualities of music or lyrics and even less plot). Pre-opening hype about *Phantom* promised a gripping story with more intrigue and characterization than its predecessors, and lushly romantic music. In general, critics agreed that the musical fulfilled this promise of a richer, more satisfying evening.

Phantom was Lloyd Webber's first serious-tone book musical since *Evita* with Tim Rice; for all three of their collaborations, *Jesus Christ Superstar, Joseph and the Amazing Technicolor Dreamcoat,* and *Evita,* Rice had supplied the concept and a detailed book as well as the lyrics. While *Cats* and *Starlight Express* had been Lloyd Webber's ideas, the hands of directors, producers, and set designers can clearly be seen not only in the books, but in the shaping of the concepts. This time, Lloyd Webber stuck close to his source material and to his own vision. He found the original Gaston Leroux novel in a used bookstore, having already been pondering it as a subject for a musical, particularly because another musical version was already running. Its creator, Ken Hill, had asked Lloyd Webber's new young wife, singer/dancer Sarah Brightman, to play the lead, but her schedule did not allow for it. The story nevertheless drew Lloyd Webber's attention because it concerned real people in historical, romantic situations—not (as Michael Walsh puts it) the "gods, demigods, cats, and trains" about which he usually wrote.[1] It had been difficult for audiences to relate to many of his heroes, including the morally ambiguous Eva Peron and the string of entertaining but nonhuman, un-romantic cats and trains. The press often extended these troublesome qualities in his characters to descriptions of him: they depicted him as aloof, distant, and shy about expressing his affection for people, even his new wife. This show, he hoped, would be his romantic declaration, a heartfelt love triangle story that appealed to him not only for its romance in plot but in its overall musical style; he felt it called for a full symphony orchestra and allowed for some complex compositional devices, especially in ensembles. It also allowed him to cast his beautiful wife with her sweet soprano voice as the ingénue Christine.

Lloyd Webber began work on *Phantom* in the fall of 1984 by reassigning some melodies he had thought to use for another work still years in the future, *Aspects of Love.* He already had some basic ideas about how the book for a *Phantom* musical should be written, even before a lyricist and director came on board. His vision was truer to the Gaston Leroux novel than many movie versions had been. The original Phantom, like Lloyd Webber's, was deformed at birth and is a composer, architect, ventriloquist, and magician. He lives, of course, in the dark subterranean lairs beneath the Paris Opéra, from which vantage point he plays the organ, tutors a young chorus singer/dancer named Christine Daaé, with whom he is infatuated, and harasses the opera's managers and patrons. Eventually his love for Christine and his need to protect his strange way of life lead him to apply his considerable talents to several clever but brutal murders.

This is the stuff of pulp horror, and Leroux's novel was well received when it appeared in 1911. He was a journalist who often uncovered juicy investigative stories by using disguises and intrigue. This led to detective novels and romantic horror stories, serialized in newspapers. After visiting the Opéra and discovering the underground lake beneath the house, as well as the iron gates blocking off sections of the cavernous dark space, he began to write *The Phantom of the Opera.* The gates were left from when the unfinished Opéra had been used as storage for supplies, and possibly prisoners, during the Franco-Prussian War.[2] There had been a long delay in building the Opéra, which Leroux reasoned would give his fictional Erik the Phantom plenty of time to design and take up residence in his secret underground home. The story did well in serial form in France, England, and the United States, but was quickly forgotten as a novel until the movie version in 1924 starring Lon Chaney; Leroux died in 1927, having enjoyed an enormous rebirth in his novel's popularity in the wake of the film.[3]

Leroux tells the story in somewhat journalistic fashion, complete with realistic documents and testimony from key players. Lloyd Webber frames his story differently; the musical opens with an aged Raoul, Vicomte de Chagny, reflecting back on the strange events concerning the Opera Ghost, and the rest of the show is one large flashback (although told not from Raoul's or any one character's perspective; the later time period is never revisited). Lloyd Webber and his creative team eliminated some tangential characters and combined others, changes common to the musicalization of any source, but the show also contains lines taken word for word from the novel.

In Lloyd Webber's version, and to a slightly lesser degree in the novel, *Phantom* is basically a beauty and the beast story, a genre which (as one journalist pointed out) can end in two ways: either the girl kisses the beast and gets a prince, or the beast sacrifices himself so that the girl may have a normal love.[4] In this version we get both the kiss (but no prince) and the sacrifice, which lends a greater sense of romance than other versions of the story. Indeed, Lloyd Webber envisioned the story as primarily romantic, with the elements of horror lending an eerie atmosphere to the main love story. Focusing on the horror, particularly that of the Phantom's face, would be difficult for the audience to see; hence in the musical the unveiling of his disfigurement takes place in public so that the reaction of the other actors could fill in what the audience could not scrutinize. But his face, cheese-like or otherwise, was never the point. This Phantom was alluring, far more seductive than menacing to Christine, more of a "possible romantic alternative" than in the novel.[5] When she kisses him, we can see that she cares for him, but he realizes it comes from compassion, not love, and he sends her away with Raoul, her love interest and champion. (See appendix H for a full plot summary.)

Lloyd Webber began assembling his team with producer Cameron Mackintosh, and they first looked for a librettist. Tim Rice was already committed to his own new project, *Chess*. The legendary Alan Jay Lerner agreed to do it, but then fell ill after writing only a few lines. Lloyd Webber and Mackintosh then brought on board Richard Stilgoe, who had contributed a few lyrics to *Cats* and then served as the librettist for *Starlight Express*. He wrote the lyrics for the single "The Phantom of the Opera" (sung by Sarah Brightman and Steve Harley), released with great success in the spring of 1985, more than a year before the London opening. Stilgoe's talents, however, were best suited to molding the plot, not to writing the poetic, romantic lyrics the story required, so Mackintosh brought in Charles Hart, a twenty-four-year-old writer whose earlier work Mackintosh had seen in a competition. Although that work did not win and was never performed, Hart nevertheless impressed Mackintosh, and eventually Lloyd Webber as well. Hart wrote most of the libretto in about three months.[6] The love duet "All I Ask of You" was also successfully released as a single, recorded by Brightman and Cliff Richard, before the show had even had a run-through.

The run-through came at the Sydmonton Festival, the testing-ground concert series Lloyd Webber held every summer on his country estate. In July 1985, a rough act 1 was performed there to the delight of many—and to the shock of director Trevor Nunn. He had already written lyrics for the melodies he heard that day, but he thought they were to have been for *Aspects of Love*. Now Nunn, having directed *Cats* and *Starlight Express* and expecting to work on *Aspects,* hoped to roll with these changes and direct *Phantom*. But despite the fact that Nunn had lent Lloyd Webber the cast of the upcoming *Les Misérables* for the run-through at Sydmonton, including Colm Wilkinson as the Phantom, Lloyd Webber apparently had no intention of giving him the project. Instead Lloyd Webber chose perhaps the only director with a more solid reputation in musical theater (at least in America) than Nunn: Harold Prince. (Nunn would recover from the rejection and eventually direct *Aspects of Love* as well as *Sunset Boulevard*.)

At the time, however, Prince's reputation was perhaps not as glowing as it had once been; he had not had a hit in eight years, since Lloyd Webber's *Evita,* which was one of his few projects to that point not written by Stephen Sondheim or another American composer. As a London journalist pointed out at the time of Prince's work on *Phantom,* Prince previously "had always been identified with the opposition, Sondheim and Bernstein and a range of other American musicals. New York was the home of the musical. Eight years on, it feels very different. The balance of power in musical theatre has tilted across the Atlantic. Prince needs Lloyd Webber, not the other way about."[7] *The Phantom of the Opera,* therefore, came to be seen as Prince's comeback vehicle.

Prince's work had an enormous impact on the development of the show as well as on its ensuing success. The director jumped at the chance to direct a romantic musical, since he felt it was something the theater needed—something along the lines of *South Pacific,* which happened to be Lloyd Webber's favorite classic.[8] For inspiration Prince visited the Paris Opéra, discovering for himself the impressive lagoon several stories below the basement, the roof decorated with gilded statues, and the endless maze of nooks throughout the building in which, it was said, several scorned lovers had hanged themselves during the nineteenth century. The house boasts several thousand doors and six miles of underground passages, and is seventeen stories high, although it seats a relatively small 2,156.[9] Leroux describes much of this in his novel, but Prince, along with set designer Maria Björnson and lighting designer Andrew Bridge, still found the visit invaluable. The chandelier, the lobby staircase, the house itself, all became key elements of the musical.

It is easy to see why the house proved so inspirational. Construction had been underway for thirteen years, including several delays, when the Opéra was finally completed in 1875. Architect Charles Garnier unintentionally hit water beneath the site, but used it to his advantage: he created a permanent lake and used it to operate hydraulic stage machinery. After the house had been in operation for several years, accidents occurred that became the stuff of fiction. One of eight counterweights to the chandelier was severed by a fire in the fly space and fell into the audience, killing a woman. The performance that night, 20 May 1896, was Collasse's *Thétis and Pelée,* and the weight fell at the end of the first act. Leroux changed the weight to the chandelier itself and the opera to *Faust;* Lloyd Webber kept the chandelier but changed the opera to the fictional Mozart-like *Il muto.* There are other tales and mysterious secrets involving the Opéra. A man, rejected by a ballet girl, killed himself and willed his skeleton to the props department so that he might stay near his beloved. There is a room with a locked door but no doorknob that was decreed to remain shut until 2007.[10]

Such eerie but romantic tales, and the sensual atmosphere of the place, helped lead Prince to his most important revelation about what the show needed:

sex. It is an erotic tale, not just a romantic one, about a man longing for a lover, for someone to touch him for the first time in his life. Around this time, Prince saw a documentary about disabled people attempting to live their lives, including their sexual lives, normally and happily. The notion of the Phantom's search for sexual fulfillment helped not only to shape the show and the performances, but the sets as well; rich fabric drapes the stage, candles and shadows abound, the lighting is often quite dim and glowing, and the arch of the stage itself is framed by gilded statues of people who, as Prince pointed out, "if you look carefully, you realize are in various stages of ecstasy."[11] The research of Prince, set designer Björnson, and lighting designer Bridge in Paris became context over which they built a sensuous look of their own imaginations.

All this atmosphere required expensive and complex set and lighting design, something for which many critics had developed a distaste; spectacle, they felt, had been taking precedence over everything from plot to actors. Musical theater seemed dominated by laser beams and ramps for roller skates. Lloyd Webber and Prince were careful to keep *Phantom* from being overwhelmed by its spectacular elements, a criticism with which Lloyd Webber was all too familiar and with which Prince tended to agree. "I was tired of what spectacle had become," said Prince. "If this was spectacle, it was another kind, a romantic show with a sense of theatrical occasion and a Victorian feel to it."[12] Although Lloyd Webber would cheerfully work again with Trevor Nunn, he shied away at the moment from Nunn's impressive but sometimes superficial use of overwhelming sets and effects. Prince grounded his designs more in the drama and meant them to help create the dark and sexual mood of the show. Critics generally found the show as high-tech as any, but with a definite purpose; in fact, the show would probably not work without the rich visual atmosphere.

There are many impressive and beautiful visual moments in the show. Hundreds of candles rise from the water to surround the boat in the Phantom's lair. The Phantom vanishes into thin air and projects his voice around the theater. He leads Christine to his lair on a descending ramp that represents miles of underground passages. Raoul, pursuing the Phantom late in the show, jumps off one of the ramps and disappears into the water below. But none of these illusions is impossible to explain; they involve, in fact, basic tricks of staging such as lighting and trap doors, done with particular skill. More impressive and central to the show's overall impact are the ways in which Prince and his designers fill the stage with ever-changing spaces and movement. As Foster Hirsch points out, Prince "sculpts theatrical space and time, from scene to scene transforming the height and depth of the playing area as he divides and rearranges space, creates frames within frames as drapes descend from the flies, reverses perspective, and fuses episodes with fades, dissolves, montage effects, or abrupt cuts."[13] Prince also eliminated what little dialogue the show had in its early drafts, explaining that "the *size* of the way the story is told does not require dialogue."[14] Like other megamusicals, *Phantom* had a grand, epic feel as well as seamless, constantly underscored action that made dialogue seem out of place most of the time.

Lloyd Webber, Prince, and their team made several brilliant casting decisions that in true Lloyd Webber fashion helped in promoting the show. Casting Christine was never an issue; Lloyd Webber had composed the role for his new wife, Sarah Brightman. For the Phantom, the team made the surprising choice of Michael Crawford. Largely known for his comic roles on television and stage in England, Crawford had done his share of musicals, including *Barnum,* but was not considered a serious musical theater performer. Yet he had extensive formal vocal training, and his powerful acting would prove one of the highlights of the show. The role of Raoul went to American actor Steve Barton, whom the show's choreographer, Gillian Lynne, had recommended.

Lloyd Webber and his production team had hoped to open *Phantom* at the Palace Theatre in London, which, along with several other West End venues, Lloyd Webber now owned. But he had already promised the Palace to Cameron Mackintosh's *Les Misérables* when it moved out of the Barbican Theatre and into the West End. Lloyd Webber kept his deal with *Les Misérables* (and earned profits as the owner), and chose instead Her Majesty's Theatre for *Phantom*. As Lloyd Webber biographer Michael Coveney puts it, this resulted in the "triple whammy" of *Cats, Phantom,* and *Les Misérables* all in the West End together, as they would remain into the twenty-first century; they were "the three most successful musicals in history and the cultural indicator of the Thatcher boom years."[15]

Opening Nights and Sarah II

Opening night, 9 October 1986 at Her Majesty's Theatre, was greeted with an enthusiastic audience reception and generally good reviews. The cast album, released in January 1987, went platinum in a very impressive ten days. Advance sales boomed. The show won the Larry at that season's Laurence Olivier Awards, and another Larry went to star Michael Crawford, whose performance as the Phantom critics on both sides of the Atlantic generally hailed as brilliant. Sarah Brightman, nominated for her own Larry, lost.

Perhaps it would have helped coming events had she won. One of the key factors that made *Phantom* a megamusical was its pre-opening buzz, generated not just by marketing or the success of Lloyd Webber's previous shows, but by gossip, scandal, and casting problems. Brightman's presence in the role of Christine created an international scandal when Lloyd Webber and Mackintosh began planning the move to Broadway. The American Council of the Actors' Equity Association barred Brightman from playing her role in New York because it would contradict their policy of allowing only proven international stars to move with a production from a foreign country to New York. If the actor in a lead role was not internationally renowned, Actor's Equity could ban the performer and insist on an American (whether famous or not) in the role, so that an American could have the first crack at a potentially star-making or career-boosting turn. Michael Crawford, famous enough in both countries for a number of years, had no problem getting similar permission. Steve Barton was an American and so there was no issue. But Brightman, basically unknown in the United States as anything other than Lloyd Webber's wife, was not considered by Actors' Equity to be a big enough star to take such a plum role away from an American performer.

It was by no means the first time that Brightman had caused a scandal, at least in England. Known as "Sarah II" to the media there, she was Lloyd Webber's second wife; he had rather suddenly left his first wife, Sarah Hugill—dubbed "Sarah I"—for Brightman. Brightman and Lloyd Webber became regular tabloid subjects, their activities reported the way those of pop music and movie stars are in the United States. She was already working her way up the ladder in the theater at the time, but it was *Phantom* that launched her as a musical star. Casting her in the lead role was a bold move.

Lloyd Webber and Prince were furious with Actors' Equity for blocking Brightman's performance in New York; Lloyd Webber reportedly threatened to cancel the production. The conflict made the front page of the *New York Times* in June 1987, by which time Actors' Equity had already denied Brightman twice. Actors' Equity continued to argue that such a star-making role should go to an American, while Lloyd Webber and Prince argued that the role had been written for Brightman specifically and that she had performed it with great success in London. Prince even attempted to prove his point by holding auditions with dozens of women and then reasserting that Brightman was the best of the lot. Eventually Actors' Equity, knowing what a boon the show would be for the industry, gave in, but with stipulations. Brightman could play New York for six months, and the producers would have to give a leading role in a new London production to an American sometime in the next three years.[16]

Just as the conflict was nearing resolution, an influential and familiar voice entered the picture: Frank Rich, chief theater critic for the *New York Times*. He had already reviewed the London production which, true to form regarding Lloyd Webber, he found generally unfavorable, although he praised Prince. Neither he nor anyone else would review the New York opening for another seven months. But having seen in London both Brightman and her replacement, who played the role for two of the eight shows a week, he weighed in on the difference between the two women: "There wasn't any." The show continued to sell out in London without Brightman, and the real stars, Rich asserted, were Crawford and the sets. "So why has everyone been in such a tizzy about a casting question that will have no effect on the artistic or economic health of a production? I would list the following factors (not necessarily in order of importance): Ego, marital devotion, xenophobia, labor-management negotiating tactics."[17] It came down to power, Rich argued. The producers assumed their leading lady was everyone's star, and American Actors' Equity did not want to be manipulated or bullied. He felt it was also about international rivalry: the Americans resented the recent dominance of British musicals on home turf, and the British pushed to make their control more complete. The case of Sarah Brightman became a miniature version of the larger co-dependent rivalry between New York and London that had arisen in the 1980s. Rich correctly predicted that the show would indeed open, and open with Brightman, because everyone would lose too much money if it did not open at all, or if the now-famous Brightman did not come with it. In the end, the whole scandal fell into the no-publicity-is-bad-publicity category, with the exception of some pre-formed biases against Brightman's performance.

Previews in New York began on 9 January 1988, with opening night on 26 January at the Shubert-owned Majestic Theater. The show had already taken in about $16 million in pre-sales, breaking the record of *Les Misérables* by a good four million dollars, thanks to a massive publicity campaign engineered by Mackintosh. *Phantom* landed on the covers of *Time* and *New York* and gained a great deal of television time. The show broke first-day ticket sales records, and by opening night not a seat was available for almost a year; at present writing, the house sells out regularly and tickets are virtually never offered at a discount. Since its opening, it has run in sixty cities in fourteen countries, earning about two billion dollars.[18] It won seven Tony Awards, including Best Musical, Best Actor in a Musical (Crawford), and Best Director (Prince, his record-breaking sixteenth Tony). Sarah Brightman did not receive a nomination.[19]

The Score: Help Me Make the Music of the Night; or, What Do We Mean by Opera, Anyway?

OPERATIC FEATURES, OPERA SCENES

Andrew Lloyd Webber expressed ambivalence about the use of the word "opera" in regard to both *The Phantom of the Opera* and to new musical theater generally. Nevertheless, the word hovered around pre-opening discussions of *Phantom* and remained prominent in reviews. Several characteristics make *Phantom* seem operatic, both to those who know opera and to those who do not. The score, like all of Lloyd Webber's up to this point, features very little dialogue; a few short conversations transpire over underscoring, but almost everything is sung. As discussed regarding *Jesus Christ Superstar,* the lack of spoken dialogue does not make a show an opera, but it generally makes the show feel more like an opera than a musical comedy to most critics and audiences. The cast also features several operatic voices. Scenes and songs often run together, becoming large complexes of numbers with unclear beginnings and ends, a technique that served Puccini well. Motifs and recurring musical themes, ranging from the catchy and transparent to the complex and dissonant, tie together numbers, sections, and whole scenes, and most of the fragments undergo significant changes in context, form, or meaning. Such devices bring Wagner to mind. Several ensemble numbers grow from one player to two, then three, until eventually seven characters express seven different texts simultaneously, very much like ensembles in Verdi's or Mozart's operas.

But perhaps most important, two factors caused the word "opera" to hover around *Phantom.* First, the pre-opening hype and the ensuing reviews all commented on an apparent leap in sophistication that Lloyd Webber had made. The media hailed the show as his most mature, well-crafted work to date, and not just because it told a human love story rather than a children's tale like *Starlight Express.* Critics, even those not particularly well trained in music, understood that the score was more musically rich than Lloyd Webber's others, with its motifs, polyphonic ensembles, and large scene structures. Critics and scholars made a link, therefore, between "sophisticated" and "opera." The use of operatic elements in the score may have simply been coincidental to the maturing of Lloyd Webber's style, but the two notions were irrevocably linked. One critic noted the "shift toward classical seriousness" that this show, along with Lloyd Webber's *Variations* and *Requiem,* demonstrated.[20]

Critics debated whether *Phantom* could be considered a new opera, and whether musical theater generally was a modern take on the operatic tradition.

Lloyd Webber made his view clear: "What do we mean by opera, anyway? And where does that put *Phantom*? Obviously there is a world of difference between *Phantom* and something like *Sugar Babies*. But there is no difference today between opera and serious musical theater."[21] If *Sugar Babies* represented nonserious musical theater, by which Lloyd Webber implies a more traditionally structured stop-and-sing musical comedy, then his new definition of opera/serious musical theater helps his effort to win critical respect. This category of opera-like "serious musical theater" would include not only *Phantom* and perhaps his *Jesus Christ Superstar* and *Evita*, but also *Les Misérables* and many sung-through, serious-minded megamusicals yet to come. Lloyd Webber agreed *Phantom* was basically an opera, but he preferred to have it stand as a Broadway show, as that had always been his field, and he chose the devils he knew (theater critics) over those he did not (opera critics).[22]

Theater critics, even those who did not fully embrace *Phantom*, agreed the score was Lloyd Webber's most sophisticated and "serious" to date, embracing Lloyd Webber's link between sung-through musicals and (according to Lloyd Webber) the parallel sophistication of opera. Biographer Michael Walsh declares that the score "represents such a leap beyond anything he had done to that point that it can only be explained as one of those periodic quantum leaps that every real artist makes in his art."[23] Mark Steyn argues that *Phantom* is Lloyd Webber's best score because the material suited his musical style so well: "Greatest score? Yes, because this story and these characters were perfectly matched to his broad, sweeping, soaring melodies. *Aspects* needed someone more cynical, *Sunset* someone more psychological; but *Phantom* was made for him: Lloyd Webber made the show sing, full-throated and open-vowelled."[24]

Steyn has a point, in that Lloyd Webber had always been drawn to romantic nineteenth-century opera, especially Puccini, as in his deliberate Puccini parody in "Growltiger's Last Stand" from *Cats*. The nineteenth-century Parisian setting of *Phantom* allowed Lloyd Webber to give full vent to his taste for romantic melody, true love, and lush orchestration. Critics began to talk not of pastiche, but of a new Lloyd Webber style, one that was his own, built up from elements of other styles in a sophisticated, integrated way. A critic for *Opera News* explained,

> Lloyd Webber's emotional, well-orchestrated score is his most satisfying to date, and his richest. He has absorbed the eclectic nineteenth-century opera idiom and built upon it a personal one that is at once fresh and appropriate to the period setting, supporting the drama on a stream of melodic inspiration that Broadway and the opera would have thirsted for. . . . Lloyd Webber unabashedly

follows his lyrical impulse and develops his thematic material with artistic integrity and craftsmanship along traditional lines of serious composition.[25]

Walsh calls *Phantom* "the gauntlet that Lloyd Webber has thrown down to challenge his critics to take him seriously,"[26] and for the most part, they did.

The second and more obvious reason that the idea of opera seems important in *Phantom* is that the musical takes place in the Paris Opéra in 1861, so the show is steeped in the atmosphere of French Romantic opera. The story concerns an opera singer/dancer, surrounded by other performers, the house's managers, and the opera house itself. Their world is the world of opera. Also, the score provides the audience with three performances by the opera company, so we actually see them at work, presenting a scene from a fairly contemporaneous grand opera, another from an Italian eighteenth-century *opera buffa,* and a third from a new opera written by the Phantom.

So Lloyd Webber wrote pastiches. He dove into that most risky of territories, and wrote scenes as close to the style of operatic tradition as he could. The theater critics, generally not as versed in opera as Lloyd Webber, rarely understood whom he parodied, and usually dismissed these scenes as frivolous, but they actually work quite well as operatic pastiches. When critics did bring up the word "pastiche," it was often in conjunction with a melody from the score that reminded them of another Broadway showtune; the opening of "The Music of the Night," for example, seemed to many remarkably like the opening of "Come to Me, Bend to Me" from *Brigadoon.*[27]

When the setting first shifts from the opening scene at the auction to the opera house in its glory days of 1861, the first thing we see is a scene from the grand opera *Hannibal* by a fictional French composer, Chalumeau. Carlotta, the diva of the company playing the Queen of Carthage, sings a flowery cadenza while holding a severed and bleeding head—a gift from her lover, Hannibal. He is returning to Carthage to free it from the conquering Romans, and the head suggests he has been victorious thus far. Carlotta's coloratura is overblown and shrill, characteristics that hold true for her vocal style throughout the show, whether she is performing in an opera or not.

French grand opera is reflected here in the elaborate sets and large ensemble, complete with ballet dancing slave girls, among them Meg and Christine. The backdrop features a desert landscape with palm trees and two enormous sphinx-like statues of animal-gods. When the character of Piangi enters playing the role of Hannibal, he rides a huge mechanical elephant. Lloyd Webber compresses a number of musical elements into this one scene, items that would each, in an actual grand opera, make up entire numbers. Piangi sings a recitative, then the slave girls launch into a ballet, and everyone offers choral comments. Piangi and Carlotta share a florid moment of duet, and the whole thing drives to a triumphant finish in honor of Hannibal with a final stage picture. But this is just a rehearsal, so when the scene finishes, everyone falls out of character and the elephant, which we can now see is being operated by two stagehands sitting inside it, is rolled offstage. As Walsh points out, Lloyd Webber surely found satisfaction in writing like Meyerbeer: "The charge of being a pastiche artist had dogged Lloyd Webber for so long that it must have amused him to embrace it wholeheartedly in a work that, paradoxically, turned out to be his most original score. The *Hannibal* scene is mock-Meyerbeer (an inside joke since Meyerbeer is practically synonymous with second-rate, overblown opera)."[28]

The new managers of the opera house, Messieurs Firmin and André, ask La Carlotta to sing an aria from act 3 of *Hannibal,* and she begins "Think of Me." Musically, the song seems out of step with what we have heard of this opera so far, with its gentle melody and tasteful decorative touches. It is definitely more parlor chanson than operatic aria.[29] But it serves mostly as a plot point, to allow Carlotta to be replaced by Christine (for whose voice the song is, conveniently, much better suited, especially when transposed down a major third for her) and thereafter to allow Christine to move from rehearsal to successful performance.

The second opera parody comes at the end of *Phantom's* first act. *Il muto,* by the supposedly well known (but fictional) Italian composer Albrizzio, is an *opera buffa* in the style of Mozart or Salieri. In terms of plot, it bears a strong resemblance to Mozart's *The Marriage of Figaro,* with which some *Phantom* audience members would be familiar, but the plot devices were common enough in other *buffa* works of the time as well. Several scholars argue that Salieri is Lloyd Webber's more likely target, for two reasons: his modern-day reputation as a second-rate Mozart makes him a more likely subject for parody, and—in something of a reversal of the previous point—Salieri was popular at the Paris Opéra in the late eighteenth and early nineteenth century.[30]

Despite the Phantom's explicit demand that Christine play the lead, the opera's managers cast Carlotta as the Countess, and Christine, as the mute of the opera's title, plays a trouser role, the Countess's young pageboy Serafimo (similar to Mozart's Cherubino in *The Marriage of Figaro*). The scene we see also features a lady friend of the Countess, two foppish male companions—a hairdresser and a jeweler—and the jeweler's assistant, played by Meg. The Countess sports an aristocratic lace-covered ensemble with an enormous skirt, and her two male friends preen in powdered wigs and shiny knee breeches. Christine wears a maid's dress over her pageboy costume, as she is currently in disguise to fool the Countess's husband, Don Attilio, played by the Italian star tenor Piangi.

To the accompaniment of a stately, dotted-rhythm orchestral introduction, the rising curtain reveals a fancy salon with a bed at the back. After a brief vamp introduction, the group snickers about the escapades in which they engage under the unsuspecting nose of the Count. Upon his entrance, the Count and the Countess exchange some recitative, both *secco* and accompanied, during which the Count announces he must depart on a trip. The Countess plans to use the opportunity to have an affair with young Serafimo, but the Count, not as foolish as everyone suspects, has actually set up a test of loyalty; he plans to hide and observe his wife's antics. (This testing of loyalty resembles another Mozart *opera buffa, Così fan tutte.*) After a flourish of "addio, addio" in decorated recitative, the Count exits, and Carlotta sings a brief recitative before launching into her aria, "Poor Fool, He Makes Me Laugh" (see ex. 5.1). The musical style certainly recalls classical norms, with typical shifts of harmony in the recitative, accompanied by a harpsichord and occasional string comments, and the aria's generally square phrase pattern. The introductory orchestral vamp, still popular through Verdi's day, leads to a bouncy *buffa* melody. Carlotta's coloratura is reminiscent of the vocal acrobatics of, for example, the evil Queen of the Night in Mozart's German *singspiel, The Magic Flute,* but in this much lighter context the virtuosic nature of the passage reflects both Carlotta and her role. As in *Hannibal,* Lloyd Webber compresses musical events, bringing the chorus into what otherwise might have been a full-length aria.

But the ensemble barely has time to settle in when the annoyed Phantom interrupts them. His disembodied voice reminds the performers, as well as the managers and Raoul, that Raoul is occupying his private box in the audience—and that Carlotta is playing Christine's role. Carlotta regains her composure and begins the aria again, but she becomes the locus of the Phantom's threats when she makes a loud croaking sound in the middle of a line. When the croaking continues, Carlotta's performance falls apart, as do the other performances and eventually the set—which reveals the dead body of the stagehand Buquet. We get no more of *Il muto;* when Christine takes over for the Countess after "All I Ask of You," she sports the huge embroidered dress but is already taking her bows and then avoiding the plunging chandelier.

Carlotta and Piangi, as befits both their performance skills and their caricatured personalities, have big operatic voices throughout *Phantom,* not just in their operatic performances. Carlotta especially puts this to good use in group scenes, when she wishes to be heard (usually complaining) over the others. Christine, both because she is the ingénue and because Lloyd Webber wrote the role for Sarah Brightman, has a lighter, lyric soprano voice. Raoul is a strapping

Example 5.1. "Poor Fool, He Makes Me Laugh" from *Il muto*

Example 5.1. (*continued*)

Broadway tenor, not operatic but not pop-style either, and the Phantom himself mostly sings in the tenor range, often so high that falsetto is required. The rest of the voices resemble Raoul's in style: theater voices, big and flexible, with occasional tips toward the operatic and a complete absence of pop elements. This was a change for Lloyd Webber, whose musicals until now had been almost entirely populated by pop voices (or a mixture of pop and theater voices), but such was Sarah Brightman's influence on him. Also, the cleaner, straightforward theater voices with their light operatic flavor sounded more appropriate in the context of the story than rock-influenced singing would have. Perhaps most important, Lloyd Webber's use of "serious" voices served as one of many signals that he meant *Phantom* to be taken as his most mature and sophisticated score.

CONTINUAL AND RECURRING MUSIC

Sophistication, or at least intricacy, is indeed evident in a number of the score's features, perhaps most obvious in the fact that the music is nearly continuous throughout. Many numbers feature only vague beginnings or ends and run without pause into the next number, with the result that much of the score cannot be divided into set pieces at all. A continuous string of material moves the story from event to event. Even the true set numbers rarely allow for applause afterward, either because transitional, recitative-like music or underscoring begins immediately, or because the music gives no clear cue to the audience. *Phantom* does contain occasional, brief spoken dialogue, but almost always accompanies it with orchestral underscoring that then leads into more singing. The staging greatly reinforces this musical continuity, often accomplishing set changes in the middle of numbers; at only one point in the entire show, before the first "Notes," is there a slight pause in the score as well as a significant set change. When the music does provide full closure to a number and the audience gets the rare opportunity to interrupt the mood with applause, the set does not change; rather, the actors simply pause, then continue. Such moments occur, for example, after "The Music of the Night," "All I Ask of You," and "Wishing You Were Somehow Here Again." A similar continuity of action carries *Les Misérables* along; in fact, its creators, Schönberg and Boublil, having been influenced by Lloyd Webber's early sung-through scores, wrote a more smoothly continuous score than anything Lloyd Webber had done until *Phantom*—which followed *Les Misérables* by a year. No evidence suggests that Lloyd Webber was influenced by the structure of *Les Misérables;* he claimed not to like the show much, and he had composed parts of *Phantom* long before his exposure to the other work. Nevertheless, the structural devices the shows share are striking, and it is possible that Lloyd Webber felt the influence of *Les Mis* in some way.

Phantom's opening group of numbers, glued together by various transitional materials, carries the audience along most energetically of any section of the score. The first scene at the auction, which contains bits of singing, underscoring, and dialogue, moves into the orchestral overture quite suddenly, with a burst of light from the chandelier. The overture stops abruptly, incomplete, and Carlotta steps in immediately, with the end of her cadenza from *Hannibal.* The audience sometimes applauds the grand finish to Hannibal's entrance scene, but the actors have already broken character and the new managers begin their dialogue over orchestral underscoring. This leads into "Think of Me," during which days pass, Raoul is introduced, and the set changes from rehearsal to performance, then to a reverse view of that performance from backstage. The applause the actual audience gives Christine merges with the applause of the invisible, upstage attendants of the Paris Opéra, and Madame Giry continues the backstage scene. The Phantom's disembodied voice sings its praise for Christine's performance as she enters her dressing room, which leads immediately to "Angel of Music." This fizzles off into dialogue and underscoring, which then builds again into Christine and Raoul's singing about their fond memories of childhood stories about Little Lotte. A few lines of dialogue and some thematic transformations in the orchestra lead back into "Angel of Music," which connects without pause to "The Phantom of the Opera" thanks to a bass line that bridges the two. During the course of this number, the Phantom lures Christine through her dressing room mirror into his underground world; it takes them most of the song to descend a series of ramps through the mist and shadows. Toward the end they arrive in his lair via boat, and the Phantom encourages Christine to sing with all her might. She ends "The Phantom of the Opera" on a desperate, strangely spellbound high E, now that she is caught in his trap and will do his bidding. Before her note can fully die away, the Phantom launches into an introductory section of material that sets up "The Music of the Night."

At the soft but definitive close of this number, the audience has its first chance to applaud the show itself, rather than a show within the show. The Phantom and Christine (with the help of the lighting designer) use these few moments to show that night has passed, and Christine awakens to underscoring and lighting that suggest it is now the next morning. A series of small sections of music lead to "Stranger Than You Dreamt It," which, at long last, ends with both a clear cadence and a set change. This entire sequence of numbers carries the audience along through set changes and plot development, all smoothly conveyed through the virtually seamless combination of set pieces and linking material. In fact, this whole dramatic arc covers about half the entire first act.

In most cases, Lloyd Webber glues the more number-like material together with various kinds of recurring musical ideas. As we have seen, Lloyd Webber is well known (and often berated) for revisiting a melody several times in a show. In *Jesus Christ Superstar,* entire songs return with new words. In *Cats,* Lloyd Webber developed a technique that involved a combination of recurring songs (such as "Memory") and more flexible, changeable motifs (such as the Jellicle theme). In *The Phantom of the Opera,* the balance tips significantly toward the use of developing motif material and away from full melodic reprises. Often the recurring material is dissonant, highly altered, buried under layers of other material, or otherwise easily overlooked; very few critics or historians have commented on any but the most obvious of themes. Yet these less catchy recurring motifs carry large portions of the show and work in intricate ways. Below, we look at three kinds of recurring musical material: a few traditional reprises, several short and catchy motifs, and a number of longer, less fixed motivic ideas.

Lloyd Webber does revisit whole melodies on a few occasions, but never in the teasing way of "Memory" in *Cats* or the somewhat unjustified way of "Strange Thing, Mystifying" and "Peter's Denial" in *Jesus Christ Superstar.* Here, full reprises of melodies occur in quite traditional musical theater settings: the Phantom, for example, reprises Christine and Raoul's love song, "All I Ask of You," when he begs Christine to love him after his unmasking. The love duet also returns at the very end of the show, as Raoul and Christine float out of the Phantom's lair to begin their life together. Similarly, the Phantom revisits "Angel of Music," the song by which he flattered and seduced Christine into his world, when he attempts to win her back in the graveyard scene. Here the melody eventually blurs into the trio among the Phantom, Raoul, and Christine. Conversely, "Angel of Music" emerges from their second trio, in the Phantom's lair just before Christine kisses him. Christine begins the tune while the trio is at its point of maximum chaos, and its shape only becomes clear when the others drop out. The tune then carries her from the trio into the climactic orchestral music of their kiss. In this reversal of roles, in which Christine shows her affection for the Phantom instead of the other way around, the use of their quasi-love song makes sense. Similar instances of recurring recognizable melodies from set numbers include "The Phantom of the Opera" and "Masquerade" (see appendix I for a listing of these and all other types of recurring musical material).

Full melodic reprises, however, are few in number compared to the recurrence of two other sorts of musical material. In the first sort, Lloyd Webber provides the audience with perhaps the most recognizable and understood kind of recurring music: a short, catchy theme or motif with obvious ties to plot or character, not dissimilar to Wagner's use of motifs. The most striking motif is the Phantom's trademark chromatic scale, harmonized and usually played on the organ. It signals that he has done or is doing something violent or frightening; in fact, the motif is so obvious and uncomplicated that one must assume Lloyd Webber meant it as a kind of melodrama or horror movie reference. It is easy to imagine this motif accompanying the silent film version of this story, and it seems in keeping with the period setting of the show. In the first instance of this motif meant to suggest horror, the auctioneer in the opening scene reminds us of the strange tale of the Phantom, and the chandelier suddenly bursts into light; the organ scale accompanies the moment. Similarly, as the Phantom lures Christine through her dressing room mirror, the chromatic-scale chords introduce (and appear periodically throughout) "The Phantom of the Opera" (see ex. 5.2).

Several times, when characters fail to do the Phantom's bidding, his menacing motif interrupts the endings of their ensemble numbers, as he scolds them for their disobedience and vows retribution. "Prima Donna" ends with the ensemble in agreement about how to proceed, namely with the casting of Carlotta rather than Christine in the lead role of *Il muto,* but their final chord is overrun by the Phantom's chromatic scale, running up and down without rests, and the Phantom's voice: "So, it is to be war between us. If these demands are not met, a disaster beyond your imagination will occur!" The group reasserts its final cadence, but the Phantom and his motif have effectively shattered their good mood. The Phantom and his chromatic scale similarly step on the ending of "Masquerade," interrupting the party and presenting a new set of demands. The motif also appears when the Phantom's violence takes control of the action, such as when a falling set reveals the body of Buquet, or when the chandelier shakes and falls to the stage. The motif therefore becomes firmly associated with the Phantom's violence and anger, but also with the more melodramatic horror-story moments of the show, so that when it appears once again as Christine reveals

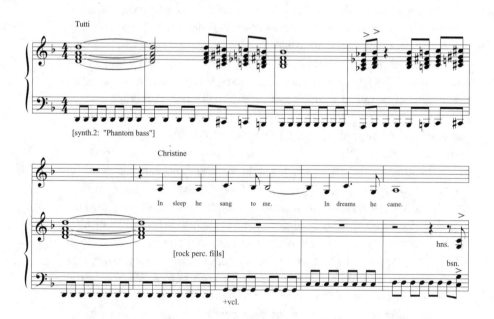

Example 5.2. "The Phantom of the Opera"

the Phantom's face to the world, it helps to trigger gasps of shock and fear. As noted, the unveiling is public because the audience cannot see the hideous face in close-up, so they take their cue from the actors. The presence of the motif that represents the evil, frightening side of the Phantom surely aids this moment greatly—it has become a musical signal for horror.

A similarly melodramatic short phrase, also tied to the horrors of the Phantom, seems to have been invented by the twittering, superstition-prone, ballet girls. They, and eventually the whole chorus, intone "He's here, the Phantom of the opera," when they feel the Phantom's presence and experience chills of apprehension (see ex. 5.3). It returns, sung by an eerie offstage chorus, during "The Phantom of the Opera," and again at moments when characters sense the Phantom's presence, such as when his disgruntled voice interrupts *Il muto.* Sharing a pounding bass line similar to that which carries the overture and "The Phantom of the Opera," this phrase from the orchestra accompanies the Phantom's disembodied voice as he booms, "Did I not instruct that Box Five was to be kept empty?" Meg then sings the phrase in her breathless young voice, in one of many places in which she, the leader of the frightened ballet girls, represents their fear. These two Phantom-related motifs are the only ones that work in such an obvious, button-pushing sort of way; clearly Lloyd Webber meant them to sound melodramatic, like an old monster movie, as well as appropriate to the more gullible, superstitious, and nervous characters in the show.

Perhaps the most complex and abundant kind of musical manipulation takes the form of more melodically disjunct, less recognizable musical material that returns, serves as transition, and mutates. Less memorable than the tunes of the set numbers, and less obvious than the catchy short motifs discussed above, these materials are less easily detected by the audience and the critics. Yet they make up a vast amount of the music at work here, and Lloyd Webber transforms them in complicated ways. The most prominent of these changeable motifs is one that I have labeled the "story motif," due to its usual association with

Example 5.3. The phrase "He's here, the Phantom of the Opera"

various kinds of narration or exposition. It often functions as a kind of recitative, not only because it furthers the plot at times, but because it sometimes has a free meter or loose tempo, allowing the lyrics to be sung in natural speech rhythms.

The story motif makes its first appearance in the first sung notes of the show, as an aged Raoul contemplates the music box said to have come from the Phantom's lair (and which has just played a tinny version of "Masquerade"):

> A collector's piece indeed.
> Every detail exactly as she said
> She often spoke of you, my friend
> Your velvet lining, and your figurine of lead
> Will you still play, when all the rest of us are dead?

From this we learn that Christine told Raoul of the figurine she saw in the Phantom's lair, and apparently that Christine has died. Next, the theme functions as exposition for Buquet, who sings it while explaining that the fallen piece of scenery which has just interrupted the *Hannibal* rehearsal is not his fault, but the opera ghost's. This inspires Meg to intone "He's there, the Phantom of the opera." Buquet sings the motif in strict time over an eerie vamp. It next appears as underscoring, in trumpet, harp, violins, and violas, as Christine dazedly reads a letter from Raoul in her dressing room while still confused by the Phantom's role in her first triumphant performance.

The next appearance of the story motif is framed by several other short recurring themes, in an excellent example of Lloyd Webber's segue technique. "The Music of the Night" has concluded, and morning comes to the Phantom's lair. The Phantom plays passages on his organ from what will become *Don Juan Triumphant,* and when he stops suddenly, the music box resting by Christine spontaneously begins to play "Masquerade," which will not be heard in full until the top of the second act. When this fizzles out, an ostinato similar to that which accompanied Buquet begins in the strings, and Christine, beginning to come to her senses after her dream-like evening with the Phantom, begins to piece things together using the story motif.

> I remember there was mist,
> Swirling mist upon a vast, glassy lake.
> There were candles all around
> And on the lake there was a boat
> And in the boat there was a man.

This cues a solo violin, symbolic of Christine's violinist father, playing "Angel of Music." Christine picks up the melody as she approaches the mysterious Phantom: "Who was that shape in the shadows? / Whose is the face in the mask?" She sneaks up behind him and unmasks him, and he rounds on her with a hollered "Damn you!" His subsequent lines present a melody that will be altered slightly to become the first theme of "Notes" in the next scene. This moment, then, features portions of "Masquerade," "Angel of Music," and "Notes," as well as a full statement of the story motif.

But several of these seemingly disjunct passages stem from the same source. Both the Phantom's "Damn you!" and the first theme of "Notes" are based on the same musical idea, derived from the story motif. The story motif outlines the interval of a perfect fifth, and briefly visits another perfect fifth, a whole step below it. Christine's vocal line (in the "I remember there was mist" section) outlines the E-B fifth and visits D-A. The Phantom's enraged reaction to his surprise unmasking more closely resembles the theme in "Notes" than the story motif, but it also serves to carry the idea of descending fifths from one home to the next. His short outburst ends with two sets of fifths a whole step apart as he yells, "Damn you! Curse you!" This simplified take on the fifths has a life of its own in the form of another motif, to which we turn in a moment.

The story motif, being the most common and changeable of linked material in the show, appears not only in its own recognizable form but in the melodies of set numbers such as "Notes" and in significantly altered forms as well. It also appears in what can be thought of as its full form, with a second consequent section added to the first (see ex. 5.4). The Phantom most often sings this form, especially when he instructs his managers and actors in his disembodied, echoing voice. The first such instance occurs during the first "Notes" number, in which the agitated André, Firmin, Raoul, Carlotta, Piangi, Madame Giry, and Meg have all assembled to sort out the enigmatic letters the Phantom has sent them. The crucial one has gone to Madame Giry, the Phantom's most loyal servant, and as she reads it, the ostinato begins and the Phantom's voice takes over for her as all gaze around in wonder. The Phantom here outlines the fifth E-B and subsides to the fifth D-A, just as Christine's version had done. The presence of the story motif in this context not only reflects the other occasions in which it is used to narrate or underscore the reading of letters, it also grows out of the first melody of the very song which it interrupts, "Notes," with its similarly paired fifths (see ex. 5.5).

The story motif appears, in sizes from tiny to full, throughout the musical. For example, the second part of the motif, with its series of steps down, appears in *Don Juan Triumphant* as well as late in the show as Christine angrily arrives in the Phantom's lair for the final time. The first phrase of the motif once appears by itself as a frantic snippet of advice: when Madame Giry sends Raoul down

Example 5.4. Story motif in Phantom's letter in "Notes"

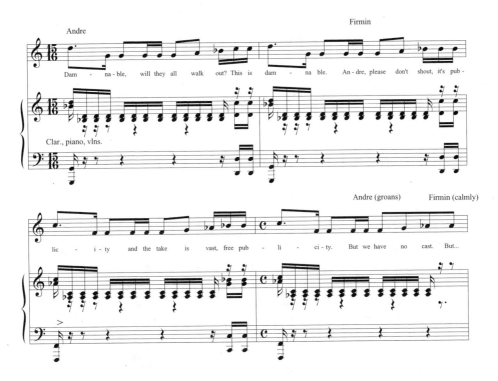

Example 5.5. Opening of "Notes"

below to hunt the Phantom, and later when Meg leads the crowd there, they remind each other, "Your hand at the level of your eyes."

The fifths on which the story motif rests reflect those used in "Notes" and in the Phantom's angry "Damn you!" to Christine. This latter instance itself varies what could be considered a separate motif, an outgrowth of the fifths of the story motif. This version, simply a descending fifth followed by another one a whole step lower, usually sets the text, "Christine, Christine." When characters plead with Christine, attempt to get her attention, or try to comfort her, this motif often helps them do it. Sometimes, the motif gains a third fifth, yet another whole or half step lower, when the Phantom echoes the first speaker in an attempt to remind her of his presence. Raoul experiences this when he tries to soothe Christine after *Il muto* has disintegrated into chaos and they have fled to the roof (see ex. 5.6).

Thus, Lloyd Webber creates a set of related ideas: the story motif with its two halves, the opening melody of "Notes," the motif that accompanies "Christine, Christine," and others. Lloyd Webber uses this highly versatile set of musical

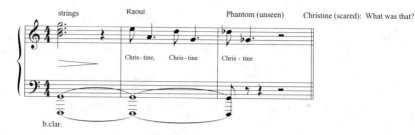

Example 5.6. Echo of "Christine"

thoughts often, but their presence could easily go unnoticed on a first listening, as their subtle, recitative-like, and functional nature makes them fundamental to the show's structure but not prominent to the listener.

Lloyd Webber provides a second set of related motifs, somewhat less complicated than the story group, and usually undergoing less mutation. This musical gesture involves a bit of recitative on one note, and/or a passage of distinct, tonally ambiguous melody, both accompanied by bold chords. Since it makes its first appearance while Christine and Raoul, recently reunited after years apart, recall stories of a character called Little Lotte that they enjoyed as children, I call this the "Little Lotte motif" (see ex. 5.7).

When the Phantom claims this music as his own, he launches immediately into its second part, using it as the introduction to "The Music of the Night."

> I have brought you to the seat of sweet music's throne,
> To this kingdom where all must pay homage to music, music.
> You have come here for one purpose and one alone.
> Since the moment I first heard you sing,
> I have needed you with me to serve me, to sing for my music, my music.

After several other appearances, this music truly becomes the Phantom's, because it appears in his opera *Don Juan Triumphant* (see ex. 5.8). In fact, the Phantom's opera contains six motifs, most of which exist also in the music outside the Phantom's score. The most significant of these is the Little Lotte music, which with a slight shift of shape becomes a central theme of the Phantom's work. This material has already moved from the dressing room scene between Christine and Raoul to the Phantom's lair, where he used it as the introduction to "The Music of the Night." He uses it similarly in his opera, to introduce the one set number of *Don Juan Triumphant*, "The Point of No Return." The lyrics even borrow a few phrases from this previous context in "The Music of the Night." But the music also appears earlier in the Phantom's opera, before he makes his appearance.

Example 5.7. "Little Lotte" music

Example 5.7. (*continued*)

Don Juan Triumphant opens with a loud, tonally uncentered choral explanation of the plot in violent and lewd terms: young Aminta, sexually inexperienced and curious, will soon arrive and have to "pay the bill" for her bold
behavior by becoming Don Juan's latest conquest. When "tables, plans, and
maids are laid," Don Juan will have his triumph. The first section of this music
is derived from the story motif, now harmonized with angry dissonances. The
chorus then moves on to two other motifs associated with the Phantom's opera,
the first of which involves dissonant block chords, and the second of which has
a shape that steps down, then up, within the outline of a perfect fourth. Finally,
the chorus climaxes on the *Don Juan* version of the Little Lotte music (see ex.
5.8).

While much of the *Don Juan* music appears elsewhere in the show, the
Phantom's opera relies much more heavily on harsh-sounding harmonies and
unpredictable melodies and rhythms than does the rest of Lloyd Webber's score.
Lloyd Webber explains the appeal of the opportunity to compose the Phantom's
opera, for musical as well as story-driven reasons: "I decided that if we adapted

Example 5.8. Chorus in *Don Juan Triumphant*

Example 5.8. (*continued*)

Example 5.8. (*continued*)

Example 5.8. (*continued*)

the plot to include a performance of an opera specifically composed for Christine by the Phantom, we could not only introduce a far more modern musical ingredient into the score, but could contrive a situation where the Phantom was not only unmasked in front of many characters, but on the stage of his opera house, in his own opera, in what was supposed to be his night of triumph."[31] The Phantom's opera is mentioned in Leroux's original story, but never performed. In Lloyd Webber's telling, the characters generally dislike the score they are commanded to sing; in rehearsal, Piangi cannot sing a whole-tone scale, and Carlotta complains loudly that no one in the audience will know or care if they get the notes right.[32]

During the actual performance, with the chorus's foreboding exposition out of the way, Don Juan, played by Piangi, enters. He summons his latest lover, played by Meg, who coquettishly takes his payment, kisses him, and flits off. Don Juan then reviews his plan for Aminta (played by Christine) with his servant, Passarino: they have lured Aminta there on the pretense that she will meet the servant for a tryst, but the Don, in his servant's clothes and with his face hidden, will do the seducing. The master and servant swap clothes in the tradition of Don Juan stories, although the servant, unlike Mozart's Leporello, seems just as ill-intentioned as his master here. The music that accompanies their discussion presents two more *Don Juan* motifs, both of which have already made appearances in earlier contexts. The first motif runs up, then down, steps made from two whole tone collections, usually covering the span of a ninth or more (see ex. 5.9); the second circles around itself, hovering inside a fourth (see ex. 5.10). Both find their way into several orchestra underscorings and short sung phrases, and the second will appear again, for example, in the Phantom's final lair scene ("Hounded out by everyone! Met with hatred everywhere!").

Example 5.9. Phrase from *Don Juan Triumphant*

Example 5.10. Phrase from _Don Juan Triumphant_

Next, Christine, as Aminta, enters, and Piangi as Don Juan exits to prepare for his conquest. Later the audience will realize that at this juncture the Phantom kills Piangi backstage and takes over for him, donning the cloak that hides his face. Christine enters singing a lilting phrase she will use once more (in her real life) in the final scene, and the substituted Don Juan then launches into the Little Lotte music that introduces "The Point of No Return." This number is a tango-like seduction of Aminta that the Phantom clearly means to use to sway Christine, but during its course she realizes his identity. Gradually the guards Raoul has hired realize it too, and the Phantom, giving up all pretense of acting, moves from his own composition into a heartfelt reprise of "All I Ask of You." Before his final word, Christine removes his mask, the law moves in, Piangi's body is discovered, and the Phantom vanishes with Christine.

It is quite telling that the Phantom's idea of seduction, as revealed in his opera's libretto, involves violence, male domination, and bold sexual imagery. This brings to mind Hal Prince's revelation about the psyche of the Phantom, and his inclusion of sexual imagery alongside romantic notions in the story and the sets. The Phantom seduces Christine quite gently in "The Music of the Night," but apparently this step is simply the first of many; there, she becomes used to his presence, his mask (which he has her stroke), and his strange home. By the time we arrive at _Don Juan Triumphant,_ the Phantom is ready for a real sexual relationship, and he hopes Christine will be as well; by now he has a mannequin in a wedding gown which resembles her, and he has clearly begun to envision a true romantic and sexual encounter. But his longing takes on an angry, desperate, and somewhat explosive tone in his opera, which discusses conquering women, unleashing their repressed sexual urges, and teaching them about physical pleasures in a callous, dominating way. *Don Juan Triumphant*'s harsh, jagged music reflects this and seems to serve as an outlet for this darker aspect of the Phantom's psyche. This side of the Phantom, disguised as Don Juan, fizzles quickly when he is confronted with the real thing: when Christine kisses him passionately in the final scene, she defeats him. He understands that although she is quite capable of physical love, she should be with Raoul, and he lets her go. The Phantom's sexuality—linked with the angry music of his opera—feels frightening and dangerous despite its brief airing.

THE STRUCTURE OF AN OPERA-LIKE ENSEMBLE, "NOTES/PRIMA DONNA"

The Don Juan plot is not Lloyd Webber's only borrowing from Mozart's operatic world. Besides the more general operatic features already mentioned above, several numbers in *The Phantom of the Opera* are reminiscent of Mozart in their structure. Lloyd Webber wrote many more ensembles, ranging from trios to septets, in this show than in any previous one, and several of them function in a distinctly Mozartean manner, in that they build up one voice at a time as characters enter. Then, in a structure that refers to Verdi as much as Mozart, the characters sing distinct lines simultaneously, with different melodies and lyrics, while the basic mood and message of each line remain clear. Sections of action alternate with sections of reflection. The act 3 quartet from Verdi's *Rigoletto,* for example, works similarly, as does the act 2 finale of Mozart's *The Marriage of Figaro* and the act 2 sextet in *Don Giovanni* (to name a few of Mozart's many ensembles in which he adds layers of character, information, and melody as the scene progresses). The most sprawling and impressive example of this cumulative and polyphonic ensemble style in *Phantom* is the first "Notes," which becomes "Prima Donna."

"Notes" begins with the Opéra's co-manager, Firmin, reading about Christine's successful debut and subsequent disappearance in the papers, and reflecting on the profitability of scandal. His partner André enters, and they share the notes written to them by the Opera Ghost. Just as their verse ends, Raoul barges in demanding to know Christine's location and brandishing his own threatening note from the Ghost. His entrance is marked by a descending fifth, reminiscent of the "Christine, Christine" echoes (which, as we have seen, is logical since both the first melody of "Notes" and the echoes of Christine's name relate to the story motif). Next Carlotta, returned from having temporarily quit in fury and humiliation, returns with Piangi in tow, rattling a note threatening her not to perform lest a "great misfortune" ensue. Finally Madame Giry enters with her daughter Meg, and the mood shifts to a quieter and more menacing one. Madame Giry's note is quoted in example 5.4, the Phantom's disembodied voice doing most of the reading. In the eerie silence after he finishes, Meg murmurs the "Christine, Christine" motif, echoed by a furious Carlotta.

This initiates a new section of the ensemble; now that everyone has had their individual say, they all comment on the tense situation simultaneously. Carlotta shrieks "O traditori! O mentitori!" André and Firmin attempt to pacify her: "Please signora, we beseech you." Madame Giry reminds everyone, "The angel sees, the angel knows." Raoul wonders to himself, "Why did Christine fly from my arms?" Meg occasionally joins him in support, wondering where Christine went. This *tutti* passage covers only twelve measures, climaxing in a unison "What new surprises lie in store?" but it lays the groundwork for the longer ensemble passage to follow.

"Prima Donna" proper begins next; André and Firmin charm, flatter, and woo Carlotta: "Can you deny us the triumph in store? / Sing, prima donna, once more." Carlotta then picks up the thread, singing of her glories, and soon all seven voices join in. André and Firmin note wryly that all this high drama reminds them of opera, while Meg, Madame Giry, and Raoul ponder the nature of this angel or ghost. The melody changes hands, as does a faster-moving line with an almost patter feel to its lyrics, and anyone not singing one of these two items sings his or her own material. All of the voices unite ("Sing, prima donna, once more") and then the Phantom, as usual, steps on their climactic finish, vowing disastrous consequences should Carlotta indeed sing. The number is both funny and chaotic, and although the lyrics are largely lost, the import of each character's message is clear. One of the most effective and complex ensembles in the show, "Prima Donna" manages to further the plot and unite most of the main characters in a structure reminiscent of earlier operatic ensembles.[33]

SET NUMBERS THAT DEFINE MOMENTS OF DRAMA

In *Cats,* Lloyd Webber assigned each solo cat a musical genre; to a certain extent, he assigned styles to characters in *Jesus Christ Superstar* as well. *Phantom* has a much more consistent musical style to it; set numbers usually sound less different in style and tone than in Lloyd Webber's earlier works. In fact—in another interesting similarity to *Les Misérables*—*Phantom* uses most of its set numbers as fodder for manipulation and recurrence, rather than as character-defining signature tunes.

"The Music of the Night" ranks as Lloyd Webber's biggest hit from *Phantom,* although its success pales in comparison to "Memory" from *Cats* or "Don't Cry for Me, Argentina" from *Evita.* It never quite became the pop standard that those songs did, but it does continue to enjoy a healthy life as a concert piece, for Michael Crawford (whose performance of the number in the show appears to be largely responsible for its ensuing success), Sarah Brightman, and a host of other Broadway talents. The Phantom uses the song to cast a hazy spell over Christine, imploring her to trust him, touch him, and allow the power of his music to enter her mind. He reinforces the magical atmosphere of the moment with a gentle final phrase, rounded out by five soft chords that have a shimmering, seductive quality (see ex. 5.11).

The same five chords will close the show, as the Phantom sings a brief reprise of the number before vanishing. The chords also introduce "All I Ask of You," functioning there as a shift from a tense, fast-paced mood to one of calm happiness. The two songs share a stronger connection as well: their final sung phrases are virtually the same. This resemblance is not particularly noticeable until the last moments of the show, in which the departing Raoul and Christine sing the first three lines of the chorus of "All I Ask of You," and the Phantom sings the fourth and fifth lines, but uses lyrics that refer to the "Music of the Night" version instead of the "All I Ask of You" version of the phrase.

> *Raoul and Christine:* Say you'll share with me one love, one lifetime
> Say the word and I will follow you.
> Share each day with me, each night, each morning
> *Phantom:* You alone can make my song take flight
> It's over now, the music of the night.

"All I Ask of You" is a warm, comforting love duet, and its traditional musical comedy quality (Michael Walsh points out its Richard Rodgers feel) comes

Example 5.11. The end of "The Music of the Night"

as a relief after the visual and musical chaos of *Il muto*.[34] A quite traditional Entr'acte features both "All I Ask of You" and "The Music of the Night," and opens with "Angel of Music."

In its home early in the second act, "Angel of Music" wonderfully conveys the sense of excitement, uncertainty, and magic in the air that Christine, who has not yet seen her new vocal coach, experiences. Harp, light strings, clarinet, and flute make Christine's explanation of the Angel of Music sound not only angelic, but child-like, for it was her father who told her the stories of him. Rather giddily, she explains:

> Here in this room, he calls me softly, somewhere inside, hiding.
> Somehow I know he's always with me. He, the unseen genius.

After Meg departs, Christine shares her Little Lotte moment with Raoul, and "Angel of Music" resumes with the Phantom's voice filling Christine's dressing room. Christine, ecstatic about coming to know this mysterious figure, calls to him in reverent, obedient terms:

> Angel of Music, guide and guardian, grant to me your glory.
> Angel of Music, hide no longer. Come to me, strange angel.

The light texture gives way to the throbbing bass, which moves the score directly into "The Phantom of the Opera," the show's only pop song. It comes as no surprise that this song was chosen for music video treatment, not only because of its steady rock beat, but also because the action takes on a cinematic, montage feel with a recorded, processed sound. Throughout the first two-thirds of the song, the Phantom leads Christine down a winding set of shadowy ramps and paths set far back from the audience, while the audience hears their voices blasted over the sound system, intimately close to their microphones.[35] The orchestra becomes dominated, just this once, by a synthesized drum track and electric keyboards that really sound electronic, rather than synthesizing acoustic instruments. Soon, the two arrive in the Phantom's lair and the sound reverts to its more normal acoustic space (still heavily miked, but obviously emanating from the bodies onstage). The number, despite being the only rock tune in the show, grows organically and realistically out of the tense throbbing of "Angel of Music," and carries the murky stage images effectively. Once Christine and the Phantom arrive in his lair, he bids her to sing, and she launches into a high coloratura based on the motif "He's here, the Phantom of the opera." As the Phantom draws her out ("Sing, my angel!"), Christine climbs higher and higher, the song stepping up in key twice and ending abruptly on Christine's high E.

"Masquerade," the only true chorus number (as opposed to ensembles sung by principal players) in the show, is notable for its orchestration. Taking place at a masquerade ball to celebrate the new operatic season and the newly replaced chandelier, as well as the absence of the opera ghost of late, the number relies heavily on percussion. The masked chorus features all the principal players, but also a number of colorfully dressed *commedia dell'arte*–like players, in stylized costumes reminiscent of the circus. Four of these figures play percussion instruments onstage; these include a genie-like man with a tambourine, a court jester with hand bells, and cymbals played by a girl in a monkey costume not unlike the figure on the Phantom's music box. The scoring of the song features these percussion instruments and a host of others in the orchestra pit, including an insistent bass drum, as well as a synthesized barrel organ, frequent pizzicato strings, and a general absence of a bass line and low instruments. At one point the orchestra imitates a music box, and the choral texture becomes light and clipped (see ex. 5.12). While the principal characters rejoice in the recent peace, the chorus refers to sinister, concealing masks and the truths they can hide. The distinctive orchestration and the strange, freakish costumes combine to make "Masquerade" a strong conveyor of this tensely charged moment of respite before another Phantom-inspired storm.

The Phantom of the Opera, like *Cats,* creates a world of its own, yet it relies less on its sets to achieve this theatrical escapism; the multifaceted, lush score does a great deal of the transporting that an audience experiences. The seamlessness of the transitions, the unity of the sound, and the consistency of the rich romantic atmosphere make *The Phantom of the Opera* Lloyd Webber's most satisfying score to study not only for its musical qualities, but its emotional ones too. The characters, despite their melodramatic situations, have discussions, fall in love, and express fear and grief. Lloyd Webber provides them with a unified, interesting, complicated, seductive score with which to carry out this drama.

Reviews: "This Is Subtle. This Is Bold. This Is Theater."

The pre-opening buzz in both London and New York was massive for *The Phantom of the Opera. Cats* had proven Andrew Lloyd Webber as a reliable, crowd-pleasing commodity, but it had also solidified his position as many critics' least favorite composer. *Starlight Express,* with even more spectacle and even less plot than *Cats,* only served to prove to critics that they had been right. As noted, *Phantom* was meant to be Lloyd Webber's adult statement, his mature musical both in compositional style and in content. For the most part, his plan succeeded.

Example 5.12. "Masquerade"

Reviews for *Phantom* were generally positive in London and fairly good in New York. Critics agreed that the show was lovely to look at, the spectacle in this case serving an enjoyably romantic story rather than simply impressing the eye. Praise for director Hal Prince, designer Maria Björnson, and actor Michael Crawford was consistent. But Lloyd Webber's music received from some critics the usual share of snide and dismissive remarks. At this crucial point in his career, when he hoped to move from pop music into something more critically admired, when he hoped to have himself evaluated as a composer rather than a song-writer, the critics only partially helped him get there. While some admired his melodies, techniques, structures, and orchestration, others found his style (as they had before) overly melody-centered and simple. *Phantom* certainly paved the way stylistically for his next steps, *Aspects of Love* and *Sunset Boulevard,* but it did not entirely redeem his critical reputation, nor has any other show since done so.

Lloyd Webber has rarely championed his work as the complex, deep sort that critics might like. Speaking about *Phantom* long after the critics had had their say, he noted, "I started from the premise of wanting to write something that was a high romance. It doesn't stand up to huge intellectual scrutiny. . . . At the end of the day, it's overwhelmingly high romance."[36] Still, it mattered deeply to Lloyd Webber what the critics said, and their takes on *Phantom,* while not hurting the show economically, could surely have helped its reputation.

Frank Rich of the *New York Times,* the one source to which people might turn before deciding whether to see the show, told his readers to see it. He managed to do this while actually disliking the show rather strongly. Interestingly, he seems to have enjoyed his evening despite himself and his general objections to Lloyd Webber's music. His review opened on a seemingly positive note: "It may be possible to have a terrible time at 'The Phantom of the Opera,' but you'll have to work at it. Only a terminal prig would let the avalanche of pre-opening publicity poison his enjoyment of this show, which usually wants nothing more than to shower the audience with fantasy and fun, and which often succeeds, at any price."[37] The "at any price" pointed to Rich's basic problem with Lloyd Webber: he writes catchy pop tunes highlighted so brightly that the show comes to a halt to showcase them. The tunes are too pop-like and could be sung by anyone, since the lyrics are generic and the melodies do not reflect the characters' personalities or states of mind. The show did not, despite its hype, make Lloyd Webber the next Richard Rodgers; it was simply a "characteristic Lloyd Webber project—long on pop professionalism and melody, impoverished of artistic per-sonality and passion" that the admirable work of Prince, Björnson, and Crawford elevated to enjoyable and respectable heights. Prince and Björnson's visual cre-ations, and Mackintosh's panache with marketing, overcame Lloyd Webber's faults: it was "as much a victory of dynamic stagecraft over musical kitsch as it is a triumph of merchandising über alles." Prince and Björnson's dark images were so heartfelt, Rich maintains, that their passion for the theater itself was the real romance here. Even as he praised the look of it—the roof, lake, gondola, drapes, all timed and directed well—he found the premise laughable: "The lake, awash in dry-ice fog and illuminated by dozens of candelabra, is a masterpiece of campy phallic Hollywood iconography—it's Liberace's vision of hell."

The engrossing sets overcame the paltry book, Rich said, which is a simple story of beast meeting and losing beauty, set among "disposable" secondary characters among whom only Carlotta (Judy Kaye) held much interest. This weak story was filled out by plenty of pauses in the action for the catchier songs, forcing the show to "cool its heels while he [Lloyd Webber] hawks his wares." These were nevertheless "lovely tunes, arguably his best yet" and featured wonderful orchestration, but of course they returned too often. Rich made an exception for "Music of the Night," which he found particularly moving as it seemed to "express from its author's gut a desperate longing for acceptance." He was of course referring to Lloyd Webber, who did not write the lyrics but presumably had a strong say as to the general point of the song, which does indeed focus on the Phantom's longing to be accepted by Christine. Rich found the three opera parodies (including the Phantom's own work) "self-indulgently windy" and not particularly funny, aimed as they were at "such less than riotous targets as Meyerbeer."

Crawford received high praise; Rich labeled him "mesmerizing," "moving," and the source of "most of what emotional heat" the show had. Despite the handicap of having his face covered by a mask, his voice and hands were very expressive of his desire for Christine, especially in the powerful "Music of the Night," which, as he bewitches her, becomes "as much a rape as a seduction." He was just as impressive by the end, when without his mask he becomes a "crestfallen, sweaty, cadaverous misfit."

Rich offered no such praise for Brightman, whose performance he had already disliked in London. Although her voice is lush and strong, she cannot act, he asserted. Despite her long history in the role, "she still simulates fear and affection alike by screwing her face into bug-eyed, chipmunk-cheeked poses more appropriate to the Lon Chaney film version." His criticism, echoed by many, was that while her voice was sweet and pleasing, her acting came across as stiff and less heartfelt than the more nuanced Phantom. Rich quickly dismissed Steve Barton as Raoul as "an affable professional escort with unconvincingly bright hair."

In conclusion, Rich conceded a significant point: Lloyd Webber was vastly influential in the theater and should not be dismissed. *The Phantom of the Opera* became for Rich a window into the workings and appeal of the megamusical:

> Yet for now, if not forever [a reference to *Cats*], Mr. Lloyd Webber is a genuine phenomenon—not an invention of the press or ticket scalpers—and 'Phantom' is worth seeing not only for its punch as high-gloss entertainment but also as a fascinating key to what the phenomenon is about. Mr. Lloyd Webber's esthetic has never been more baldly stated than in this show, which favors the decorative trappings of art over the troublesome substance of culture and finds more eroticism in rococo opulence and conspicuous consumption than in love or sex. Mr. Lloyd Webber is a creature, perhaps even a prisoner, of his time; with 'The Phantom of the Opera,' he remakes La Belle Epoque in the image of our own Gilded Age. If by any chance this musical doesn't prove Mr. Lloyd Webber's most popular, it won't be his fault, but another sign that times are changing and that our boom era, like the opera house's chandelier, is poised to go bust.

Rich seemed to understand that he had lost touch with audience taste, while Lloyd Webber understood it perfectly. Though Rich maintained that his own minority view was the correct one, that current theatrical styles were not admirable, he nevertheless acknowledged not only Lloyd Webber's talent at audience-pleasing, but his staying power.

Another review opened with an obvious joke:

> Andrew Lloyd Webber's new musical is, he says, "About a man who is hideously ugly who falls hopelessly in love with this girl and is only able to express himself through music."
>
> Only those of a very cruel frame of mind would suggest the musical was at all autobiographical.[38]

A few critics took a particularly snide tone. John Simon of *New York* magazine summarized, "The only areas in which *The Phantom of the Opera* is deficient are book, music, and lyrics." He later added Brightman's performance to his list.[39] Michael Feingold of the *Village Voice* clarified his moral objections: "Yes, yes, I know. The semi-educated middle-class world loves Andrew Lloyd Webber best of all theater composers, and the *Phantom* is already a financial triumph, no matter what any critic may say, with an $18 million advance sale. . . . Nevertheless, the educated world knows by now that Andrew Lloyd Webber is not a real composer, but a secondhand music peddler, whose pathetic aural imagination was outpaced years ago by his apparently exhaustive memory."[40] This last comment, about Lloyd Webber's memory, refers to what Feingold felt was an inexcusable series of brief quotations from other composers, never integrated into a whole but simply butted up against one another. He offered a few examples, extremely brief and obscure, with only vague pointers as to where in the show he heard them. He wrote what he has always written on Lloyd Webber's music, in his usual trendy, anti-establishment stance: Lloyd Webber's popularity makes him worthless, and only the "semi-educated middle class" would be fooled by his music, which is clearly not even composed.

Walter Kerr in the *New York Times* focused on the variously satisfying and disappointing ways in which the show realized the book's chills and frights. Kerr was drawn to the story by the falling chandelier, the Phantom as Red Death, the boat, and all the other juicy thrills, and he felt some of these were staged fulfillingly. Oddly, he spent much of his review analyzing the importance and effectiveness of these moments of melodrama, but then goes on to complain that the show is nothing but these moments.[41]

William A. Henry III in *Time* attributed the show's effectiveness to powerful theatrical magic, in words almost exactly the same as those Rich had used in describing a similar quality in *Cats:* "The show apparently taps into yearnings for a transporting sensory and mystical experience: in a word, for magic. On that primal level, despite considerable and embarrassing shortcomings, *Phantom* powerfully delivers."[42] Henry seemed at first not to mind the sketchily drawn characters or the "muddled" story; he found the journey delightful, full of safe scares and lovely sights. Yet he went on to analyze the plot and, in an odd shift, seemed to convince himself that the magic doesn't work after all. The similarity he saw between "The Music of the Night" and "Come to Me, Bend to Me" from *Brigadoon* inspired him to take back his statement that the show "powerfully delivers" its magic; *Brigadoon* had "true magic, fantasy and romance" which Lloyd Webber "has not come close to matching." His change of heart in mid-review seemed to result from his discussion of the psychological makeup of the characters, which itself went off track. He argued that Christine's dilemma lies in choosing between the outward beauty of Raoul and the inner beauty of the Phantom, but the show never suggests that Raoul is not a good person, despite being handsome, and the Phantom's inner beauty must surely be marred by his murderous tendencies. Henry became even more creative when he speculated that Christine chooses between being a rich man's wife and a performer, but again, nothing suggests Raoul would make her stop performing; in fact, he admires her talent repeatedly. Henry did raise an interesting point: that Lloyd Webber and the Phantom seem to be conducting simultaneous reshapings of musical theater in their own times.[43]

A number of fairly important New York critics showed great enthusiasm for *Phantom*. Howard Kissel of the *Daily News* enjoyed the nineteenth-century sensibility created by Prince and Björnson in the "breathtaking, witty, sensual" staging and design, and he welcomed the rare chance to see a love story.[44] Though he found the characters shallow, the plot melodramatic, and the lyrics forgettable, the whole added up to a good time, an evening of harmless fun. Like so many critics before him, he accused Lloyd Webber of writing music that sounded "borrowed" without citing anything specific, yet he enjoyed Lloyd Webber's sound in this show: "He seems to be borrowing from better sources, and he has much greater sophistication about putting it all together." Jack Kroll of *Newsweek* admired the show's overall structure, especially in the moving series of numbers that begins the first act. It was as if everyone on the creative team had worked out a perfect series of events, highlighted by Lloyd Webber's "purely romantic, indeed erotic, group of songs" from "Angel of Music" through "The Music of the Night."[45] Kroll declared, "These songs, with their reaching, yearning, impassioned melodies, are the most effective Lloyd Webber has ever written."

Clive Barnes of the *New York Post* wrote a glowing, if slightly over-the-top, rave. Using words like "phabulous," "phantastic," and the "biggest-ever, superheated megahit," he declared that it fully lived up to its hype.[46] This was the way to create a megamusical, he believed; of all the "spectacular theatrical extravaganzas" that Lloyd Webber and other British composers have made their own, this one worked best at creating an accord among "theme, music and staging." Prince's vision of the story, and Björnson's fulfillment of it, had a great impact, especially when telling a beauty and the beast story that no one can resist. Lloyd Webber's music, borrowing for parodic purposes with great skill here, "is smart enough to give pastiche a good name." Here, at last, Lloyd Webber had found a voice of his own, Barnes believed. "His scores . . . have always seemed like imitations of opera and operetta. . . . But with 'Phantom,' Lloyd Webber's style comes into its own, and gives itself carte blanche. . . . This music just couldn't be more appropriate." And the music, in turn, was at its best when expertly serving the drama; Barnes pointed specifically to the moment after Christine kisses the Phantom, and the orchestra, led by the soft snare drum, sneaks back into the silence. "This is subtle," he declared. "This is bold. This is theater."

On balance critics in London were slightly more enthusiastic than those in New York, since Lloyd Webber was a homegrown hero that Brits were proud to champion. Michael Coveney of London's *Financial Times* wrote an all-out rave: *Phantom* "restores sex and romance to the modern musical, with a full quota of pulsating melodramatic tension."[47] He found the ending of the story "almost unbearably moving" and advised bringing tissues. Lloyd Webber's score, he felt, used older operatic styles, linking motifs, and his own "idiosyncratic sound" in interesting ways.

Michael Billington of London's *Guardian* agreed with many that the spectacle, though abundant, was put "to the service of an exciting story" made all the more gripping by effective music.[48] The story was corny but in an irresistible and sincere way: "It may be hokum but it is hokum here treated with hand on heart rather than tongue in cheek." Responding to the very same sentiments that Prince and Lloyd Webber had hoped to convey when they began the project, Billington found it "refreshing to find a musical that pins its faith in people, narrative and traditional illusion." Lloyd Webber's "lush, romantic, string-filled" style nicely mixed with the opera scenes and the comic numbers, and *Don Juan Triumphant* sounded effectively like "1860s avant-garde." Billington rounded out his unabashed rave with praise for lyricist Charles Hart, a sentiment shared by few fellow critics, including most of the enthusiastic ones.

Irving Wardle of the London *Times* offered a review with a more negative slant than most of his English peers. Although a few moments from the story were beautifully and frighteningly embodied here, the show overall was not as scary as Wardle wished; he was annoyed by the emphasis on the love story rather than on the unrealized but potentially thrilling frights.[49]

If the London and New York critics did not quite agree on the value of the staging or the score, they did mostly concur when rating the performances. All praised Michael Crawford as the Phantom. "Reasserting his pre-eminence as the outstanding star of our musical theatre," he carried the show and made England proud.[50] Most of the critics found Sarah Brightman's work adequate, although several echoed Frank Rich's negative assessment of her acting. *Time*'s William A. Henry III declared that "as an actress she has learned almost nothing from her years in the role,"[51] and Joel Siegel on WABC said she "couldn't act scared on the IRT at four o'clock in the morning."[52] Mimi Kramer in the *New Yorker* saw parallels between the way the Phantom threatened and controlled the opera company into giving Christine the lead in his opera and the way Lloyd Webber threatened and cajoled Actors' Equity into giving Brightman the lead in New York.[53] Many reviewers, however, amid such well-publicized derision, found Brightman's performance enjoyable; Clive Barnes of the *Post* and Douglas Watt of the *Daily News* in particular admired her.[54] Steve Barton as Raoul was generally considered to be talented but underused in a role that called for him to do little more than portray a "stick-hero in [a] yellow wig."[55]

Later History

It was a competitive year at the Tony Awards in 1988. Also nominated was Stephen Sondheim's most commercially successful musical, *Into the Woods,* which had also been critically acclaimed. In the end Sondheim took the Tony for Best Score over Lloyd Webber, but *Phantom* beat *Into the Woods* for Best Musical. *Phantom* also won Tonys for Michael Crawford, Judy Kaye, Hal Prince, Maria Björnson (for both costumes and scenic design), and Andrew Bridge (for lighting). *Into the Woods* also won for its book and for Best Actress, the category in which Sarah Brightman was conspicuously not nominated.

It took a little over a year for *Phantom* to recoup its initial Broadway investment, and the show has turned a profit ever since. At this writing, it continues to run both in London and New York, and like *Cats* and *Les Misérables* before it, the show opened all over the world, starting with Toronto, Tokyo, Vienna, and Stockholm. While the show remains one of the most coveted tickets in any city in which it opens, it also costs a great deal to maintain; nevertheless, Lloyd Webber's Really Useful Group has deftly balanced profits with losses from other productions and *Phantom* appears untouchable.[56]

When the show's run reached ten years in London, Lloyd Webber played "The Music of the Night" onstage while Sarah Brightman—now his ex-wife— sang it in a mini-concert; reminding the British papers why he is such a favorite source of gossip, both the first and third (then current) Mrs. Lloyd Webbers attended. It made for more effective publicity.

By 2004, two new *Phantom* enterprises were in the works, giving the show fresh life. A film version, based on the Broadway staging, premiered amid strong publicity and moderate critical success. And the Venetian Hotel and Casino in Las Vegas announced that a new version of *Phantom* would take up permanent residence in a specially built theater there in 2006. This version of *Phantom* was to be restaged on a new set and directed by Hal Prince, with the score trimmed to ninety minutes by the composer. In carrying the story, the *New York Times* noted that since *Phantom* opened in London in 1986, it had made $3.2 billion—and continues to tour the United States and several foreign countries.[57]

Despite some negative reviews, *Phantom* remains Lloyd Webber's most enduring mature work. His next hit, *Sunset Boulevard,* received good notices, but *Phantom* is Lloyd Webber's only musical currently running on Broadway in its original production. Like *Les Misérables,* but unlike a number of other musicals, *Phantom* weathered the disastrous drop in ticket sales after the tragedy of 11 September 2001. The show may have annoyed a few Lloyd Webber haters as much as *Cats* had, but *Phantom* won over some skeptics and rightly gained the composer a small amount of the respectability for which he had always hoped. Its influence and success were brought home in January 2006 when it passed Lloyd Webber's other institution, *Cats,* to become the longest-running show in

Broadway history. *Phantom,* perhaps more than any other megamusical with the possible exception of *Les Misérables,* set the bar for future Broadway composers. It is remarkable how many musicals of the 1990s and 2000s have drawn their inspiration from *Phantom*'s tone, style, and techniques.

"A Model of Decorum and Tranquility"

Other Megamusicals in the 1980s

In May 1986, *New York Times* critic Frank Rich reported from London on several new musicals. He used the opportunity to summarize the current state of musical theater, both in London and New York. In short, he lamented the megamusical's takeover of the theater scene in both cities. Though he did not use the word, which had not yet come into circulation, his transatlantic excursion led him to the realization that the era of the British megamusical was undeniably in full swing: "The unthinkable has finally happened—London, an erstwhile also-ran in the contemporary musical theater, threatens to surpass New York as a production center for musical extravaganzas." Rich counted nine shows that qualified as (what we now call) megamusicals, ones which "adhere to the form of pop-rock opera that, as perfected by the now severed team of Andrew Lloyd Webber and Tim Rice, is England's latter-day claim to the Gilbert and Sullivan tradition."[1]

Only a month later, he updated his conclusions: London no longer "threatens to surpass," but

> now surpasses Broadway as a manufacturer of musical extravaganzas. What's more, a distinctive London musical theater style has emerged—one that consolidates and coarsens the Disneyland-ride format of "Cats." As with that commercial smash, English musicals now tend to be deafening soft-rock operettas, in which lavish environmental sets (often designed by John Napier, of "Cats," and usually replicated in an elaborate line of merchandised knickknacks) take precedence over story, dancing or characters.[2]

Rich noted that although London was mounting few new plays, many of its slew of new musicals were expected to go to Broadway. Of these offerings, he argued, "Only 'Chess,' whose London reception will likely mandate improvements for a New York edition, resembles a Broadway product." Whether he meant *Chess* was like a more typical Broadway musical or it was worthy of appearing on Broadway, the point is clear: the British invasion could not be ignored. The other two shows he discussed in his report from London, *Starlight Express* and *Time,* both focused heavily on spectacle, for which the former would suffer in New York. *Time* never made it to Broadway, instead becoming a famous flop thanks to its bizarre features, including an overwhelming laser-filled planetarium set by megamusical designer Napier and the disembodied head of an alien Laurence Olivier.[3]

This chapter discusses megamusicals not embraced by critics or audiences, as well as the state of musical theater in general in the 1980s. What distinguished megamusicals other than the Big Three of *Cats, Les Misérables,* and *The Phantom of the Opera*? And what room was left for musicals of other styles, by different creators?

Stephen Oliver and Tim Rice's *Blondel*

Tim Rice's first show without Andrew Lloyd Webber, *Blondel,* was—as he notes in the liner notes to *Blondel*'s recording—"my first commercial failure."[4] It ran briefly in London but never arrived on Broadway. He takes much of the responsibility, suggesting that the problems lay in the book (which, like all three of his collaborations with Lloyd Webber, had been his idea, but became the work of many hands) and an overly large and somewhat unsuccessful staging. He expresses great admiration for the music, by opera composer Stephen Oliver, and hopes that someday a smaller, light-hearted production will honor the composer's only foray into musicals.

Blondel is, indeed, a romp. The two-CD original cast recording includes virtually every word of the show, and from it one gets a strong sense of the gleefully anachronistic, occasionally topical humor. The story takes place in the year 1189, when King Richard of England leaves his country in the hands of his smarmy brother John to lead the Crusades. A court minstrel, Blondel, hoping both to honor his beloved king and make it big in show business, treks all over Europe in pursuit of Richard, whom he eventually discovers imprisoned in Austria. Blondel's long-suffering girlfriend, Fiona, joins the search, and helps thwart a bumbling assassin that Prince John has sent after his brother. There is never any real danger; the show is all jokes, biting social commentary, clever puns, and running about. Blondel's song to honor King Richard, with which he drives everyone mad by playing all over Europe, is a 1960s-style doo-wop complete with backup girls (the Blondettes) called "I'm a Monarchist." It receives an elaborate, celebratory performance at the end of the show.

Rice's hand in the score is strongly felt, not only in the lyrics. The show's mood is quite similar to that of *Joseph and the Amazing Technicolor Dreamcoat,* which also engaged in joyous anachronisms of musical style and textual tone. Both shows also share a few quiet, still moments, when things turn melancholy—in the case of *Blondel,* these moments are reserved for Blondel and Fiona's struggle to make their relationship work. He is a driven but perpetually poor artist, she a rebellious serf with no patience for his slow-building career nor her own hopeless social circumstances. But his song saves Richard in the end, and she bargains for her freedom.

Rice's lyrics occasionally date the show, but in ways that would be virtually unnoticeable in new productions. Fiona storms the Ministry of Feudal Affairs, demanding her freedom, and eventually creates such a ruckus that King Richard himself comes out to investigate. When she asks her king why she should have to buy her freedom, his explanation covers not only the feudal system, but England in the 1980s.

> My dear, have you heard about balancing books?
> Are you by chance a sociology student?
> Running this joint's not as cheap as it looks
> Grants must be cut—like the housewife we're prudent
> All who work hard will have their reward
> Remember that through any years of austerity
> Earn what you spend then you can afford
> Trinkets and treats on the road to prosperity.[5]

Now read the first letter of each of these eight lines, going down—it's an acrostic that spells "Margaret." Richard's second verse, naturally, spells "Thatcher." This is completely undetectable in performance (unless one were to highlight it by, say, having the cast hold up big letters, a technique I have always hoped to try if given the chance to stage this work) and would be virtually undetectable as printed text as well, except that in the CD booklet, the first letter is set aside, with a space after it. Rice reveals his private joke.

The show is narrated by a group of monks, singing in tight harmony that touches on styles of chant, barbershop, and doo wop. "Come back with us to the Middle Ages," they invite, to hear the story of Blondel. Later, Prince John commands Blondel to write a new song, honoring him rather than his brother Richard; his reasoning includes the handy point that there is "No Rhyme for Richard." Fiona expresses her uncertainty about her relationship with Blondel in "Running Back for More," a distinctly 1980s-style ballad, though it features Stephen Oliver's interestingly wide-ranging melody.

Blondel opened in Bath in September 1983, where local audiences received it with great enthusiasm. After three weeks there and two weeks in Manchester, it moved to London, where its opening was largely overshadowed by the theater in which it appeared. The famous Old Vic had just been completely restored, and since *Blondel* was its first occupant, many critics talked more about the look of the theater than the show itself. Audiences seemed to enjoy themselves, although apparently not as energetically as they had during out-of-town tryouts; apparently the theater was distracting because of its new look and overwhelming because of its gilded hugeness. Michael Coveney, generally a supporter of Rice's work (and megamusicals in general), gave *Blondel* a mixed review. He called it a "sprightly enough opening show" for the theater, but it "suffers from a devastatingly trite, almost non-existent, book." He praised Rice's lyrics, which had "his customary lyrical agility, mixing anachronistic phrases with several clever point numbers and sly digs at pop song mannerisms." He liked some songs but not others, some cast members but not others.[6] Similarly mixed reviews, mostly lamenting the thin story, came from most of the other important London papers, with one strong rave from John Barber in the *Daily Telegraph*.[7]

Blondel remains popular with English school groups and local amateur and professional groups, especially if it is not overwhelmed by a megamusical-style staging. The lyrics go by far too fast, and the jokes are too wordy and subtle for a distracting staging. Rice is correct that an intimate, score-focused staging suits the show best; it would even do well on Broadway or in a big house if the over-the-top visuals were reserved for the big numbers like "I'm a Monarchist," and the rest was kept within the realm of realism—a staging similar to that of *The Producers*, which is also full of silly, wordy jokes and small bits of business, bursting into huge visuals only a few times. Rice, however, was still a lyricist of the 1980s, and still fond of the megamusical, which he had, after all, been fundamental in creating.

Chess

> How sad to see
> A model of decorum and tranquility
> Become like any other sport:
> A battleground for rival ideologies to slug it out with glee.

Rice's next major project, like every one that had come before, was his own idea. *Chess,* however, was his first concept for a show that took place in the mid-1980s. It is a Cold War story of espionage and politics played out in the arena of championship chess. The book (and with it, the music and lyrics) underwent massive rewrites between the show's London opening and its Broadway premiere, but the story centered on the same basic idea. A woman, Florence, works as a "second" to an American chess champion (called Freddie in the Broadway version). They used to date, but Freddie's obnoxious, grandstanding ways have brought Florence to her senses, so now she is all business with this John McEnroe-like hothead. His main opponent is the Russian (called Anatoly), whose life is controlled largely by the KGB, just as—we learn—Freddie's is monitored by the CIA. Florence and Anatoly fall in love, and he, despite a love for his country but driven by a distaste for being a political pawn, defects. But the politicians and spies conspire to doom their relationship in the interest of accomplishing some political maneuvers. First, the Russians bring Anatoly's estranged wife Svetlana to drag him home—she and the family have been suffering since his shameful defection. Next—continuing with the Broadway version, since it differs from the London one—we learn that Florence's long-lost father may be alive. She was born in Hungary, and as a young child in 1956, after being taught to play chess by her father, she lost track of him in the Hungarian uprising and has since presumed him dead. Molokov, the Russian political operative, introduces Florence to an old man who sings her a lullaby she remembers; she is sure he is her father. Anatoly is told that she can only be with her father if Anatoly returns to Russia. Wishing for his beloved to have a family at last, he purposefully throws the final chess match and returns in shame to the Soviet Union. Only then does Florence learn that the old man was not her father, but rather a CIA operative held captive—the USSR had exchanged him for Anatoly.

The musical ends with her sobbing, alone, on the ground. It is perhaps the most depressing ending of any musical. Other shows may feature more dead bodies, more crying, more war, but they usually offer some uplifting glimmer of hope for the future. *Les Misérables,* for example, has an enormous body count but ends with such a joyous vision of heaven and such a rousing anthem of hope for the world that audiences leave talking of redemption, not death. But *Chess* is an odd megamusical in this sense—its story, fundamentally, only suggests the scope of the typical megamusical. It is basically a human drama about four people, with an epic-sized backdrop and a hopeless ending. The emotions of Florence and Anatoly are at least meant to be realistic, not melodramatic like those of, say, the Phantom and Christine.

In all other ways, *Chess* is a megamusical, complete with an almost entirely sung-through score full of pop-rock belting and intense emotions, a staging (both in London and in New York) of enormous size and technical wizardry, and a vast amount of pre-opening hype and publicity. Unfortunately, this worthy show could not overcome its obstacles and played only sixty-eight Broadway performances, from April to June 1988.

Chess contains some of Rice's most personal, emotional lyrics to that point. Typically clever, ironic lines are reserved for secondary characters like calculating merchandisers selling chess-related products; the lead characters sometimes speak bitterly, but never cutely and always realistically, about love and politics. The music was composed by an unlikely duo: Benny Andersson and Björn Ulvaeus, the two B's from the 1970s Swedish pop sensation ABBA. Though successful pop composers, they had been looking for a chance to try their hand at theater, and the result is an original, distinct sound. *Chess* has a score that sounds like no other megamusical; it exhibits the pop-based, ballad-heavy megamusical style in general, but in the details it stands alone. The frequent use of dissonant, leaping vocal lines is particularly unusual, especially when paired with unpredictable rhythms and uneven phrase lengths; the song "How Many Women," for Florence and Freddie early in the first act, perhaps best demonstrates these features. Florence has grown angry with her job, which has become little more than babysitting her ill-tempered charge; her leaping line, complete with prominent tritone, and her pointed words convey this side of her character clearly, in under two minutes.

> How many women—articulate women
> With something to shout about—
> Spend their time
> Playing a game in which silence is golden
> And speaking a crime?[8]

Early in the show, Anatoly too is frustrated, though also quite pessimistic that he has a way out of his position as Russian pawn. In the second verse of "Where I Want to Be," he describes the sneaky way in which "they" have taken over his life.

> Then they move in
> Oh, so discreetly
> Slowly at first
> Smiling too sweetly
> I opened doors
> They walked right through them
> Called me their friend
> I hardly knew them.

The music here is sinuous, a flowing waltz which gains a high string countermelody in this verse—the light, seemingly polite treads of the KGB. Beautifully orchestrated by Anders Eljas, the verses suggest a music box, soft, mechanical, and haunting. But the choruses burst out with full orchestral and rock forces, as

Anatoly's thoughts run away with him in a bit of honest, uncensored stream of consciousness: "Now I'm where I want to be and who I want to be and doing what I always said I would and yet I feel I haven't won at all."

Florence and Anatoly begin to take an interest in each other during "Terrace Duet," one of several songs built on bits of recurring musical phrases rather than a verse-chorus rock structure. Fairly free in form, the duet loops back on itself several times, revisiting melody and lyrics, as their conversation progresses. By the end of the number, the pair has constructed a musical phrase that will become—in a somewhat altered form—central to their bittersweet love duet, "You and I." This later song undergoes its own transformations as it returns, several times, throughout the second act. Andersson and Ulvaeus, despite being pop composers with no theatrical experience, know how theater music works. These mobile, changeable musical ideas operate in manners similar to those found in other megamusicals, especially *Evita* and *Les Misérables*. Despite a certain similarity of form, however, the musical material itself retains its unique sound. "You and I" contains a few unpredictable turns of phrase, pivoting away from more obvious square forms toward unexpected leaps and resolutions.

When Anatoly resolves to defect, he closes the first act with the appropriately named "Anthem." He sings of his love for his country, but not its current political methods, in a ballad that rises to an enormous belted climax. Like similar songs meant to lift audiences up out of their seats with emotion, "Anthem" is manipulative in all the best theatrical ways. "Let man's petty nations tear themselves apart," Anatoly declares. "My land's only borders lie around my heart." (Having been one of the few people fortunate to see *Chess* during its brief Broadway run, I can add that the song was made all the more effective by David Carroll's performance; he stood downstage center, unmoving, with tears streaming down his face. By the end of the second act, Judy Kuhn's face was also covered in real tears—as were the faces of most of the audience.)

The song "Quartet (A Model of Decorum and Tranquility)" offers more sustained polyphony than in most musicals. (The only somewhat similar moments in recent Broadway history come from *The Phantom of the Opera,* which opened just three months before *Chess.*) The quartet takes place early in the show, after Freddie has accused Anatoly of cheating during a match and then stormed off. Florence, attempting to speak for Freddie, tries to resolve the squabble with Anatoly, Molokov (Anatoly's second), and the very self-assured arbiter of the match. The quartet begins with a delicate waltz, recalling "Where I Want to Be." Molokov begins politely, with short, slow phrases. Florence, agitated, joins the fray in a flurry of words and faster rhythms. Anatoly stands removed from much of the activity, only getting involved in order to ask Florence how such a nice girl got stuck helping a second-place "nut" like Freddie. Several times, all four join in to express their dismay over the degenerated state of chess:

Florence and Anatoly: *Molokov and Arbiter, simultaneously:*
How sad   It's very sad to see
To see   The ancient and distinguished game that used to be
           All:
           A model of decorum and tranquility
           Become like any other sport
           A battleground for rival ideologies
           To slug it out with glee.

By the end of the quartet, this refrain spins off into something of a fantasia, as the counterpoint grows more active in a rather impressively Baroque manner. The four voices join only to cry "slug it out with glee!" at the end. The quartet, though complicated, also clearly conveys the different emotions of all four characters (much like Verdi's polyphonic ensembles), and injects a much-needed touch of humor into the drama. Rice's words are particularly well matched to Ulvaeus and Andersson's musical style here. And Rice is particularly well suited to making phrases like "a model of decorum and tranquility" and "a battleground for rival ideologies" both singable and realistic.

    The score also contains a few stand-alone ballads and pop songs, ones which made little sense out of context but were catchy enough to work well as singles. Rice and his new team, having learned from the megamusical tradition of *Superstar* and *Evita*, sent two singles up the pop charts before the show even began rehearsals in London. The first was "One Night in Bangkok," a techno-rap (sung by Freddie as he tours Bangkok's seedier areas before a chess match) that was in the top ten in the United States in 1985. Despite the endless chess puns and allusions in the song, few teenagers likely knew that it was from a musical, much less one about chess (and many now-thirty-somethings, still unaware of who wrote the song or why, can still rap along). The second single, "I Know Him So Well," is a bittersweet duet for Florence and Svetlana. Freddie's "Pity the Child," a rock ballad in which he laments his broken home as a child, failed to win over critics, but requires some impressive belting. Florence has perhaps the two best pop solos. In the up-tempo "Nobody's Side," Florence (in typical Rice form) doubts that anyone is ever truthful or loyal: "Better learn to go it alone / Recognize you're out on your own / Nobody's on nobody's side." In the gentler "Someone Else's Story," the best song added for the New York premiere, she resolves to stop working for Freddie. This number particularly showcased Judy Kuhn's remarkable, clear-as-a-bell voice, happily heard on the Broadway cast recording. The theater-style music, with its recurring musical ideas, rousing ballads, catchy pop songs, and unpredictable melodies and rhythms, all added up to a score with megamusical outlines but an unusual, effective sound.

In early 1986, just as rehearsals were about to get underway in London, *Chess* experienced its first major obstacle, one that would reverberate through the rest of the history of the show and help seal its fate. Director Michael Bennett, who had conceived and directed the extremely successful *A Chorus Line* (it was the longest-running musical on Broadway at the time, later topped by *Cats*), had to leave the production for health reasons. Trevor Nunn, already the leading director of megamusicals—*Cats* was running both in London and New York, and *Les Misérables* was a hit in London and on its way to Broadway—stepped in. He therefore inherited Bennett's concept, basic stage design, and cast, and had to make the best of it while trying to assert his own vision as well.[9] The result was a show that did not quite know if it was a personal drama or a giant metaphor—in London, the two male leads were simply called the American and the Russian, and the idea that life was a chess game in which everyone is a pawn dominated not only the story and the tone, but the set design, which featured a huge tilting chess board with video screens in each square as the floor.

Frank Rich, reporting from London, admired some things about the London production (he called the music "enjoyable," although it sounded like Lloyd Webber to him) but found it overly metaphorical and therefore lacking a strong book or character development. *Chess* reminded him of *Evita,* with its rather cold subject matter and staging, its pop-rock music, and its hit singles. British critics mostly gave the show mixed reviews, and fans of the already-released double album embraced the production.

But Rice, Andersson, Ulvaeus, Nunn, and the show's producers were concerned enough to undertake a radical rewrite before opening in New York, particularly because of the problems with the book and character development, as several critics had commented. Nunn also could not resist the temptation to direct his own staging from the ground up. Some songs remained, but others were cut and new ones written. The sung-through score gained some spoken dialogue and a more plot-driven, less ethereal book, rewritten by Rice and playwright Richard Nelson. The main characters remained, but they all gained actual names, back stories, and more complex personalities. Florence's back story, involving her father and her childhood in war-torn Hungary, became central. A new prologue ("The Story of Chess") depicted little Florence's father explaining the history of chess before going off to die (presumably) in the uprising. In London, the two main rounds of chess had taken place in Italy and then Bangkok. Now, the first match was in Bangkok (since "One Night in Bangkok" was a hit) and the second was in Budapest, to bring Florence's story to a climax.

With a more developed book, added twists, and characters more human than symbolic, the story felt more grounded. What had been a concept musical, or at least a sort of hybrid of concept and megamusical, was now a drama—still full of politics, but also driven by a love story and many tears. The chessboard set had been replaced by one equally huge but one that many felt failed to reflect the new version of the story. Designer Robin Wagner (of *Jesus Christ Superstar, A Chorus Line, The Producers,* and *The Boy From Oz,* to name a fraction of his work) created a number of fairly realistic sets—a hotel room, an airport lounge—but surrounded them with twelve three-sided columns, huge gray towers that revolved on their own axes as well as around one another. These became walls behind people, but also (when set in motion) became the winding streets of Budapest or simply scary monolithic barriers to be dodged. Many critics felt they overwhelmed the actors, and despite the very clear symbolism that the world was somehow controlling these individuals, pushing them about, forcing them to move and duck lest they be run over, the giant towers were more distracting than effective.

By the time *Chess* opened on Broadway, however, the controversial new set design was only one factor in the show's negative buzz. Originally planned for a spring 1987 opening, the rewrites, technical aspects, and schedules of the creative team (especially Nunn) pushed the date back until May 1988; the *New York Times* then announced an indefinite postponement, then a fall 1988 open-ing, and finally a return to May 1988. About six months before this opening, when the date was still unclear, Rice told the *Times* that he had hoped to open promptly but did not mind waiting for Nunn; meanwhile, the London version continued to run to strong audiences and was well on its way to recouping its investment.[10] This positive spin helped to displace only some of the doubt sur-rounding the show's rocky road to its New York opening.

Rice, talking to the *Times* again for their customary pre-opening feature, continued to cheer the changes. He also recalled that when he and Lloyd Webber started out, they knew far more about pop music than theater music (especially Rice), and now he found himself working with two pop experts who knew even less about theater music than he did. He added that no theater composer would have written "One Night in Bangkok." (This would no longer be true—one is reminded of "Today 4 U" from Jonathan Larson's *Rent*—but in 1984, the techno-rap sound stood out in the theater.) Rice offered a clear description of the show's themes—involving Cold War politics more than pawns and queens—and summarized what perhaps made *Chess* so depressing: the complete lack of control any character has over his or her life.

> What seems clear to me in international politics is that nobody really knows what's going on except the players. The show's most obvious message is that most people on the sidelines are watching the game and can't really do anything about it. It's not just because they aren't playing but because they don't know what the next move is going to be or why the last move was made. Another point the show makes is that if you get to the top of any field you inevitably get caught up in politics. It even happens to songwriters.[11]

The title of the interview, " 'Chess' Seeks To Shed Its Checkered Past," summarized the problem *Chess* faced on opening night. Critics, whether or not they took the show's strange history into account, nearly all agreed that the concept and/or its execution did not work. Frank Rich pointed out a number of issues which other critics echoed, although he was generally harsher, having been sorely disappointed. He found the show far too full of yelling (thanks to overly emotional directing as well as a loud sound system) and temper tantrums. The politics, which could have had real bite, instead seemed to make both sides equally duplicitous and interchangeable, with unspecific agendas. He felt that the book and lyrics were "pompous pretensions," repeating too often the life-is-a-chess-game metaphor, and the score somehow managed to be "sometimes tuneful but always characterless." He had good things to say about the three leading actors: Judy Kuhn (the first American Cosette in *Les Misérables*) as Florence, David Carroll as Anatoly, and Philip Casnoff as Freddie. The new prologue, featuring a war-torn Budapest, reminded Rich of Nunn's *Les Misérables,* which he liked far better.[12]

In *Newsweek,* Jack Kroll sensed a similar tone—an attempt at a serious mood had resulted instead in self-importance, and the show attempted to overwhelm rather than develop characters. Kroll took this as a sign that the megamusical had gone too far: "With 'Chess,' the first crack in Broadway's Chinese wall of blockbuster overseas musicals appears—and it is a big, festering fissure." The sets dwarfed the actors, the book was weak, the score sounded like bland international pop, and the whole thing felt cobbled together like Frankenstein's monster. Kroll then combined one monstrous giant beast image with another: he noted that while *Les Misérables, Starlight Express,* or *The Phantom of the Opera* might have debatable merits, "each of them delivers something, *some thing,* to its audience. With the $6 million 'Chess' the entire apparatus of these high-tech, huge-concept, giant-scale shows breaks loose from its moorings, like King Kong, and flails about, stomping and crushing everything in its way."[13]

Although their opinions would not do much good, a few critics raved about the show, most notably William A. Henry III in *Time*. He found the show challenging to the viewer, psychologically complex, and emotionally weighty. The show featured a "clear narrative drive, Nunn's trademark cinematic staging, three superb leading performances by actors willing to be complex and unlikable and one of the best rock scores ever produced in the theater. This is an angry, difficult, demanding and rewarding show, one that pushes the boundaries of the form."[14] He even praised the gray pillars, which made everything look appropriately the same, in a "triumph of a soulless international pragmatism."

Clive Barnes felt that the transformation of *Chess* from an "ambitious attempt to symbolize life and politics as a chess game" into a sentimental love story with a political backdrop worked better as a show, but only because its goal was less bold. What kept the show from succeeding was its overly serious tone, which demanded complete believability from the characters and a strict non-offensive stance. He pointed out, as many others did, that it was incredibly unlikely that Anatoly would be allowed to play chess in an Eastern bloc country (Hungary) after having defected so recently, but he found the story of the "tortured love quartet" to be "surprisingly convincing, and Anatoly's doubts, fears and difficulties on his defection are precisely those encountered by every defector I have ever known." He praised the cast and the pillars, and advised his readers to go see it (with earplugs), but—in the inevitable comparison to Lloyd Webber which virtually every megamusical encounters, with or without Rice's presence on the creative team—noted that the score "could be characterized as Andrew Lloyd Webber without the tunes, which is not the best of news."[15]

While a number of critics mentioned the similarly conniving attitudes of the American and Soviet politicians in the show, few pointed directly to the show's bleak ending as a cause of its unpopularity or weakness as a drama. They spoke of the two sides' vague causes and the blindingly obvious metaphor that the main characters were pawns in an international chess game. But after the show had been running a few weeks, Michael Kimmelman of the *New York Times* came perhaps the closest to putting his finger on the problem of *Chess*. He pointed out that the show (along with several others that dealt with the Cold War) depicted quite realistically how the two nations were "locked in a poisonous and unfathomable embrace." The real-life stand-off between the United States and the Soviet Union felt both hopeless and pointless; the result was a generation of young people who expected the world to be full of enemies and tension. This show, then, spoke "directly to an affluent generation of young, politically unmotivated viewers." If they were politically unmotivated, perhaps they were not particularly interested in being an audience for this show either. Perhaps it did not seem like entertainment to watch worthy but powerless people be destroyed by the system in which, despite the glimmer of glasnost on the horizon, we were all still living. This show, then, was "neatly tailored to the apathetic 80's," as Kimmelman described it at the time. Apathetic about politics, and perhaps theater too.[16] Other megamusicals were full of doom and death, but those—*Les Misérables, The Phantom of the Opera, Cats*—displayed two key differences. First, as mentioned, they offered at least sparks of hope for the future and for a present that involves some sense of family or community: Jean Valjean is welcomed by loved ones into heaven, as the people of France march resolutely toward the dawn; Grizabella is welcomed into the Jellicle community, then reborn into a better life; the Phantom sacrifices himself, nobly, so that Christine can have a happy life and family. But by the end of *Chess,* we are left with a man who has been forced through a series of despicable deceptions to return to a loveless marriage and an oppressive country, and a woman who has lost, within minutes, her true love and the father who turns out not to be her father after all. Most important, both have lost—been betrayed by, and abandoned by—their countries. There is no welcome into a better life, no group with whom to march. Florence ends the show alone, sobbing. Despite the megamusical qualities of the show, the ending was atypical of the genre, and an apathetic audience of depressed Americans saw only reality rather than escape or hope.

After the opening, the creative team made some cuts to trim the show to just under three hours rather than just over—better for audiences, and also for the show's budget. Because of union rules for performers, instrumentalists, and backstage staff, any show that runs past three hours runs into overtime pay; the cuts helped them save ten minutes per night and therefore $25,000 per week.[17] None of the changes could sustain the Broadway run, however. When it was all over, *Chess* received only two Tony nominations—for performers David Carroll and Judy Kuhn.

It is quite possible that the time of *Chess* has not yet come, and that with distance from the mid-1980s, when the show can be rendered as a period piece, it will be more of an emotional thrill and less of a depressing reminder of the world outside the theater. When the generation of teens who loved "One Night in Bangkok" raises its own teenagers, the time would perhaps be ripe for a revival. It could work with either a megamusical-style staging or a small, intimate one. And whatever the complaints, a bleak ending can certainly make for a satisfying evening at the theater. This particular story's bleak ending may have been too timely back in 1986, but twenty or thirty years later it might deliver the dramatic punch for which its creative team had hoped.

Andrew Lloyd Webber's (or Trevor Nunn's?) *Starlight Express*

A year before Tim Rice brought *Chess* to New York, his former partner Andrew Lloyd Webber brought *Starlight Express. Cats* had been running for five years when *Starlight Express* arrived, so expectations were high. The new show, however, failed to live up to one of the key features of the 1980s megamusical: it did not last "forever." Instead, *Starlight Express,* despite a very long run in London, ran less than two years in New York, from March 1987 to January 1989, for a total of 761 performances. This would have been a very respectable run by any other standard, but for a megamusical by Andrew Lloyd Webber it was a disappointment.

What limited its success was that it tipped the delicate balance between grand emotion and flashy spectacle, landing with a thud on the spectacle side. *Starlight Express,* as virtually every critic on both sides of the Atlantic agreed, had no heart. What they meant was that it had no real characters; the show told the story of male train engines, engaging in a series of races and attempting to win the love of female train cars—all of which actually takes place in the imagination of an unseen little boy playing with his train toys. The actors roller-skated around the elaborate set, but they rarely demonstrated any emotions other than those befitting cartoons. This could have been great fun; the roller skating and the huge set were impressive, and had the boy's story made more sense, or allowed for some pathos or true love or other believable emotions, it could have added up to a successful entertainment. But Lloyd Webber's score is his weakest to date; the songs had a dated, new wave pop sound even in 1987. Instead of the soaring or slinky or unpredictable melodies of *Cats* or *Superstar,* he offered short-breathed, repetitive, four-square songs orchestrated as teenage bubble gum pop. This was the show that proved—although some critics refuse to believe it—that audiences, at least those in New York, are not entertained merely by a fancy set. *Starlight Express* boasted the fanciest of all sets, and although these sets and loyalty to Lloyd Webber helped it run in London for an astounding eighteen years, the Broadway production was far less successful.

The idea for the story was Lloyd Webber's own. He had always been a fan of trains, especially old-fashioned ones, and had shared this interest with his children. They were fond of stories about Thomas the Tank Engine, a hero of British children's books. Trevor Nunn, who had been so fundamental to the concept, themes, and even the writing of *Cats,* directed *Starlight Express* with his customary large-scale taste. The roller skates were his idea, as was the set: in London's Apollo Victoria Theatre, Nunn and set designer John Napier took out nearly half the seats, turned the stage into an enormous concave bowl, and built a huge moving bridge upstage. They put tracks, on several different levels, around and through the house; the actors skated right through and behind the audience, on all three levels of the theater. Nunn meant for the show to be interactive, surrounding the audience as if they were on a ride.

Starlight Express opened in London in March 1984 to reviews that praised the entertaining set and visual experience, but dismissed much of the rest of the show. Robert Hewison, in the *Sunday Times,* thought the set an impressive accomplishment and admired the hard-working cast, but declared that the show had no plot, boring music, and no heart. He spent the whole show riveted, because he was sure someone would fall and get hurt.[18] The novelty of the show was apparently enough to sustain it in London, though this included some major overhauling.

It took longer than usual for *Starlight Express* to make the move from London to New York, mostly because of requirements of the set. In the end, the show took up residence at the Gershwin Theatre, where the most expensive design to that point in Broadway history—$2.5 million—gave viewers a computer-run bridge, a revolving stage, nearly a mile of skating track, and bodies of water that glowed in the dark.[19] Despite this, many critics would note that because of restrictions of the theater, the set design was not nearly as interactive and surrounding as it was in London, which make the show more like watching other people go on a ride rather than sharing in the experience.

The set led to inevitable backlash against spectacle in general. The situation would surely have been different had the score or the story won audiences or critics over, but with little else to talk about besides the set, it became the hot topic of the day. The architecture critic of the *New York Times*, Paul Goldberger, wrote an article about the tendency toward "overdesign" which was currently plaguing theater pieces and everything else—he mentioned *Starlight Express*, Franco Zeffirelli's production of *Turandot* at the Metropolitan Opera, and George Lucas's films *Star Wars* and *Raiders of the Lost Ark,* among other culprits. He exempted *Les Misérables:* the sets were big but simple in design, and unlike the other examples, they served the plot. In the end, he blamed the Ronald Reagan era for a society that cared more about how things looked than how they actually were.[20]

Lloyd Webber, for his part, had already caught on to this backlash. Though he would rarely give up spectacle, he would be acutely aware that it had to serve the drama (and that there had to be a strong drama to begin with) from now on. But he had his realization—that *Starlight Express* had gone too far in the spectacle direction—in a much too public manner. He disowned the show, blaming Nunn's directing for the production's size and overall mood. Not only did he lament in interviews the loss of his (supposedly) intimate children's musical about trains, he put a disclaimer in the actual Broadway program that each audience member received. "I hope Trevor and my other collaborators will forgive me for saying that despite the commercial success the show has had in London, something of the joy and sense of pure fun that was the original intention seemed to get lost and *Starlight Express* was not quite what we intended."[21] With this, Lloyd Webber practically invited critics to pan the show. They did not disappoint.

Frank Rich echoed virtually all his opinions from his review of the London production three years earlier. At that time he wrote that the sets were entertaining, but that's all there was; the rest of the show "is a dud," with a plot that rips off *Cats.* He predicted that the show would do less well in America, where children cared less about trains than in England, and where Disneyworld offered them much more thrilling rides they could actually experience. He also pointed out that the story and lyrics (by Richard Stilgoe) contained numerous sexist and racist problems; a number of these would be changed later. The girl dining car, for example, describes herself as "fast and cheap and quick"—and she, like all the female train cars, has no engine of her own but must hook herself to a male engine. Rich did not go into detail about the racial problems, but he is surely referring to the fact that the steam engines were black and the diesel ones white, so when they battle, the fights contain clear segregation and racial tension. Rich summarized the overall problem: "Money substitutes for creativity; machinery and deafening noise replace theatrical magic." This is a telling choice of words, because "theatrical magic" was exactly what he had found, and admired, in *Cats.*[22]

In *New York* magazine, John Simon shared Rich's (and virtually everyone's) view that the show lacked emotion or a sense of humanity; he noted that the little boy playing with his trains booms out his lines in a clearly pre-recorded, unspontaneous way.[23] William A. Henry noted in *Time* that the creators of the show had made a revealing comment: they hoped that the show would be compared to Disneyland, not *Sweeney Todd.* The Lloyd Webber vs. Sondheim argument was thus raised, as it usually is, to point out that Lloyd Webber demands less of his audience or offers shows that are more fun and less intellectual. This is often a specious contrast, but in this case actually made sense. Henry pointed out, however, that *Starlight Express* was not nearly as much fun as Disneyland.[24] Ironically, the critics' and creators' doom-filled references to all things Disney would actually come be realized when Disney jumped into the Broadway game in the mid-1990s. With Disney on Broadway, spectacle would be here to stay.

Few critics had much to say about the cast, other than that they all seemed to be working hard to skate, sing, and dance. The only recognizable name was Andrea McArdle, who had been the first Little Orphan Annie in *Annie;* no stars were made from this show (though some found success later, such as Jane Krakowski).

Michael Walsh wrote that no matter how much Lloyd Webber tried to protest that *Starlight Express* was intended for kids, this did not make it good kids' entertainment like *Joseph and the Amazing Technicolor Dreamcoat.* Walsh listed the show's faults, including lyrics that were either dumb or overly sexual (sometimes sexist), a weak plot, and a weak score too full of what he calls "genre" songs in different styles.[25]

Some of these problems were solved in 1992, when Lloyd Webber rewrote large sections of the show. While keeping the same basic plot, set, and many of the songs, he cut five of the more problematic numbers, added three new ones, and engaged Don Black to rework many of the old lyrics and pen new ones. The result was a musical called *The New Starlight Express.* The changes were implemented in all the productions running around the world at that time, including in London, and a new cast album was released. Soon after, in April 1993, *Starlight Express* became the second-longest-running musical in London (behind *Cats*), and it would run there for nearly another decade. It was already long forgotten in New York, where *Cats* and *Phantom* were the shows most associated with their composer. Meanwhile, *The New Starlight Express* continues to tour the United States and the world.

Other Musicals in the 1980s

Broadway took more chances on new musicals in the 1980s than in the 1990s. Revivals, though numerous, rarely ran for more than a year and a half—a fine run for a revival, but nothing like what some new musicals (especially megamusicals) experienced. Most of the shows chosen were safe Golden Era choices: Bernstein and Sondheim's *West Side Story,* Rodgers and Hammerstein's *The King and I,* and Lerner and Loewe's *Brigadoon* and *My Fair Lady.* A few revivals with longer runs were not so high on the list of perennial favorites: Cole Porter's *Anything Goes,* Rodgers and Hart's *On Your Toes,* and Colman and Fields's *Sweet Charity* (based on the film). An excellent production of Gilbert and Sullivan's *The Pirates of Penzance,* featuring Kevin Kline, Linda Ronstadt, George Rose, and Rex Smith (as well as several future members of the cast of *Cats*), ran for nearly two years starting in December 1980 (happily, a pre-Broadway staging in Central Park in summer 1980 of this very funny, warm production is available on video).

But otherwise, Broadway seemed largely interested in new, unusual works. This would not be the case in the 1990s, when revivals abounded and new works were much more often based on known entities like films. But the 1980s saw successful first runs of some influential musicals: Jerry Herman's *La Cage aux Folles, Dreamgirls* by composer Henry Krieger and lyricist Tom Eyen, and the Twain-inspired *Big River* by Roger Miller, among others.

The 1980s was also the decade in which composer/lyricist Stephen Sondheim achieved his greatest critical and commercial successes so far. He has always had supporters among critics and audiences, and though his shows never run for decades like megamusicals, a number of them have been well received and at least somewhat financially successful. Popular lore tells us that Sondheim's shows are too intellectual and complex to be audience favorites, and it is left to the critics and musicologists to appreciate his greatness. There is some truth to this; his lyrics are often intricate and wordy, his music sometimes angular and very rarely sentimental. His plots tend to involve unhappy romances and personal struggles, rarely ending in a standard union of lead characters. One can see why the media often sets him up in opposition to Lloyd Webber, known for his lush romanticism (both musically and in terms of story). But the dichotomy often goes too far, making Sondheim out to be a rarefied, secret genius and Lloyd Webber a crowd-pleasing hack. Compare Sondheim's *Follies* to Lloyd Webber's *Cats,* and the differences do indeed seem striking. But compare Sondheim's *Sweeney Todd* to Lloyd Webber's *Evita,* and the differences become much less apparent. Both shows are quite dark and gruesome in their subject matter; Hal Prince adeptly directed both productions (in fact both in 1979); and both feature scores that use dissonant, harsh music to reflect characters' true feelings and more tuneful music to reflect dissembling. Note, for example, the lovely insincerity of "Don't Cry for Me, Argentina" and a similar false calm demonstrated by the murderous Sweeney Todd in "Pretty Women."

The megamusical bears the distinct stamp of the 1980s in many ways. As we saw in chapter 3, *Cats* especially seemed stuck, mostly stylistically, in 1981; by the 1990s those leg warmers had become appealing kitsch. The next decade brought with it new twists on the megamusical, in new works by both the originators of the genre and by a second generation of composers and lyricists that learned their crafts during the first megamusical heyday of the 1980s. The genre morphed in various ways, retaining certain elements, altering others, dropping a few here and there. But it did not go away. Despite many critics' objections, the large, flashy, highly hyped megamusical remained strong, adapting to the times and finding new ways to be innovative and original. Some megamusicals flopped, as some new musicals always do, but others took their place as semi-permanent institutions on Broadway alongside *Cats, Les Misérables,* and *The Phantom of the Opera.* Those three stalwarts would survive the entire decade, but a few others running alongside them will probably yet surpass them in longevity and success.

"New Music"

The Megamusical in the 1990s

The 1990s saw the premieres of megamusicals by those who had helped to create the form in the 1970s and 1980s, and also by a new generation of composers, lyricists, directors, and producers who had been influenced by the earlier megamusicals. By the end of the decade, many of the original creators of the genre were no longer clearly leading the pack. Indeed, the megamusical itself, having dominated the Broadway musical in the 1980s, would share the stage with a host of other styles by the end of the century. Creators began to stretch the elements of the megamusical in new directions; for example, megamusicals no longer needed to be sung from beginning to end or based on a romantic, melodramatic plot. Still other features of the 1980s megamusical began to find their way into shows outside the genre or to fall by the wayside altogether.

Nevertheless, the megamusical clearly matured and adjusted through the 1990s. First, we look at the megamusical offerings from those who led the field in the 1980s, beginning with the team of Schönberg and Boublil and then Andrew Lloyd Webber. Then we move on to megamusicals and megamusical-influenced shows created by new teams, most of whom were composed of Americans, New York having chipped away at London's dominance. This chapter is more inclusive and less detailed than the previous chapters on the 1980s, not only because there were fewer iconic works in the 1990s, but also because the megamusical's influence grew increasingly far-reaching and diversified. By the end of the decade, the megamusical was still going strong in new forms and helped give rise to a number of related styles.

Schönberg and Boublil in the 1990s: *Miss Saigon*

Miss Saigon is a quintessential megamusical. Most of the shows discussed so far, especially those written after the first wave of the 1980s, demonstrate many but not all the features of a megamusical. But *Miss Saigon* has it all. It features a sung-through score from the creators of *Les Misérables,* Claude-Michel Schönberg and Alain Boublil. It was produced by the leading force behind the megamusical, Cameron Mackintosh. It featured expensive, elaborate sets, including one hugely famous *coup de théâtre,* a helicopter that landed onstage and flew away again. John Napier designed the sets, as he did for *Cats, Starlight Express, Les Misérables,* and *Sunset Boulevard.* Costume designer Andreane Neofitou and lighting designer David Hersey had worked on *Les Misérables,* as did most of the other key players on the creative team. The plot had all the epic, emotional qualities that megamusical audiences expected, with a plot drawn from Puccini's *Madama Butterfly,* an opera with smaller dimensions but equally romantic, exaggerated emotions. (*Miss Saigon* was the first of a mini-wave of Broadway productions based on operas, followed by Jonathan Larson's *Rent,* based on Puccini's *La Bohème;* Elton John and Tim Rice's *Aida,* based on Verdi; and *La Bohème* itself, in a trendy staging by Baz Luhrmann.) It was the biggest of Mackintosh's "high-tech spectacular 'event' musicals" so far, yet one with a personal, somewhat realistic story.[1]

Miss Saigon takes place in Vietnam in April 1975, as the last American troops are being pulled out of the war, just before Saigon falls and Ho Chi Minh takes control. Kim, a seventeen-year-old girl whose family of rice farmers has been killed in the war, has just arrived in Saigon and is working her first night as a "bar-girl" in the sleazy nightclub Dreamland. It is run by a half-French, half-Vietnamese man known as the Engineer, who makes shady deals, pimps his employees, and cares for nothing but his own profit. Kim, full of charming wide-eyed innocence, falls immediately for Chris, a tired marine stationed at the American embassy in Saigon. Despite the desperate urgings of Chris's fellow soldier John, Chris spends the last tense days of the American presence holed up in blissful love with Kim. They even participate in a ceremony that Kim considers a wedding.

Unlike Pinkerton in *Madama Butterfly,* Chris does not intentionally leave Kim behind. Saigon falls, the embassy is evacuated, and Chris and Kim are separated in the chaos. We learn this only later, in a flashback in the second act. But by the end of the first act, three years have gone by, and Kim is now struggling to keep herself alive—as well as her young son, Tam, whom Chris never knew he had fathered. In fact, having been unable to find Kim after a year of searching, he presumed her dead and returned to America, marrying his back-home sweetheart, Ellen. Ellen is aware that she does not have Chris's whole heart; eventually Chris tells her about Kim.

Kim has a back-home sweetheart of sorts as well, Thuy, who was pledged to Kim when they were children and who has since taken up with the victorious North Vietnamese. When Thuy tracks Kim down and threatens to kill her illegitimate son, she shoots him. With the help of the ever-present Engineer, Kim and her son become boat people and flee Vietnam. They dream of going to America, but make it only as far as Bangkok. Chris's old friend John now works as an advocate for the *bui doi,* the children of soldiers and Vietnamese women who are often ignored by their American families. Through his work, he finds Kim in Bangkok and takes Chris and Ellen there. Kim then accidentally meets Ellen before she can be reunited with Chris. The Engineer still dreams of the good life in America, which he plans to win by continuing to hook himself to Kim and her half-American son. But Kim is only interested in giving Tam a better life. Believing that Chris will honor his second marriage to Ellen and that Tam's best hope is to go to America with his father, Kim shoots herself. The show ends with Chris weeping over her body.

The story obviously called for a nearly all-Asian cast. The creative team mounted a far-reaching search for suitable actor/singer/dancers of Asian descent to play the bar girls and local Vietnamese. After extensive searches in London, New York, Los Angeles, and Hawaii, they finally found their Kim in Manila, a teenager who was also a theater veteran, Lea Salonga. In fact, the London cast featured a number of Filipinos along with English performers (both white and not).[2] For the Engineer, Mackintosh and the creative team chose English actor Jonathan Pryce. No one thought anything was controversial about this choice at the time. Pryce was a well-known theater and film actor who would garner rave reviews for capturing the smarmy, slithering Engineer—a character who was more a product of the ongoing war and his own opportunism than that of either his Vietnamese or French parentage.

Schönberg and Boublil explained that their inspiration for *Miss Saigon* came from a photograph they saw of a child being given up by her Vietnamese mother to be taken to an American father that the girl had never seen. This reminded them of the sacrifice in *Madama Butterfly,* so they combined elements of that plot with the backdrop of actual events in Vietnam. Schönberg noted that they used Puccini merely for inspiration, and that the show was meant to be as far from the opera as *West Side Story* is from *Romeo and Juliet.*[3] Schönberg, in fact, was less enthusiastic about using the *Madama Butterfly* story as an inspiration until he came across Pierre Loti's novel *Madame Chrysanthemum,* with a similar but less tragic East/West backdrop. This made it seem as if *Miss Saigon* would be part of a tradition of telling stories of conflict between cultures (and using such stories as fodder for romantic plots) rather than simply retelling Puccini.[4] Certainly many other operas and musicals tread similar ground, such as Rodgers and Hammerstein's *South Pacific* and *The King and I.*

The composer and lyricist worked for months on the book before writing any of the score, paying great attention to the dramatic arc of the plot and the details of the characters. Mackintosh, on board now as their producer, had been a bit wary at first about such a modern, volatile subject, so different from their previous show. But he slowly came to believe in the dramatic power of the story and then to admire the music. He was not accustomed to the duo's working methods. Unlike Lloyd Webber, who often visits his drawer full of tunes when he begins a new project or when he needs to find a song to add to a show, Schönberg focuses first on the book with Boublil and then retreats to compose. Certainly the fact that *Les Misérables* and *Miss Saigon* have nothing in common in terms of setting or mood would make it difficult to use a melody cut from one show in the other. Whatever their differences from Lloyd Webber, Mackintosh eventually found that Schönberg and Boublil had at least something in common with a number of famous American musical composers and lyricists (even if Schönberg knew virtually nothing about Richard Rodgers): "They're not Parisians. They're good Jewish boys—like most writers of the theatre."[5]

Mackintosh's search for a director began, not surprisingly, with Trevor Nunn. But Mackintosh feared that Nunn's sensibilities lay more with historical epics than modern love stories, and he searched for other options. At the same time, Lloyd Webber was considering Nunn for *Aspects of Love,* and Nunn was engaged in the New York reworking of Tim Rice's *Chess.* (The megamusical, for all its hugeness, was still quite a small world; Lloyd Webber, Rice, Nunn, Mackintosh, Napier, Schönberg, and Boublil perpetually rearranged themselves in new combinations, bringing along many of the same team members in slightly shifted groups.) Lloyd Webber thought the young, relatively unknown director Nicholas Hytner might be good for *Aspects of Love,* though Nunn promised everyone that he could do both that show and *Miss Saigon.* But Mackintosh was not convinced, and in the end, Lloyd Webber got Nunn for *Aspects* and Mackintosh got Hytner for *Miss Saigon.*[6] Choreographer Bob Avian, another American on this French/British creative team (he had worked alongside Michael Bennett on Sondheim's *Follies*), came on board, as did the entire design team from *Les Misérables.* Boublil, much more confident in his ability to write English lyrics than he was at the time of *Les Mis,* now had a partner instead of a translator: Richard Maltby Jr., who had directed Lloyd Webber's *Song and Dance* (and many musicals since), worked with Boublil on translations both poetic and colloquial.

Mackintosh had originally intended to take *Miss Saigon* to New York first, but when a suitable theater proved difficult to find, he went the traditional megamusical route and opened in London in September 1989. In typical Mackintosh fashion, the show boasted big numbers: it cost $5 million to stage, had advance sales of $8 million, and was sold out for six months.

The show earned very strong reviews from critics and raves from audiences, and Lea Salonga became an overnight star. The show settled in for a ten-year run.

With the show proving an immediate success, talk resumed about bringing it to New York, and the usual rumors arose—speculation about which theater would win the bidding war, for example. The show soon broke the record for the largest advance ticket sales in New York, at an astounding $24 million, and it wasn't even scheduled to open until March 1991.

But then a controversy descended on *Miss Saigon* that would become better known than any other aspect of the show (except for the helicopter). Megamusicals have often, intentionally or not, attracted publicity from casting controversies; in the case of *Miss Saigon* the issues were not merely the stuff of gossip but involved politics and race relations, and led to changes in how producers and directors thought about casting. The scandal also retained an element of behind-the-scenes gossip, which gave the show even more free publicity.

In July 1990, the Asian division of the ethnic minorities committee of Actors' Equity, the union of Broadway performers, filed a complaint with their parent organization. The complaint, spearheaded by playwright David Henry Hwang and actor B. D. Wong, alleged that the casting of Jonathan Pryce, a white man, as the half-Asian Engineer, was offensive. Pryce had won the Olivier Award for his performance in London, and Actors' Equity had granted him "star status" to bring the role to New York. British Equity pointed out that they had searched for an Asian-English actor to play the Engineer, but when they did not find a suitable one, cast Pryce and received no complaints from their union members or the Asian community. Pryce wore a subtle make-up design when the show first opened, suggesting his character was of color and had Asian eyes, which again garnered no protest until the American controversy began. Pryce then ceased using the make-up.

Hwang had won a Tony for his play *M. Butterfly* in 1988, as had B. D. Wong for Best Actor in that play. (*M. Butterfly* also drew inspiration from the Puccini opera, in this case with a gender-bending twist.) Both Hwang and Wong were strong advocates for more opportunity for Asian-American performers, in roles meant for Asians or for nonspecific roles. Actors' Equity supported this policy, as did the theater community at large—but when it came to this particular example, players were sharply divided. Actors' Equity, quick to back the views of its protestors from within, condemned the casting of Pryce, a white man "painted yellow," in their words. Mackintosh responded that the casting director had seen countless actors in open calls, not only in New York but also in Hawaii, Los Angeles, other California cities, and Manila. None had the talent or reputation of Pryce. Mackintosh did not see the offense in having the half-white character be white rather than Asian; in fact, he declared it a double standard. "Ironically," he noted, "in the current Broadway production of 'Phantom' we have an Amerasian actor of tremendous ability playing the lead role of [Raoul,] the Vicomte de Chagny. Why is it quite proper for him to play a European aristocrat and not for Jonathan Pryce to play a Eurasian?" He accused Actors' Equity of being far more interested in protecting American jobs than Asian-American ones, and since they could not deny Pryce star status, they hoped to block him this way instead.[7] Mackintosh immediately threatened to cancel the show if he could not bring Pryce.

With this, the controversy erupted into front-page news, moving beyond the gossip of the New York theater scene to become a national debate. Could a white man play a man of color without offending the ethnic minority he portrayed? Why, then, could a man of color play a role intended for a white man, including everything from Raoul in *Phantom* to roles in Shakespeare? Why shouldn't the union fight to give the role to an Asian-American? This was the union's job—to fight for its own, both minorities and Americans in general, and the Engineer was a potentially star-making role. Equity, through its spokesperson and executive secretary, Alan Eisenberg, responded to Mackintosh's accusation of a double standard by explaining affirmative action: colorblind casting is intended to give unspecific or even white roles to minority actors, not to give minority roles to white actors.

But many of Equity's own members did not support the barring of Pryce or even the principle behind Wong and Hwang's protest. *Miss Saigon* would bring fifty jobs to actors, at least thirty-four of which would be filled by minorities. If Mackintosh were to cancel this show as a result of Equity's standing on the principle of having one Asian-American actor get one role, all thirty-four would be out of work. So would all the white actors, all the stage workers in sibling unions, all the replacement actors that would work if the production ran for years, all the potential employees of tours, and so on. Then, just as it looked like the members of Equity might overrule their own administration, Mackintosh cancelled the show. Within hours, members of Equity had signed a petition that forced their governing board to reconsider barring Pryce.[8]

The controversy made news in the *New York Times* nearly every day during the summer of 1990. It became clear that the majority of Equity members felt that colorblind casting should be a two-way street, and that more important, New York needed this show. But a few did support the principle behind the original protest: Asian roles should be filled by Asian actors. Pryce, from London, said that he felt as if he were being called a racist, when all he hoped to do was a good job. "I've never had any doubts or qualms about playing the Engineer," he noted. "What is appropriate is that the best person for the job play the role, and I think it's completely valid that I play the role. If the character is half Asian and half European, you've got to drop down on one side of the fence or the other, and I'm choosing to drop down on the European side."[9] As the controversy raged, Pryce's air of general calm about the whole thing continued; to him, acting was acting. "Changing our appearance is what we do as actors," he pointed out. "I'm Welsh, and in 18 years of working, I've never played a Welshman. Does that mean that every time I appear, I'm offending the acting community?"[10]

Frank Rich, reporting in the *New York Times* about the London production, made an even stronger case for the Engineer's being cast with a white man: it did not matter, really, that the role was only half-Asian. Fundamentally, the role was not even a real person. Similar to the role of the Emcee in *Cabaret,* the Engineer's job was to "personify the spirit of the war in Vietnam itself—of warped ideals, bottomless corruption, unspeakable atrocities, hypocritical politicians (East and West) and moral chaos. He's not really an Engineer, but rather a parasitic fixer." It did not matter in the slightest what race the actor was— but it mattered completely that the role be played by Pryce. Rich declared it one of the two best performances he had seen in thirty years in London, and he felt that Mackintosh was absolutely right not to bring the show to New York without him, since he carried and saved a production that otherwise would suffer from what Rich saw as its dull, bloated sections. Rich supported the idea of colorblind casting no matter the direction, and declared Equity's decision "hypocritical reverse racism." But even if he could understand that Equity was making a stand in favor of helping minorities, they chose the worst possible example with which to do so. The Engineer is half French and half Vietnamese because the setting of the show makes it appropriate for him to be so, but he is "in reality a theatrical device, a chorus, an eternal camp follower—alternately American and satanic in personality, a character without a proper name and without an ethnic or national identity of any recognizable sort in the text or on stage."[11]

Indeed, not only was the Engineer's ethnicity unclear (he speaks of learning various life lessons from various groups but aligns himself with none), he rarely interacts with the other characters in any realistic way. He makes events happen, he schemes, but he has few human emotions other than greed. He often speaks to the audience, not to the other characters, about his cynical beliefs and goals. Thanks partly to Pryce's effective performance, the big eleven o'clock number was not Kim's self-sacrifice, but the Engineer's twisted fantasy about what he hopes to find in America when he wheedles his way there with Kim and her son. In "The American Dream," the audience sees the Engineer's vision come to colorful life. He begins with a reminder of his multicultural, hard-luck childhood: his mother was a whore for whom he pimped as a child. But when the Americans came to Vietnam, he found new ways to earn money: "I can sell shit, and get thanks. / That's what I learned from the Yanks."[12] He feels that he is an American at heart, because of the opportunity one can find there.

> What's that I smell in the air?
> The American dream
> Sweet as a suite in Bel-Air
> The American dream
> Girls can buy tits by the pair
> The American dream
> Bald people think they'll grow hair
> The American dream
> Bums there have money to spare
> The American dream . . .
> Schlitz down the drain
> Pop the champagne
> It's time we all entertain
> My American dream!

As he becomes more enthralled by the fantasy he spins, the stage transforms into a cartoonish vision of his America. The Asian girls he used to employ now enter in Vegas-style sequined showgirl costumes and very fake blonde wigs. Dancing men in sparkling tuxedos frolic about. And, in the middle, a huge pink Cadillac convertible carries a girl in a Statue of Liberty costume. The Engineer throws himself onto its hood amid a fit of sexual ecstasy. The song reaches a peak of volume and intensity, but it gets there slowly, building from a soft Kander and Ebb-style vamp and a rather vaudevillian sensibility.

It became clear to the board of Actors' Equity that they had made an ill-informed decision, supporting the protest of Hwang and Wong and barring Pryce without realizing the backlash it would receive from many of its members, minority and not. Equity had seventy-nine voting members at the time, and only about half had voted (in a very close count) on the question of barring Pryce from coming to New York. They represented about 39,000 performers. Now, with hundreds of Equity members demanding that the decision be reconsidered so that they all might have the chance to work, Equity was forced to reconvene. Statements were released, meetings were called, editorials for both sides abounded. Finally, Equity's board voted again, reversed their decision, and invited Pryce to New York. Their statement said they had "applied an honest and moral principle in an inappropriate manner."[13]

At this juncture, Mackintosh made an ingenious—or perhaps diabolical—move. He did not immediately cheer the decision and agree to bring his show to New York. Instead, he made a new demand: that he have complete creative control over any future decisions, including those of casting. Rumors suggested that he feared Lea Salonga, the Filipino actress, would be blocked by Equity. But what he explained publicly was that he did not want to bring the show to New York under the cloud of a hostile working environment. He wanted assurance that, although he would be perfectly happy to cast any person of any race in any role, the ultimate criterion had to be talent, and the final decision his.[14]

A fresh round of discussions sprang up. The *New York Times* and other papers ran not just editorials, but features about the history of Asians in entertainment. If Wong and Hwang's primary goal had been awareness, they had achieved it. Equity released a statement saying that they had reached an agreement with Mackintosh, the details of which were kept secret—but the show would go on.[15] Casting began; many hundreds of Asian-American and other actors of color flocked to the open calls in New York and Los Angeles.

But, as expected, Mackintosh had one more round of fighting to go. He asked Equity for special permission to bring Salonga to New York. He had auditioned over 1,200 women, he argued, and not one had both the youth and the range of talent that Salonga brought to the role. Equity could not justify the exception by declaring Salonga an international star, since this was her first high-profile role, so they had to be convinced that no American could do the job. Equity rejected Mackintosh's request, Mackintosh took the next step of seeking outside arbitration, and finally—with *Miss Saigon*'s advance rising to a new record of $34 million—Equity granted Salonga permission to come to New York.[16] (Taking over the strenuous role for occasional performances was an Asian-American woman from Allentown, Pennsylvania.)

By this time, Mackintosh had become a star in his own right, more famous than he had been for his work on *Cats* or *Les Misérables*. In the *New York Times Magazine*, Mervyn Rothstein wrote a long article about the controversial producer in which he used a then-unfamiliar term to describe his shows; *Cats*, he opined, was "the first of the British megamusicals." Rothstein offered interesting insights into Mackintosh's working methods, including his commitment to getting investors their money back as soon as possible; his persuasive techniques that involve a mix of charm, ego, and temper; his admiration for Lloyd Webber; his hands-on involvement in everything his company does, including a single advertising slogan in a newspaper; and his earlier biography.[17]

With so much attention paid to the casting, the role of the Engineer, and the power of Mackintosh, few critics or historians have looked at the score. "The American Dream" is the Engineer's only big number, and he otherwise sings while engaged in various deals or scams. Kim, on the other hand, carries a great deal of the music, as does Chris. They sing several duets, including the delicate "Sun and Moon" and the equally crystalline "Wedding Ceremony (Dju Vui Vai)." These numbers, like many of Kim's, feature flute and other delicate, high instruments, though for their duet, "The Last Night of the World," they are given a soft-rock saxophone and a more pop-oriented, less theater-like number.

Kim also belts out several anthems; for "I Still Believe," she is joined (from the other side of the planet) by Ellen. As Kim remains hopeful for Chris's return, Ellen attempts to understand why he remains troubled after three years at home. The act 1 finale, "I'd Give My Life for You," begins with Kim softly pledging to protect her son, but slowly builds and then merges, in a chilling dramatic effect, with the dirge-like march of the boat people as they trudge hopelessly off to a different life.

The use of the chorus, in fact, is one of the most effective elements in *Miss Saigon,* as it had been in *Les Misérables.* Serving as poor bar girls and patrons ("The Heat Is On in Saigon"), then as dispirited disenfranchised Vietnamese, then as victorious soldiers ("The Morning of the Dragon"), the chorus surrounds and saturates the love story with its moody context.

In terms of form, the score works much like that of *Les Misérables,* with scenes made up of interlocking sections of song and recitative-like material. Overall, however, the score relies far more on set numbers than on amorphous binding material, and contains fewer revisitings and reworkings of moveable musical ideas.

With the casting controversies finally settled, *Miss Saigon* opened on Broadway on 11 April 1991. In true megamusical fashion, it easily overcame mixed reviews with publicity and extremely positive word of mouth from audiences. But unlike *Cats,* for example, *Miss Saigon* received fairly level-headed reviews, without much of the open hostility or snide remarks that megamusicals sometimes inspire. Most critics found the show worth seeing, even if they had a number of criticisms.

Frank Rich, having already weighed in with his view that Jonathan Pryce was a must for the show, told his *New York Times* readers to go see it, now that it had finally arrived. Interestingly, Rich cast *Miss Saigon* in a non-mega-musical light, finding that it had much more in common with older American musicals than with the newer British imports. He saw the influence of *Follies, Pacific Overtures, Oliver!, South Pacific, The King and I, West Side Story,* and *Fiddler on the Roof,* among others. The first two shows on this list are Sondheim's—not normally a name that springs to mind when critics consider the megamusical. But this was Rich's point: *Miss Saigon* has "lush melodies" like Rodgers and Hammerstein's works, excellent star-making performances rather than undefined ensembles, and despite the "inane" helicopter moment, this is the most "intimate" and "least spectacular" of the imports from the West End. In fact, he argued, it only goes astray when it tries to be more like the mega-musical. This happened in two ways. First, the spectacle moments seemed point-less (and in fact the flashy Bangkok set reminded Rich of a similar moment in the ill-fated *Chess*). Second, *Miss Saigon* shared the fatal flaw of all megamus-icals: they all demonstrate "their creators' utter bewilderment about what hap-pens between men and women emotionally, psychologically and sexually." Ellen drew inadvertent laughs, and Chris came across as bland. Many earlier mega-musicals got away with not addressing intimacy because they were almost com-pletely lacking in a traditional love story (*Jesus Christ Superstar, Evita, Cats, Starlight Express*), but this one faced the problem head-on. Rich found the results rather embarrassing. But Salonga, Pryce, and the seedier, moodier sections that did not deal directly with the love story sold the show for Rich; he also praised (as all others did) Hinton Battle as Chris's friend John, who delivered the corny "Bui Doi" with a passion that stopped the show. The show might not say any-thing new about the war, noted Rich, but it "still manages to plunge the audience back into the quagmire of a generation ago, stirring up feelings of anguish and rage that run even deeper" than the recent casting controversy.[18]

Understandably, most critics compared *Miss Saigon* to earlier megamusicals, although here in 1991, they were each still making up their own labels: British imports, spectaculars, and so on. Some found the spectacle impressive and well-integrated; others found it gratuitous and responsible for the new high in ticket prices (regular seats went for $60, and Mackintosh sold a few select spots for a record-breaking $100). Some thought the music tuneful, others a bland wash of Euro-pop. Douglas Watt, in the New York *Daily News,* found the score less successful than that of *Les Misérables,* made up of "trifling melodies punctuated by downward crashing Andrew Lloyd Webberisms" (though he neither defines the term nor cites examples).[19] For *Time* magazine, William A. Henry III wrote an enthusiastic rave, finding the show "relevant and thought provoking" as well as full of deeper meanings: Kim's fate was "a paradigm for all the promises that Western powers made but failed to keep in Vietnam and other colonies." Linda Winer in *Newsday* admired the staging, sets, and performances, but was put off by the very element that Henry found so moving: the message and subject matter. She found the photos of actual Vietnamese children, projected during "Bui Doi," offensive; the show "dances on a sliver of a line between exploitation and the show-biz equivalent of passionate commentary about exploitation." She declared that the team had "created a big, slick, entertaining, sentimental yet cynical melodrama that plays pat and loose with political history and charges up to $100 for people to feel guilty about orphans left by American servicemen."[20] Her tone was similar to that of Michael Feingold in his review of *Les Misérables;* both sense a lack of sincerity in the creative team, and a manipulation of the audience, tapping into their upper-middle-class guilt about those less fortunate. Neither show, it is safe to say, intends this. Nothing suggests that anyone on the creative team for *Miss Saigon* (or *Les Misérables*) used the subject matter for its ability to evoke guilt. If audiences were moved, the goal was reached; if some of them went out to make the world a better place, the goal was surpassed. But, in increasingly cynical times, it is understandable that critics may find grand emotions and naïve, sincere characters hard to swallow, and therefore decide that the creators could not have been sincere.

Even those who disliked certain aspects of the show found others to praise, and no major newspaper panned the show completely.[21] It scarcely mattered, since the publicity (especially from the casting dispute) was more than enough to keep the show running for some months, and by then, good word of mouth from audiences handed the show a healthy ten-year run, until January 2001, for a total of 4,092 performances.

Lea Salonga, Jonathan Pryce, and Hinton Battle all won Tony Awards for their work. The entire creative team was nominated in their respective categories, but lost most of their Tonys to *The Will Rogers Follies* (which also beat *The Secret Garden* in many categories). The media, which had run a *Miss Saigon* story nearly every day for much of the summer in 1990, and which had covered the show's opening with great attention, left it alone until Mackintosh announced its closing. Originally announced for 31 December 2000, the date would be moved a month later, thanks to a last-minute boost in ticket sales; Mackintosh did the same shift with the closing date of *Cats* (which finally shut down around the same time, in September 2000). By the time of *Miss Saigon*'s closing, it had grossed $1.3 billion worldwide, which for a musical is enormous but for a megamusical is quite average—unlike *Les Misérables, Miss Saigon* had by then opened in "only" seven foreign countries. A feature in the *New York Times* noted that the show had done wonders for minorities, especially Asians, by keeping hundreds of people steadily employed—and the worldwide productions, plus two U.S. tours, would continue.[22]

Andrew Lloyd Webber in the 1990s

Andrew Lloyd Webber chose a different path—or at least attempted to—when he followed *The Phantom of the Opera* with *Aspects of Love. Phantom* was not only immensely popular, it was also far better received by critics than many of his previous works. But Lloyd Webber wanted to write something other than a megamusical. He knew the formula was not infallible; *Cats* had been an unprecedented hit, but there had also been *Starlight Express.* And Lloyd Webber was never one to rest on his laurels or rely on a formula, in any strict sense; despite his two big hits of the 1980s sharing certain megamusical qualities (a sung-through score, elaborate sets, enormous marketing campaigns and publicity), they also demonstrated strong differences. *Cats* was heavy on theme and light on plot and character, and was told almost entirely through dance and movement; *Phantom* was a character-based book musical revolving around a love story.

Braving a new experiment once again, Lloyd Webber turned to *Aspects of Love.* Having long been criticized (or at least known) for writing musicals lacking in realism or fully developed love stories and emotions, Lloyd Webber set out to write an earthbound story about love. Based on a 1955 novella by David Garnett, the story revolves around Rose, an actress, and her young admirer, Alex. They impulsively begin an affair and run off to a villa owned by Alex's uncle, George. George must interrupt his tryst with his lover, Giulietta, a sculptor, to investigate what young Alex has been doing at his villa. There he is immediately taken with Rose, much younger than himself but much older than Alex. When Rose is called to work and Alex to his duties as a soldier, their affair ends. Two years later, Alex is stunned to find that Rose has taken up with George. Rose meets Giulietta (George is still seeing her as well as Rose) and the two women become friends, bonded by their love for George and by a (mostly implied) homosexual experimentation. George and Rose eventually marry and have a daughter, Jenny. Act 2 opens twelve years later; Rose has become a huge success. Upon seeing Alex for the first time in all these years, both she and Alex abandon their current unimportant love interests (no one is entirely faithful to anyone) and return to George's villa, where Alex befriends young Jenny, the daughter of George and Rose. By the time the girl is fourteen, she and Alex have developed an illicit attraction for each other, the stress of which eventually leads George to have a fatal heart attack. Giulietta, after delivering a rousing eulogy for George, suggests to Alex that she become his lover, at least until Jenny is of age. At the end, Rose fears loneliness.

By no means a traditional love story, the plot nevertheless involved realistic human characters engaging in mostly everyday discussions, from declarations of love to (as many critics would note) ordering drinks, all set to music. The sung-through score made *Aspects of Love* seem like a megamusical, but also, thanks to an earthbound (if occasionally melodramatic) romantic plot, like an opera. Indeed, Lloyd Webber spoke of it as a chamber opera, on a Mozartean scale, and resisted huge sets.[23] Perhaps it was inevitable that the show would drift toward the megamusical, though, especially when Lloyd Webber chose Trevor Nunn to direct it. This was a rather surprising choice, given their recent history. Lloyd Webber had disowned *Starlight Express,* publicly blaming the show's mega-sizing, and its resulting failure in New York, on Nunn. Then he passed over Nunn in favor of Harold Prince to direct *The Phantom of the Opera,* and rejected the lyrics Nunn had written for melodies that were originally intended for *Aspects* but ended up in *Phantom.* And finally, Lloyd Webber had been considering young director Nicholas Hytner for *Aspects* before settling on Nunn instead. Despite this rocky history, Nunn was enthusiastic about the project and was already its director during the tryout at Lloyd Webber's Sydmonton Festival in July 1988.

Lloyd Webber, who had been interested in creating a musical from Garnett's short novel since about 1980, shaped the basics of the book himself. He also took on the role of producer; the Really Useful Group funded the entire venture. Lloyd Webber's days of handing over the responsibility for the money, publicity, and other business tasks to Cameron Mackintosh were over. He chose two lyricists: Charles Hart of *Phantom,* who worked on the more romantic sections, and Don Black of Lloyd Webber's one-woman show *Tell Me on a Sunday,* who wrote the bulk of the lyrics, especially the lighter sections. Once the score was well underway, Lloyd Webber released a single, in his usual fashion; this was "Love Changes Everything," the anthem that frames the entire story, sung by Michael Ball. (Ball, famous as London's first Marius in *Les Misérables,* played Alex from the Sydmonton Festival onward.) Thanks to some fairly general lyrics and Ball's young, dashing, full-throated belting, the song hit number two in England, but no concept album was released.[24] In preparation for the London opening, Lloyd Webber paid his debt to American Actors' Equity. In exchange for their allowing Sarah Brightman to play Christine in *Phantom* in New York, Lloyd Webber cast not one but two American actresses in his London cast: Ann Crumb as Rose and Kathleen Rowe McAllen as Giulietta.

Perhaps Nunn's visions are always large. Or perhaps Lloyd Webber, who has an instinct toward largeness just like Nunn, could not entirely hold firm to his small-scale intention. In any case, Nunn's production had a distinctly megamusical look: large sets and constant motion. While the main set pieces were rather drab—a back wall and floor made of lumpy tan brick, a distant view of the Pyrenees, George's vine-covered house—they flew in and out along with the more elaborate settings of café, garden, and train. Despite these megamusical-style visual stimulants, some qualities in Lloyd Webber's writing that had not been emphasized before now seemed to shine through. Critics, both in London and in New York, noted especially the use of recurring musical ideas—not just melodies but motifs, recitative ideas, and other seemingly more sophisticated techniques. Critics also acknowledged the realistic emotions, although many found the story distasteful and the characters somewhat unlikable. In London, many critics admired not only the complex score and the interesting characters, but the drab (if big and numerous) sets which were usually quite unobtrusive and well integrated.

John Peter of the London *Sunday Times* led the way with a fairly encouraging mixed review, in which he noted but did not entirely admire the use of recurring motifs. As so many critics do, Peter compared Lloyd Webber to Sondheim, in a way that suggested that Lloyd Webber's increasing sophistication made him more like Sondheim, and that this was a noble goal. Peter wrote, "As with some of Sondheim's songs, the point is not whether it's a tune you can hum on the way home, but whether the music is in tune with the feeling of the moment. I don't think you have to be steeped in classical opera to respond to this; and if this is the new direction of Lloyd Webber's work then we have a lot to look forward to."[25] The score is indeed filled with phrases and shapes that return and carry meaning, but probably no more often than in *Phantom,* and in any case Lloyd Webber had used recurring motifs since *Jesus Christ Superstar.* Critics, primed by the advertising for something like a chamber opera, were simply more inclined to notice these techniques in *Aspects of Love.* British audiences also seemed to understand and enjoy this new venture of Lloyd Webber's, and gave *Aspects* a healthy run of over three years.

Audiences in New York did not embrace *Aspects of Love* as they had most of Lloyd Webber's earlier imports; apparently the odd mix of megamusical, opera, and book musical, with its somewhat unpleasant characters, failed to resonate. It ran on Broadway from 8 April 1990 to 2 March 1991, 377 performances, and lost about $8 million. Michael Walsh offers an interestingly contradictory explanation for why the show failed in New York, both blaming and pardoning the audience for the show's fate. He separates the audience into two groups; the first is smart enough to realize the value of the score, and the second (apparently larger) expects spectacle. "Sophisticated theatergoers mostly recognized it for what it was, Lloyd Webber's best, most well-integrated score. But the New Jersey day-trippers and the tourists from Kansas City couldn't figure it out; for them *Aspects* really was, as one London wag put it, a musical about 'rather selfish middle-class people bonking each other.' It was not a must-see, like *Cats* or *Phantom;* why, the sets didn't even levitate!"[26] And yet Walsh ignores the fact that (presumably unsophisticated) audiences did not embrace *Starlight Express*— surely the shiniest of all musicals—because despite its entertaining set, it offered virtually no other rewards. Audiences failed to embrace *Aspects of Love* for different reasons, perhaps most prominently because it lacked satisfactorily moving characters (as Walsh himself implies); spectacle would not have added much.

For *Aspects of Love,* Frank Rich wrote his most hostile pan of a Lloyd Webber production to date. The *New York Times* critic felt that Lloyd Webber's foray into the human heart "generates about as much heated passion as a visit to the bank," and trying to follow all of the liaisons over seventeen years was baffling and eventually ridiculous, especially when one couple (Alex and Giulietta at the very end) finally engages in a literal roll in the hay. The lyrics, "translated from the original Hallmark," do not help to clarify anyone's emotions, he felt. Rich found the book, mostly Lloyd Webber's doing, particularly troubling thanks to rampant misogyny: "Both heroines of 'Aspects of Love' frequently behave like bitches and whores, to use the epithets of the male characters." And Maria Björnson's dark sets, so effective for *Phantom,* did not serve this show well. With regard to the score, Rich, who had so often raised the charge of pastiche and accused Lloyd Webber of borrowing from other composers, here found a new musical influence: "But this time the composer's usual Puccini-isms have been supplanted by a naked Sondheim envy." Rich does not define what makes the music sound like Sondheim, but like Walsh, he is probably referring to the use of angular, moveable bits of melody. The technique is as much Puccini as Sondheim, generally speaking, but perhaps the mere presence of regular humans having conversations about relationships was enough to invoke images of Sondheim, no matter the musical technique. Rich noted, finally, that the whole show would have been better on roller skates.[27]

Two critics who usually disliked megamusicals embraced a few aspects of *Aspects*, perhaps because the megamusical qualities were toned down. John Simon of *New York* gave high praise to the sets, which although in constant motion were still simple and necessary to the drama. Michael Feingold of the *Village Voice* praised Trevor Nunn's work, which he admitted surprised him; he enjoyed the stage pictures and the justified movement. Both panned Lloyd Webber's contributions; Feingold, true to form, declared that Lloyd Webber was not actually a composer at all.[28]

William A. Henry's rave review in *Time* could not stem the flow of negativity. Nevertheless, his take on the mood of the show was perhaps the most insightful of any major critic: "Events are often melodramatic, but the tone is rueful and autumnal." He enjoyed the recurring music, and found it daring that Lloyd Webber presented the best tune ("Love Changes Everything") first and then found interesting ways to repeat it.[29]

Biographer Michael Coveney notes that the innovations in the score of *Aspects* are clear. Lloyd Webber, continuing to write sung-through scores with some recurring music, had also hit upon new ways to carry the drama with this show (although these innovations contained much that he learned in *Phantom*). "The music in *Aspects*," explains Coveney, "never stands still but curls round the narrative like wreaths of smoke, signaling a quite different way of writing to that of the barbarous recitative in *Superstar* or the segregated pastiche styles in *Starlight*."[30] He is right that no character in *Aspects* is assigned a unique musical style; rather, they all share the same set of musical ideas, using different ones (the childlike music of "Chanson d'Enfance," the declarations about new and uncertain love made with "Seeing Is Believing") when the drama suits them. Characters even dissemble with melody; when Jenny tries to persuade Alex to give in to his feelings for her, she uses his own melody, "Love Changes Everything," which for him is a sincere statement of truth but for her is a tool of manipulation. The emotional conflicts reach a peak in the quartet "Falling," which twists four lines of music into dissonant crashes and dead ends rarely heard on Broadway.

When *Aspects of Love* closed in New York, an article in the *New York Times* speculated about "whether the show's failure indicates that the expensive, over-produced British musical extravaganza has lost its luster with audiences."[31] But this was not entirely the right question. *Aspects* was indeed somewhat over-produced and would have fared better in a smaller theater on a smaller set. But by the nature of its plot, *Aspects* was not entirely a megamusical—not, as the phrase "British musical extravaganza" tries to assert, meant to be considered in the same breath as *Cats* or *Les Mis*. What *Aspects* needs is a bit of book tweaking, and then a revival that bills it with appropriate expectations to size and plot. Mark Steyn is more on track when he explains the failure of *Aspects* not as the failure of a megamusical but simply as a misunderstanding; he argues that *Aspects* is not a megamusical, a reality for which people were unprepared given that it was a Lloyd Webber show. Instead, *Aspects* was like just another musical that any composer might have written, and Lloyd Webber's name on the marquee merely caused false expectations and disappointment.[32]

According to Walsh, *Sunset Boulevard*, Lloyd Webber's next work, "marked a return for the composer to the realm of the megamusical."[33] But, as we have seen with each new Lloyd Webber show, this one featured a number of innovations and changes to the genre. Most obviously, *Sunset Boulevard* differs in that it has dialogue. It works in some ways like an old-fashioned book musical, with conversations among characters landing on a song cue. There are also entire scenes that have underscoring as people speak, and a few sections that work like *Aspects* or *Phantom*, with recitative-like singing or a reliance on motifs. But for the most part, dialogue leads to set piece in this show, and the musical recurrences are closer to reprises than motivic reworkings. Theater historian Mark Steyn particularly admires Lloyd Webber's compositional technique in this show, because he recognizes some Golden Era techniques effectively deployed here. He notes, for example, that the songs usually begin and end, as set numbers, and that they arise naturally from the dialogue, to embody one idea or emotion in song. This is certainly true in many cases; "Too Much in Love to Care," for example, neatly embodies Joe and Betty's youthful, pure feelings for each other, in a distinctly Rodgers and Hammerstein vein. For Norma, Lloyd Webber created yearning ballads—"With One Look," "New Ways to Dream"—which sound sincere and normal inside Norma's head but, from Joe's (and our) perspective are sometimes pathetic and creepy. Steyn especially admires Lloyd Webber's music for Norma because it contrasts with that of Joes's young Hollywood peers:

> For Norma, he's written a silent film score: she sounds, musically, like a creature from another world, conjured by clean, spare, almost translucent 4/4 ballads, whose eerie strings and woodwinds hover like the soundtrack to a trance. The orchestrations are elusive, ambiguous—a surprisingly psychological score from a composer we've come to associate with lush operetta certainties. But it's not just music, with [lyricists] Black and Hampton playing [librettists] Giacosa and Illica to Britain's Puccini wannabe: with this score, we're back, at last, to *song* ideas.[34]

Despite this bold change in compositional style to a more song-based, dialogue-inspired form, *Sunset Boulevard* had all the other trappings of a megamusical. Based on the well-known Billy Wilder film, it tells the story of the larger-than-life Norma Desmond, a former silent film star, now a middle-aged and somewhat deranged woman alone in her enormous mansion, waiting for her comeback. Struggling screenwriter Joe Gillis stumbles into her world, and eventually his distaste toward her turns to pity and something like attraction. As he gets sucked into her strange psyche, he pulls away from his sweet young girlfriend, Betty Schaefer. When Norma's dreams of renewed fame on the screen are shattered once and for all, she drops over the edge into psychosis and takes Joe with her. The musical, like the movie, begins after Norma has shot Joe, and he narrates the story as a flashback from beyond the dead.

Most of the characters are normal, and they talk and sing realistically— much more like in *Aspects of Love* than the thoroughly romantic *Phantom*. The lyrics came from Don Black, who had just written the dialogue-like lyrics for *Aspects of Love,* and screenwriter Christopher Hampton. But the mere presence of Norma Desmond, who delivers her lines in a state of perpetual grandness, as if she were always onscreen, tips the whole show away from the everyday and toward the megamusical. Her mansion, with its giant staircase coming down from the back wall, seals the deal; veteran megamusical set designer John Napier built a gilded, fading, cavernous home for Norma that at one point rises off the stage floor to reveal the much humbler dwelling of Joe's friends. With Trevor Nunn again on board, the scope of the story and of Nunn's predictably large-scale vision were an excellent match. The entire undertaking was again produced by Lloyd Webber's Really Useful Theatre Company.

As with *The Phantom of the Opera* and, for somewhat different reasons, *Miss Saigon, Sunset Boulevard* garnered enormous pre-opening publicity because of casting issues prior to the New York opening. *Sunset Boulevard* opened at the Adelphi in London on 12 July 1993, where it received fairly favorable if mixed reviews from critics and strong support from audiences. Patti LuPone, the American theater star who had been Broadway's first Evita and London's first Fantine in *Les Misérables,* received strong notices as Norma Desmond. In fact, the only critic with a negative reaction to LuPone's bold, scenery-chewing performance was Frank Rich, reporting for the *New York Times* from London. He admired both her acting and singing, but thought her miscast: she was too young and perky for the role of the washed-up actress. Amazingly, Rich declared the score Lloyd Webber's best to date and gave the show a level-headed mixed review, quite a change from the vitriol he released on *Aspects of Love* and most of Lloyd Webber's other shows.[35]

Before the Broadway production, Lloyd Webber decided to give *Sunset Boulevard* an out-of-town opening in Los Angeles; it was more than a tryout, given the enormous publicity the Really Useful Group unleashed on L.A., but it was still considered a kinder critical audience than New York. It was also culturally appropriate to open in L.A. given the show's Hollywood subject matter and film inspiration. Patti LuPone, soon to end her run in London, had been signed to open with the show in New York. But for this engagement in California, film actress Glenn Close was cast as Norma.

A surprising thing happened: Glenn Close, known for her acting but not considered much of a singer, received rave reviews. Critics, while acknowledging her somewhat small singing voice, were completely taken by her acting. They even liked how she managed to compensate for imperfect singing with convincing emotions, using her voice to demonstrate vulnerabilities within Norma Desmond rather than any possible weaknesses of her own. Lloyd Webber, characteristically quick to seize an opportunity when he saw one, announced that Close would open in the New York production instead of LuPone.

The press had a field day, especially when LuPone made it clear that she was heartbroken and angry—plus, she already had a contract. Rumors proliferated over the dollar amounts being discussed in the settlement; eventually Lloyd Webber bought her out for reportedly between one and two million dollars.[36] Back in Los Angeles, Glenn Close was finishing her run and preparing to move on to New York, and Lloyd Webber and his production team cast another film actress, Faye Dunaway, as the next L.A. Norma Desmond. But after several weeks of rehearsals with Dunaway, a previously enthusiastic Lloyd Webber and team had to admit that she could not sing the role (not even well enough to carry it along with some fudging), and rather than find a last-minute replacement, announced that the Los Angeles production would close.

The publicity generated from not one but two casting scandals, with outraged divas at the center, made the New York opening of *Sunset Boulevard* a huge media event. Dunaway, publicly humiliated, sued and won a huge settlement. An article in the *New York Times* speculated about Lloyd Webber's ability to offend two divas, and whether either firing had been a sincere move based on the needs of the show, or had been pure publicity stunts. Friends said he was shy, sensitive, and misunderstood, but others found him to have a "chilling temper, an aloof personality and, after so much power and money over the years, indifference to the sensitivities and needs of performers with fragile egos."[37]

If the goal had indeed been publicity, it worked, for there was no one who had not heard that Lloyd Webber had a new show coming to Broadway. Advance ticket sales threatened previous records, reaching $32 million. It would barely matter what the critics had to say about Glenn Close or any other aspect of the show, because *Sunset Boulevard* looked sure to have a respectably long run. As it turned out, Lloyd Webber and his team need not have worried, if they had at all: the critics were kind to *Sunset Boulevard,* with reviews ranging from enthusiastic raves to insult-free mixed opinions.

David Richards, who replaced Frank Rich as theater critic at the *New York Times,* submitted his only review of a Lloyd Webber show, and it was quite enthusiastic. He admired Glenn Close's risk-taking performance, the cast overall, the show's dark mood, and the set, including Norma's house, which managed to be grand and claustrophobic at the same time. He admired the music but thought some tunes were reprised too often, and was unimpressed with the pedestrian, clichéd lyrics. He noted that the comedy and irony of the film were largely lost, replaced by elements of the megamusical: "Machinery and the voracious public appetite for spectacle are remaking the contemporary theater." But he did not seem to mind, and for the first time since Rich joined the *New York Times,* the most important paper in the Broadway world gave a Lloyd Webber show a great review.[38] Clive Barnes of the *New York Post* also wrote a positive review, and the bulk of the other notices fell into the mixed category, with only one hostile pan, from (predictably) Michael Feingold of the *Village Voice.*[39]

Surprisingly, despite the positive reviews and the enormous advance, *Sunset Boulevard* failed to recoup its full investment, running just over two years. It closed in March 1997, with the London version following a month later. But overall the show can be considered a success, given the fairly long London run, tours in the United States, and European productions that began to spring up, even though the New York run was shorter than expected. *Sunset Boulevard* did win all the major Tony Awards, in an admittedly weak year: best musical, book, score, lighting, sets, and lead actress for Close.

Part of the problem with sustaining a New York run was that, thanks to the leading lady scandals, the show was considered a star vehicle, and Close's performance had gained so much attention that it was hard to follow, at least in terms of generating excitement and ticket sales. Betty Buckley, Broadway's first Grizabella in *Cats,* became known among *Sunset Boulevard* connoisseurs as the best Norma Desmond—Glenn Close could act the role and Patti LuPone could sing it, but Betty Buckley could do both.[40] Buckley found a slightly more tender, less grotesque side of Norma, and she had a true Broadway voice. Following her turn in the Broadway run was Elaine Paige, the London star (*Evita, Grizabella, Florence* in *Chess*) making her Broadway debut. Critics admired both Buckley and Paige, finding new nuances to the character in both performances, but it was not enough to sustain interest in the show, which became prohibitively expensive to maintain once the advance began to dry up.

Frank Wildhorn

The megamusical did not dominate Broadway in the 1990s as it had in the previous decade; other shows attracted their share of attention, including revivals (some fresh and innovative, others safe family fare), smaller-scale original ventures (Sondheim's *Passion,* often compared to Lloyd Webber's *Aspects of Love*), dance revues, and musicals based on films. But in the latter half of the decade, the megamusical reasserted its position when composer Frank Wildhorn stormed Broadway with three musicals in a row—for a brief time, all three were running simultaneously. The first, *Jekyll and Hyde,* was an instant hit with audiences, and in megamusical fashion overcame negative reviews to become not just a Broadway hit, but its own industry, with tours and merchandise. Reporters and critics talked about the new Andrew Lloyd Webber, a home-grown and critic-proof composer who clearly had his finger on the pulse of audience taste. *The Scarlet Pimpernel,* Wildhorn's second megamusical, opened a mere seven months after *Jekyll and Hyde*—then closed, and opened again, twice. His third show, *The Civil War,* was less successful and barely registered on the megamusical radar screen.

    Jekyll and Hyde, with music by Wildhorn and lyrics and book by Leslie Bricusse (creator of *Stop the World—I Want to Get Off*), opened in April 1997 and had a very successful run of nearly four years, with 1,543 performances. Like megamusicals of the 1980s, the show opened with a great deal of hype, some songs having already been released and a buzz surrounding the casting. The song "This Is the Moment," during which Dr. Jekyll gathers his courage to conduct experiments on himself (ostensibly for the sake of his ill father), had already become a hit single, used in such anthem-friendly contexts as the Miss America pageant, the Olympics, and the 1996 Democratic National Convention. Unlike "Memory" from *Cats,* which had cryptic lyrics for a pop hit, and *Evita*'s "Don't Cry for Me, Argentina," which had strong markers of its context within the show, "This Is the Moment" boasted rather general inspirational lyrics and no bitterness or irony, and so was a ready-made hit.[41] Even before *Jekyll and Hyde* reached Broadway, it garnered a loyal group of fans known as Jekkies, whose ranks grew during a series of out-of-town tryouts.

    Jekyll and Hyde received reviews ranging from fairly positive mixed reactions to flat-out pans. Ben Brantley of the *New York Times,* though inclined toward megamusicals, found in this case little to like but much of which to make fun. The most over-the-top, melodramatic moment comes in "Confrontation" late in the second act, when the main character is torn between his Jekyll side and his Hyde side; he demonstrates this by fighting with himself, snapping his head from side to side as he sings and yells. The side of his head with the slicked-back hair in a ponytail is Jekyll, and the side with the wild animal hair is Hyde. "I'll live inside you forever!" vows Hyde. "No!" snaps Jekyll. "With Satan himself by my side!" "No!"[42] It can indeed be laughable, but it features quick, effective lighting changes and a moment for the actor to chew the scenery. Brantley enjoyed the number, calling it "about the only original element in this plastic monster assembly kit of a musical." Labeling it, quite accurately, as a "leaden, solemnly campy" musical, he implied that it would have worked better had it embraced its melodramatic extravagances with a sense of fun or irony, rather than present them straight.[43] Robert Cuccioli, in the title roles, got better marks from critics as Hyde, when he could lope about and gleefully kill deserving people. Bricusse's book uses Robert Louis Stevenson's novel as its basis but gives Jekyll a noble motivation for his experiments and another noble motivation for killing people: he kills closed-minded purse-string holders who block him from conducting his research. Meanwhile, he is torn between two women, his noble, long-suffering, upper-crust fiancée and an earthy nightclub singer in need of rescue.

Wildhorn brought to Broadway a pop music style that made little effort to sound like, or work like, theater music. The pop elements present in Lloyd Webber's or Schönberg's music had always (to varying degrees) been framed by a theater sensibility in the music. Their scores were replete with recurring motifs, moments of recitative, operatic voices, large arch structures. Wildhorn is not nearly as interested in such devices, and considers himself primarily a pop composer. Like Lloyd Webber, Wildhorn released concept albums of his shows before they opened, but unlike Lloyd Webber's, these albums were often incomplete versions, subject to major changes before opening night—and they were sung by pop stars, not theater singers. In an interview, Wildhorn explained that he hoped to bridge the gap between theater music and the songs most people listen to every day; a reporter noted, "He makes no bones about believing that a musical should be easy to understand and that it should appeal to as many people as possible."[44]

This is one side of the megamusical legacy, taken to its extreme. Where Lloyd Webber and Rice were interested in appealing to audiences, they also felt the importance of creating a complete, artistic, even challenging work. Wildhorn certainly seems to care about his shows as shows, not just a collection of pop songs, but his overriding interest in accessibility and mass appeal tips the scales. His scores bear little consideration for context, so that many songs sound like pop ballads of the 1970s or 1980s regardless of the time period or the character's personality. Indeed, there seems to be a sense that he prides himself on being a from-the-gut pop composer, rather than a trained one like Lloyd Webber, Schönberg, or Sondheim: "He does not claim to be a sophisticated tunesmith. He composes by playing into a tape recorder and someone else writes down the notes later."[45] But some of his results are great pop ballads, and in the case of *Jekyll and Hyde,* many are moody and contextualized enough to serve the story.

Nevertheless, Brantley summarized many critics' reactions to this pop-heavy take on the megamusical formula: the score "makes 'Sunset Boulevard' sound like 'Parsifal.' " The score contained far too many "shivery" vamps and songs that ended with a "generic inspirational swell." Brantley went on to disparage most of the other elements of the show, including the chorus, whose choreography "seems to consist largely of bending over and pointing portentously."

Michael Feingold of the *Village Voice,* like Brantley, found the score too pop-oriented and too full of pointless climaxes.[46] His chief complaint, since the days of *Les Misérables,* had been the depressing, unpleasant stories on which megamusicals are based, and he found this one equally grim.

Other critics, best exemplified by Howard Kissel in the *Daily News,* embraced the overly broad show with a cheerful escapist attitude that the show itself lacked. Describing the show as "very much in the British mold"—that is to say, a megamusical—Kissel enjoyed the "sometimes syrupy, sometimes grandiose but always melodic music" and the excellent performances. Indeed, it's campy, he concluded—but it "has its own power."[47] He likened it to a nineteenth-century melodrama that the theater temporarily outgrew, but that clearly audiences still enjoy.

A certain sense of campy fun that might have helped critics enjoy *Jekyll and Hyde* actually became the chief ingredient of Wildhorn's next musical, *The Scarlet Pimpernel.* Like its predecessor, it is based on a well-known novel (about intrigue during the French Revolution, by the Baroness Orczy) that easily lent itself to musicalization. With a book and lyrics by Broadway newcomer Nan Knighton, *The Scarlet Pimpernel* told the story of Sir Percy Blakeney, an English nobleman newly married to a French actress, Marguerite, whom he learns may be spying for the leaders of the French Terror. Percy and his fellow noblemen disguise themselves as frivolous fops (and here we get the campy element at its silliest) and make trips to France to undermine the attempts of a Terror leader, Chauvelin, to behead English and French rebels. Chauvelin, an unabashed villain and former lover to Marguerite, is eventually outwitted, and the now happy couple (who have spent the entire show lying to one another and donning disguises) can trust each other.

The Scarlet Pimpernel, therefore, had the makings of a strong and unusual show, with far more comedy than most megamusicals despite its thoroughly epic-style megamusical plot. But its production history is like few others, and this strange series of events seems to have precipitated its ultimately lukewarm reception on Broadway. The show opened in November 1997 and ran for nearly a year. It then went dark for a little over a week, and reopened in October 1998 in a new version, with a radically rewritten book, some musical changes, and a different cast. After a run of seven months, this second version was shut down, and a third version opened four months later, in a new theater, running for nearly four months. A run of 772 performances total would have been respectable, but the run was made up of, essentially, three different shows. The second one was by far the most successful as a piece of theater.

Ben Brantley reviewed all three versions. He found the first lacking considerably in energy, made up of frozen tableaux and a lackluster cast. Douglass Sills, as Percy, was Brantley's notable exception; indeed, the sense of boyish fun that Sills brought to the role won over most critics, and he would be the only lead actor to survive into the second incarnation of the show. Brantley described the "pulpy pop score" as having an easy listening style, with large ensemble numbers that never "catch fire."[48]

He did not, however, directly address the overwhelmingly obvious problem of the first version: the characters had no motivation for any of their actions. Knighton's book launched us into the world of Percy and Marguerite too late in their relationship, after suspicions have set in, such that we have no way of knowing whether we too are meant to be suspicious or not. We never really know whether to like Marguerite, or whether she loves Percy. This problem was almost entirely resolved in the second version, which opens with Marguerite's farewell performance at the Comédie Française. There she appropriately sets the stage for a lighthearted romp by inviting us all to hear a tale of love, in "Storybook." This song works much better than in its former position in the second act. Also very effectively reassigned is the duet "You Are My Home," first placed late in the second act for an imprisoned Marguerite and her brother, now transformed into a genuine love song at the wedding of Percy and Marguerite near the start of act 1. With this, we now know how to feel about their relationship— clearly they do indeed love each other, but their whirlwind courtship has been so quick and unexpected that their doubts about one another are understandable. This prepares the entire show with a solid foundation of back story and character motivation. It also helps us to understand that Percy's fop act is indeed an act. When he and his men mince their way through "The Creation of Man" (about the importance of fashion in a man's life) and "They Seek Him Here" (about the comings and goings of the mysterious Pimpernel), the audience understands how much effort Percy is actually putting into his false front. Even the rousing marching anthem "Into the Fire," in which Percy rounds up his aristocratic friends and leads them into battle, works better with more background information; now, the audience could move through the stresses and confusions of the first few scenes with Percy rather than being thrust into the situation partway through.

Brantley found the transformation of the show "astounding," comparing it to the sort of major rewrites that might happen during out-of-town tryouts but rarely on Broadway. The result was like bringing a corpse to life. Brantley conceded that the show was no *My Fair Lady* nor "even" *The Phantom of the Opera,* but it now worked as a "pleasant diversion" for the family, which was accomplishment enough on Broadway these days.[49] Christine Andreas was replaced by Rachel York as Marguerite, and the more energetic Rex Smith took over for Broadway veteran Terrence Mann (the Rum Tum Tugger in *Cats,* Javert in *Les Misérables,* the Beast in *Beauty and the Beast*), whom many had felt was merely going through the paces of yet another heartsick villain role. With Sills's carefree spirit of adventure still intact, the whole show gained energy and a cohesive mood.

This lighthearted mood was, unfortunately, lost again in the third incarnation of the show. Apparently not satisfied with the fairly positive notices and the decent attendance, Wildhorn and his creative team shut the show down and reopened it in a drastically scaled-down, supposedly more personal version. With an all-new (and much smaller) cast, reduced sets, and a smaller theater, this *Scarlet Pimpernel* was meant to be more realistic, psychological, and serious. For Brantley, this eradicated everything good about the second version; in a show that is meant to be "rendered in exaggerated postures and declamations," subtlety doesn't work. It was much more entertaining to see the cast "winking" at the melodrama rather than taking it seriously.[50]

The show continues to tour, despite fizzling out in its third version after only a few months, using the much-improved book from the second version. But apparently Wildhorn was not as critic-proof as he seemed at first. *The Scarlet Pimpernel* also did not generate nearly as much of a fan base as *Jekyll and Hyde,* though it did have its own loyal followers who supported each version (several critics dubbed them "Pimpies").

Wildhorn's juggernaut, slowed significantly by the problems of *The Scarlet Pimpernel,* came to an abrupt halt with *The Civil War,* which ran for only sixty-one performances, from April to June 1999. Working with a new lyricist, Jack Murphy, and co-writing the book with Gregory Boyd, Wildhorn created a musical that was not really a musical. It was more like a revue or a song cycle of extremely similar songs on the same topic, with characters whose names remained unclear and whose causes and ideals—despite different uniforms—seemed interchangeable. The score also dove head-first into a gospel and R&B-flavored pop style that his other shows had merely hinted at; while it gave singers a chance to wail, it was inappropriate for most characters and the time period in general.

This time around, audiences agreed with critics, and even loyal Wildhorn fans could not help the show continue. Ben Brantley at least gave Wildhorn credit for breaking into a business that only one composer before him had dominated. Although Wildhorn "these days bestrides Broadway with the colossus-like status once belonging to Andrew Lloyd Webber," he felt the music in this show failed to stick in the mind like the catchy, powerful ones of his predecessor. Brantley found the show to have no plot, no characters, and nothing original to say about the history it examines—instead, both sides speak of honor, kill each other without ever having names of their own, and sing of dark nights and hopes for bright mornings.[51] In all, Wildhorn had only a few years (and two musicals, or maybe one and a half) to enjoy his status as the new critic-proof composer in the Lloyd Webber vein. His latest show, *Dracula: The Musical,* received unanimous pans and ran only four and a half months starting in August 2004.

Maury Yeston's *Titanic*

Following in the megamusical tradition in a number of ways, *Titanic* had a respectable Broadway run of nearly two years (804 performances from April 1997), yet received decidedly low critical notices. Initially positive audience reception gave the show momentum, but unlike other megamusicals with poor reviews, *Titanic* did not have enough positive buzz to carry on for ten or fifteen years. The subject, though, is pure megamusical: a plot followed the doomed cruise liner and a large assortment of characters on board, rich and poor, historically accurate and invented, passengers and crew. Both music and lyrics were written by Maury Yeston, who also wrote *Nine* (Broadway premiere 1982, and a well-received revival in 2003) and *Grand Hotel* (1989). *Titanic* took home five Tony Awards—for best musical, score, book (Peter Stone, whose earlier work included *1776* and *The Will Rogers Follies*), scenic design (Stewart Laing), and orchestration (Jonathan Tunick)—which probably had much to with the show continuing as long as it did, despite a sizeable drop-off in attendance.

Ben Brantley, offering a mixed review tipping distinctly toward the negative, put his finger on the problem: the characters all came across as two-dimensional stereotypes, each marking a tidy spot in the world's social order and never springing to life. While he found it "an admirably efficient piece of narrative," it failed to deliver the two best qualities that come built in to the true story on which it was based: "sentimentality and suspense."[52] Indeed, since we know exactly what will happen to the ship, the show should have created excitement among the characters, but instead, the most thrilling, alarming moment occurred when the furniture slid offstage left as the set tilted ever more angularly. Brantley found Yeston's score lacking in confidence, though he admired a few songs and the cast overall. Other critics were similarly disappointed by the way the book and score failed to flesh out the characters; Michael Feingold called the show "data-bound and devoid of humanity."[53] He was also put off by the story, interpreting it as a tale of how human greed led to technology that killed people.

For those who do embrace such tales, the problem with *Titanic* sprang not from its story (which has always been popular and was at the time of the musical's opening also enjoying unprecedented success in the movie version) but the distance that it placed between us and the characters. Not unlike Wildhorn's mistake with *The Civil War*, the problem here was too many characters drawn too quickly, such that we have no opportunity to know them and therefore be genuinely moved when peril descends. The set, with its many levels arranged by economic rank and its gradual list to one side, is fascinating—but one should not cheer for the iceberg and its aftereffects, as it were. Brantley admired the song that perhaps best embodies this problem of superficial sentimentality offered in the place of genuine sentiment. In "The Proposal/The Night Was Alive," a sailor sends a telegram home to his beloved, asking to marry her, and the radio man (in a laughable lyric expressed with over-the-top earnestness) sings as he taps: "dit dit-dah-dit dah-dit." The score works better when it relies (as it often does) on large choral numbers, declaring the beauty of the ship in passages such as the recurring "There She Is."

Disney Comes to Broadway

Rarely are musicals grouped by producer. Cameron Mackintosh may be a notable exception, but we still speak almost exclusively of Lloyd Webber shows, Schön-berg/Boublil shows, Hal Prince shows. With the arrival of Disney on Broadway, however, the producer was nearly all any critic or audience member could talk about. Despite having entirely different teams of creators, *Beauty and the Beast* and *The Lion King* are almost always discussed in the same breath, compared and contrasted, since both are Disney entities. Of course it was not simply that the Walt Disney Company funded these musicals—both were also based on popular Disney feature-length cartoons and were brought to Broadway with massive pre-opening hype, advertising, and merchandising. It was as if some critics' nightmare had come to pass. For nearly two decades, critics had been complaining that the megamusical was the Disneyfication of musicals, with product tie-ins, aggressive ad campaigns, and expensive and elaborate stagings. The comparison was meant as an insult; now, with Disney becoming a force in American musical theater, some even predicted the end of the genre. The doomsayers foresaw a Broadway dominated by shows featuring only live-action versions of children's cartoons, which would become unstoppable box office juggernauts due to the established popularity of the source movies and theme park shows. Indeed, the director of *Beauty and the Beast,* Robert Jess Roth, came to the project after having staged numerous revues and reenactments of Disney films at their theme parks.

At first, it looked like the wary critics might be right: *Beauty and the Beast,* or as the title actually runs, *Disney's Beauty and the Beast,* stuck extremely close to its film source material. Some thought it a well-done adaptation, others found it a predictable disappointment. But Disney's second effort on Broadway, *The Lion King,* surprised everyone. Apparently having taken to heart the criticism leveled at the literal-minded *Beauty and the Beast,* the Disney leaders (including CEO Michael Eisner, who was quite involved in Disney on Broadway) chose fringe theater director Julie Taymor to adapt the film through the filter of her own idiosyncratic vision. The result, virtually every critic declared, was not only a creative adaptation of the film, but great theater. As of this writing, both shows are still running.

The film version of *Beauty and the Beast* perhaps lent itself particularly well to the form of a staged musical because it was basically one already. Like many of the best Disney films, *Beauty and the Beast* has a handful of clever, theatrical songs written by theater veterans—in this case, composer Alan Menken and lyricist Howard Ashman, who had had great success with the off-Broadway *Little Shop of Horrors* (which eventually became a film and more recently a Broadway show). Ashman passed away before *Beauty and the Beast* reached Broadway, so Tim Rice stepped in and wrote lyrics for some new Menken songs. (This would mark the beginning of Rice's affiliation with Disney, which continued through *The Lion King* and *Aida.*) The story ran just as it had in the film, with a bookworm heroine, Belle, and a blustery, tenderhearted Beast eventually finding love. The Beast, having been cursed for an earlier act of unkindness, lives in his gloomy house with formerly human servants that have all become the objects of their trade; the cook, for instance, is now a singing, dancing teapot.

Beauty and the Beast opened in April 1994. David Richards, briefly the chief theater critic for the *New York Times,* offered an opinion that many critics shared: "It is hardly a triumph of art, but it'll probably be a whale of a tourist attraction."[54] The spectacle, while certainly appropriate considering the fairy-tale and kid-friendly mood, often overwhelmed a very strong score. Richards found that one gaped at the show throughout, marveling at effects such as the Beast's transformation into a handsome prince or the castle that rotates to allow the viewer to follow the action as in a movie. But the result was a show that left nothing to the imagination, such that Richards marveled at Disney's impressive technical know-how and endless financial resources rather than the ostensible point, "the redemptive power of love." The most discussed song, "Be Our Guest," involved the dishes and silverware dancing about, enticing Belle to stay for dinner with the Beast. This song "knows no shame," Richards noted, going all-out to give us the hard sell. It was as if Busby Berkeley had gotten high, and this was his hallucinogenic vision: "Its lavishness is close to delirium, its giddiness beyond camp." Like many critics, Richards had little time left for discussing the cast, all of whom came in for good notices; they included Susan Egan, then a Broadway newcomer, as Belle; as the Beast, veteran Terrence Mann; and Gary Beach as the candelabrum Lumière, who had been on Broadway for decades but would not achieve major notice until he originated the role of Roger De Bris in *The Producers.* (Beach's Lumière, by the way, came across as distinctly and ridiculously effeminate, not unlike Roger De Bris.)

The other reviews focused mostly on the staging and effects, and what it meant that Disney had arrived, and few were impressed overall. Linda Winer, like many, thought it was nice to have a musical to take the kids to see, but she put it in its context quite neatly: as a "contender in the real world of Broadway megamusicals, this is pretty tacky stuff."[55] It is important to note that the megamusical had come so far by this point that it was not only an accepted term, but there was a canon of megamusicals against which new contenders had to be measured. Like most critics, Winer feared the influence of Disney, wary of franchising and thrill-ride musicals. But she praised the cast and the ingenious human/object costumes by Ann Hould-Ward (whose work was also successful in Sondheim's *Sunday in the Park with George* and *Into the Woods,* among others).

Howard Kissel of the *Daily News* found it sad that Disney had not taken the opportunity to do something imaginative and daring, but instead catered to what was already Broadway's main audiences at the time: tourists and children. This was a predictable megamusical, in the British mold but with less "refined" elements, including the set (by Stan Meyer); Kissel and other critics compared the Beast's castle to the huge mansion in the forthcoming *Sunset Boulevard* (which would open on Broadway seven months later), and found the former quite unimpressive and two-dimensional.[56] John Simon, rarely a fan of the megamusical, noted that it would not matter what he or any critic said, since the Disney name and the audience's familiarity with both the story and the cartoon version would sell the show. Therefore, he was free to declare that the show "bored the pants off me," although he enjoyed many of the special effects and most of the cast.[57] Clive Barnes thought the show fine for what it was: a Disney entertainment, with no pretensions toward affecting the future of musical theater. His low expectations encompassed every element of the show; the staging, sets, costumes, cast, both old and newly written songs, and the dancing all worked "extremely well on their own terms."[58] He fully expected a show that simply acted out a popular cartoon, and was happy enough to report that the show did exactly that.

Disney bankrolled the entire production itself, without the usual outside investors or "angels" from whom a producer normally raises funds. The company announced the cost to be $10 million (a Broadway record at the time), but rumor put it closer to $12 million, and some speculated it was as high as $20 million. The mere fact that the production was so expensive marked it as a Disney venture; editorials enjoyed describing the evil empire and its takeover of 42nd Street. (Indeed, Disney bought the New Amsterdam Theatre, which after a complete refurbishing would house *The Lion King;* the street sign reads "New 42nd Street.") Disney chief Michael Eisner spoke of his interest in making this show and Broadway in general a family experience. It used to be the case, he pointed out, that going to the theater was what a family did on a birthday or special occasion; now they attend movies, and Broadway was suffering as a result. He spoke about the idea of community, of a family or group venturing out into the world together, sharing experiences, no matter the venue: "The point is—and our rides are built this way—you all go on together."[59]

The success of *Beauty and the Beast* led everyone to expect a similar product from Disney for its next show off the assembly line, but their expectations were thwarted by *The Lion King.* Instead of simply acting out the cartoon in three dimensions, translating the visuals into a staged rendering, the creative team thoroughly reworked the material. Except for a few comedic roles, the characters onstage looked little like their cartoon counterparts, and the sets, rather than being pale copies of what animation can do, are clever and entirely theater-based creations. Director, costume designer, and puppet creator Julie Taymor worked from the script, not the film, and therefore invented solutions to, for example, an onstage stampede or a magical manifestation of a lion in heaven that were entirely her own creation. Critics were thrilled. Here was a creative director with a quirky, often dark style of creating theater (both with puppets and humans) that until now had rarely been performed in mainstream venues, who was able to transform a rather typical Disney story into an atmospheric visual masterpiece. New songs, many of them with a tip toward African musical styles, also helped immensely in bringing *The Lion King* into the world of fresh theater.

The film contained five songs composed by Elton John, with lyrics by Tim Rice. John and Rice would go on to compose the thoroughly adult score for *Aida,* also produced by Disney, though with no history as a Disney story. The staged *Lion King* featured a host of new songs largely by African composer Lebo M, who supplied ethnic-sounding, mood-setting chants and calls as well as set pieces. John and Rice also wrote three new songs, and four other people (Mark Mancina, Jay Rifkin, Hans Zimmer, and Julie Taymor) contributed to the new music as well. Considering the many hands at work on the score, it works fairly well as a whole thanks to a balance of comic and grand as well as the unifying chorus-based sound. The music swings smoothly back and forth between light, kid-friendly numbers and somewhat darker, atmospheric ones. It surely helped that Taymor's concept of the entire show governed every step of the creative process.

The story is a typical Disney coming-of-age adventure: Simba, destined to assume his father Mufasa's role as king of the Pridelands' diverse animal culture someday, is set up by his evil uncle Scar (who gets Mufasa killed and then blames Simba). Simba flees and grows up with the help of some cute sidekicks, but eventually he faces his destiny and returns to reclaim his throne. His return and the restoration of the Pridelands are both aided greatly by the work of Nala, first a childhood friend of Simba's, later a group leader as well as his love interest.

The score, while receiving less attention than the design elements, carries the story along more effectively than is the case in many kid-oriented musicals or animated films. The African-inspired music gives a whole series of numbers a similar musical language involving tight choral harmonies and a darker mood than the cute kid songs. These numbers include the powerful "Rafiki Mourns," in which Rafiki (a monkey, but more of a priestess) and the lionesses mourn the death of Mufasa; and "Shadowland," in which a now-grown Nala vows to go find a way to help her homeland, over choral support. (The role of Nala was originated by Heather Headley, who would become a star in John and Rice's *Aida*.) The evil Scar and his three goofy hyena helpers receive clever, funny lyrics from Rice, who as usual reserves his flashier lines for comedy and villains. Simba goes from spunky kid ("I Just Can't Wait to Be King" by John and Rice) to young man longing for guidance from his father ("Endless Night," by Lebo M, Hans Zimmer, Jay Rifkin, and Julie Taymor).

The visual elements of the show dominate it entirely—a positive attribute given the rather thin plot. Taymor's costumes/puppets are fascinating and rarely distracting. The lions wear masks that hover above their faces, which are always in view. It becomes clear that their lion selves emerge when they are in public, or angry—they lean forward, and the masks drop over their faces. But in tender moments, the masks float harmlessly above their human/inner selves or are occasionally removed altogether. When Simba flees to the jungle, he celebrates the "Hakuna Matata" (worry-free) lifestyle with Timon the meerkat, a full puppet who looks just like the film version and is controlled by a singing, dancing puppeteer just behind him, and Pumbaa the warthog, whose body is part human, part puppet. The human/puppet combinations, often with double heads, work remarkably well at presenting the characters' look and personality in one.

The creative design extended to the set as well. Many critics noted the impressive stampede of animals, rolling in ever-larger groups directly toward the audience. This simple, elegant trick was created by mounting different-size animal masks on revolving cylinders, and engaging them in sequence, closer and closer to the audience. The simplest design elements, though often overlooked by critics more concerned with flashy moments, were often the most theatrical and shiver-inducing. When the Pridelands experience a drought, it is represented by a huge but completely plain circle of blue fabric on the stage floor, gradually pulled through a central hole in the floor, such that the diameter of the circle—the symbolic lake—becomes shriveled and ever smaller.

But the part of the show about which virtually every critic raved was the opening ten minutes, when the animals all gather at Pride Rock to honor Mufasa's new son, Simba. (Indeed, Disney had long known the power of this moment, having used the cartoon version, shown in full and without other clips, as the preview in theaters before the film opened.) With Elton John's hit song "Circle of Life" moving through verses and choruses, Taymor's animals assembled, many of them walking through the aisles—giraffes with stilt legs, papier-mâché elephants, antelopes perched on the arms and heads of leaping dancers, birds being swung on the ends of bowed sticks.

The "transporting magic" of this opening, raved Ben Brantley, suggests that Taymor's translation of the film is full of "astonishment and promise."[60] Fintan O'Toole in the *Daily News* found that the visual element "takes the breath away without numbing the mind," something that other megamusicals had failed to achieve. At last the "big Broadway spectacular" had been transformed into art, O'Toole declared.[61] Even Michael Feingold was completely charmed—but this was partly due to the apparent victory of Taymor (a fringe artist the *Village Voice* is inclined to support) over Disney (the evil empire). Taymor "faced the corporate gorgon and survived," Feingold cheered.[62] In fact, Taymor reported that her dealings with Disney were congenial, and that she had been given free creative reign.[63]

These raves for Taymor's work did not mean that every element of the story came in for untempered praise. Ben Brantley, while enthralled with the design that bore elements of "divinity," noted that Taymor did not develop individual characters particularly well—she was all big picture. As a result, the show lacked some of the personal "suspense and poignancy" of the film. Feingold defended the show and attacked Brantley and the *Times* (though coyly, not by name): "And to think there are people, or whatever we call those pitiable objects writing for the daily papers, who complain that her work lacks the 'suspense and poignancy' of some through-the-mill mass-market movie. Well, maybe they were dropped on their heads at an early age." It is quite an achievement that this one show could please critics and audiences, fans of the mainstream and the fringe, and those who liked the movie and those who did not.[64]

Jonathan Larson's *Rent*

As noted, musicals of the 1990s took some elements of the 1980s megamusical and adapted them to changing styles. *The Lion King* embraced the megamusical's notion of spectacle but with a distinct twist. Wildhorn's *Jekyll and Hyde*, while slightly less design-driven, demonstrated the megamusical's epic pseudo-historical plot and heightened emotion. In creating *Rent,* Jonathan Larson took an approach that few others did: he combined the idea of a romantic, melodramatic plot with the idea of a rock opera. Like *Miss Saigon, Rent* borrows its plot from a Puccini opera, in this case *La Bohème.* And like *Jesus Christ Superstar, Rent* has a score based in rock—not the lighter pop of *Les Misérables,* but actual rock music—though it makes use of pop and theater styles as well. Larson thought of *Rent* as a *Hair* for the 1990s, which is certainly a fitting parallel given that the plot centers on a group of disenfranchised young people living in Greenwich Village. But unlike *Hair, Rent* is strongly book-driven, with Puccini's dramatic arc as its underpinnings; structurally, then, the show works more like *Superstar* (or any other story-based megamusical) than *Hair.* Also, unlike many musicals of the 1990s, but like most megamusicals, *Rent* is sung from beginning to end.

Rent tells the story of a group of struggling artists and friends; each main character has a direct parallel in the Puccini original, and some sections of the musical ("Light My Candle," for example) translate bits of the Italian libretto nearly word for word.[65] But the plot abandons Puccini at times as Larson invents new incidents. Mark, a filmmaker, is a stand-in for Larson himself; a middle-class kid drawn to the romantic bohemian artistic lifestyle, he becomes the audience's guide through this world while staying somewhat removed from it himself. The central plot revolves around Mark's roommate Roger, a rock guitarist and song-writer, and his girlfriend Mimi (retaining her *Bohème* name), both of whom have AIDS, which complicates their tempestuous relationship. Mimi seemingly dies from her illness in the final moments of the show, only to return seconds later, thus subverting the tragic ending. But Larson has already supplied plenty of loss by introducing Angel, a cross-dressing, free-spirited street musician, and his love interest Collins, both of whom also have AIDS. Angel dies partway through the second act, and this event becomes the temporary undoing of the group. Puccini's Musetta is here Maureen, a former girlfriend of Mark's who now dates a woman. Maureen is a performance artist; Musetta's famous waltz is replaced by a hilar-ious piece of theater which she stages in order to protest the loss of her down-town performance space to the landlord Benny. The melody of Musetta's waltz appears several times, as Roger plucks it out on his electric guitar when he doesn't know what else to play; later it becomes the strangely anti-climactic moment in the eleven o'clock song, "Your Eyes."

Rent began in a very humble setting, at the small New York Theater Work-shop on East 4th Street—appropriately, downtown. Just as *Rent* was about to open off-Broadway in January 1996, Jonathan Larson died suddenly from an aortic aneurysm. It was a bizarre and sad turn of events that surely (as cynics pointed out) granted the show far more attention than it would have otherwise had. Within months, *Rent* had won the Pulitzer Prize for drama and moved into a Broadway house, where critics continued to laud it. *Rent* took the Tony for best book, score, and musical, and Wilson Jermaine Heredia also won for his role as Angel; in addition, there were nominations for Idina Menzel as Maureen (she would win for her lead role in *Wicked* in 2004), Adam Pascal, later of *Aida*, as Roger, Daphne Rubin-Vega as Mimi, and director Michael Greif. *Rent* continues to run on Broadway to strong houses, where it has gradually become less of a contemporary look at social issues such as poverty and AIDS, and more of a period piece about life in the 1990s, though of course the issues remain.

Virtually all critics praised *Rent* when it arrived on Broadway on 29 April 1996. All mentioned the tragic loss of Larson and pondered what else this prom-ising thirty-five-year-old composer and lyricist might have produced. (A few years later, colleagues would finish and stage a musical Larson had written before *Rent, Tick, Tick, Boom!*) Most critics were reminded of *Hair* because of the story and very loud rock music. The singers are actually accompanied by a rock combo that sits stage right; there is no orchestra or orchestra pit. This, and the simple set of raw, industrial-looking scaffolding and a drab gray backdrop, made *Rent* look like the opposite of a megamusical. Certainly the lyrics, full of cursing, jokes, and slang, also lent the show a much more contemporary feel than the long-ago tone of most megamusicals. But the influence of *Superstar*, especially in the score's mix of hard-rock numbers ("Rent," "Out Tonight") with softer pop-styled songs ("Without You") and even a few pastiches of far-removed styles ("Tango Maureen," "Santa Fe"), is clear. The score also featured a few Broadway-style belted anthems, especially "Seasons of Love," a stand-alone song with no direct role in the story. It delivers a catchy melody, an excellent rousing use of chorus and R&B wailing, and effective reprises throughout the second act. It even be-came a pop hit, released as a single in a new recording with Stevie Wonder joining the cast.

Michael Feingold gave *Rent* one of his few rave reviews. Both Feingold and the *Village Voice* in general have always taken a counter-culture stance on artistic issues, supporting endeavors outside the mainstream and (in Feingold's case) dismissing everything mainstream or popular as artistically void. But *Rent* is a musical about the very people the *Voice* writes for; the newspaper is even men-tioned as one of the many bohemian items the group embraces in their bouncy act 1 finale, "La Vie Boheme." The group, ostensibly toasting the death of bo-hemia, toasts the *Village Voice* (it rhymes with "choice") along with Sondheim, leather, yogurt, "any passing fad," *Carmina Burana*, "hating convention, hating pretension," masturbation, "Ginsberg, Dylan, Cunningham and Cage," and hun-dreds of other items, people, and concepts.[66] Feingold declared *Rent* one of the most important rock musicals since *Hair*, and admired how Larson used rock music to make a point, within a context of show music. He detected Sondheim's influence (Sondheim was indeed a mentor of Larson's, and the influence is clear, though perhaps more in the lyrics than the music) and admired Larson's use of different musical styles, a trait he usually criticizes.[67]

Ben Brantley enjoyed the score and cast of *Rent* just as much as he had downtown, but found that the show did not fit well into its new oversized Broadway home. The theater, which in a move reminiscent of *Cats* was decorated throughout to look like the shabby set, made it seem as if one were entering a theme park that Brantley named East Village Land. Brantley particularly admired how this contemporary show strove not for hipness, but instead for a sentimental, Rodgers and Hammerstein mood, demonstrating the "extraordinary spirit of hope-ful defiance and humanity."[68] John Simon, on the other hand, panned the show thanks to what he saw as its pretentious need to be trendy, arty, and hip. References to Heidegger and *Carmina Burana*, meant to "slay us with their so-phistication," failed to impress, he argued: "All in all, *Rent* is a musical for the politically correct, the terminally trendy, the believers in everything the media tell them, and those who set stock by that most discredited of prizes, the theatrical Pulitzer."[69] Howard Kissel's review fell somewhere between Feingold's and Simon's; he admired the show's blending of rock and theater music, but he noted that transvestites, performance artists, and homeless people are not the romantic or exotic figures the show suggests, and that for all the show's disdain for "bourgeois values," Bloomingdale's was about to open a *Rent* boutique.[70] He made note of an issue that screams for attention: many of these young people have parents who call them, leaving repeated messages on their answering machines, offering to help and support them. The parents are a joke in the show, but most of them seem quite loving and willing to help; why starve while ignoring those who love you and raised you? Roger and Mimi both have drug and health problems, which might explain their distance from their families, but nothing in the book quite explains why Mark ignores his friendly (if ditsy) mother.

Small quibbles aside, *Rent* brought Broadway a fresh, unusual combination of music theater elements, some drawn from the megamusical. Perhaps most important, it opened Broadway up to new subject matter, facing the AIDS crisis head-on for the first time in a Broadway musical; it also dealt boldly with drug addiction, homosexuality, homelessness, violence, and artistic freedom. Critics and local audiences were not particularly shocked by this back in 1996, but even ten years later some areas of the country still find the subject matter offensive or shocking.[71] This is partly what Larson had in mind, by depicting the realities—but also the romantic hopefulness—of life in the Village in the 1990s.

Flaherty and Ahrens's *Ragtime*

> Giving the nation a
> New syncopation, the
> People called it "ragtime"

One of the salient differences between large-scale musicals of the 1980s and those of the 1990s was that the productions were more firmly in the hands of Americans in the latter decade. The topics of the second generation of megamusicals reflected this; even grand, thoroughly megamusical subjects often had an American setting, as in *Rent*. Other shows, however, remained in the megamusical tradition with plots that took place in far-off or long-ago lands (all three Disney musicals, and Wildhorn's *Jekyll and Hyde* and *The Scarlet Pimpernel*, for example).

Ragtime best combined the features of the megamusical that still seemed viable in the late 1990s with a strong sense of being a home-grown, American musical; indeed, *Ragtime* reminded a number of critics of the Golden Era musicals from forty or fifty years earlier. It was almost entirely sung, and the dialogue often featured underscoring. Its sets were innovative, fascinating, and well integrated into the story. The plot spanned several years and dozens of characters, both fictional and historical. It had all the sweep, emotion, and epic gestures that audiences had embraced back in the 1980s, but with some distinctly quirky, American twists that made *Ragtime* an excellent model of the megamusical for the future. Set at the beginning of the twentieth century and opening at the very end of it, it neatly pointed the way toward the next century. And it arrived on Broadway in megamusical style, backed by strong publicity and a concept album.

Ragtime is based on the 1975 novel by E. L. Doctorow. The musical's book, adapted by playwright Terrence McNally, retains most of the huge cast of characters and main events, as well as some elements of the novel's unusual style. Doctorow's novel is full of short, direct sentences that announce events with a sort of ironic distance; in the musical, characters often speak about themselves directly to the audience, in the third person. This has the odd but interesting effect of placing the characters both within the events as they actually take place and beyond it, as if speaking to us from the future. The musical has an overwhelming air of nostalgia, reminding the audience that although the events depicted are dramatic, indeed sometimes horrifying, at least some of the characters will survive and most (even those that speak to us from beyond their deaths) will find some peace.

The story revolves around three different families whose lives eventually clash and blend. In upper-middle-class New Rochelle, New York, a woman simply known as Mother lives with her husband, Father, and her son, Mother's Little Boy. She has a polite, distant relationship with her husband. "She . . . often told herself how fortunate she was to be so protected and provided for by her husband," she tells us, in a way that suggests her feelings will change, or may have already.[72] Mother's Younger Brother is, as he explains to the audience about himself, "a young man in search of something to believe in." He first lavishes his unfocused energies on the scandalous vaudeville star Evelyn Nesbit, and then on social activist Emma Goldman; these are but two of the historical figures who drift in and out of the fictional characters' lives, in a series of encounters that are sometimes real, sometimes dreamed or imagined.

The second family is headed by Coalhouse Walker Jr., an African American rag pianist in Harlem, and his sometime-girlfriend, Sarah. She has just given birth to their child and, after trying to kill it by burying it in Mother's garden (she is a maid in the white neighborhood), she and the infant are taken in by Mother. Coalhouse, having been something of a free-loving cad, comes calling on Sarah and the two reunite. Hence he meets Mother and her family.

The third family is composed of Tateh (Yiddish for daddy) and Tateh's Little Girl, Eastern European Jewish immigrants who settle on the poor Lower East Side, where Tateh attempts to eke out a living cutting silhouettes of famous stars and passers-by. Harry Houdini is his role model; a Jew who achieved fame and fortune, he appears to Tateh in moments of doubt.

The musical tells its story on two levels: the first depicts the lives of the main characters, and the second describes America's turbulent, uncertain years around 1910. The historical characters bridge the two. For example, Henry Ford exemplifies the machine age, turning workers on his assembly line into cogs in his machine, but also creating a car that Coalhouse Walker can afford and use to court Sarah. But the car becomes a point of contention when Coalhouse drives it through New Rochelle and encounters a group of bigoted Irish firemen. A series of racist incidents eventually turns Coalhouse into a violent vigilante, and leads to Sarah's inadvertent death as well as his own.

Tateh faces his own racism, unable to make a living either as an artist or a factory worker; he encounters the anarchist Emma Goldman, who fights for workers' rights. Mother's Younger Brother encounters her as well; in "The Night that Goldman Spoke in Union Square," he feels as if (and the audience sees the scene as if) she speaks directly to him at a rally. The transition from reality to the fantastic experience inside Younger Brother's mind is seamless and virtually impossible to pull off, but *Ragtime*'s score and staging deftly carry the audience into his psyche and out again. Still talking of himself, Younger Brother exclaims, "He thought he heard her say—" "Poor young rich boy!" bellows Emma along with those at the rally. Later Younger Brother joins Coalhouse's rebellion.

Mother's life is transformed by the arrivals of Sarah and Coalhouse, and eventually she breaks out of her decorous social role and falls in love with Tateh, who has become a successful film director. Eventually, a new family is formed: Mother, Tateh, their two children, and Coalhouse and Sarah's orphaned son. Their story becomes an example of what happened in America at the time, including not only the clash of cultures but the tentative first steps toward peaceful cultural diversity.

Coalhouse plays ragtime music in Harlem and in the genteel parlor of Mother's home, but the music also becomes a recurring motif with multiple meanings. For example, the immigrants arrive in America wearing rags, on "rag ships." More broadly, the ragged syncopation comes to symbolize a world slightly off-kilter, rushing ahead of itself, unsure of its own pulse. When Father hears

Coalhouse play, he understands that he does not understand this music, or Coalhouse, or the age in which he lives. He and Mother sing, "I thought I knew what love was / But these lovers play / New music." Ironically, Father is singing along with what Coalhouse plays; he sings the new music but does not live in it as Coalhouse does, and as his estranged wife now seems to be doing.

Composer Stephen Flaherty provides a few delicate, Joplinesque ragtime melodies for the score, and these become the material of the opening scene ("Prologue") and "New Music," among other numbers. But he also writes blues-tinged ballads for Sarah ("Your Daddy's Son"), a perky march for Henry Ford, and minor-key ethnic references for Tateh ("A Shtetl Iz Amereke," "Success"). Like Lloyd Webber, Flaherty engages in pastiche, here employed to evoke the ragtime era (as Lloyd Webber did with the 1940s Hollywood sound in *Sunset Boulevard*). The pastiches also suggest Sondheim's use of the technique, seen in the rhythm and instrumentation of the song "Henry Ford." In *Assassins*, Sondheim evokes a time period just a few years earlier than that of *Ragtime*, with his song "The Ballad of Czolgosz." Both songs use their music and snappy lyrics to portray early-twentieth-century America with a sense of irony and foreboding: this wonderful time was not nearly as wonderful as the sunny surface of the music would have us believe.

Ragtime was produced in the megamusical tradition with one powerful producer at the helm, Canadian Garth Drabinsky. Often referred to as an impresario, Drabinsky, with his production company, Livent, brought *Ragtime* to a new theater, the Ford Center for the Performing Arts, which had just been built using parts of the old Lyric and Apollo theaters on 42nd Street. (The coincidence of the theater's namesake and a character in the theater's first show was not lost on anyone.) Livent brought with it enormous financial resources and grand artistic goals, but by the end of 1998, when it produced *Parade*, the company would be in financial jeopardy. *Ragtime*, despite generally good reviews and strong word of mouth, would not run long enough to become a financial success; it closed almost exactly two years after opening in January 1998.

The staging of *Ragtime*, by the team of director Frank Galati, choreographer (given credit for "musical staging") Graciela Daniele, and set designer Eugene Lee, demonstrated an interesting mix of megamusical style and simple, nearly bare moments. When Tateh and fellow immigrants arrive in America, they rush forward through a series of ever-larger, ever-closer gates at Ellis Island; the design gives not only a cinematic account of what moving through the process of arriving might have been like, but also a stop-and-start, emotional rhythm that mirrors the desperation of the immigrants. Atlantic City, where Mother meets a now-successful Tateh, positively glows with clean air and blue skies. A ragtime band

and a slew of extras bound across the stage in sped-up, jerky motions, which soon is explained by the presence of film director Tateh and his movie crew—for a moment, we have seen the world through his lens. But soon after, when Mother declares that the changes in her life mean she can never go "Back to Before," the boardwalk and other set pieces simply sink away, and she stands alone on a bare stage. The entire proscenium is framed by an arch and large clock modeled on Penn Station; its architect, Stanford White, appears briefly in "Prologue," reenacting his affair with Evelyn Nesbit and becoming her husband's murder victim. Silhouettes and distant images appear throughout the show, a device which helps create the Doctorow-like separation from the events we see. Racists destroy Coalhouse's Model T Ford in silhouette. Mother's house has a full-size living room, but is also seen as if from far off, dollhouse-size. Mother's Little Boy shows the audience the house through his stereopticon. At the end, the boy runs a film projector, and all the characters stream across the stage, posing and making silhouette shapes against a simple glowing background. The set design, matched well with the unusual tone and idiosyncratic narrative devices, makes *Ragtime* unique—a word not to be taken lightly.

Ben Brantley admired many features of the show, but found the whole "utterly resistible." The opening "Prologue" captivated him in the way that it introduced the three juxtaposed families and the larger ethnic groups which they represented, but this "allegorical" opening never turned into a real story for him. This is entirely in keeping with the tone of Doctorow's novel, so clearly transferred onstage by the third-person narration and the magical encounters with historical figures. Some critics embraced this unusual tone, but Brantley wanted something other than Doctorow's "omniscient, distanced quality." Like virtually all other critics, Brantley noted that much of the novel's wit had been lost, replaced by earnest anthems and calls for justice.[73] (Other critics would note especially that the sex in the novel, which was both raunchy and disturbing, was absent here.)

Brantley's mixed review rated a bit lower than most; Clive Barnes, by contrast, turned in one of his most enthusiastic reviews ever: "You might have thought it couldn't have been done in this day and age—a totally (well, totally enough) successful, traditional all-American Broadway musical. Well, it has been done." His pointed praise for the show's American quality may have been meant to disparage imported megamusicals, though sometimes he enjoyed these too. Director Frank Galati "achieved miracles," Barnes went on, in putting all of the disparate, potentially confusing characters and plot lines together in a smooth whole. (Barnes, among others, noted that the 1981 film version of the novel failed in this regard; the film is not a musical but has an interesting score by Randy Newman and a host of current and rising stars, including Mandy Patinkin as Tateh.) Drabinsky could not have asked for a better review than Barnes's final words: "No one in their right minds will want to miss this."[74]

In the *Daily News,* Fintan O'Toole argued that *Ragtime* reflected the present day, though the show never makes this explicit. "It is a tough and truthful parable for our own times. It hums to the tune of history, but beats with the living pulse of contemporary America," O'Toole wrote.[75] Michael Feingold also saw *Ragtime* as a reflection of our present day, though he interpreted it as a symbol of the downfall of theater in the last thirty years. The Golden Era ended in the early 1960s, he argued, and since then neither home-grown American composers nor the imported megamusical has been much good. The musical has been "a very unhappy art form" since the late 1970s, "its artiness (à la Sondheim) getting ever more rarefied and convoluted, while its popular appeal, once its principal strength, has been left to European clotpolls." Feingold found that *Ragtime* did not restore the American musical to greatness; it simply announced a new phase that, while less horrible than the last few decades had been, was no Golden Era. It was, then, the first musical of a Silver Era: apparently this is "the best we can do" today. This bleak outlook aside, Feingold found much to admire in *Ragtime,* including the well-adapted plot, the negatives (bigotry, the industrial age) interestingly balanced out by positives ("fair-mindedness" and convincing characters). Had he not declared all American musical theater doomed to mediocrity, this would have qualified as a positive review.[76]

On to the Twenty-first Century

The megamusical, having adapted in various ways and integrated itself into the creative work of mostly American teams, marched boldly into the new century. With plots somewhat less epic and more human, scores that made room for occasional dialogue, and fresh teams of composers, lyricists, directors, and producers, the megamusical was in a strong position to continue, which it has. Just as *Cats* handed off to *The Lion King*—it would not be at all surprising if eventually *The Lion King* becomes Broadway's longest-running musical—a third generation of megamusical-inspired shows arose in the new century, and it is possible that one of these will become the next semi-permanent Broadway institution.

8

"Everything Is Show Biz"

The Megamusical and Broadway in the Twenty-first Century

Today, there are virtually no new musicals that, at first glance, fit the 1980s definition of the megamusical. But there are also no new musicals that do not, in at least some ways, reflect the influence of the 1980s megamusical. Without *The Phantom of the Opera*, *Wicked* would not be the same show, nor would *The Producers*. Some musicals are sung from beginning to end, or at least mostly sung. Others feature elaborate sets and spectacle. Some arrive on Broadway amid a great deal of pre-opening hype and publicity, or with substantial advance sales thanks to concept albums. Some are marketed using one simple, distinct logo. Some tell melodramatic, emotional stories; others make fun of such stories. In every case, one can trace a musical's stylistic history back through the megamusical and beyond. A show might seem more Sondheim than Lloyd Webber, or more Golden Era than megamusical, but this too is an influence. Whatever one's opinion of the megamusical—and we have seen that many people have strong opinions—the influence has been unavoidable and the legacy is felt in every new show.

Elton John and Tim Rice's *Aida*

Tim Rice, perhaps one of the three most influential forces in the creation of the early megamusical, returned to Broadway as the lyricist for *Aida*—or, as its full title runs, *Elton John and Tim Rice's Aida*. John composed the music, having been inspired to write a new version of the story after reading a children's book based on it by opera star (and legendary Aida) Leontyne Price. Linda Woolverton, Robert Falls, and David Henry Hwang wrote the musical's book with the Price version in mind, as well as Verdi's famous opera, but they diverged from the opera's plot significantly. In this version, the story begins earlier: we see Aida arrive as a slave in ancient Egypt, having been taken from Nubia with many compatriots by the army leader Radames. It is clear to Radames that Aida is no ordinary slave, thanks to her self-assured bearing, but only later does he learn that she is Nubia's princess. Aida becomes a handmaiden to the lovely princess Amneris, who is betrothed to Radames but cannot seem to win his sincere affection. Aida falls in love with Radames despite herself, and suffers the conflict of being torn between love for one man and love (and responsibility) for her country and its people. Meanwhile, the Pharaoh, Amneris's father, is slowly being poisoned by Zoser, the evil prime minister who is also Radames's father. Zoser has visions of a day when his son will marry Amneris and take over the country. Radames, disgusted by his cruel, power-hungry father and now regretful of Egypt's invasion of Nubia, tries to help Aida and her people. She and Radames conspire to free her father the king, and both are sentenced to death for their actions. With no hope of preventing Radames's execution and realizing that his love for Aida is genuine, Amneris asks that he and the Nubian princess be allowed to share their last moments of life together in a tomb. Amneris's request indicates her sympathy for the doomed couple's plight and highlights her transformation: whereas earlier she was concerned only with her appearance and social status, now she becomes a wise ruler and puts an end to the attacks on Nubia.

Aida arrived on Broadway in megamusical style. The music relies on rock and pop styles primarily, though John wrote in an impressively wide range of styles, including blues, gospel, and songs much closer to theater music than to any pop genre. His mere association with the project gave *Aida* enormous amounts of pre-opening publicity; it received even more, though of the negative variety, when an early tryout in Atlanta in 1998 was a dismal failure. The creative team undertook major rewrites and were joined at this point by playwright David Henry Hwang and director Robert Falls. A large moving pyramid, central to the set design at first but difficult to work, was scrapped. The new set design, by Bob Crowley, featured simple but striking ideas. After another tryout and a few more rewrites in Chicago, the show moved to Broadway. Further attention fell on the show when John stormed out of a preview there in what the *New York Times* called a "diva-sized huff." He was apparently angered by some dance arrangements of his music that had been done without his knowledge, but admitted to the *Times* that walking out demoralized the cast. He actually wrote, in something of a creative frenzy, most of the instrumental music himself, unlike some Broadway composers. "Disney said not for me to say this," he told the *Times,* "but I wrote it in 21 days, including the instrumental music." He explained that the challenge inspired him, because here was a romantic, adult story, with the intimidating ghost of Verdi lurking behind it, and no association with a children's cartoon. His work on *The Lion King* and a few other animated films had made for welcome diversions from his solo pop song career, but he was grateful for this task to write something more substantial and grown-up. Disney, the sole producer of *Aida*, hoped to make it clear that *Aida* was not a musical for children and produced it under the name of a new branch, Hyperion Theatricals.[1] Part of John's ease and speed in composing also came from a lyrics-first working method; John had always set other people's lyrics to music, and this became his working method with Rice, though Rice had more often worked in a melody-first method, at least with Lloyd Webber.

All this pre-opening hype, even the negative, was of course good for business. What probably did not help business much was the concept album released about a year before the Broadway opening. Instead of having the cast sing some of the songs, John and other pop stars sang them all, with no consideration for which characters would sing which songs onstage. The album—featuring Sting, Shania Twain, Tina Turner, Lenny Kravitz, James Taylor, and Janet Jackson, among others—did not sell well, nor did it give much of a sense of what the musical would be like. Frank Wildhorn had released similar albums, notably a recording of *The Civil War* featuring country artists; both Wildhorn and John might have fared much better had they used the Lloyd Webber/Rice model for concept albums, releasing something as close to a cast recording as possible.

Tim Rice penned perhaps some of his finest lyrics for *Aida*. As had been his habit since the days of *Joseph and the Amazing Technicolor Dreamcoat* and *Jesus Christ Superstar,* he saved his more comic, clever lyrics for lighter moments and villains. In "Another Pyramid," the conniving Zoser attempts to explain to an unwilling Radames what the future holds for them now that the Pharaoh is ailing.

> According to the hawk god, Horus,
> Our most regal invalid
> Is not that much longer for us
> Build another pyramid![2]

The very blonde and ditzy Amneris has her first big number while lounging by her swimming pool with her maidens; in an applause-worthy moment of staging, Bob Crowley tips the pool upright as the back wall, and girls "swim" through it suspended from wires. Amneris, whom many critics took to be a stand-in for John's friend Princess Diana, begins the show with nothing on her mind but fashion. Later, she will explain that this is partly a defense against being perpetually dismissed as "cute," but here she sings the praises of lovely clothes with gusto. The song is reminiscent of the Supremes, with the handmaidens providing peppy harmonized backup vocals. Critics, both pro and con, quoted parts of this song's lyric as an example of Rice's work.

> From your cradle via trousseau
> To your deathbed, you're on view, so
> Never compromise, accept no substitute
> I would rather wear a barrel
> Than conservative apparel
> For dress has always been my strongest suit.

"My Strongest Suit" soon becomes a ridiculous, over-the-top fashion show as Amneris and her maidens model space-age gowns and hats. It is entirely gratuitous comic relief, except for reinforcing Amneris's preoccupation with fashion, and critics were divided about whether it made for good fun or dragged the pace to a halt.

Much of the score is Aida's; she sings several songs about being torn between her country and her own desires, swinging from feeling frightened by her responsibilities to being angrily resentful of them. The best of these is "Dance of the Robe," in which Aida visits an internment camp for Nubian slaves. They ask her to lead them and give them hope, and they present her with a royal robe they have made from scraps. She concludes rather desperately that if she can at least "rekindle our ancestors' dreams, it's enough." The first act ends with the rousing spiritual anthem, "The Gods Love Nubia," in which Aida reminds her people of their homeland's greatness. It ranks among the best send-offs into intermission in any megamusical (or even any musical).

In the mouths of Aida, Amneris, and the chorus, the music sounds very little like Elton John. When sung by Radames and Zoser, however, John's style is blatant. The contrast is not necessarily problematic, though it does occasionally break the illusion of the show when one is reminded of a favorite Elton John pop song. Radames's music with Aida is closer to theater music. Their recurring duet, "Elaborate Lives," has no proper chorus, but consists of several very long, rather meandering verses and one bridge section. One can sense that Radames, who begins the song, is realizing his ideas as he sings them, stringing them together as they form in his mind.

The creative team gave *Aida* a frame story; the musical opens in modern times, in an Egyptian exhibit in a museum. The actor playing Radames and the actress playing Aida mill about, separately, among other visitors. On display, among other relics, is the square tomb in which Aida and Radames are buried, and the robes of a royal woman. The robes move, and in them Amneris turns around, delivering "Every Story Is a Love Story." Rice, as usual reluctant to characterize love as entirely happy, has Amneris explain that all stories are "tales of human failing / All are tales of love, at heart." Amneris then sets the scene, telling the audience about the importance of the Nile River and Egypt's battles to control it. When "Every Story Is a Love Story" returns at the end, we are back in the museum, with Amneris singing of a love that "never dies." The modern-day Radames and Aida, milling about in the museum, now meet by chance in front of the tomb exhibit and stare at each other with some sort of understanding. This is certainly a more hopeful ending than Verdi's, in which Amneris undergoes much less of a transformation and the lovers die together only because Aida sneaks into Radames's tomb; in the musical version, the frame story implies reincarnation and the reunion of the lovers.

The idea of the show as a legend is reinforced by Bob Crowley's sets, which are more suggestive than literal. The design relies heavily on color: rich reds and yellows, royal purples, and in the frame story, virtually nothing but white. The river can be represented by several large sheets of billowing fabric, or by the silhouette of a line of trees against a sunset sky, with a reflection of itself just below, upside down. There are some distinctly flashy moments, like Amneris's swimming pool, but also a trio for the main characters ("A Step Too Far") featuring nothing but a starry sky and a lopsided triangle made of thin beams of white light, suggesting a pyramid.

Aida opened on Broadway on 23 March 2000 and made a star out of Heather Headley, who received nearly unanimous praise in the title role. She had played Nala, Simba's love interest, in *The Lion King* on Broadway, but this new role made huge demands on both her acting and singing, and critics and audiences agreed that she triumphed. Adam Pascal (the original Roger in *Rent*) as Radames fared less well; certainly his rock-oriented voice contrasted with Headley's enormous belting theater voice. Sherie René Scott, as Amneris, had more of a traditional theater voice and received high marks. In the *New York Times,* Ben Brantley found a host of problems in *Aida,* although he opened with high praise for Headley. He argued that the show could not settle on one mood or tone, a problem which he blamed on the creative team: "Like many Broadway mega-musicals today, it has the disconnected, sterile feeling that suggests it has been assembled, piecemeal, by committee." Noting that this was a Disney-sponsored production, he imagined that it would work better as a cartoon; he even found parallels with typical Disney characters. One of the Nubian slaves, Mereb, is a young man who helps Aida reunite with her people; Brantley cast him as the "sly, ingratiating and ultimately heroic sidekick, usually represented in Disney films by a cute, small animal like a guppy or a monkey."[3] In *Newsweek,* Jack

Kroll and Veronica Chambers likewise began with a rave for Headley, but then went on to praise virtually all other aspects of the show. For them, both the comic and the dramatic worked. They praised Rice's work and Scott's delivery in "My Strongest Suit," and admired the sets.[4]

Fintan O'Toole in the *Daily News* neatly delivered a review in between these two extremes, admiring the show's ingredients—an excellent cast, singing, smooth directing, lovely sets, a good composer—but concluding that it did not quite work due to the problem in tone. O'Toole concluded that the show "hovers somewhere between camp extravaganza and historical parable without ever landing firmly on either side." He pointed out, as few others did, that *Aida* was cast with an eye toward race: Aida, the Nubian, is black, as are most of her compatriots. Radames, Amneris, the Pharaoh, and Zoser, along with most of the Egyptians, are white. As the show continued to run, replacement casts maintained this division. Thus a strong correlation is made: the slaves are people of color, the rulers are white. O'Toole hoped the show would make more of what he saw as a reference to American slavery, but the mere visual element makes the battle between rulers and captives painfully clear.[5]

Heather Headley won the Tony for 2000 (interrupting the winning streak of Audra McDonald), while John and Rice won for Best Score. Despite this recognition, *Aida* was not even nominated for Best Musical. (The controversial winner that year was *Contact,* a wonderful piece of dance-based theater, but not strictly speaking a musical. It has no live singing and uses recordings of previously released classical and pop music.)

Aida exemplifies a successful twenty-first century megamusical. Overcoming mixed reviews to settle in for a healthy run of four and a half years (it closed in September 2004), it used some megamusical elements (pop music, an emotional long-ago plot) and smoothly combined them with fresh elements (plenty of comedy, beautiful but simple sets dominated by color and style rather than technology).

Mel Brooks's *The Producers*

The Producers is a backstage musical—a show about putting on a show. It is also a mock megamusical, making fun of many of the megamusical's most controversial and recognizable elements while relying heavily on those same elements. The result is comedy rather than melodrama. What makes *The Producers* especially important in this regard is that, were we not all so familiar with the conventions of the megamusical, many of the jokes would not be so funny.

The show tells the story of washed-up Broadway producer Max Bialystock and his wimpy, straight-laced accountant, Leo Bloom. When Leo comes to Max's office to balance his books, he muses out loud that a flop could make a producer more money than a hit, if he were to raise far more than he needed to put on a show; when the show flops, the investors would assume all their money was lost. Max's interest is piqued, and a scam is born. He convinces Leo, who has secretly always wanted to live the glamorous lifestyle of a producer, to help carry out the plan, after which they can abscond with the never-spent funds. The only risk would be if the show is a hit, in which case it would be revealed that the show was oversold to its investors, and the producers would land in jail for fraud. So their first step is to find a sure-fire flop to produce; they find it in the musical *Springtime for Hitler: A Gay Romp with Adolf and Eva at Berchtesgaden,* written by a loony neo-Nazi named Franz Liebkind. They hire ridiculously gay director Roger De Bris, who, with a man named Carmen Ghia, referred to as Roger's "common law assistant," envisions the musical as an uplifting extravaganza—a megamusical, in essence—in which Hitler wins the war. They all agree that musicals are too serious lately, and vow to, as the song goes, "keep it happy, keep it snappy, keep it gay."[6] This is a direct comment on megamusicals, especially those of Lloyd Webber, which Mel Brooks repeatedly pointed out are painfully lacking in laughs. Max and Leo hire a sweet-hearted Swedish bimbo named Ulla to be their secretary. Max raises the money—far too much money—from a bevy of sex-starved little old ladies.

Springtime for Hitler opens, starring the director Roger De Bris as Hitler, and we see a big production number from the show, also called "Springtime for Hitler." Then the worst happens: the press declares it a "satiric masterpiece," and it's an enormous smash. Little Leo flees with Ulla, now his girlfriend, to Rio, but returns to take half the blame with Max. Both end up in jail, write a new musical called *Prisoners of Love,* which is also a hit, and are set free to go on being successful producers.

Mel Brooks wrote all the music and lyrics and shaped the book (with help from Thomas Meehan), based on his 1968 movie of the same name. The musical is far lighter and sillier than the movie, which has a dark, biting sensibility. But like its predecessor, the show does not hold back in its offenses—it makes crass, politically incorrect jokes about Nazis, Jews, Germans, homosexuals, blondes, the elderly, Irish policemen, and producers, to name a few of the targets. But many critics felt it was all done quite sweetly, and with such a goofy Mel Brooks sensibility that it's too funny and too all-offending to be offensive. In the *New York Times,* Ben Brantley called it a "sublimely ridiculous spectacle" and particularly admired that the show, while satirizing earlier musicals, also pays loving tribute to them.[7] Indeed, there are moments boldly and intentionally reminiscent of *Fiddler on the Roof, Gypsy, A Chorus Line, Kiss Me Kate, 42nd Street,* and *Follies,* among others. Virtually every other critic followed Brantley in praising the show, declaring it great fun, and admiring its innovative staging, hilarious lyrics, and warm heart. Director Susan Stroman, the creative choreographer behind *Contact,* shaped the look of the show and invented such over-the-top production numbers as the old ladies tap dancing with their walkers in "Along Came Bialy." She also created the extravaganza from the show within the show, "Springtime for Hitler," featuring dancing Nazis, a decidedly effeminate Hitler who sounds like Judy Garland and Ethel Merman, and a bevy of chorus girls in skimpy outfits singing backup for this Führer who is "causing a furor."

No critic writing for a mainstream paper, magazine, or television show was offended. Why? Apparently our society is quite hard to shock. Frank Rich, now a columnist for the *Times,* wrote that we are beyond the age of political correctness, and we are desensitized to offensive, crude material: "Culture cops of the left and right alike may sense that their day is finally waning," likening the popularity of the show to that of rapper Eminem or television's *The Sopranos.*[8] In fact, another *Times* columnist, Margo Jefferson, wanted *The Producers* to be "more outrageous, given its premise: to challenge the laughter comfort zone."[9] A handful of people—but no critics—did indeed have their laughter comfort zones challenged.[10]

By far the most outrageous part of the show, its very obvious climax, and the only part to garner any real protest, was the song "Springtime for Hitler." The number opens with a chorus of Bavarian-costumed peasants and then a young, handsome Nazi stormtrooper who introduces Hitler. The young stormtrooper is probably a reference to the waiters' song "Tomorrow Belongs to Me" from Kander and Ebb's *Cabaret*—he is blonde and handsome, and he has the most glorious tenor solo in the entire show. Brooks and Stroman have talked about shows which their script and staging make reference to, and neither has ever mentioned *Cabaret;* nevertheless, the allusion to a blonde handsome tenor Nazi leading a sweet song, whether they did it consciously or not, is boldly present. The stormtrooper sings:

> Springtime for Hitler and Germany
> Deutschland is happy and gay!
> We're marching to a faster pace
> Look out, here comes the master race!
> Springtime for Hitler and Germany

Rhineland's a fine land once more!
Springtime for Hitler and Germany
Watch out, Europe, we're going on tour!

Next we meet a line of Ziegfeld-like chorus girls dressed as symbols of Germany, each with giant objects on her head and covering her breasts—a huge beer stein, horns, and a breastplate like Brunhilde, a twisted pretzel, and an enormous sausage. Finally, Hitler makes his entrance and, bringing the mood of the house to a quieter level for a moment, sits on the edge of the stage like Judy at the Palace for his solo, "Heil Myself."

I was just a paper hanger
No one more obscurer
Got a phone call from the Reichstag
Told me I was Fuhrer
Germany was blue
What, oh, what to do?
Hitched up my pants
And conquered France
Now Deutschland's smiling through!

Momentum builds, the chorus returns, and eventually the stage is filled with marching Nazi stormtroopers, some of them real dancers, others life-size dolls attached to those dancers by poles and pulleys so that they move along with their live neighbors. The line advances on the audience, then forms the most outrageous image of all: a kick line shaped like a giant swastika, which rotates slowly around Hitler in the center. The image is reflected via an overhead mirror to the audience, à la Busby Berkeley or *A Chorus Line*. The final tableau involves a stage filled with soldiers and symbols of the war that Hitler has just declared. Chorus girls enter wearing tank costumes, a veiled reference to *The Lion King*'s elaborate animal puppets; bombs rain down; paratroopers drop and then hang suspended and singing. It is a mock megamusical, staged in full megamusical fashion.

So what are Mel Brooks and Susan Stroman doing here? Brooks had first-hand experience with Nazis, war, and the Holocaust, and his method for dealing with it, even then, was laughter. The *New Yorker* described it thus: "As a foot soldier tromping through Germany at the end of the Second World War, Brooks was the platoon cutup; he sang all the time and was never one to brood about the dead bodies around him, or the prospect of becoming one of them. . . . He used to tell the troops, 'Nobody dies—it's all made up.' He explained, 'Otherwise, we'd all get hysterical.' "[11] To avoid death, or the hysteria of living in constant fear of death, laughter (with a healthy dose of denial) was Brooks's therapy. But

"Springtime for Hitler" revels not just in laughs, but laughs at Hitler's expense. Brooks explains, "You can't compete with a despot on a soapbox. The best thing is to make him ludicrous."[12] It is safe to say that "ludicrous" is achieved here by making Hitler a very silly, very gay egomaniac giddy from his own power. But another side of Hitler is revealed: Hitler is a showman, a performer, a creature of the theater. He and his company of singers and dancers use theater metaphors to describe the Nazi takeover of neighboring countries: "Look out, Europe, we're going on tour," playing the "big room" versus the "lounge." As Hitler notes during "Heil Myself":

> It ain't no mystery, if it's politics or history.
> The thing you gotta know is, everything is show biz.

Brooks, then, is likening Hitler and his Nazis to the cast of a musical comedy, in which even the most serious or far-reaching acts of politics, war, or genocide somehow become show biz. *New York Times* critic Anthony Tommasini saw the parallel: "Mr. Brooks and his co-author, Thomas Meehan, realize that the very idea of 'Springtime for Hitler' will offend some people. But wasn't the real Hitler, in the most warped way imaginable, like the self-made star of some Continental production number, with gargantuan sets, pompously silly costumes, marching choristers and cheering throngs who fell for it?"[13] Or, as Michael Feingold of the *Village Voice* put it with a bit more bitterness: "If you leave aside the brutality, horror, devastation, and mass slaughter that it caused, Nazism was nothing but showbiz."[14]

Brooks is in fact intentionally revealing how Nazism worked, why people went along with it, how they got seduced into following. It was not simple passivity, as Captain Von Trapp's friend Max in Rodgers and Hammerstein's *The Sound of Music* or *Cabaret*'s Sally Bowles would argue. It's show biz. It's manipulative, calculated theater, meant to seduce its audience into believing it and singing along. This undoing of the power of the Nazi movement, this lifting of the curtain to reveal the mechanics behind the intimidating leader's façade, is a powerful political act. Now, we can not only laugh at Hitler, we can explain why earlier, more gullible audiences did not laugh—they were dazzled by his production values. His trickery is revealed, his magical powers deflated.

The day after *The Producers* opened, it broke the record for one-day ticket sales, selling more than $3 million worth, topping *The Lion King*. It helped, though, that a single regular ticket cost more than for any show in the history of Broadway—$100.[15] Later, a group of fifty seats would sell for a ridiculous $480 each, in an effort to undermine the profits being made by scalpers making nearly twice that much. The show recouped its initial $11 million investment in a quick thirty-six weeks, which meant the producers, unlike Max and Leo, could pay off their backers and then some. It was nominated for a record number of Tonys and won twelve, which was the most it could have won, given that the show had multiple nominees in some categories. When Brooks accepted one of his many awards, he said, "I want to thank Hitler for being such a funny guy . . . on stage."[16] Already, the show has become part of the cultural consciousness; in an editorial about Middle Eastern politics, the *Washington Post* called Yasser Arafat "the Max Bialystock of revolutionaries."[17]

The megamusical had been around for so long by the time of *The Producers* that jokes making fun of it generated big laughs. Putting these regular guys, Max and Leo, not to mention Hitler, in megamusical-style settings allowed Brooks both to mock the megamusical and to make his political point. It is testament to the megamusical's full integration into our shared culture that this show works so well.

Broadway after 11 September 2001

Following the terrorist attacks on the World Trade Center, New York mayor Rudolph Giuliani, then an almost constant presence on television and a source of both information and comfort to locals, urged the city to reopen only three major institutions on 13 September: City Hall, the New York Stock Exchange, and Broadway theaters. He encouraged people to get on with their lives, go to restaurants and museums, though many of these—as well as concert venues, movie theaters, and indeed almost all the city's subway lines, bridges, and tunnels— remained closed for a week or more. But in keeping with the mayor's request, Broadway theaters opened on the thirteenth. Almost no one came, but considering the proximity to the attacks, it was remarkable that anyone was in the audience at all. Before the curtains went up, the marquee lights at every Broadway house were dimmed, and after most performances, casts led the few audience members in patriotic songs. At *The Producers,* stars Matthew Broderick and Nathan Lane led the sing-along. The *New York Times* quoted Lane as saying, "They shouldn't rob us of our right to have a good time."[18]

Besides a "show must go on" philosophy, Broadway has also begun to respond to the attacks directly. There have been show tunes written by Broadway composers and lyricists about the events, as well as plays that use the attacks as their backdrop to tell smaller stories. There has not yet been a full-length musical that reflects 9/11, but there surely will be. Although Broadway musicals—especially megamusicals—have a reputation for being escapist, transporting fun, Broadway has never failed to reflect, address, even shape current events, including the most tragic or horrific.

By 11 September 2001, *The Producers* had been running for five months. That show boasted the only nearly full house two nights later, and for many weeks thereafter it had by far the most populated audience. But audiences came, even in those first few weeks, to all the musicals. There had been two places to buy same-day half-price tickets in the city: at the TKTS booth in the middle of Times Square, and at a booth in the World Trade Center. A temporary booth was set up on 13 September in Duffy Square, and it did brisk business, mostly from tourists stranded in Manhattan with nothing to occupy their time and no means of leaving. "We just wanted to do something, to have something to do," stuttered one tourist in line that first day.[19] A few days after the attacks, a businessman—who had seen the second plane hit the South Tower—took fifteen of his buddies to *The Producers.* They had bought the tickets nine months earlier. "I was determined to go," he told the *New York Times.* "I was determined to laugh and determined to make my life as normal as possible. And [seeing *The Producers*] was a big element of that."[20]

Others came not just to keep busy or to bring their lives some element of normalcy, but as a political statement. On 20 September, only a handful of the 1,636 seats at *The Phantom of the Opera* were filled, a tiny audience of people who attended with what the *New York Times* called "a sense of urgency." They came "as a gesture of support for the theater, as a demonstration that the terrorists could not paralyze the culture industry or kill theatergoers' spirit."[21] A couple came from Waterbury, Connecticut, to celebrate the husband's fifty-third birthday: "We decided over the weekend that coming to the theater and having a good time, despite what was going on, was important to encourage business. If we didn't, we would be kind of giving in to them."[22] This was the fourteenth time they had seen *The Phantom of the Opera;* they had seen it once a year. Other audience members told reporters that they brought their children to *Phantom, Les Mis, The Lion King,* and other long-running megamusicals in order to teach them not to be afraid to go out, and to show them that life went on beyond the horror of what they were seeing on television. Because these megamusicals were now institutions, they proved the most popular destinations for families seeking diversion and reassurance, and as a group they weathered the crisis better than many other musicals.

A number of shows, especially revivals and smaller-scale pieces, never made it out of those first few weeks after the attacks due to the disastrous drop-off in attendance. Four shows closed almost immediately, including the successful revival of *Kiss Me, Kate.* A production of Andrew Lloyd Webber's small-scale musical *By Jeeves,* slated to open in the fall of 2001, was cancelled when jittery investors pulled out. But Lloyd Webber stepped in and funded the show himself, saying, "We believe very strongly in Broadway. And Broadway has been very good to me."[23] Another Broadway show planned for that fall, Stephen Sondheim's *Assassins* (which had previously played only in a short-lived off-Broadway staging in 1990), was cancelled. The subject matter—a concept musical about presidential assassinations or attempted assassinations—was deemed inappropriate. It finally arrived, to critical acclaim and several Tony Awards, in March 2004, but ran only until that July.

The question about the appropriateness of certain topics reached so broadly in the first weeks after 9/11 that people began to speculate about whether it was acceptable to attend the theater at all. Not surprisingly, *The Producers* was the title floated most often in this discussion, not only because of its touchy subject matter but because of its overwhelming popularity. One Broadway fan said on 13 September, "I mean, they can start up again today for all intents and purposes, but are people going to want to get back into the theater after such a horrible event? Will the comedies be funny? Will we laugh at 'The Producers' anymore? (Can we even think to laugh at Hitler anymore?)."[24] Roger Bart, playing the role of Carmen Ghia, told the *New York Times* on 20 September: "I remember thinking how strange it was to hear an anchorman on TV say this and that would remain closed but that Broadway shows would open again. I felt a little embarrassed."[25]

Slowly, Broadway attendance began to rebuild. Six months after the attacks, in March 2002, Broadway was enjoying a very healthy season, with sales down only 5 percent from that of the previous March. As the *New York Times* pointed out, "Who came to the rescue? Locals."[26] People from the tri-state area flocked to Broadway, lured by the desire to support their city, the strong set of shows running, and several intense publicity and marketing campaigns designed to do exactly this—draw the locals back to Broadway. By the peak of the season in May 2002, records had been broken. But even as of this writing, the tourists still have not fully returned. Group tours, especially international ones, are booking a fraction of what they used to. Houses are full only because so many people buy same-day tickets at discounted prices. What this means is that only the most popular, stable shows have any kind of security, with an advance sale strong enough to ensure investors and producers that it can survive another month. At first, most of the secure shows were megamusicals, including 1980s holdovers *The Phantom of the Opera* and *Les Misérables,* as well as more recent megamusical hits like *The Lion King* and that anti-megamusical, *The Producers.*

There were a number of strategies to rejuvenate attendance that helped

Broadway turn a profit in these difficult months, something few could have expected given the circumstances. Within a week of the attacks, the League of American Theaters and Producers, the governing body of Broadway, met to discuss temporary adjustments and cost-cutting measures. Theater owners waived rent. Actors, stagehands, and musicians at a handful of successful shows took a 25 percent pay cut for a month. Grumbling—anonymous grumbling—arose immediately about the injustice of hard-working actors and backstage workers taking pay cuts while producers, who had made millions off these shows, gave up nothing.[27]

The League's next move was a television commercial filmed on Broadway, in the middle of Times Square. The full casts of every musical running at the time, led by Broadway's reigning diva, Bernadette Peters, sang Kander and Ebb's "New York, New York." Nathan Lane and Matthew Broderick were placed conspicuously just behind Peters, near all the other stars who might be recognizable to an audience beyond the New York area. The commercial ran in twenty countries around the world.

The League also accepted—with a great show of probably fake reluctance—financial help from both the city and the state. In a campaign called "Spend Your Regards to Broadway," the city of New York bought 50,000 tickets for $2.5 million, and then gave them away in pairs to anyone who spent $500 in certain stores. It was good for Broadway and for retail, and it worked. The city gave 15,000 of the tickets away for free, to the Twin Towers Fund for firefighters, police officers, rescue workers, and victims' families. Mayor Giuliani made it very clear that Broadway was a crucial New York cultural, economic, and artistic institution that required support. He had always been close with the leadership of the League of American Theaters and Producers, and in the end the effort to help Broadway bounce back was so successful that the League gave a million dollars back to the city.[28]

The importance of Broadway—not just theater anywhere in New York—as a symbol was so powerful that these were the only theaters to receive any help from the government. The city offered no aid to off-Broadway houses, many of which are below 14th Street and were directly affected by the attacks. A number of their critically well-received and relatively secure shows closed. Unfortunately, this sort of treatment is the norm for off-Broadway; they are not members of the League, they are much less organized as an institution, they do not have close ties to the mayor's office (past or present), they cannot afford to rebuild their own theaters or film their own international television commercials, much less give to the mayor's election campaign, as the League has done.

It is irrefutable, then, that Broadway as an institution has become a cultural touchstone, representing New York to the rest of the country and to the world. The mere act of returning to shows on the thirteenth, the performers and the audiences using the theater as a venue for political defiance and life-affirming activity, was itself a performance. I do not question the sincerity of the dedicated audience, of which I was one—but as we ourselves made clear, attendance was itself an act of defiance, like a sit-in with its own floor show. We were putting on an act that we hoped the enemy would see. This is why Mayor Giuliani sent the casts back to work—as a show, a message, that he hoped would resonate around the world. The partial recovery of the Broadway economy has done nothing to help the war on terrorism, but it has done wonders for the economy of New York, the morale of the American people, and the healthy cultural image America projects to the world. The most effective way to convey this message is through performance, by both casts and audiences. When Broadway went back to work on the thirteenth, casts led the audience in singing of "God Bless America," a song written by Broadway composer Irving Berlin. He originally intended it as the big, stirring finale of a musical, and it was so effective that most do not even realize that it is being used in the same context today.

Recent Megamusicals

Several seasons after the attacks, the Broadway scene settled back into its usual routine: some months boasted excellent economic health and a flock of popular new musicals, others featured poor ticket sales and a few weak musicals getting bad reviews. The latest megamusicals, which one may now consider a generation or two removed from their main models of the 1980s, can still find great success, but they also share Broadway with a host of other styles. At the 2004 Tony Awards, most of the theater community was shocked when *Avenue Q* beat *Wicked* for Best Musical. *Avenue Q*, a small-scale musical by Robert Lopez and Jeff Marx, features a small cast of twenty-something people and Muppet-style puppets pondering their lives and futures. These are wise-cracking, foul-mouthed puppets in a satirical, funny musical that managed to transfer from off-Broadway and become both a popular and critical hit. Still, it came as a surprise when *Avenue Q* took Best Book, Score, and Musical; *Wicked* won in some technical categories, as well as for lead actress Idina Menzel. Many cheered this turn of events, interpreting it as an underdog's victory over a megamusical villain. What it really means is that Broadway now has room for various types of musicals, including the large and epic as well as the small and satiric (another example of which was the hit show *Urinetown*). The megamusical's stranglehold on theater has eased considerably in the last five years, and while the genre will continue to influence new shows, it was refreshing to see both musicals recognized for different achievements. The 2004 Tony Awards also brought attention to the critically well-received musical *Caroline, or Change,* and the long overdue and highly praised revival of Sondheim's *Assassins,* directed, like *Wicked,* by Joe Mantello.

Wicked does indeed fit the definition of a megamusical, but only in its twenty-first-century guise. It includes plenty of humor and irony; in fact, many critics felt that the entire tone of the show was one of satire, using a well-known cast of fantasy characters as a parallel for political life today. This is a far cry from the earnest, straightforward grand emotions of the 1980s megamusical. But *Wicked* does demonstrate a number of recognizable megamusical features, both within the show and in its socio-theatrical context.

Based on the novel by Gregory Maguire, *Wicked* tells the story of *The Wizard of Oz*'s Wicked Witch of the West and the good witch Glinda, long before Dorothy enters the picture. Elphaba, born green and perpetually shunned and mocked for it, is a smart, withdrawn girl. Her college roommate, Glinda, befriends her and draws her out a bit, but thanks to some evil doings in Oz—by the Wizard himself, in part—Elphaba ends up on the wrong side of right and wrong, eventually embracing the wickedness that, as Glinda notes, was thrust upon her. The music and lyrics, by Stephen Schwartz (*Godspell, Pippin*), feature a number of light theater songs mixed with many pop-rock belters and a few emotional duets. The book, adapted by Winnie Holzman from the novel, has to convey an enormous amount of plot in a show that features a fair amount of dialogue. Much of the attention *Wicked* received in the press went to its two leading ladies: Idina Menzel, the original Maureen in *Rent,* as Elphaba, and Kristin Chenoweth, a Tony winner as Sally in *You're a Good Man, Charlie Brown,* as Glinda. Critics noted that it was unusual for a musical to center on the friendship of two women, rather than on a romantic plot or a plot following one main character's rise and fall; many detected a distinct feminist tone in the show as a result.[29]

With a large, complicated set design by Eugene Lee (*Ragtime*), featuring many wheels and cogs, a big dragon, and much flying and floating by witches and evil monkeys, *Wicked* certainly looks like a megamusical. And the substantial pre-opening buzz made its arrival on Broadway an event in megamusical style. But the show's unusual tone of irony and self-mocking satire—though it comes and goes—makes the show something of a post-megamusical.

Some felt this tone did not quite work. Ben Brantley found the "bloated" show to be too heavy-handed in its politics and message, reminding us in far too blatant terms of the problems of championing style over substance, photo opportunities over actual good deeds. This mixed awkwardly, he felt, with the more comedic moments. The score, his comments imply, is too megamusical; he described it as a "swirling pop-eretta score" with too many "generically impassioned songs, which have that to-the-barricades sound of the ominously underscored anthems of 'Les Misérables.' " He did admire the large set. But his only enthusiastic praise was reserved for Chenoweth, who he felt stole the show, unbalancing the story but providing an astounding performance.[30] Elysa Gardner of *USA Today* saw in the tone of the show exactly what Brantley did not: it "juggles winning irreverence with thoughtfulness and heart." She found the score hummable, not bombastic, and praised the whole cast.[31] In the *New Yorker,* John Lahr too saw a show full of "high camp" and "irony," and praised the book's handling of the story and the clever, invented words used in the land of Oz. He also greatly admired both leading ladies, but found the score's songs unmemorable, which led him to conclude that despite many excellent qualities, the show overall did not quite work. He noted, however, that the audience gave the show a standing ovation.[32]

The plot, though quite complicated, does carry the audience from the comic numbers to the emotional peaks and back again. Glinda's song "Popular," which she sings while giving Elphaba a makeover in order to help her fit in, features clever rhymes and just enough off-beat rhythmic play to keep it bouncy and interesting yet digestible. The gradual build-up to Elphaba's embracing of her supposedly wicked side moves smoothly away from the tone of "Popular" toward, among others, Elphaba's tour-de-force anthem, "Defying Gravity." The earthbound comedic tone set earlier makes Elphaba seem like a real person, not an idealized romantic heroine, so that by the time she belts out these high notes she has reached the top but not gone over it.

In an article in the *New York Times* written seven months after *Wicked* opened, music critic Stephen Holden made a point of noting the underlying layers of *Wicked* that, especially upon multiple hearings of the cast recording, reveal that the "show is much smarter than it lets on." The modern parallels, revealed especially through Schwartz's clever, "barbed" lyrics, prove Oz to be like a "21st-century America clenched in post-9/11 apprehension." For Holden, Schwartz's score combined the megamusical with rock, leading to numbers sometimes too large for their "lyrics' considerable wit." Schwartz "infuses the lumbering grandiosity of an 80's spectacle by Andrew Lloyd Webber with the pounding declamation of late-70's-early-80's power ballads by rock groups like Journey and Styx."[33] Like *Aida, Wicked* serves as a prime example of the third generation of the megamusical, adjusting and selecting elements from its ancestors and collecting them all in a show with a current sensibility.

The 2003–2004 season saw one other megamusical reach Broadway, the first since *Sunset Boulevard* that featured contributions by Andrew Lloyd Webber. In the case of *Bombay Dreams*, however, Lloyd Webber played only a small role; he helped "conceive" the idea of the show, and his Really Useful Group produced the London version before it came to New York. The music is by composer A. R. Rahman and the lyrics are by veteran megamusical lyricist Don Black; when the book and lyrics underwent some rewriting for New York, Thomas Meehan (*The Producers*) and David Yazbek (*The Full Monty*) contributed. *Bombay Dreams* follows a young man's struggle to become a famous performer in musicals in "Bollywood," the center of the Indian film industry. Like countless backstage musicals before it, *Bombay Dreams* features a few show-within-a-show scenes, when the audience gets to see the film's big production numbers. The show's unusual setting and story at first seemed to be overcoming a distinctly mixed critical reception upon its opening (29 April 2004), but it ran less than a year.

Of course, the first few years of the twenty-first century saw its share of megamusical flops. Perhaps the highest-profile of these was *Dance of the Vampires*, because it marked the return of Michael Crawford, the original Phantom, to Broadway. Based on a Roman Polanski film, the show had a score by Jim Steinman, the pop song writer who had written the lyrics for Lloyd Webber's *Whistle Down the Wind*. Critics and audiences alike were unmoved by the odd nineteenth-century vampire story, Crawford's performance, the score, and the complex sets full of technical wizardry; the show closed less than two months after its December 2002 opening.

The Megamusical's Twenty-first Century Context

In the 1990s, we saw that the megamusical loosened its stranglehold on Broadway, and other genres once again made their mark. This continues today, although many new musicals not particularly megamusical-like fall into fairly safe categories. For example, musicals based on familiar pop hits abound: the dance revue *Movin' Out*, and *Taboo* and *Mamma Mia!* to name a few. *Mamma Mia!* has been one of the few solid hits so far this century (along with *Aida*, *The Producers*, and *Wicked*), featuring an original book involving a reunion of old friends. Its score comes from hits of the Swedish pop group ABBA, composed by Benny Andersson and Björn Ulvaeus, whose last foray into the Broadway musical, *Chess*, resulted in a fascinating score but an overall flop. It makes for a strange twist that they would have a hit with a show for which they wrote no new music. Audiences sing along with the familiar tunes, which are clearly a large part of the show's appeal.

Another trend in recent years, resulting in a similar mix of hits and flops despite the seeming safeness of the undertaking, involves adapting familiar films to the stage. *Hairspray*, based on the John Waters film, has a score by Marc Shaiman (a film composer whose credits include the songs in the *South Park* movie musical) and Scott Wittman, with a book by Thomas Meehan (*The Producers*) and Mark O'Donnell. *Thoroughly Modern Millie*, based on the 1967 film, was a musical in that form already. The stage musical uses much of the film's story and songs, with some additions and changes in the score and book. Several movies failed to make the transition to musical quite as successfully, including *Footloose* and *Saturday Night Fever*, both of which opened in the final years of the last century and closed in 2000. This might have indicated that the movie-to-musical trend was waning had not *The Producers*, *Hairspray*, and *Thoroughly Modern Millie* all come along afterward. What *Footloose* and *Saturday Night Fever* suffered from the most was literal-mindedness; their adaptations kept very close to their source material, making them seem like pale copies of films rather than creative, fresh stage works.

The influence of the megamusical of course continues, in similar as well as opposing forms of shows. Just as the megamusical's innovations had their roots in earlier forms of music theater, but recombined them in ways that required its own label, so too the shows being written today reflect the unprecedented successes of the megamusical.

I will demonstrate the cultural currency of the megamusical with this anecdote: when I was in middle school (in the early 1980s), it was of course unacceptable to like anything. We had to be sarcastic at every turn; eye-rolling proliferated. What better way to display utter disdain for something than with a reference to *Cats*? That show had already, in the mid-1980s, become such a part of our culture that it became synonymous with the uncool. Today, many people my age still use this phrase when expressing disdain for something new. Did you like that new book, movie, event, or musical? people ask us.

Oh, *sure*, we answer. I laughed, I cried, it was better than *Cats*.

Appendix A: Jesus Christ Superstar *Plot Summary and List of Recurring Musical Material*

Each section of the score is listed below. In the cases in which a number refers musically to another number, that reference is listed in brackets. Following each title is a description of the plot during that section.

1. Overture ["Trial Before Pilate"]
2. "Heaven on Their Minds"
   Judas reveals his disappointment in the way his friend, Jesus, is currently handling their social movement. Judas feels that Jesus has allowed the adoration of the crowds to convince him that he might be God, and Judas fears the wrath of the Roman occupiers if any more attention is drawn their way. Already, Judas is disillusioned by this turn away from their formerly quiet, controlled activities.
3. "What's the Buzz?"
   Jesus fields questions from his enthusiastic but naïve apostles, who are overly eager to act. Mary Magdalene attempts to soothe an annoyed and tense Jesus.
4. "Strange Thing Mystifying"
   Judas scolds Jesus for spending time with Mary, whose reputation could bring him harm, but Jesus, frustrated, turns on Judas and the rest of the apostles, declaring that none of them understand him. (In the 1973 film version only, a song for the evil Priests, "Then We Are Decided," follows, in which they agree strong action must be taken against Jesus.)
5. "Everything's Alright"
   Mary attempts to calm Jesus, but he and Judas debate Mary's place, what the group should be doing with their money, and whether people appreciate Jesus while they still can. This trio for Mary, Jesus, and Judas also includes the apostles and some women, who eventually help calm Jesus.
6. "This Jesus Must Die" ["Trial Before Pilate"]
   The scene shifts to the Jewish Priests, led by Caiaphas and his sidekick Annas; they all agree that Jesus and his adoring crowds of supporters threaten their leadership, and they resolve that Jesus must be stopped.
7. "Hosanna"
   Jesus and his crowd come on the scene. Jesus smiles at Caiaphas's attempt to quiet them, and he joins happily in the crowd's singing; it is the most pleasant time for Jesus in the musical, but it is tainted when the crowd's adulation changes to a fleeting call for his death on their behalf.
8. "Simon Zealotes/Poor Jerusalem" ["Pilate's Dream"]
   The crowd's political goals become pronounced, as Simon encourages Jesus to use his power to lead a revolution against the Romans; the crowd gets whipped up into

Simon's frenzy. Jesus tries to explain that this is not the way to help Jerusalem, that they do not understand power, but his manner is already defeated; it seems they may never understand.

9. "Pilate's Dream"

Pilate, the Roman leader in Jerusalem, sings alone, recounting a dream that fore-shadows his meeting with Jesus; he envisions that he will be blamed for Jesus' death.

10. "The Temple" ["Gethsemane"]

The scene moves to the Temple, where crowds sell, buy, and gamble for all manner of sinful goods and services. Jesus, infuriated, clears them out, but soon loses his energy and feels defeated. One by one, then in a surging mob, people come to Jesus, begging for help and healing. Overwhelmed, Jesus shrieks that there are too many of them, that they should heal themselves.

11. "I Don't Know How to Love Him" [introduction: "Everything's Alright"]

Mary Magdalene comes on the scene and soothes Jesus, then reflects on her love for this strange man, so different than the others she has known.

12. "Damned for All Time/Blood Money" ["This Jesus Must Die"]

Judas goes to the Priests, tormented by his conflict: he loves Jesus and their move-ment, but he feels Jesus cannot control it any longer, and despite his fear of eternal damnation, he is driven to talk to the Priests. They offer him silver for his information, which he refuses, but eventually, in defeat, he accepts it and reveals that Jesus will be in the Garden of Gethsemane.

13. "The Last Supper" ["Everything's Alright," "Superstar"]

The second act begins with "The Last Supper," at which the shallow and mindless apostles relax and imagine how Jesus will make them famous one day. Jesus knows the end is near; he offers them bread and wine, hoping they will remember him when they eat and drink. Then he rounds on both Judas and Peter, until Judas and Jesus erupt into a shouting match. Jesus urges Judas to go betray him; he seems to know what Judas has done, just as he knows that Peter will deny him three times. Judas flees and the apostles drift drunkenly to sleep.

14. "Gethsemane (I Only Want to Say)"

Jesus, alone, questions God, demanding to know why so much is being asked of him, whether his death will do any good, why God will not reveal Himself to Jesus. Finally, he angrily agrees to die, although he still has no answers.

15. "The Arrest" ["What's the Buzz?" "The Temple," choral section of "Strange Thing Mystifying"]

Judas returns with the Priests' guards and, after kissing Jesus, sees his friend arrested. The crowd, now turned against their leader, taunt him as they lead him to Caiaphas, then Pilate.

16. "Peter's Denial" ["Strange Thing Mystifying"]

Peter, confronted about knowing the famous leader who was taken away, denies it three times. Mary is saddened by Peter's actions, but marvels that Jesus knew it would happen.

17. "Pilate and Christ" ["Trial Before Pilate," "Hosanna"]

Jesus appears before Pilate for the first of two times; a flippant Pilate passes him off on Herod, King of Galilee.

18. "King Herod's Song"

Herod turns out to be far more interested in seeing Jesus perform tricks and miracles than anything else, and when he gets no response to his taunts and demands, he sends Jesus back to Pilate.

19. "Could We Start Again, Please?"
    In a moment of quieter reflection, Mary, joined by Peter and the other apostles, expresses her confusion about how the situation got out of hand, and longs to see Jesus again. (This number was added to the show after the concept album.)

20. "Judas's Death" ["This Jesus Must Die," "Damned for All Time," "I Don't Know How to Love Him," "Heaven on Their Minds"]
    Judas arrives at the Priests' door for a second time, furious that Jesus is being treated so badly. The Priests point out that Judas saved Israel, that he will always be remembered. Judas, tortured by his love for Jesus, his anger at having his actions so misunderstood, and his fear of eternal retribution, lurches to an anguished suicide, sobbing that Jesus has murdered him.

21. "Trial Before Pilate"
    Pilate attempts repeatedly to understand Jesus and to placate the crowd, which calls for Jesus' crucifixion. He fails in both regards; Jesus does little to defend himself, and the crowd is beyond reason. Jesus has committed no crime, Pilate points out, but to attempt to assuage the bloodthirsty mob, he has Jesus whipped thirty-nine times. Jesus continues to assert that everything is fixed, nothing can be done, and Pilate, angry now, lets Jesus go to his fate.

22. "Superstar"
    Judas appears, from the dead or the future, to question Jesus' actions one last time. He wants to know if Jesus really is God, if he meant to die, and why he chose to appear at that time and place. No answers are forthcoming.

23. "Crucifixion"
    Jesus talks to God in weakened tones during his crucifixion, which the jeering crowd and mourning apostles witness.

24. "John Nineteen Forty-One" ["Gethsemane"]
    After Jesus' death, the orchestra offers a slow postlude.

Evita opens on 26 July 1952, the day Eva Peron died. In a movie theater, the film is interrupted by an announcement that the First Lady has passed away; the chorus erupts into wails and the scene shifts to her funeral. It is an elaborate, emotional affair, the people of Argentina mourning loudly in Latin. Only Che stands apart from it, explaining directly to the audience that the whole affair looks more like show business than politics to him ("Requiem for Evita/Oh What a Circus"). Eva's voice floats over the funeral, reminding her people that she is ordinary, that the mourning should be for Argentina, not for her.

The scene now flashes back to 1934 and the town of Junin, where Eva Duarte, age fifteen, is in a nightclub with her family. A tango singer, Augustin Magaldi, is wrapping up his set with a rather corny number ("On This Night of a Thousand Stars"). It becomes clear that Eva has seduced him, and now wants him to take her to Buenos Aires, the big city, so her real life can begin. He resists, but Che points out to him that it's hopeless; she will get what she wants. She expresses hatred for the middle class, and she reveals a bitter edge and cunning that quickly outwit Magaldi ("Eva and Magaldi"). He attempts to dissuade her from her big city ambitions ("Eva Beware of the City") but before he has even finished his final note, the scene shifts to Buenos Aires. Eva has arrived ("Buenos Aires"). She boldly declares her star quality and wills the dirty city to take her on and take her in. Che hovers nearby and updates us on the news in Buenos Aires.

Having set up shop, Eva now begins climbing her way through the ranks of show business, a process presented in a montage of lovers coming and going ("Goodnight and Thank You"). Che, with some amusement, narrates the tale of Eva's string of lovers as he escorts each one out of her life. After Magaldi she moves on to one who can get her photographed as a model and another who can get her acting jobs on the radio. Between dalliances, Eva and Che reflect that everyone uses other people for their own gain. A rising star now, she focuses her ambitions even higher.

The scene shifts to the rise in power of Juan Peron, chosen from a group of military leaders as the next leader of Argentina ("The Art of the Possible"). The right-wing leaders had seized power several years before, and it is Peron who rises to the surface to lead them and perhaps the nation. While the officers vie for power, Eva speaks on the radio about how she, as one of the people, would like to see a government which would help them. (This song does not appear on the concept album; instead, Che explains Peron's rise, as well as his own foray into insecticides, in the rock number "The Lady's Got Potential," a reworked version of which appears in the film adaptation.)

In 1944, there is a charity concert that the film actress Eva Duarte and the politician Juan Peron both attend. Peron makes a rousing speech to the cheering crowds, vowing to use his power to speak for the people. Eva seduces him quickly, not only with her beauty but with her sound reasoning: the two of them are in positions to help one another in their ambitions ("Charity Concert/I'd Be Surprisingly Good for You"). Eva accompanies

Peron home, where she tosses out Peron's young mistress; the girl sings the only solo in the show not sung by one of the three leads, as she contemplates in a world-weary way what will become of her now ("Another Suitcase In Another Hall"). Che hovers nearby, in sympathy.

Two groups deeply resent the rise of Eva to the role of Peron's wife and, if Peron should come to power, First Lady of Argentina. The military wonders why Peron does not simply keep her in bed, the proper place for pretty lovers, and the aristocracy worries over how such a low-class woman could have come to be respected ("Peron's Latest Flame"). The soldiers sing their march with machismo and aggression, while the aristocrats tiptoe, uptight. Che, amused, fuels their anger and agitation. He approaches Eva in the guise of a reporter, representing the media attention Eva is now receiving; when his questions become too personal, heavies hustle him off.

By 1945, the government has no clear leader, but Peron and Eva have won the support of the lower-class workers. Peron expresses doubt about his ability to grab the reigns of the country, but Eva insists he is the man for the job. She goes before the people, declaring Peron's support for them, until they are whipped up into a frenzy of enthusiasm for Peron and for his effective spokeswoman ("A New Argentina"). Only Che remains unmoved, and is again set upon by heavies who silence his dissenting voice. The whole sequence culminates in the stirring chorus declaring that the voices of the people can no longer be ignored.

The second act opens just after Peron has won a sweeping victory in the presidential election of 1946. He appears before his ecstatic people, vowing as always to support their causes, and introduces, to even greater cheers, the new First Lady ("On the Balcony of the Casa Rosada/Don't Cry for Me, Argentina"). As Evita emerges onto the balcony to greet her people, Che feigns enthusiasm for the sake of nearby heavies who suspect he is less than thrilled by her presence. Eva, ever the actress, takes the stage and sings the now-famous song of her love for her people, and of her (supposedly) unexpected rise to fame and wealth. At one point she breaks down in tears, and the crowd rallies to support her. The moment her back is turned to her people, she notes snidely that she is loved, that a low-class girl has risen to the greatest power. The crowd chants for her frantically.

Che reflects on the strange nature of stardom, and on what this angry woman can possibly do now that she has achieved all she wanted at age twenty-six ("High Flying, Adored"). The song suggests Che may have more understanding for Eva than his usual hostility would imply. Eva decides to show the world the glamour and power of the new Peronist government. She gets her team of beauty consultants and fashion designers to perfect her image ("Rainbow High") and embarks on a tour of Europe ("Rainbow Tour"). Her travels are narrated by Che, who points out that while she was a rousing success in Spain, Italy was less than impressed, and by the time she reached France she looked tired. Che insinuates himself into the action. Eva returns home in semi-defeat. Although the aristocracy gloats over her failure, she vows never to give in to them, never to become one of them ("The Actress Hasn't Learned the Lines [You'd Like to Hear]"). Che asks her how it can be that, if she is so supportive of the poor, they have received no help at all from her. She announces the creation of her new foundation which gives money to the lower class.

Che narrates the story of Eva's handling of money; it seems that she has been taking "donations" by force from her people, and a good deal of this money has found its way into her own coffers ("And the Money Kept Rolling In [and Out]"). The people are blissfully unaware of her mishandling of funds, and joyously accept her gifts of cash to them. The children of Argentina bless and praise Eva in a hymn, and they are joined by the workers who declare her a saint ("Santa Evita"). Che points out that she seems to have chosen sainthood over the job of running her country.

This leads to the only extended confrontation between Eva and Che ("Waltz for Eva and Che"). He demands to know how she can justify eliminating all dissenting voices, how she can abuse her position, how she can avoid doing anything humanitarian with her power. She argues that she is simply playing the politics game, that she is happy to please her people for the time being, and that evil is an integral part of government. After dismissing Che, she reflects, alone, on her frustration regarding her failing health.

Now begins a series of events which lead to the end of the show. Peron ponders Eva's role in his government, admiring her ability to project her glamorous image ("She Is a Diamond"). His military critics remain unimpressed by both Eva and Peron. Che, angry now, spits out some facts: a formerly wealthy Argentina is bankrupt, food is being rationed, most newspapers and all dissenting voices have been silenced. Beginning to lose his grip on the country, Peron tries to persuade Eva to quit while they still can, before a coup robs them of their power and perhaps their lives ("Dice Are Rolling"). Eva continues to argue that the people will support them, but Peron knows they are fickle. Besides, Eva's illness is sapping her of energy, beauty, and power. Eva insists that she is fine, that her role will be even stronger when she becomes vice president ("Eva's Sonnet").

Eventually bowing to the inevitable, Eva agrees to one last radio broadcast as she steps down from the public eye ("Eva's Final Broadcast"). In a partial reprise of "Don't Cry for Me, Argentina," she declines all future governmental positions but vows always to love and represent the people. She is weak, and her broadcast is brief and somewhat disjointed. In her final hours, she recalls moments from her life in a number that reprises bits and pieces from earlier numbers ("Montage"), and she reflects on the choices she made ("Lament"). She does not regret that she chose to live fast and hard, rather than having a slow, anonymous, boring life, but she does wonder about the children she never had. As she dies, embalmers move in to preserve her glamorous look forever. Che adds softly that although a monument was built for Eva, the body disappeared for seventeen years. The music fades away, unresolved and unsettling.

Appendix C: Joseph and the Amazing Technicolor Dreamcoat *Plot Summary*

This summary describes *Joseph* in the form of its Broadway run in 1982, which is the version most widely known and the one which is generally performed today. It contains all the extensions and additions made over the years. *Joseph* opens with the Narrator (a woman, for our purposes) singing to the audience about dreamers, and one dreamer in particular whose story she will tell us tonight ("Prologue: You Are What You Feel"). This moves directly into "Jacob and Sons," which introduces Jacob, father of Israel, and his twelve boisterous sons. They are farmers and sheep herders. Joseph is Jacob's favorite.

In "Joseph's Coat (The Coat of Many Colors)," Jacob tells us that Joseph's mother was his favorite wife, so he loves Joseph the best, and to prove it he gives Joseph a stunning multicolored coat. Joseph is thrilled, and gloats and models his coat rather obnoxiously; his brothers are jealous and bitter. The Narrator tells us that Jacob could not see beyond his love for Joseph to the problems he was creating. The full company (Narrator, Joseph, Jacob, brothers, and chorus of women) lists the many, many colors in Joseph's coat in a rousing finish.

Joseph's brothers are annoyed not only by his coat, but by the dreams he has, which inevitably feature representations of his brothers bowing down to him ("Joseph's Dreams"). The brothers begin to wonder if Joseph knows something about the future, and decide the best solution is to get rid of him. They do so in "Poor, Poor Joseph" by selling him into slavery to a group of Ishmaelites bound for Egypt. They slaughter a goat and cover Joseph's coat in its blood to prove to Jacob that he is dead. This sad news is delivered via a silly country-western song, "One More Angel." The brothers tell Jacob that Joseph bravely fought a goat and died in the process, which Jacob buys.

The scene shifts to Egypt, where Potiphar, Joseph's master, tells the audience of his great wealth and his boy-crazy wife ("Potiphar"). Potiphar finds that Joseph makes for an excellent slave, and promotes him to the top ranks. Mrs. Potiphar attempts to seduce him and, despite his resistance, Potiphar catches them together and throws Joseph in jail.

The show now settles down from its energetic pace for a moment, as Joseph sits in jail ("Close Every Door"). Joseph declares that it does not matter what becomes of him, he is only one man. What matters is that he is of Israel, he has brothers and sisters, and someday they will have a land of their own. The Narrator enters the scene and tells us that Joseph, although feeling down, will end up just fine ("Go Go Go Joseph"). Joseph gains two new roommates, whose dreams he interprets: a butler whose dream signifies that he will soon be free, and a baker whose future is much less promising. The chorus joins the Narrator in a celebration of Joseph's renewed optimism and assuredly bright future.

The second act opens similarly to the first, with the Narrator catching us up on the latest events ("Pharaoh's Story"). She introduces the Pharaoh, whose sleep has been disturbed lately by troubling dreams. She hints broadly that a man who knows how to interpret dreams might fare well. In "Poor, Poor Pharaoh," Joseph's old friend, the now-freed butler, points out that he knows a man in jail who might be able to help Pharaoh. Joseph is summoned before Pharaoh.

In an Elvis-style rock number ("Song of the King"), a hip-wiggling Pharaoh tells Joseph of his dreams: he saw seven fat cows, then seven thin, among other things. Joseph declares that what Pharaoh has dreamed is a premonition about the weather and the future of Egypt: there will be seven years of prodigious crops, then seven years of famine ("Pharaoh's Dream Explained"). Joseph, gaining confidence, points out that what Pharaoh needs is someone to organize the rationing, so that Egypt can survive the coming lean years. Pharaoh appoints Joseph to the task, and the fourteen years go by smoothly ("Stone the Crows"). Joseph becomes a favorite of the Pharaoh and is beloved by Egyptian maidens. But the Narrator steps in to remind us that we might wonder what became of Joseph's brothers back home.

"Those Canaan Days" is the answer: in this parody of a French chanson, we learn that the brothers, unprepared (like the rest of Canaan) for the famine, are starving and miserable. They even begin to miss Joseph and his dreams. They decide to go to Egypt, where there is food ("The Brothers Come to Egypt") and find themselves begging before Pharaoh's right-hand man ("Grovel, Grovel"). Joseph recognizes his brothers, but they have no idea that this is their long-lost brother in this fine Egyptian setting. He decides to test them, to see if they have changed from the cruel, selfish men they used to be. He plants a gold cup in the sack of Benjamin, his youngest brother, and then rounds on the group demanding they confess ("Who's the Thief?"). When the cup is found in Benjamin's sack, the brothers immediately rush to his defense in (for no reason other than good fun) a calypso number ("Benjamin Calypso").

Convinced of their sincerity, Joseph reveals who he is, and the twelve brothers joyously reunite ("Joseph All the Time"). They send for Jacob, who arrives in style for a happy reunion ("Jacob in Egypt"). The relentless pace pauses again for the closing number, in which Joseph reflects that any dream is better than none ("Any Dream Will Do"). The point, it seems, is not so much in the fulfillment of the dream but in simply having a dream—in Joseph's case, the dream of his beloved coat, now returned to him in all its glory.

Appendix D: Cats *Plot Summary and Table of Recurring Musical Material*

Number	Musical Material Used
Act 1	
1. Overture The cats take hiding places in their junk heap.	• Jellicle theme (and Jellicle theme fragments)
2. "Jellicle Songs for Jellicle Cats" The company tells the audience about the nature of being a Jellicle cat.	
3. "The Naming of Cats" The cats describe the importance of a cat's three names.	• Jellicle theme (and Jellicle theme fragments)
4. "Invitation to the Jellicle Ball" Munkustrap, a Jellicle leader, explains that tonight, at the Jellicle Ball, one cat will be chosen to be reborn.	• Jellicle theme
5. "The Old Gumbie Cat" Munkustrap introduces Jennyanydots, who oversees the activities of a group of mice and insects; the cast joins her in acting this out.	• transitional fanfare
6. "The Rum Tum Tugger" The swaggering Rum Tum Tugger introduces himself and his demanding habits to the audience. Female cats swoon in appreciation.	
7. "Grizabella the Glamour Cat" Grizabella's entrance interrupts the Rum Tum Tugger's revelry; her arrival is met with hostility. Demeter and Bombalurina recount how this once-glamorous cat has fallen on hard times.	• first occurrence of Grizabella's ground bass
8. "Bustopher Jones" We meet Bustopher Jones, dapper cat about town.	• melody of hymn section of "Jellicle Songs for Jellicle Cats"
9. "Mungojerrie and Rumpelteazer" A sudden loud crash causes much	• Macavity's motif

confusion; it is Macavity, the evil, dangerous cat, lurking about. The cast scatters, and two petty thieves take advantage of the quiet to celebrate their exploits.

10. "Old Deuteronomy"
The cast reassembles and their attention is turned to the arrival of their honored leader. After he is praised and welcomed, Munkustrap reminds us that the big night is close at hand.

11. "The Pekes and the Pollicles"
Munkustrap recounts the legend of a fight between two groups of dogs, broken up by the famous Rumpuscat. A few words from Old Deuteronomy turns the mood somber, then Macavity's crash reappears.
   - transitional fanfare
   - Macavity's motif

12. "The Jellicle Ball"
The cats sing, dance, and revel at the Ball.
   - Jellicle theme and Jellicle theme fragments
   - "Old Deuteronomy"
   - "Jellicle Songs for Jellicle Cats"

13. "Grizabella, the Glamour Cat" reprise
Grizabella, having watched from a distance, staggers into view once more, and all scatter. Thinking she is alone, although Old Deuteronomy keeps a protective eye on her, Grizabella ponders her outsider state with a preview of "Memory."
   - Grizabella's ground bass
   - "Jellicle songs for Jellicle Cats"
   - "Memory"
   - Jellicle theme

Act 2

14. "The Moments of Happiness"
The second act opens with a philosophical musing from Old Deuteronomy and another quick visit from "Memory," sung this time by a kitten, Sillabub.
   - Jellicle theme
   - "Old Deuteronomy"
   - "Memory"

15. "Gus the Theatre Cat" and "Growltiger's Last Stand"
Next we meet Gus, who reminisces about his days as a theater actor. He recalls his role as the pirate cat Growltiger, and we see an extended scene from that production in flashback (this is "Growltiger's Last

Stand"). Back in the present, a melancholy Gus exits.

16. "Skimbleshanks, the Railway Cat"
We meet Skimble, who works on trains. The cats help him act out his tasks and build a pretend train.

17. "Macavity" and "Macavity's Fight"
Skimble's revelries are interrupted by Macavity's crash, and by the appearance of Macavity himself, who kidnaps Old Deuteronomy. Two of the sexy female cats, Demeter and Bombalurina, step forward to tell us of the notorious criminal's evil ways. Macavity, disguised as Old Deuteronomy, reappears; a fight ensues, but not even the powerful Munkustrap can hurt Macavity, who escapes by seeming to electrocute himself.

- Macavity's motif
- "Old Deuteronomy"
- "Jellicle Songs for Jellicle Cats"
- Jellicle theme and theme fragments

18. "The Magical Mr. Mistoffelees"
The Rum Tum Tugger suggests that the group ask Mr. Mistoffelees to help find their leader, and we are introduced to this cat who can perform magical feats of all sorts. For his big finale, Mr. Mistoffelees does indeed make Old Deuteronomy reappear, and all are delighted.

- contains fanfare usually used for transition

19. "Memory"
Munkustrap again reminds us that a cat has yet to be chosen for rebirth, just as Grizabella enters. She describes her longing for a new day and her desire to be welcomed, despite her current sorry state.

- Jellicle theme
- Grizabella's ground bass

20. "Journey to the Heaviside Layer"
One by one, the cats embrace and accept Grizabella, and Old Deuteronomy leads her to the Heaviside Layer, where she will be reborn.

- transitional fanfare
- "Jellicle Songs for Jellicle Cats," hymn section

21. "The Ad-dressing of Cats"
Old Deuteronomy and company, having sent Grizabella on her way, now turn to us and remind us of the lessons we have learned about cat nature.

Appendix E: Sources of Lyrics in Cats

Most of the poems taken from T. S. Eliot's *Old Possum's Book of Practical Cats* underwent minor changes for the stage. These included things like the occasional cutting of a stanza, the adjusting of pronouns to fit the speakers, and a bit of rearranging of a couplet here and there, but in general the lyrics are very close to Eliot's original.

"Jellicle Songs for Jellicle Cats"
- Sections of Eliot's unpublished poem "Pollicle Dogs and Jellicle Cats" with additional text by Trevor Nunn

"The Naming of Cats"
- Eliot's *Old Possum's Book of Practical Cats*

"The Invitation to the Jellicle Ball"
- a quatrain from "The Song of the Jellicles" from *Old Possum*, then a verse by Nunn

"The Old Gumbie Cat"
- Eliot's *Old Possum*

"The Rum Tum Tugger"
- Eliot's *Old Possum*

"Grizabella the Glamour Cat"
- Introduction is taken from Eliot's poem "Rhapsody on a Windy Night" and combines a verse about a fallen woman with a reference to a cat; then the unpublished Eliot fragment "Grizabella the Glamour Cat"

"Bustopher Jones"
- Eliot's *Old Possum*

"Mungojerrie and Rumpelteazer"
- Eliot's *Old Possum*

"Old Deuteronomy"
- Eliot's *Old Possum*

"The Pekes and the Pollicles"
- Eliot's *Old Possum*, plus an insertion from Eliot's poem "The Marching Song of the Pollicle Dogs"

"The Jellicle Ball"
- Eliot's "The Song of the Jellicles" from *Old Possum*

"The Moments of Happiness"
- From Eliot's poem "The Dry Salvages" from *Four Quartets*

"Gus the Theatre Cat"
- Eliot's *Old Possum*, plus a new tag line for segue purposes

"Growltiger's Last Stand"
- Eliot's *Old Possum*, and the insertion of a verse in Italian

"Skimbleshanks the Railway Cat"
- Eliot's *Old Possum*

"Macavity"
- Eliot's *Old Possum*

"The Magical Mr. Mistoffelees"
- Eliot's *Old Possum*

"Memory"
- Bits of Eliot's "Rhapsody on a Windy Night," mixed with lyrics by Nunn

"Journey to the Heaviside Layer"
- From an Eliot letter; Nunn added a few words

"The Ad-dressing of Cats"
- Eliot's *Old Possum*

Appendix F: Les Misérables *Plot Summary and List of Numbers*

1. "Prologue": It is 1815, in Digne. The lights come up on a prison chain gang, sweating in the sun and bemoaning their fate as they break invisible rocks with invisible tools. Inspector Javert arrives and paroles prisoner number 24601, Jean Valjean, who has served five years for stealing a loaf of bread to feed his starving family, and another fourteen for an attempted escape. Javert warns Valjean not to forget him. Valjean rejoins the world, but finds that his parole papers prevent him from earning a decent living or receiving fair treatment. Valjean moves through a series of encounters. He is shortchanged for his work by a farmer and rejected by an innkeeper, and grows increasingly bitter. A kindly bishop offers him food and shelter, and an incredulous Valjean repays this kindness by stealing the man's silver and fleeing into the night. The police catch him and return him to the bishop who, to Valjean's amazement, declares that he had given the poor man the silver and offers more. The bishop explains to Valjean that he must use the silver to become an honest man, that his soul is now God's. Valjean, ashamed of his actions and amazed by the bishop's kindness and his own dawning sense of spirituality, declares his old life over and, shredding his parole papers in his final illegal act, begins a new life.
2. "At the End of the Day": Eight years later, in Montreuil-sur-Mer, a group of poor factory workers express hopelessness and bitterness. Fantine, one of the workers, is teased by the other women for having an illegitimate daughter, who now lives with an innkeeper to whom Fantine sends her meager wages. A tussle breaks out; the owner of the factory, who is also the mayor of the town, arrives. It is Jean Valjean, living an upstanding life under another name.
3. "I Dreamed a Dream": The stage clears and Fantine, having been fired by the factory foreman for her supposed troublemaking, recalls her sweet affair with her daughter's father and gives in to hopelessness.
4. "Lovely Ladies": The scene shifts to the docks, where whores and sailors bawdily interact. Fantine sells first her necklace, then her hair, and eventually her body to pay for her daughter, Cosette. The whores welcome a weary Fantine into their ranks. She resists an abusive customer, drawing the attention of the local police inspector, who happens to be Javert (a subsection sometimes referred to as "Fantine's Arrest"). Valjean, known to Javert only as the respectable mayor, intercedes on Fantine's behalf and sends her to the hospital.
5. "The Runaway Cart": Suddenly, an out-of-control cart laden with goods rolls by, pinning a man beneath it. When onlookers fear to get near, Valjean lifts it off the grateful man. Javert, amazed by Valjean's show of strength, is reminded of prisoner 24601 from years ago—but this cannot be him, for the man has been recaptured and comes to trial today.
6. "Who Am I?": Alone on a bare stage, Valjean reflects on this development. Can he

allow another man to go to jail for him? If he admits who he is, how will he care for Fantine and the people in his town? Valjean concludes that, since his soul belongs to God now, he can face the truth. He reveals to Javert and the startled crowd that he is prisoner 24601. He then informs Javert he will be at the hospital, and flees.

7. "Fantine's Death/The Confrontation": Fantine, dying, rests in a hospital bed, speaking to an absent Cosette. Valjean arrives and pledges that he will raise Cosette as his own, and Fantine dies at peace. When Javert catches up to Valjean, the two men argue heatedly. Valjean begs for three days to settle Cosette's affairs, but when Javert refuses to budge, Valjean knocks him over and flees.

8. "Castle on a Cloud": Young Cosette, a frail, dirty, adorable little girl, sweeps up the closed inn in Montfermeil where she lives with Thénardier, Mme. Thénardier, and their spoiled little daughter Eponine. Alone at first, Cosette imagines a happy world of children, peace, and a mother figure. Mme. Thénardier, big, brash, and obnoxious, yells at Cosette and sends her out into the woods to fetch water.

9. "Master of the House": The inn opens for business, and Thénardier shares with us his methods of fleecing his guests, serving them substandard food, and enjoying his nefarious ways. The scene rotates to the woods outside, where Valjean encounters Cosette and gently befriends her.

10. "The Bargain/Waltz of Treachery": Valjean explains to the Thénardiers that he must keep his promise to Fantine, and will compensate them. The Thénardiers, with mock sorrow, immediately begin jacking up the price, and Valjean, in disgust, eventually pays them off and leaves with an optimistic Cosette.

11. "Look Down" and "The Robbery": Nine years later, in 1832, in Paris, we meet the inhabitants of the slums, who bitterly beg for money and snap at one another. Among those living in this urban squalor are Gavroche, a streetwise urchin, and the Thénardiers, who have fallen on hard times. Their daughter, Eponine, now a young woman, has become a fellow con artist with her family, but has also befriended a young student, Marius. He and other students, led by Enjorlas, speak of a government which does nothing for them or for the poor. Valjean enters with his daughter, Cosette, now grown, and they give charity to the poor. Cosette and Marius spot one another, and it is love at first sight. But Thénardier recognizes Valjean and confusion ensues, during which Valjean flees with Cosette while Javert—now an inspector here in Paris—arrives. Thénardier tips off Javert that an ex-con is about (Thénardier has seen the numbers tattooed on Valjean's chest) and Javert wonders if this could possibly be the man for whom he has hunted all these years.

12. "Stars": The crowd clears and Javert, standing on a bridge over the river at night, reflects on his life's mission. His is the righteous path, he declares, and he will bring this fallen man to justice, so that God and the law may punish him.

13. "Eponine's Errand": Back on the ramshackle poor side of town, Eponine realizes that the girl Cosette, whom she saw briefly in the street, must be the child who lived with her family. Marius enters and, oblivious to Eponine's feelings of love for him, asks the streetwise girl to track down the mysterious young woman he saw that day.

14 and 15. "Red and Black" and "Do You Hear the People Sing?": At a café, the students gather to ponder ways to rally the people to their cause, so that they might mount a large demonstration calling for freedoms and rights ("Red and Black"). When Gavroche arrives with the news that their only governmental supporter, General La-

marque, has died, Enjorlas finds the occasion he seeks: this tragedy will incite the people to action. He stirs the students and, eventually, the entire chorus into a revolutionary frenzy ("Do You Hear the People Sing?").

16. "In My Life": Onstage appears a large iron gate set into an ivy-covered wall; it is the garden of Valjean's house, where Cosette sits musing on her unknown true love.

17. "A Heart Full of Love": Eponine leads Marius to the gate and watches sadly as the two introduce themselves and tentatively acknowledge their feelings of love.

18. "The Attack on the Rue Plumet": Thénardier and his cronies enter, having also tracked down Valjean's house and intending to rob him as payback for taking Cosette. Eponine, despite her jealousy, knows that Cosette and her father are innocent, and screams in warning. Chaos erupts and everyone flees; Valjean assumes the noise was Javert, come to find him at last. He tells Cosette they must move away.

19. "One Day More": All the plotlines come together in the act 1 finale. Valjean resolves to move on, Cosette and Marius express their love, and Eponine regrets that Marius has never noticed her. Enjorlas rallies the students, and eventually Marius joins them. The Thénardiers know trouble is coming, and hope they can loot some valuables as a result. Javert, knowing the students are about to riot, resolves to quash their activities. Tomorrow, the group sings, we will see what God has planned for us.

20. "At the Barricade": Act 2 opens with Enjorlas assembling his ragged but committed forces in the street, where they will make their stand. Javert, disguised as a rebel, joins their ranks, as does Eponine, dressed like a boy. Marius sends her to Cosette's house with a letter for his beloved. Eponine delivers it grudgingly to a protective Valjean instead; he reads it and discovers not only that Cosette has a new love, but that the young man may die in the rebellion tomorrow.

21. "On My Own": Eponine wanders the darkened streets and longs for Marius's love.

22. "Building the Barricade/Javert's Arrival": In a brief instrumental interlude, we watch as the doorways, ladders, crates, and beams that represented the streets of the poor slowly flip and merge, and become the barricade. The students pledge to defend it, and Javert arrives to feed them false information about the "enemy" plan.

23. "Little People": Gavroche, who knows everyone around the area, blows Javert's cover and delights in his streetwise abilities. The students tie Javert up.

24. "A Little Fall of Rain": Shots from the enemy (from upstage, invisible behind the barricade) follow someone climbing over the barricade toward the students; it is Eponine, come to rejoin Marius, who discovers that she was hit by the soldiers' fire. They share their fondness for each other as Eponine quietly dies in Marius's arms. The students vow to fight in her honor.

25. "Night of Anguish/First Attack": Another person arrives over the barricade: it is Valjean, come to volunteer and to meet the mysterious young man with whom his daughter has fallen in love. The students welcome him warily, having already been betrayed by the volunteer Javert. But when the soldiers attack, Valjean proves his worth by shooting a sniper. As thanks, Valjean asks to kill the prisoner Javert, but when they cannot be heard, he frees the inspector instead. He tells Javert that he understands fulfilling one's duty and bears no grudge; if he survives, Javert can find him at home. Javert stumbles away in confusion.

26. "Drink With Me": The students relax for the night, and Marius longs for Cosette, thereby revealing his identity to Valjean.

27. "Bring Him Home": As the others sleep, Valjean prays to God for Marius's protection.

28. "Second Attack": In the morning, the soldiers attack again, and when the students run short on ammunition, Gavroche scrambles over the barricade to retrieve bullets from the dead (and we follow him over, with help from the revolve, which spins the barricade completely around to the enemy side). Mercilessly, the unseen enemy shoots Gavroche three times, finally killing him just as he tosses a bag of bullets up to his friends.

29. "Final Battle": The final battle commences and, one by one, each student is killed. Eventually, quiet settles, and during an orchestral interlude, the barricade spins slowly around, showing us who fell on both sides. Valjean stirs and discovers that Marius is barely alive; he hauls the young man's body through the floor into the sewers. Javert arrives in search of Valjean and soon realizes the man must have escaped to the tunnels below the streets.

30. "Dog Eat Dog": We join them underground, and find also Thénardier, looting gold teeth and watches from the dead and sharing his philosophy that no one will punish him for this; God is dead. Valjean trudges by with Marius in tow, encountering Javert, who, surprisingly, lets him go so that he might help Marius, but promising to find him once again.

31. "Javert's Suicide": But Javert's hunt is over, his faith in his mission rocked by Valjean's freeing of him. He returns to the bridge over the river, under the stars which used to reassure him. Unable to live knowing that he owes Valjean his life, and unable to reconcile Valjean's actions with his own sense of justice, he leaps into the river.

32. "Turning": The next morning, the women friends of the students reflect on their fruitless efforts.

33. "Empty Chairs at Empty Tables": Time passes, and Marius is nearly recovered physically, but tormented emotionally by the loss of his friends and the burden of being the only one who survived. Cosette cheers him and they reflect on their love for each other.

34. "Valjean's Confession": With Marius and Cosette's wedding coming, Valjean, looking older and weaker now, confesses to Marius that he is an ex-con and a parole jumper, and that he must go away to keep shame from Cosette.

35. "Wedding Chorale/Beggars at the Feast": Marius and Cosette are wed in a grand affair, but the reception is marred by the arrival of the Thénardiers, failing completely to fit in with their gaudy mock-formal fashions. They have come to tell Marius several secrets, in exchange for money; they know that Cosette's "father" is an ex-con, which is not news to Marius, but they also know that he is the man who saved Marius the night the barricade fell, which is surprising and wonderful news. Marius rushes off with Cosette to see Valjean. The Thénardiers linger at the party, enjoying their brush with the aristocracy and stealing as much silver as possible.

36. "Epilogue": Valjean, alone and quite frail, prays for Marius and Cosette, and for his own death. Fantine, peacefully appearing from beyond, begins to welcome Valjean, but Cosette and Marius rush in to beg Valjean to stay with them, so that they may honor and love him as he deserves. Valjean gives Cosette a letter, telling her his life story, then he joins Fantine and Eponine in the bright white light of heaven. As the chorus reprises "Do You Hear the People Sing?" Cosette reads her father's letter and weeps; eventually, the entire company, living and dead, joins in the rousing chorus.

Appendix G: List of Recurring Musical Material *in* Les Misérables

- The **dotted chords** which open the show appear in several other places, including the top of act 2, during the building of the barricade, and softly just after Eponine's death. They also link "Do You Hear the People Sing?" with "In My Life."
- The melodies and vamp of **"Look Down"** are shared by the prisoners' song and the Valjean/Javert exchange during the "Prologue," and in "Confrontation." The main melody is sung briefly several other times, and the orchestra uses the "Look Down" material as underscoring numerous times.
- The melody of **"Fantine's Death,"** which is the same as "On My Own," also appears as Valjean is dying and Eponine and Fantine arrive, and in the orchestra in several places. Valjean also uses a small portion of the melody as he leaves prison and wonders "what this new world will do for me," and again as he vows to help Fantine ("I will see it done"). Enjorlas sings his own variation of this line several times.
- Marius's act 2 solo **"Empty Chairs at Empty Tables"** provides the bishop with his solo sections in the "Prologue."
- The **recitative-style "encounter music"** appears during a number of encounters: Valjean and the farmer, then Valjean and the innkeeper, during the "Prologue"; Fantine's three encounters during "Lovely Ladies," plus the pimp's solo, in tempo; Fantine and her violent customer; Valjean and the victim of the runaway cart; Javert and Valjean immediately after the runaway cart scene; Madame Thénardier and Cosette as the woman taunts and bosses the child; Valjean and Cosette between "The Attack on the Rue Plumet" and "One Day More"; and Valjean and Javert as Valjean frees the inspector from his student captors.
- **Valjean uses a distinct recitative-style vocal line** (which begins with "Now every door is closed to me") to express feelings and situations several times: he laments his restricted freedom in the "Prologue," he confronts Javert on Fantine's behalf, then again on the wrongly accused prisoner's behalf, and he confronts the Thénardiers with it when he arrives at the inn with Cosette.
- The **"accusation music,"** first heard when Valjean is accused of stealing from the bishop ("Tell His Reverence your story"), occurs also during these moments of accusation: Javert breaks up the scuffle between Fantine and her violent customer, Javert questions Valjean about the history and whereabouts of prisoner 24601 after the runaway cart scene, Javert's intervention during the Thénardiers' robbery during "Look Down," Gavroche's tag on "Stars," and the hostile exchange between Javert and the students after they have captured him.
- The **introduction section of "Javert's Suicide,"** with its pulsing chords in the orchestra and then its frantic vocal line, appears a number of times before it finally lands in Javert's death scene. It introduces Valjean's soliloquy during the prologue, and in fact Valjean foreshadows much of the music of Javert's number. The music appears again

as the segue between the courtroom and the hospital. It intersects the accusation music as Javert disrupts the beggars in "Javert's Intervention," and Thénardier uses the same music at the top of "The Attack on the Rue Plumet." Also, Javert arrives at the barricade to a variation of this music.

- The **arpeggiated figure** which introduces "At the End of the Day" runs throughout "Who Am I?" and "One Day More" as well as "Valjean's Confession." It also signals the moment in which Marius and Cosette first see each other.
- **Eponine has a pair of melodic shapes** with which she voices her feelings and banters with Marius, initially heard at her first entrance.
- Gavroche reprises his number, **"Little People,"** as he scavenges for bullets and is shot.
- The **introductory section to "Fantine's Death"** ("Cosette, it's turned so cold") appears several times, including "Epilogue."
- The **women's chorus in stacked thirds,** as in "Turning," also appears as counterpoint in "Lovely Ladies."
- **"Red and Black"** emerges in small pieces during a number of scenes at the barricade, including battles and students' vows to hold the barricade.
- A **brass fanfare** serves as a warning of impending attack several times.
- **"Drink With Me"** is reprised as the women leave the barricade area.
- **"Bring Him Home"** receives orchestral treatment as the barricade displays its dead, and Valjean reprises a small portion of the song as he awaits his own death in "Epilogue."
- Cosette revisits **"Castle on a Cloud"** several times, including her wordless contrapuntal duet with Valjean. The orchestra also uses it as a segue between "Drink with Me" and "Second Attack."
- **"Master of the House"** becomes reworked as "Beggars at the Feast."
- **"Do You Hear the People Sing?"** becomes orchestral fodder for the busy music of all three attack scenes. Javert also uses it several times to deliver false news of the enemy to the students, and it is reprised in the final moments of the show.
- **"I Dreamed a Dream"** receives a contrapuntal line when Valjean and Javert end their "Confrontation," and again when Valjean explains to the Thénardiers that he must raise Cosette. Marius sings the melody of the second line of the verse when he spies Cosette for the first time, to the accompaniment of the cascading arpeggiated figure. Several other brief references appear.
- The Thénardiers' **"Waltz of Treachery"** reappears as they beg for food from Valjean during "The Robbery," and again when they confront Marius at his wedding.
- **Thénardier uses a jagged, aggressive vocal line to rob Valjean,** first in the square during "The Robbery" ("Everyone here?/You know your place") and again during "The Attack on the Rue Plumet."
- **"Stars"** reappears in the orchestra as the closing of "Javert's Suicide."
- There are several returns to Valjean's **introduction section of "Who Am I?"** ("He thinks that man is me,/he knew him at a glance"), including when Valjean first appears at the barricade.
- Portions of the melody of **"At the End of the Day"** recur in several places during "Lovely Ladies" and "The Runaway Cart," and the orchestra occasionally uses its material for underscoring.
- Marius and Cosette reprise their love duet **"A Heart Full of Love"** during Marius's recovery from his injuries.
- A **recitative shape, mostly sung on one note,** allows Cosette to express her feelings

before "In My Life," and Marius and Valjean use this same shape on several occasions, including Valjean's reading of Marius's letter to Cosette, and as Marius and Valjean discuss gratitude and departure in "Valjean's Confession."

- **"A Little Fall of Rain"** is first heard as Marius asks Eponine to help him find Cosette's house, and the orchestra reprises it as Eponine's body is carried offstage.
- **"One Day More"** brings together a number of musical ideas from elsewhere; see chapter 4 for a complete description.

Appendix H: The Phantom of the Opera
Plot Summary and List of Numbers

In 1905, on the dark dustcloth-covered stage of the Paris Opéra, an auction is being held ("Prologue"). Artifacts from earlier glory days are being sold, some of them to an aged Raoul, Vicomte de Chagny. They come from productions by Meyerbeer and the fictional Chalumeau, among others. Raoul buys a mechanical monkey that plays the cymbals and ponders how much it looks the way "she" described it. Soon the bidding turns to the chandelier, lying now in a dusty heap beneath a cloth, but which figured (so the auctioneer tells us) in the still-mysterious business of the Phantom of the Opera. As he opens the bidding, the chandelier illuminates and rises, slowly, until it is hanging in all its glory above the first few rows of the house ("Overture").

The Phantom, or (as he likes to call himself) the Opera Ghost, is a mysterious presence well known to those who work in the Opéra already. Unaware of him, however, are the Opéra's new managers, Firmin and André, who are just taking over their positions from a fearful, fleeing former manager as the musical begins. The first thing we see, after Raoul has reminisced us back in time to 1861, is a rehearsal in mid-cadenza; Carlotta, the reigning and obnoxious Italian diva, is singing from *Hannibal* by Chalumeau. The chorus girls, Christine Daaé and Meg Giry among them, practice their singing and dancing with Carlotta, and while Meg (the managers agree) is quite good, Christine is distracted and disruptive. The new managers ask La Carlotta to sing an aria from the opera ("Think of Me"), but after her first few lines, a backdrop falls, for no apparent reason, loudly across the stage. The ballet girls twitter that it is the Ghost. Madame Giry, who is Meg's mother and also the formidable ballet mistress, helps Meg push Christine into singing the aria in place of Carlotta, who has stormed off in a huff. Christine admits she does not know who has been teaching her, but she steps timidly forward to sing. In the middle of the number, the stage is transformed into a performance, and Christine, more confident now, is a roaring success. Among her admirers is Raoul, a childhood friend and now a wealthy opera patron, cheering in a box seat.

After her applause has died down and she hears her strange teacher's voice whispering "bravissima," she talks with her friend Meg about the Angel of Music who has been coaching her ("Angel of Music"). Her late father, a violinist, used to tell her of such an Angel, who would come to her and inspire her; she supposes this new teacher is this Angel of Music, some sort of embodiment of her father or messenger from him. Christine and Raoul are reunited and happily recall their childhood times, especially the stories her father told them of this Angel, but she does not have a chance to explain to Raoul that she thinks the Angel is real. He leaves, and the Phantom's voice booms through her dressing room, mesmerizing her, luring her into his world. She follows the flattering, seductive voice willingly, first through her mirror and then down many levels to his boat on the underground lake ("The Phantom of the Opera"). We see him now, dashing in his tuxedo and half mask. He rows their gondola into his lair, where hundreds of candles emerge through the mist. His home is a strange one, and features the mechanical monkey from "Prologue" as well as a pipe organ. He teaches her, gently, to trust him, to touch him, to enjoy his dark world ("The Music of the Night"). Later, still dazed, she awakes and allows curiosity to take over, ripping the mask from his face. She sees him, we do not. He is furious at first, then defeated and shy, and she returns his mask ("I Remember/ Stranger than You Dreamt It").

A brief scene features Buquet, an old stagehand who, like Madame Giry, is well versed in the ways of the Ghost; he teases the young opera dancers with his tales ("Magical Lasso"). We join the opera managers in their office, who have received mysterious letters from "O.G.," the Opera Ghost, demanding his salary and praising Christine's debut. An ensemble emerges, as characters enter with letters of their own ("Notes"). Raoul's note warns him to stay away from Christine, Carlotta's forbids her from singing the lead in the next production because the Phantom means for Christine to have it, and Madame Giry—who has received letters before and has full faith in the Ghost—finds that her letter is a threat to carry out his demands lest trouble should ensue. The managers wish Carlotta to play the lead and woo her back with flattery, while the others reflect on the strange situation ("Prima Donna"). The performance in question, an opera buffa called *Il muto,* begins with Carlotta singing the lead and Christine as the mute pageboy ("Poor Fool, He Makes Me Laugh"). The Phantom, true to his threats, gleefully causes Carlotta to croak like a toad as she tries to sing. This minor problem escalates into a serious one when the chandelier begins swinging and blinking, until finally total chaos erupts when the body of Buquet falls from the rafters onto the stage. Christine and Raoul flee to the roof ("Why Have You Brought Me Here/Raoul, I've Been There"), where after debating the true nature of Christine's strange experience they find a moment of respite and sing of the peaceful, sunny life they hope to have together ("All I Ask of You"). Having overheard this romantic encounter from his hiding place among the roof's gilded statues, the Phantom, feeling betrayed, promises Christine will be sorry for being disloyal to him. We see her taking bows, now in Carlotta's costume, as the Phantom, from high above, causes the huge chandelier to fall and land onstage at her feet.

Act 2 opens six months later, in the great lobby of the Opéra, where a strange but celebratory masquerade ball finds everyone in good spirits ("Masquerade"). The Phantom has not been heard from, the season is going well, and Christine and Raoul are secretly engaged. The party is interrupted by the Phantom, dressed menacingly as Red Death, descending the curving staircase ("Why So Silent"). He presents his new composition, an opera called *Don Juan Triumphant,* that he expects the company to mount. He rips Christine's engagement ring from the chain around her neck, telling her she is still his. Raoul, finally willing to believe this strange man has threatening powers, demands that Madame Giry tell him what she knows. She tells him that the Phantom, deformed since birth, had once traveled in a freak show, but was a scholar, architect, musician, and inventor. He escaped and apparently took up residence in the Opéra some years ago.

Another mostly humorous ensemble of letters from the Opera Ghost follows ("Notes"); in this one, he makes demands about training or replacing the performers and musicians, noting especially that Carlotta must be taught to act and that Piangi, the leading tenor, must lose weight. Everyone's outrage builds until Raoul and the managers hatch a plan: they will perform his opera and catch the Ghost when he comes up to see it, sitting as he always does in box five. Christine resists the plan, believing he is too clever and dangerous, but eventually concedes ("Twisted Every Way").

Rehearsals are not going well; Piangi cannot sing the Phantom's strange dissonant music and nerves are frayed. The piano then begins to play the score by itself and the company sings, dazedly, along with it. Christine moves off and finds her way to her father's grave, a large mausoleum in a dark mossy area. She wishes her father were still with her, to return her to her previously safe, warm life ("Wishing You Were Somehow Here Again"). The Phantom enters ("Wandering Child") and she is confused, calling him angel, father, friend, Phantom. Raoul rushes in, and all three battle for mental control of the situation as each man tries to lure Christine away from the other ("Bravo, Monsieur"). She eventually runs to Raoul, while the Phantom hurls fireballs at them. They flee and the Phantom declares war on them both.

Before the opening of *Don Juan Triumphant*, Raoul checks that the armed guards are in place all over the theater. The performance begins. Don Juan, played by Piangi, is hatching a plan with his servant to woo Aminta, a plan that involves switching outfits with one another. They exit and Christine, as Aminta, enters; when Don Juan returns, the part is being played not by Piangi, but by the Phantom. The two sing of their coming union ("The Point of No Return"), and it becomes clear to Christine that this is the Phantom. As he drops his pretense and asks Christine to be his, she puts on the ring he offers, then she rips the mask from his face for all to see. Chaos erupts, the body of Piangi is seen upstage, and the Phantom disappears with Christine. They emerge in his underground home, where she tells him that the problem lies not in his face, but his soul. The offstage crowd, meanwhile, is attempting to find them ("Down Once More/Track Down This Murderer"). Raoul finds his way down to them, and the Phantom captures him in a magic lasso suspended from nothing. All three battle for control of the situation. Eventually Christine's voice wins out, and she goes slowly to the Phantom. She kisses him, full and lingeringly, on the mouth. His world is shattered.

He frees Raoul and sends him away with Christine, as the mob of angry opera staff and audience grows closer to his lair. Christine returns and gives the ring back to the Phantom, then rushes away again. The Phantom, alone and defeated, sits in his chair, singing that his music is over, then vanishes. Meg, leading the arriving crowd, finds only his mask left.

Appendix I: List of Recurring Musical Material in The Phantom of the Opera

"Masquerade"

- on music box in prologue
- on music box in Phantom's lair, as Christine awakens after "The Phantom of the Opera"
- a short reference in orchestra as Christine and Raoul flee to roof after *Il muto*
- orchestral segue out of "All I Ask of You," then sung by Christine (*"I must go, they'll wonder where I am"*)
- the complete song "Masquerade," at the top of act 2
- on music box, in the Phantom's final moments

The Phantom's chromatic scale

- throughout overture
- throughout "The Phantom of the Opera"
- interrupted ending of "Prima Donna" (runs up and down without rests)
- as Buquet's body is revealed during *Il muto*
- as chandelier shakes and falls, end of act 1
- segue from entr'acte to act 2
- interrupted ending of "Masquerade"
- segue between "Twisted Every Way" and *Don Juan Triumphant* rehearsal, Raoul borrows "Prima Donna" melody with same interrupted ending (no rests)
- as Christine reveals Phantom's face to all

Vocal melody of "The Phantom of the Opera"

- throughout overture
- the song "The Phantom of the Opera"
- as Raoul and Christine arrive on roof after *Il muto* (*"Why have you brought us here?"*)
- in orchestra, over *Don Juan Triumphant* music, as Christine wanders out of rehearsal and into "Wishing You Were Somehow Here Again"
- in orchestra as Piangi's body is revealed after *Don Juan Triumphant,* ensuing chaos, Giry leads Raoul to Phantom's lair
- several times as chorus comes down to lair at end of act 2 (*"Track down this murderer"*)

"He's here, the Phantom of the opera" phrase

- interrupts Carlotta's "Think of Me," Meg again a moment later
- in orchestra, prepares for Phantom's voice in Christine's dressing room

- Phantom's *"I am your Angel"* variation, between "Angel of Music" and "The Phantom of the Opera"
- during "The Phantom of the Opera," from offstage chorus and orchestra
- Meg, when Phantom interrupts *Il muto*
- Phantom's *"I am your Angel"* version, in graveyard as he lures Christine back to him
- Phantom's voice from different parts of the theater before *Don Juan Triumphant* (*"I'm here, the Phantom of the opera"*)
- as chorus searches for Phantom's lair, end of act 2

Descending 5th echo "Christine, Christine" [related to story motif]

- Meg and Phantom, in Christine's dressing room
- the Phantom's *"Damn you! Curse you!"* variation as Christine unmasks him, before "Stranger than You Dreamt It"
- Meg, then Carlotta, segue info part two of "Notes I"
- Phantom echoes Raoul as he comforts Christine on roof after *Il muto*
- Raoul comforts Christine during "Notes II"
- Phantom as he drags Christine to lair final time
- Raoul pleading with Phantom in lair

"Angel of Music"

- the complete song part 1, in Christine's dressing room, Christine and Meg
- as Christine tries to explain the Phantom to Raoul, in orchestra, which becomes . . .
- the song part 2, as Phantom lures Christine through mirror
- as Christine moves to see Phantom's face when she awakes in his lair
- Entr'acte
- Phantom joins Christine in graveyard, almost a full reprise
- Christine's part in final trio in Phantom's lair, leading into kiss

"Think of Me"

- Carlotta, then Christine, perform the song
- in "Masquerade" Christine and Raoul discuss their secret engagement

"All I Ask of You"

- quick preview and complete song, on roof after *Il muto*
- up-tempo reprise immediately following
- Phantom's reprise, plus Raoul and Christine from afar, in final moments of act 1
- Entr'acte
- as Phantom drops his Don Juan façade and begs Christine to love him, during *Don Juan Triumphant*
- in final moments of act 2 as Raoul and Christine float away in distance, Phantom in his lair

"Christine, I love you" phrase [derived from ending of "Masquerade" vocal line]

- Raoul to Christine on roof, as segue between "Masquerade" and "All I Ask of You" reprise
- in its "Masquerade" form, in orchestra
- Phantom alone in lair, again as segue between "Masquerade" and "All I Ask of You"

Little Lotte music

- in Christine's dressing room, as Raoul and Christine discuss Little Lotte, in orchestra, then voices
- Phantom's introduction to "The Music of the Night"
- Christine tries to explain things to Raoul on roof after *Il muto*
- in orchestra during "Masquerade" dance
- in orchestra, then voices, as Christine ponders the plan to put on *Don Juan Triumphant,* just before "Twisted Every Way"
- Christine chants but there are no Little Lotte chords beneath, in introduction to "Wishing You Were Somehow Here Again"
- Little Lotte music becomes *Don Juan Triumphant* music, in rehearsals and performance of Phantom's opera
- Phantom's introduction to "Point of No Return," repeated by Christine during the song
- Phantom celebrates snaring Raoul in lasso in final confrontation in Phantom's lair

"The Music of the Night"

- the complete song "The Music of the Night"
- bridge of the song, as Christine explains her visit to Phantom's lair to Raoul on roof after *Il muto*
- Entr'acte
- bridge of the song, as Phantom drags Christine to lair for final time
- Phantom to Christine in lair final time, as he explains the burden of being deformed
- Phantom's last words, then in orchestra, to end the show

The five chords that close "The Music of the Night"

- end of "The Music of the Night"
- start of "All I Ask of You"
- end of the "Music of the Night/All I Ask of You" combination that closes the show

"Stranger Than You Dreamt It"

- the complete song, after Christine has unmasked the Phantom in his lair
- in "Notes II" as Phantom's voice discusses Christine's role in *Don Juan Triumphant*
- Phantom's voice commands his opera to start, just before *Don Juan Triumphant*
- Phantom welcomes Raoul to lair, moves in with magic lasso, during final confrontation in lair

"Prima Donna"

- the complete song
- Raoul persuades Christine to perform in *Don Juan Triumphant,* just after "Twisted Every Way"

"Yet in his eyes" phrase

- in orchestra, as Christine returns Phantom's mask after first unmasking him in his lair
- in orchestra, as Raoul and Christine arrive on roof after *Il muto*
- Christine explains Phantom to Raoul on roof (*"Yet in his eyes, all the sadness of the world"*)
- Raoul persuades Christine to perform in *Don Juan Triumphant* (*"You said yourself he was nothing but a man"*)
- Christine to Phantom in final lair scene, just before Raoul arrives (*"This haunted face holds no horror for me now"*)

"Notes" melodies A and B

- Phantom to Christine after she unmasks him in his lair (*"Damn you! You little prying Pandora!"*) (tune A)
- the songs "Notes I" and "Notes II"
- André and Firmin, introduction to "Masquerade" (tune B)
- Raoul's part in graveyard trio [in more recent version of trio, updated since the show opened] (*"Leave her, you have no claim on her"*) (tune A)
- Raoul to Phantom in lair, during final confrontation (*"Free her, do what you like"*)

Christine's two "No thoughts within her head" phrases

- as she enters her *Don Juan Triumphant* scene (*"No thoughts within her head but thoughts of love"*)
- Christine turns on Phantom during final confrontation (*"The tears I might have shed for your dark fate"*)

The melody of Raoul's plan to catch Phantom

- Raoul's plan to catch Phantom during performance of his opera (*"We have all been blind, and yet the answer is staring us in the face"*)
- Phantom sees Raoul approaching lair for final confrontation (*"Wait, I think my dear, we have a guest"*)

"Point of No Return"

- the complete song
- in orchestra and in Phantom' vocal line, during final trio in Phantom's lair, leading up to the kiss

themes a, b, c d, e, f, from *Don Juan Triumphant*

- Phantom plays his organ in the morning, after "The Music of the Night" (theme e, plus the Little Lotte/*Don Juan* shared music)
- in orchestra under Phantom's outburst when Christine unmasks him in lair (*"Curse you!"*) (theme b)
- a quick phrase (theme b) as Buquet prepares to tell the ballet girls ghost stories
- in orchestra, as Christine and Raoul flee the chaos after Buquet's body is revealed (themes b, c)
- in orchestra, as Raoul and Christine arrive on roof after *Il muto* and sing melody of "Phantom of the Opera" reprise (theme b)
- in orchestra, after "Masquerade," as Giry begins to tell Raoul the Phantom's story (theme b)
- in orchestra, in "Notes II" as Phantom talks of his opera (themes a, b)
- rehearsal for *Don Juan Triumphant* (themes a, b, d in voices, c in orchestra); also, phrase c gets normalized and incorporated into Christine's reprise of "Phantom of the Opera"
- orchestra tunes up to perform *Don Juan Triumphant* (themes a, b, c)
- *Don Juan Triumphant* performed, all six phrases
- Phantom yells at Christine as they descend to lair for final time (*"Why, you ask, was I bound and chained"*) (theme f), (*"Hounded out by everyone"*) (theme c)

the story motif [all are the first part of the tune except where noted]

- Raoul, then orchestra, in prologue (*"A collector's piece indeed"*)
- Buquet swears he was not at his post after falling set interrupts *Hannibal*
- in orchestra, as Christine reads Raoul's note in her dressing room
- as Christine awakens in Phantom's lair (*"I remember there was mist"*)
- Buquet tells tales to ballet girls and Giry scolds (*"Like yellow parchment is his skin"*)
- in "Notes I," Phantom's voice reads letter (*"Christine Daaé has returned to you"*); this also contains the second part of this motif (*"The role which Miss Daaé plays calls for charm and appeal"*)
- Phantom's interruption of "Masquerade" (*"Why so silent, good monsieurs?"*)
- as Giry and Raoul discuss Phantom's past after "Masquerade"; both parts of the motif, then moves to orchestra
- in "Notes II," Phantom's voice reads letter (*"Fondest greetings to you all"*)
- as Phantom hurls fireballs in graveyard (*"Bravo, Monsieur, such spirited words"*); second part in orchestra
- story motif is the same as theme a of *Don Juan Triumphant,* appears in rehearsal and performance (*"Here the sire may serve the dam"*)
- second part only, as Phantom appears on the opera's stage playing Don Juan (*"Passarino, go away, for the trap is set . . ."*)
- Giry and chorus as they search for the Phantom through end of act 2 (*"Your hand at the level of your eyes"*)
- second part only, as Christine arrives in lair for final time (*"Have you gorged yourself at last"*)
- Phantom's response to Christine (*"That fate that condemns me to wallow in blood"*)
- after the kiss, Phantom sends Raoul and Christine away (*"Take her, forget me"*), has tune of "Phantom of the Opera" as counterpoint

Notes

Introduction

1. For musicological examples of defining the subgenres of musical theater, see Edith Boroff, "Origin of Species: Conflicting Views of American Musical Theater History," *American Music* 2, no. 4 (Winter 1984): 101–11; Paul Wittke, "The American Musical Theater (with an Aside on Popular Music)," *Musical Quarterly* 68, no. 2 (April 1982): 274–86; and Larry Stempel, "The Musical Play Expands," *American Music* 10, no. 2 (Summer 1992): 136–69. For an example of a canon and its justification, see Geoffrey Block, "The Broadway Canon from *Show Boat* to *West Side Story* and the European Operatic Ideal," *Journal of Musicology* 11, no. 4 (Fall 1993): 525–44. Block's book, *Enchanted Evenings,* offers a nice start toward a methodology of evaluating musicals. Had he carried it through to musicals of recent years, the megamusical would have been addressed, probably with great success. Instead, he canonizes fourteen shows before 1970, and then devotes a chapter to Sondheim. He describes Lloyd Webber as "probably underrated, certainly underestimated and understudied" (275), yet devotes no attention to him. Geoffrey Block, *Enchanted Evenings: The Broadway Musical from* Show Boat *to Sondheim* (New York: Oxford University Press, 1997).

2. I attended a panel at the meeting of the Society for American Music in March 2000 that drove this point home: my colleague Professor Paul Laird presented a canon of one hundred musicals to be used for teaching, the first canon I had seen which included megamusicals. Virtually the only shows that came under any sort of fire for their inclusion were Lloyd Webber's. Some of my colleagues do not deny the financial success of megamusicals, nor even their influence on shows that have followed; they just resent them. I must say, though, that when I presented a paper on *Cats* at this same meeting, it was received with great warmth by these very people (and a rather large crowd of scholars in other areas)—my investigation into *Cats* as a phenomenon, and even as a show and a score, was taken as valuable. Scholars remain conflicted, apparently. Professor Laird, with William A. Everett, recently included the megamusical (even using this term) as a chapter in their *Cambridge Companion to the Musical* (Cambridge: Cambridge University Press, 2002). Despite the book devoting only nineteen pages to the megamusical (a perfectly reasonable number given the book's breadth of material), and despite the fact that *Cats* merits far less discussion than most other musicals in the chapter, a large photo from *Cats* adorns the cover; as we see in chapter 3, *Cats* sells.

3. Michael Walsh, *Andrew Lloyd Webber: His Life and Works,* updated and enlarged ed. (New York: Harry N. Abrams, 1997), 256.

1. "Why'd You Choose Such a Backward Time and Such a Strange Land?"

1. Sheridan Morley, *Spread a Little Happiness: The First Hundred Years of the British Musical* (London: Thames and Hudson, 1987), 176, 181.

2. For more on the 1940s and 1950s, see Richard Kislan, *The Musical: A Look at the American Musical Theater,* rev. ed. (New York: Applause, 1995); Kurt Gänzl, *The Musical: A Concise History* (Boston: Northeastern University Press, 1997); Denny Martin Flinn, *Musical! A Grand Tour: The Rise, Glory, and Fall of an American Institution* (New York: Schirmer, 1997); and Hans Heinsheimer, "Splendour and Misery of the American Musical," *The World of Music* 12, no. 2 (1970): 44–56. For more on defining genres of musical theater and the integrated musical, see Geoffrey Block, "Gershwin's Buzzard and Other Mythological Creatures," *Opera Quarterly* 7, no. 2 (1990): 74–82; Geoffrey Block, "The Broadway Canon from *Show Boat* to *West Side Story* and the European Operatic Ideal," *Journal of Musicology* 11, no. 4 (1993): 525–44; Larry Stempel, "The Musical Play Expands," *American Music* 10, no. 2 (1992): 136–69; Edith Boroff, "Origin of Species: Conflicting Views of American Musical Theater History," *American Music* 2, no. 4 (1984): 101–11; Paul Wittke, "The American Musical Theater (with an Aside on Popular Music)," *Musical Quarterly* 67, no. 2 (1982): 274–86; Wilfrid Mellers, "Are Musicals Musical?" *Musical Times* 132, no. 1782 (1991): 380.

3. Gerald Bordman, for example, calls *Fiddler* "the last of the great masterworks of the era," in *American Musical Theatre: A Chronicle* (Oxford: Oxford University Press, 2001), 693.

4. For more on the troubled 1960s, see especially Heinsheimer, "Splendour and Misery," as well as the general histories listed above.

5. Ibid., 53.

6. Morley, *Spread a Little Happiness,* 154.

7. Ibid., 166. For a study of what the British musical was doing while America's Golden Era was going on, see John Snelson, " 'We Said We Wouldn't Look Back': British Musical Theatre, 1935–1960," in *The Cambridge Companion to the Musical,* ed. William A. Everett and Paul R. Laird (Cambridge: Cambridge University Press, 2002). Snelson examines why almost all of the 127 new shows of these twenty-five years received only one staging and then were largely forgotten.

8. Theater scholar Barbara Lee Horn argues that *Hair* was the first "concept musical," a term which would later be coined to explain, among other shows, Sondheim's musicals of the 1970s. Like those shows, she argues, *Hair* is more about an idea than a conventional plot like a love story. This is a helpful way to look at *Hair,* although it remains more atmosphere than idea. However, Horn, in championing the influence of *Hair,* incorrectly states that Lloyd Webber and Rice decided to write a "rock show" after seeing it. Her odd source for this is an interview with Martin Gottfried, at the time the theater critic for *Women's Wear Daily,* later a Sondheim historian. There is no other proof that Lloyd Webber and Rice saw the show, although they were certainly familiar with it and worked hard to make clear that their show would not resemble it much. Barbara Lee Horn, *The Age of Hair: Evolution and Impact of Broadway's First Rock Musical* (New York: Greenwood, 1991), 66.

9. Gänzl, *The Musical,* 333.

10. Walter Kerr, " 'Hair': Not in Fear, But in Delight," *New York Times,* 19 May 1968. Among Kerr's complaints about O'Horgan's additions was his distributing of dialogue

among many actors such that the sentences became unintelligible, an especially vexing habit when it ruined good jokes.

11. Clive Barnes, "Theater: 'Hair'—It's Fresh and Frank," *New York Times,* 30 April 1968. See also Barnes's review of the show in its original off-Broadway staging and in a follow-up review a year after the Broadway opening: "The Theater: 'Hair,' a Love-Rock Musical, Inaugurates Shakespeare Festival's Anspacher Playhouse," *New York Times,* 30 October 1967; " 'Hair' Holds Up Under Second Look," *New York Times,* 5 February 1969.

12. Mark Steyn, *Broadway Babies Say Goodnight: Musicals Then and Now* (New York: Routledge, 1997), 220.

13. Clive Barnes enjoyed the music and the energetic cast, but had the same problem with the premise that he would have with *Jesus Christ Superstar.* Regarding *Godspell,* he wrote, "I found its whole concept of whimsy, and of Jesus's being a regular fellow, too coy and knowing." It reminded him of *Superstar* (known to him in album form at this time) plus the circus. Walter Kerr liked it better, except for a tacked-on serious ending, although he made it clear that the show "isn't 'Jesus Christ Superstar,' a much more ambitious, musically complex, in fact, superior piece of work." Clive Barnes, "The Theater: 'Godspell,' " *New York Times,* 18 May 1971; Walter Kerr, "Why Make St. Matthew Dance? For the Fun of It," *New York Times,* 30 May 1971.

14. As quoted in Ellis Nassour and Richard Broderick, *Rock Opera: The Creation of Jesus Christ Superstar, from Record Album to Broadway Show and Motion Picture* (New York: Hawthorn Books, 1973), 25.

15. For more on the Jesus Rock movement, see George Gent, "Rock Music Turns to Spiritual Ideas," *New York Times,* 24 November 1970; Bill Bender and Timothy Foote, "Gold Rush to Golgotha," *Time,* 25 October 1971; Claude Hall, "Trade Gets R 'n' R(eligion)," *Billboard,* 7 November 1970, 1, 12; Michael Walsh, *Andrew Lloyd Webber: His Life and Works* (New York: Harry N. Abrams, 1989), 63; and Michael Coveney, *Cats on a Chandelier: The Andrew Lloyd Webber Story* (London: Hutchinson, 1999), 51.

16. These songs are by Dee Mullins, The Sweet Revival, and The Byrds, respectively.

17. Bender and Foote, "Gold Rush."

18. A note about the name Lloyd Webber. W. S. L. Webber, Andrew's father, changed his third Christian name to the first half of his last name in order to distinguish himself from a classmate, W. G. Webber. His sons, Andrew and Julian, were baptized with the double but unhyphenated last name Lloyd Webber. Now, most critics and scholars understand this, but a large number of writings refer to the composer as Webber. To avoid frequent interruption of quotations, I have allowed "Webber" to stand without *sic.*

19. This basic biographical information can be found in several sources, including Walsh, *Andrew Lloyd Webber,* and McKnight's early biography, which although told rather breezily like fiction is based partly on interviews with Lloyd Webber and recounts his childhood and early years in some detail. Gerald McKnight, *Andrew Lloyd Webber* (New York: St. Martin's, 1984). Walsh's book is the best resource on Lloyd Webber overall. Disguised as a coffee table book full of glossy photos, it actually discusses the shows and surrounding issues with relative thoroughness. Walsh deals in some detail with the score of each show, although without notated examples or much technical analysis. He also recounts Lloyd Webber's biography with less sensation than other sources. There is in addition Kurt Gänzl's brief summary in *The British Musical Theater* (London: Macmillan, 1986), and the almost entirely plagiarized (mostly from Walsh) retelling in Keith Richmond, *The Musicals of Andrew Lloyd Webber* (London: Virgin, 1995). More recently, Michael Coveney's *Cats on a Chandelier* largely summarizes what others have already recounted,

although as a theater critic he offers occasional fresh insights. Finally, a note about Nassour and Broderick's *Rock Opera:* the authors were insiders at the MCA record company, which lends a certain credibility to their recounting of the facts, since they were directly involved. It also gives the whole book a distinct slant toward the importance of the record company in the lives of Lloyd Webber and Rice. Richard Broderick was a vice president at MCA (owner of Decca) at the time of the recording; the main author, Ellis Nassour, was a publicist for MCA at some undefined time in the past and was a journalist when the book was published in 1973. Their first-hand knowledge of many events does not make for reliable scholarship, however; the authors offer a vast majority of their facts, quotes, and concepts without citation of any kind. It is often implied that Lloyd Webber's words were spoken directly to the authors in interviews, but there is no proof of this.

20. As reproduced by Rice in *Oh, What a Circus: The Autobiography: 1944–1978* (London: Hodder and Stoughton, 1999, 2000), 97.

21. Lloyd Webber would often seem embarrassed to discuss money or the fact that he was making so much of it, an embarrassment which seemed to stem both from a genuine lack of interest in money, in contrast to the artistic drive that motivated him, and from a need to cover up the fact that he did indeed like the money but felt pressure to look as if the art were always more important. Rice, on the other hand, had a healthy ambition to succeed artistically, but unabashedly embraced the money that came with it. When asked, just after *Jesus Christ Superstar* opened on Broadway, if they would now be millionaires, Lloyd Webber gasped, "Heavens no!" Rice cheerfully disagreed: "We'll make an absolute packet." Rice was right. Guy Flatley, "They Wrote It—and They're Glad," *New York Times,* 31 October 1971.

22. Information on the single can be found in Walsh, *Andrew Lloyd Webber,* 62, and Nassour and Broderick, *Rock Opera,* 22–24.

23. Apparently this was said directly to Nassour and Broderick, as quoted by them in *Rock Opera,* 21.

24. Walsh, *Andrew Lloyd Webber,* 62. Walsh simply says that Lloyd Webber said this "ingenuously" to "the press" and gives no specific citation.

25. Rice, *Oh, What a Circus,* 172. Rice says that he and Lloyd Webber always knew the single would be sung by Judas, and that calling him an Everyman simply made more sense for a stand-alone single.

26. Walsh, *Andrew Lloyd Webber,* 63.

27. Flatley, "They Wrote It."

28. Ibid.

29. Ibid. Rice, demonstrating his irreverence toward the subject they had chosen, apparently joked about calling the show *Christ!* in the spirit of *Oliver!* Walsh, *Andrew Lloyd Webber,* 61.

30. Joseph Swain classifies *Superstar* as a historical musical, which means it has a well-known plot and therefore allows for full character development. A similar but less successful use of a historical plot propels *Evita,* according to Swain, and also Sherman Edwards's *1776.* Joseph P. Swain, *The Broadway Musical: A Critical and Musical Survey* (New York: Oxford University Press, 1990). One could also add Maury Yetson's *Titanic* (a well-known true story with some fictional additions) and Jason Robert Brown's *Parade* (a relatively unknown true story) and familiar but fictional tales like Frank Wildhorn's *Jekyll and Hyde.*

31. Walsh, *Andrew Lloyd Webber,* 65. Walsh seems to be quoting a press release or other prepared statement; it is implied that Lloyd Webber did not improvise these words.

32. Rice, *Oh, What a Circus,* 201.

33. Flatley, "They Wrote It." See also Nassour and Broderick, *Rock Opera,* 191.

34. Nassour and Broderick, *Rock Opera,* 37, and Walsh, *Andrew Lloyd Webber,* 78.

35. Nassour and Broderick, *Rock Opera,* 49.

36. Walsh, *Andrew Lloyd Webber,* 66, and Nassour and Broderick, *Rock Opera,* 48. Tim Rice got himself cast as Priest 2 on the album, as well as both the soldier and the old man (whose voice is particularly funny) who accuse Peter of knowing Jesus. See Rice, *Oh, What a Circus,* 210.

37. Advertisement by Decca Records, "Jesus Christ Superstar: A Rock Opera," *Record World,* 14 November 1970.

38. William Bender, "Rock Passion," *Time,* 9 November 1970.

39. Ibid. Other classical borrowings, in this case mentioned by Walsh, include Grieg and Ligeti, and he agrees that there is Orff and Prokofiev. Walsh, *Andrew Lloyd Webber,* 67, 69, 70. Also, Nassour and Broderick, *Rock Opera,* 61, say various writers, unnamed, also heard Bizet, Bach, Weill, Bernstein, Coward, and Rodgers.

40. Hubert Saal, "Pop Testament," *Newsweek,* 16 November 1970. For other raves, see *Billboard,* 14 November 1970; Thomas Willis, "It Could Be the 'Rock' of Ages," *Chicago Tribune,* 8 November 1970; and Jack Shadoian, "Jesus Christ Superstar," *Rolling Stone,* 4 March 1971. Theater historian Mark Steyn agrees that Lloyd Webber uses a broad definition of rock music and that the musical styles serve the drama: "*Superstar* is that rare thing: a rock musical which tries to use rock to differentiate character, an ambitious undertaking in which Lloyd Webber succeeds more effectively than in later scores." Steyn, *Broadway Babies,* 221.

41. Alan Rich, " 'Superstar' Supersuds," *New York,* 7 December 1970.

42. Carl LaFong, "Notes from the Underground: 'Jesus Christ' All-Time Seller?" *Record World,* 14 November 1970.

43. For more on this, see the bewildering passage in Nassour and Broderick, *Rock Opera,* 37–38.

44. Meyer Kantor, "Is 'Superstar' About Christ—or Us?" *New York Times,* 23 September 1973. Other authors that show parallels to modern social leaders include Bender and Foote, "Gold Rush"; Bender, "Rock Passion"; Swain, *The Broadway Musical,* 294; and Scott Miller, *From Assassins to West Side Story: The Director's Guide to Musical Theater* (Portsmouth, N.H.: Heinemann, 1996), 128.

45. Saal, "Pop Testament."

46. It is Equity's policy to give starring roles to American actors, instead of allowing foreign performers into New York, in order to keep as many Americans employed as possible, and, it is hoped, to make stars out of some of them. Exceptions are occasionally made for foreign stars of international fame. Murray Head, who is British, was well liked by Lloyd Webber and Rice but asked for too much money, so the battle with Equity to try to get him in never had to be fought. This issue arises often with imported shows, and particularly with Lloyd Webber; the fight over Sarah Brightman in *The Phantom of the Opera* (see chapter 5) would make the front page of the *New York Times.*

47. Early in the casting process, in December 1969, newspapers reported that John Lennon was being considered for the role of Jesus, and that he was interested, and hoped also to have Yoko Ono cast as Mary. The entire story was retracted by all the papers the following day, all of it having been created by the *Daily Express.* A reporter had asked Lloyd Webber and Rice, and then Lennon, if they were interested in casting the rock icon, and everyone involved had politely agreed it was an interesting idea, but nothing ever

came of it. Lloyd Webber and Rice had wanted an unknown from the beginning. The rumor nevertheless probably helped sales. Walsh, *Andrew Lloyd Webber,* 64–65.

48. Bender and Foote, "Gold Rush."

49. Nassour and Broderick, *Rock Opera,* 117.

50. John Gruen, " 'Do You Mind Critics Calling You Cheap, Decadent, Sensation-alistic, Gimmicky, Vulgar, Overinflated, Megalomaniacal?' 'I Don't Read Reviews Very Much,' Answers Tom O'Horgan," *New York Times,* 2 January 1972.

51. Hal Prince, an established (and soon to be legendary) director, expressed interest in the job, but his telegram went to London when Lloyd Webber was in New York and the chance was lost. Walsh speculates that Lloyd Webber would have jumped at the chance to hire Prince, which indeed he later did, for *Evita* and *The Phantom of the Opera.* Walsh, *Andrew Lloyd Webber,* 75. Another director, Frank Corsaro, was actually hired before O'Horgan, but Stigwood replaced him. See Nassour and Broderick, *Rock Opera,* 100 and 114.

52. Walsh, *Andrew Lloyd Webber,* 75.

53. Mel Gussow, " 'Superstar' and 'On the Town' Start Out—With a Past," *New York Times,* 1 September 1971.

54. Sidebar to Bender and Foote, "Gold Rush," and Nassour and Broderick, *Rock Opera,* 117.

55. Other preview problems are discussed in Mel Gussow, " 'Superstar' a Hit Before Opening," *New York Times,* 12 October 1971.

56. The statement as quoted in Lawrence Van Gelder, "Two Jewish Organizations Are Critical of 'Superstar,' " *New York Times,* 13 October 1971. One is reminded of similar complaints voiced about Mel Gibson's 2004 film *The Passion of the Christ.*

57. Rabbi Marc H. Tannenbaum, one of the American Jewish Committee's spokes-people, as quoted in Van Gelder, "Two Jewish Organizations."

58. See Walsh, *Andrew Lloyd Webber,* 77.

59. As quoted in Van Gelder, "Two Jewish Organizations."

60. Both quotes in Flatley, "They Wrote It."

61. Bender and Foote, "Gold Rush."

62. Walsh, *Andrew Lloyd Webber,* 77.

63. For more on the protests, see George Gent, " 'Superstar': The Cheers and Jeers Build," *New York Times,* 14 October 1971; "Drama Mailbag: Do They Ridicule Religion?" *New York Times,* 12 December 1971; Jack Kroll, "Theater," *Newsweek,* 25 October 1971; Flatley, "They Wrote It"; Bender and Foote, "Gold Rush." Rice cheerfully dismissed the protestors: "On the opening night itself a motley collection of placard-carrying religious maniacs picketed the theatre, but as most of them loudly denied ever having soiled themselves by listening to the album or by attending a preview, their campaign lacked a certain amount of authority." Rice, *Oh, What a Circus,* 263.

64. Swain, *The Broadway Musical,* 302. Listeners occasionally point out the similarity between the groove of "Everything's Alright" and that of Dave Brubeck's piece *Take 5,* though the two pieces differ strongly in most other ways; there is no evidence that Lloyd Webber knew or was inspired by Brubeck's work, but the two do have sections that flow in a somewhat similar rhythmic vein. Swain and Walsh offer some useful musical analysis of *Superstar,* a rare find with Lloyd Webber. Swain's interpretation lingers on one idea to the detriment of many other techniques at work in the score. He spends the majority of his analysis discussing the "contrafactum" technique, which reuses melodies with new lyrics. He traces the tunes through the show (which is certainly worth noting,

as is done above, but other elements are also important). Swain believes that this method arose from an inexperienced operating procedure that Lloyd Webber and Rice were using. Citing an unreferenced press release in *Rock Opera* (Nassour and Broderick, 46), Swain notes that Rice describes the creative process as based on song types. They needed a ballad here, a vaudeville there, something agitated to link them, and so on. Lloyd Webber would write a tune, then Rice would add lyrics. Swain concludes that if they are operating on the "naïve belief that a kind of music is analogous to a kind of dramatic action, it is all too easy to see how they could decide that one dramatic situation might be similar in character to another, so why not use the same music again, with different words?" (Swain, *The Broadway Musical, 302*). While Swain is right to say that most dramatic situations are not so tidy as to require always the same type of music, his conclusion that it is simple-minded to link certain dramatic moments through shared music is disproven by the score itself. Some very subtle, otherwise unspoken links are made through shared music. (Swain, in something of a contradiction, does grant that some of the contrafacta are dramatically justified and interesting.) Also, there is no reason to assume that Lloyd Webber and Rice were incapable of creating more than one ballad or vaudeville or agitated number; it is much more likely, and in keeping with Lloyd Webber's later practice, that they chose purposely to repeat music in order to lend unity to a score full of many musical styles.

65. Swain, *The Broadway Musical*, 303.

66. Swain is disappointed by this ending to an otherwise brilliant song, saying that Lloyd Webber "resorts to the recording industry's all-purpose answer for composers who cannot end their songs properly: the fade-out" (ibid., 305). While it is entirely possible that Lloyd Webber's thoughts were more pop-oriented, especially since he was writing at the time for an album, with distant hopes of the stage, the fade-out section can be quite effective in performance. It gives Mary and Jesus a long time to be close to one another, while the others become lost in their own repeated musings. Most productions, however, use definitive alternate endings provided in the score, instead of recreating the concept album's fade-outs.

67. In the first of many such instances in his career, Lloyd Webber here used a tune he had already written. Here and there in his shows are songs which were originally meant to go in other shows, both completed and incomplete, or were simply tunes he had written in the hopes of finding a home for them someday. In this case, however, the song had actually already lived a full life under a different guise: called "Kansas Morning," Lloyd Webber and Rice had sold it, and their agent David Land had bought back the rights for its use here. Walsh, *Andrew Lloyd Webber*, 66. See also Rice's autobiography, in which he sheepishly quotes his poor first lyrics and praises Lloyd Webber's melody, the beauty of which is fully revealed by what he feels are the quite appropriate, direct lyrics of "I Don't Know How to Love Him." Rice, *Oh, What a Circus*, 189, 206.

68. Swain, *The Broadway Musical*, 305.

69. Rice, *Oh, What a Circus*, 208.

70. Swain calls it a rondo form, which indeed it is, in a general way. Audiences at least surely feel the three repeats of the apostles' song at the beginning, middle, and end. Swain, *The Broadway Musical*, 305.

71. Walsh, *Andrew Lloyd Webber*, 68. Somewhat simplistically, though, Walsh reduces the "dilemma" to damned if Judas does, damned if he doesn't.

72. Ibid., 68.

73. Ibid., 69.

74. Theater historian Kurt Gänzl finds the voicing here particularly effective. The priests, one scraping the lowest recesses of the male range, another "twittering horribly" above the staff in a rock tenor (which Gänzl labels countertenor), combine for "a novel and effective piece of part-writing." Gänzl, *The Musical,* 341–42.

75. Another recycled Lloyd Webber tune: with different lyrics, this tune, then called "Try It and See," had won a prize in the Eurovision song contest in 1969. Then it was placed tentatively into a show that the team never wrote, about the Crusades, where it was equally as campy but meant to be sung by King Richard I. Walsh, *Andrew Lloyd Webber,* 67. Rice would later write, with composer Stephen Oliver, his Crusades comedy *Blondel,* with a different campy song for King Richard.

76. Miller, *Director's Guide,* 135. Miller does not of course speak for everyone, but certainly many agreed. He feels the number doesn't work at all and prefers a rock remake used in a 1994 production.

77. Swain, *The Broadway Musical,* 305.

78. Walsh, *Andrew Lloyd Webber,* 70.

79. As quoted in McKnight, *Andrew Lloyd Webber,* 231.

80. Clive Barnes, "Theater: Christ's Passion Transported to the Stage in Guise of Serious Pop," *New York Times,* 13 October 1971.

81. Alan Rich, "The Selling of the Savior," *New York,* 25 October 1971.

82. John Simon, "Jesus Christ Superclub-Star," *New York,* 25 October 1971.

83. Richard Watts, "The Passion in a Rock Beat," *New York Post,* 13 October 1971. Martin Gottfried agreed that it was lifeless. It reminded him of watching a very expensive jukebox play the album. Martin Gottfried, "Jesus Christ Superstar . . . 'Easter Show at the Music Hall,'" *Women's Wear Daily,* 14 October 1971.

84. Dick Brukenfield, "Save a Few Nails for the Producer," *Village Voice,* 21 October 1971. Other reviews came from three local television stations, whose reviews were beginning to count more and more, although their reviews were extremely short and rather shallow. WCBS was quite positive, WABC slightly less so, and WNBC panned the look of the show, skipping music and lyrics. The reviewers were Leonard Harris, Kevin Sanders, and Leonard Probst, respectively, and all three reviews aired on 12 October 1971. As transcribed in the *New York Critics' Theatre Reviews,* 1971.

85. Douglas Watt, "'Jesus Christ Superstar' is Full of Life, Vibrant with Reverence," *New York Daily News,* 13 October 1971.

86. George Melloan, "The Theater," *Wall Street Journal,* 14 October 1971.

87. Gruen, "Tom O'Horgan."

88. Miller, *Director's Guide,* 137.

89. These descriptions come from Nassour and Broderick, *Rock Opera,* 141–62, a source which is often unreliable, but in this case (because of the authors' proximity to events and because they are not critics) offers the most objective take on what O'Horgan thought he was doing. Critics will of course have their own ways of describing what they saw.

90. Apparently a paraphrase of O'Horgan's words by Nassour and Broderick, *Rock Opera,* 144.

91. Ibid., 155.

92. Ibid., 157.

93. Kurt Gänzl claims audiences apparently did not mind O'Horgan's production as much as critics did, although this may be due to their incoming positive bias toward the score. Gänzl, *The British Musical Theatre,* 941. They certainly did not fully embrace the

production, as its somewhat limited New York run (but success in other productions) shows. For an interesting interview with O'Horgan in which he claims imagery about insects was fundamental to his concept for *Superstar,* see Lawrence Thelen, *The Show Makers: Great Directors of the American Musical Theatre* (New York: Routledge, 2000).

94. Barnes, "Christ's Passion."

95. Walter Kerr, " 'Jesus Christ Superstar'—Two Views: A Critic Likes the Opera, Loathes the Production," *New York Times,* 24 October 1971. Brendan Gill of the *New Yorker* agreed with Kerr that the problem was making a modest, relatively intimate story into a self-promoting spectacle. Brendan Gill, "Alien Corn," *New Yorker,* 23 October 1971.

96. Bender and Foote, "Gold Rush."

97. Simon, "Jesus Christ Superclub-Star." On the idea of Herod having the best song, Sheridan Morley agrees, saying that the devil often does. Morley, *Spread a Little Happiness,* 181.

98. Brukenfield, "Save a Few Nails."

99. Kroll, "Theater."

100. Flinn, *Musical! A Grand Tour,* 316.

101. Gottfried, "Jesus Christ Superstar."

102. All exchanges between Lloyd Webber and Rice from Flatley, "They Wrote It."

103. Walsh, *Andrew Lloyd Webber,* 78.

104. Barnes, "Christ's Passion." Richard Watts agreed, calling the music "agreeable" and "ordinary and decidedly not exciting." Watts, "Passion in a Rock Beat."

105. Kerr, "Two Views: A Critic."

106. Bender and Foote, "Gold Rush." Two others who liked the virtuosity and range in this generally rock work were Melloan, "The Theater," and Watt, "Jesus Christ Superstar." Tim Rice gives Lloyd Webber's music a rave review: "I believe that Andrew barely put a foot, or note, wrong when he wrote the music of *Superstar* and . . . his orchestrations were flawless and ensured that the work was never boring." Rice, *Oh, What a Circus,* 193.

107. Barnes, "Christ's Passion."

108. Kerr, "Two Views: A Critic," Melloan (in "The Theater") also praises Rice's vernacular, as do Bender and Foote ("Gold Rush"). The only pan of Rice was Gottfried, "Jesus Christ Superstar," which is a rather inadequate review in any case, and simply dismisses Rice's lyrics as "inane."

109. Barnes, "Christ's Passion."

110. Rich, "Selling of the Savior." Rich's co-worker, John Simon, *New York* magazine's theater critic, had a similar reaction: he felt this Jesus was rather too human, and people's responses too shallow. Simon, "Jesus Christ Superclub-Star." One of the strongest negative reactions to the interpretation of the story came from Malcolm Boyd, a priest, whose review ran in a prominent position: parallel to that of Walter Kerr's in the *Times.* He found this Jesus too weak, petulant, and depressed, but Boyd's main problem was the sexuality which he felt intruded "again and again and again" into the story. O'Horgan's hippie-minded instructions to his actors clearly baffled Boyd, who questioned Jesus' sexual orientation and at the same time was disturbed by his obviously physical relationship with Mary. Malcolm Boyd, " 'Jesus Christ Superstar'—Two Views: A Priest Says, 'It Doesn't Have a Soul,' " *New York Times,* 24 October 1971. To Walsh, one of the most prominent things about O'Horgan's production was the "pronounced gay sensibility," but few saw it at the time, or at least chose not to speak about it. Walsh, *Andrew Lloyd Webber,* 78. It is certainly possible to see why Walsh sees this in the production, but it seems more a

product of an air of sexuality than a particularly homosexual bent; Walsh's example of Christ staged like a phallic symbol need not express orientation. The subject did come up once at the time: the *New York Times* mentioned to Lloyd Webber and Rice that an audience member had gotten the impression that this Jesus was the leader of a pack of gay men. "That man's an idiot!" Rice responded. Flatley, "They Wrote It."

111. Lloyd Webber was also unimpressed by Fenholt. "That boy Jeff," he told the *New York Times,* "has a lovely singing voice. But my personal image of Jesus was some-body like Mick Jagger. Somebody with tremendous charisma and power." He suggested Murray Head, the Judas of the album. His chance to write for a Jagger-like personality would come in *Cats,* in the character of the Rum Tum Tugger. Flatley, "They Wrote It."

112. Gill, "Alien Corn."

113. Nassour and Broderick, *Rock Opera,* 195.

114. See Walsh, *Andrew Lloyd Webber,* 79–80, and Nassour and Broderick, *Rock Opera,* 195.

115. See Walsh, *Andrew Lloyd Webber,* 80; Nassour and Broderick, *Rock Opera,* 199; Gänzl, *The British Musical Theatre,* 945.

116. Irving Wardle, "Little Here for Card-Carrying Christians," *Times* (London), 10 August 1972. Similarly, see Arthur Thirkell, "No Miracle, but Jesus is a Real Superstar," *Daily Mirror* (London), 10 August 1972. John Barber of the *Daily Telegraph* found the show disturbing and compelling at once; clearly unprepared for the hard rock element, he found the music far more upsetting than the lyrics, especially when Judas "shouts himself hoarse," and Jesus could be heard "yelling himself silly." John Barber, " 'Superstar' Star-tling and Nauseating," *Daily Telegraph* (London), 10 August 1972.

117. Harold Hobson, "Book Learning," *Sunday Times* (London), 13 August 1972.

118. Derek Jewell, "Superstar Subdued," *Sunday Times* (London), 13 August 1972.

119. See Lewis Funke, "Jesus Christ Superstar," *New York Times,* 30 May 1971.

120. See Terence Smith, "Israeli Government Moves to Dissociate Itself from 'Jesus Christ Superstar,' " *New York Times,* 14 July 1973.

121. Kantor, "Is 'Superstar' About Christ—or About Us?" For more on the film's controversial references to modern times and perhaps modern Jews, see Smith, "Israeli Government."

122. Nassour and Broderick, *Rock Opera,* 226, no citation for the quote.

123. Statement as quoted in Irving Spiegel, "Jewish Unit Call Movie 'Insidious,' " *New York Times,* 24 June 1973. For more protests and discussion see also Sanka Knox, "Jewish Group Charges Anti-Semitism in Movie," *New York Times,* 9 August 1973.

124. Linda Greenhouse, " 'Superstar' Film Renews Disputes," *New York Times,* 8 August 1973.

125. Howard Thompson, "Mod-Pop 'Superstar' Comes to Screen," *New York Times,* 9 August 1973.

126. Coveney, *Cats on a Chandelier,* 59.

127. Rice, *Oh, What a Circus,* 225.

2. "Humming the Scenery"

1. Tim Rice, *Oh, What a Circus: The Autobiography: 1944–1978* (London: Hodder and Stoughton, 1999), 1.

2. Coveney recounting the story as told to him by Julian, in *Cats on a Chandelier: The Andrew Lloyd Webber Story* (London: Hutchinson, 1999), 56–57. Albums celebrating

Lloyd Webber's greatest hits are numerous; there are dozens of compilations, excerpts, orchestral arrangements, and cover albums of Lloyd Webber's music, selling briskly.

3. Coveney, *Cats on a Chandelier,* 60.

4. For more on these events of the 1970s, see Gerald McKnight, *Andrew Lloyd Webber* (New York: St. Martin's, 1984), 143–45; Coveney, *Cats on a Chandelier,* 69; Michael Walsh, *Andrew Lloyd Webber: His Life and Works,* 2nd ed. (New York: Harry N. Abrams, 1997), 82 and 111–12; and Keith Richmond, *The Musicals of Andrew Lloyd Webber* (London: Virgin, 1995), 112. The name of the Really Useful Company derives from the British children's stories of Thomas the Tank Engine by the Reverend W. Awdry, stories not unlike the American Little Engine That Could. Lloyd Webber had always adored trains and these stories, and would eventually be inspired to write a musical about them, *Starlight Express.*

5. For more on Lloyd Webber's finances, see Coveney, *Cats on a Chandelier,* 68; McKnight, *Andrew Lloyd Webber,* 10; Richmond, *Musicals of Lloyd Webber,* 116–17; Walsh, *Andrew Lloyd Webber,* 179–80; and John Rockwell, "Andrew Lloyd Webber Superstar," *New York Times,* 20 December 1987. It is thought that the total income of all British theater composers combined would not total half of what Lloyd Webber was worth in 1986; see Sheridan Morley, *Spread a Little Happiness: The First Hundred Years of the British Musical* (London: Thames and Hudson, 1987), 8. Walsh asserts that Lloyd Webber has "earned more money from his music than any theater composer who ever lived." See Walsh, *Andrew Lloyd Webber,* 9. For more on Lloyd Webber's respected status as a knowledgeable and influential art collector, see John Russell, "What a Few Hummable Tunes Will Buy," *New York Times Magazine,* 10 December 1995.

6. Walsh, *Andrew Lloyd Webber,* 155.

7. Coveney recounts several comings and goings of partners in Lloyd Webber's company, examples of Lloyd Webber's tendency to drop people after years of friendship. One who dropped out of the whole enterprise was founding member Brian Brolly, which (along with other insider troubles) inspired board member Tim Rice to resign. Coveney, *Cats on a Chandelier,* 142.

8. Ibid., 139.

9. Lloyd Webber's theater purchases are chronicled in Warren Hoge, "A Major New Role As Theater Mogul For Lloyd Webber," *New York Times,* 10 January 2000.

10. The title "Lord" requires hyphenating the name Lloyd-Webber, which is just now beginning to be used by some writers, but even Coveney, who explains the hyphen, does not use it. For the sake of consistency, and since he was not yet Lord Lloyd-Webber at the time of the shows discussed here, I have chosen not to use it. Coveney, *Cats on a Chandelier,* 4. Lloyd Webber and his third (and current) wife Madeleine have three children, and Madeleine's career as a horse rider and breeder inspired Lloyd Webber to convert many of Sydmonton's thousands of acres into horse country.

11. Ibid., 225–28. For more on Lloyd Webber and food, among other nonmusical pursuits, see Coveney's chapter 12 in *Cats on a Chandelier.*

12. As recounted, with no hint that Lerner could have been making it up, by Mark Steyn, *Broadway Babies Say Goodnight: Musicals Then and Now* (New York: Routledge, 1997), 273. Coveney declares the dialogue bunk, but he passes it along anyway, a temptation I could not resist either. Coveney, *Cats on a Chandelier,* 129.

13. Walsh, *Andrew Lloyd Webber,* 12.

14. Fausto Torrefranca, *Giacomo Puccini e l'opera internazionale* (Turin, 1912), vii; Alexandra Wilson's translation, as quoted in her article "Torrefranca vs. Puccini: Embodying a Decadent Italy," *Cambridge Opera Journal* 13, no. 1 (March 2001): 31.

15. Arthur Groos and Roger Parker, *Giacomo Puccini: La bohème,* in the series *Cambridge Opera Handbooks* (Cambridge: Cambridge University Press, 1986), 131.

16. Wilson, "Torrefranca vs. Puccini," 31.

17. Richard Kislan, *The Musical: A Look at the American Musical Theater,* rev. ed. (New York: Applause, 1995), 273.

18. Steyn, *Broadway Babies,* 165.

19. Walsh concurs: "In less than twenty years, he has gone in critical estimation from being the exciting, and penniless, young firebrand who was bringing a fresh new voice to a tired genre to the millionaire hack whose overwrought works are emblematic of what ails Broadway. And all this before he turned forty." Walsh, *Andrew Lloyd Webber,* 14. See also Rockwell, "Andrew Lloyd Webber Superstar."

20. Coveney, *Cats on a Chandelier,* 194. Coveney defends both Lloyd Webber and the audience, arguing that *Cats* does have content and that the label "megamusical" is derogatory and inappropriate for Lloyd Webber. "It has become fashionable to say that you don't have to understand what is going on in *Cats* to have a good time. This is as popular and misleading a myth as the one about Lloyd Webber being only a mega-musical man, or the other one about his shows being obvious commercial propositions before they even open." Coveney, *Cats on a Chandelier,* 97.

21. See Bernard Rosenberg and Ernest Harburg, *The Broadway Musical: Collaboration in Commerce and Art* (New York: New York University Press, 1993), 197.

22. Upon reading Rich's review of *Aspects,* Lloyd Webber declared, "This is a man who knows nothing about love," and he is rumored to have said far worse in private. Rich, for his part, declared that Lloyd Webber was "emblematic of all that was wrong with the contemporary music theater" (a paraphrase by Walsh) and often used Lloyd Webber as a negative comparison in reviews of other people's shows (such as in his review of *Miss Saigon*). Walsh, *Andrew Lloyd Webber,* 219 and 235.

23. Nunn writes of this in a coffee table book of photos and lyrics from *Cats,* ostensibly authored by Andrew Lloyd Webber and T. S. Eliot, *Cats: The Book of the Musical* (New York: Harcourt Brace, 1983), 12. For more thoughts on critics see Stephen Citron, *The Musical from the Inside Out,* rev. ed. (Chicago: Ivan R. Dee, 1997), 273; and Rosenberg and Harburg, *Collaboration,* 188.

24. What we need, of course, is a theater critic trained in theater and in music. There are only a handful of musicologists studying musical theater, virtually none of whom address the megamusical. See Geoffrey Block, "The Broadway Canon from *Show Boat* to *West Side Story* and the European Operatic Ideal," *Journal of Musicology* 11, no. 4 (Fall 1993): 528, for more on musicology's general disinterest in musicals. See also McKnight, *Andrew Lloyd Webber,* 138, for more on the qualifications of various critics.

25. Michael Walsh, "Magician of the Musical," *Time,* 18 January 1988. For an anecdote about how the well-educated understand that Lloyd Webber is worthy only of disdain, see John Eaton, "Andrew Lloyd Webber: That 'Cats' Meow Is a Phantom Talent," *Washington Post,* 31 January 1988. Eaton recounts telling an audience at a Smithsonian lecture that "Memory" from *Cats* is "an outrageous piece of fakery" and receiving applause. This is an extreme example of the gleefully mean tone that Lloyd Webber haters tend to take. I must counter his anecdote with my own. I myself stood behind a podium and discussed "Memory" at a meeting of the Society for American Music. I did not defend it, but I certainly treated it as "real" music; my task was to demonstrate its effectiveness in its context within the show, and my point was cheerfully received by all present, even

those who did not like the song as such. A few eminent scholars later confessed to getting choked up by the emotion and beauty of the song.

26. Coveney, *Cats on a Chandelier,* 137.

27. Walsh, *Andrew Lloyd Webber,* 219. See also Geoffrey Block, *Enchanted Evenings: The Broadway Musical from* Show Boat *to Sondheim* (New York: Oxford University Press, 1997), 275, which discusses the idea that critics dislike Lloyd Webber precisely because he is so popular. Block argues that Lloyd Webber's shows deserve far more scholarly attention than they have gotten, but like many others, he fails to give the shows much attention at all. Coveney, too, argues that "so much seems to get in the way of dispassionate assessment" that the music goes undiscussed, but he too fails to discuss it beyond the most basic level (nor is this particularly his goal; he makes it clear that his focus lies where most everyone else's does: on Lloyd Webber's life, reputation, and cultural impact). Coveney, *Cats on a Chandelier,* 13.

28. Walsh, *Andrew Lloyd Webber,* 14.

29. This is Frank Rich's favorite example of the idea that he has no power. In Rosenberg and Harburg, *Collaboration,* 200.

30. For a particularly vitriolic rant against Lloyd Webber as the cause of musicals becoming commerce rather than art, see Denny Martin Flinn, *Musical! A Grand Tour: The Rise, Glory, and Fall of an American Institution* (New York: Schirmer, 1997), 474 and 484.

31. A notion reinforced by Wilfrid Mellers, "Platform: Are Musicals Musical?" *Musical Times* 132, no. 1782 (August 1991).

32. A theater columnist for the *New York Post,* as quoted in Myrna Katz Frommer and Harvey Frommer, *It Happened on Broadway: An Oral History of the Great White Way* (New York: Harcourt Brace, 1998), 279. For an interesting, if wildly opinionated, discussion of Lloyd Webber, opera, and high versus low culture, see Anthony Tommasini, "Woe to Shows that Put on Operatic Airs," *New York Times,* 20 July 1997. For a similarly biased opinion, see Harold C. Schonberg, "J. C. Superstar—No Rock of Ages," *New York Times,* 24 October 1971. Schonberg believes that no rock or pop music can be meaningful or lasting, since its only goal is commercial success. A letter to the editor pointed out his strange bias toward all things old and stuffy ("Music Mailbag: Is Only Classical Music 'Good'?" *New York Times,* 14 November 1971).

33. For more on how the Tony Awards work and a complete listing of past winners, see Isabelle Stevenson, ed., *The Tony Award: A Complete Listing with a History of the American Theatre Wing* (Portsmouth, N.H.: Heinemann, 1994). For the most recent years, see www.tonys.org.

34. Morley, *Spread a Little Happiness,* 11.

35. Walsh, *Andrew Lloyd Webber,* 205. See also Steyn, *Broadway Babies,* 171.

36. Morley, *Spread a Little Happiness,* 13, 203, and 210.

37. Steyn, *Broadway Babies,* 231.

38. Ibid., 34.

39. The first television ad for a Broadway show, most agree, was for *Pippin* in 1973, run by producer Stuart Ostrow; see Ostrow, *A Producer's Broadway Journey* (Westport, Conn., and London: Praeger, 1999), xvi, and also Flinn, *Musical! A Grand Tour,* 305. The ad successfully boosted sagging ticket sales and the show ran another four years. Ostrow, however, deeply regrets being responsible for what he sees as a shift in focus from producing a good show to producing a good commercial. Indeed, television ads are

a requirement now, and not just for megamusicals; virtually every show on Broadway, including plays, runs television ads.

40. As quoted in Walsh, "Magician of the Musical."

41. McKnight, *Andrew Lloyd Webber,* 14. Steyn points out that although Lloyd Webber will, at any given time and with total sincerity, claim to be completely uninterested in publicity, he will embrace the hype which surrounds him soon after. "The thing about Lloyd Webber," Steyn opines, "is that he talks a lot of bunk which, at the time, is apparently heartfelt, but which he'll cheerfully contradict a few weeks later." Steyn, *Broadway Babies,* 274.

42. Lloyd Webber to Walsh, in "Magician of the Musical."

43. As quoted in Ellis Nassour and Richard Broderick, *Rock Opera: The Creation of Jesus Christ Superstar, from Record Album to Broadway Show and Motion Picture* (New York: Hawthorn Books, 1973), 192.

44. Ostrow, *Producer's Journey,* 136.

45. Ibid., 136. This is still true to a great extent today. Recently at a performance of John and Rice's *Aida,* I sat next to a miserable husband who was there with his wife and her mother. He fought to stay awake; the wife and mother loved the show. At matinees of *Cats,* children celebrating birthdays abounded. At *Jekyll and Hyde,* a young woman marveled at her husband's gesture of buying the tickets for their anniversary. At *Phantom,* I was once surrounded by dozens of Japanese businessmen, following the plot by using a summary in Japanese printed off the internet. Also, in the six months before *Cats* closed, I hosted four separate groups of family and friends who were motivated to see it before it was too late, somehow having missed their opportunity to do so in the first seventeen and a half years of its run. Similarly, acquiring tickets to *The Lion King* or *The Producers* was quite a social coup, especially early in their runs.

46. Howard Kissel, *New York Daily News* critic, as quoted in Frommer and Frommer, *It Happened on Broadway,* 278.

47. Mimi Kramer, "The Phantom of Broadway," *New Yorker,* 8 February 1988. For a similar view, see, among others, Ostrow, *Producer's Journey,* 135.

48. Steyn, *Broadway Babies,* 23, 26. Steyn offers some examples of spectacle over the history of musical theater which make a falling chandelier seem downright dull. Mary Martin flying in *Peter Pan* is a perfect example of a spectacular feat of theatrical staging which is nevertheless entirely in keeping with the story.

49. Ibid., 127.

50. Rosenberg and Harburg, *Collaboration,* 19–21. By the early 1990s, almost every house on Broadway was owned either by the Shubert Organization or the Nederlander Organization, with only the Jujamcyn Theaters holding a distant third place.

51. Ibid., 34. For more on the dilemma of musicals being produced by lawyers and bankers, see Ostrow, *Producer's Journey,* xvii; and Steyn, *Broadway Babies,* 270.

52. Walsh, "Magician of the Musical"; agreement on this can be found in Rockwell, "Andrew Lloyd Webber Superstar," as well as Frank Rich, "London Readies Some Bundles for Broadway," *New York Times,* 18 July 1982.

53. Steyn, *Broadway Babies,* 167.

54. Morley's thoughts contained in this paragraph come from *Spread a Little Happiness,* 173–74, 189, 191, and 200.

55. For more on Mackintosh's background, see Edward Behr, *Les Misérables: History in the Making,* updated ed. (New York: Arcade, 1996), 51–58.

56. Dennis McGowen and Deborah Grace Winer, *Sing Out, Louise! 150 Stars of the*

Musical Theatre Remember 50 Years on Broadway (New York: Schirmer, 1993), 210. This book's hostility continues for several pages, where it boldly states that the sour grapes are justified because the music is bad, and it is prerecorded and lip-synched, which is of course untrue. In an even stranger example of resentment toward the British invasion, Steyn, normally opinionated but at least rational, blames the invasion on AIDS. This "virus of British musicals," as he tastelessly puts it, would never have happened had the competition not died. He claims the best shows in town are AIDS benefits and memorials. Steyn, *Broadway Babies*, 211.

57. Kislan, *The Musical*, 269–70. Kislan's assessment of the British invasion, while technically accurate up to a point, drips with bitterness and implies a distinct lack of interest in creativity on behalf of the three men. According to him, money was clearly their goal: "Andrew Lloyd Webber emerged as a major international songwriter just as his colleagues Trevor Nunn and Cameron Mackintosh discovered how to fill the Broadway vacuum with established theatrical properties. Their formula for success: Produce heavily capitalized shows in London at an estimated third of New York production costs, test market the product abroad for quality, then position the production for a low-risk go at Broadway. Almost immediately, the balance of trade in his musicals between New York and London experienced a startling reversal."

58. Kroll's views can be found in a two-part article. Jack Kroll and Constance Guthrie, "A Show of All Shows," and Kroll, "The Transatlantic Gold Rush," both in *Newsweek*, 30 March 1987.

59. Morley, *Spread a Little Happiness*, 218. For more on cross-fertilization, see Rich, "London Readies Some Bundles."

60. Coveney, *Cats on a Chandelier*, 10.

61. See Coveney, *Cats on a Chandelier*, 24–30. Lloyd Webber saw *Tosca* when he was fifteen, at which time he realized that Puccini, until then considered rather low-brow by critics, was being given a position of much greater respect thanks to Maria Callas's performance. Already he had begun to ponder the standing of composers who were too popular to be taken seriously, a position in which he would spend much of his career, and already his love of Puccini was in place. He always felt moved to "total tears" by Puccini, and had never cared about Puccini's critical standing, although he would care a great deal about his own. See McKnight, *Andrew Lloyd Webber*, 67.

62. Lloyd Webber to Rockwell, in "Andrew Lloyd Webber Superstar." For more on why "Memory" sounds like Puccini, see chapter 3.

63. Michael Feingold, "The Ghosts of Music Past," *Village Voice*, 2 February 1988.

64. M. Owen Lee, "Recordings: The Phantom of the Opera. Andrew Lloyd Webber," *Opera Quarterly* 6, no. 1 (Autumn 1988): 150.

65. Walsh, *Andrew Lloyd Webber*, 13.

66. Ibid., 12. Coveney agrees, and makes a point of saying of course no one writes in a vacuum, and even Walsh's well-intentioned hunt for any quotes is unnecessary. Coveney, *Cats on a Chandelier*, 50 and 198–99. Lee, in "Recordings," offers us moments when Kern directly quotes Puccini, Loewe quotes Tchaikovsky, and Rodgers quotes Beethoven and Brahms. Yet Lee argues that the other composers integrated the quotes better while Lloyd Webber's work "remains an imperfectly homogenized pastiche." Rice says Lloyd Webber borrowed more heavily from classical composers when he was very young, but mixed it with plenty of original material, and it worked fine. Rice, *Oh, What a Circus*, 125.

67. As quoted in Jesse McKinley, "Jury Vindicates Andrew Lloyd Webber," *New*

York Times, 16 December 1998. For the whole Repp story, see this article and those before it: William Grimes, "A $78 Song vs. a Lloyd Webber Work," *New York Times,* 16 Sem-tember 1996; Dinita Smith, "Who Copied Whom? Ruling Implies Neither," *New York Times,* 5 December 1996; and Jesse McKinley, "Andrew Lloyd Webber's Latest Audience: A Jury in Federal District Court," *New York Times,* 15 December 1998. Also, in 1988, amateur songwriter John Brett filed suit claiming that "Angel of Music" and "The Phantom of the Opera" were stolen from demo tapes he had sent to Tim Rice in 1985, but the case was quickly thrown out when Lloyd Webber pointed out that the melodies had already been used in a different context at the Sydmonton Festival several years before. Walsh, *Andrew Lloyd Webber,* 182; and Coveney, *Cats on a Chandelier,* 199.

68. Lloyd Webber to McKnight, *Andrew Lloyd Webber,* 245.

69. Rice, *Oh, What a Circus,* 370.

70. As quoted in Rockwell, "Andrew Lloyd Webber Superstar." Citron, in *The Musical from the Inside Out,* 207–208, also discusses the ideas of themes and leitmotifs and tunes reused with new words, although he becomes rather lost in his own definitions. Walsh argues in a *New York Times* article that Lloyd Webber writes melodies that any "composer would kill to have written," but it is just as true that Lloyd Webber is a great architect of dramatic flow, and revisits melodies with "heightened and transformed emotional power." Walsh compares this technique to that of Verdi in *Don Carlos,* when the melody which represented the bond between Carlos and Posa returns (as Posa is dying) in a fragmented, emotionally loaded new context. Michael Walsh, "Lloyd Webber: Now, but Forever?" *New York Times,* 9 April 2000.

71. Walsh, "Magician of the Musical."

72. Walsh, *Andrew Lloyd Webber,* 13.

73. Caddick in Chris Pasles, "Andrew Lloyd Webber and the Phantom: A new kind of opera?" *Opera Canada* 30, no. 3 (Fall 1989): 17.

74. Lloyd Webber to McKnight, *Andrew Lloyd Webber,* 244. See also Glenn Loney, "Don't Cry for Andrew Lloyd Webber," *Opera News* 45, no. 17 (4 April 1981): 14. Coveney devotes a great deal of space to supporters of Lloyd Webber, allowing them to defend his talent. Coveney, *Cats on a Chandelier,* 198 and 207–10. McKnight also waxes poetic about the brilliance of Andrew Lloyd Webber, citing unnamed experts: "In the cautious opinion of distinguished musical contemporaries, his feeling for melody is exceptionally gifted, his mastery of theatrical effect extraordinary, and the use he makes of every known form of musical expression demonstrates a catholicity and adventurous courage which has become the Lloyd Webber keynote." McKnight, *Andrew Lloyd Webber,* 195–96.

75. In Loney, "Don't Cry for Lloyd Webber."

76. Walsh, "Magician of the Musical."

77. The terms through-sung, sung-through, and through-composed are often bandied about loosely. Technically, through-composed means never repeating, like a long spun-out melody; the term relevant to the megamusical is through-sung (or sung-through), meaning simply sung throughout.

78. Loney, "Don't Cry for Lloyd Webber." See also Kurt Gänzl, *The British Musical Theatre* (London: Macmillan, 1986), 2: 945.

79. Black's comments can be found in Steyn, *Broadway Babies,* 279. See also Foster Hirsch, *Harold Prince and the American Musical Theatre* (Cambridge: Cambridge University Press, 1989), 157, on how Lloyd Webber makes song and recitative take the place of dialogue.

80. Flinn, *Musical! A Grand Tour,* 475–81.

81. Steyn's thoughts can be found in *Broadway Babies,* 20, 103, and 277–80.

82. Walsh, "Now, but Forever?" Walsh goes on to argue that there are plenty of good musicals and plenty of bad operas, so arguing the difference based on artistic merit is not helpful. The two terms simply imply a level of class, without actually fulfilling the implication.

83. For more on vocal types, see Citron, *Musical from the Inside Out,* 78; and Flinn, *Musical! A Grand Tour,* 477.

84. Citron, *Musical from the Inside Out,* 204–205.

85. Steyn, *Broadway Babies,* 45 and 277. Steyn makes an extensive, and only somewhat flippant, comparison between Lloyd Webber and the composer Steyn sees as his most closely connected predecessor, Lehár. Lloyd Webber has more in common with Lehár than anything that has come in the decades since him, Steyn argues, making Broadway's heyday seem like "a blip, a freak, an agreeable detour" on the way back to the "luxuriant tunes, emotional generalities, operetta certainties" of Lehár and Lloyd Webber. Steyn adds that Strauss and Viennese operetta can be added to the family tree before Lehár. *Broadway Babies,* 30–34.

86. Loney, "Don't Cry for Lloyd Webber."

87. See Carol Ilson, *Harold Prince: From* Pajama Game *to* Phantom of the Opera, *and Beyond,* 2nd ed. (New York: Limelight Editions, 1992), 271. A personal anecdote: While I was studying Lloyd Webber's scores at the Really Useful Group's headquarters in London, I was privileged to be working in the heart of the office, among the executives in charge of publishing, tours, and the like. (The numbers I heard bandied about on the phones—licensing fees, profits—were dumbfounding.) The office was disrupted by the news that Lloyd Webber, just returned from Italy, had closed a deal to have *The Phantom of the Opera* performed at La Scala in Milan. The staff reacted with resigned shrugs, and it occurred to me that their lack of jubilation revolved around money. I asked how many performances the opera house was planning to do. Eight, I was told, within the regular season. And how many performances does it take to break even, when a new production of *Phantom* opens in a foreign city? Five hundred, they told me. And who was going to lose all that money? Lord Lloyd Webber himself, they said, grinning now, because he's so dedicated to winning respectability.

88. Steyn, *Broadway Babies,* 220.

89. For more discussion of rock music, see Scott Miller, *From* Assassins *to* West Side Story: *The Director's Guide to Musical Theater* (Portsmouth, N.H.: Heinemann, 1996), 124; Joseph P. Swain, *The Broadway Musical: A Critical and Musical Survey* (New York: Oxford University Press, 1990), 360; Steyn, *Broadway Babies,* 220–23; Ethan C. Mordden, "The Once and Future American Opera," *Opera News* 40, no. 2 (August 1975); and Robert Palmer, "The Pop Life: Writing Musicals Attuned to Rock Era," *New York Times,* 10 February 1982.

90. Rice, *Oh, What a Circus,* 422–23.

91. Coveney, *Cats on a Chandelier,* 34.

92. Rice, *Oh, What a Circus,* 2.

93. Ibid., 27.

94. In *Oh, What a Circus,* 32, Rice notes that Mackintosh had been inspired by that same production of *Salad Days* to be in musical theater: "Maybe Cameron was the noisy little pest in front of me who kept jumping out of his seat."

95. Rice, *Oh, What a Circus,* 85 and 90.

96. Ibid., 109.

97. The tale of Rice's firing from the law firm is hilarious; see Rice, *Oh, What a Circus,* 99.

98. Ibid., 340.

99. Rice complains, only half-jestingly, in his autobiography that Lloyd Webber occasionally implied to the press that he was forced to work on other things while waiting for Rice to write lyrics. Rice makes the point several times that lyrics often take longer than music, especially when working with a composer who already has a store of tunes just waiting to be used, and when that tune can easily be repeated for multiple verses. Rice, *Oh, What a Circus,* 402.

100. Ibid., 369.

101. Ibid., 421.

102. On *Jeeves,* see Walsh, *Andrew Lloyd Webber,* 83; McKnight, *Andrew Lloyd Webber,* 150–60; Gänzl, *British Musical Theatre,* 995–97; and Rice, *Oh, What a Circus,* 306. It is of course a lovely parallel that Wodehouse himself was a British writer who achieved great success as a theater lyricist in America. Despite all the talk about Broadway as a fundamentally American endeavor, which was corrupted only by the invasion of the Brits in the 1970s, the groundwork had been laid long ago: "Andrew Lloyd Webber isn't the first British subject to remake the American musical in his own image: P. G. Wodehouse did it 60 years earlier." Steyn, *Broadway Babies,* 51.

103. Rice, *Oh, What a Circus,* 322.

104. Rice to Michael Owen, "A London Hit Arrives—With a Controversial Heroine," *New York Times,* 23 September 1979.

105. Rice, *Oh, What a Circus,* 319–20.

106. Walsh tells us that Lloyd Webber was inspired by seeing a frail, aging Judy Garland stumbling her way through "Over the Rainbow" in concert. He also sees parallels to Mimi's reprise of "Mi chiamano Mimi" in *La Bohème,* a logical inspiration since Lloyd Webber knows his Puccini. Walsh, *Andrew Lloyd Webber,* 97. Coveney's interview with Lloyd Webber revealed that Lloyd Webber's interest in Eva was partly grounded in her early death, which must have infuriated this ambitious woman. "Puccini would have loved her," he said to Coveney. *Cats on a Chandelier,* 70.

107. Gänzl, in a notion similar to that of Catherine Clément in *Opera, or the Undoing of Women,* notes that Eva outsings everyone and is only silenced by death. Kurt Gänzl, *The Musical: A Concise History* (Boston: Northeastern University Press, 1997), 374.

108. For more on the recording of *Evita,* see Rice, *Oh, What a Circus;* and Walsh, *Andrew Lloyd Webber.* On *Evita's* journey to the stage, see Walsh and Rice, and also Owen, "A London Hit Arrives." On Prince, see Hirsch, *Harold Prince,* and Lawrence Thelen, *The Show Makers: Great Directors of the American Musical Theatre* (New York: Routledge, 2000).

109. Rice, *Oh, What a Circus,* 412.

110. *Evita's* trip to New York is recounted in Walsh, *Andrew Lloyd Webber;* Ilson, *Harold Prince;* Frommer and Frommer, *It Happened on Broadway,* 255; and Owen, "A London Hit Arrives."

111. Rice, *Oh, What a Circus,* 419.

112. Swain's analysis is in *Broadway Musical,* 298–307. Other than this handy point, he mostly talks about the "contrafacta," which is his usual topic of choice, and some problems he sees in the score, which in general he likes much less well than *Superstar.*

113. Coveney, *Cats on a Chandelier,* 73–74.

114. John Simon, "Gilding the Argentine," *New York,* 8 October 1979.

115. An uncredited quote in Walsh, *Andrew Lloyd Webber*, 105.

116. Owen, "A London Hit Arrives."

117. Loney, "Don't Cry for Lloyd Webber."

118. Mel Gussow, "London to Broadway: How a Culture Shapes a Show," *New York Times*, 3 February 1980.

119. The article in question is Owen, "A London Hit Arrives." For more on the whole debate, see John Corry, "New Casts Change Broadway Chemistry," *New York Times*, 21 March 1980; Russell Baker, "Broadway Prefers Politicians Who Sing and Dance," *New York Times*, 10 August 1980; Loney, "Don't Cry for Lloyd Webber"; Gänzl, *Concise History*, 375; Coveney, *Cats on a Chandelier*, 80; and Morley, *Spread a Little Happiness*, 191. Also, Walsh's defense is that the glamour and the hideousness are both fully explored in the music, and the problem is that critics are too dumb about music to hear it. The grisly piece of work was fully there; critics just did not see past her mere presence on the stage. It would be like saying Shakespeare supported Macbeth's murderous ways simply by staging them, he argues. Walsh, *Andrew Lloyd Webber*, 108. For a range of reviews of *Evita*'s London opening, see John Peter, "Evita: Glitter of Evil . . ." *Sunday Times* (London), 25 June 1978; Derek Jewell, ". . . and Shimmer of Art," *Sunday Times* (London), 25 June 1978; Robert Cushman, "But what about Argentina?" *Observer*, 25 June 1978; Frank Rich, reporting from London for *Time*, in "Eva Perón, Superstar," *Time*, 21 August 1978; Irving Wardle, "A Puccini heroine captivated by her own dream," *Times* (London), 22 June 1978; and Michael Billington, "For Evita a Prince of quicksilver fluency," *Guardian*, 22 June 1978. Coveney, by the way, claims that *Evita* was particularly relevant in England at the time, thanks to a lack of strong governmental leadership and a generally volatile mood, but no British critics seem to have picked up on the modern parallels. Coveney, *Cats on a Chandelier*, 80–81. However, when *Evita* went to Hungary in the 1980s, the political parallels were widely recognized, and it actually inspired two local rock musicians to write a politically charged show of their own, *King Stephen*, in 1989; it was a massive hit. See Steyn, *Broadway Babies*, 157.

120. Walter Kerr, "Stage: 'Evita,' a Musical Perón," *New York Times*, 26 September 1979; and Kerr, " 'Evita'—A Bold Step Backward," *New York Times*, 7 October 1979.

121. Julius Novick, " 'Evita': Si!" *Village Voice*, 8 October 1979. For a mixed review, see Howard Kissel, "Evita," *Women's Wear Daily*, 26 September 1979. Reviews of *Evita* in New York other than those already mentioned: Douglas Watt, " 'Evita' equals empty and is vulgar to boot," *New York Daily News*, 26 September 1979; Clive Barnes, "A stunning 'Evita' seduces with its gloss," *New York Post*, 26 September 1979; Joel Siegel, "Evita," review on WABC, 26 September 1979, transcribed in *New York Critics' Theatre Reviews;* Edwin Wilson, "Dazzling Production of a Muddled Story," *Wall Street Journal*, 26 September 1979; Jack Kroll, "Evita in Soft Focus," *Newsweek*, 8 October 1979; T. E. Kalem, "Vogue of the Age: Carrion Chic," *Time*, 8 October 1979.

122. Rice, *Oh, What a Circus*, 133–36.

123. Carol Lawson, " 'Joseph,' Rock Musical, Is Returning," *New York Times*, 31 December 1980.

124. Rice, *Oh, What a Circus*, 292.

125. For *Joseph* on Broadway, see Carol Lawson, "Broadway," *New York Times*, 11 December 1981; Alvin Klein, "At 26, Producing 'Joseph' on Broadway," *New York Times*, 3 October 1982; Rice, *Oh, What a Circus;* and Walsh, *Andrew Lloyd Webber.*

126. See John Corry, "Broadway," *New York Times*, 2 April 1982.

127. John Simon, "Save Me from the 'Waltz,' " *New York*, 30 November 1981.

128. Mel Gussow, "Theater: 'Joseph and the Dreamcoat,' " *New York Times,* 19 November 1981.

129. Clive Barnes, " 'Technicolor Dreamcoat' has faded," *New York Post,* 19 November 1981. Other reviews include Don Nelsen, " 'Joseph' is a youthful dream," *New York Daily News,* 19 November 1981; Christopher Sharp, "Full-Length 'Joseph,' " *Women's Wear Daily,* 20 November 1981; Dennis Cunningham, "Joseph and the Amazing Technicolor Dreamcoat," review on WCBS, 18 November 1981, transcribed in *New York Theatre Critics' Reviews,* 1981; Carol Cooper, "Joseph and the Amazing Technicolor Dreamcoat," *Village Voice,* 16–22 December 1981; and Gerald Clarke, "In the Beginning," *Time,* 7 December 1981.

130. Rice, when confronted with the charges of antisemitism in *Superstar,* often cited "Close Every Door" as an example of a song that addresses the fate of the Jews (which the songs in *Superstar,* despite the charges, largely do not). It is a beautiful, and entirely modern, statement in favor of Jews and the nation of Israel. Rice, *Oh, What a Circus,* 140.

131. Ibid., 141. Paul Simon would eventually try his own hand at lyrics for the theater, and the music as well, with his musical *The Capeman.* The lyrics were in true Simon form: unusual, fuzzy, poetic, not always functional. The show was a rather disastrous flop, largely due to its depressing plot.

132. Peter Marks, "Climbing Tooth and Claw to the Top of the Heap," *New York Times,* 15 June 1997.

133. Walsh, *Andrew Lloyd Webber,* 231.

134. Howard Kissel, "Song & Dance," *Women's Wear Daily,* 19 September 1985.

3. "Well, the Theatre Is Certainly Not What It Was"

1. The chapter epigraph comes from Peter Marks, "Climbing Tooth and Claw to the Top of the Heap," *New York Times,* 15 June 1997. David Letterman made the same joke, as cited in Michael Walsh, *Andrew Lloyd Webber: His Life and Works,* 2nd ed. (New York: Harry N. Abrams, 1997), 122, and as cited by John Rockwell, "Andrew Lloyd Webber Superstar," *New York Times,* 20 December 1987. A similar joke—"Is that a promise or a threat?"—is made by Dennis McGowen and Deborah Grace Winer in *Sing Out Louise! 150 Stars of the Musical Theatre Remember 50 Years on Broadway* (New York: Schirmer, 1993), 109. See also Jesse McKinley, " 'Cats,' Broadway's Longevity Champ, to Close," *New York Times,* 20 February 2000.

2. As recounted in Mark Steyn, *Broadway Babies Say Goodnight: Musicals Then and Now* (New York: Routledge, 1997), 281. Steyn gives credit to David Letterman, who was indeed the unofficial leader of the *Cats*-as-cultural-icon movement, but Norm MacDonald told the same joke on "Saturday Night Live," so Steyn may be wrong about this reference. Letterman offered several Top Ten lists concerning *Cats* over the years, and honored its long run by seeing how many cat-costumed people could fit in a coffee shop. *Cats* references have abounded on television shows, including *NYPD Blue, Caroline in the City* (on which the wacky neighbor was a cast member), and *Will and Grace.* For more, see Bruce Weber, "Suit says 'Cats' Character Was Much Too Frisky," *New York Times,* 1 February 1997; and Gerald McKnight, *Andrew Lloyd Webber* (New York: St. Martin's, 1984), 17.

3. Bruce Handy, "Endpaper: Kitty Litter," *New York Times,* 6 March 1994.

4. McKnight, *Andrew Lloyd Webber,* 5.

5. This and the above quote from Walsh, *Andrew Lloyd Webber,* 115.

6. Rockwell, "Andrew Lloyd Webber Superstar."

7. Steyn, *Broadway Babies*, 163.

8. See *Cats: The Book of the Musical* (no authors listed other than Andrew Lloyd Webber and T. S. Eliot) (New York: Harcourt Brace, 1983), 9.

9. Nunn writing in *Cats: The Book*, 10.

10. Walsh, *Andrew Lloyd Webber*, 116.

11. Eliot's widow Valerie Eliot writing in *Cats: The Book*, 7–8.

12. On Valerie Eliot, see Walsh, *Andrew Lloyd Webber*, 117–18.

13. Nunn to Steve Lawson, "Trevor Nunn Reshapes 'Cats' for Broadway," *New York Times*, 3 October 1982. Hal Prince, hoping to work with Lloyd Webber again, was apparently found unsuitable when he failed to grasp the concept behind the show. An amusing, possibly apocryphal exchange has been passed along concerning the possibility of Prince taking the job. Prince asked, "Is it a metaphor? Is one of these cats Disraeli? Gladstone? Queen Victoria? Is this about British politics?" Lloyd Webber responded, "Hal, it's about cats!" In Keith Richmond, *The Musicals of Andrew Lloyd Webber* (London: Virgin, 1995), 73; and Michael Coveney, *Cats on a Chandelier: The Andrew Lloyd Webber Story* (London: Hutchinson, 1999), 88.

14. *Cats: The Book*, 10.

15. See Benedict Nightingale, "A Designer Makes Maverick Worlds," *New York Times*, 2 January 1983.

16. On financing, see Mervyn Rothstein, "For 'Cats,' Nine is the One to Celebrate," *New York Times*, 7 October 1991; and Walsh, *Andrew Lloyd Webber*, 120.

17. The characters in *A Chorus Line* have far more riding on the choice than those in *Cats*, who are not particularly hoping to be reborn and are not actually "auditioning" for the opportunity. On the other hand, at the end of *A Chorus Line*, the entire cast returns for the final number, despite half of them having been cut, so the full ensemble remains intact, as in *Cats*. A reporter for the *New York Times* spotted the similarity in plot and labeled *Cats* "conventional" and "conservative" despite its innovative sheen. Marks, "Tooth and Claw."

18. On Eliot's and Nunn's lyrics, see Eleanor Blau, "Redoing London's 'Cats' for Broadway Opening," *New York Times*, 17 August 1982; Rothstein, "Nine is the One," and Walsh, *Andrew Lloyd Webber*, 118–20. See appendix E for a full listing of text sources.

19. "Eliot's 'Cats' Enjoys Spurt of New Interest," *New York Times*, 8 October 1982.

20. Sheridan Morley, *Spread a Little Happiness: The First Hundred Years of the British Musical* (London: Thames and Hudson, 1987), 201.

21. Walsh, *Andrew Lloyd Webber*, 119.

22. Ibid., 121. Walsh gives no indication of where he got this conversation, and it is rather far-fetched. Why would Bill use dollars? But it is probably true that Andrew Lloyd Webber had a moment of doubt. Coveney claims that "Memory" was meant to be Leoncavallo's work, not Puccini's, in Lloyd Webber's imagined musical on the two composers. It is unclear how he comes to think this, but it is possible that Lloyd Webber had never officially decided the matter, and had simply written a melody in the general style of the era. Coveney, *Cats on a Chandelier*, 90.

23. Coveney, *Cats on a Chandelier*, 120. Also recounted by Nunn himself in McKnight, *Andrew Lloyd Webber*, 209. Mark Steyn agrees that the song fulfills its intended purpose; he labels "Memory" a "take-home song," one which stops the show and which audiences will leave humming, and will live on as a song, separate from its context. Steyn, *Broadway Babies*, 273.

24. On Rice, see Walsh, *Andrew Lloyd Webber,* 120–21. Nunn recounts Rice's role in events in a less flattering light, and his own role is portrayed as a rather noble and long-suffering one, in McKnight, *Andrew Lloyd Webber,* 210–18. Coveney weighs in with a slightly different version from all of the above, in which Rice half-jestingly laments the loss of decades' worth of potential royalties; Coveney, *Cats on a Chandelier,* 92.

25. *Cats: The Book,* 11. For Elaine Paige's story, see also Walsh, *Andrew Lloyd Webber,* 121.

26. Richmond, *Musicals of Lloyd Webber,* 77.

27. Robert Cushman, "The cat's whiskers," *Observer* (London), 17 May 1981.

28. Sheridan Morley, "Possum Power," *Punch* (England), 20 May 1981, 798. While British critics were consistently impressed with both the dancing and the choreography, Frank Rich, reviewing the show for the *New York Times,* reviewed the choreography just as his American peers would do when the show arrived there: it was rather dull and lacked a consistent style that a Bob Fosse, a Tommy Tune, or a Michael Bennett might have brought to it. "For some reason," Rich wrote, "the British generally don't have a knack for pop, showbiz choreography." Frank Rich, "London Readies Some Bundles for Broadway," *New York Times,* 18 July 1982.

29. Cushman, "Cat's whiskers."

30. Michael Billington, "Cats," *Guardian,* 12 May 1981.

31. Derek Jewell, "The Cats' Whiskers," *Sunday Times* (London), 17 May 1981.

32. Irving Wardle, "Flash Cats and Little Sense," *Times* (London), 12 May 1981.

33. James Fenton, "How Mr Eliot's doodles got into a catsuit," *Sunday Times* (London), 17 May 1981.

34. Richmond, *Musicals of Lloyd Webber,* 77.

35. Betty Buckley recounts her tale in Myrna Katz Frommer and Harvey Frommer, *It Happened on Broadway: An Oral History of the Great White Way* (New York: Harcourt Brace, 1998), 9. For more on casting, see "British Musical 'Cats' is Cast for Broadway," *New York Times,* 5 August 1982.

36. Blau, "Redoing London's 'Cats.' "

37. On casting, see also Lawson, "Nunn Reshapes 'Cats' "; McKnight, *Andrew Lloyd Webber,* 6; and *Cats: The Book,* 12.

38. See " 'Cats,' a Hit in London, Sets Broadway Dates," *New York Times,* 21 April 1982; and Walsh, *Andrew Lloyd Webber,* 126.

39. For changes to the theater and the score, see Blau, "Redoing London's 'Cats' "; Lawson, "Nunn Reshapes 'Cats' "; Walsh, *Andrew Lloyd Webber,* 127; and also Jack Kroll with Constance Guthrie, "The 'Cats' Meow on Broadway," *Newsweek,* 11 October 1982.

40. Walsh, *Andrew Lloyd Webber,* 126.

41. Streisand's rendition of "Memory" entered *Billboard*'s Hot 100 chart on 20 February 1982, and reached its peak at number 52 on 27 March.

42. An example of the unusual practice of marketing the composer and other creators, but not the stars: on the first preview day, Nunn and Lynne were on "Good Morning America," and on the opening day, Lloyd Webber and Valerie Eliot appeared on the same program. No performers appeared. Leslie Bennetts, "How Tickets to 'Cats' Became a 'Must,' " *New York Times,* 13 October 1982.

43. Jim Davis, Garfield's cartoonist, had four cartoon anthologies on the *New York Times* paperback bestseller list in the last few weeks of September 1982. Four books at once was a record for any author, but he outdid himself: the *Times*'s list of 10 October,

two days after *Cats* opened on Broadway, featured a fifth Garfield book, which entered the list at number one.

44. On marketing, see Bennetts, "Tickets to 'Cats' "; Walsh, *Andrew Lloyd Webber,* 126; Bernard Rosenberg and Ernest Harburg, *The Broadway Musical: Collaboration in Commerce and Art* (New York: New York University Press, 1993), 200; and McKinley, "Broadway's Longevity Champ."

45. William Grimes, "With 6,138 Lives, 'Cats' Sets Broadway Mark," *New York Times,* 19 June 1997. At a 1999 performance, I was hard pressed to find one English-speaking audience member. Granted, it was also the night the Yankees won the World Series, but it was still a rather odd experience. The house was perhaps half full, and no one but me seemed to know when to applaud. Since I was unable to gather information from those around me, as is my usual habit, I grilled the bartender and the woman selling T-shirts and recordings: they estimated that in recent years, about 70 to 90 percent of the audience was foreign.

46. Grimes, "6,138 Lives." See also Marks, "Tooth and Claw," on marketing.

47. *Cats: The Book,* 10.

48. Ibid., 11.

49. Nunn in Kroll, "The 'Cats' Meow."

50. As is Lloyd Webber's wont, *Cats* has one true rock song which suggests an era of by-gone music. Like Herod's honky-tonk in *Superstar,* and especially like the Elvis-styled Pharaoh in *Joseph,* this is a fun stand-out song. In many productions, and most notably on the 1998 video version of *Cats,* the Rum Tum Tugger suggests not only Mick Jagger, but swaggering rock stars in general and a bit of the *Rocky Horror Picture Show*'s Sweet Transvestite from Transsexual Transylvania.

51. Michael Walsh, it should be noted, is the only scholar to write about the music of *Cats* in any sort of extended way; morning-after critics are the only others who offered any sort of musical commentary or analysis. This might explain why almost every critic, and Walsh himself, dwells far more on the songs about individual cats and their various styles than on the songs about the cats in general, which account for about half the show. Also, after one hearing it is certainly more challenging to comment on the long, complex pieces which make up the Jellicles' self-defining numbers than on the much catchier, explicable singular songs. Nevertheless, Walsh, who clearly had access to a score of some sort, dwells much more at length on the lighter individual songs than on the richer, more rewarding music of the Jellicle numbers. Also, he is not overly fond of the score as a whole, and has a somewhat dismissive attitude toward it throughout his discussion. Sounding much more stodgy than usual, he calls the show "a triumph of special effects and marketing over content and emotion." His distaste leads him to some flippant and erroneous generalizations. He contends, for example, that the score is too often in 4/4 time and in the key of B-flat major. While it is true that the Jellicle theme almost always appears in B-flat major, that key is used in almost no other location (with the exception of "Memory"). Also, while most of the numbers about individual cats are in 4/4 time, virtually none of the others are; 6/8 abounds, for example. Walsh, *Andrew Lloyd Webber,* 122.

52. *Cats: The Book,* 13.

53. As an example of Walsh's bias, here he points out that this ecclesiastical section is in B-flat major (Walsh, *Andrew Lloyd Webber,* 123). This is indeed the case, but it is part of a remarkable key scheme (which Walsh fails to notice) that runs throughout the

piece: it opens in E minor and climbs, dwelling in almost every key along the way, straight up the scale to end in D major.

54. Even Walsh agrees that "Old Deuteronomy" is a lovely song, a "flowing F-major meditation in 6/8"—for him, F major is better than B-flat major, and 6/8 better than 4/4. He calls it the "most memorable" tune besides "Memory."

55. Walsh, his bitterness toward *Cats* showing once again, describes Old Deuteronomy's music as "plodding basso music . . . squarely in the tradition of such operatic holy bores as Mozart's Sarastro and Verdi's Padre Guardiano, although not nearly as distinguished." Walsh, *Andrew Lloyd Webber*, 123. Perhaps "The Moments of Happiness" is somewhat boring, and is not helped by basically nonsensical lyrics. Still, it is brief, and serves its function as mood-setter adequately.

56. This cartoonish sort of sneaky motif reminded more than one writer of Henry Mancini's "Pink Panther" theme. See Kevin Kelly, "The performers are wonderful, but 'Cats' is a dog," *Boston Globe*, 17 October 1982; and Walsh, *Andrew Lloyd Webber*, 123.

57. Michael Feingold, "Kitty Litter," *Village Voice*, 26 October 1982.

58. John Simon, "Mayhem in the Cat(h)edral," *New York*, 18 October 1982.

59. Kevin Kelly of the *Boston Globe* argued that Mozart and Sondheim, for example, are "identifiable through a generalized sound," while Lloyd Webber simply "repeats limited devices." This makes it, Kelly argued, unoriginal but still enjoyable music. How does this work? Sondheim and Lloyd Webber are both simply borrowing stylistic techniques from themselves, and indeed, it seems that Lloyd Webber uses a variety of musical styles whereas Sondheim (if we follow the argument out) always sounds the same. Why is it better that, no matter the dramatic situation, Sondheim always sounds like Sondheim? See Kelly, " 'Cats' is a dog."

60. Walsh, *Andrew Lloyd Webber*, 125–26.

61. As Lynne argues in *Cats: The Book*, 13.

62. Kurt Gänzl, *The Musical: A Concise History* (Boston: Northeastern University Press, 1997), 380.

63. Demeter now participates in this number, and appears also on the British video, but originally Cassandra apparently rounded out the trio, for it is she on the original Broadway cast recording and in the score I received for study from The Really Useful Group. Demeter makes more sense, character-wise.

64. The brief refrain, sung to the text "Skimbleshanks the Railway Cat, the cat of the railway train," is in 13/8 and is quite tricky. Walsh asserts that this promising start leads to disappointment when "the composer loses his nerve and regresses to 4/4." Walsh, *Andrew Lloyd Webber*, 123. Of course it would have been theoretically possible for Lloyd Webber to have continued the 13/8 throughout the piece or to have varied the poetry's inherent meter in some other way, but the train rhythm is so overwhelming in the text that it is hard to fault Lloyd Webber for "losing his nerve" when he bows to the text's demands.

65. *Cats: The Book*, 9.

66. Walsh, as always inclined to dislike the more serious parts of the show, describes the moment this way: Grizabella "comes trudging on, carrying her heavy load of existential angst, over a dotted-rhythm ground bass." But her entrance is "just a passing shudder" this time and we move on. Walsh, *Andrew Lloyd Webber*, 123.

67. All of these Sillabub moments are assigned to others on the original Broadway cast CD: Tantomile sings the first reprise of "Memory," Victoria the second. But in the production today, as is made clear in the program, all these sections are given to Sillabub,

and on the video they are given to her British counterpart, Jemima. Apparently these items were reassigned over the years.

68. See Walsh, *Andrew Lloyd Webber,* 124.

69. Stuart Ostrow, *A Producer's Broadway Journey* (Westport, Conn.: Praeger, 1999), 140.

70. Simon, "Mayhem in the Cat(h)edral."

71. Cushman, "Cat's Whiskers."

72. M. Owen Lee, "Recordings: *The Phantom of the Opera.* Andrew Lloyd Webber," *Opera Quarterly* 6, no. 1 (Autumn 1988): 149. A few others have pointed out to me a possible similarity between "Memory" and *Bolero* over the years, but they acknowledge that the resemblance is fleeting and without significance.

73. Handy, "Kitty Litter," and Walsh, *Andrew Lloyd Webber,* 123.

74. Rich, "Bundles for Broadway."

75. Frank Rich, "Lloyd Webber's 'Cats,' " *New York Times,* 8 October 1982.

76. Regarding Rich's review, Mackintosh reported, apparently directly to Gerald McKnight, "That may not be a great review but it will sell seats. Andrew, I think, is very happy." The idea that the best thing about *Cats,* the thing that makes it worth seeing, is its magical ability to transport the audience, became a battle cry of Lloyd Webber supporters. Biographer McKnight on why *Cats* worked: "What has taken root in the universal consciousness, it seems, is an appetite for magic." McKnight, *Andrew Lloyd Webber,* 19–20.

77. Walter Kerr, "The Spectacle of 'Cats,' Or Inflation Beyond Reason," *New York Times,* 17 October 1982. A similar view to Kerr's is extolled by Robert Brustein, "This 'Money-got, Mechanic Age,' " *New Republic,* 15 November 1982.

78. Theater historian Denny Martin Flinn, generally hostile toward megamusicals and Lloyd Webber, also strongly disliked Lynne's choreography in *Cats.* "Theatre dance could have made the show immensely more exciting," he stated bluntly. Jerome Robbins, Michael Bennett, Michael Kidd, or Bob Fosse all could have brought more personal style and more cat style to the dancing. Instead, Lynne used "the tap, modern, and ballet vocabularies that the American musical gave up in the 1940s, and she staged the numbers like the musical pastiches they are, denying the show a style of its own." Denny Martin Flinn, *Musical! A Grand Tour: The Rise, Glory, and Fall of an American Institution* (New York: Schirmer, 1997), 478. As with so many other critics, Flinn ignores the huge portions of the show that are not pastiche numbers.

79. Feingold, "Kitty Litter." For two other negative (though less hostile) reviews, see Kelly, " 'Cats' is a dog," who admired the cast but little else; and Joel Siegel, who praised only the score, in his television review on WABC, 7 October 1982, as transcribed in *The New York Theatre Critics' Reviews,* 1982.

80. This was a book of rather mean-spirited anti-cat activities by Simon Bond. It had occupied the number one spot on the bestseller list for ten weeks the previous summer, and had remained on the chart for a year. Even before *Cats,* then, the culture's cat trend already had experienced a backlash.

81. Clive Barnes, " 'Cats': It's quite a musical but hardly purr-fect," *New York Post,* 8 October 1982. Several years later, Barnes would declare *Cats* Lloyd Webber's best work to that point, and would admit to being rather too tough on his shows in general, although he still had his reservations. As told to McKnight, *Andrew Lloyd Webber,* 141.

82. Simon, "Mayhem in the Cat(h)edral." Edwin Wilson of the *Wall Street Journal* echoed Simon point for point, finding the numbers overly dazzling and large, and the

music delightful but too much for Eliot's texts. Edwin Wilson, "Tim Webber [*sic*] Brings His Curious 'Cats' to Broadway," *Wall Street Journal,* 8 October 1982. Similar mixed reviews praising the cast but finding the concept overblown include Howard Kissel, "Cats," *Women's Wear Daily,* 8 October 1982; Douglas Watt, " 'Cats': Not quite purr-fect," *New York Daily News,* 8 October 1982; and T. E. Kalem, "O That Anthropomorphical Rag," *Time,* 18 October 1982.

83. Brendan Gill, "Homage to Cats," *New Yorker,* 18 October 1982.

84. Kroll, "The 'Cats' Meow." Another full-out rave, which basically listed all the show's elements and then said they were all great, came from Dennis Cunningham, television review on WCBS, 7 October 1982, as transcribed in *The New York Theatre Critics' Reviews,* 1982.

85. The *New York Times* noted that being dead for eighteen years had not been a handicap in Eliot's writing of lyrics and book for a new musical, and implied with pleasure that it was quite in keeping with the sorts of people (somehow "dead") who wrote and produced musicals and voted for Tonys. Russell Baker, "And His Mouth So Prim," *New York Times,* 25 May 1983.

86. Rosenberg and Harburg, *Collaboration,* 63.

87. Bennetts, "Tickets to 'Cats.' "

88. Walsh, *Andrew Lloyd Webber,* 128.

89. Leslie Bennetts, "The Hazardous Lives of Cats on Broadway," *New York Times,* 29 August 1983; and Nina Darnton, "When Every Night Has to Be Opening Night," *New York Times,* 14 July 1985.

90. Peter Marks, "Broadway's Anonymous Stars," *New York Times,* 2 February 1996.

91. Vincent Canby, "Two on the Aisle, Yes, but Which Aisle?" *New York Times,* 6 March 1994.

92. Peter Marks, "5,001 Broadway Nights: Shows With 9 Lives," *New York Times,* 17 January 1997.

93. Lawson, "Trevor Nunn."

94. Handy, "Kitty Litter."

95. Rothstein, "Nine is the One."

96. Glenn Collins, "Cats with 10 Lives," *New York Times,* 4 October 1992.

97. Daniel B. Schneider, "The 15 Lives of 'Cats,' " *New York Times,* 6 October 1996.

98. Weber, "Much Too Frisky."

99. Marks, "Tooth and Claw."

100. William Grimes, "Purring Over a New Broadway Record," *New York Times,* 20 June 1997.

101. William Grimes, "On Stage, and Off," *New York Times,* 14 March 1997, and Grimes, "Purring."

102. For more thoughts on the video, see Stephen Holden, "More Intimate 'Cats,' " *New York Times,* 1 November 1998; and Peter Marks, "Broadway's 'Cats': Restaged for Eternity," *New York Times* television guide, 1 November 1998.

103. See McKinley, "Broadway's Longevity Champ"; Alan Feuer, "18 Years of 'Cats,' but Ticket Demand Surges for Final Shows," *New York Times,* 22 February 2000; and Jesse McKinley, "On Stage and Off: A 10th Life for 'Cats'?" *New York Times,* 25 February 2000. For other features on the closing, see Rick Marin, "Four City Mice Who Had to See 'Cats,' "

New York Times, 5 March 2000; Joyce Wadler, "A Cat Now and for 17 Years (Nearly Forever)," *New York Times,* 25 February 2000; and Robin Pogrebin, "Nine Lives, Nine Memories," *New York Times,* 21 April 2000.

104. *Cats: The Book,* 12.

105. Flinn, *Musical! A Grand Tour,* 479.

106. Grimes, "6,138 Lives."

107. Steyn, *Broadway Babies,* 164.

108. Walsh, *Andrew Lloyd Webber,* 118. Walsh exaggerates to make his point—for example, a Beatles tribute show (similar to the "jukebox shows" currently popular) called *Beatlemania* opened in 1977—but Lloyd Webber's work did embody a youthfulness few could deny.

109. Ibid., 125.

110. "It is simply not true that the musical did not travel well," writes Walsh. "It was the *book* musical, whose disappearance the American drama critics were forever bemoaning, that was difficult to export." Walsh, *Andrew Lloyd Webber,* 125.

111. Ibid., 125.

112. Barnes, "Hardly purr-fect."

113. McKnight, *Andrew Lloyd Webber,* 233.

4. "To Love Another Person Is to See the Face of God"

1. Gradually, the show became known in most print media as *Les Miz* rather than *Les Mis.* The *New York Times* made the switch almost two years into the show's run, switched back two years later, and settled once again on *Miz* the year after that. Edward Behr, author of the only full-length book on this show, calls it *Les Mis.* Producer Stuart Ostrow gives the credit for *Miz* to *Variety,* which seems plausible. See Edward Behr, *Les Misérables: History in the Making,* updated ed. (New York: Arcade, 1996); Mervyn Rothstein, "To Avoid Scalpers, Try the Box Office," *New York Times,* 24 January 1989; Alan Riding, "Parisians Flock To See 'Les Mis,' " *New York Times,* 30 October 1991; Alan Riding, " 'Les Miz': Of and By But Not For the French," *New York Times,* 16 May 1992; and Stuart Ostrow, *A Producer's Broadway Journey* (Westport, Conn.: Praeger, 1999), 145.

2. Behr, *History in the Making,* 47. Behr's book serves a similar function for *Les Mis* as Michael Walsh's book on Lloyd Webber; while sometimes chatty and clearly intended for the coffee table, it features interviews with all the key players and gathers a good deal of information (though without citations of any kind) in one place.

3. On Schönberg, see Behr, *History in the Making,* 47. Schönberg is distantly related to composer Arnold Schönberg.

4. Ibid., 47.

5. Ibid., 50.

6. Leslie Bennetts, " 'Les Misérables' Ready For Its American Debut," *New York Times,* 20 May 1986.

7. Behr, *History in the Making,* 21.

8. Sidebar to Jeremy Gerard, "The Hunter and the Hunted," *New York Times,* 8 March 1987.

9. See Behr, *History in the Making,* 149–51.

10. Ibid., 50–51. Behr notes that Jean-Marc Natel helped with the lyrics and received credit as co-writer, but Behr does not define his contributions.

11. Ibid., 51. For more on the lithograph, see Behr, 192.

12. Ibid., 62–63.

13. Jeremy Gerard, "A Trans-Atlantic Producer Calls the Tune," *New York Times,* 7 December 1986.

14. Nunn speaks of his ideas about commercial theater in "The Magician Theatre Angels Love," *Observer* (London), 13 October 1985.

15. Behr, *History in the Making,* 67; for more on the RSC, see 63–67.

16. See ibid., 71–78.

17. Michael Coveney, *Cats on a Chandelier: The Andrew Lloyd Webber Story* (London: Hutchinson, 1999), 91.

18. Behr, *History in the Making,* 83; for more on Kretzmer's work, see 79–82.

19. Kretzmer as quoted in ibid., 86.

20. Nunn as quoted in ibid., 87.

21. Ibid., 87. As Behr notes (143), large sections lost between the Barbican and the Palace included most of Gavroche's song "Little People," which made sense—as Caird points out, it is not appropriate (or funny) for Gavroche to sing about the joys of being short "on the eve of an insurrection." But Caird regrets, rightly, the loss of the meeting between Valjean and Cosette, featuring the beautiful contrapuntal "Castle on a Cloud." The complete symphonic recording includes this number.

22. Ibid., 106; on casting, see also 94–95.

23. Jack Kroll, "A Show of All Shows," *Newsweek,* 30 March 1987. See also Behr, *History in the Making,* 98, 103.

24. I confess that I am more partial to this effect than others; in 2004 some of my students at Carnegie Mellon University, including those engaged in intensive graduate scenic design studies, described this moment as Javert leaping into a giant flushing toilet. Thanks to the revolving floor, the river does indeed have a bit of a circular swirl to it.

25. Behr, *History in the Making,* 140–42.

26. Irving Wardle, "Spectacular Boldness," *Times* (London), 10 October 1985.

27. Michael Billington, "Fugitives from a Chain-Gang Melodrama," *Guardian,* 10 October 1985.

28. Michael Ratcliffe, "Victor Hugo on the Garbage Dump," *Observer,* 13 October 1985. For one more rather negative mixed review, see Benedict Nightingale, "Come To-gether," *New Statesman,* 18 October 1985.

29. John Peter, "Adult Spectacle," *Sunday Times* (London), 13 October 1985.

30. Michael Coveney, "Les Misérables," *Financial Times,* 9 October 1985. Coveney, as we have seen, enjoys megamusicals, and would later write *Cats on a Chandelier,* a biography of Andrew Lloyd Webber already familiar from previous chapters of this work.

31. Sheridan Morley, " 'Les Misérables': Blazing Theatricality," *International Herald Tribune,* 16 October 1985. Two other positive reviews of the London opening came from visiting American critics, and both would help pave a smooth way for *Les Mis* to transfer to Broadway. Frank Rich of the *New York Times,* not a fan of Lloyd Webber's megamusicals thus far, enjoyed *Les Mis* specifically because it had a new sound, less pop-driven and more operatic than Lloyd Webber's. Like most, Rich admired the staging. Also, William A. Henry III of *Time* delivered a strong rave, praising the show's style, score, storytelling, staging, and emotional impact. See Frank Rich, "The Stage: Three London Musicals," *New York Times,* 20 May 1986; and William A. Henry III, "A Jubilant Cry from the Gutter," *Time,* 21 October 1985.

32. Sheridan Morley, *Spread a Little Happiness: The First Hundred Years of the British*

Musical (London: Thames and Hudson, 1987), 205–206. Theater historian Denny Martin Flinn had the exact opposite reaction to the London opening of *Les Mis,* declaring it "the dullest seen on a musical stage in years." Never one to be persuaded of a megamusical's charms, Flinn finds *Les Mis* just as annoying as almost every other musical of the 1980s. Denny Martin Flinn, *Musical! A Grand Tour: The Rise, Glory, and Fall of an American Institution* (New York: Schirmer, 1997), 479–80.

33. Gerard, "Trans-Atlantic Producer."

34. Brooke Kroeger, "Raising a Million for 'Les Mis,' " *New York Times,* 19 July 1987.

35. As quoted in Geraldine Fabrikant, " 'Misérables' Already a Financial Hit," *New York Times,* 2 March 1987.

36. Behr, *History in the Making,* 144.

37. See Jeremy Gerard, "The Hunter and the Hunted."

38. Jeremy Gerard, "Already, 'Misérables' Is a Box-Office Marve," *New York Times,* 17 January 1987.

39. Fabrikant, "Financial Hit."

40. This chapter discusses some of the highlights of the recurring musical ideas; for a more complete listing, see appendix G.

41. Stephen Citron agrees that Valjean's voice stretches toward God, and adds that the melody feels particularly risky and vulnerable because of its opening octave leap into the upper register. Stephen Citron, *The Musical from the Inside Out,* rev. ed. (Chicago: Ivan R. Dee, 1992), 82.

42. For more on voice types in *Les Mis,* see Kurt Gänzl, *The Musical: A Concise History* (Boston: Northeastern University Press, 1997), 395–96.

43. Frank Rich, "Stage: 'Misérables,' Musical Version Opens on Broadway," *New York Times,* 19 March 1987.

44. Jack Kroll, "Revolution on Broadway," *Newsweek,* 23 March 1987.

45. William A. Henry III, "An Epic of the Downtrodden," *Time,* 23 March 1987. For other raves, see John Beaufort, " 'Les Misérables' on stage: spectacle and more," *Christian Science Monitor,* 13 March 1987; Jack Curry, " 'Les Miz' sends spirits soaring," *USA Today,* 13 March 1987; and Joel Siegel, "Les Misérables," review on WABC, 12 March 1987, transcribed in the *New York Theatre Critics' Reviews,* 1987.

46. Clive Barnes, "Smashing!" *New York Post,* 13 March 1987.

47. John Simon, "Victor Victorious," *New York,* 23 March 1987. Other mixed reviews include Edwin Wilson, "The Trouble With High Tech," *Wall Street Journal,* 16 March 1987; and Alan Wallach, " 'Les Miserables' Arrives as Pop Opera," *New York Newsday,* 13 March 1987.

48. Michael Feingold, "Hugo Your Way, I'll Go Mine," *Village Voice,* 24 March 1987. For other (less hostile) pans, see Edith Oliver, "Tous Les Misérables," *New Yorker,* 23 March 1987; Howard Kissel, "A Rabble Rouser," *New York Daily News,* 13 March 1987; and David Lida, " 'Les Miserables'—a review," *Women's Wear Daily,* 13 March 1987.

49. As quoted in Victoria Churchville, " 'Les Miz' Plays to Its Toughest Critics," *Washington Post,* 8 September 1988. See also Michael Wines, " 'Les Mis' Brightens Day for Outcasts," *New York Times,* 18 May 1988.

50. Leslie Bennetts, "Marketing 'Les Misérables,' Or, Maneuvering Behind a Hit," *New York Times,* 20 August 1987.

51. Behr, *History in the Making,* 144–45.

52. Ibid., 153.

53. See Alan Riding's two articles in the *New York Times,* mentioned in note 1 above.

54. Mark Steyn, *Broadway Babies Say Goodnight: Musicals Then and Now* (New York: Routledge, 1997), 157. Hugo's characters had already found political lives outside the novel, at least in France: when workers in Paris rebelled in an uprising in 1871, the conservative government killed thousands, shouting, "Down with Jean Valjean." Behr, *History in the Making,* 24. A modern usage: the *Washington Post* featured an article on the nature of a new kind of political gathering, the "Noble Crowd," a descendant of protesting crowds throughout history. The article ran under a sizeable Cosette drawing, altered so that she sported a Chinese headband. Charles Paul Freund, "Rise of the Noble Crowd: The Legacy of Tiananmen Square," *Washington Post,* 4 June 1989.

55. As quoted in Behr, *History in the Making,* 159.

56. Behr, for example, cites the *Tampa Tribune,* which declares *Les Mis* the "best theatre on the road." Behr, *History in the Making,* 146–47.

57. Joe Brown, "McMiz: Mass Marketing the 'Musical Sensation,' " *Washington Post,* 3 July 1988. Recently, local groups have been granted the rights to apply for a license to perform *Les Mis,* and Music Theatre International even offers a "school version." According to Behr, 3,000 theaters and schools applied for the rights before they even became available.

58. Frank Rich, " 'Fences' and 'Les Mis': After a Year's Run, Changes and Constants," *New York Times,* 16 March 1988.

59. See Mervyn Rothstein, "To Avoid Scalpers, Try the Box Office," *New York Times,* 24 January 1989.

60. Mel Gussow, "From 'Les Misérables' To Just Plain Miserable," *New York Times,* 30 October 1996.

61. Peter Marks, "Act IV, Years Later: The Cast Battles Time," *New York Times,* 5 November 1996.

62. The saga of the recasting includes the two articles above, as well as William Grimes, "After 10 Years, 'Miz' Is Replacing Cast," *New York Times,* 29 October 1996; William Grimes, "Union Kept 'Miz' Cast In the Dark On Change," *New York Times,* 2 November 1996; and Peter Marks, "A Happier 'Les Misérables,' " *New York Times,* 13 March 1997. See also Elizabeth Sharland, *The British on Broadway: Backstage and Beyond—The Early Years* (Somerset, England: Barbican, 1999), 59.

63. Brown, "McMiz."

64. Behr, *History in the Making,* 156–59.

65. Ibid., 160.

66. Mackintosh, who wrote the foreword to Behr's *History in the Making,* 7.

67. As quoted in Behr, *History in the Making,* 39 and 42.

68. Joe Brown, " 'Les Miz's' Grand Reprise," *Washington Post,* 11 July 1988.

5. "The Angel of Music Sings Songs in My Head"

1. Michael Walsh, *Andrew Lloyd Webber: His Life and Works,* updated and enlarged ed. (New York: Harry N. Abrams, 1997), 173.

2. Prisoners, says George C. Perry, *The Complete Phantom of the Opera* (New York: Henry Holt, 1988), 28. The perhaps more qualified Leonard Wolf asserts that the French used the Opéra for storing food. Leonard Wolf, *The Essential Phantom of the Opera* (New York: Plume, 1996), 26. Wolf's book contains Leroux's full novel, nicely annotated.

3. Perry, *The Complete Phantom of the Opera,* 30.

4. Mel Gussow, "The Phantom's Many Faces Over the Years," *New York Times,* 30 January 1988.

5. Ibid.

6. Walsh, *Andrew Lloyd Webber,* 178. For more on the competition and Hart's contributions, see Michael Coveney, *Cats on a Chandelier: The Andrew Lloyd Webber Story* (London: Hutchinson, 1999), 129–30.

7. Tom Sutcliffe, "Prince, the Phantom and the opera," *Guardian,* 10 October 1986. On Prince's comeback, see also Carol Ilson, *Harold Prince: From* Pajama Game *to* Phantom of the Opera, *and Beyond,* 2nd ed. (New York: Limelight Editions, 1992), 2.

8. Ilson, *Harold Prince,* 344.

9. Walsh, *Andrew Lloyd Webber,* 177.

10. These statistics and tales of the opera house are gathered from Perry, *The Complete Phantom of the Opera,* 11, 21; and Walsh, *Andrew Lloyd Webber,* 177–78, 183. There was also an actual chandelier incident, at the Theatre Lyrique; the chandelier itself fell during a play on a man, killing him, on 22 November 1888. Recounted in Wolf, *The Essential Phantom of the Opera,* 122.

11. Harold Prince in an interview with Benedict Nightingale, "Conjuring an Eerie World for the Phantom," *New York Times,* 24 January 1988. See also Ilson, *Harold Prince,* 347.

12. Prince to Nightingale, "Conjuring an Eerie World."

13. Foster Hirsch, *Harold Prince and the American Musical Theatre* (Cambridge: Cambridge University Press, 1989), 166.

14. Ibid., 168.

15. Coveney, *Cats on a Chandelier,* 124.

16. The *New York Times* monitored the entire affair with close attention in a series of articles by Jeremy Gerard and in smaller updates. They are found on 24 June 1987, 25 June 1987, 26 June 1987, 1 July 1987, 2 July 1987, and 3 July 1987. See also Walsh, *Andrew Lloyd Webber,* 206. The bargain was fulfilled when Lloyd Webber cast two American women as the leads in the original London cast of *Aspects of Love.*

17. Frank Rich, "When British Push Comes to Broadway Shove," *New York Times,* 2 July 1987.

18. It usually takes millions of dollars for a theater to prepare for a touring company of *Phantom,* but the hosting city will gain millions back in ticket sales and related income. Also, now that Lloyd Webber has learned the value of producing and managing his own productions, and with the Really Useful Group running things, quality control is extremely strong in tours.

19. For these and other statistics, see Mervyn Rothstein, " 'Phantom of Opera' Wins Seven Tonys; Best Play: 'Butterfly,' " *New York Times,* 6 June 1988; Dinitia Smith, "The Chandelier That Earned $1.5 Billion," *New York Times,* 18 October 1995; Nadine Brozan, "Chronicle," *New York Times,* 11 October 1996; and Michael Walsh, "Magician of the Musical," *Time,* 18 January 1988.

20. John Rockwell, "Andrew Lloyd Webber Superstar," *New York Times,* 20 December 1987.

21. Lloyd Webber to Walsh, "Magician of the Musical." For more on whether *Phantom* is strictly an opera, especially because of its sung-through score, see Chris Pasles, "Andrew Lloyd Webber and The Phantom: A new kind of opera?" *Opera Canada* 30, no. 3 (Fall 1989): 19; Steven Suskin, *Show Tunes 1905–1991: The Songs, Shows and Careers*

of Broadway's Major Composers, rev. ed. (New York: Limelight, 1992), 603; and Stephen Citron, *The Musical from the Inside Out,* rev. ed. (Chicago: Ivan R. Dee, 1992), 37, 80–81.

22. Rockwell, "Andrew Lloyd Webber Superstar."

23. Walsh, *Andrew Lloyd Webber,* 202. As usual with Walsh, his reasons for feeling this way largely involve Lloyd Webber's key structure.

24. Mark Steyn, *Broadway Babies Say Goodnight: Musicals Then and Now* (New York: Routledge, 1997), 286.

25. Barrymore Laurence Scherer, "In Review: from around the world," *Opera News* 52, no. 17 (June 1988): 32.

26. Walsh, "Magician of the Musical."

27. It is true that the first four notes do echo those in *Brigadoon,* but the two songs then diverge completely, and they embody (as Walsh points out) such different moods and contexts that the similarity is not particularly interesting. Walsh, *Andrew Lloyd Webber,* 13. On this, see also Gussow, "The Phantom's Many Faces," and Denny Martin Flinn, *Musical! A Grand Tour: The Rise, Glory, and Fall of an American Institution* (New York: Schirmer, 1997), 474. For other composers from whom critics feel Lloyd Webber borrowed, see M. Owen Lee, "Recordings: *The Phantom of the Opera.* Andrew Lloyd Webber," *Opera Quarterly* 6, no. 1 (Autumn 1988): 150. (Lee suggests, without citing any places in the score, Puccini, Bach, Humperdinck, Rodgers, and Loewe.)

28. Walsh, *Andrew Lloyd Webber,* 180. Similarly, George Perry senses Lloyd Webber's delight in "faking part of a Meyerbeer-esque grand opera, *Hannibal,* with a scenic elephant, a demented soprano and a chorus line of slave girls." Perry, *The Complete Phantom of the Opera,* 78. Perry notes (11) that Meyerbeer's *Le Prophète* features roller skating, meant to simulate outdoor ice skating. In *Phantom,* Lloyd Webber parodies Meyerbeer, but his previous show, *Starlight Express,* featured roller skating—meant to simulate trains—as its main attraction.

29. Michael Feingold of the *Village Voice* was particularly offended by this stylistic inconsistency; he points out that "the reigning diva absurdly warbles, not mock Massenet or Saint-Saens, but a tacky 1850s-style parlor song of the Balfé or Stephen Foster kind, which gets even absurder when a huge cadenza is tacked onto the end of it, like a silk brocade train on a Benetton tennis dress." Feingold, "The Ghosts of Music Past," *Village Voice,* 2 February 1988. For the record, the cadenza is quite brief (at least in Christine's rendition; one can only wonder what Carlotta's would have sounded like), and neither Massenet nor Saint-Saëns had made their mark on opera by 1861, so an 1850s style is quite appropriate, even if it diverges from Meyerbeer's.

30. On this see, for example, George Perry, *The Complete Phantom of the Opera,* 11.

31. As quoted in ibid., 70.

32. Several writers find that *Don Juan Triumphant* reminds them of Britten, and one thinks of Stravinsky's *The Rake's Progress.* See Walsh, *Andrew Lloyd Webber,* 184; Lee, "Recordings"; and Michael Ratcliffe, "Tinsel terror at the Opera," *Observer* (London), 12 October 1986.

33. Admirers of "Prima Donna" and the other large ensembles with operatic features such as "Notes II" include Lee, "Recordings"; Perry, *The Complete Phantom of the Opera,* 78; and Kurt Gänzl, *The Musical: A Concise History* (Boston: Northeastern University Press, 1997), 386.

34. Walsh, *Andrew Lloyd Webber,* 183. Walsh, as usual, focuses most of his musical analysis on the keys of each set number, pointing out Lloyd Webber's use of D-flat major

for important numbers ("All I Ask of You" and "The Music of the Night," although the latter is notated in C-sharp major), but also the mood-setting effects of a multitude of dark flat keys and the quite frequent use of chromatic and whole-tone scales, which often renders the tonality vague. For a few other comments on the music, largely focusing on song forms, see Citron, *The Musical from the Inside Out.*

35. I have always assumed that the actors playing the Phantom and Christine actually sing this portion of the song backstage, and body doubles walk along the dark ramps, although Lloyd Webber's production staff remains silent on the point. Practical motivations abound for such an idea; the ramps are dark and dangerous, and the song is strenuous. The only drawback to this staging solution is the noticeable shift in sound quality.

36. Lloyd Webber, quoted by Smith, "Chandelier."

37. This and all subsequent quotes from Rich's review come from Frank Rich, "Stage: 'Phantom of the Opera,' " *New York Times,* 27 January 1988.

38. David Shannon of London's *Today,* as quoted in Walsh, *Andrew Lloyd Webber,* 204. For similar suggestions that Lloyd Webber engaged in autobiography, see Rockwell, "Andrew Lloyd Webber Superstar"; Hirsch, *Harold Prince,* 171; and Steyn, *Broadway Babies,* 285–86.

39. John Simon, "What Price Majesty?" *New York,* 8 February 1988.

40. Feingold, "The Ghosts of Music Past." For another hostile negative review, see John Peter, "There Is a World Elsewhere," *Sunday Times* (London), 12 October 1986.

41. Walter Kerr, "Now, About That Chandelier That Goes Crashing," *New York Times,* 14 February 1988.

42. William A. Henry III, "Music of the Night," *Time,* 8 February 1988.

43. For other mixed reviews, see David Lida, *Women's Wear Daily,* 27 January 1988; David Patrick Stearns, "Masked man steals 'Phantom,' " *USA Today,* 27 January 1988; and Mimi Kramer, "The Phantom of Broadway," *New Yorker,* 8 February 1988.

44. Howard Kissel, "A Grand 'Opera': 'Phantom' is Phun," *New York Daily News,* 27 January 1988.

45. Jack Kroll, "The 'Phantom' Hits Broadway," *Newsweek,* 8 February 1988.

46. Clive Barnes, "Phabulous 'Phantom,' " *New York Post,* 27 January 1988. More raves: Allan Wallach, "Manifold Delights in the 'Phantom,' " *New York Newsday,* 27 January 1988; Doug Watt, " 'Phantom': Close, But No Opera," *New York Daily News,* 27 January 1988; David Richards, "The Seductive Spell of 'Phantom,' " *Washington Post,* 27 January 1988; Joel Siegel, review on WABC, 26 January 1988, transcribed in *The New York Theatre Critics' Reviews,* 1988; and John Beaufort, "Why 'Phantom' is an immediate hit," *Christian Science Monitor,* 27 January 1988.

47. Michael Coveney, "The Phantom of the Opera/Her Majesty's," *Financial Times,* 10 October 1986.

48. Michael Billington, "The murders in Leroux's morgue," *Guardian,* 11 October 1986. For another glowing review, see Sheridan Morley, "A Fright at the Opera," *Punch,* 22 October 1986.

49. Irving Wardle, "God's gift to musical theatre," *London Times,* 10 October 1986.

50. Coveney, "The Phantom of the Opera." Crawford also receives praise in Ratcliffe, "Tinsel Terror," and Morley, "A Fright at the Opera."

51. Henry, "Music of the Night."

52. Siegel, television review.

53. Kramer, "The Phantom of Broadway."

54. Respectively, Barnes, "Phabulous 'Phantom,' " and Watt, "Close, But No Opera." Others who found Brightman fine include Kroll, Kramer, Kissel, and Wallach.

55. Ratcliffe, "Tinsel Terror."

56. Biographer Coveney notes that expenses for dry ice and light bulbs alone are formidable, and he felt that things may have gotten more lax in recent years; when he saw a performance around 1999, he noted that there seemed to be a shortage of make-up for the Phantom, making him look like "Bart Simpson covered in chocolate." Coveney, *Cats on a Chandelier,* 255.

57. See Jesse McKinley, "Revised 'Phantom' Going to Las Vegas," *New York Times,* 25 July 2004.

6. "A Model of Decorum and Tranquility"

1. Frank Rich, "The Stage: Three London Musicals," *New York Times,* 20 May 1986.

2. Frank Rich, "In London, Theater That Mirrors Britain Today," *New York Times,* 15 June 1986.

3. *Time* was written by Dave Clark, and starred Cliff Richard. On *Time,* see Sheridan Morley, *Spread a Little Happiness: The First Hundred Years of the British Musical* (London: Thames and Hudson, 1987), 212.

4. Rice's liner notes to the *Blondel* CD, by Stephen Oliver and Tim Rice (MCA Records, MCD11486, copyright 1983, CD released 1996).

5. Tim Rice, lyrics included in CD booklet with 1996 release.

6. Michael Coveney, "Blondel/Old Vic," *Financial Times,* 11 November 1983.

7. See [AP], "Old Vic Show Criticized," *New York Times,* 13 November 1983.

8. This and all lyrics from *Chess* can be found in the booklet that accompanies *Chess: Original Broadway Cast Recording* (RCA Victor, 7700-2-RC, 1988).

9. For background on *Chess* in London, see Samuel G. Freedman, "Shuberts Win Battle For the Musical 'Chess,' " *New York Times,* 11 September 1985; Nan Robertson, "Michael Bennett Leaves Musical," *New York Times,* 23 January 1986; and Dena Kleiman, "Trevor Nunn to Direct 'Chess,' " *New York Times,* 28 January 1986.

10. Jeremy Gerard, "Musical 'Chess' Postponed Indefinitely," *New York Times,* 31 December 1987.

11. As quoted in Stephen Holden, " 'Chess' Seeks To Shed Its Checkered Past," *New York Times,* 24 April 1988.

12. Frank Rich, "In Trevor Nunn's Musical 'Chess,' East Faces West Across a Board," *New York Times,* 29 April 1988.

13. Jack Kroll, "Checkmate in Two Acts," *Newsweek,* 9 May 1988.

14. William A. Henry III, "Bold Gambit by a Grand Master," *Time,* 9 May 1988. For another mostly positive review, see Linda Winer, "For Broadway, 'Chess' Is a Love Match," *New York Newsday,* 29 April 1988.

15. Clive Barnes, "Checkered musical of chess," *New York Post,* 29 April 1988. For other (mostly mixed) reviews, see Howard Kissel, " 'Chess' Bored," *New York Daily News,* 29 April 1988; Douglas Watt, "Few Good Moves in 'Chess,' " *New York Daily News,* 6 May 1988; David Patrick Stearns, "This match is a stalemate," *USA Today,* 29 April 1988; Edwin Wilson, [no title], *Wall Street Journal,* 4 May 1988; and Joel Siegel, review of *Chess* on WABC, 28 April 1988. Interestingly, Siegel noted that in a musical in which an entire act took place in Bangkok, the cast contained only two Asian-American actors. With the

coming of *Miss Saigon* several years later, such casting issues would become an extremely contested topic.

16. Michael Kimmelman, "Broadway's New Realpolitik," *New York Times,* 22 May 1988.

17. Mervyn Rothstein, "Trims Are Made in 'Chess,' Saving Time and Money," *New York Times,* 5 May 1988.

18. Robert Hewison, "Meccano Musical," *Sunday Times* (London), 1 April 1984. For more reviews from London, most of them in the mixed-to-low category, see Irving Wardle, "Monument to the power of steam," *Times* (London), 28 March 1984; Michael Ratcliffe, "Rollermouse rock," *Observer,* 1 April 1984; Michael Coveney [no title], *Financial Times,* 28 March 1984; and Michael Billington, "The blockbuster that ran out of steam," *Guardian,* 28 March 1984. The only rave came from Derek Jewell, who could be relied on to like everything Lloyd Webber and/or Rice wrote, because he had discovered them back in the *Joseph* days. Derek Jewell, "The Art of Writing Hits," *Sunday Times* (London), 1 April 1984. Michael Walsh points out that at this point, Jewell seems to have lost all objectivity because of his role in Lloyd Webber's career, apparently not considering the possibility that Jewell genuinely liked the show. See Michael Walsh, *Andrew Lloyd Webber: His Life and Works,* 2nd ed. (New York: Harry N. Abrams, 1993), 162.

19. Dena Kleiman, "Preparing for Arrival of 'Starlight Express,'" *New York Times,* 23 December 1986. For more on the set, as well as issues of advertising and money, see Stephen Holden, " 'Starlight Express' Rolls to Market With a Rock Beat," *New York Times,* 1 March 1987.

20. Paul Goldberger, "Design: The Risks of Razzle-Dazzle," *New York Times,* 12 April 1987.

21. As quoted in Walsh, *Andrew Lloyd Webber,* 165.

22. The review from London: Frank Rich, "The Theater: 'Starlight' and an 'Animal Farm,'" *New York Times,* 25 July 1984. The New York review: Frank Rich, "Stage: Andrew Lloyd Webber's 'Starlight Express,'" *New York Times,* 16 March 1987.

23. John Simon, "Railway Disaster," *New York,* 30 March 1987.

24. William A. Henry III, "Toward the Freight Yards of Fiasco," *Time,* 30 March 1987. For mixed reviews, see Edwin Wilson, "The Trouble With High Tech," *Wall Street Journal,* 16 March 1987; and Allan Wallach, " 'Express': It's The Musical On Wheels," *New York Newsday,* 16 March 1987. For pans, see Edith Oliver, "The Theatre: Staggerlee and Company," *New Yorker,* 30 March 1987; Erika Munk, "Out of Service," *Village Voice,* 24 March 1987; Howard Kissel, " 'Express' Heading Nowhere," *New York Daily News,* 16 March 1987; Douglas Watt, "Oh, for a Good Two-Character Comedy: 'Starlight' Leaves You Skate Bored," *New York Daily News,* 20 March 1987; and Clive Barnes, "Roller 'Disney,'" *New York Post,* 16 March 1987. The only rave came from John Beaufort, "Wow! Roller-skating extravaganza bids for audiences of all ages," *Christian Science Monitor,* 18 March 1987.

25. Walsh, *Andrew Lloyd Webber,* 162–63.

7. "New Music"

1. Hilary de Vries, "From the Paris Sewers to Vietnam's Streets," *New York Times,* 17 September 1989.

2. For a detailed account of the casting for the London staging, see Edward Behr

and Mark Steyn, *The Story of Miss Saigon* (New York: Arcade, 1991), 141ff. Behr, who wrote the handy (if not academically minded) companion book for *Les Misérables,* became an unofficial consultant on *Miss Saigon* and therefore offers an interesting insider's view. He had been a reporter in Vietnam during the war and could describe Saigon, especially the Americans' place in the city; he also had some first-hand experience with bar girls in Saigon. Robert Stone, in the *New York Times*'s pre-opening feature article (the sort that until recently featured a Hirschfeld drawing), offered a historically grounded insight and also summarized what actually happened during the final exit via helicopters of American soldiers from Saigon at the end of April 1975. See Robert Stone, " 'Miss Saigon' Flirts With Art and Reality," *New York Times,* 7 April 1991.

3. De Vries, "Vietnam's Streets."

4. Behr and Steyn, *The Story of Miss Saigon,* 27.

5. Ibid., 33. When asked about his influences, Schönberg cites, among others, Offenbach, much admired for his use of recitative. Schönberg describes both Offenbach's and his own recitative in similar terms: they contain little "treasures of melody" that can be developed into whole songs, or may just exist as perfect one-off moments (ibid., 36). Behr and Steyn offer some quirky musical analysis (40ff.), including interesting comments from orchestrator Bill Brohn (one of a number of Americans working on this supposedly British musical), the use of instruments from a number of Asian cultures, and an extensive discussion about Maltby's work in both translating and Americanizing the lyrics.

6. Behr and Steyn recount the messy negotiations, with no small amount of gossip, in chapter 9 of *The Story of Miss Saigon.* The end result suited each show well, but led to a disastrous falling-out between Mackintosh and Nunn.

7. Both of the above quotes from Alex Witchel, "Actors' Equity Attacks Casting of 'Miss Saigon,' " *New York Times,* 26 July 1990. On casting, see also Alex Witchel, "Union Weighs 'Miss Saigon' Casting," *New York Times,* 25 July 1990. Also, Behr and Steyn give credit not to Hwang and Wong for the first volley, although theirs was the first within Equity. A complaint several weeks earlier reached Equity from Tisa Chang, artistic director of the Pan Asian Repertory Theatre. Behr and Steyn, *The Story of Miss Saigon,* 181.

8. See Mervyn Rothstein, "Union Bars White in Asian Role; Broadway May Lose 'Miss Saigon,' " *New York Times,* 8 August 1990.

9. As quoted in Mervyn Rothstein, "Producer Cancels 'Miss Saigon'; 140 Members Challenge Equity," *New York Times,* 9 August 1990.

10. Alex Witchel, "British Star Talks of Racial Harmony and Disillusionment With Equity," *New York Times,* 11 August 1990.

11. Frank Rich, "Jonathan Pryce, 'Miss Saigon' and Equity's Decision," *New York Times,* 10 August 1990.

12. This and all quotes from *Miss Saigon* are from the libretto included with *The Complete Recording of Boublil and Schönberg's* Miss Saigon (London: First Night Records, KIM CD 1, 1995).

13. As quoted in Mervyn Rothstein, "Equity Reverses 'Saigon' Vote And Welcomes English Star," *New York Times,* 17 August 1990.

14. Mervyn Rothstein, "Producer Demands A Free Hand to Cast 'Miss Saigon' Roles," *New York Times,* 22 August 1990.

15. Mervyn Rothstein, "Dispute Settled, 'Miss Saigon' Is Broadway Bound," *New York Times,* 19 September 1990.

16. On Salonga's casting, see Mervyn Rothstein, " 'Miss Saigon' Takes On Equity Again," *New York Times,* 5 December 1990; and Mervyn Rothstein, "Filipino Actress

Allowed in 'Saigon,' " *New York Times*, 8 January 1991. For an interesting interview with Salonga and her very protective mother, see Alex Witchel, "The Iron Butterfly Within Miss Saigon," *New York Times*, 17 March 1991.

17. Mervyn Rothstein, "The Musical Is Money To His Ears," *New York Times Magazine*, 9 December 1990.

18. Frank Rich, " 'Miss Saigon' Arrives, From the Old School," *New York Times*, 12 April 1991.

19. Douglas Watt, "Pryce is right, but 'Saigon' is no bargain," *New York Daily News*, 19 April 1991.

20. William A. Henry III, "Memories of a World on Fire," *Time*, 22 April 1991; Linda Winer, " 'Miss Saigon' Arrives: The year's most anticipated musical is finally here . . . ," *New York Newsday*, 12 April 1991.

21. Positive reviews came from Joel Siegel, review on WABC, 11 April 1991, transcribed in the *New York Theatre Critics' Reviews*, 1991; David Patrick Stearns, "Poor score can't make 'Saigon' fall," *USA Today*, 12 April 1991; and Edwin Wilson, "Old-Fashioned Entertainment," *Wall Street Journal*, 12 April 1991. Mixed reviews, including those with very few complaints and those with many: Clive Barnes, "A little amiss in 'Saigon,' " *New York Post*, 12 April 1991; Jack Kroll, "Good Evening, 'Miss Saigon,' " *Newsweek*, 22 April 1991; John Simon, "Leaden Butterfly," *New York*, 22 April 1991; Howard Kissel, "Viet Numb!" *New York Daily News*, 12 April 1991; and David Richards, "The 'Saigon' Picture Is Worth 1,000 Words," *New York Times*, 21 April 1991.

22. Robin Pogrebin, "For 'Miss Saigon,' Light at the End," *New York Times*, 25 August 2000.

23. Michael Walsh, *Andrew Lloyd Webber: His Life and Works*, 2nd ed. (New York: Harry N. Abrams, 1997), 223. A coffee table book devoted to *Aspects of Love*, by theater historian Kurt Gänzl, discusses David Garnett and the creation of the musical, including many details of set and costume design, casting, writing, and rehearsing. It ends with London's opening night, barely mentioning the critical or popular reaction. Kurt Gänzl, *The Complete Aspects of Love* (New York: Viking Studio Books, 1990).

24. For more on the early stages of the show, see Walsh, *Andrew Lloyd Webber*, 219–22.

25. John Peter, "How to Wrap an Opera in Musical Wallpaper," *Sunday Times* (London), 23 April 1989. For other mixed reviews, see Michael Billington, "The tender touch," *Guardian*, 18 April 1989; and Michael Ratcliffe, "Sing a song of love," *Observer*, 23 April 1989. For far more positive reviews, see Michael Coveney, "Aspects of Love," *Financial Times*, 18 April 1989; and Irving Wardle, "Hedonistic experiment," *Times* (London), 18 April 1989.

26. Walsh, *Andrew Lloyd Webber*, 238. No citation of the London wag.

27. Frank Rich, "Lloyd Webber's 'Aspects of Love,' " *New York Times*, 9 April 1990.

28. John Simon, "No Cats, No Skates, No Nothin'," *New York*, 23 April 1990; Michael Feingold, "Call it Macaroni," *Village Voice*, 17 April 1990. For another pan that amounted more to heated hostility than critical review, see Mimi Kramer, "The Theatre: Aspects of Vulgarity," *New Yorker*, 23 April 1990. Other pans include Howard Kissel, "Anything but 'Love,' " *New York Daily News*, 9 April 1990; Douglas Watt, "Webber grilled on 'Aspects,' " *New York Daily News*, 13 April 1990; Edwin Wilson, "Theater: 'Aspects of Love,' " *Wall Street Journal*, 11 April 1990.

29. William A. Henry III, " ''Romance, Mostly Misguided," *Time*, 16 April 1990. Other raves include Jack Kroll, "Falling in Love with Love," *Newsweek*, 16 April 1990; and Clive

Barnes, " 'Aspects' has the right sound, look, atmosphere," *New York Post,* 9 April 1990. For mixed reviews, see Linda Winer, "Lloyd Webber's 'Aspects' Of Being Grown-Up," *New York Newsday,* 9 April 1990; and David Richards, " 'Aspects of Love,' Palpitations On a Theme," *Washington Post,* 9 April 1990.

30. Michael Coveney, *Cats on a Chandelier: The Andrew Lloyd Webber Story* (London: Hutchinson, 1999), 151.

31. Richard Bernstein, " 'Aspects,' the Musical That Had Everything, And Lost Everything," *New York Times,* 7 March 1991.

32. Mark Steyn, *Broadway Babies Say Goodnight: Musicals Then and Now* (New York: Routledge, 1997), 289.

33. Walsh, *Andrew Lloyd Webber,* 258.

34. Steyn, *Broadway Babies,* 281. A coffee table book on the making of *Sunset Boulevard* features interesting sections on the silent film era and on Billy Wilder's film version, and some background on how the London staging took shape (including many details of set and costume design, with photos). It ends with the London opening, so the show's fate in the United States is unaddressed. George Perry, *Sunset Boulevard: From Movie to Musical* (New York: Henry Holt, 1993).

35. Frank Rich, "Upstaging a New Lloyd Webber Musical," *New York Times,* 14 July 1993. For two glowing reviews in British papers, see Benedict Nightingale, "Gorgeous to look at, enchanting to hear," *Times* (London), 13 July 1993; and Michael Coveney, "Boulevard of broken dreams," *Observer,* 18 July 1993. For mixed reviews, see Hugh Canning, "Sunset that will not fade: The music," *Times* (London), 18 July 1993; Robert Hewison, "Sunset that will not fade: The play," *Times* (London), 18 July 1993; Michael Billington, "Wilder's wit turned to romanticism in Lloyd Webber's Hollywood dream," *Guardian,* 13 July 1993; Malcolm Rutherford, "Sunset Boulevard," *Financial Times,* 13 July 1993; and William A. Henry III, "A Hollywood Opera Noir," *Time,* 26 July 1993.

36. On the Patti LuPone casting scandal, see Bernard Weintraub, "Hollywood Braces For Look Into Mirror Of 'Sunset Boulevard,' " *New York Times,* 9 December 1993; Bruce Weber, "Close Is Given LuPone's Place in 'Sunset' Cast for Broadway," *New York Times,* 18 February 1994; "LuPone Settlement on 'Sunset,' " *New York Times,* 18 May 1994; and Bernard Weintraub, "When Egos Collide: Twilight at 'Sunset,' " *New York Times,* 5 July 1994.

37. Weintraub, "When Egos Collide." For more on the Dunaway scandal, see "Dunaway Gets 'Sunset' Role," *New York Times,* 6 May 1994; " 'Sunset Boulevard' To Close in Los Angeles," *New York Times,* 24 June 1994; "Dunaway Sues Lloyd Webber," *New York Times,* 27 August 1994; and [Reuters], "Lloyd Webber and Dunaway Settle," *New York Times,* 17 January 1995. Frank Rich, for one, felt that both casting scandals had been stunts to sell tickets in New York, so that the show would have a healthy run no matter what critics had to say. Frank Rich, "Trashing for Dollars," *New York Times,* 9 October 1994.

38. David Richards, "Boulevard of Broken Dreams," *New York Times,* 18 November 1994.

39. Feingold had little to say that was new about this show; he even repeated his joke about how the music was "like Philip Glass, only repetitive," from his *Aspects of Love* review. He continued to maintain that Lloyd Webber did not, in fact, compose, and he derided David Richards for his positive review. Michael Feingold, "What Entertain Meant," *Village Voice,* 29 November 1994. For Barnes's strong review, see Clive Barnes,

"The Sun Won't Set on the *Boulevard,*" *New York Post,* 18 November 1994. For other glowing reviews, see Donald Lyons, "Webber's Masterpiece," *Wall Street Journal,* 19 November 1994; Michael Walsh, "As If We Never Said Goodbye," *Time,* 28 November 1994; and Vincent Canby, "A Glittering 'Sunset' Rises," *New York Times,* 27 November 1994. For mixed reviews, see John Simon, "Promises, Promises," *New York,* 28 November 1994; John Lahr, "Cinéma un-vérité," *New Yorker,* 5 December 1994; David Patrick Stearn [*sic:* Stearns], "Sunset Sells Its Soul for Spectacle," *USA Today,* 18 November 1994; Howard Kissel, "Scenery Steals the Show," *New York Daily News,* 18 November 1994; Linda Winer, "The Diva Drives Sunset Boulevard," *New York Newsday,* 18 November 1994; and Jeremy Gerard, "Sunset Boulevard," *Variety,* 21 November 1994.

40. For an example of this view, see Denny Martin Flinn, *Musical! A Grand Tour: The Rise, Glory, and Fall of an American Institution* (New York: Schirmer, 1997), 484.

41. It is worth noting that Lloyd Webber's music was and is often used at similar events in England, such as sporting events and occasions of national pageantry or politics, but for almost all of these, he wrote new, context-appropriate songs.

42. From the libretto included with the original Broadway cast recording of Frank Wildhorn's *Jekyll and Hyde* (Atlantic 82976-2, 1997).

43. Ben Brantley, "Jekyll, Torn Between 2 Women and, Yes, 2 Men," *New York Times,* 29 April 1997.

44. Robin Pogrebin, "Broadway's Critic-Proof Composer Says This Is (Still) His Moment; Like His 'Scarlet Pimpernel,' Frank Wildhorn Keeps on Going," *New York Times,* 6 October 1999.

45. Ibid.

46. Michael Feingold, "Musical Muddlings," *Village Voice,* 6 May 1997.

47. Howard Kissel, "A Ticket to 'Hyde': Creature Comforts Sell Us on 'Jekyll,' as Musical Supplies the Beast of Both Worlds," *New York Daily News,* 29 April 1997.

48. Ben Brantley, "Two Faces, and Both In Trouble," *New York Times,* 10 November 1997.

49. Ben Brantley, "Recovered, Restuffed, Otherwise Unchanged," *New York Times,* 5 November 1998.

50. Ben Brantley, "Derring-Do Redone, Once More," *New York Times,* 28 September 1999.

51. Ben Brantley, "History Soldiering On," *New York Times,* 23 April 1999.

52. Ben Brantley, " 'Titanic,' the Musical, Is Finally Launched, and the News Is It's Still Afloat," *New York Times,* 24 April 1997.

53. Michael Feingold, "Musical Muddlings," *Village Voice,* 6 May 1997. See also Howard Kissel, "A 'Titanic' Letdown: New B'way Musical Is No Disaster, But Skimpy Sets & Story Are Disappointing," *New York Daily News,* 24 April 1997.

54. David Richards, "Disney Does Broadway, Dancing Spoons and All," *New York Times,* 19 April 1994.

55. Linda Winer, "Disney's B'way Beast," *New York Newsday,* 19 April 1994.

56. Howard Kissel, "Little Beauty in the Eyes of This Beholder," *New York Daily News,* 19 April 1994.

57. John Simon, "Hairy Fairy Tale," *New York,* 2 May 1994.

58. Clive Barnes, "Fable for Our Times," *New York Post,* 19 April 1994. For other mixed reviews, see William A. Henry III, "Disenchanting Kingdom," *Time,* 2 May 1994; John Lahr, "The Shock of the Neutral," *New Yorker,* 2 May 1994; Jeremy Gerard, "Beauty

and the Beast," *Variety*, 25 April 1994; David Patrick Stearns, "Ingratiation Replaces Animation in Staged *Beauty*," *USA Today*, 19 April 1994; and Edwin Wilson, "A Bit of Disneyland Comes to Broadway," *Wall Street Journal*, 19 April 1994.

59. Lahr, "The Shock of the Neutral."

60. Ben Brantley, "Cub Comes of Age: A Twice-Told Cosmic Tale," *New York Times*, 14 November 1997.

61. Fintan O'Toole, "Mane Event is Spectacular: Adaptation of Disney Film Reigns Supreme as Musical Theater," *New York Daily News*, 14 November 1997.

62. Michael Feingold, "Spectacle and Spirit," *Village Voice*, 25 November 1997.

63. Disney "asked me to do the show so I would do what I do," reported Taymor. She was grateful for the unlimited budget and the potential for a long run, two things her work in less mainstream theaters had rarely enjoyed. As quoted in Eileen Blumenthal, "Queen of the Jungle," *Village Voice*, 18 November 1997.

64. For other raves or near-raves (there are no pans to report), see Vincent Canby, " 'The Lion King' Earns Its Roars Of Approval," *New York Times*, 23 November 1997; Jack Kroll, "A Magic Kingdom," *Newsweek*, 24 November 1997; and Richard Zoglin, "Stand Up and Roar," *Time*, 24 November 1997.

65. For more on how *Rent* parallels the Puccini version, see Leighton Kramer, "Downtown Arias: Assessing the Opera in *Rent*," *Village Voice*, 19 March 1996.

66. For a complete libretto, see the booklet published with *Rent: Original Broadway Cast Recording* (Dreamworks Records, DRMD2-50003, 1996). The double CD set also contains the remix of "Seasons of Love."

67. Michael Feingold, "Long-Term Lease," *Village Voice*, 20 February 1996. Other rave reviews include Jeremy Gerard, [no title], *Variety*, 6 May 1996; and Clive Barnes, "It Pays to *Rent*," *New York Post*, 30 April 1996. For more on whether the music of *Rent* is opera, rock, or theater, see Bernard Holland, "Flaws Aside, 'Rent' Lives and Breathes," *New York Times*, 17 March 1996; and Jon Pareles, "Can Rock Play to the Broadway Crowd?" *New York Times*, 28 April 1996. For more background on how Rent came to be, see Anthony Tommasini, "The Seven-Year Odyssey That Led to 'Rent,' " *New York Times*, 17 March 1996.

68. Ben Brantley, [no title], *New York Times*, 30 April 1996.

69. John Simon, [no title], *New York*, 13 May 1996. Simon seems to find the Pulitzer an unreliable measure of theatrical achievement; some critics agree it tends to go to popular shows or shows that take few risks. Winners are almost always straight plays, not musicals.

70. Howard Kissel, "*Rent* Comes Due on Broadway," *New York Daily News*, 30 April 1996.

71. I recently took a group of college students from a small western Pennsylvania town to see a touring company of *Rent* in Pittsburgh; about a third of them reported being shocked or offended by the story.

72. This and all quotations from *Ragtime* come from the libretto included with *Ragtime: The Musical*, original Broadway cast recording (RCA Victor, 09026 63167-2, 1998).

73. Ben Brantley, " 'Ragtime': A Diorama With Nostalgia Rampant," *New York Times*, 19 January 1998. For another mixed review, see John Simon, "Maple Leaf *Rag*," *New York*, 2 February 1998.

74. Clive Barnes, " 'Ragtime' Hits All the Right Notes," *New York Post*, 19 January 1998.

75. Fintan O'Toole, " 'Ragtime' to Riches: Three Divergent Worlds Collide in a Mosaic

of Stunning Power," *New York Daily News,* 19 January 1998. For other enthusiastic, if tempered, reviews, see Vincent Canby, "Big and Beautiful, 'Ragtime' Never Quite Sings," *New York Times,* 25 January 1998; and Jack Kroll, "Turn-of-the-Century Blues," *Newsweek,* 26 January 1998.

76. Michael Feingold, "Silver Threads," *Village Voice,* 3 February 1998.

8. "Everything Is Show Biz"

1. This background and the interview with John both appear in the *Times*'s pre-opening feature article. Alex Witchel, "An 'Aida' Born of Ecstasies and Explosions," *New York Times,* 19 March 2000.

2. This and all quotations from *Aida* can be found in the booklet that accompanies *Elton John and Tim Rice's Aida: Original Broadway Cast Recording* (Hyperion Theatricals, 60671-7, 2000). I have made a few alterations in the punctuation and line breaks, for clarity of scansion.

3. Ben Brantley, "Destiny and Duty, Nile Style," *New York Times,* 24 March 2000. For two other negative reviews, both more hostile than Brantley's fairly moderate one, see Jim Farber, "Rocket Man Runs Outta Fuel," *New York Daily News,* 24 March 2000; and Michael Feingold, "Power Steering," *Village Voice,* 4 April 2000. Feingold argues dismissively that *Aida* barely qualifies as being written at all, and devotes little space to it.

4. Jack Kroll and Veronica Chambers, "Star Over Egypt," *Newsweek,* 3 April 2000. For another glowing review, see Nancy Franklin, "Pop Goes Aida," *New Yorker,* 10 April 2000.

5. Fintan O'Toole, "Desert 'Aida' Beautiful but Empty," *New York Daily News,* 24 March 2000. For another mixed review, see Lloyd Rose, "Disney's 'Aida': Close Your Eyes and Enjoy," *Washington Post,* 24 March 2000.

6. This and all lyrics from *The Producers* can be found in a funny, handy coffee table book by the authors themselves. Mel Brooks and Thomas Meehan, *The Producers: The Book, Lyrics, and Story behind the Biggest Hit in Broadway History! How We Did It* (New York: Roundtable, 2001).

7. Ben Brantley, " 'The Producers': A Scam That'll Knock 'Em Dead," *New York Times,* 20 April 2001.

8. Frank Rich, "Journal: Springtime for Adolf and Tony," *New York Times,* 12 May 2001.

9. Margo Jefferson, "Theater: Broadway Choices: Old World Edivice Or Sleek Machine," *New York Times,* 13 May 2001.

10. See, for example, Phil Jacobs, "Dreading 'Springtime,' " published on *Jewish-Times.com,* 18 May 2001, viewed 12 February 2003; and Ted Hoover, "The Producers/Falsettos/The Region/And Miss Reardon Drinks a Little: Musically Challenged," *CP: Pittsburgh City Paper,* 25 September–2 October 2002.

11. John Lahr, "Gold Rush: Mel Brooks is back, mit a bing, mit a bang, mit a boom," *New Yorker,* 7 May 2001.

12. As quoted in Richard Zoglin with Amy Lennard Goehner, "Brush Up Your Goose Step," *Time,* 16 April 2001.

13. Anthony Tommasini, "Writing Musical Scores Like They Used To," *New York Times,* 20 May 2001.

14. Michael Feingold, "Glitzkrieg," *Village Voice,* 1 May 2001.

15. See Robin Pogrebin, "Ticket Sales for 'Producers' Set a Broadway Record," *New*

York Times, 21 April 2001; and Patricia O'Haire and Robert Dominguez, "$480 Seats Music to Producers' Ears," *New York Daily News*, 27 October 2001.

16. On the 2001 Tony Awards, 3 June 2001, PBS and CBS television. See also Robin Pogrebin, " 'Producers' Shatters Tony Award Record with 12 Prizes; 'Proof' Takes Best Play and 2 Other Awards," *New York Times*, 4 June 2001.

17. Jim Hoagland, "Fresh Out of Sympathy for Arafat," *Washington Post*, 7 June 2001.

18. In Dan Barry, "After the Attacks: The Scene: Normality Proves Elusive Amid Bomb Scares and Transit Woes," *New York Times*, 14 September 2001.

19. As quoted in Jesse McKinley, "New York's Theaters and Museums Open in a Bold Resolve to Persevere," *New York Times*, 14 September 2001.

20. Jesse McKinley, "Lights On, Broadway Dispels the Dark," *New York Times*, 15 September 2001.

21. Robin Pogrebin, "At 'Phantom,' Empty Seats and Defiance," *New York Times*, 20 September 2001.

22. As quoted in Pogrebin, "Empty Seats and Defiance."

23. As quoted in Jesse McKinley, "Broadway is in the War All the Way," *New York Times*, 21 September 2001.

24. As quoted in McKinley, "Bold Resolve to Persevere."

25. As quoted in Peter Marks, "Voices Not Silenced, Feet Not Stilled; As They Return to Work, Artists Talk Performing in a Time of Tragedy," *New York Times*, 20 September 2001.

26. Jesse McKinley, "Shows Must, and Did, Go On," *New York Times*, 8 March 2002.

27. See McKinley, "Broadway is in the War."

28. See McKinley, "Shows Must, and Did, Go On"; Robin Pogrebin, "How Broadway Bounced Back After 9/11," *New York Times*, 22 May 2002; and Jesse McKinley, "Broadway Getting Jitters as Advance Ticket Sales Fall," *New York Times*, 4 August 2002.

29. See, for example, the pre-opening feature in the *New York Times*, which talks almost exclusively about the two women, their backgrounds, their contrasting styles and personalities, and the feminist implications of the show. Bruce Weber, "The Wicked Young Witches," *New York Times*, 26 October 2003.

30. Ben Brantley, "There's Trouble in Emerald City," *New York Times*, 31 October 2003. For two other reviews—both of them far more negative than Brantley's—see How-ard Kissel, "The Girl from Oz: It's Such a 'Wicked' Waste of Talent," *New York Daily News*, 31 October 2003; and Michael Feingold, "Green Witch, Mean Time," *Village Voice*, 11 November 2003.

31. Elysa Gardner, "Something 'Wicked' Comes to Broadway," *USA Today*, 31 October 2003. For another positive review, see Richard Zoglin, "Which Witch was Wicked?" *Time*, 17 November 2003.

32. John Lahr, "Ulterior Motives in 'Cat on a Hot Tin Roof' and 'Wicked,' " *New Yorker*, 10 November 2003.

33. Stephen Holden, "Yellow Brick Road Leads Show Tunes Down a New Path," *New York Times*, 28 May 2004. This article on cast albums offers interesting insights into *Wicked* and also *Assassins, Taboo, Avenue Q, Bombay Dreams, The Boy from Oz, Caroline, or Change, Gypsy*, and *Wonderful Town*.

Bibliography

American Newspapers and Periodicals

Billboard
Christian Science Monitor
New York
New York Daily News
New York Post
New York Times
New Yorker
Newsweek
Record World
Time
USA Today
Variety
Village Voice
Wall Street Journal
Washington Post
Women's Wear Daily

British Newspapers

Daily Mirror
Daily Telegraph
Financial Times
Guardian
Observer
Times and *Sunday Times*

Books and Journals

Altman, Rick, ed. *Genre: The Musical: A Reader.* London: Routledge and Kegan Paul, 1981.
Banfield, Stephen. *Sondheim's Broadway Musicals.* Ann Arbor: University of Michigan Press, 1993.
Behr, Edward. *Les Misérables: History in the Making.* Updated ed. New York: Arcade, 1996.
Behr, Edward, and Mark Steyn. *The Story of Miss Saigon.* New York: Arcade, 1991.
Block, Geoffrey. "The Broadway Canon from *Show Boat* to *West Side Story* and the European Operatic Ideal." *Journal of Musicology* 11, no. 4 (Fall 1993): 525–44.
———. *Enchanted Evenings: The Broadway Musical from* Show Boat *to* Sondheim. New York: Oxford University Press, 1997.

———. "Gershwin's Buzzard and Other Mythological Creatures." *Opera Quarterly* 7, no. 2 (Summer 1990): 74–82.

Bloom, Ken. *American Song: The Complete Musical Theatre Companion.* New York: Schirmer Books, 1996.

———. *Broadway.* New York: Facts on File, 1991.

Bordman, Gerald Martin. *American Musical Theatre: A Chronicle.* 3rd ed. New York: Oxford University Press, 2001.

———. *American Operetta from "H.M.S. Pinafore" to "Sweeney Todd."* New York: Oxford University Press, 1981.

Borroff, Edith. "Origin of Species: Conflicting Views of American Musical Theater History." *American Music* 2, no. 4 (Winter 1984): 101–11.

Bowers, Dwight Blocker. *American Musical Theater.* Washington, D.C.: Smithsonian Institution Press, 1989.

Brahms, Caryl, and Ned Sherrin. *Song by Song: The Lives and Work of Fourteen Great Lyric Writers.* Bolton, England: Ross Anderson, 1984.

Brooks, Mel, and Tom Meehan. *The Producers: The Book, Lyrics, and Story Behind the Biggest Hit in Broadway History! How We Did It.* New York: Roundtable, 2001.

Brown, Gene. *Show Time: A Chronology of Broadway and the Theatre from Its Beginnings to the Present.* New York: Macmillan, 1997.

Citron, Stephen. *The Musical from the Inside Out.* 2nd ed. Chicago: Ivan R. Dee, 1997.

———. *Sondheim and Lloyd-Webber: The New Musical.* Oxford: Oxford University Press, 2001.

Coven, Brenda, et al., eds. *David Merrick and Hal Prince: An Annotated Bibliography.* New York: Garland, 1993.

Coveney, Michael. *Cats on a Chandelier: The Andrew Lloyd Webber Story.* London: Hutchinson, 1999.

DiGaetani, John L., and Josef P. Sirefman. *Opera and the Golden West: The Past, Present, and Future of Opera in the U.S.A.* London and Toronto: Associated University Presses, 1994.

Everett, William A., and Paul R. Laird. *The Cambridge Companion to the Musical.* Cambridge: Cambridge University Press, 2002.

Flinn, Denny Martin. *Musical! A Grand Tour: The Rise, Glory, and Fall of an American Institution.* New York: Schirmer Books, 1997.

Frommer, Myrna Katz, and Harvey Frommer. *It Happened on Broadway: An Oral History of the Great White Way.* New York: Harcourt Brace and Co., 1998.

Gänzl, Kurt. *The British Musical Theatre.* 2 vols. London: Macmillan, 1986.

———. *The Complete Aspects of Love.* New York: Viking Studio Books, 1990.

———. *An Encyclopedia of the Musical Theater.* New York: Schirmer Books, 1994.

———. *Gänzl's Book of the Broadway Musical.* New York: Schirmer Books, 1995.

———. *The Musical: A Concise History.* Boston: Northeastern University Press, 1997.

Garebian, Keith. *The Making of West Side Story.* Toronto: E C W, 1995.

Goodhart, Sandor, ed. *Reading Stephen Sondheim: A Collection of Critical Essays.* New York: Garland, 2000.

Gordon, Joanne. *Art Isn't Easy: The Theatre of Stephen Sondheim.* 2nd ed. New York: Da Capo, 1992.

———, ed. *Stephen Sondheim: A Casebook.* New York: Garland, 1997.

Gottfried, Martin. *Sondheim.* New York: Harry N. Abrams, 1993.

Green, Stanley. *Broadway Musicals Show by Show.* 5th ed. Milwaukee: Hal Leonard Books, 1996.

————. *The World of Musical Comedy.* 4th ed. New York: Da Capo, 1980; rev. ed., 1984.

Groos, Arthur, and Roger Parker. *Giacomo Puccini: La bohème. Cambridge Opera Handbooks.* Cambridge: Cambridge University Press, 1986.

Hanan, Stephen Mo. *A Cat's Diary: How the Broadway Production of* Cats *Was Born.* Hanover, N.H.: Smith and Kraus, 2001.

Headington, Christopher. *The Performing World of the Musician.* New Jersey: Silver Burdett, 1981.

Heinsheimer, Hans. "Splendour and Misery of the American Musical." *The World of Music* 12, no. 2 (1970): 44–56.

Henderson, Amy, and Dwight Blocker Bowers. *Red, Hot, and Blue: A Smithsonian Salute to the American Musical.* Washington, D.C.: Smithsonian Institution Press, 1996.

Hirsch, Foster. *Harold Prince and the American Musical Theatre.* Cambridge: Cambridge University Press, 1989.

Horn, Barbara Lee. *The Age of Hair: Evolution and Impact of Broadway's First Rock Musical.* New York: Greenwood, 1991.

Horowitz, Mark Eden. *Sondheim on Music: Minor Details and Major Decisions.* Lanham, Md.: Scarecrow, 2003.

Huber, Eugene Robert. "Stephen Sondheim and Harold Prince: Collaborative Contributions to the Development of the Modern Concept Musical, 1970–1981." Ph.D. dissertation, New York University, 1990.

Ilson, Carol. *Harold Prince: From* Pajama Game *to* Phantom of the Opera*, and Beyond.* 2nd ed. New York: Limelight Editions, 1992.

Jones, John Bush. *Our Musicals, Ourselves: A Social History of the American Musical Theatre.* Hanover, N.H.: Brandeis University Press, 2003.

Kasha, Al. *Notes on Broadway: Intimate Conversations with Broadway's Greatest Songwriters.* New York: Simon and Schuster, 1987.

Kislan, Richard. *The Musical: A Look at the American Musical Theater.* Rev. ed. New York: Applause, 1995.

Kreuger, Miles. *Show Boat: The Story of a Classic American Musical.* 2nd ed. New York: Da Capo, 1990.

Lamb, Andrew. *150 Years of Popular Musical Theatre.* New Haven: Yale University Press, 2000.

Lassell, Michael. *Elton John and Tim Rice's* Aida: *The Making of the Broadway Musical.* New York: Disney Editions, 2000.

Laufe, Abe. *Broadway's Greatest Musicals.* Rev. ed. New York: Funk and Wagnalls, 1977.

Lawson-Peebles, Robert, ed. *Approaches to the American Musical.* Exeter, Devon, England: University of Exeter Press, 1996.

Lee, M. Owen. "Recordings: The Phantom of the Opera. Andrew Lloyd Webber." *Opera Quarterly* 6, no. 1 (Autumn 1988): 150.

Lerner, Alan Jay. *The Musical Theatre.* New York: Da Capo, 1989.

Levine, Lawrence. *Highbrow/Lowbrow: The Emergence of a Cultural Hierarchy in America.* Cambridge, Mass.: Harvard University Press, 1988.

Lewis, David H. *Broadway Musicals: A Hundred Year History.* Jefferson, N.C.: McFarland, 2002.

[Lloyd Webber, Andrew, and T. S. Eliot.] *Cats: The Book of the Musical.* New York: Harcourt Brace and Co., 1983.

Lloyd Webber, Andrew, and Tim Rice. *Evita: The Legend of Eva Peron.* New York: Drama Book Specialists, 1978.

Loney, Glenn. "A Conversation with Hal Prince." *Dramatics* (Jan. 1989): 18–23.

———. "Crossing Over: Prince Hal: Broadway and opera director and NIMT chief speaks out as a fierce champion of the musical as a serious art form." *Opera News* 50, no. 4 (Oct. 1985): 50–51, 54.

———. "Don't Cry for Andrew Lloyd Webber." *Opera News* 45, no. 17 (Apr. 4, 1981): 12–14, 27.

Mantle, Jonathan. *Fanfare: The Unauthorized Biography of Andrew Lloyd Webber.* London: Michael Joseph Ltd., 1989.

Marx, Robert. *Contemporary American Musical Theater, Opera, and Experimental Music Theater: An Overview of Current Conditions and Future Trends.* Washington, D.C.: National Endowment for the Arts, 1985.

Mast, Gerald. *Can't Help Singin': The American Musical on Stage and Screen.* Woodstock, N.Y.: Overlook, 1987.

Mates, Julian. *America's Musical Stage: Two Hundred Years of Musical Theatre.* New York: Praeger, 1987.

McDonnell, Evelyn, and Katherine Silberger. *Rent.* New York: Rob Weisbach Books, 1997.

McGowan, Dennis, and Deborah Grace Winer. *Sing Out, Louise! 150 Stars of the Musical Theatre Remember 50 Years on Broadway.* New York: Schirmer Books, 1993.

McKnight, Gerald. *Andrew Lloyd Webber.* New York: St. Martin's, 1984.

Mellers, Wilfrid. "Platform: Are Musicals Musical?" *Musical Times* 132, no. 1782 (Aug. 1991): 380.

Miller, D. A. *Place for Us: Essay on the Broadway Musical.* Cambridge, Mass.: Harvard University Press, 1998.

Miller, Scott. *Deconstructing Harold Hill: An Insider's Guide to Musical Theatre.* Portsmouth, N.H.: Heinemann, 2000.

———. *From Assassins to West Side Story: The Director's Guide to Musical Theater.* Portsmouth, N.H.: Heinemann, 1996.

Milnes, Rodney. "Towards the great American opera." *Opera* 39, no. 10 (Oct. 1988): 1167–73.

Mordden, Ethan. *Better Foot Forward: The History of American Musical Theatre.* New York: Oxford University Press, 1983.

———. "The Once and Future American Opera: As the U.S. enters the Bicentennial, what are its options for music theater?" *Opera News* 40, no. 2 (Aug. 1975): 16–21.

———. *One More Kiss: The Broadway Musical in the 1970s.* New York: Palgrave Macmillan, 2003.

———. *Open a New Window: The Broadway Musical in the 1960s.* New York: Palgrave Macmillan, 2001.

Morley, Sheridan. *Spread a Little Happiness: The First Hundred Years of the British Musical.* London: Thames and Hudson, 1987.

Nassour, Ellis, and Richard Broderick. *Rock Opera: The Creation of Jesus Christ Superstar, from Record Album to Broadway Show and Motion Picture.* New York: Hawthorn Books, 1973.

Novak, Elaine A., and Deborah Novak. *Staging Musical Theatre: A Complete Guide for Directors, Choreographers and Producers.* Cincinnati: Betterway Books, 1996.

Ostrow, Stuart. *A Producer's Broadway Journey.* Westport, Conn.: Praeger, 1999.

Parker, Alan. *The Making of Evita.* New York: Collins, 1996.

Pasles, Chris. "Andrew Lloyd Webber and The Phantom: A new kind of opera?" *Opera Canada* 30, no. 3 (Fall 1989): 17–19.

Perry, George C. *The Complete Phantom of the Opera.* New York: Henry Holt, 1988.
————. *Sunset Boulevard: From Movie to Musical.* New York: Henry Holt, 1993.
Porter, Steven. *The American Musical Theatre: A Complete Musical Theatre Course.* 2nd ed. Studio City, Calif.: Phantom, 1997.
Rice, Tim. *Oh, What a Circus. The Autobiography: 1944–1978.* London: Hodder and Stoughton, 1999.
Richmond, Keith. *The Musicals of Andrew Lloyd Webber.* London: Virgin, 1995.
Rosenberg, Bernard, and Ernest Harburg. *The Broadway Musical: Collaboration in Commerce and Art.* New York: New York University Press, 1993.
Salem, James M. *A Guide to Critical Reviews: Part II: The Musical, 1909–1989.* 3rd ed. Metuchen, N.J.: Scarecrow, 1991.
Sams, Jeremy. "Sondheim's operatic overtures." *Opera* 38, no. 9 (Sept. 1987): 1002–1007.
Secrest, Meryle. *Stephen Sondheim: A Life.* New York: Alfred A. Knopf, 1998.
Sharland, Elizabeth. *The British on Broadway: Backstage and Beyond—The Early Years.* Somerset, England: Barbican, 1999.
Simas, Rick. *The Musicals No One Came to See.* New York: Garland, 1987.
Singer, Barry. *Ever After: The Last Years of Musical Theater and Beyond.* New York: Applause Books, 2004.
Smith, Cecil, and Glenn Litton. *Musical Comedy in America.* 2nd ed. New York: Theatre Arts Books, 1981.
Stempel, Larry. "The Musical Play Expands." *American Music* 10, no. 2 (Summer 1992): 136–69.
Stevenson, Isabelle. *The Tony Award: A Complete Listing with a History of the American Theatre Wing.* Portsmouth, N.H.: Heinemann, 2001.
Steyn, Mark. *Broadway Babies Say Goodnight: Musicals Then and Now.* New York: Routledge, 1997.
Stubblebine, Donald J. *Broadway Sheet Music: A Comprehensive Listing of Published Music from Broadway and Other Stage Shows, 1918–1993.* Jefferson, N.C.: McFarland, 1996.
Suskin, Steven. *Show Tunes 1905–1991: The Songs, Shows and Careers of Broadway's Major Composers.* Rev. ed. New York: Limelight, 1992.
Sutcliffe, Tom. "Sondheim and the Musical." *Musical Times* 128, no. 1735 (Sept. 1987): 487–90.
Swain, Joseph P. *The Broadway Musical: A Critical and Musical Survey.* Rev. ed. Lanham, Md.: Scarecrow, 2002.
Taubman, Howard. *The Pleasures of Their Company: A Reminiscence.* Portland, Ore.: Amadeus, 1994.
Thelen, Lawrence. *The Show Makers: Great Directors of the American Musical Theatre.* New York: Routledge, 2000.
Walsh, Michael. *Andrew Lloyd Webber: His Life and Works.* Updated and enlarged ed. New York: Harry N. Abrams, 1997.
Wildbihler, Hubert, and Sonja Völklein. *The Musical: An International Annotated Bibliography.* New York: Saur, 1986.
Wilk, Max. *OK! The Story of "Oklahoma!"* New York: Grove, 1993.
Wilson, Alexandra. "Torrefranca vs. Puccini: Embodying a Decadent Italy." *Cambridge Opera Journal* 13, no. 1 (Mar. 2001): 29–53.
Wittke, Paul. "The American Musical Theater (with an Aside on Popular Music)." *Musical Quarterly* 68, no. 2 (Apr. 1982): 274–86.

Wolf, Leonard, ed. *The Essential Phantom of the Opera.* New York: Plume, 1996.

Wolf, Stacy. *A Problem like Maria: Gender and Sexuality in the American Musical.* Ann Arbor: University of Michigan Press, 2002.

Zadan, Craig. *Sondheim & Co.* 2nd ed. New York: Da Capo, 1994.

Index

techniques in, 92–93; post-opening Broadway history of, 219–21; September 11th and, 345–46; set of, 80–81; Tony Awards and, 217

Miss Saigon (Schönberg and Boublil), 1, 7, 117, 222, 293–304, 310, 325; analysis of, 299, 301; background and creation of, 293–96; casting controversies in, 296–301; later history of, 303–304; reviews of, 301–303; set of, 80; Tony Awards and, 303

Morris, Gary, 221

The Most Happy Fella (Loesser), 10, 90

Mostel, Joshua, 64–65

Mozart, Wolfgang Amadeus, 91, 93, 215; *Aspects of Love* and, 305; *The Phantom of the Opera* and, 86, 229, 234, 237–38, 257, 259

Murphy, Jack. *See The Civil War*

The Music Man (Wilson), 128

My Fair Lady (Lerner and Loewe), 10, 289, 317; Tim Rice and, 95

Napier, John, 273. *See also Cats; Les Misérables; Miss Saigon; Starlight Express; Sunset Boulevard*

Nederlander (producers), 174, 179, 188

Neeley, Ted, 63–65

Neofitou, Andreane, 184, 217, 293

Nicholas, Paul, 64, 119

Nunn, Trevor, 74, 83, 228, 230, 295; "British Invasion" of the megamusical and, 83–85; *Cricket* and, 98. *See also Aspects of Love; Cats; Chess; Les Misérables; Starlight Express; Sunset Boulevard*

Odessa File, The (film), 68

Oh! Calcutta!, 170

O'Horgan, Tom, 12, 24, 59, 102. *See also Jesus Christ Superstar*

Oklahoma! (Rodgers and Hammerstein), 5, 10

Oliver! (Bart), 11, 83, 176, 187, 188, 302

Oliver, Stephen. *See Blondel*

opera, 2; French grand opera, 2, 236–37; Lloyd Webber's use of techniques from, 90–93; operatic voices in the megamus-ical, 92. *See also Cats; Les Misérables; The Phantom of the Opera*

Pacific Overtures (Sondheim), 302

Page, Ken, 171

Paige, Elaine, 97, 102, 103, 120, 171, 312

Parade (Brown), 90, 102, 331

Pascal, Adam, 326, 338

Passion (Sondheim), 313

Patinkin, Mandy, 103, 332

The Phantom of the Opera (Lloyd Webber, Hart, and Stilgoe), 1, 2, 3, 5, 6–7, 28, 70, 71, 75, 78, 108, 117, 204, 217, 221, 225–72, 274, 277, 283, 285, 289, 291, 297, 304, 305, 307, 309, 310, 317, 334; background and creation of, 225–31; film version of, 71, 271; London and New York reviews of, 263, 265–70; London opening of, 231; marketing and, 77–80; melody in, 89; musical analysis of, 190, 191, 193, 234–64, 279, 306; New York casting controversy surrounding, 232–33; operatic techniques in, 91–92, 234–41, 259–60; pastiche in, 86–88; post-Broadway history of, 270–72; September 11th and, 345–46; set of, 80–81; Tony Awards and, 76, 233, 270–71

Porter, Cole, 5, 10

Previn, Andre, 64

Prince, Hal, 63, 75, 305, 319. *See also Cabaret; Company; Evita; Kiss of the Spider Woman; A Little Night Music; Parade; The Phantom of the Opera; Show Boat; Sweeney Todd*

The Producers (Brooks), 7, 276, 282, 321, 334, 352; analysis of, 339–43; September 11th and, 345–46; success of, 343–44

Pryce, Jonathan, 294, 296–300, 302, 304

Puccini, Giacomo, 21, 72, 87, 91, 307; *La Bohème*, 293, 325; *Cats* and, 119–20, 166; *Madama Butterfly*, 202, 293, 294, 296; *The Phantom of the Opera* and, 234, 235; *Tosca*, 86; *Turandot*, 287. *See also Miss Saigon, Rent*

Quast, Philip, 221

Ulvaeus, Björn. *See Chess*

Variations (Lloyd Webber), 68, 98, 234
Verdi, Giuseppe, 28, 91, 93, 187, 216, 234, 259, 334, 338. *See also Aida*
Vereen, Ben, 24, 62

Wagner, Richard, 93, 234, 243
Wagner, Robin, 282
West Side Story (Bernstein and Sondheim), 10, 85, 176, 216, 289, 294, 302
Whistle Down the Wind (Lloyd Webber and Steinman), 70, 90

Wicked (Schwartz), 326, 334, 348–50
Wildhorn, Frank. *See Jekyll and Hyde; The Scarlet Pimpernel; The Civil War*
Wilkinson, Colm, 182–83, 187, 189, 214, 215, 217, 222, 228
The Woman in White (Lloyd Webber and Zippel), 71
Wong, B. D., 296–97, 299, 300
Woolverton, Linda, 334

Yeston, Maury. *See Titanic*
York, Rachel, 317

JESSICA STERNFELD is a lifelong musical theater fan and performer. She earned her Ph.D. in musicology from Princeton University, and teaches the history and cultural contexts of musical theater, opera, pop genres, and Western Classical and Romantic musics. She is currently Assistant Professor of Music at Rhode Island College, and has a new chapter in the forthcoming second edition of the *Cambridge Companion to the Musical.*